W9-CHV-021

Conducting Educational Research

Fifth Edition

Conducting Educational Research

Fifth Edition

Bruce W. Tuckman
The Ohio State University

WADSWORTH

THOMSON LEARNING

Australia • Canada • Mexico • Singapore • Spain • United Kingdom • United States

Publisher	Earl McPeek
Acquisitions Editor	Carol Wada
Market Strategist	Laura Brennan
Project Editor	Angela Williams Urquhart
Art Director	Sue Hart
Production Manager	Andrea A. Johnson

ISBN: 0-15-505477-5

Library of Congress Catalog Card Number: 98-86589

Wadsworth Group/Thomson Learning
10 Davis Drive
Belmont CA 94002-3098
USA

For information about our products, contact us:
Thomson Learning Academic Resource Center
1-800-423-0563
http://www.wadsworth.com

For permission to use material from this text, contact us by
Web: http://www.thomsonrights.com
Fax: 1-800-730-2215
Phone: 1-800-730-2214

Printed in the United States of America

10 9 8 7 6 5 4 3 2

To Blair and Bret,
as they go through life's passages.

BRIEF CONTENTS

Contents

PREFACE

Many aspects of research design and methodology have changed very little in the quarter-century since this book first appeared. The challenge of formulating a researchable problem and labeling and operationalizing the variables that make up that problem remains today as it was then. The research designs, their graphic representation, and their sources of validity and invalidity, initially popularized in the first edition of this book, remain largely unchanged as well. The bases for evaluating measuring instruments, many of the statistical tests, and the format for reporting research show little difference from the versions presented in the initial appearance of this textbook.

But this fifth edition of *Conducting Educational Research* reflects two dramatic areas of change and a number of other changes of lesser note. While graduate students were learning to do research to complete theses and dissertations and then advance to become themselves the practitioners and researchers of today (and while my children, to whom, incidentally, every edition of this book has been dedicated, were growing up), we have been experiencing a technological revolution. This revolution has had its impact in educational research as in virtually all areas of life. When this book first appeared, statistical tests were mostly laboriously performed on "high-speed" desk calculators, which, like the dinosaur, have become extinct. The computer age, however, was in its infancy and most of us were learning how to run data on mainframe computers using punched cards and program control language.

Today, the availability and easy use of statistical software packages for use on personal computers enable researchers to remain at their desks and run any number of statistical analyses from simple tests to sophisticated analyses. In this edition of *CER*, instructions and descriptions for running the different statistical tests described in previous editions are now presented for personal computer software. In keeping with my strong belief that instruction in research methods should be as concrete and applications-oriented as possible, the process of carrying out statistical tests by computer is not presented in a general way, but in terms of the specific operations required to perform a number of the most commonly used statistical tests, using the Statistical Package for the Social Sciences (SPSS). This software program has been chosen because of its common familiarity and widespread use throughout the research world.

New technological developments have also transformed the process of literature searching, and new updates have been added to every *CER* edition, this latest one being no exception. The Internet has exploded into the everyday world, and only a new edition every year could keep up with its burgeoning development.

The second major change area in educational research has been the growing interest in and use of qualitative data to study and understand educational phenomena. While the first edition of *CER* described methods for collecting interview and observational data, it was not until the third edition that a full chapter was added to cover qualitative research. This chapter has been considerably expanded in this edition to include more background on the nature and characteristics of the qualitative approach, more specifics on the "mechanics" of its procedures, and special sections on techniques for interviewing children, analyzing taped interview transcripts, and doing analysis of think-aloud verbal protocols, all of which reflect the increasing emphasis on exactness and objectivity in collection and analysis of qualitative data.

Smaller changes in the text reflect developments and growing and changing emphases in educational research methodology. These alterations cover a wide range of subjects, beginning with an expansion of the detail in the discussion of researchers' ethical requirements, reflecting the growing concern with the welfare of participants in research. Additional new material addresses issues regarding the validity of meta-analysis and controversies about some of the conclusions it has spawned. The text also covers techniques for employing a wider range of research designs, including single-subject, cross-sectional, and longitudinal designs, the latter two specifically intended to study developmental change.

All of the editions, including this one, focus on teaching researchers-to-be and practitioners alike to be astute and critical readers and users of research. As the universe of knowledge expands, critical evaluation of what one can and cannot accept as good research becomes a progressively more necessary yet more challenging task.

I would like to acknowledge the people who have helped me in the preparation of this edition. Foremost among them is Dr. Andy Palmer, one of my former doctoral students, who made a major contribution to the revision of the chapter on statistics. One can learn much, I am often reminded, from the very people one teaches. In this same spirit, my current doctoral student, Dennis Abry, has been most helpful. I am also gratified to be able to include the work on protocol analysis by my colleague, K. Anders Ericsson. Finally, I offer my thanks to those who assisted me by reviewing the fourth edition and offering suggestions for its improvement, including Dr. Michael Pressley, University of Notre Dame; Dr. Alan Klockars, University of Washington; and Dr. John Taccarino, De Paul University.

As always, I am grateful to my colleagues in the field who have used *CER* as a text for teaching educational research methods, and to the many students who have pored over its pages in an effort to discover the "mysteries" of research.

Bruce W. Tuckman

Part 1

INTRODUCTION

Chapter 1

THE ROLE OF RESEARCH

Objectives

▶ Identify the role of internal validity.

▶ Identify the role of external validity.

▶ Describe the relationship between internal validity and external validity.

▶ Describe the characteristics of the research process.

▶ Identify the sequence of steps in the research process.

▶ Describe the ethical rights of participants in research studies.

WHAT IS RESEARCH?

Research is a systematic attempt to provide answers to questions. It may yield abstract and general answers, as basic research often does, or it may give extremely concrete and specific answers, as demonstration or applied research often does. In both kinds of research, the investigator uncovers facts and then formulates a generalization based on an interpretation of those facts.

Basic research is concerned with the relationship between two or more variables. It is carried out by identifying a problem, examining selected relevant variables through a literature review, constructing a hypothesis where possible, creating a research design to investigate the problem, collecting and analyzing appropriate data, and then drawing conclusions about the relationships of the variables. Basic research does not often provide information with an immediate application for altering the environment. Its purpose, rather, is to develop a model, or theory, that identifies all the relevant variables in a particular environment and hypothesizes about their relationships. Using the findings of basic research, it is possible to develop a product—a concept that includes, for example, a given curriculum, a particular teacher-training program, a textbook, or an audiovisual aid.

A further step, often called *demonstration,* is to test the product. This activity is the province of applied research, which is, in effect, a test or tryout of the application that includes systematic evaluation.

VALIDITY IN RESEARCH

Achieving validity in research is not an easy task, as the following examples demonstrate.

A science educator is designing a new instructional program for fifth-grade science. He has at his disposal films, textbooks, lecture text, lab experiments, and computer software, and he needs to decide which of these approaches to use and in what combination. To make this decision, he plans to teach the first unit, on force, using the lecture-textbook approach; he will teach the second unit, on motion, using films. He can then see which method has the better effect and guide later efforts according to this judgment. But the science educator has created logical pitfalls for himself.

Suppose that the unit on force were easier to understand than the unit on motion. Students might perform better on the end-of-unit test for the force material simply because they could more easily grasp the concepts covered in the unit. It is possible, too, that films are particularly good tools for teaching motion, because of the nature of the subject matter, but poor tools for teaching force. Therefore, any generalization about the advantage of films beyond the teaching of motion would lack validity. It is also possible that the particular film the science educator has chosen for teaching motion is a poor one, and its failure to instruct would not entitle him generally to condemn films for instruction in elementary science. Of additional concern, the students' learning about force might help them to learn about motion, thereby predisposing them to do better on the second unit, regardless of pedagogical technique. Even if the two units were independent in subject matter, the sophistication gained in the first unit might help students to master the second unit. Furthermore, one of the end-of-unit tests might be easier or more representative of the learning material than the other. Finally, the outcomes of the two instructional methods might occur once but have little likelihood of recurring. Either might simply be an unstable outcome due to chance.

How is a researcher to deal with these potential pitfalls? Let us dig the holes a bit deeper with another example before trying to fill them.

A graduate student is interested in exploring the similarities and differences between teachers and inner-city students in matters of motivation and values. She plans to collect data from two groups—150 inner-city students and 150 teachers—all of whom are attending a university summer institute. Findings will consist of verbatim reports of the subjects' responses to open-ended questions supplemented by attempts to detect any generalities or trends without any system for data analysis.

Needless to say, the representativeness of the two samples is in serious doubt. Students and teachers who have the motivation to attend a summer program at a university probably differ in their perceptions and values from those who do not attend such programs. The plan to draw conclusions based on visual inspection of some 300 responses suffers from its own flaws. Aside from the obvious difficulty and tediousness of such an approach, it creates a strong likelihood that the conclusions would reflect the initial biases of the researcher; she may tend to see exactly what she is looking for in the data.

One final example at this point may be helpful. A faculty group is interested in assessing the effectiveness of a new teacher-education program for college seniors. The group is specifically interested in how much students in the program identify with the teaching profession. The students are asked to complete a questionnaire dealing with occupational identification during their junior year (prior to beginning the program) and again at the end of their senior year (after completing the program). Unfortunately, the outcome is as likely to be a function of the students' maturing over the intervening year as it is a function of the program.

Another university with a desire to evaluate a similar new program was fortunate in having two campuses. Because only one campus was to implement the new program, an experiment compared the identification of the students in that program with the identification of the students in the old program at the end of their senior year. Sadly, however, it is impossible to be sure that the research began with similar groups, because the students on the two campuses were known to differ in many ways.

In the real world—as opposed to the laboratory—educational researchers are confronted by such situations as those described in these examples. Because they often lack opportunities to control what is to happen and to whom it is to happen, they often proceed as did the researchers in the examples. It is the contention in this book, however, that the research process, when properly understood, provides a basis for dealing with such situations in a more adequate and logical way.

INTERNAL AND EXTERNAL VALIDITY

To understand the shortcomings in the above research situations and the advantages of overcoming them, consider two principles: internal validity and external validity.

A study has *internal validity* if its outcome is a function of the program or approach being tested rather than the result of other causes not systematically dealt with in the study. Internal validity affects observers' certainty that the research results can be accepted, based on the design of the study.

A study has *external validity* if the results obtained would apply in the real world to other similar programs and approaches. External validity affects observers' ability to credit the research results with *generality* based on the procedures used.

The process of carrying out an experiment—that is, exercising some control over the environment—contributes to internal validity while producing some limitation in external validity. As the researcher regulates and controls the circumstances of inquiry, as occurs in an experiment, he or she increases the probability that the phenomena under study are producing the outcomes attained (enhancing internal validity). Simultaneously, however, he or she decreases the probability that the conclusions will hold in the absence of the experimental manipulations (reducing external validity). Without procedures to provide some degree of internal validity, one may never know what has caused observed effects to occur. Thus, external validity is of little value without some reasonable degree of internal validity, which gives confidence in a study's conclusions before one attempts to generalize from them.[1]

Consider again the example of the science educator who was designing a new program for fifth graders. For several reasons, his experiment lacked internal validity. To begin with, he should have applied his different teaching techniques to the same material to avoid the pitfall that some material is more easily learned than other material. He might rather have taught both units to one group of students using the lecture approach and both units to another group of students using films. Doing so would help to offset the danger that films might be especially

---

[1] I am not denying the value of naturalistic observations made outside a designed study. However, I am suggesting that from a logical perspective, such observations could not justify the same degree of confidence in one's conclusions as the controlled study. Often, naturalistic observations provide a good source of insight and a basis for generating expectations and theories that can then be tested by experiments.

appropriate tools for a single unit, because this special appropriateness would be less likely to apply to two units than to one. By using two different films and two different lectures, he would also minimize the possibility that the effect was solely a function of the merits of a specific film; it is less likely that *both* films will be outstanding (or poor) than that one will be. In repeating the experiment, the science teacher should be extremely cautious in composing his two groups; if one group contains more bright students than the other, obviously that group's advantage would affect the results. (However, the use of two groups is the best way to ensure that one teaching approach does not benefit from the advantage of being applied last.) The educator should also, of course, ensure that his end-of-unit tests are representative of the learning material; because both groups will get the same tests, however, their relative difficulty ceases to be as important as it was in the original plan.

The second example of research about attitude differences between inner-city students and teachers poses some important problems in external validity. Both the student group and the teacher group are unrepresentative of the universe of teachers and that of inner-city students. Thus, it would be difficult to draw general conclusions from this investigation beyond the specific teachers and students studied. With such a limitation, the study might not be worth undertaking. The study as described also poses some problems with internal validity. Converting subjects' answers into data is an important part of the research process. In effect, the researcher creates a measuring *instrument* to accomplish this conversion. This instrument, like the instruments used in the physical sciences, must possess some consistency. It must generate the same readings when read by different people and when read by the same person at different points in time. If, however, the instrument reflects the researcher's own biases or hypotheses, it may allow her to overlook some relevant occurrences, to the detriment of internal validity.

The final example of a study of identification by college seniors with the teaching profession illustrates a common problem in achieving internal validity: Human beings change over time in the normal course of development and as they acquire experience. If a study involves the passage of time, then the researcher must use a research design that separates changes resulting from normal human development from changes resulting from the special experiences of the experimental treatment. It is tempting indeed for a researcher to take measures at Time 1 and Time 2 and conclude that any change was a function of conditions intentionally introduced during the interim period. If, however, the researcher cannot prove that the change was a result of the treatment tested in the experiment rather than a natural change over time, then the researcher cannot claim to have discovered a change agent.

Evaluating Changes Over Time

When examining data from two points in time, researchers may be misled by overevaluating or underevaluating the effect of an intervening experimental manipulation. The data from Time 1 may itself be the result of unusual circumstances that render it nonrepresentative of the prevailing conditions. Moreover, phenomena other than the manipulation may account for any change that occurs. Data from more than Time 1 and Time 2 should be examined to evaluate any manipulation between them.

This approach is illustrated by a possible but fictitious example study. The research is intended to evaluate the effect of a policy requiring classroom discussions of all violent incidents in Holmes Middle School, based on the number of violent incidents that occurred. Figure 1.1 shows the number of violent incidents at Holmes in the 1986–1987 school year, before the new policy was introduced (Time 1), and in the 1987–1988 school year, after the policy was introduced (Time 2). The results tempt researchers to conclude that the act of introducing the policy requiring class discussion of all violent incidents in the school yielded a spectacular decline in school violence.

Figure 1.2 shows that a simple explanation of data from just two separate years can be misleading: The reduction in school year 1987–1988 was followed by a dramatic and continuing upturn thereafter. Thus, an examination of data from 1985–1986 to 1992–1993 shows that the decline in 1987–1988 might have been a statistical artifact or else a temporary effect of the policy in one school. Moreover, another useful comparison might contrast the trends at Holmes, the one middle school in the district using the new policy, and Westside, a neighboring district's middle school that introduced the same policy a year earlier, with the average of the remaining three middle schools in the district not using the policy. This comparison shows that violent incidents grew faster with the new policy than without it.

FIGURE 1.1   **TRENDS IN VIOLENT INCIDENTS AT HOLMES MIDDLE SCHOOL (FICTITIOUS DATA)**

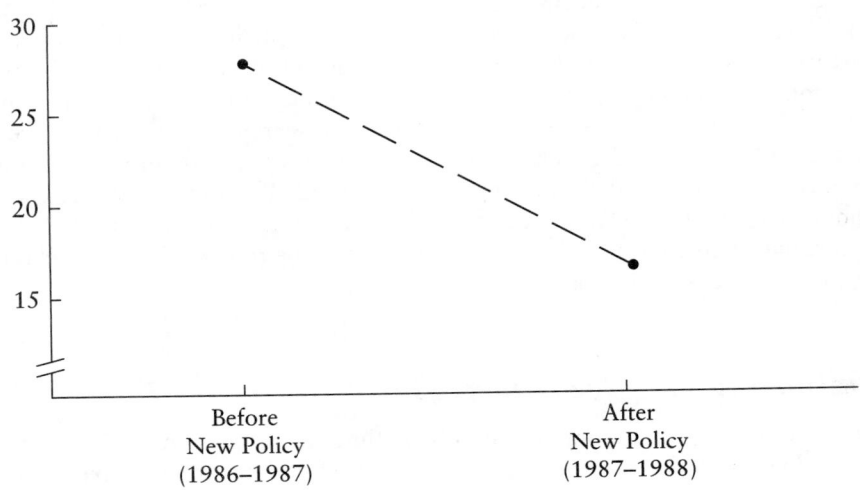

Clearly, one must put time changes in a proper context. Certain changes will normally occur over time, having little to do with conditions one has imposed on the situation. One must distinguish between such ordinary changes over time and those caused by an intervention.

Comparing Groups

A problem common to most experiments is the assignment of experimental participants to groups. Internal validity depends, in part, on the condition that the effect attributed to a treatment is a function of the treatment itself, rather than a

Trends in Violent Incidents at Holmes, Westside, and Other Schools (Fictitious Data)

FIGURE 1.2

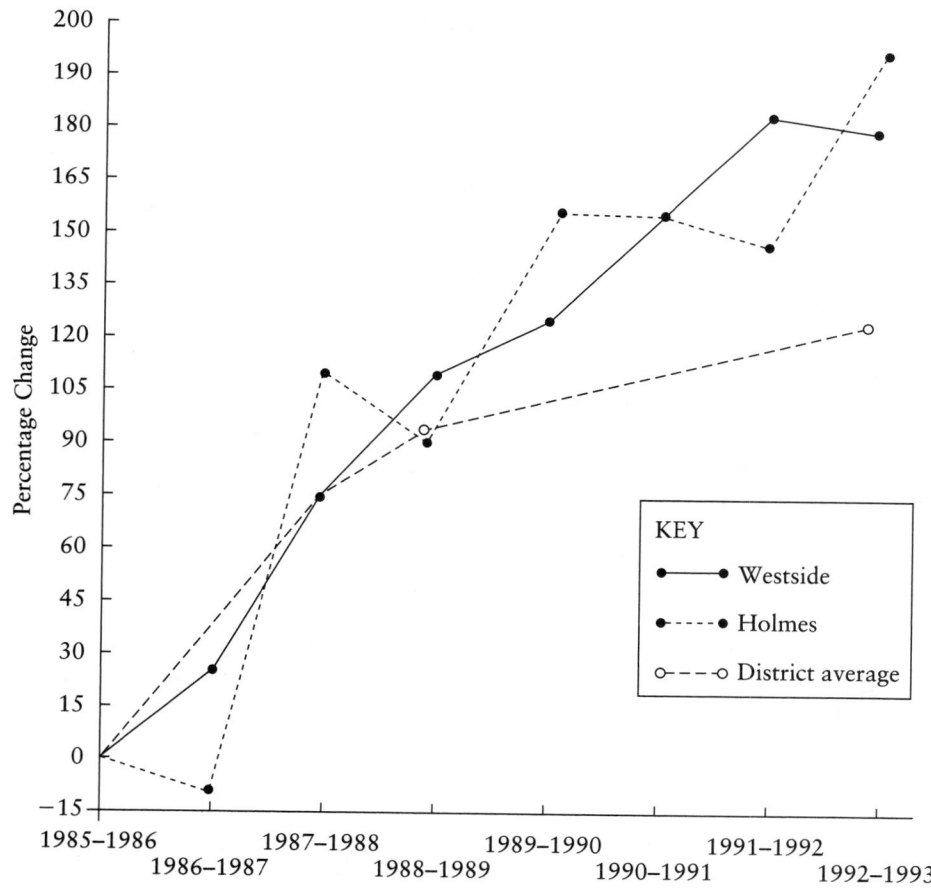

function of some other unmeasured and uncontrolled differences between treated and untreated persons.[2] Validity requires that an equivalent control group must share the same composition as the group receiving the treatment. Before Teacher A can say that a teaching technique works on her students based on a comparison of their performance to that of Teacher B's students, she must take into account the fact that her students may be more intelligent, more motivated, or more something else than B's students. It could be these other factors, alone or in combination, rather than the teaching approach per se that account for the superior performance of A's students.

In setting up a research project, it is necessary to strike a balance between the two sets of validity demands, establishing enough internal validity so that an experiment can be conclusive while remaining sufficiently within reality to yield representative and generalizable results.

DEALING WITH REALITY

The demands of internal validity, or *certainty*, are most easily met by confining research to a laboratory, where the researcher can control or eliminate the irrelevant variables and manipulate the relevant ones. However, elimination of many variables, regardless of their centrality to the problem in question, may limit the external validity, or *generality*, of the findings. Success in the laboratory may not indicate success in the real world, where activities are subject to the influence of real variables that have been shut out of the laboratory. Thus, many research problems require field settings to ensure external validity. The crux of the problem is to operate in the field and still achieve internal validity.

In some situations in the field, however, it is impossible to apply fully the rules of internal validity. Often, for example, any proposed improvements in a school must ethically be made at the same time for the whole school rather than just for certain experimental groups. To evaluate the effects of such changes, the researcher must choose some approach other than the recommended one of applying the change to and withholding it from equivalent groups. To deal with such a situation, the time-series design, illustrated in the violent incidents study, can be used.

An incontrovertible fact remains, however, that research, even that carried out in the field rather than in the laboratory, must impose some artificialities and restrictions on the situation being studied. It is often this aspect that administrators find most objectionable. J. P. Campbell and Dunnette react to such criticism as follows:

---

[2] The term *treatment* is used here to label that technique or approach being tested or evaluated in the study.

There are at least two possible replies to the perceived sterility of controlled systematic research. On the one hand, it is an unfortunate fact of scientific life that the reduction of ambiguity in behavioral data to tolerable levels demands systematic observations, measurement, and control. Often the unwanted result seems to be a dehumanization of the behavior being studied. That is, achieving unambiguous results may generate dependent variables that are somewhat removed from the original objectives of the development program and seem, thereby, to lack relevant content. This is not an unfamiliar problem in psychological research. As always, the constructive solution is to increase the effort and ingenuity devoted to developing criteria that are *both* meaningful and amenable to controlled observation and measurement. (Campbell and Dunnette, 1968, p. 101)

SURVEY RESEARCH

A particular kind of research that frequently appears in the educational milieu is survey research. In a school survey, a procedure common in education, variables frequently are studied using a simple counting procedure, with little or no attempt to determine in a systematic fashion the relationship between those and other relevant variables. Such analysis would require comparison data, and often none are collected.

For instance, a school district is concerned with the kinds of students who enroll in high school vocational education programs. A researcher goes into high school vocational education classes with some form of questionnaire or interview schedule and collects data, compiling them together in frequency counts, and making statements such as "75 percent of the students who go into vocational education also hold down jobs after school." Does this statement indicate that holding down a job after school is a necessary prerequisite and predisposing factor to entrance into vocational education classes? The data do not necessarily justify this conclusion, because this illustrative research study has used an incorrect design. Were the researcher to ask the same questions of a comparable group of high school students who are not enrolled in vocational education classes, the results might reveal that both groups include the same percentage of students who hold after-school jobs. Therefore, although this precondition characterized the vocational students, it might, in fact, be equally true of other students, too, so it could not be considered to be a predisposing factor. The survey gets answers that match the questions asked, but the interpretations of the answers may be misleading without a basis for comparison. By including a control or comparison group of students who have not had the experience being evaluated, the researcher can discover whether the interpretations of data correspond to the real situation.

Another type of research that often suffers from the absence of a designed comparison is the follow-up survey. For example, studies of incomes and projected lifetime earnings of students who attend college suggest considerable economic gains from a college education. However, to properly evaluate the economic benefits of a college education, it would be necessary to *compare* the projected incomes of students who attended college for less than 4 years to the incomes of high school graduates in order to determine whether any advantage accrues to the college student. Because earnings depend in some degree on other factors besides, or in addition to, the program of study taken by students, a researcher should not draw conclusions based on an examination of the graduates of only one program. Such a conclusion requires *comparisons* between students who experience different types of education. The term *comparison* should be stressed, because survey research limited to a single group often leads to invalid conclusions about cause-and-effect relationships.

Perhaps because of its simplicity, survey research abounds in education. A potentially useful technique in education, as it is in public opinion polling and the social sciences, the survey has undeniable value as a means of gathering data. It is recommended, however, that surveys be undertaken within a research design utilizing comparison groups. When properly constructed and when employed within a proper design, questionnaires and interviews may be used to great advantage. This book discusses the survey as a research instrument in Chapter 10.

CHARACTERISTICS OF THE RESEARCH PROCESS

Based on the preceding discussion, it is possible to list a set of properties that characterize the research process, at least in its ideal form.

RESEARCH IS A SYSTEMATIC PROCESS   Because research is a structured process (that is, researchers conform to rules in carrying it out), it follows that it is also a systematic process. The rules include procedural specifications for identifying and defining variables, for designing studies to examine these variables and determine their effects on other variables, and for relating the data thus collected to the originally stated problem and hypothesis. (Other equally systematic processes, such as deduction, can be used for arriving at conclusions, but processes such as "guesstimation" and intuition lack the systematic quality that characterizes research.)

RESEARCH IS A LOGICAL ACTIVITY   Research follows a system that employs logic at many points. By logical examination of the procedures employed in an experiment relative to the requirements of internal validity, the researcher can check the validity of the conclusions drawn. Applying logic, he or she may also check generalizations in the context of external validity. The logic of valid research makes it a valuable tool for decision making, certainly far superior to intuition or using "off-the-top-of-the-head" observations for data.

RESEARCH IS AN EMPIRICAL UNDERTAKING   Research has a reality-referent. Much abstract deduction may precede research, but data are its end result. The collection of data identifies research as an empirical undertaking. To determine the extent to which empirical findings can be generalized beyond the immediate research situation, the researcher must evaluate the external validity of the data. Other processes involved in understanding the world or in making decisions within it may equal research in their logic, but they fail to match its empirical quality.

RESEARCH IS A REDUCTIVE PROCESS   A researcher applies analytic procedures to the data collected to reduce the confusion of particular events and objects by grouping them into more general and understandable conceptual categories. The researcher sacrifices some of the specificity and uniqueness associated with the individual objects or events, but she or he gains power to identify general relationships, a process that requires conceptualization. This process of reduction translates empirical reality to an abstract or conceptual state in an attempt to understand the relationships between events and predict how these relationships might operate in other contexts. Reductionism thus enables research to explain rather than simply describe.

RESEARCH IS A REPLICABLE AND TRANSMITTABLE PROCEDURE
Because it is recorded, generalized, and replicated, research generates results considerably less transitory than those of other problem-solving processes. Thus, individuals other than the researcher may use the results of a study, and one researcher may build upon the results of another. Moreover, the process and procedures are themselves transmittable, enabling others to replicate them and assess their validity. This transmittable property of research is critical to its roles both in extending knowledge and in decision making.

SOME ETHICAL CONSIDERATIONS

The matter of ethics is important for educational researchers. Because the subjects of their studies are the learning and behavior of human beings, often children, research may embarrass, hurt, frighten, impose on, or otherwise negatively affect the lives of the participants. To deal with this problem, the federal government has promulgated a Code of Federal Regulations for the Protection of Human Subjects (U.S. Department of Health and Human Services, 1991). This code sets forth specifications for Institutional Review Boards to review research proposals and ensure that they provide adequate protection for participants under guidelines set forth in the code. These protections are on the following pages.

Of course, one may ask, "Why do research at all if even one person might be compromised?" However, the educational researcher must begin by asserting, and accepting the assertion, that research has the potential to help people improve their lives. Therefore it must remain an integral part of human endeavor. Accepting the assertion that research has value in contributing to knowledge and, ultimately, to human betterment, it is still necessary to ask, "What ethical considerations *must* the researcher take into account in designing experiments that do not interfere with human rights?" The following sections review these considerations and suggest guidelines for dealing with them.

The Right to Informed Consent

First and foremost, a person has the full right not to participate at all in a study. To exercise this right, prospective participants must be informed about the research, and their formal consent to participate must be obtained. As set forth in the federal code, informed consent requires that prospective participants be provided with the following information:

1. An explanation of the purposes of the research, its expected duration, and a description of the procedures, including those that are experimental
2. A description of possible risks or discomforts
3. A description of possible benefits, to the participant or others, resulting from the research
4. A statement about confidentiality of records (See the following sections on The Right to Privacy and The Right to Remain Anonymous.)
5. An explanation of the availability of medical assistance (in studies of more than minimal risk)
6. A statement indicating that participation is voluntary and may be discontinued at any time, and that nonparticipation or discontinuance of participation will not be penalized
7. An indication of whom to contact for more information about the research or in case of research-related harm (either physical or psychological)
8. A statement of the approximate number of subjects who will be participating in the research and how they are being recruited.

A sample informed consent form appears in Figure 1.3.

When prospective research participants are children, the code requires that researchers solicit their assent in instances when they are deemed capable of providing it. In addition, permission must be obtained from a parent or guardian.

A Sample Informed Consent Form

FIGURE 1.3

I voluntarily and of my own free will consent to be a participant in the research project entitled "A Study of the Relationship Between Attribution Beliefs and School Success." This research is being conducted by Luther Mahoney, Ph.D., who is Professor of Education at East State University. I understand that the purpose of the research is to determine whether the beliefs that college students hold about causes for events influence their success in school.

I understand that if I participate in the research, I will be asked questions about my beliefs regarding causes of events, and I have agreed to provide the researcher access to my college grades. My participation will require filling out a questionnaire that will take no more than 20 minutes. In exchange for doing this, and granting access to my school records, I (along with the other 99 students who volunteer) will receive 10 extra credit points on the next Educational Psychology examination.

I understand that there will be no penalty should I choose not to participate in this research, and I may discontinue at any time without penalty. I also have been assured that all my answers and information from my records will be kept entirely confidential and will be identified by a code number. My name will never appear on any research document, and no individual question answers will be reported. Only group findings will be reported.

I understand that this research may help us learn more about how college students may attain greater success in college, and I retain the right to ask and have answered any questions I have about the research. Any questions I have asked have been satisfactorily answered. I also retain the right to receive a summary of the research results after the project has been completed if I so request. These assurances have been provided to me by Dr. Mahoney.

I have read and understand this consent form.

Participant _____   Date _____

The Right to Privacy

All participants in a study enjoy the right to keep from the public certain information about themselves. For example, many people would perceive invasion of privacy in test items in psychological inventories that ask about religious convictions or personal feelings about parents. To safeguard the privacy of the subjects, the researcher should (1) avoid asking unnecessary questions, (2) avoid recording individual item responses if possible, and, most importantly, (3) obtain direct consent for participation from adult subjects and from parents and teachers for participation by children.

The Right to Remain Anonymous

All participants in human research have the right to remain anonymous, that is, the right to insist that their individual identities not be salient features of the research. To ensure anonymity, many researchers employ two approaches. First, they usually want to group data rather than recording individual data; thus scores obtained from individuals in a study are pooled or grouped together and reported as averages. Because an individual's scores cannot be identified, such a reporting process provides each participant with anonymity. Second, wherever possible, subjects are identified by number rather than by name.

Before starting any testing, it is wise to explain to the subjects that they have not been singled out as individuals for study. Rather, they should understand that they have been randomly selected in an attempt to study the population of which they are representatives. This information should reassure them that the researcher has no reason to compromise their right to anonymity.

The Right to Confidentiality

Similar to the concerns over privacy and anonymity is the concern over confidentiality: Who will have access to a study's data? In school studies, students and teachers both may be concerned that others could gain access to research data and use them to make judgments of individual character or performance. Certainly, participants have every right to insist that data collected from them be treated with confidentiality. To guarantee this protection, the researcher should (1) roster all data by number rather than by name, (2) destroy the original test protocols as soon as the study is completed, and, when possible, (3) provide participants with stamped, self-addressed envelopes to return questionnaires directly (rather than turning them in to a teacher or principal).

The Right to Expect Experimenter Responsibility

Finally, every participant in a study has the right to expect that the researcher will display sensitivity to human dignity. Researchers should particularly reassure potential participants that they will not be hurt by their participation. Although some studies, by their very nature, require that their true purposes be camouflaged (or at least not divulged) before their completion, participants have the right to insist that the researcher explain a study to them after it is completed. This is a particularly important protection to overcome any negative effects that might result from participation.

STEPS IN THE RESEARCH PROCESS

The research process described in this book applies the scientific method: Pose a problem to be solved, construct a hypothesis or potential solution to that problem, state the hypothesis in a testable form, and then attempt to verify the hypothesis by means of experimentation and observation. The purpose of this book is to provide the potential researcher with the skills necessary to carry out this research process. This section lists and briefly describes the steps in the research process, which are discussed in detail in subsequent chapters.

IDENTIFYING A PROBLEM   Identifying a problem can be the most difficult step in the research process. One must discover and define for study not only a general problem area but also a specific problem within that area. Chapter 2 presents sample models for helping to identify and define problem areas and problems for potential study.

REVIEWING THE LITERATURE   The steps of selecting variables and constructing hypotheses (discussed below) draw heavily on significant work in the field preceding the proposed study. Chapter 3 describes procedures for identifying and examining relevant prior studies.

CONSTRUCTING A HYPOTHESIS   After identifying a problem, the researcher often employs the logical processes of deduction and induction to formulate an expectation for the outcome of the study. That is, he or she conjectures or hypothesizes about the relationships between the concepts identified in the problem. This process is the topic of Chapter 4.

IDENTIFYING AND LABELING VARIABLES   After formulating a hypothesis, the researcher must identify and label the variables to be studied both in the hypothesis and elsewhere in the write-up of the study. Chapter 5 reviews independent, dependent, moderator, control, and intervening variables.

CONSTRUCTING OPERATIONAL DEFINITIONS   Because research is a series of operations, it is necessary to convert each variable from an abstract or conceptual form to an operational form. *Operationalizing variables* means stating them in observable and measurable terms, making them available for manipulation, control, and examination. After establishing the need for operational definitions, Chapter 6 presents methods for defining variables and discusses the criteria that guide researchers in constructing operational definitions.

MANIPULATING AND CONTROLLING VARIABLES   To study the relationships between variables, a researcher undertakes both manipulation and control. The concepts of internal and external validity, discussed in detail in Chapter 7, are basic to this undertaking.

CONSTRUCTING A RESEARCH DESIGN   A research design specifies operations for testing a hypothesis under a given set of conditions. Chapter 8 describes specific types of true, quasi-experimental, and ex post facto designs. The chapter also diagrams them in the context of internal and external validity.

IDENTIFYING AND CONSTRUCTING DEVICES FOR OBSERVATION AND MEASUREMENT   After operationally defining the variables in a study and choosing a design, a researcher must adopt or construct devices for measuring selected variables. Chapter 9 enumerates types of standardized tests and presents techniques for developing achievement and attitude measures. Basic measurement concepts are also covered.

CONSTRUCTING QUESTIONNAIRES AND INTERVIEW SCHEDULES Many studies in education and allied fields rely on questionnaires and interviews as their main sources of data. Chapter 10 describes techniques for constructing and using these measurement devices.

CARRYING OUT STATISTICAL ANALYSES   A researcher uses measuring devices to collect data to test hypotheses. Once data have been collected, they must be reduced by statistical analysis so that conclusions or generalizations can be drawn from them (that is, so that hypotheses can be tested). Chapter 11 provides computer techniques for conducting six basic statistical tests and a model for selecting a suitable test for a given situation.

WRITING A RESEARCH REPORT   Chapter 12 deals in detail with report writing, providing instruction and examples. Its sections cover the construction of each section of a research proposal and the construction of a final research report, with recommendations on structure and format.[3] Information about the construction of tables and graphs is also presented.

CONDUCTING EVALUATION STUDIES   Although evaluation is not a discrete step in the research process, today's educational researcher must have a clear grasp of the technique. The two types of evaluation, formative and summative evaluation, are described in Chapter 13, with an emphasis on the latter, because this type of evaluation is part of the demonstration process.

CONDUCTING QUALITATIVE RESEARCH   Some research is carried out using observation, interviewing, and analysis of recorded documents as its primary methodologies. The written results of these methodologies become such a study's data. Chapter 14 describes this qualitative or case study approach and how to carry it out.

---

[3] Before continuing this book, the reader might find it useful to read parts of Chapter 12, particularly the procedures for writing the introduction and the method sections of a research proposal.

ANALYZING AND CRITIQUING A RESEARCH STUDY   Since professionals are users or "consumers" of research, they must be able to read and understand articles that appear in journals covering their areas of interest. They must also evaluate the quality of these articles in order to determine how seriously they should take the results. Chapter 15 provides a model for this analysis and critique process along with a detailed example.

SAMPLE STUDIES AND SELF-EVALUATIONS

To provide examples for each of the steps in the research process (Chapters 2 through 12), sample studies have been selected from the published literature and placed in Appendix A of this book. Within each chapter, where appropriate, illustrations drawn from Sample Studies I and II appear in boxes.[4] The reader is encouraged to read the first two sample studies before proceeding with the remainder of this book. (See Box 1 for a brief summary of them.) Familiarity with the sample studies will give more meaning to the illustrations drawn from them. Sample Studies III and IV are used in conjunction with the performance evaluation worksheets and are described below.

This book includes two sets of procedures for self-evaluation, that is, for measuring and improving your learning of its content and for mastering its objectives. The first set includes the Competency Test Exercises that appear at the end of every chapter. Its exercises correspond to the objectives listed at the beginning of the chapter, and answers appear at the end of the book. If you complete these exercises and check your answers, you can monitor your progress through the book.

The second self-evaluation procedure is the Performance Evaluation Worksheets in Appendix B. These 11 worksheets correspond to the steps required to analyze and critique a piece of research, as described in detail in Chapter 15. The worksheets can be applied to any research study in accordance with the instructions for their use that begin Appendix B. For purposes of self-evaluation, these 11 worksheets have been applied to Sample Studies III and IV from Appendix A; the resulting "answers" appear at the end of Appendix D. You can complete the worksheets for Sample Studies III and IV and then check your answers against those given at the end of Appendix D. In this way, you can evaluate your own performance. This is a particularly useful self-evaluative activity to complete after reading Chapter 15.

---

[4] Chapter 15 also presents a "sample" study to illustrate the processes of analyzing and evaluating a research study.

BOX 1

ILLUSTRATIONS FROM THE SAMPLE STUDIES

The chapters that follow will include boxes containing illustrations drawn from Sample Studies I and II of the concepts presented. The reader is encouraged to read these studies in their entirety, as they appear in Appendix A, before proceeding. However, to provide both immediate familiarity and an opportunity to refresh memory prior to reading the chapter boxes, both studies will be summarized here.

Sample Study I is a study of the effect of encouragement on (1) students' performance on a task, and (2) their belief in their ability to perform on the task (called *self-efficacy*). Encouragement or encouraging feedback was represented by positive statements about performance, designed to make half of the 64 class members (chosen at random) feel better about their performance capability. It was given to them on their feedback forms. The research compared the results of this treatment to that of neutral feedback statements given to 32 other students. The task was to write test items on the material being covered as homework in a college course. Writing items was voluntary, but grade bonuses were offered based on the number of items a student wrote relative to the number written by other students. Items were written and feedback given on a weekly basis for 10 weeks. Self-efficacy was measured each week. Measures of procrastination tendency, outcome importance, and outcome expectation were obtained at the start and used as covariates to control for any initial differences between the groups. Recipients of encouraging feedback were found to achieve higher performance and higher self-efficacy than recipients of neutral feedback. Growth in self-efficacy paralleled performance gains, suggesting its role as a mediator between feedback and performance.

Sample Study II is a study of how good and poor readers behave in classrooms, particularly in regard to their engagement in classroom learning activities. The three best and worst readers from each of three regular classrooms at each of six grade levels were observed under natural conditions to determine the following behaviors: (1) seconds to start, (2) materials missing, (3) noise created, (4) out of place movement, (5) unacceptable physical contact or destruction, (6) off-task activity, and (7) volunteering. Across all grade levels, differences between good and poor readers were found only on two measures: (a) poor readers were off task more than good readers, and (b) good readers volunteered more than poor readers.

SUMMARY

1. Basic research is concerned with the relationship between two or more variables. When it results in a product, it may be followed by applied research, also called a *demonstration*.
2. A research study has internal validity or certainty if its outcome is a function of the approach being tested rather than of other causes not systematically controlled for in the research design.
3. A research study has external validity or generality if its results will apply in the real world.
4. In evaluating changes over time, researchers must distinguish between those that have been caused by their intervention and those that occur naturally.
5. To establish certainty, it is important to compare results from treatment and nontreatment groups whose members have been initially assigned to ensure equivalence.
6. To establish generality, it is important to operate a study under conditions that are as real to life as possible.
7. Survey research, although a popular tool, lacks certainty, because it usually fails to incorporate a comparison group into its design.
8. In its ideal form, research is systematic (completed according to a prescribed set of rules), logical, empirical (data-based), reductive or analytical, replicable, and transmittable.
9. Anyone asked to participate in a research study has a right to decline. Anyone willing to participate has a right to privacy, confidentiality, and anonymity. Participants also have a right to expect experimenter responsibility.
10. The research process includes the following steps: (1) identifying a problem, (2) reviewing the literature, (3) constructing a hypothesis, (4) identifying and labeling variables, (5) constructing operational definitions, (6) manipulating and controlling variables, (7) constructing a research design, (8) identifying and constructing devices for observation and measurement, (9) constructing questionnaires and interview schedules, (10) carrying out statistical analyses, and (11) writing a research report. In addition to experimental and ex post facto studies, researchers may conduct evaluation studies and qualitative studies. In addition to conducting research, professionals often need to analyze and evaluate published reports of research.

COMPETENCY TEST EXERCISES

1. Consider the following experiment:
   Research focuses on two first-grade classes in a particular school. One first grade was taught readiness and then sight reading, while the second was

given a pre-primer and then a primer using the phonics method. The second group earned higher scores at the end of the year on the Davis Reading Test.

Below are five statements applicable to this experiment. Some represent threats to internal validity; some represent threats to external validity; some do not represent threats at all. Write *i* next to threats to internal validity, *e* next to threats to external validity, and nothing next to all others.

   a. No attempt to establish group equivalence.
   b. Reading gain due to maturation.
   c. Groups not representative of all first graders.
   d. Teachers of the two classes have different styles.
   e. Combinations of treatments are contrived.

2. Which one of the following definitions best describes internal validity, and which one best describes external validity?
   a. Ensuring that an experiment is reasonably representative of reality.
   b. Ensuring that the results really occurred.
   c. Ensuring that the experimenter followed the rules.
   d. Ensuring that the results were really a function of the experimental treatment.

3. Which of the following statements best describes the relationship between internal and external validity?
   a. If an experiment lacks internal validity, it cannot achieve external validity.
   b. Without external validity in an experiment, it cannot achieve internal validity.
   c. Internal validity and external validity are essentially unrelated.

4. I have just read about an experiment. I cannot apply the results, because I cannot believe that the results are a function of the research treatment. The conclusions do not seem warranted based on the design of the experiment. The experiment lacks _____ (internal, external) validity.

5. Describe (in one sentence) each of the following characteristics of the research process:
   a. Systematic.
   b. Logical.
   c. Empirical.
   d. Reductive.
   e. Transmittable.

6. Some of the following statements represent steps in the research process. Write numbers next to those statements to indicate their places in the sequence of the research process.
   a. Constructing operational definitions.
   b. Carrying out data analysis.

c. Teaching students how to teach.
d. Identifying a problem.
e. Writing a final report.
f. Constructing devices for measurement.
g. Resolving discipline problems.
h. Identifying and labeling variables.
i. Constructing an experimental design.
j. Adjusting individual initiative.
k. Constructing a hypothesis.
l. Reviewing the literature.

7. Describe in one sentence each of the four individual ethical rights of a participant in an experiment.

RECOMMENDED REFERENCES

Sieber, J. E. (1992). *Planning ethically responsible research.* Newbury Park, CA: Sage.

Part 2

LOGICAL STAGES

From Problem-Posing to Predicting

Chapter 2

SELECTING A PROBLEM

Objectives

▶ State a research problem as the relationship between two or more variables.

▶ Select a research problem characterized by both practicality and interest.

▶ Restate a research problem in clear terms.

▶ Evaluate a research problem according to five criteria.

CHARACTERISTICS OF A PROBLEM

Although the task of selecting a research problem is often one of the most difficult steps in the research process, it is unfortunately the one for which the least guidance can be given. Problem selection is not subject to specific, technical rules or requirements like those that govern research design, measurement techniques, and statistics. Fortunately, however, some guidelines can be offered.

A good problem statement displays the following characteristics:

1. It should ask about a relationship between two or more variables.
2. It should be clearly and unambiguously stated.
3. It should be stated in question form (or, alternatively, in the form of an implicit question such as, The purpose of this study was to determine whether . . .).
4. It should be testable by empirical methods; that is, it should be possible to collect data to answer the question(s) asked.
5. It should not represent a moral or ethical position.

Relationship Between Variables

The type of problem addressed in this book examines a relationship between two or more variables. In this kind of problem, the researcher manipulates or measures a minimum of one variable to determine its effect on other variables. In contrast, a purely descriptive study requires the researcher to observe, count, or in some way measure the frequency of a particular variable in a particular setting. For instance, a descriptive study might state a problem as, How many students in School X have IQs in excess of 120? This problem requires only simple recording of observed frequencies of IQ scores higher than 120; it makes no attempt to deal with a relationship between variables. The problem might be worded in a different way, however: Are boys more likely than girls to have IQs in excess of 120? The research would then involve the relationship between the variables gender and IQ score.

For purposes of this book, a problem statement will require specification of at least two variables and their relationship. The examples given in the next subsection illustrate this point.

Stated in Question Form

A research problem is best stated in the form of a question (as distinct from declarative statements of the hypotheses derived from the problem; see Chapter 4). Consider some examples:

- What is the relationship between IQ and achievement?
- Do students learn more from a directive teacher or a nondirective teacher?
- Does any relationship hold between racial background and dropout rate?
- Do more students continue in training programs offering job placement services or in programs not offering those services?
- Can students who have completed pretraining be taught a learning task more quickly than those who have not experienced pretraining?
- Does the repetitious use of prompting in instructional materials impair the effectiveness of those materials?
- Do students who are described unfavorably by their teachers tend to describe themselves more unfavorably than students described favorably by teachers?

Often, a problem is stated in the form of an implicit question:

- The purpose of the study was to discover the relationship between rote learning ability and socioeconomic status.
- The study investigated whether the ability to discriminate among parts of speech increased with chronological age and education level.
- The study examined whether students taught by the phonics method achieved higher reading scores than those taught by the whole language approach.

Empirical Testability

A research problem should be testable by empirical methods—that is, through collecting data. In other words, it should be possible to construct a potential solution to the problem that can be verified by the collection of certain evidence or disconfirmed by the collection of other evidence. The nature of the variables included in a problem statement is a good clue to its testability. An example suggests the kind of problem that wise researchers avoid: Does an extended experience in isolated living improve a person's outlook on life? For such a problem, the variables ("extended experience in isolated living" and "improved outlook on life") are complex and vague, making them difficult to define, measure, and manipulate.

Avoidance of Moral or Ethical Judgments

Questions about ideals or values are often more difficult to study than questions about attitudes or performance. Some examples show problems that would be difficult to test: Should people disguise their feelings? Should children be seen and not heard? Some problems represent moral and ethical issues, such as: Are all philosophies equally inspiring? Should students avoid cheating under all circumstances? These types of questions should be avoided. After completing Chapter 6 on operational definitions, you may feel that you can bring some ethical questions into the range of solvable problems, but in general they are best avoided.

NARROWING THE RANGE OF PROBLEMS

Schemes for Classifying and Selecting a Problem

From the infinite number of potential problems for study, it is wise for researchers to narrow the range of possibilities to problems that correspond to their interests and skills. To accomplish this goal, some scheme for classifying problems provides useful help. Two such schemes are offered in Figures 2.1 and 2.2.

FIGURE 2.1   **A THREE-DIMENSIONAL MODEL FOR PROBLEM CONSIDERATION**

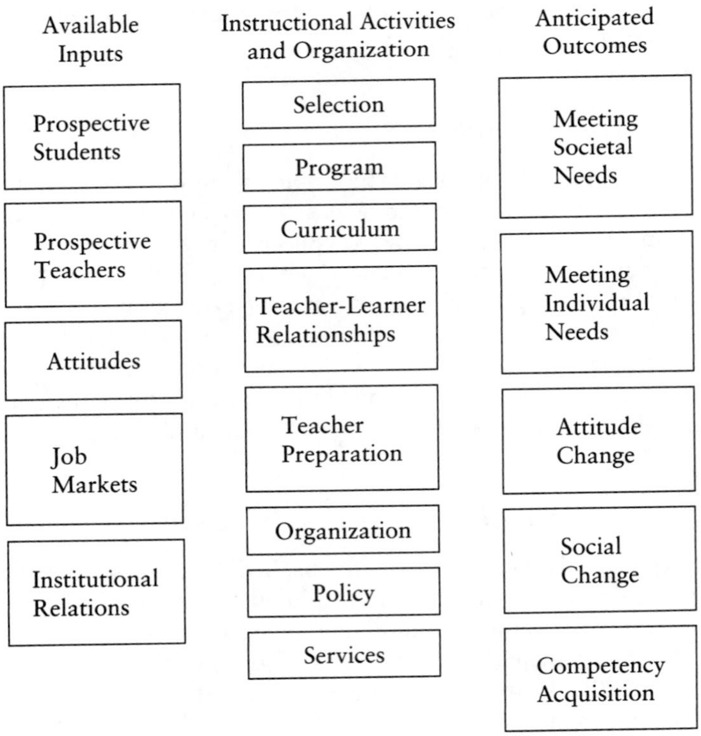

Available Inputs	Instructional Activities and Organization	Anticipated Outcomes
Prospective Students	Selection	Meeting Societal Needs
	Program	
Prospective Teachers	Curriculum	Meeting Individual Needs
	Teacher-Learner Relationships	
Attitudes		
	Teacher Preparation	Attitude Change
Job Markets	Organization	Social Change
	Policy	
Institutional Relations	Services	Competency Acquisition

(These are only basic illustrations; you should feel free to use any other scheme that more clearly fits your frame of reference.)[1]

To use Figure 2.1, identify an area of interest in Column 1 and link it to interests in Columns 2 and 3. However, you need not begin with Column 1 or use all three columns. You may begin in any column and use only two. Thus, if your major interest is career development (possibly a subcategory of meeting individual needs shown in Column 3), you might link it to services (Column 2) and then further refine services to highlight a particular interest of your own, such as group guidance. Thus, you might ask: Is group guidance as effective as individual guidance in facilitating appropriate career choices? Bringing in the first column (prospective students), you might ask: Is group guidance more effective in facilitating appropriate career choices among students with clearly defined goals or among students without clearly defined goals?

Figure 2.2 identifies different sets or classes of variables that may be linked in their effects on outcomes in a school setting. You might look at such teacher-related variables as amount of education, knowledge of subject, or teaching style and relate each variable to outcomes, or you might consider them in conjunction with such student variables as socioeconomic status, intelligence, or prior achievement. If your interest is context variables, you might look at class size, amount of funding, or school climate. If your interest is content variables, you might look at the nature and scope of the curriculum. Choosing instruction variables would mean looking at such aspects as time-on-task, the model of instruction employed by the teacher, or the use or nonuse of computers. Outcomes might cover a wide variety of learner areas, perhaps also dealing with changes in any of the other categories (for example, teacher variables).

AN INQUIRY MODEL PATTERNED AFTER ONE PROPOSED BY CRUIKSHANK (1984)

FIGURE 2.2

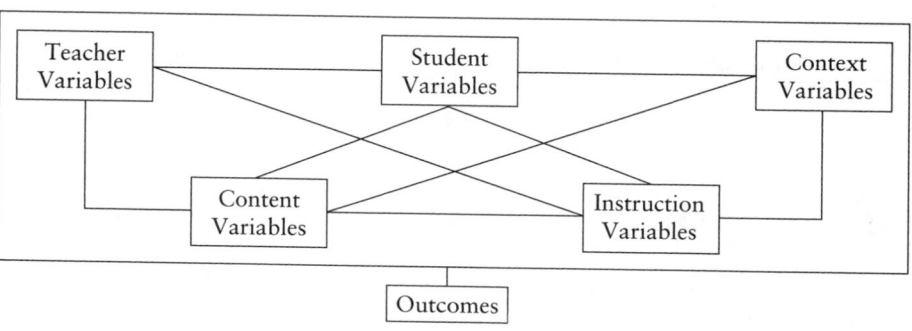

---

[1] A third scheme for classifying problems, one relevant to the activities of the literature search, is shown in the next chapter as Figure 3.4.

On the basis of this model, you could identify a large number of prospective studies and then evaluate each based on the conceptual considerations discussed in the next subsection. Models such as these, or others, may help you to narrow the range of problems you want to consider.

Using Conceptual Models

A conceptual model is more than either a general classification scheme for variables or a proposed set of linkages between classes of variables, like those shown in Figures 2.1 and 2.2. A *conceptual model* is a proposed set of linkages between specific variables, often along a path from input to process to outcome, with the expressed purpose of predicting or accounting for specific outcomes. In other words, it is a complex proposal of all the variables and their interconnections that make a particular outcome, such as learning or liking oneself or delinquent behavior, happen. The example of such a model, appearing in Figure 2.3, is aimed at predicting decisions to drop out of school by nontraditional students.

A conceptual model supplies more than a set of variables to consider for further research. It also provides specific instances of these variables and expectations about relationships between them. From such a model, any number of researchable problems may be identified. From the model shown in Figure 2.3, for example, the following problem statements might be formulated:

- Are students aged 55 and older more likely to drop out of college than students between the ages of 30 and 40?
- Is the relationship between age and dropping-out behavior affected by the student's perception of the utility of the program to his or her future needs?
- Do women over 40 find the return to school more or less stressful than men over 40?
- Do institutions with more extensive adult course offerings encounter lower proportions of adult dropouts than institutions with less extensive offerings?
- Do students who are given training to improve study habits earn higher GPAs than those not given such training?

CLASSROOM RESEARCH PROBLEMS

A considerable amount of educational research, particularly in the study of teaching and learning, involves classroom activities. Much of it focuses on obtaining answers to the general question of whether one instructional method is more effective than another at improving learning or attitudes under a given set of circumstances. Researchers might group various methods, means, or styles of

A CONCEPTUAL MODEL OF NONTRADITIONAL STUDENT ATTRITION

FIGURE 2.3

*From Bean &
Metzner (1985).
Reprinted with
permission of the
authors and
publisher.*

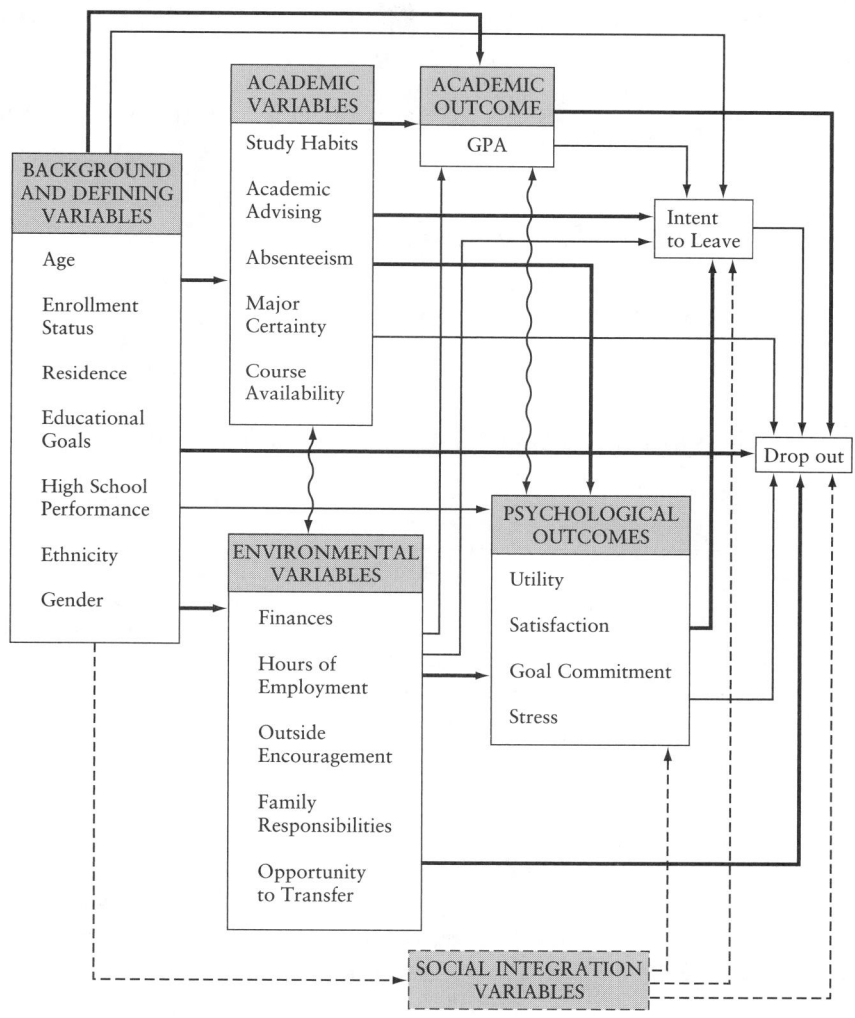

carrying out instruction in a classroom under the term *characteristics of instruction,* and a wide range of these characteristics may be the subject of study. The circumstances under which instruction is given, ranging from student and teacher characteristics to subject matter, can be considered the *components of instruction.* The aspects of student performance on which the effects of instruction might be measured are termed *student outcomes.* Taken together, these three categories for classifying variables can serve as a model for generating researchable problems, as seen in Figure 2.4.

Characteristics of Instruction

A list of sample input variable categories (characteristics of instruction) is shown in Figure 2.4. In classroom research, a major subset of all educational research,

FIGURE 2.4   **Setting Up Variables for Classroom Research**

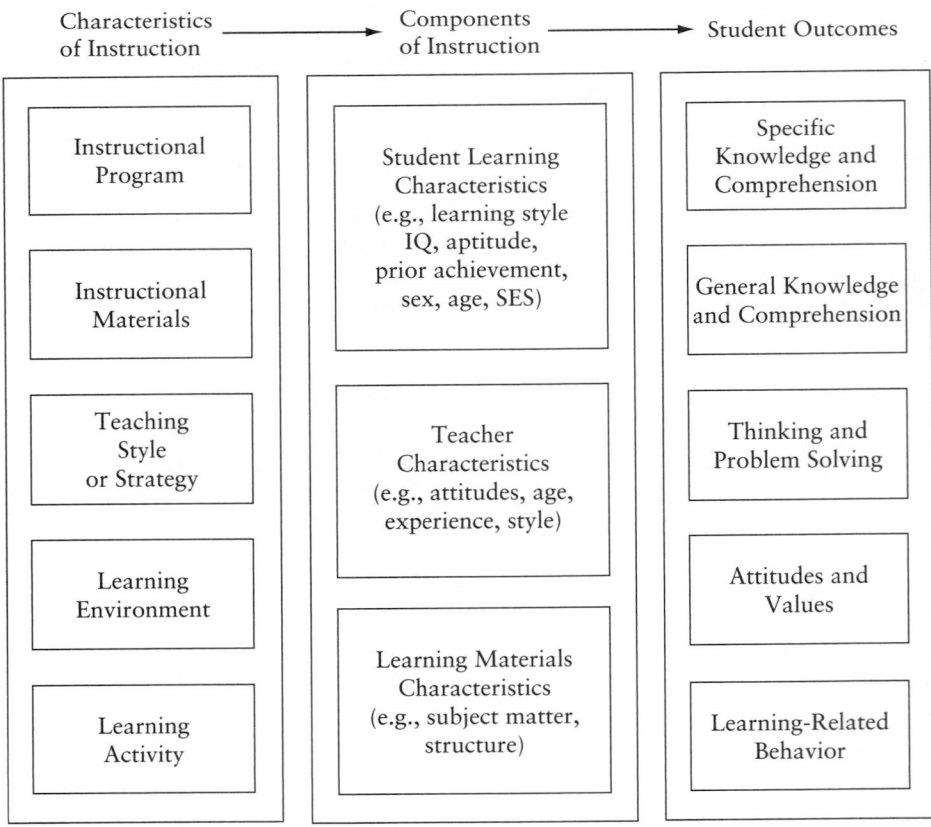

these categories focus on instructional procedures or interventions introduced for purposes of study. Treatment A may take the form of individualized instruction, direct instruction, team teaching, increased time on task, or any of a wide variety of alternatives; often, the interventions represent instructional innovations. Treatment B, by contrast, is usually typical, group-oriented instruction methods within a self-contained, teacher-controlled classroom. Such instructional alternatives are operationalized by accurately and completely describing the essential activities that must be instituted to put them into operation.

By properly operationalizing variables, classroom research can examine an overall instructional program, such as individually guided education (IGE) or individually prescribed instruction (IPI). An *instructional program* is a total approach to instruction, often in a comprehensive, packaged form. It includes variables not only of materials (or a curriculum) but also of equipment and of the philosophy or plan for instructional management embodied in the teacher's guide.

Instructional materials may include the following kinds of resources:

- Published print (textbooks, readers, workbooks)
- Unpublished print (handouts)
- Multimedia resources (films, tapes, TV)
- Technological resources (computer-assisted, programmed)
- Participatory activities (games, simulations)
- Manipulable devices (apparatus, machines)
- Observable elements (displays, exhibits)

Some teachers use *teaching styles* that are student-centered, some rely more on lecturing; some teachers display warm attitudes, some more formal ones; some are task-oriented, others emphasize social-emotional interactions. Important sources of variability in classroom research are (1) the teacher's philosophy or orientation, (2) the manner in which the teacher manages the classroom, and (3) how the teacher behaves toward students. Variables of teaching style and strategy concern the teacher's instructional role; in contrast, the variables of instructional approach focus primarily on formal materials and systems.

Learning environment refers to the way in which the classroom is organized and the ways in which students interact with the sources of instruction. Variables in the learning environment category focus not on the teacher or on materials but on such considerations as the arrangement of the classroom, the use of space and time, and the bases for decision making.

Learning activity refers to discrete and specific learning behaviors. Examples include student question answering, time spent on a particular instructional activity, amount of homework assignments completed, the extent of use of particular instructional materials, student persistence at a task, and engaging in selected art projects.

For example, in a learning activity study of college students, King (1990) compared the results of using a reciprocal peer-questioning procedure to those of a discussion approach for learning material originally presented in lectures. In the reciprocal questioning approach, students developed questions individually and then worked in groups, answering those posed by other students. In the discussion approach, group members simply discussed the lectures. Results showed that reciprocal peer questioning as a learning activity led students to ask more critical questions, give more explanations, and achieve better on tests than students whose learning activity involved participating in discussions. Hence, the research demonstrated that the learning activity of asking peers challenging questions about the content of a lecture can be an important factor in improving student outcomes.

Components of Instruction

The general categories that define the three principal components of an instructional system are student, teacher, and materials (Figure 2.4). The complexity of classroom activity and the fact that students, teachers, and materials may all affect outcomes suggest strongly that researchers should simultaneously study two or possibly all three of these sources. The variable of principal interest becomes the characteristic of instruction, while the secondary and tertiary variables, that is, the components of instruction, allow the researcher to extend the focus of a study from a single cause to multiple potential causes.

Student characteristics that influence the learning process include aptitude, ability, prior achievement, IQ, learning rate, age, gender, personality, learning style, and social class. Some students learn faster than others do. Still others bring more prior experience in the instructional area and greater prior achievement to a learning situation. Either characteristic will affect learning outcomes apart from any qualities of the teacher or instructional materials. Moreover, a concern with individual differences, coupled with a realization of their extent and importance, should compel an examination of at least one individual difference measure in each classroom study.

Teacher characteristics are often included in research studies as variables. These may include such background information on the teacher as years of teaching experience, degrees held, amount of specialized training, and age. An alternative profile might cover teacher attitudes, beliefs, perceptions, or philosophies as measured by a test completed by the teachers themselves. A third category of teacher traits addresses the styles or behaviors that characterize their teaching; that is, the observed behavior of the teachers in contrast to their own self-descriptions. A sample instrument for reporting on a teacher's style as observed by students is the Tuckman Teacher Feedback Form shown later in the book in Figures 9.7 and 9.8.

The kinds of *learning materials* used in a classroom and the subject matter taught may affect instructional outcomes. The same instructional approach may vary in effectiveness for teaching social studies as compared to teaching science, for teaching factual content as compared to teaching conceptual content, for teaching unfamiliar materials as compared to teaching familiar materials, or for teaching materials organized by topic as compared to teaching unorganized material.

Rather than making the overgeneralization that Treatment A is better than Treatment B for teaching anything, classroom researchers must restrict their generalizations to the kinds of materials used in their studies or to particular content or subject matter. To extend these generalizations, they can choose to examine more than one type of learning material.

Student Outcomes

Figure 2.4 lists five categories of student outcomes (which are similar to the categories listed by Gagné, 1985). The proposed categories have two noteworthy features. First, they relate to the ultimate recipient of influence in the classroom—the student. They represent areas in which students may be expected to change or gain as a result of classroom experiences (the input). Second, they represent a more complete set of differentiated outcomes than the single category of outcome that is often the exclusive target of classroom intervention research, namely, subject matter achievement. Hence, the categories reflect a more complete range of possible effects of classroom programs on students.

Specific knowledge and comprehension, the first category of student outcomes, is also the most traditional and most-often measured category. It includes both the facts that the student has acquired and the student's understanding of those facts. Facts often make up the bulk of the subject matter that is transmitted in a classroom experiment, which typically varies alternative programs or approaches. Student acquisition of facts is measured by an achievement test, either a published one or one developed by the teacher.

Such an achievement test reflects the content or objectives of the instruction. If not, Treatment A may be more effective than an alternative but produce lower scores on the test! For this reason, the researcher must ensure that an achievement test leaves no instructional objective unmeasured and contains no item that measures something other than a given instructional objective. (This concept, called *content validity,* is discussed in detail in Chapters 9 and 13.)

Another category of student classroom outcome, *general knowledge and comprehension,* includes such variables as intelligence, general mental or academic ability, and academic or scholastic aptitude. These qualities are more general than subject matter achievement and hence more difficult to alter by means of classroom interventions or treatments (except perhaps in the earliest grades). They represent more stable and enduring qualities than specific achievements, so researchers often treat them as components of instruction rather than as outcomes.

The activities regarded as higher cognitive processes, *thinking and problem solving,* are often goal areas of classroom instruction. Due to difficulties of measurement, however, they are usually neglected as outcome measures in classroom research. Problem solving is the ability of students to identify and describe solutions to problem situations they have not encountered before; the solutions therefore cannot be simply recalled from memory. Such novel problem situations typically call for skills in analysis and synthesis. Researchers studying the kinds of instructional innovation that transfer learning management responsibility from teacher to student should include a problem-solving measure if they can identify one germane to the situation in which it is used—the measure should be of unfamiliar but relevant material.

In classroom research, the area of *attitudes and values* focuses primarily on attitudes toward the instructional approaches under study. This variable may take the form of attitudes toward school if the approaches under study dominate the whole school experience—as they may at the elementary level. At the high school or college level, this variable may take the form of attitudes toward the subject matter, the course, or instructor. (See, for example, Figures 9.4 and 10.5.)

Measures of self-concept are also relevant in some studies of classroom effects. Attitudes toward self are relatively enduring characteristics and hence are harder to affect than are attitudes toward school, particularly by instructional treatments, or instructors.

Many classroom studies overlook the satisfaction (or lack of it) that students derive from an instructional approach. However, student preference is an important ingredient of learning in the long run, and how students feel about the way they are taught is an important outcome in a classroom study. An instructional approach may need to affect student satisfaction before it can generate learning gains. (See, for example, Figure 10.6.)

The final area of student outcomes covers the variety of *learning-related behaviors* that occur in or relate to the classroom. Some of these behaviors can be recorded fairly automatically, such as attendance, tardiness, or disciplinary actions. Other behaviors still allow reasonably objective measurement, although they are less obvious than the first group. These include performance in a simulated situation, time devoted to learning (so-called *time on task)*, number of questions asked, and the like. Finally, other behaviors require highly judgmental interpretations, including evidences of self-discipline, motivation, initiative, responsibility, and cooperation, to name a few. Measurement of these types of behaviors requires the construction of scales or coding systems and the establishment of rater reliability, as described in Chapter 9.

Behavioral outcomes can represent important instructional effects, which instructional designers are hoping to maximize and classroom researchers would do well to study. Although the study of these outcomes may pose some methodological difficulties, these can be overcome through available observational rating and coding procedures and instruments. A study might also use teachers' judgments of student behavior, which are often reported on report cards. In such an evaluation, however, the issue of reliability of judgment mentioned above becomes an important consideration.

ANOTHER PROBLEM FRAMEWORK

Another way to evaluate potential research problems involves the three categories of variables shown in Table 2.1. Situational variables refer to conditions present in the environment, surrounding or defining the task to be performed, and the social background of that performance. Tasks can vary in their familiarity, meaningfulness, difficulty and complexity, and on the training, practice, and feedback that may be provided. They can also be performed alone or in groups, and groups may vary in size, leadership, roles, and norms.

Dispositional variables refer to characteristics of the individuals under study, potentially varying across a wide number of categories, as Table 2.1 shows. Finally, a number of resulting behaviors may be studied as the joint results of the nature of a situation and the disposition or characteristics of the people studied.

Suppose, for example, that you are interested in stress among high school athletes, particularly as they approach the performance of their events. What conditions would you choose to evaluate in the situation that may affect stress levels? In the Situational Variables column of Table 2.1, perhaps *training* would be a good choice. Can you find a training program that seems

ANOTHER PROBLEM FRAMEWORK   TABLE 2.1

SITUATIONAL VARIABLES	DISPOSITIONAL VARIABLES	BEHAVIORS
Task Characteristics		
Familiarity	Intellectual (e.g., intelligence)	Choice of activity
Meaningfulness		Persistence
Difficulty	Emotional (e.g., anxiety)	Performance
Complexity	Personality (e.g., introversion)	Productivity
Importance		Arousal
Training	Interpersonal (e.g., honesty)	Satisfaction
Practice	Artistic (e.g., musicality)	
Feedback		
Social Characteristics	Intrapersonal (e.g., self-confidence)	
Alone	Psychomotor (e.g., coordination)	
With other		
Group size		
Leadership		
Roles		
Norms		

likely to make athletes experience low stress? If so, then you can compare its effect to results without the program. Perhaps you feel that the social condition of training determines stress levels. If so, you can compare training *alone* to training *with others*. Finally, you would want to look at tasks or events with high *importance* for athletes, because those are the ones that seem likely to generate the most stress.

Now you are ready to choose a dispositional variable. Which aspect of an athlete's disposition seems most likely to affect his or her level of stress? From studying the table, the *emotional* category seems most relevant, particularly the athletes' anxiety levels. Remember that dispositional variables refer to relatively stable personal characteristics of individuals, so anxiety as a dispositional variable refers to a person's typical or everyday anxiety level (not how anxious she or he may feel in a particular stressful situation). The choice would suggest a comparison of athletes who are particularly anxious on a regular basis to those who are not.

The last decision is to choose the behavior or behaviors you want to affect. Do you want to apply a treatment intended to make the athletes less anxious before competing? If so, choose *arousal* as the behavior variable to study. You may also want to improve their *performance*, so choose that one, as well. You are not limited to one variable from each column.

Clearly, models constructed to classify variables can be helpful in choosing variables to study. Such models not only suggest numbers of possible variables; they also suggest which variables may be particular sources of influence on others. In other words, they suggest possible connections between variables that make them worth studying.

PROGRAMMATIC RESEARCH AS A SOURCE OF PROBLEMS

Most researchers do not pursue isolated studies; they carry out related studies within larger programs of research, giving rise to the term *programmatic research*. Programmatic research defines an underlying theme or communality, partly conceptual and partly methodological, for component studies. Conceptual communality identifies a common idea or phenomenon that runs through all the studies in the series or research program. Methodological communality defines a similar approach for component studies, often typified by reliance on a single research setting or way of operationalizing variables. Studies built around reinforcement theory, for example, shared this common conceptual framework and the common methodology of the Skinner Box to study the effects of varying reinforcers or schedules of reinforcement on the strength of the bar-pressing response.

Within programmatic research, one can generate individual studies by introducing new situational, dispositional, or behavioral variables or new characteristics of instruction, components of instruction, or student outcomes, to use terms from Table 2.1 and Figure 2.4, respectively. After determining the conceptual base and methodological approach of a study, numerous research problems can be identified. Students undertaking research for the first time can facilitate the process of generating a research problem by identifying an ongoing program of research and "spinning off" a problem that fits within it.

Consider the following example, taken from this author's own work. The original research problem was to determine ways of helping college students to learn from text resources, an important practical problem, since college students are expected to learn much of the content of their courses by reading textbooks. The obvious outcome choice would focus on course achievement, as measured by scores on examinations. A review of the research literature on learning from text revealed three important text-processing strategies, called *coding, elaborating,* and *organizing* (or *outlining*). In the initial study, students were taught to use a combination of all three strategies, termed the *coded elaborative outline,* or CEO (Tuckman, 1993), in contrast to the traditional form of outlining that most students have learned to do. Two studies followed closely from this original one. In the first, students were taught only one of the strategies, and the three, taken singly, were compared (O'Connor, 1995). In the second follow-up study, the CEO method was compared to a method requiring students to construct test items on the chapter topics or write papers about them; also, an additional outcome measure, reading achievement, was added (Sahari, Tuckman, & Fletcher, 1996).

The original research idea also gave rise to another stream of research based on the question of whether or not students already knew how to process text but failed to do so because they lacked motivation. To this end, new research examined the "spotquiz," a seven-item test on each chapter, in contrast to a basic text-processing strategy of identifying key terms, defining them, and creating an example for each (called *TDE).* A comparison of spotquiz and TDE approaches was done, first across all students, and then by distinguishing students at different levels of grade point average (Tuckman, 1996a). A second study, similar to the first, distinguished students who differed in their tendency to procrastinate (Tuckman, 1996b). Another study about to begin will compare results for students given both the spotquizzes and the TDE homework against those for students given only the spotquizzes. This last study should shed more light on the importance of motivation versus text-processing strategy.

All the studies used the most constant possible student population, course, content, and outcome measures. In an effort to test for generalizations, one study compared the spotquiz approach to a homework approach among eighth-grade science students (Tuckman and Trimble, 1997). After each study was completed, questions were raised that gave rise to new studies, thus enabling the research program to expand.

SPECIFIC CONSIDERATIONS IN CHOOSING A PROBLEM

This section lists and discusses some critical criteria to apply to a chosen problem before going ahead with a study of it. Try these questions out on your potential problem statements.

1. *Workability.* Does the contemplated study remain within the limits of your resource and time constraints? Will you have access to the neces-

---

BOX 2

ILLUSTRATIONS FROM THE SAMPLE STUDIES

Sample Study I evaluates the effect of encouragement on college students' self-beliefs in their ability to perform a task and on their actual performance of that task. One group of students received encouragement, while the other got neutral feedback. The study appears in Appendix A and is discussed in each chapter to illustrate the concepts presented there.

The problem statement, on the article's second page, reads as follows:

The purpose of the present study was to see if encouragement or feedback praising the quality of college students' performance on a given educational task would (1) increase their self-efficacy and (2) motivate them to increase the extent to which they performed that task, or their self-regulated performance.

It is clear from this statement that the study is aimed at finding out whether encouragement causes students to gain confidence in themselves and to increase their task performance. This statement does not indicate that the study actually compared results from encouraging feedback to those from neutral feedback, although that point is established elsewhere in the surrounding text.

Analyzed according to the classroom research model in Figure 2.4, this study looked at the effect of two aspects of the *learning environment,* namely encouraging feedback and neutral feedback, among students who differed in initial self-efficacy (another name for self-confidence) and other related *student characteristics,* on their *attitudes* (self-efficacy) and their *learning-related behavior.*

The results of this study should be useful both in theory and in application. It will increase understanding of how students can be motivated to perform, in turn helping teachers to increase the effectiveness of their motivation techniques. This research has the potential size and complex-

sary sample in the numbers required? Can you come up with an answer to the problem? Is the required methodology manageable and understandable to you?

2. *Critical mass.* Is the problem of sufficient magnitude and scope to fulfill the requirement that motivated the study in the first place? Does the study target enough variables? Has it identified enough potential results? Will it give enough to write about?

3. *Interest.* Are you interested in the problem area, specific problem, and potential solution? Does it relate to your background? To your career

---

ity to be a major study; at the same time, it is reasonably workable, particularly since it employed a class of students as part of an ongoing college course.

Sample Study II (which also appears in Appendix A) is a comparison of classroom behaviors exhibited by good and poor readers across the full range of public school grade levels. The behaviors studied relate to the engagement of students in the learning activities of their classrooms. Like Sample Study I, this study is discussed for illustrative purposes throughout this book.

The problem statement that appears in the last sentence of the introductory section reads as follows:

> The present research attempts to provide consistency by investigating a single set of objectively observable behaviors of both good and poor readers in classroom settings from Grades 1 through 11.

This statement clearly indicates that good and poor readers from a wide range of grade levels were compared on a set of behaviors, but it gives no information about what those behaviors were. According to the model in Figure 2.4, the study looked at two of the three dimensions, components of instruction (namely *student learning characteristics*) and student outcomes (namely *learning-related behavior*); it did not address the third dimension, characteristics of instruction.

The study manifested sufficient scope and magnitude for publication, primarily because of the effort required to measure the classroom behaviors. While it has implications for the practice of teaching, suggesting difficulties inherent in keeping poor readers on task, it does not do so in a theoretical context. However, the research article is short, and therefore easy to process and apply for illustrative purposes, as in this chapter.

interests? Does it enthuse you? Will you learn useful skills from pursuing the study? Will others be interested in it?

4. *Theoretical value.* Does the problem fill a gap in the literature? Will others recognize its importance? Will it contribute to advancement in your field? Does it improve upon the state of the art? Will it lead to a publishable report? Does it help explain *why* something happened?

5. *Practical value.* Will the solution to the problem improve educational practice? Are practitioners likely to be interested in the results? Will education be changed by the outcome? Will your own educational practices likely change as a result?

In more general terms, the choice of a research problem depends on practicality and payoff. *Practicality* means that the study is neither too big for your resources and schedule or too small to satisfy the requirements for which you are considering completing it. To make judgments of practicality, it is useful to read other studies that have had to meet the same set of requirements—such as doctoral dissertations, master's theses, or journal articles—to develop a sense of size and practicality. How many research questions are investigated? How many variables are measured? How many subjects participate? How complex is the design? Note the range into which the answers to these questions fall, so that you can develop a sense of the appropriate range for your own purposes.

To make judgments of *payoff* from a proposed study, you must rely primarily on information discovered in a literature review (covered in the next chapter) and on your own experience. Your goal should be to carry out a study that can provide answers to questions with importance in both theory and application. Of all possible research problems, you should seek one that you expect will yield a relationship between the variables of choice; such a study gives more definitive results than come from one that finds no relationship. A no-relationship finding may reflect a weakness in some aspect of the methodology rather than a verifiable outcome.

SUMMARY

1. A research problem should clearly and unambiguously ask a question (implicit or explicit) about the relationship between two or more variables. It should not represent an ethical or moral question, but one that can be tested empirically (that is, by collecting data).

2. Researchers employ schemes for narrowing the range of problems for consideration. Among these tools, certain conceptual models lay out proposed sets of linkages between specific variables. The input-process-output model is one model.

3. Classroom research models typically classify variables as representing (a) characteristics of instruction (such as instructional materials), (b) components of instruction (such as teacher or student characteristics), and (c) student outcomes (such as learning-related behaviors).

4. Another problem framework involves (a) situational variables (such as task or social characteristics), and (b) dispositional variables (such as intelligence or anxiety), as they affect (c) behaviors such as performance or satisfaction.

5. In choosing a problem, pay particular attention to its (1) workability or demands, (2) critical mass or size and complexity, (3) interest to you and others, (4) theoretical value or potential contribution to our understanding of a phenomenon, and (5) practical value or potential contribution to the practice of education.

COMPETENCY TEST EXERCISES

1. Consider the research report *Evaluating Developmental Instruction,* a long abstract of which appears at the end of Chapter 13. What problem would you say this study investigates?

2. Assume that you are a classroom teacher teaching two sections of the same course (choose any course you like at any level). Think about a piece of classroom research that you might be interested in doing with those classes. Consider a study involving an extracurricular activity, such as homework, or an in-class instructional approach, such as individualization. State a problem that you might choose to study with these two classes.

3. Critique each of the research problems in Exercises 1 and 2 in terms of:
   a. Its interest to you
   b. Its practicality as a researchable problem

4. Show how the research problem you stated in Exercise 1 fits into the three-dimensional model in Figure 2.1.

5. Show how the classroom research problem you stated in Exercise 2 fits into the classroom research model in Figure 2.4.

6. Construct a problem statement with at least three variables that fits the inquiry model shown in Figure 2.2. Label the category into which each variable falls.

7. Construct a problem statement with at least three variables that fits the attrition model shown in Figure 2.3. Label the category into which each variable falls.

8. Critique the research problems constructed in Exercises 6 and 7 in terms of their:
   a. Theoretical value
   b. Practical value

RECOMMENDED REFERENCES

Cronbach, L. J., & Snow, R. E. (1981). *Aptitudes and instructional methods* (2nd ed.). New York: Irvington.

Chapter 3

REVIEWING THE LITERATURE

Objectives

▶ Describe purposes and strategies for searching the literature.

▶ Identify literature sources and their characteristics: for example, ERIC, PsycLIT, indexes, abstracts, reviews, and journals.

▶ Describe procedures for conducting a literature search, that is, for locating relevant titles, abstracts, and primary source documents.

▶ Demonstrate the technique of reviewing and abstracting.

▶ Evaluate a literature review.

THE PURPOSE OF THE REVIEW

Research begins with ideas and concepts that are related to one another through hypotheses about their expected relationships. These expectations are then tested by transforming or operationalizing the concepts into procedures for collecting data. Findings based on these data are then interpreted and extended by converting them into new concepts. (This sequence, called the *research spectrum*, is displayed later in the book in Figure 6.1.)

But where do researchers find the original ideas and concepts, and how can they link those elements to form hypotheses? To some extent the ideas come out of the researchers' heads, but to a large extent they come from the collective body of prior work referred to as *the literature* of a field. For example, reference to relevant studies helps to uncover and provide:

- Ideas about variables that have proved important or unimportant in a given field of study.
- Information about work that has already been done and that can be meaningfully extended or applied.
- The status of work in a field, reflecting established conclusions and potential hypotheses.
- Meanings of and relationships between variables chosen for study and hypotheses.
- A basis for establishing the context of a problem.
- A basis for establishing the significance of a problem.

Every serious research project includes a review of relevant literature. Although some may regard this activity as relatively meaningless and treat it lightly, it is in fact a significant and necessary part of the research process.

Discovering Important Variables

It is often difficult to formulate a researchable problem, that is, to select variables to study that are within the scope of a particular set of interests and resources and that will extend the field in meaningful ways. One may be able to specify a general interest area, such as teacher education or science instruction, without forming a clear idea of variables operating within that area that are either amenable to study or of potential importance. An examination of the literature often provides helpful ideas about defining and operationalizing key variables. A literature survey can reveal variables and their relationships that are identified in relevant research as conceptually and practically important.

An examination of the current literature also provides an indication of areas that currently hold the interest of researchers and, presumably therefore, educators. One such list results from an informal examination of the contents over the past few years of an important educational journal that publishes both quantitative and qualitative studies spanning a wide variety of content areas:

- Bilingual education
- Cooperative learning
- Cultural differences/multicultural education
- Educational goals/goal setting
- Grouping for instruction
- Mathematics learning and achievement
- Preschool interventions
- Reading instruction
- Restructuring schools/shared decision making
- School climate
- Self-regulated learning
- Teacher as researcher
- Teacher efficacy
- Teacher preservice training
- Writing instruction

This list reflects an interest in classroom diversity brought on by the growing number of ethnic and language groups in school classrooms and by different educational strategies for dealing with this diversity. It also includes the "three *R*s" which never seem to lose their currency, especially given the growth in diversity. Locating variables of interest in these areas would ensure a degree of currency to one's research work. Reading current journals such as those listed later in the chapter in Figure 3.3 is a good way to keep abreast of interest trends in broad areas of education.

Distinguishing What Has Been Done From What Needs to Be Done

In situations that call for original research, it is necessary to survey past work in order to avoid repeating it. More importantly, past work can and should be viewed as a springboard into subsequent work, the later studies building upon and extending earlier ones. A careful examination of major studies in a field of interest may suggest a number of directions worth pursuing to interpret prior findings, to choose between alternative explanations, or to indicate useful applications. Many studies, for example, conclude with the researchers' suggestions for further research. The mere fact that a study has never been done before does not automatically justify its worth, though. Prior work should suggest and support the value of a study not previously undertaken. This point will be discussed further in Chapter 4.

Synthesizing and Gaining Perspective

A researcher can acquire much valuable insight by summarizing the past work in a field and bringing it up to date. Often, such activity yields useful conclusions about the phenomena in question and suggests how those conclusions may be applied in practice. Many researchers choose to review literature specifically to reduce the enormous and growing body of knowledge to a smaller number of workable conclusions that can then be made available to subsequent researchers and practitioners. The constantly expanding body of knowledge can retain its value if it is collated and synthesized—a process that enables others to see significant overlaps as well as gaps and to give direction to a field.

Determining and Supporting Meanings and Relationships

Variables must be named, defined, and joined into problems and hypotheses. This is a large task, made both more meaningful and more manageable when undertaken in a broader context than a single research situation. That context comes from the literature relevant to a chosen area of study. If every researcher were to start anew, constructing entirely original meanings and definitions of variables and creating his or her own hypothetical links between them, knowledge would become chaotic rather than a summative undertaking. Synthesis and application would become difficult if not impossible to achieve. The mere act of creating all these original thoughts itself subjects one to enormous difficulty, especially for the novice. To do a meaningful study, prior relationships between variables in the chosen area must be explored, examined, and reviewed in order to build both a context and a case for a subsequent investigation with potential merit and applicability. Such a review process will help both in understanding the phenomena in question and in explaining them to a report's readers. It will also be an invaluable asset in suggesting relationships to expect or to seek. It will provide useful definitions, suggest possible hypotheses, and even offer ideas about how to construct and carry out the study itself. It will save much unnecessary invention while providing insight into methods for applying critical inventiveness in building upon and extending past work.

A brief example may be helpful. Sutton (1991) reviewed and synthesized a series of studies on gender differences in computer access and attitudes toward computers from 1984 to 1990. The relationship between gender and access as reflected in 15 studies is shown in Table 3.1.

As the last two columns of the table show, three comparisons had determined that boys had significantly more access than girls to computers in school, and they had significantly more access to computers at home in 10 of the comparisons. This synthesis reflects a clear relationship between student gender and computer access during this period—a balance shifted in favor of boys.

A subsequent figure later in the same article depicted the results of 43 studies (reporting 48 comparisons) relating student gender to attitudes toward technology, using the same format as Table 3.1. Of the 48 comparisons, 26 showed significantly more positive attitudes by boys than by girls. Considering those results together with those in Table 3.1 suggests a possible explanation that attitudes toward new technologies like computers are based on access to them. The

TABLE 3.1

SUMMARY OF RESEARCH ON GENDER DIFFERENCES IN COMPUTER ACCESS IN SCHOOL AND AT HOME

From Sutton (1991). Reprinted with permission of the author and publisher.

				SIGNIFICANCE	
STUDY	LOCATION	TOTAL N	GRADE	SCHOOL ACCESS	HOME ACCESS
Anderson, Welch, & Harris, 1984	U.S.A.	15,000	3rd, 7th, 11th	0	
Becker & Sterling, 1987	U.S.A.	265#	K-6th Middle High school	+ + +	
Martinez & Mead, 1988	U.S.A.	24,000	3rd 7th 11th	+ + +	+ + +
Chen, 1986	California	1,138	High school	0	*
Linn, 1985a	California	51,481	High school	+	
Fetler, 1985	California	7,343 4,800	6th 12th		* *
Miura, 1986	California	400	6th–8th		*
Swadener & Jarrett, 1986	Colorado	259	4th–8th	*	+
Campbell, 1989	Oklahoma and Kansas	1,067	7th–12th		*
Arenz & Lee, 1990	Wisconsin	306	Middle		*
Collis, Kass, & Kieren, 1989	Canada	3,000	11th	*	*
Colbourn & Light, 1987	Britain	56	Middle		*
Culley, 1988	Britain	984	High school		*
Johnson, 1987	Britain	144	High school		+
Levin & Gordon, 1989	Israel	222	8th–10th	*	*

0 No significant difference
+ Data favoring boys, no significance reported
* Significant differences favoring boys
# Sample size is of teachers, not students

results presented in this review have the potential for generating a number of hypotheses for further research.

Establishing the Context of a Problem

The context of a research problem is the frame of reference orienting the reader to the area in which the problem is found and justifying or explaining why the phenomenon is, in fact, a problem. This information appears in the opening statement of any research report, and it may draw upon or refer to prior published or unpublished work. This reference appears, not to justify specific hypotheses, but to identify the general setting from which the problem has been drawn.

Establishing the Significance of a Problem

The statement of a problem should ordinarily be enhanced by a theoretical justification, an applied justification, or both. Researchers usually refer to the justification of a problem as its *significance,* and research articles on the subject may use literature citations in support of the justification. Sometimes prior studies suggest the applicability of research yet to be carried out; this information may help uncover a problem and may support judgments about its significance, as well.

LITERATURE REVIEW SOURCES

The Educational Resources Information Center

The Educational Resources Information Center (ERIC) is a national network of decentralized information centers. It is a major repository of documents on education, primarily unpublished ones, furnishing copies of documents in either microfiche (reduced-size film plates) or paper form at nominal cost. It provides interpretive summaries, bibliographies, and research reviews on selected topics. It also furnishes lists of titles and abstracts (searches) on request, also at a cost. ERIC is currently supported by the U.S. Department of Education. It is composed of clearinghouses in different parts of the country (primarily at universities), that cover the following 16 areas: career education; counseling and personnel services; early childhood education; educational management; education of handicapped and gifted children; higher education; information resources; junior colleges; languages and linguistics; reading and communication skills; rural education and small schools; science, mathematics, and environmental education; social studies/social science education; teacher education; tests, measurement, and evaluation; and urban education.

Most major libraries have access to the entire ERIC file and subscribe to a publication that catalogs newly added documents. This publication, *Resources in Education (RIE),* is published monthly, with cumulative indexes issued semiannually in the middle and at the end of each year. *RIE* identifies all documents identified by ED numbers, listing them in numerical order in the Documents Résumé section. The number listings are accompanied by short abstracts and sets of *descriptors,* key words that identify their essential subject matter to aid searches and retrieval. These descriptors are taken from the *Thesaurus of ERIC Descriptors,* which lists and defines all descriptors used by the system. *RIE* also catalogs each entry into a subject index (by major descriptor), an author index, and an institution index. A sample entry appears in Figure 3.1.

SAMPLE ERIC ENTRY

FIGURE 3.1

ED 331 860   TM 016 383

Tuckman, Bruce W.   Sexton, Thomas L.

Motivating Student Performance: The Influence of Grading Criteria and Assignment Length Limit.

Pub Date—Apr 91

Note—15p.; Paper presented at the Annual Meeting of the American Educational Research Association (Chicago, IL, April 3–7, 1991).

Pub   Type—Reports-Research   (143)— Speeches/Meeting Papers (150)

EDRS Price-MF01/PC01 Plus Postage.

Descriptors—Analysis of Variance, Assignments, *College Students, Comparative Analysis, *Education Majors, *Grading, Higher Education, *Performance Factors, Predictor Variables, Self Efficacy, *Self Motivation, *Student Motivation, Test Items

Identifiers—*Self Regulation

Two studies of influences on self-regulated performance were conducted. The purpose of the first was to determine if the level of performance of college students would be higher if the allowable length of the assignment was greater or smaller. Subjects were 126 education majors at a large state university participating in an extra-credit program called the Voluntary Homework System (VHS) as part of a course in educational psychology. The maximum number of test items prepared for extra credit that could be submitted each week was set at 100 for one group and 25 for a second group. Students gave self reports of their own competence. Analysis of variance indicated that length limit and perceived self-competence level affected performance, with a significantly lower level of performance produced by the 100-item limit. In a second study, 63 students from the same course had a 25-item length limit and were graded according to preset criteria of 300 points for a single bonus and 450 points for a double bonus. Other aspects of the VHS were identical. The grading criteria tended to affect performance differently for the different self-competence levels. Its overall impact was not great, but students low in perceived self-competence tended to receive the greatest motivational boost. Implications for instruction are discussed. Four tables present study data. (SLD)

Each major descriptor in ERIC is identified by an asterisk. For example, the descriptor "*Student Motivation" appears next to last in Figure 3.1. Any document classified by this descriptor might also be cross-referenced by some of the following related descriptors, taken from the thesaurus: Academic Aspiration, Student Attitudes, Student Characteristics, or Student Interests.

You can search the ERIC file by paging through semiannual index issues of *RIE* and looking up entries under a major descriptor that corresponds to your area of interest. Such a search yields a list of titles and ED numbers classified under the major descriptor you have chosen. You can then look up ED numbers in the specified monthly issues of *RIE* and read their document résumés to determine which are most relevant to your needs. Those that seem particularly valuable can be ordered in either microfiche or paper copy from the central supplier using the form at the back of *RIE*, or they can come directly from your library if it has the necessary duplication capability. (In many cases you will find the document résumés in *RIE* sufficient for your purposes.)

Because ERIC is an enormous collection of documents, you may find such manual searching an unwieldy process. For example, a recent issue of *RIE* lists three documents under the heading "Student Motivation" added in only a 1-month period. It is also difficult to do a manual search if you wish to review more than one descriptor at a time, a recommended procedure to maximize the relevance of the documents located to your specific area of interest and to increase the likelihood of stumbling on something good.

More practical than a manual search is a computer search using the resources of the library in which the ERIC file is housed. For a fee, you can obtain a listing of all titles in the file classified according to a given set of descriptors. The list includes a short abstract and a list of descriptors accompanying each title. Adding descriptors within a *simultaneous* search reduces the list of titles and returns more documents relevant to your needs. For a larger fee, the search can include full résumés of each document listed.[1] In some libraries, you can avoid the fee by doing an online search yourself using a computer that has been dedicated to this use or a personal computer equipped with a modem.

The computer search is a highly practical and affordable approach if you are able to provide a number of descriptors that result in combination in a list of reasonable length and relevance. (Single-descriptor lists usually number well into the hundreds of titles.) Less refined searches are time-consuming and may discover many documents of no relevance to the searcher. You may find fewer than half of the documents located under a single descriptor to be useful because of the breadth of the descriptor categories (for example, Teacher Education). Another searching strategy is to use descriptors that are narrow in their scope. For example, the descriptor Self Motivation in Figure 3.1 is cross-referenced with no other descriptors, so it will yield fewer documents than the descriptor Student Motivation.

---

[1] As a financial safeguard, you might prefer to limit your search request to the 100 most recent, relevant documents.

Remember that virtually all documents submitted to an ERIC clearinghouse are classified into the system with little or no screening for quality. However, the vast ERIC file contains documents rarely cataloged elsewhere; thus, the serious researcher cannot disregard its contents.

Abstracts

ERIC may be the principal abstracting service relevant to educational research, but it is not the only one. The Council for Exceptional Children, based in Reston, Virginia, publishes the quarterly *Exceptional Child Education Resources* (formerly *Exceptional Child Education Abstracts),* which includes abstracts of articles in almost 200 journals devoted to exceptional child education.

Fields of specialization related to education also have their own abstract collections. Unlike ERIC, these abstract collections cover published rather than unpublished articles (since journal publication is a conventional route for dissemination of research results in these fields). Listings include reference citations along with abstracts of the articles themselves. Located in the library's reference section, these abstract collections include *Psychological Abstracts* (Washington, DC: American Psychological Association, 1927–), *Sociological Abstracts* (New York: Sociological Abstracts, Inc., 1954–), and *Child Development Abstracts* (Washington, DC: National Research Council of the Society for Research in Child Development, 1927–). In the past, these collections allowed only manual searches, but now computer searches can provide (at a cost) lists of titles and abstracts based on specified subject descriptors.

Other organizations are joining the information dissemination field to meet the rising demand. The Smithsonian Science Information Exchange offers services in the behavioral sciences, including education, allowing customized literature searches of its file (at a cost) based on specified descriptors. It also sells up-to-date research information packages and completed searches (complete with titles and abstracts) on specific topics such as intelligence and intelligence testing, computer-assisted instruction, and environmental education. These prerun searches are less costly than customized ones and give broad and complete coverage of common fields of interest.

A major research source in education is the doctoral dissertation, accounting for an estimated one-third to one-half of all educational research. Because of its size, researchers cannot ignore this important source, which they may access through *Dissertation Abstracts International* (Ann Arbor, MI: University Microfilms, 1938–; University Microfilms is a subsidiary of Xerox). Educational studies are cataloged under Item IIA on the Humanities List, and education dissertations are sorted into 39 subject categories (for example, middle school, social sciences, theory and practice) that replace the descriptors of the other systems. Titles, abstracts, and order numbers are provided. Volumes of these abstracts appear monthly, with cumulative author indexes spanning a year. Computerized searches of dissertation abstracts are provided through DATRIX (the computer retrieval service of University Microfilms) guided by *key words,* which match words appearing in the titles or subject headings of the dissertations. Compounds of these key words allow researchers to limit searches to specific information. Such a search returns a list of dissertation titles and order numbers fitting the key words. Dissertations on the list may then be ordered from University Microfilms.

PsycLIT

PsycLIT is a computerized version of the printed index *Psychological Abstracts.* Its database contains summaries of the world's serial literature in psychology and related disciplines, compiled from the PsycINFO database and copyrighted by the American Psychological Association in 1990. This source covers over 1,300 journals in 27 languages from approximately 50 countries. The files are stored on two discs, one covering 1974 through 1982, and another from 1983 through the current (quarterly) update.

In the database, each reference to an article is called a *record.* Each record is divided into categories of information called *fields.* A typical record includes the following fields (also illustrated in Figure 3.2): (1) article title (TI), (2) author(s)/editor(s) (AU), (3) author affiliation (IN), (4) journal name, date, page (JN), (5) journal code number (IS), (6) language (LA), (7) publication year (PY), (8) abstract (AB), (9) key phrase (KP), (10) descriptors (DE), (11) classification codes (CC), (12) population (PO), (13) age group (AG), (14) update code (UD), (15) *Psychological Abstracts* volume and abstract number (AN), (16) journal code (JC), and (17) record number within the set of records found on the subject.

PsycLIT is available in most university libraries, where students can receive instructions for simple searching (limited to a single word, phrase, or descriptor), advanced searching (further limiting the search to a specific field), and complex searching (using multiple terms or descriptors). Each of the two available discs may be searched, and results may be viewed, printed, or downloaded to a disc. An available thesaurus lists possible descriptors. PsycLIT provides high-speed searching of a vast, potentially relevant literature.

Indexes

A research index lists study titles cataloged according to headings or descriptors, but it does not provide abstracts or any other descriptions of the documents. The *Education Index* (New York: H. W. Wilson Co., 1929–), for example, appears monthly, listing studies under headings (for example, CLASSROOM MANAGEMENT), subheadings (for example, Research), and occasionally sub-subheadings, titles, and references. This source covers all articles in approximately 200 educational journals and magazines. A search of the May 1989 issue combining the example headings above discovers the following entry:

SAMPLE RECORD FROM PsycLIT

FIGURE 3.2

17.

2 of 10

1. TI: The benefits of in-class bibliographic instruction.
2. AU: Baxter,-Pam-M.
3. IN: Purdue U, Psychological Sciences Library, West Lafayette
4. JN: Teaching-of-Psychology; 1986 Feb Vol 13(I) 40–41
5. IS: 00986283
6. LA: English
7. PY: 1986
8. AB: Discusses students' needs for knowledge of reference tools and the utility of bibliographic instruction by librarians in the psychology classroom. Advantages of such instruction include (1) introduction of basic reference tools, (2) maximization of general skills by presenting a logical process of topic definition, and (3) introduction of the librarian as an intermediary/interpreter. (PsycLIT Database Copyright 1987 American Psychological Assn. all rights reserved)
9. KP: need for reference & bibliographic instruction by librarians; college students in psychology classes
10. DE: COLLEGE-STUDENTS; PSYCHOLOGY-EDUCATION; SCHOOL-LIBRARIES; INFORMATION-SEEKING; SCIENTIFIC-COMMUNICATION; EXPERIMENTATION-; ADULTHOOD-
11. CC: 3530; 35
12. PO: Human
13. AG: Adult
14. UD: 8707
15. AN: 74-20100
16. JC: 1921

Discipline [assertive discipline; symposium] bibl *Educ Leadership* 46:72–75+ Mr '89

This citation indicates an article and bibliography on pages 72–75, with continuation on later pages, of the March 1989 issue (Volume 46) of the magazine *Educational Leadership*. Major categories are likely to contain lengthy lists of titles. In June of each year a cumulated volume appears, indexing all entries covering the 12 months from the preceding July. In both monthly and yearly volumes, entries are indexed both by subject and by author.

A useful monthly index is the *Current Index to Journals in Education* (Phoenix, AZ: The Oryx Press, 1969–). Set up in a manner parallel to *RIE* (including descriptors and one-sentence abstracts), this source indexes the contents of almost 800 journals and magazines devoted to education and related fields from all over the world. By using the *Thesaurus of ERIC Descriptors,* this index allows coordinated literature searching of published and unpublished sources. Volumes of *CIJE* appear monthly with cumulated volumes appearing semiannually in June and December.

A useful index for tracing the influence or for following the work of a given author is the *Social Sciences Citation Index* (Philadelphia: Institute for Scientific Information, 1973–). This index lists published documents that reference or cite a given work by a given author. If you find an important study in your area of interest that was completed a few years before, you may want to see if any follow-up work has been done by the same or other authors. You can do this by looking up the important study (by its author's name) in the *Citation Index,* where you will discover titles of later documents that have referred to it. You can then track down these more recent articles. This index is the only resource for tracking connections between articles forward in time.

Finally, Xerox's *Comprehensive Dissertation Index* lists dissertation titles indexed by title and coordinated with *Dissertation Abstracts International* and DATRIX.

Reviews

Reviews are articles that report on and synthesize work done by researchers in an area of interest over a period of time. Reviewers locate articles relevant to their topics; organize them by content; describe, compare, and often critique their findings; and offer conclusions and generalizations. Of course, such a review includes full references of all articles on which it reports.

The principal review journal in education is the quarterly *Review of Educational Research* (Washington, DC: American Educational Research Association, 1931–). This journal presents comprehensive reviews of a wide variety of educational topics, with an emphasis on synthesis and updating. As an example of its coverage, a recent issue contains the following titles:

- Questioning in classrooms: A sociolinguistic perspective
- Learning with media
- The instructional effect of feedback in test-like events
- Research on reading comprehension instruction

The article on gender and computer access discussed on pages 50–51 came from this review journal.

Review articles are excellent sources for researchers who wish to locate the bulk of work in an area of interest without having to search it out themselves. Many disciplines related to education have their own review journals (for example, the *Psychological Bulletin;* Washington, DC: American Psychological Association, 1904–).

Review articles are found not only in review journals but also in handbooks, yearbooks, and encyclopedias. The best-known of these resources for education and cognate fields are:

- *Annual Review of Psychology* (Palo Alto, CA: Annual Reviews, Inc., 1950–)
- *Current Research in Elementary School Science* and *Current Research in Elementary School Mathematics* (New York: Macmillan, 1971–)
- *Encyclopedia of Education* (New York: Macmillan and Free Press, 1971)
- *Encyclopedia of Educational Evaluation* (San Francisco: Jossey-Bass, 1973–)
- *Encyclopedia of Educational Research* (London: Macmillan, 1941–)
- *Handbook of Academic Evaluation* (San Francisco: Jossey-Bass, 1976)
- *Handbook of Research on Teaching* (Chicago: Rand McNally, 1973–)
- *Handbook on Formative and Summative Evaluation of Student Learning* (New York: McGraw-Hill, 1971)
- *Mental Measurements Yearbook* (Lincoln, NE: University of Nebraska Press, 1938–)
- *Report of the International Clearinghouse on Science and Mathematics Curricular Developments* (College Park, MD: University of Maryland, 1962–)
- *Review of Educational Research* (Washington, DC: American Educational Research Association, 1931–)
- *Review of Research in Education* (Itasca, IL: F. E. Peacock Publishers, 1973–)
- *Yearbook of the National Society for the Study of Education* (Chicago: University of Chicago Press, 1902–)

Journals and Books

Journals and books are primary sources in educational research. They contain the original work, or "raw materials," for secondary sources like reviews. Ultimately, researchers should consult the primary sources to which abstracts and reviews have led them. Also, these primary sources themselves contain literature reviews (although often short ones) in which researchers will find useful input for their own planned work. Moreover, as educational research proliferates, increasing numbers of books attempt to review, synthesize, and suggest applications of the work in an area.

One distinction separates research journals from other types of journals or magazines. A *research journal* publishes reports of original research studies, including detailed statements of methodology and results. These journals are *refereed;* that is, prior to publication, articles are reviewed and critiqued by other researchers in the area, whose judgments guide decisions about inclusion and exclusion (or improvement) of submissions. Because they maintain such high standards, these journals usually reject at least half of the manuscripts they receive. Nonrefereed journals usually contain discursive articles with occasional reviews or primary research articles included, but these reports may be written in a less technical manner than research journal articles to meet the needs of their readers. Researchers interested in technical accounts and actual research results should consult research journals for information about studies that interest them. A partial list of research journals in educational areas appears in Figure 3.3.

FIGURE 3.3 WIDELY REFERENCED RESEARCH JOURNALS IN EDUCATIONAL AREAS

- *Anthropology and Education Quarterly* (Washington, D.C.: American Anthropology Association, 1977–)
- *American Educational Research Journal* (Washington, D.C.: American Educational Research Association, 1964–)
- *Educational Administration Quarterly* (Columbus, Ohio: University Counsel for Educational Administration, 1965–)
- *The Elementary School Journal* (Chicago: University of Chicago Press, 1900–)
- *Journal of Counseling Psychology* (Washington, D.C.: American Psychological Association, 1954–)
- *Journal of Educational Psychology* (Washington, D.C.: American Psychological Association, 1910–)
- *Journal of Educational Research* (Washington, D.C.: HELDREF Publications, 1920–)
- *Journal of Experimental Education* (Washington, D.C.: HELDREF Publications, 1932–)
- *Journal of Reading Behavior* (Bloomington, Ind.: National Reading Conference, 1969–)
- *Journal of Research in Science Teaching* (New York: Wiley, 1964–)
- *Psychology in the Schools* (Brandon, Vt.: Clinical Psychology Publishing Co., 1964–)
- *Reading Research Quarterly* (Newark, Del.: International Reading Association, 1965–)
- *Research in the Teaching of English* (Urbana, Ill.: National Council of Teachers of English, 1967–)
- *Science Education* (New York: Wiley, 1916–)
- *Sociology of Education* (Albany, N.Y.: American Sociological Association, 1927–)

The Internet

The Internet is a global network linking together thousands of computer networks that share a common language and procedures so they can communicate. Users obtain information over the Internet by accessing servers through a client computer. A part of the Internet that enables clients to access graphically oriented information is the World Wide Web (WWW). The Web is made up of Web sites that provide information from individual sources.

To gain access to the Web, a user needs a particular kind of software called a *browser.* The most popular browser is a program called *Netscape Navigator.* Using the browser, a client computer can access a Web site much as a person would locate a book in a library. Every Web site has a unique address, just as books in a library have unique numbers. The address enables the client to gain access to the specific Web site.

Some Web sites offer access to research literature in specific areas of interest, functioning like ERIC does for the wide area of research in education. For example, titles of articles and abstracts that cover adolescent health and pregnancy prevention can be accessed at a Web site provided by Sociometrics Corporation at the address http://www.socio.com. This site also includes information on aging, drug abuse, and AIDS.

Information about research grants can also be obtained from Web sites. For example, information on grants in science education from the National Science Foundation can be found at http://www.nsf.gov. All government organizations' Web site addresses end with the designation or domain name ".gov" while addresses for all educational institutions end with ".edu" and those for commercial organizations end with ".com."

CONDUCTING A LITERATURE SEARCH

The process for a literature search involves (1) choosing interest areas and descriptors, (2) searching for relevant titles and abstracts, and (3) locating important primary source documents.

Choosing Interest Areas and Descriptors

A successful literature search requires a direction and a focus. As a search becomes more general, its outcome usually becomes less useful. Therefore, an important first step is to identify an interest area and the descriptors within it. Interest areas are themselves fairly general when considered individually, but they become more specific when you combine two or more. If interest and subinterest areas are stated as descriptors (from within the *Thesaurus of ERIC Descriptors*), their simultaneous consideration will narrow the focus of the literature search.

The matrix of interest areas shown in Figure 3.4 illustrates one simple way of considering at least two interest areas at once.

For example, consider a researcher studying incentives for changing the instructional behavior of elementary school teachers as a function of their personalities. A search of the ERIC system on the Elementary School descriptor by itself would locate titles numbering in the thousands; such a general search would be a waste of time and money. Instead, a researcher could request a search of all articles that simultaneously contained the descriptor Elementary School (or Elementary School Teachers) plus various combinations of the following descriptors: Behavior Change, Changing Attitudes, Change Strategies, Change Agents, Intervention, Incentive Systems, Locus of Control, Credibility, Beliefs, Personality, Reinforcement, and Diffusion. The resulting search yielded 69 titles, most of which were highly relevant to the study under consideration.

FIGURE 3.4   A MATRIX OF POSSIBLE INTEREST AREAS DEFINED BY THE INTERSECTION OF TWO SETS OF DESCRIPTORS

	1. Elementary Education	2. Secondary Education	3. Higher Education	4. Vocational and Technical Education	5. Special Education	6. Bilingual Education	7. Early Childhood Education	8. Reading, Language, English	9. Mathematics and Science	10. Social Studies/ Social Science	11. Arts and Music	12. Physical Education	13. Adult Education	14. International Education	15. General
1. Philosophy															
2. Administration															
3. Teaching and Learning															
4. Instructional Approaches															
5. Student Personnel Services															
6. Climate and Context															
7. Measurement and Evaluation															
8. Development and Socialization															
9. Teacher Education															
10. Finance and Facilities															

The key is the choice of descriptors—in various combinations. Begin with interest areas, such as those shown in Figure 3.4, and then consider two major sources of descriptors: relevant concepts (for example, Reinforcement, Behavior Change) and variables (for example, Personality, Locus of Control). Generate as many relevant descriptors as possible. Be sure to consider the potential variables of your study as a basis for selecting descriptors.

Consider another example where the use of multiple descriptors greatly narrows the range of articles located, making for more useful and manageable search results. Suppose you were interested in a topic in health education such as using counseling as a means of reducing students' school-related stress. If you were to do a search of titles using one of the three relevant descriptors: (1) Stress, (2) Counseling or (3) Health, you would obtain a list represented by one of the three circles below.

If, however, you were to combine two of the descriptors, such as (1) Stress plus (2) Counseling, the search result would be much smaller and more on target, reflected by the shaded area where the two circles below overlap. Using all three descriptors at once would yield an even smaller and even more relevant set of articles, as reflected by the overlapping part of the three circles below.

Searching for Relevant Titles and Abstracts

A good search should include three major categories of documents: (1) published articles, (2) unpublished articles, and (3) dissertations.[2] An ERIC search is a must, because it provides access not only to the ERIC file of unpublished documents (which are identified by ED numbers) but also to journal articles (that is, published papers) cataloged in the *Current Index to Journals in Education* (CIJE; identified by EJ numbers). For example, the 69 titles discovered in the search on teacher change and personality included 13 articles and 56 unpublished documents. Although the journal article titles can be located via a manual search using the *Educational Index, Psychological Abstracts, Sociological Abstracts,* and so forth, or by

---

[2] Another useful source, meta-analysis, is described in the next chapter.

searching through issues of *CIJE*, this slow and tedious process still would not yield unpublished documents, which are largely inaccessible from any source other than ERIC. Hence, the second step in the search after selecting descriptors should be to conduct a computerized search of the ERIC file including *CIJE*.

The next step should be to carry out a dissertation search. After you contact DATRIX and input a set of key words (its counterpart of descriptors), it will generate a list of relevant dissertation titles. Again, remember that the cost of a search is a function of the number of titles located; to minimize this cost, combine descriptors or key words rather than searching for single matches. Specificity increases relevance and reduces cost.

The last step in the general search process is to locate handbooks, yearbooks, and encyclopedias in the reference section of the library and read the relevant sections, taking particular notice of the references provided. The *Review of Educational Research* is a particularly useful source of this kind of reference material on specific topics; starting about 5 years before the current issue, read through the index of all titles to locate any review articles that seem relevant to your subject. Locate these articles and select from them the references most relevant to your area of interest. These references will primarily cite journal articles that previous reviewers have selected for their relevance.

Locating Important Primary Source Documents

Titles and abstracts provide limited information about past work. The ERIC search provides titles and very short (often single-sentence) abstracts. The DATRIX search provides only titles. Review articles provide titles of sources they discuss along with descriptions (also usually of limited length) in their text. Both ERIC and DATRIX provide document identification numbers that can lead you to full abstracts in *RIE* and in *Dissertation Abstracts International*, respectively. However, the only complete description of a resource is to be found in the original (or primary) source document itself.

Expense and time constraints prevent full consideration of all the titles yielded by the various searches. The researcher must be selective, choosing titles that seem most relevant for further examination. Consulting abstracts, where available, will help in identifying the most potentially useful and relevant articles. These articles must then be located or obtained. Unpublished documents identified through the ERIC search can be purchased either in microfiche or on paper from the ERIC Document Reproduction Service; simply fill in the form and follow the procedures described in the back of *RIE*. Often, these documents can also be obtained from a library housing the complete ERIC collection. Microfiche copies are considerably less costly than paper copies, and they may, in fact, be the only ones available from the library.

Dissertations chosen for further examination can be ordered in microfiche or on paper from University Microfilms, Inc., Ann Arbor, Michigan. Paper copies are convenient but costly; thus, one should avoid purchasing a large number of them. Journal articles must be located directly in the journals in which they appeared. Libraries are the major sources of journal collections (although reprints of recent articles can often be obtained by writing directly to their authors). Once a search locates articles, a researcher can photocopy them for convenient access.

Of the three types of documents—journal articles, dissertations, and unpublished reports—journal articles are the most concise and the most technically valuable sources, because they have satisfied the high requirements for journal publication. Dissertations are lengthy documents, but supervision by faculty committees helps to ensure good information. Unpublished reports are usually lengthy and typically are the poorest of the three types in quality—although conversely of the greatest usefulness to the practitioner, in contrast to the researcher (Vockell and Asher, 1974). Hence, journal sources should be examined most closely and completely in the literature review.

Primary documents reveal not only potentially useful methodologies and findings but also additional references to relevant articles. This interconnectedness of significant articles on a topical area enables a researcher to backtrack from one relevant study to others that preceded it. This backtracking process often leads to the richest sources of useful and important work in the area of interest, leading to studies that have been singled out by other researchers for review and inclusion. Hence, one researcher builds a study on his or her previous work as well as on that of other researchers, adding to the research in an area. Finding your way into this collection of interlocking research often delivers the whole collection for your discovery and review. This access is the payoff of the literature review process—enabling you to fit your own work into the context of important past research.

Dissertation searching can also have its payoff. Because a dissertation commonly contains an extensive review of the literature of its subject, locating a relevant dissertation can provide you with a lengthy list of significant titles. These can be tracked down and examined for inclusion in your own review.

Using Primary Documents as Literature Sources

Another viable strategy for searching the literature is to start with a journal article, review article, or dissertation highly relevant to your area of interest and then search out, locate, and read all of the sources in its reference list. In this way, you can find the most relevant ones. Each will include a list of references which can then be located and read, and you can continue following up references in each of the next batch of articles. Cooper (1982) calls this model of tracking backward to locate antecedent studies the *ancestry approach*.

Another approach, mentioned previously, is to locate an important article of interest, and then to locate all of the articles that cite it in their reference lists using the *Social Sciences Citation Index (SSCI)*. Cooper (1982) calls this method the *descendancy approach,* since it focuses on the studies that have "descended" from a major one. For example, when Tuckman and Jensen (1977) were asked to determine the impact of Tuckman's (1965) theory of small-group development on the field, they went to *SSCI* to locate all the subsequent studies that had cited the original article. The researchers then reviewed the findings of those later studies.

REVIEWING AND ABSTRACTING

All primary documents located in a literature search should not necessarily be included in a literature review. Slavin (1986) recommends a process of *best-evidence synthesis,* which chooses only best-evidence articles for inclusion. He identifies best-evidence studies on the basis of the following criteria: (1) germaneness to the issue at hand; (2) minimization of the methodological biases that cause a reduction in internal validity or certainty, as discussed in Chapter 7; (3) maximization of external validity or generality, also discussed in Chapter 7. Literature reviewers should clearly state their criteria for including studies.

After thoroughly reading a document or article and deciding to include it in your literature review, it is useful to prepare your own abstract to summarize the methodology and findings of the study it reports in a way germane to your own needs and interests. Most journal articles are preceded by short abstracts of 100 to 200 words. Although you may incorporate this information into your own abstract, for an important article, it is preferable to prepare a more detailed version.

The abstract should be headed by the full reference exactly as it will appear in your final reference list. (Reference format is described in Chapter 12.) The abstract itself should be divided into the following three sections: (1) purpose and hypotheses, (2) methodology, and (3) findings and conclusions. You will probably not use all of this information in writing your review, but because you do not know what and how much you will need, it is wise to have it all (particularly if you borrow copies of the articles and have to return them). Identify and summarize in a sentence or two the purpose of the study you are reviewing. Then locate the hypotheses or research questions, and record them verbatim if they are not too long. If they are lengthy, summarize them. Underline the names of the variables.

In the second paragraph of your abstract, briefly describe the methodology of the research, including sample characteristics and size, methods for measuring or manipulating the variables, design, and statistics.

The final paragraph should include a brief summary of each finding and a clear, concise statement of the paper's conclusion. Do not trust to memory for recalling important details of the article. Because you will be reviewing many studies, their details will become blurred in your memory. Any information that seems important should be put in the abstract.

Because you will ultimately want to categorize the study when writing up your literature review, it is useful at this time to generate a category system.

Categories usually reflect the variables of the proposed study or the descriptors used in locating the source document. Write this category name at the top of the card, and file it accordingly for easy use. A sample review abstract of a journal article is shown in Figure 3.5.

Writing the Literature Review

The literature review appears as part of the introductory section of a research report. (See Chapter 12 for additional details.) In addition to helping support and justify the researcher's selection of variables and hypotheses, literature citations also help to establish both the context of the problem and its significance.

When writing a literature review, make sure to satisfy several important criteria: (1) Adequacy: Is the review sufficiently thorough? (2) Clarity:

A Sample Review Abstract of a Journal Article   FIGURE 3.5

VARIABLES AFFECTING MOTIVATION

Tuckman, B.W. (1990a). Group versus goal-setting effects on the self-regulated performance of students differing in self-efficacy. *Journal of Experimental Education, 58*, 291–298.

Purpose and Hypotheses. This study compared the effect of (a) underline{working in groups}, to those of (b) setting goals, and to (c) doing neither on the self-regulated or self-motivated performance of students at high, middle, and low levels of self-efficacy (or self-confidence). Students at middle and low levels of self-efficacy were expected to perform more in both group and goal-setting conditions.

Methodology. A self-regulated performance task called Voluntary Homework System or VHS offered 126 college students the opportunity to write different types of test items for extra credit bonuses in an educational psychology course, the amounts of the rewards depending on the magnitudes of their performance relative to that of their classmates. Top-third performers got double bonuses, middle-third single bonuses, and low-third no bonuses. Self-efficacy was measured at the start of the 4-week performance period.

Findings and Conclusions. Although no performance differences were found among the three conditions overall, the data revealed a strong interaction between performance condition and individual level of self-efficacy. The group condition showed the greatest enhancement of middle self-efficacy level students relative to the other conditions, whereas goal-setting had its greatest effect on the performance of low self-efficacy students relative to the other conditions. Neither condition affected the performance of high self-efficacy students. It was concluded that students' self-beliefs must be taken into account when choosing a condition to function as a performance motivator.

BOX 3

AN ILLUSTRATION FROM SAMPLE STUDY I

This study reports an evaluation of the effect of encouragement on students' self-beliefs in their ability to perform a task and on their subsequent task performance. The introductory section of the article includes 11 paragraphs. The first three establish the context of the study by introducing its three major variables: self-regulated performance, self-efficacy, and encouragement. The first paragraph establishes that self-regulated performance is a reflection of motivation rather than learning. The second paragraph indicates that self-regulated performance, particularly when it is successful, is influenced by, and in turn influences, self-efficacy. The third paragraph argues that success is communicated in the form of the response to the performance.

The fourth, seventh, and eighth paragraphs review literature relative to the point that feedback affects performance, while the sixth and ninth paragraphs establish the distinction between pure informational feedback and feedback that encourages or gives credit for good performance. (The fifth paragraph is the problem statement.)

The literature review in this study is relatively small, even for a journal article constrained by space limitations. Ordinarily, more literature would be cited, particularly in regard to feedback.

Are the important points clearly made? (3) Empirical orientation: Are actual findings cited rather than just opinions? (4) Recency: Are the citations up to date? (5) Relevance: Do the citations bear on the variables and hypotheses? (6) Organization: Is the presentation of the literature review well-organized with a clear introduction, subheadings, and summaries? (7) Convincing argument: Does the literature help in making a case for the proposed study?

IN CONCLUSION

The literature search should be a systematic review aimed at both relevance and completeness. An effort should be made not to overlook any material that might be important to the purpose of the review. Fortuitous findings are likely, but on the whole systematic planning yields better results than luck does. The process begins with the smallest traces of past work—titles—and then expands to more detailed abstracts and then to the complete articles and documents themselves. Finally, these complete sources are reduced to relevant review abstracts that you yourself

THE LITERATURE REVIEW PROCESS IN SCHEMATIC   <u>FIGURE 3.6</u>

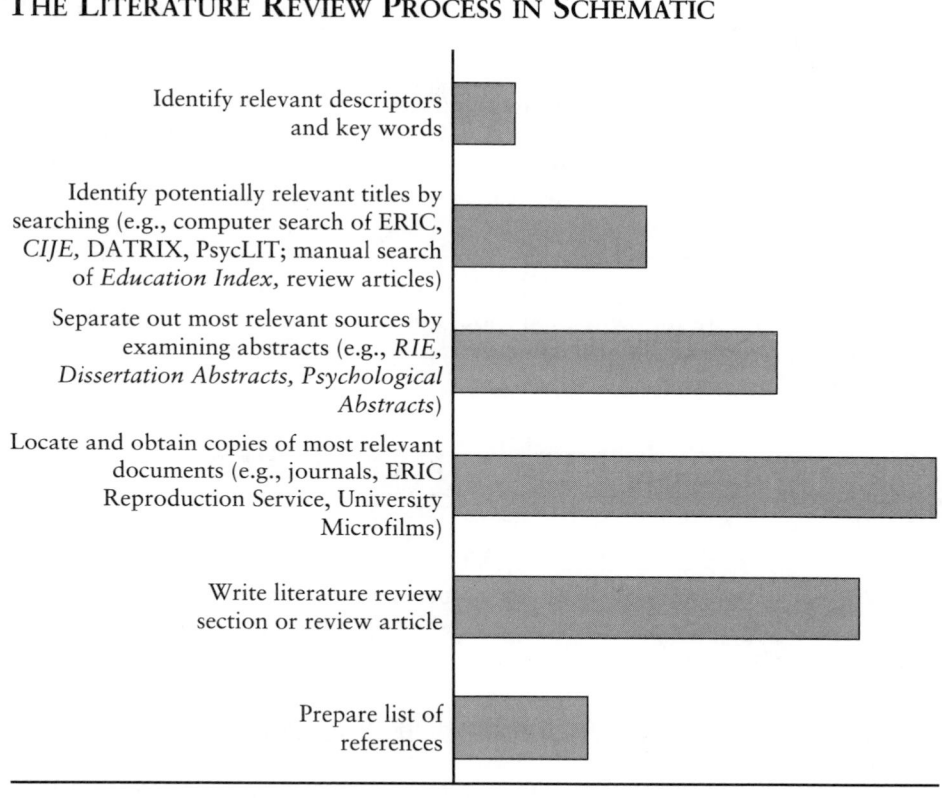

Identify relevant descriptors and key words

Identify potentially relevant titles by searching (e.g., computer search of ERIC, *CIJE*, DATRIX, PsycLIT; manual search of *Education Index*, review articles)

Separate out most relevant sources by examining abstracts (e.g., *RIE, Dissertation Abstracts, Psychological Abstracts*)

Locate and obtain copies of most relevant documents (e.g., journals, ERIC Reproduction Service, University Microfilms)

Write literature review section or review article

Prepare list of references

Level of Information or Detail

write in preparation for a review article, if that is your purpose. The final reduction produces a set of references, which appear at the end of your report.

A schematic portraying the entire sequence appears in Figure 3.6. (Procedures for writing the literature review and for preparing the list of references are described in Chapter 12 as part of preparing the proposal or research report.)

SUMMARY

1. The literature review provides ideas about variables of interest based on prior work that has contributed to an understanding of those variables. Prior work contributes to the development of new hypotheses.
2. Literature sources include major computerized collections of abstracts such as ERIC for education, PsycLIT for psychology, and DATRIX for dissertations. Additional sources include indexes such as the *Education Index* and

Citation Index, review journals such as the *Review of Educational Research* and *Annual Review of Psychology,* and original source documents such as journals and books.

3. To conduct a literature search, follow these steps: (1) Choose interest areas and descriptors (that is, variable names or labels that classify studies in literature collections such as ERIC). (2) Search by hand or computer for relevant titles and abstracts. (3) Locate, read, and abstract relevant articles in primary sources.

4. In preparing an abstract of a research article, briefly describe its purpose and hypotheses, methodology, and findings and conclusions.

5. A good literature review section should be sufficient in its coverage of the field, clear, empirical, up to date, relevant to the study's problem, well-organized, and supportive of the study's hypotheses.

COMPETENCY TEST EXERCISES

1. State six purposes for conducting a literature search.

2. Why do you presume a researcher prepares a literature review—separate from any experimental research he or she might be engaged in—like those found in such review journals as the *Review of Educational Research?*

3. Match the literature source on the left with the kind of information it provides on the right.

1. ERIC	a. Lists titles and reference information for journal articles
2. *Resources in Education*	b. Journal index for ERIC
3. PsycLIT	c. Provides full texts of dissertations
4. DATRIX	d. Lists documents that reference given pieces of work
5. CIJE	e. Provides lists of relevant dissertation titles
6. *Education Index*	f. A catalog of ERIC documents
7. *Citation Index*	g. A repository for educational documents
	h. Abstracts of psychological documents

4. a. List three review publications, handbooks, or encyclopedias in education or related fields.
   b. List three research journals in educational areas.

5. Suppose that your area of research interest is the teaching of high school liberal arts subjects and the characteristics of teachers who are effective for this teaching. Describe the procedure you would use for identifying relevant search descriptors, and list five descriptors you might choose.

6. Starting out with the five descriptors listed in Exercise 5, describe (in detail) three searches you would make to locate articles relevant to those descriptors.

7. Starting with the searches described in Exercise 6, describe procedures for obtaining primary source documents.

8. Turn to the end of Chapter 13, and find the long abstract of a study entitled, *Evaluating Developmental Instruction.* Prepare a 100-word abstract of this study.

RECOMMENDED REFERENCES

Ackerman, E. (1995). *Learning to use the Internet.* Wilsonville, OR: Franklin Beedle.

Cooper, H. M. (1989). *Integrating research: A guide for literature reviews* (2nd ed.). Newbury Park, CA: Sage.

Cooper, H. M., & Hedges, L. V. (Eds.). (1994). *The handbook of research synthesis.* New York: Russell Sage Foundation.

4 Chapter

CONSTRUCTING HYPOTHESES

Objectives

▶ Identify specific and general hypotheses and observations,
and describe their differences.

▶ Construct alternative directional hypotheses
from a problem statement.

▶ Determine the appropriateness of a hypothesis
using deduction and induction.

▶ Given operational statements, identify concepts
that can aid in generating hypotheses.

▶ Identify testable hypotheses based on the results of meta-analyses.

▶ Construct a null hypothesis from a hypothesis
given in directional form.

FORMULATING HYPOTHESES

What is a hypothesis?

The next step in the research process after selecting a problem is to state a hypothesis (or hypotheses). A hypothesis, a suggested answer to the selected problem, has the following characteristics:

- It should conjecture about the direction of the relationship between two or more variables.
- It should be stated clearly and unambiguously in the form of a declarative sentence.
- It should be testable; that is, it should allow restatement in an operational form that can then be evaluated based on data. (This subject is addressed in Chapter 6.)

Thus, hypotheses that might have been derived from the problem statements listed on page 29 are:

- IQ and achievement are positively related.
- Directive teachers give more effective instruction than nondirective teachers.
- The dropout rate is higher for black students than for white students.
- Programs offering stipends are more successful at retaining students than are programs that do not offer stipends.
- Speed of learning a task is directly proportional to the amount of pre-training that learners complete.
- Repetitious prompting in a learning process impairs the effectiveness of programmed materials.
- As a teacher's descriptions of a student become increasingly unfavorable, the student's self-description becomes increasingly unfavorable, as well.
- Error rate in a rote learning task is inversely related to socioeconomic status; that is, middle-class youngsters make fewer errors in a rote learning task than lower-class youngsters make.
- The ability to discriminate among parts of speech increases with chronological age and educational level.
- Students taught by the phonics method achieve higher reading scores than those taught by the whole language approach.

Observations Versus Specific and General Hypotheses

Hypotheses are often confused with observations. These terms refer, however, to quite different things. *Observation* refers to *what is*—that is, to what can be seen. Thus, researchers may look around in a school and observe that most of the students are performing above their grade levels.

From that observation, they may then *infer* that the school is located in a middle-class neighborhood. Though the researchers do not *know* that the neighborhood is middle-class (that is, they have no data on income level), they expect that most people living there are of moderate means. By making explicit their expectation that schools of advanced learners are in middle-class neighborhoods, the researchers make a *specific hypothesis* setting forth an anticipated relationship between two variables—academic performance and income level.[1]

To test this specific hypothesis, the researchers could walk around the neighborhood, observe the homes, and ask the residents to reveal their income levels. (They would also need an operational definition of moderate income level to guide this judgment; see Chapter 6.) After making the observations needed to evaluate their specific hypothesis, the researchers might make a *general hypothesis*: Areas containing high concentrations of good learners are characterized by high incidences of moderate incomes. The second hypothesis represents a generalization from the first, and researchers must test it separately by making observations, as they did for the specific hypothesis. Because they could not practically (or even possibly) observe all neighborhoods, the researchers would take a sample of neighborhoods and reach conclusions on a probability basis, that is, on the likelihood that the hypothesis states a true relationship. (Researchers can test a specific hypothesis based on fewer observations than they would need to test a general hypothesis. To allow testing, they reformulate a general hypothesis to construct a more specific one.)

Formally, then, a *hypothesis* is an expectation about events based on generalizations of the assumed relationship between variables. Hypotheses are abstract statements concerned with theories and concepts, whereas the observations used to test hypotheses are specific data based on facts.

Where Do Hypotheses Come From?

Given a problem statement—Are A and B related?—researchers can construct three possible hypotheses:

1. Yes, as A increases so does B.
2. Yes, as A increases, B decreases.
3. No, A and B are unrelated.

Of course, as more variables are simultaneously considered, the number of possible hypotheses dramatically increases. Also, these basic possibilities are limited to simple linear relationships; refinements could conceivably produce more possibilities, perhaps as A increases, B initially increases and then levels off.

---

[1] Chapter 6 introduces the term *prediction* as an alternative for this meaning of a *specific hypothesis*. The two terms have the same meaning.

After deciding that the research problem will focus on the relationship between Variables A and B, the researcher can draw upon two logical processes in developing a hypothesis: deduction and induction.

Deduction proceeds from the general to the specific. In deduction, general expectations about events (based on presumed relationships between variables) give rise to more specific expectations (or anticipated observations). For example, consider two general statements:

1. People spend *less* time on activities they perform well.
2. People spend *more* time on activities they perform well.

From the first statement, the researcher may, for example, deduce the specific hypothesis that people spend less time doing whatever they do well because they achieve efficiency at that activity. From the second general statement, the researcher may instead deduce that people spend more time doing what they do well because they enjoy doing it. The specific hypothesis deduced depends on the more general assumptions or theoretical position from which the researcher begins.

In *induction,* in contrast, the researcher starts with specific observations and combines them to produce a more general statement of a relationship, namely a hypothesis. Many researchers begin by searching the literature for relevant specific findings from which to induce hypotheses (a process considered in detail in Chapter 3). Others run exploratory studies before attempting to induce hypothetical[2] statements about the relationships between the variables in question. One example of induction began with research findings that obese people eat as much immediately after meals as they do some hours after meals, that they eat much less unappealing food than appealing food, and that they eat when they think it's time for dinner even if little time has elapsed since eating last. These observations led a researcher to induce that for obese people, hunger is controlled externally rather than internally, as it is for people of normal weight.

Induction begins with data and observations (empirical events) and proceeds toward hypotheses and theories; deduction begins with theories and general hypotheses and proceeds toward specific hypotheses (or anticipated observations).

Constructing Alternative Hypotheses

From any problem statement, it is generally possible to derive more than one hypothesis. As an example, consider a study based on the problem statement: What is the combined effect of student personality and instructional procedure on the amount of learning achieved? Three possible hypotheses that can be generated from this statement are:

---

[2] The terms *hypothetical, conceptual,* and *theoretical* are used interchangeably to refer to inferred or anticipated events or relationships.

1. More structured instructional procedures will provoke comparably greater achievement among students most comfortable with concrete concepts, while less structured approaches will provoke comparably greater achievement among students most comfortable with abstract concepts.
2. Less structured instructional procedures will provoke comparably greater achievement among students most comfortable with concrete concepts, while more structured approaches will provoke comparably greater achievement among students most comfortable with abstract concepts.
3. More structured and less structured instructional procedures will provoke equal achievement among students most comfortable with abstract concepts and those most comfortable with concrete concepts.

Both induction and deduction are needed to choose among these possibilities. Many theories, both psychological and educational ones, deal with the relationship between student personality and the effectiveness of different teaching techniques. The match-mismatch model described by Tuckman (1992a) suggests that when teaching approaches are consistent with students' personalities, students learn more from the experiences. Because a student most comfortable with concrete learning prefers structure, and one most comfortable with abstract learning prefers ambiguity, the logical *deduction* is that Hypothesis 1 is the most "appropriate" expectation of the three. Moreover, observation tends to confirm a strong relationship between what students like and their personalities. In other words, empirical evidence provides support for the *induction* that Hypothesis 1 is the most appropriate choice.

Consider a study based on a problem to determine the effect of group-contingent rewards in modifying aggressive classroom behaviors. (Group-contingent rewards result from an arrangement that aggressive action by one group member causes rewards to be withheld from all members.) At first glance, these three hypotheses might be offered:

1. Group-contingent rewards will decrease aggressive classroom behaviors.
2. Group-contingent rewards will increase aggressive classroom behaviors.
3. Group-contingent rewards will not affect aggressive classroom behaviors.

Ample evidence from previous laboratory studies suggests that group-contingent rewards effectively reduce aggressive behavior (Hypothesis 1). Induction from the laboratory findings that substantiate a relationship between group-contingent rewards and behavior change, combined with deduction from the assumption that the effects of group-contingent rewards observed in laboratory settings will apply also (though perhaps more subtly) in real classroom settings, leads to the logical conclusion that group-contingent rewards will indeed demonstrably reduce aggressive classroom behaviors.

Consider one further example of a choice among possible hypotheses. A researcher interested in the possible relationship between birth order and achievement motivation asks: Are firstborn children more likely to pursue higher education than later-born children? Three possible hypotheses may result:

1. Firstborns are more likely to pursue higher education than later-born children.
2. Firstborns are less likely to pursue higher education than later-borns.
3. Firstborns and later-borns are equally likely to pursue higher education.

Available data indicate that, in specific studies, firstborn children sought parental approval more than later-borns. Moreover, the researcher has observed specific occasions when educational accomplishment was a source of parental approval: Parents were likely both to approve and to reward the educational attainments of their children. Based on the specific observations that firstborns seek parental approval and that such approval may be gained from educational pursuits, the researcher induces the more general expectation that firstborns are more education-oriented than later-borns (Hypothesis 1). From this general hypothesis, arrived at inductively, the researcher may deduce that this year's graduating class at Harvard will include more firstborns than later-borns.

Researchers formulate hypotheses using deduction and induction, thus giving due consideration both to potentially relevant theory and to prior research findings. Because one goal of research is to contribute to generalizable bodies of theory that will provide *answers* to practical problems, any researcher should try, where possible, to work both out of and toward a general theoretical base. Hypothesis construction and testing enable researchers to generalize their findings beyond the specific conditions in which they obtained those results.

The decision to pursue a particular study is usually based on considerations of the potential importance of definitive findings and the likelihood of obtaining them. Because hypotheses are formulations of anticipated findings, researchers are advised to develop hypotheses as a means of demonstrating to themselves and their readers the importance and achievability of their studies. Moreover, by helping to integrate relevant research and logic, the formulation of hypotheses helps researchers to introduce their studies and discuss their findings.

HYPOTHESES BASED ON CONCEPTUALIZING

Researchers deal with reality on two levels, the operational level and the conceptual level. On the *operational* level, they must define events in observable terms in order to operate with the reality necessary to do research. On the *conceptual* level they must define events in terms of underlying communality (usually causal relationships) with other events. At a conceptual level, researchers abstract from single, specific instances to general ones and thus begin to understand how phenomena operate and variables interrelate. The formulation of a hypothesis very frequently requires movement from the operational (concrete) level to the conceptual (abstract) level. This movement to the conceptual level allows generalization of the results of research beyond the specific conditions of a particular study, giving the research wider applicability.

Research requires the ability to move from the operational to the conceptual level and vice versa. This ability influences not only the process of constructing experiments but also that of applying their findings.

Consider the following hypothetical study. The staff development department of a large school district has decided to run three in-service workshops for all the schools in the district. The purpose of the workshops is to help teachers and administrators work together in establishing priorities and programs for helping inner city students develop communication and problem-solving skills.

Label these Workshops A, B, and C. At first glance, the research problem might seem to compare the relative success of each workshop in helping participants to plan programs. However, the researchers may set more ambitious goals than merely concluding that one workshop was more successful than the others; they may want to determine *how* the workshops differed in order to discover what characteristics of one led to its superior effectiveness.

Two dimensions or concepts were identified to classify these workshops. The first was the concept of *structure*, that is, predesignated specification of what was to happen, when, and for what purpose.

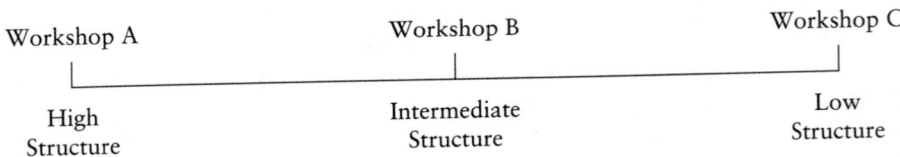

The second concept dealt with the *task orientation* of the workshops, that is, what kinds of problems they addressed. The researchers distinguished between *cognitive* problems (those dealing with thinking and problem-solving) and *affective* problems (those dealing with feelings and attitudes).

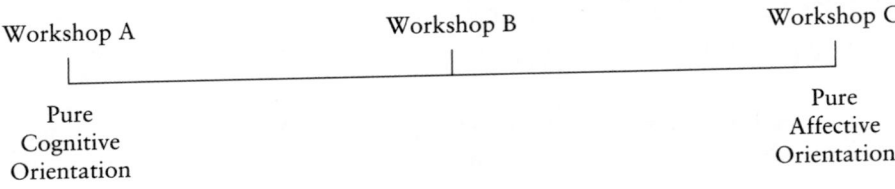

Workshop A used a very traditional approach, marked by a highly developed agenda and focusing on generating solutions to preordained, real-world, cognitive problems. Workshop C was almost entirely oriented toward human relations and followed no set agenda. Participants dealt with emotional and attitudinal (affective) problems as they emerged. Workshop B was in the middle, dealing with both "in-the-head" and "in-the-heart" problems and observing a somewhat specific agenda.

The study hypothesized that Workshop B would be the most effective one, because it provided structure without eliminating the possibility for changes in the agenda, and because it dealt with both cognitive and affective concerns. Confirmation of this hypothesis would suggest that moderate levels of structure and a mixed orientation are most conducive to success in such sessions, so developers of very different kinds of workshops and other training programs may be able to apply the results to their situations. They could generalize beyond the specifics of each workshop to the underlying dimensions on which the workshops differed. Generalizability depends in part on conceptualization.

Consider a second example of a study comparing computer-assisted instruction to traditional instruction. *Computer-assisted instruction* and *traditional instruction* are operational terms. To enhance the ability to generalize results, these operational terms should be examined for underlying conceptual similarities and differences. (This process of making conceptual contrasts between operational programs is called *conceptualizing* or *dimensionalizing*.) Dimensions useful for contrasting computer-assisted and traditional instruction might be degree of feedback, rate of positive reinforcement, uniqueness of presentation format, control of pacing, size of instructional units, and influence of student performance feedback on instructional design. These six dimensions or concepts could apply to any classification of an instructional model and comparison to other models. Such classification and comparison of dimensions at this abstract level would help with construction of a hypothesis about whether Instructional Model A will be more effective than Model B on certain specific criteria. This classification and comparison would also help theorists to begin to understand *why* Model A would give better results and thus to build its strengths into other instructional procedures.

GOING FROM THEORY TO HYPOTHESES: AN EXAMPLE

The theory of mastery learning (Bloom, 1976) states that if learners possess the necessary cognitive and affective entry behaviors for a new learning task, and if the quality of instruction is adequate, then they should all learn the task. The theory can be diagrammed as follows:

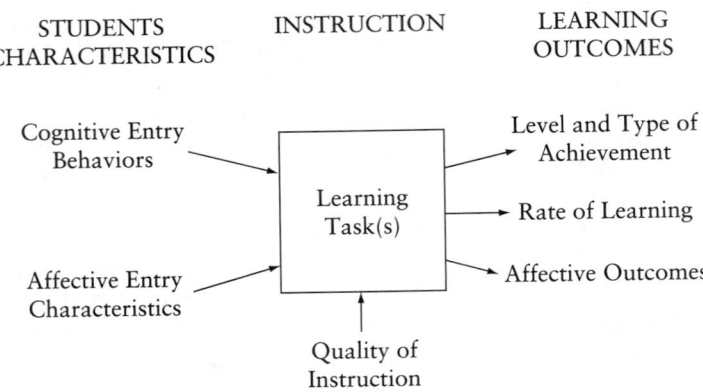

Hypotheses can be generated by identifying one set of student characteristics and linking them to one learning outcome to get examples such as:

- Achievement at any point in time is related to prior achievement.
- Aptitudes developed prior to instruction are consistent predictors of achievement following instruction.
- Academic self-concept prior to instruction predicts subsequent achievement.

However, researchers are more interested in the hypothesized impact of quality of instruction on the link between cognitive entry behaviors and achievement. Therefore, they construct alternative hypotheses:

- Following corrective instruction (mastery learning), the relationship between original learning and corrected learning will be zero.
- Given equal prior learning, corrective instruction (mastery learning) will produce greater achievement than noncorrective instruction.

In fact, a number of studies have tested these hypotheses (e.g., Slavin and Karweit, 1984; see pages 104–105, 119).

Thus, with its multiple components and theoretical linkages and connections, a theory is a bountiful source of hypotheses for researchers to test. The collective result of their inquiries serves as a test of the validity of the theory. Theory, therefore, represents a good source from which hypotheses can be derived. Its benefits come from helping to ensure a reasonable basis for hypotheses and because tests of the hypotheses confirm, elaborate, or disconfirm the theory.

META-ANALYSIS: CONSTRUCTING HYPOTHESES BY SYNTHESIZING PAST RESEARCH

Meta-analysis refers to any method that combines the probabilities, outcomes, or effects from two or more studies testing essentially the same directional hypothesis to help reveal the overall effect size or likelihood of relationship between the tested variables. In other words, meta-analysis is an analysis of other analyses. Glass, McGaw, and Smith (1981, p. 21) describe the process as follows:

> The approach of research integration referred to as meta-analysis is nothing more than the attitude of data analysis applied to quantitative summaries of individual experiments. By recording the properties of studies and their findings in quantitative terms, the meta-analysis of research invites one who would integrate numerous and diverse findings to apply the full power of statistical methods to the task. Thus it is not a technique; rather it is a perspective that uses many techniques of measurement and statistical analysis.

Meta-analysis, therefore, is a systematic, quantitative way of summarizing or integrating a body of literature about the relationships between a set of variables. It includes the following three steps:

1. Conducting a complete literature search to locate all previously published studies that have investigated the relationships between the variables in question
2. Describing and coding the studies to determine those with appropriate designs to merit inclusion
3. Either summarizing the statistical results of the different studies in tabular form (for visual comparison) or, more typically, computing and presenting the results of each study in terms of its *effect size*. In this second method, the analyst divides the mean difference between treatment and control groups by the standard deviation of the control group (Glass, 1977; Cohen, 1988), and then summarizes or averages effect sizes across all of the studies.

An example of meta-analysis conducted by Bangert-Drowns, Kulik, Kulik, and Morgan (1991) considered the instructional effects of feedback. They report statistical results of 10 studies, shown in Table 4.1, confirming that feedback following an incorrect response consistently improves subsequent performance. (Note all the pluses in the last column of the figure.) On the other hand, feedback following a correct response has little effect on subsequent performance (indicated by relatively few pluses in the third column).

TABLE 4.1

COMPARISON OF PROBABILITIES OF CORRECT ANSWERS ON CRITERION-ITEM-GIVEN-CORRECT OR -INCORRECT ANSWERS DURING INSTRUCTION

From Bangert-Drowns, Kulik, Kulik, & Morgan (1991). Reprinted with permission of the authors and publisher.

STUDY	CORRECT DURING INSTRUCTION			INCORRECT DURING INSTRUCTION		
	FEED-BACK	NO FEED-BACK	SIGNIF[a]	FEED-BACK	NO FEED-BACK	SIGNIF[a]
Carels, 1975			?			++
Chanond, 1988	0.85	0.83	0	0.75	0.25	++
Kulhavy, Yekovich, & Dyer, 1976	0.67	0.54	++	0.56	0.41	+
Lhyle & Kulhavy, 1987						
Study 1				0.62	0.17	++
Study 1				0.49	0.21	++
Newman, Williams, & Hiller, 1974	0.76	0.83	–	0.51	0.42	+
Peeck & Tilema, 1979	0.87	0.86	0	0.53	0.13	++
Peeck, Bosch, van den, & Kreupeling, 1985	0.89	0.88	0	0.57	0.20	++
Roper, 1977						
Study 1			+			+
Study 2			+			++

[a]Statistical significance of the comparison of the feedback and no-feedback probabilities: ++ Statistically significant and positive; + Nonsignificant and positive; 0 Virtually no difference; ? Nonsignificant with no direction reported; – Nonsignificant and negative.

The same authors also report effect size values from eight studies comparing different types of feedback, as shown in Table 4.2. When subjects are informed only of whether their answers are right or wrong, effect sizes (the first column of numbers) are small and mostly negative, averaging −0.08. This figure reflects an average mean difference only 8 percent the size of the standard deviation. Since Cohen (1988) considers 0.2 to be a small effect size, 0.5 a moderate one, and 0.8 a large one, the negative average indicates essentially no effect. However, when subjects are guided to or given the correct answers when they give the wrong responses, effect sizes (the second column of numbers) are larger and positive, averaging 0.31. Adding explanations to the feedback produces varying effect sizes (the last column of figures), ranging from almost no effect (0.05) to a substantial one (1.24).

EFFECT SIZES FROM STUDIES COMPARING DIFFERENT TYPES OF FEEDBACK

STUDY	RIGHT/ WRONG	CORRECT ANSWER	REPEAT UNTIL CORRECT	EXPLANATION
Arnett, 1985				
Study 1	0.38			0.36
Study 2	−0.58			0.05
Bumgarner, 1984	−0.19	0.49		
Farragher & Szabo, 1986	−0.24			0.18
Heald, 1970			0.81	1.24
Hirsch, 1952	−0.08	0.20		
Roper, 1977	0.26	0.76		
Sassenrath & Gaverick, 1965		0.58		0.33

TABLE 4.2

From Bangert-Drowns, Kulik, Kulik, & Morgan (1991). Reprinted with permission of the authors and publisher.

Based on these and other results, the authors present the following five-stage model of learning, which suggests the varying role of feedback: (1) initial state—including prior experience and pretests, (2) activation of search and retrieval strategies, (3) construction of response, (4) evaluation of response, and (5) adjustment of cognitive state. The most positive impact of feedback has appeared in the fourth stage, when it affects the evaluation of the correctness of a response and guides changes to it, if necessary. However, the model itself can be used as a source of research hypotheses about the possible impact of feedback at different points in the learning process. For example, studies might test two hypotheses:

- The effect of feedback is greater for relatively complex content than for comparatively simple content.
- The effect of feedback is greater when students receive relatively few cues, organizers, and other instructional supports than when they receive extensive supports.

A second example is the meta-analysis conducted by Schlaefli, Rest, and Thoma (1985) to answer the question, "Does moral education improve moral judgment?" In the course of their meta-analysis of previous studies, these authors identified many variables that could be included in future research, such as (1) the specific nature of a moral education program (for example, an emphasis on peer discussion of controversial moral dilemmas versus an emphasis on self-reflection to enhance personal psychological development); (2) exposure versus no exposure to a theory of moral development within a moral education program; (3) ages of the subjects (for example, junior high, senior high, college, adult); and (4) the duration of the program (for example, 1 week versus 1 semester).

The authors found positive but modest effects of moral education, and their discussion suggests several testable hypotheses for further study, such as:

- Students who begin a moral education program with positive expectations experience a greater increase in moral judgment than do students who begin with negative expectations.
- Experiencing a moral education program produces greater moral development than does simply reading material about moral development (such as the classic philosophers).
- Experiencing a moral education course produces greater moral development than does experiencing a traditional humanities course.
- Experiencing a moral education program produces more moral real-life behavior than does experiencing a lecture program in philosophy.

A final example of the use of meta-analysis provides a basis for identifying and explaining some of the criticisms and potential pitfalls of this method of synthesizing a body of literature. Indeed, meta-analyses are not uniformly accepted; some provoke controversy, particularly when such a synthesis addresses a topic of strong theoretical interest, and the meta-analysts attempt to summarize it with a single conclusion.

Responding to the position that reward or reinforcement causes a reduction in intrinsic or internal motivation, Cameron and Pierce (1994) published a meta-analysis of the relevant literature, basing their analysis on the results of 88 studies. They reach the following conclusion (Cameron and Pierce, 1994, p. 391):

> When all types of reward are aggregated, overall, the results indicate that reward does not negatively affect intrinsic motivation on any of the four measures. . . . When rewards are subdivided into reward type . . . , reward expectancy . . . , and reward contingency, the findings demonstrate that people who receive a verbal reward spend more time on a task once the reward is withdrawn; they also show more interest and enjoyment than nonrewarded persons.

In 1996, three published articles challenged the procedures that Cameron and Pierce (1994) used in their meta-analysis. These articles do not provide incontrovertible evidence of error in the procedures or conclusions of Cameron and Pierce, but they do illustrate that the meta-analytic approach is not without pitfalls and controversies. One of these critical articles (Lepper, Keavney, and Drake, 1996), includes a list of potential pitfalls that provides a good illustration of the kinds of judgments that a presumably systematic statistical technique like meta-analysis requires:

1. *Starting with the answer.* Meta-analysis often begins with the intention to support or discredit a theoretical position rather than merely to

discover. This creates the possibility of bias (both in the meta-analysts and in the responses of critics).

2. *Selecting a straw man.* If a researcher begins with a theoretical bias, then the opposing bias becomes the straw man to be knocked down by the meta-analysis.

3. *Averaging across competing effects or different groups.* This problem is a major issue in meta-analysis, which often averages results of studies that may not be comparable, thus overstating some effects and understating others. Averaging, the core procedure in meta-analysis, can obscure contingent relationships between variables, depending on which studies are averaged. For example, if tangible rewards diminish intrinsic motivation while verbal rewards enhance it, then averaging across studies that evaluate these two conditions may give the appearance that rewards exert neither helpful or harmful effects.

4. *Selectively interpreting results.* By reporting averages of results, and even averages of averages, rather than reporting more detailed results, meta-analysis can obscure important differences.

5. *Falling prey to the quality problem.* Meta-analysts sometimes give equal weight to methodologically sound studies and those with methodological problems.

6. *Falling prey to the quantity problem.* Meta-analysts sometimes lump studies of unique variations together with those of more common variations, because the researchers cannot find enough of the former to form a group or cluster. This choice obscures the effects of unique variations and the possibility of using these results to refine the interpretations of more common variations.

7. *Combining confounding variables.* If variables are correlated or tend to occur together, then they cannot be separated. Such a situation prevents grouping treatments of specific variables in multiple studies.

8. *Disregarding psychological "effect size."* Meta-analysis should weight results according to the difficulty of obtaining them. For example, results obtained by observing real behavior under naturally occurring circumstances should carry more weight than those where the subjects merely report to the experimenter what they think they would do; the former more accurately portray real psychological processes than the latter do. (Of course, applying the weights would require that the meta-analyst make judgments, thus increasing the likelihood of bias.)

With their sharp focus on and delineation of variables across studies in a given area, and with the quantitative summaries they yield, meta-analyses can be highly useful sources of information to aid in formulating hypotheses. However, while meta-analysis was created to replace researcher judgment with a seemingly more straightforward statistical combination of results, many areas of judgment remain, sometimes rendering controversial conclusions.

SOME FURTHER ILLUSTRATIONS

Illustrations of hypotheses in this section are drawn from the classroom research setting.

Classroom Research Hypotheses

In its simplest form, a hypothesis for research in the classroom can be stated as follows:

- Treatment A will increase Learning Outcome X more than will Treatment B. Treatments A and B may take a variety of forms of interest to researchers, many of which were described in Chapter 2. Similarly, Learning Outcome X can be one of many learning outcomes of interest to researchers, also described in Chapter 2. If, for example, Treatment A were individually guided education, Treatment B were so-called *conventional classroom instruction,* and Learning Outcome X were reading achievement, the sample hypothesis would read:
- Students who receive *individually guided education* will demonstrate greater gains in *reading achievement* than students who receive *conventional instruction.*

In constructing hypotheses for classroom research, it is often desirable to formulate hypotheses that include student characteristics, as well. A researcher might elaborate upon the above example to reflect this additional consideration:

- *Poor readers* who receive *individually guided education* will demonstrate greater gains in *reading achievement* than *poor readers* who receive *conventional instruction,* while no such differences in reading achievement will occur between *good readers* who receive one or the other instructional treatment.

Stated differently:

- Among *poor readers,* those receiving *individually guided education* will outgain those receiving *conventional instruction* on *reading achievement,* while among *good readers,* no differences will occur.

The first format included two variables; the second and third included a third variable, as well.

These formats could accommodate many specific hypotheses for classroom research. A change to a specific variable also changes the hypothesis; however, the formats can be used repeatedly by inserting different variables.

TESTING A HYPOTHESIS

The purpose of testing a hypothesis is to determine the probability that it is supported by fact. However, because a hypothesis expresses a general expectation about the relationship between variables, a researcher could conceive an extremely large number of instances under which to test it. One could not practically attempt to gain support in all of those instances.

For instance, consider the hypothesis that nondirective teachers instruct students more effectively than directive teachers do. One would have to test this

---

ILLUSTRATIONS FROM THE SAMPLE STUDIES   BOX 4

In Sample Study I from Appendix A, an evaluation of the effect of encouragement on self-beliefs and performance, the authors offer the following directional hypotheses: (1) Students who receive encouragement will be persuaded to feel good about their own efforts and performance and experience a concomitant increase in self-efficacy. (2) Students who receive encouragement will produce a more extensive task response than students who receive neutral responses to their performance, reflecting stronger motivation.

The fact that the authors offer hypotheses that indicate direction suggests that they have formulated expectations based on a combination of their own experience and prior work by others. Moreover, their statements of the hypotheses have sufficient clarity to allow readers to understand the meanings, for example, that encouraging feedback will have more impact than neutral feedback on both performance and self-belief.

Support for the hypothesis comes particularly from a theoretical model offered by Bandura (1986) and from the authors' own previous work, as cited in the study. Clear and understandable logic, therefore, underlies the hypotheses. Finally, the hypotheses are consistent with the problem statement quoted in Box 2.

In Sample Study II (also from Appendix A), an investigation of the classroom behavior of good and poor readers, the authors offer no formal hypotheses. They cite prior research that shows that "poor readers, in general, although not in every case, have been characterized as tending to demonstrate maladaptive behavior." But another study found that "the classroom behavior of learning-disabled adolescents enrolled in Grades 1 through 11 is not significantly different from the behavior of their non-learning-disabled peers." Thus, the authors doubted the likelihood of one possible hypothesis—that poor readers will exhibit more off-task behaviors than good readers will exhibit—too much to offer it for consideration.

assertion for many groups of teachers, in many subjects, in many settings, and with many criteria before accepting it. If, however, on the basis of limited testing, the hypothesis fails to yield confirming results, it would be fair to reject it.

Because it is extremely difficult to obtain unequivocal support for a hypothesis, the researcher instead attempts to test and disprove its negation. The negative or "no differences" version of a hypothesis is called a *null hypothesis*.

Consider the three possible hypotheses concerning a comparison of the effectiveness of directive and nondirective teachers:

1. Nondirective teachers instruct students more effectively than do directive teachers.
2. Directive teachers instruct students more effectively than do nondirective teachers.
3. Nondirective and directive teachers instruct students with equal effectiveness.

Hypothesis 3 is the null or no-differences hypothesis. (In fact, in each of the three sets of hypotheses stated on pages 76–77, Hypothesis 3 is the null hypothesis.) Although the researcher has developed a rationale for Hypothesis 1 (nondirective teachers instruct students more effectively than do directive teachers), it *implicitly* becomes the null hypothesis (nondirective and directive teachers instruct students with equal effectiveness) to allow a statistical test of it. The null hypothesis suggests that minor differences can occur due to chance variation, so they do not represent real differences. (This concept is considered further in Chapter 11.) The null hypothesis can be rejected if tests find differences large enough to indicate real effects. That is, a researcher can conclude that it is untrue that nondirective and directive teachers instruct students with equal effectiveness if one group is shown clearly to teach more effectively than the other does. Those results would not, however, justify a conclusion affirming the directional hypothesis that nondirective teachers instruct students more effectively than do directive teachers, because variables other than the characteristics of the teachers may have contributed to the observed outcomes. Although the test allows the researcher to reject the null hypothesis and conclude that the effectiveness of the two groups of teachers is not equal, one should not then conclude that a specified hypothesis is absolutely true or false; if so, different kinds of errors may lead to acceptance of hypotheses that are false or to rejection of hypotheses that are true.

Researchers can evaluate a hypothesis without stating it in null form; for ease of discussion and understanding, they may prefer to state it in directional form. However, for purposes of statistical testing and interpretation, they always evaluate the null hypothesis.

In addition to the *null* hypothesis ($A_1 = A_2$) and each of the two possible *directional* hypotheses ($A_1 > A_2$, $A_2 > A_1$), researchers must also acknowledge what might be called a *positive* hypothesis ($A_1 \neq A_2$). This position states, unlike the null hypothesis, that the treatment levels will vary in their effects, but it differs from the directional hypotheses by not stating which treatment level will produce the greatest effect. In other words, it is a nondirectional hypothesis. As such, it adds little to a research document. Directional hypotheses are preferred because they go beyond merely saying that "something will happen;" they say exactly what will happen. This specificity helps researchers to determine that a study provides a basis for accepting or rejecting expectations of differences.

Offering directional hypotheses helps to give a rationale and a focus to a study, although statistical tests actually evaluate null hypotheses. Hypothesizing a difference without specifying its direction, as in a so-called *positive hypothesis,* adds little or nothing to the process.

This chapter's discussion of hypotheses has featured words and phrases such as *effective* and *structured instructional procedures.* As you may have recognized, words and phrases such as these do not lend themselves to experimental testing. A hypothesis, even a null hypothesis, is not directly testable in the form in which it is generally stated. Its very generality, a distinguishing characteristic, limits its direct testability. To become testable, therefore, researchers must transform it into a more specific or operationalized statement. A hypothesis is operationalized (made testable) by providing operational (testable) definitions for its terms (variables). But before variables can be defined, they must be labeled. Approaches to this task are the subject of the following chapter.

Summary

1. A hypothesis is a suggested answer to the question posed in a research problem statement. Since it represents expected outcomes, a hypothesis differs from an observation, which represents outcomes actually found.
2. A specific hypothesis is the explicit expectation that is tested in a study. A general hypothesis is the broader and more conceptual version about which the researchers draw conclusions.
3. Researchers arrive at hypotheses either by deduction, that is, deriving them from more general statements like theories, or by induction, that is, deriving them from combinations of specific observations or facts.
4. A study testing the relationship between two variables always allows three possible hypotheses: As one variable increases, so does the other; as one variable increases, the other decreases; one variable has no relationship to the other.
5. To help them formulate hypotheses, researchers conceive of variables conceptually, that is, as broad ideas, rather than operationally, or as specific manipulations or measures. Theories, which are very broad, complex systems of concepts, provide excellent bases for deriving hypotheses.
6. On the other hand, collections of prior research studies, analyzed together using a procedure known as *meta-analysis,* also provide good sources of hypotheses.

7. Researchers deal with three kinds of hypotheses. A directional hypothesis specifies that one variable will either increase or decrease when the other increases; in other words, it prespecifies the direction of the outcome. This kind of hypothesis is preferred for discussion purposes, because it gives a study direction and meaning. A positive hypothesis simply states that variables are related, without specifying direction. This kind of hypothesis has no value in research. A null hypothesis predicts no relationship between variables; researchers need not specify this expectation, because, in fact, when they apply statistical tests, it is this that is being tested in an effort to disprove it.

COMPETENCY TEST EXERCISES

1. Indicate which of the following three statements is a specific hypothesis, which is a general hypothesis, and which is an observation:
   a. Jane has never been tested, but it is expected that she has a high IQ.
   b. Girls of Jane's age have higher IQs than boys of the same age.
   c. Jane was just given an IQ test, and she obtained a high score.

2. Indicate which of the following three statements is a specific hypothesis, which is a general hypothesis, and which is an observation:
   a. The phonics approach to reading is better than any other teaching method currently in practice.
   b. The Johnson Phonics Reading Program worked better in Cleveland schools than any other tried there.
   c. The Johnson Phonics Reading Program should work better in the Martin Luther King School than any presently in use there.

3. Indicate briefly the difference between the two types of hypotheses and observations.

4. Consider a research problem to find out whether the children of parents in science-related occupations are more likely to elect science courses in high school than the children of parents in nonscience-related occupations. Construct three hypotheses based on this problem.

5. Consider a research problem to find out whether students who use this textbook will learn more about research methods than students who use the Brand X textbook. Construct three hypotheses based on this problem.

6. Evaluate two hypotheses: (1) Team teaching is more effective than individual teaching. (2) Team teaching is no more effective than individual teaching. Which of these hypotheses would you judge to be more appropriate, given the following conditions:

   a. All students cannot be expected to like all teachers.

   b. Research has shown that male models and female models are both important in socialization.

Why did you choose the hypothesis you did?

7. Which of the statements (a or b) in Exercise 6 reflects a deductive process for constructing a hypothesis? Which reflects an inductive process?

8. Rewrite the following hypotheses in null form:

   a. Youngsters who read below grade level will find school less pleasant than those who read at or above grade level.

   b. Intelligence and ordinal position of birth are positively related; that is, firstborn children are more intelligent than their later-born siblings.

   c. A combination of reading readiness training and programmed reading instruction will teach reading more effectively than will normal classroom instruction in sight reading.

RECOMMENDED REFERENCES

Hunter, J. E., Schmidt, F. L., & Jackson, G. B. (1982). *Meta-analysis: Cumulating research findings across studies.* Beverly Hills, CA: Sage Publications.

Snow, R. E. (1973). Theory construction for research on teaching. In R. M. W. Travers (Ed.), *Second handbook of research on teaching* (pp. 77–112). Chicago: Rand-McNally.

5 Chapter

IDENTIFYING AND LABELING VARIABLES

Objectives

▶ Identify variables and label them according to five types: independent, dependent, moderator, control, or intervening variables.

▶ Describe the characteristics of each type of variable.

▶ State several factors to be considered in labeling variables as one of the five types.

A HYPOTHESIS AND ITS VARIABLES

Consider the hypothesis: Among students of the same age and intelligence, skill performance is directly related to the number of practice trials, the relationship being particularly strong among boys, but also holding, though less directly, among girls. This hypothesis, which indicates that practice increases learning, involves several variables:

Independent variable: Number of practice trials

Dependent variable: Skill performance

Moderator variable: Gender

Control variables: Age, intelligence

Intervening variable: Learning

THE INDEPENDENT VARIABLE

The independent variable, a stimulus variable or input, operates either within a person or within his or her environment to affect behavior. Formally stated, the *independent variable* in a research study is the factor that is measured, manipulated, or selected by the experimenter to determine its relationship to an observed phenomenon. If a researcher studying the relationship between two variables, X and Y, asks, "What will happen to Y if I make X greater or smaller?" the question identifies Variable X as the independent variable. It is the variable that the researcher will manipulate or change to cause a change in some other variable. It is independent, because the research focuses only on how it affects another variable, not what affects it. The study treats the independent variable as an antecedent condition, a required condition preceding a particular consequence. In other words, the independent variable is the *presumed cause* of any change in the outcome. Moreover, it may be manipulated or measured.

THE DEPENDENT VARIABLE

The dependent variable is a response variable or output. It reflects an observed aspect of the behavior of an organism that has been stimulated. Formally, the *dependent variable* is the factor that is observed and measured to determine the effect of the independent variable; it is the factor that appears, disappears, or varies as the researcher introduces, removes, or varies the independent variable. When the researcher asks, "What will happen to Y if I make X greater or smaller?" Variable Y is identified as the dependent variable. It is the variable that will change as a result of variations in the independent variable. It is considered dependent because its value depends upon the value of the independent variable; its variations represent consequences of changes in the independent variable. That is, it represents the *presumed effect* of the independent variable. Researchers always measure the dependent variable and never manipulate it.

THE RELATIONSHIP BETWEEN INDEPENDENT AND DEPENDENT VARIABLES

For the purpose of explanation, this section deals solely with the relationship between a single independent variable and a single dependent variable. However, it is important to note that most experiments involve many variables, not just a single independent-dependent pair. The additional variables may be independent and dependent variables, or they may be moderator or control variables.

Many studies utilize *discrete*—that is, categorical—independent variables. Such a study looks either at the presence versus the absence of a particular treatment or approach, or at a comparison between different approaches. Other studies utilize *continuous* independent variables. The researcher's observations of such a variable may be stated in numerical terms indicating degree or amount. When two continuous variables are compared, as in correlation studies, researchers make rather arbitrary decisions which variables to call independent and which dependent ones. In fact, in such cases the variables are often not labeled as independent or dependent precisely because no real distinction, like one as cause and the other as effect, separates them.

Independent variables may be called *factors,* and their variations may be called *levels.* In a study of the effect of music instruction on ability to concentrate, the difference between an experimental treatment (music instruction) versus no experimental treatment (no music instruction) represents a single independent variable or factor (namely, amount of music instruction). The variable contains two levels: some music instruction and no music instruction. A study of teaching effectiveness might compare (1) programmed instruction versus (2) instruction by lecture alone versus (3) instruction combining lecture and discussion. This study would include a single independent variable or factor (type of instruction) that contains three levels. Be careful not to confuse a single independent variable with two levels for two independent variables, or an independent variable with three levels for three independent variables, and so on.

Figure 5.1 illustrates the relationship between a discrete independent variable and a dependent variable.

RELATIONSHIPS BETWEEN INDEPENDENT AND DEPENDENT VARIABLES

FIGURE 5.1

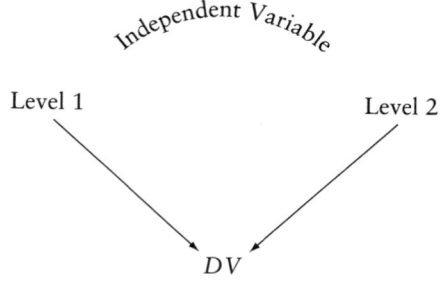

Dependent Variable

HYPOTHESIS: Dependent variable is greater with independent variable at Level 2 than at Level 1.

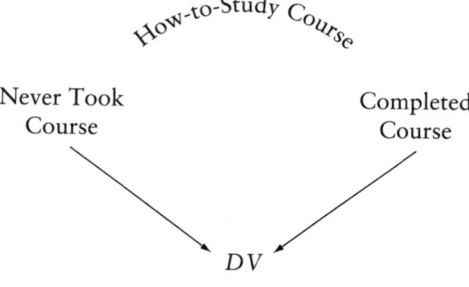

Grade-Point Average

HYPOTHESIS: Students who have completed a how-to-study course will make significantly higher grade-point averages than students who have never taken such a course.

Some Examples of Independent and Dependent Variables

The following list reports a number of hypotheses drawn from studies undertaken in a research methods course; the independent and dependent variables have been identified for each one.

- **Hypothesis 1.** Under intangible reinforcement conditions, middle-class children will learn significantly faster or more easily than lower-class children.

    Independent variable: socioeconomic status (middle-class versus lower-class)

    Dependent variable: ease or speed of learning

- **Hypothesis 2.** Girls who plan to pursue careers in science display more aggressive, less conforming, more independent attitudes, and express stronger needs for achievement than girls who do not plan such careers.

    Independent variable: career choice (science versus nonscience)

    Dependent variables: aggressiveness, conformity, independence, need for achievement[1]

- **Hypothesis 3.** In a group of children at elementary school age, those above average height are more often chosen as leaders by their classmates than are those below average height.

    Independent variable: height (above average versus below average)

    Dependent variable: selection as leader by classmates

- **Hypothesis 4.** In a middle-class, suburban, public school district in which a child is expected to meet the standards of a set curriculum, a child who is under 5 years of age upon entrance to kindergarten is less likely to be ready for first grade in 1 year than a child who is 5 years of age or more at the time of entrance to kindergarten.

    Independent variable: age upon entrance to kindergarten (under 5 versus 5 and over)

    Dependent variable: readiness for first grade

- **Hypothesis 5.** Students who are taught to read using a phonics approach will attain a higher level of reading achievement than students taught by a whole language approach.

    Independent variable: method of teaching reading (phonics versus whole language)

    Dependent variable: level of reading achievement attained

- **Hypothesis 6.** Students who receive peer counseling prior to a test will experience less test anxiety than students who receive no peer counseling.

    Independent variable: pretest peer counseling versus no peer counseling

    Dependent variable: level of test anxiety

Consider also the following two examples drawn from journal sources:

- **Hypothesis 7.** Perceptions of the characteristics of a "good" or effective teacher are in part determined by the perceiver's attitudes toward education.

    Independent variable: perceiver's attitudes toward education

---

[1] It is difficult if not impossible to determine whether career choices cause observed personality characteristics. Thus, only an arbitrary distinction separates independent and dependent variables. In such cases, research imposes no real need to label the variables other than for discussion purposes, and then labeling may be based on presumed causality.

> *Dependent variable:* perceptions of the characteristics of a "good" or effective teacher

- **Hypothesis 8.** Students who are required to take a quiz on each chapter will score higher on course examinations than students who are required to complete an outline of each chapter.

  > *Independent variable:* chapter assignment: taking quizzes versus completing outlines
  >
  > *Dependent variable:* score on course examinations

THE MODERATOR VARIABLE

The term *moderator variable* describes a special type of independent variable, a secondary independent variable selected to determine if it affects the relationship between the study's primary independent variable and its dependent variables. Formally, a *moderator variable* is a factor that is measured, manipulated, or selected by the experimenter to discover whether it modifies the relationship of the independent variable to an observed phenomenon. The word *moderator* simply acknowledges the reason that this secondary independent variable has been singled out for study. A researcher may be interested in studying the effect of Independent Variable X on Dependent Variable Y but suspects that the nature of the relationship between X and Y is altered by the level of a third factor, Z. The study may include Z in the analysis as a moderator variable.

Consider two illustrations. First, suppose that a researcher wants to compare the effectiveness of a visual approach (based mainly on pictures) to an auditory approach (based on audiotapes) for teaching a unit on ecology. The researcher suspects, however, that one method may be more effective for students who learn best in a visual mode, while the other may be more effective for those who learn best in an auditory mode. When all students are tested together for achievement at the end of the unit, the overall results of the two approaches may appear to be the same, but separating results for visual learners from those for auditory ones may show that the two approaches have different results in each subgroup. If so, the learning mode variable moderates the relationship between instructional approach (the independent variable) and teaching effectiveness (the dependent variable). This moderating relationship (usually established via analysis of variance or regression analysis) is shown graphically in Figure 5.2 (which reflects fictional data).

A second illustration (borne out by real data) comes from a study of the relationship between the conditions under which a test is taken (the independent variable) and test performance (the dependent variable). Assume that the researcher varies test conditions between ego orientation ("write your name on the paper, we're measuring you") and task orientation ("don't write your name on the paper, we're measuring the test"). The test taker's previously measured test-anxiety level, a "personality" measure characteristic, is included as a moderator variable. The combined results show that highly test-anxious people functioned better under

FIGURE 5.2   **RELATIONSHIP BETWEEN INSTRUCTIONAL APPROACH (INDEPENDENT VARIABLE) AND ACHIEVEMENT (DEPENDENT VARIABLE) AS MODERATED BY STUDENT LEARNING MODE**

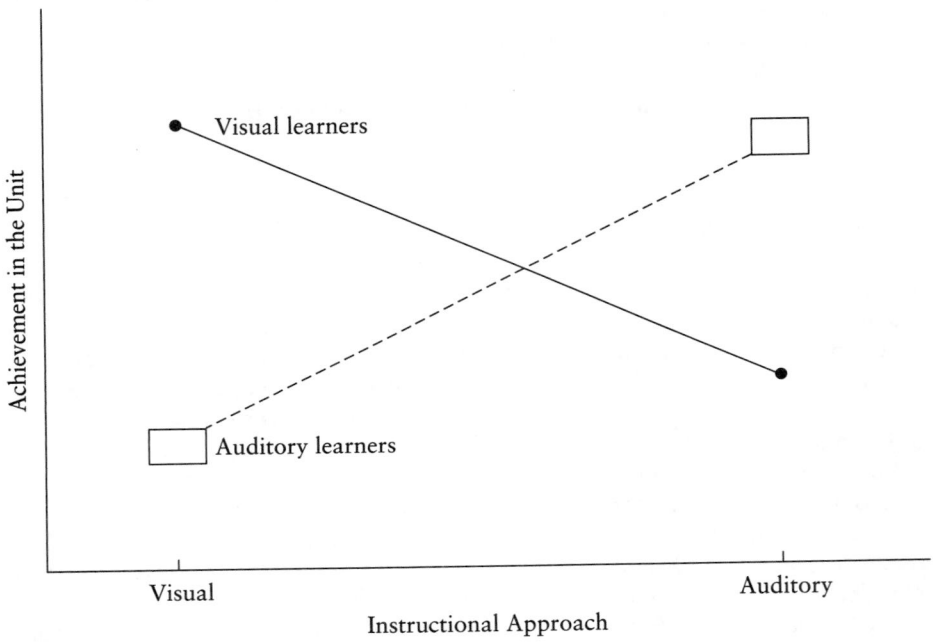

task orientation, and people of low-test anxiety functioned better under ego orientation. This interaction between the independent variable, the moderator variable, and the dependent variable is shown graphically in Figure 5.3.

Because educational research studies usually deal with highly complex situations, the inclusion of at least one moderator variable in a study is highly recommended. Often the nature of the relationship between X and Y remains poorly understood after a study because the researchers failed to single out and measure vital moderator variables such as Z, W, and so on.

Some Examples of Moderator Variables

A number of hypotheses drawn from various sources can help to illustrate the variables. The moderator variable (along with the independent and dependent variables) has been identified for each example below.

- **Hypothesis 1.** Situational pressures of morality cause nondogmatic school superintendents to innovate, whereas situational pressures of expediency cause dogmatic school superintendents to innovate.

RELATIONSHIP BETWEEN TEST CONDITIONS (INDEPENDENT VARIABLE) AND TEST PERFORMANCE (DEPENDENT VARIABLE) AS MODERATED BY TEST ANXIETY LEVEL

FIGURE 5.3

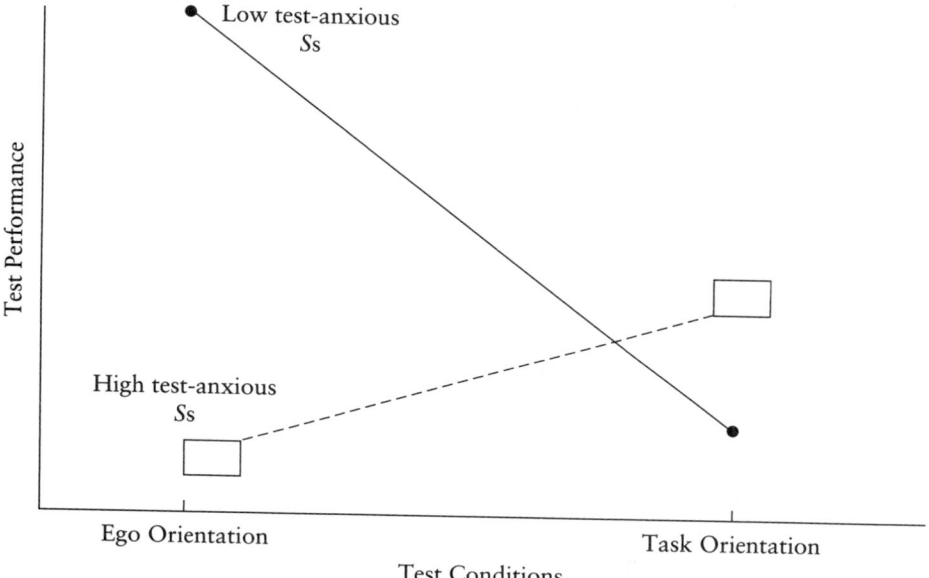

Independent variable: type of situational pressure (morality versus expediency)

Moderator variable: level of dogmatism of the school superintendent

Dependent variable: degree to which superintendent innovates

- **Hypothesis 2.** Greater differences in achievement remain between good readers and poor readers after they receive written instruction than after they receive oral instruction.

  Independent variable: type of instruction (written versus oral)

  Moderator variable: reading level (good versus poor)

  Dependent variable: achievement

- **Hypothesis 3.** Firstborn male college students with a Machiavellian orientation get higher grades than their non-Machiavellian counterparts of equal intelligence, while no such differences are found among later-borns.

  Moderator variable: It is optional whether birth order (firstborn versus later-born) or degree of Machiavellian orientation (Machiavellian versus non-Machiavellian) is considered the moderator variable; the other then becomes the independent variable.

  Dependent variable: grades

- **Hypothesis 4.** More highly structured instructional procedures will provoke greater achievement among students who practice concrete thinking, whereas less structured approaches will provoke greater achievement among students who practice abstract thinking.
     Independent variable: level of structure in instruction (more versus less)
     Moderator variable: thinking style of students (concrete versus abstract)
     Dependent variable: achievement

CONTROL VARIABLES

A single study cannot enable one to examine all of the variables in a situation (*situational* variables) or in a person (*dispositional* variables); some must be neutralized to guarantee that they will not exert differential or moderating effects on the relationship between the independent variable and the dependent variable. *Control variables* are factors controlled by the experimenter to cancel out or neutralize any effect they might otherwise have on observed phenomena. The effects of control variables are neutralized; the effects of moderator variables are studied. (As Chapter 7 will explain, the effects of control variables can be neutralized by elimination, equating across groups, or randomization.)

Certain variables appear repeatedly as control variables in educational research, although they occasionally serve as moderator variables. Gender, intelligence, and socioeconomic status are three dispositional variables that are commonly controlled; noise, task order, and task content are common situational control variables. In constructing an experiment, the researcher must always decide which variables to study and which to control. Some of the bases for this decision are discussed in the last section of this chapter.

Some Examples of Control Variables

Control variables are not necessarily specified in a hypothesis statement. Often, the choice of factors treated as control variables is discussed only in the methods section of a research report. The examples below, however, specifically list at least one control variable in each hypothesis statement.

- **Hypothesis 1.** Firstborn college students with a Machiavellian orientation get higher grades than their non-Machiavellian counterparts of equal intelligence, but no such differences are found among later-borns.
     Control variable: intelligence
- **Hypothesis 2.** Among boys, physical size is correlated with social maturity, but for girls in the same age group, these two variables show no correlation.
     Control variable: age

- **Hypothesis 3.** Task performance by high-need achievers will exceed that of low-need achievers in tasks with 50 percent subjective probability of success.

    Control variable: subjective probability of task success
- **Hypothesis 4.** Among lower-class children, tangible reinforcement conditions will produce significantly more learning than intangible reinforcement conditions.

    Control variable: social class

Each of these illustrations undoubtedly includes other variables—such as the subjects' relevant prior experiences or the noise level during treatment—that are not specified in the hypothesis statements but that must be controlled. Because they are controlled by routine design procedures, universal variables such as these are often not systematically labeled.

INTERVENING VARIABLES

All of the variable types described thus far—independent, dependent, moderator, and control variables—are concrete factors. Each independent, moderator, and control variable can be manipulated by the experimenters, and each variation can be observed as it affects the dependent variable. By manipulating these concrete variables, experimenters often want to address, not concrete phenomena, but hypothetical ones: relationships between a hypothetical underlying or intervening variable and a dependent variable. An *intervening variable* is a factor that theoretically affects observed phenomena but cannot be seen, measured, or manipulated; its effect must be inferred from the effects of the independent and moderator variables on the observed phenomena.

In writing about their studies, researchers do not always identify their intervening variables. Even less often do they label those variables as such. It would be helpful if they did explicitly state underlying variables.

Consider the roles of the intervening variables in the following hypotheses.

- **Hypothesis 1.** As task interest increases, measured task performance increases.

    Independent variable: task interest
    Intervening variable: learning
    Dependent variable: task performance
- **Hypothesis 2.** Children who are blocked from reaching their goals exhibit more aggressive acts than children not so blocked.

    Independent variable: encountering or not encountering obstacles to goals
    Intervening variable: frustration
    Dependent variable: number of aggressive acts

- **Hypothesis 3.** Teachers given many positive feedback experiences will have more positive attitudes toward children than teachers given fewer positive feedback experiences.

    Independent variable: number of positive feedback experiences for teachers
    Intervening variable: teachers' self-esteem
    Dependent variable: positive character of teachers' attitudes toward students

In these examples, the concrete, observed values of the operationalized dependent variables represent abstract characteristics or qualities affected by the independent (and moderator) variables. For example, in Hypothesis 1, increased task interest (independent variable) leads to or causes observed and measured increases in task performance (dependent variable), which in turn reflect a *presumed* increase in learning. The study directly measures task performance, not learning, but the researcher infers that learning has occurred and has affected task performance.

Researchers must operationalize variables in order to study them, and they must conceptualize variables in order to generalize from them. Researchers often use the labels *independent, dependent, moderator,* and *control* to describe operational statements of their variables. The term *intervening variable,* however, always refers to a conceptual variable—a factor affected by the independent, moderator, and control variables that, in turn, affects the dependent variable.

For example, suppose that a researcher plans to contrast the techniques of presenting a lesson on closed-circuit TV versus presenting it via a live lecture. The independent variable is mode of presentation; the dependent variable is some measure of learning. The choice of an intervening variable emerges from the question, "What underlying characteristic of the two modes of presentation should lead one to be more effective than the other?" This question amounts to asking what the intervening variable is. The likely answer (likely but not certain, because intervening variables are neither visible or directly measurable) is *attention.* Closed-circuit TV will not present more or less information, but it may stimulate more or less attention. Thus, the increased attention could lead to better learning.

Why bother to identify intervening variables? Researchers take this step to allow them to generalize about *causes* rather than simply pointing out mutual variations among variables. If the researcher in the example identifies attention as the intervening variable, then the study must examine how this factor affects learning, and the data function as a means to generalize to other situations and other modes of presentation. Researchers must concern themselves with *why* as well as what and how.

Consider the following statements:

1. Students taught by discovery (a_1) will perform better on a new but related task *(c)* than students taught by rote (a_2).

2. Students taught by discovery (a_1) will develop a search strategy (b_1)—an approach to finding solutions—that will enable them to perform better on a new but related task *(c)*, while students taught by rote will learn solutions but not strategies (b_2), thus limiting their ability to solve transfer problems *(c)*.

The symbols a_1 and a_2 refer to the two levels of the independent variable, whereas *c* refers to the dependent variable. The intervening variable (presence or absence of a search strategy) is identified as b_1 and b_2 in the second statement.

Intervening variables can often be discovered by examining a hypothesis and asking the question, "What characteristic of the independent variable will cause the predicted outcome?"

THE COMBINED VARIABLES

The relationship between the five types of variables described in this chapter is illustrated in Figure 5.4. Note that independent, moderator, and control variables

THE COMBINED VARIABLES

FIGURE 5.4

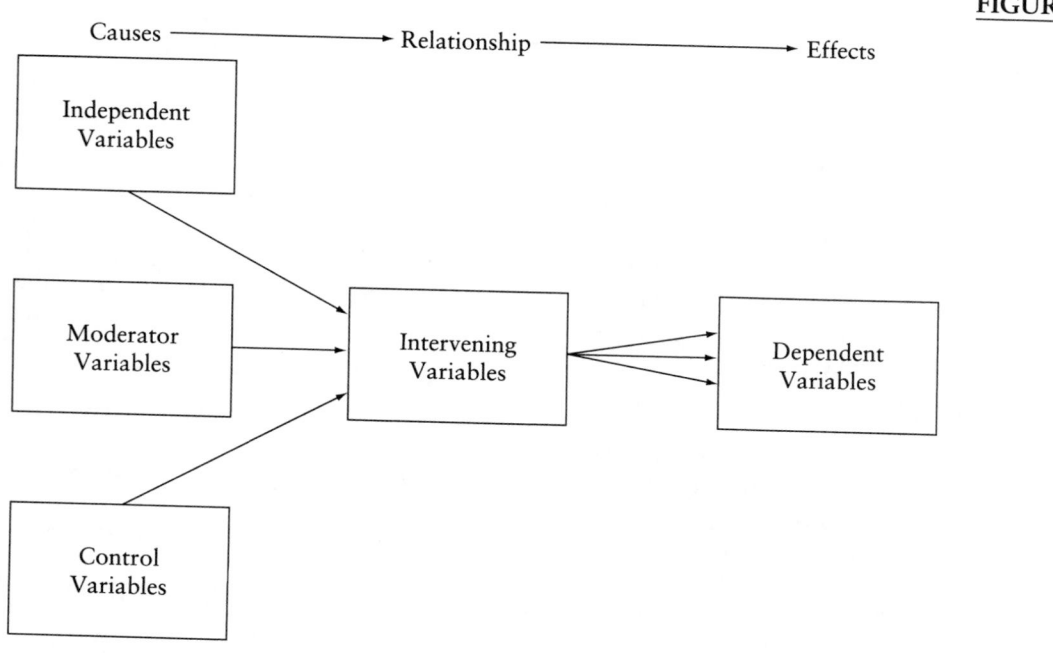

are inputs or causes: the first two types are the causes being studied in the research whereas the third represents causes neutralized or "eliminated" from influence. At the other end of the figure, dependent variables represent effects, while intervening variables are conceptual assumptions that intervene between operationally stated causes and operationally stated effects.

Example 1

Consider a study by Tuckman (1996a) of the difference in achievement in a course between two groups of college students. Members of one group are motivated to study by the presence of an incentive, but they are not taught any learning strategy; students in the other group are taught a learning strategy and required to use it, but they receive no motivation to study. In addition, students are classified for analysis purposes according to high, medium, and low prior academic achievement in college.

- The *independent variable* is the condition: incentive motivation versus learning strategy.
- The *moderator variable* is prior academic achievement in college.
- The *control variable* is education level: college students.
- The *dependent variable* is achievement in a course.
- The *intervening variables* are the desire to gain an incentive and the quality of information processing. (The study includes two, because each condition provokes one state and not the other.)

Example 2

Consider another study of the impacts of a mastery learning instructional model and a student team learning instructional model, separately and combined, on mathematics achievement among urban ninth graders. The hypothesis states that the mastery learning approach will be more effective when combined with the student team approach than when used alone, particularly among students of low prior achievement.

- One *independent variable* is instructional approach regarding mastery. It contains two levels: mastery versus nonmastery.
- The second *independent variable* is instructional approach regarding teams, also with two levels: teams versus no teams.
- The *moderator variable* is student prior achievement, with three levels: low, middle, and high achievement.
- The *control variables*, while not necessarily spelled out in the hypothesis, are grade level, urban or rural residence, quality and content of instruction, subject-matter area, and instructional time. The urban context

yielded low scholastic achievement and a predominately minority sample.

- The *dependent variable* is how much of the appropriate mathematics content students achieve.
- The *intervening variables* include ability to understand instruction (the key feature of mastery learning) and the incentive to persevere (the key feature of student teaming).

Example 3

Consider a study designed to provide feedback for teachers about their in-class behavior from (1) students, (2) supervisors, (3) both students and supervisors, and (4) neither. Students' judgments are again obtained after 12 weeks to determine whether teachers given feedback from different sources have shown differential changes of behavior in the directions advocated by the feedback. Differential outcomes are also considered based on years of teaching experience of each teacher.

- The *independent variable* is source of feedback. Note that this single independent variable or factor includes four levels, each corresponding to a condition (labeled 1, 2, 3, and 4).
- The *moderator variable* is years of teaching experience. This single factor includes three levels (1 to 3 years of teaching experience, 4 to 10 years, and 11 or more years).
- *Control variables* are students' grade level (10th, 11th, or 12th grade), students' curricular major (vocational only), teachers' subject (vocational only), and class size (approximately 15 students).
- The *dependent variable* is change in teachers' behavior (as perceived by students). The purpose of the study is to see how feedback from different sources affects teachers' behavior.
- The *intervening variable* could be identified as the responsiveness of the teacher to feedback from varying sources, based on the perceived motivation and perceived value of feedback for each teacher.

Example 4

Consider a research study reported by Tuckman (1990a, p. 291) "to compare the effect of working in groups, goal-setting, and a control condition on the self-regulated performance of (college) subjects at high, middle, and low levels of self-efficacy." (An abstract of a journal article reporting this study appeared in Chapter 3 as Figure 3.5.)

- The *independent variable* is working condition, with three levels: (1) in groups, (2) with goal-setting, and (3) with neither (the control group).

BOX 5

ILLUSTRATIONS FROM THE SAMPLE STUDIES

Consider Sample Study I in Appendix A. It addresses the question, "Does teacher encouragement lead to increases in self-efficacy and in subsequent task performance, in comparison to neutral or nonencouraging feedback?"

- The *independent variable* is the type of teacher feedback. It includes two levels: encouraging and neutral feedback.
- The study includes no *moderator variables*, although any of the control variables could conceivably have served as moderator variables.
- The *control variables* are: (1) initial self-efficacy, (2) initial outcome expectation, (3) initial outcome importance, (4) procrastination tendency, and (5) grade level. The problem statement should probably have read: Among college students of equivalent self-efficacy, outcome expectation, outcome importance, and procrastination tendency, does teacher encouragement . . . ?
- The *dependent variables* are (1) final self-efficacy and (2) task performance.
- The *intervening variable* for final self-efficacy might be the sense of success that the encouragement conveys, while the *intervening variable* for task performance might be growth in self-efficacy. The "Discussion" section of the article argues for this interpretation.

Consider Sample Study II in Appendix A. Do good and poor readers at Grade Levels 1, 3, 5, 7, 9, and 11 differ on the amounts of the following classroom behaviors: seconds to start, materials missing, noise, out-of-place movement, physical contact or destruction, off-task movement, and volunteering?

- The *independent variable* is reading level: good versus poor.
- The *moderator variable* is grade level: 1, 3, 5, 7, 9, and 11.
- No *control variables* are mentioned, although gender would be a possible one.
- Each of the seven classroom behaviors mentioned was a separate *dependent variable*.
- The *intervening variable* might be student attentiveness. Lack of attentiveness may contribute to both poor reading skills and a number of the dependent variables.

- The *moderator variable* is level of self-efficacy, with three levels: (1) high, (2) middle, and (3) low self-efficacy.
- The only *control variable* identified in the hypothesis statement is subjects' level of education: college.
- The *dependent variable* is amount of self-regulated performance.
- The *intervening variable* might be structure or assistance required for motivation.

SOME CONSIDERATIONS FOR VARIABLE CHOICE

After selecting independent and dependent variables for a study, the researcher must decide which factors to include as moderator variables and which to exclude or hold constant as control variables. He or she must decide how to treat the total pool of other variables (other than the independent) that might affect the dependent variable. In deciding which variables to include and which to exclude, the researcher should take into account theoretical, design, and practical considerations.

Theoretical Considerations

In treating a variable as a moderator variable, the researcher seeks to learn how it interacts with the independent variable to produce differential effects on the dependent variable. The theoretical base from which the researcher is working and the information he or she is trying to gain in a particular experiment often suggest certain variables that seem highly qualified as moderator variables. In choosing a moderator variable, the researcher should ask:

- Is the variable related to the theory with which I'm working?
- How helpful would information about any interaction be? That is, would this result affect my theoretical interpretations and applications?
- How likely is such an interaction to occur?

Design Considerations

Beyond the questions already cited, a researcher might ask questions that relate to the experimental design chosen and its adequacy for controlling for sources of bias. The list should include the question:

- Have my decisions about moderator and control variables met the requirements of experimental design for dealing with sources of invalidity?

Practical Considerations

A researcher can study only so many variables at one time. Human and financial resources limit this choice, as do deadline pressures. By their nature, some variables are harder to study than to neutralize, while others are as easily studied as neutralized. Although researchers are bound by design considerations, they usually find enough freedom of choice that practical concerns come into play. In dealing with practical considerations, the researcher must ask questions like these:

- What difficulties might arise from a decision to make a variable a moderator as opposed to a control variable?
- What kinds of resources are available, and what kinds are required to create and evaluate moderator variables?
- How much control do I have over the experimental situation?

This last concern is a highly significant one. Educational researchers often have less control over their situations than design and theoretical considerations alone might necessitate. Thus, researchers must take practical considerations into account when selecting variables.

SUMMARY

1. An independent variable, sometimes also called a *factor,* is a condition selected for manipulation or measurement by the researcher to determine its relationship to an observed phenomenon or outcome. It is the presumed cause of the outcome, and manipulation creates discrete levels. (Measurement may also enable the researcher to divide it into discrete levels.)
2. A dependent variable is an outcome observed or measured following manipulation or measurement of the independent variable to determine the presumed effect of the independent variable. It is usually a continuous quantity.
3. A moderator variable is a secondary independent variable, selected for study to see if it affects the relationship between the primary independent variable and the dependent variable. It is usually measured, and it often represents a characteristic of the study participants (for example, gender or grade level or ability level). It too is often divided into levels.
4. A control variable is a characteristic of the situation or person that the researcher chooses *not* to study. Its presence and potential impact on the dependent variable must be canceled out or neutralized.
5. An intervening variable is a factor that theoretically explains the reason why the independent variable affects the dependent variable as it does. This concept is created or influenced by the independent variable that enables it to have its effect. It is a hypothetical variable rather than a real one, as the other types are.

6. Independent, moderator, and control variables all may affect the dependent variable, presumably by first affecting an intervening variable.
7. Researchers must decide how to deal with potentially influential variables other than the independent variable. No variable that may affect the dependent variable can be ignored. Each must be treated as either a moderator variable, and hence studied, or a control variable, and hence eliminated.
8. Choosing to treat a variable as a moderator variable is based on (a) theoretical considerations (How likely is the variable to affect the independent variable-dependent variable relationship?), (b) design considerations (Will the choice allow adequate control?), and (c) practical considerations (Can the researcher call on sufficient resources and manageable techniques for accomplishing it?).

COMPETENCY TEST EXERCISES

1. Connect the terms in Column A with those in Column B.

COLUMN A	COLUMN B
a. Independent variable	1. Avoided
b. Dependent variable	2. Inferred
c. Moderator variable	3. Cause
d. Control variable	4. Modifier
e. Intervening variable	5. Effect

2. Consider a study of the relationship between parents' occupations in a science or nonscience field and the tendency to elect science courses in high school by males and females. In this study, identify the:
   a. Independent variable
   b. Moderator variable
   c. Control variable
   d. Dependent variable
   e. Intervening variable

3. Suggest an additional moderator variable for the study in Exercise 2. Also:
   a. State a theoretical consideration that might lead a researcher to include or exclude this variable as a moderator.
   b. State a practical consideration that might lead a researcher to include or exclude this variable as a moderator.

4. Hypothesis: Holding age constant, left-handed children with perceptual-motor training will perform better on eye-hand coordination tasks than left-handed children without this training, whereas such differences will not appear among right-handed children.

   a. Independent variable: _____

    b. Moderator variable: _____

    c. Control variable: _____

    d. Dependent variable: _____

    e. Intervening variable: _____

5. Hypothesis: Inexperienced social studies teachers are more likely to change their attitudes toward teaching after receiving televised feedback than without receiving feedback, whereas experienced social studies teachers are equally likely to maintain their attitudes either with or without televised feedback.

    a. Independent variable: _____

    b. Moderator variable: _____

    c. Control variable: _____

    d. Dependent variable: _____

    e. Intervening variable: _____

RECOMMENDED REFERENCES

Martin, D. W. (1991). *Doing psychology experiments* (3rd ed.). Monterey, CA: Brooks/Cole.

Chapter 6

Constructing Operational Definitions of Variables

Objectives

▶ Identify reasons and situations that justify constructing operational definitions of variables.

▶ Distinguish between operational definitions and other types of definitions.

▶ State minimal observable criteria to include in an operational definition.

▶ Construct three different types of operational definitions.

▶ Distinguish between operational definitions according to their exclusiveness.

▶ Construct predictions from hypotheses.

WHY HAVE OPERATIONAL DEFINITIONS?

"You say I was speeding?"

"Yes, you were going over 15 miles per hour. The speed limit is 15 miles per hour in a school zone; according to the radar gun, you were going 20."

"The children are all in school, and no child was along the street. How could my speed have been unsafe?"

"The law is the law. Here is your ticket."

An everyday situation may involve operational definitions of terms. The officer is correct that the law defines "speeding in a school zone" as: *A car moving at more than 15 miles per hour in an area marked by appropriate signs*. The law guides the officer's judgment. Determination of a violation depends only on simple observation of the cars moving within a marked school zone and measurement of their speeds; if they exceed 15 miles per hour, the driver receives a speeding ticket.

In contrast, the driver tries to use a different operational definition of speeding in a school zone: *In a marked school zone, a car is speeding only if the speed exceeds 15 miles per hour when children are near or on the street*. According to the driver, a car is speeding in a school zone if (1) its speed exceeds 15 miles per hour, and (2) children are near or on the street. The driver believes that the speed of the car is important only when children are present.

Another operational definition, but an impractical one, might define speeding in a school zone on the basis of outcome after the fact: *If a car going at any speed in a school zone hits a child and hurts him or her, then the car was speeding*. Thus, if a child hit by a car is injured, the car was speeding, but if the child gets up and walks away uninjured, the car was not speeding, even though it ran into a child. For obvious reasons, this operational definition does not provide a useful criterion for judgments of speeding in a school zone.

Consider an illustration nearer to the subject at hand. Suppose that you are the school principal and a teacher asks you to remove a youngster from the class due to aggressiveness. Suppose also that you respond by indicating that you like aggressive learners and you feel that *aggressiveness* (that is, active challenging of the relevance of instructional experiences) is a useful quality to bring to the learning situation. The teacher responds by saying that *aggressiveness* means being "filled with hate and potentially violent."

These illustrations suggest some conclusions:

1. Some situations require operational definitions.
2. An operational definition identifies observable criteria for that which is being defined.
3. A concept or object may have more than one operational definition.
4. An operational definition may apply exclusively only in the situation for which it is created.

The examples described so far illustrate communication problems; the same word or phrase can have different meanings for different people. Research is a communication process, although some think of it in different ways. A researcher employs certain techniques to find out something about the world and then attempts to communicate these findings to others. This communication requires a precision of language far more exacting than that demanded of a novelist, poet, or everyday conversationalist. A novelist or poet often tries purposely to evoke a *range* of reactions to selected words and images, while participants in everyday conversations often share a common language background. A researcher, however, must convey meanings in sufficiently precise language so that any reader from any background understands *exactly* what is being said and in sufficient detail to allow replication of the research.

BASING AN OPERATIONAL DEFINITION ON OBSERVABLE CRITERIA

People can develop a variety of ways to define something. Many definitions simply give synonymous names; others state conceptual understandings, providing hypothetical descriptions of what or why something is. Formally stated, an *operational definition* is a characterization based on the observable traits of the object being defined. The word *observable* is the significant element of this definition. If a researcher can make some relatively stable observations of an object or phenomenon, then others can repeat those observations, thus enabling them to identify the object so defined. The important standard for this process comes from the nature of the observations upon which operational definitions are based, how they are made, and how they are measured.

A *conceptual definition,* on the other hand, identifies something based on conceptual or hypothetical criteria rather than observable ones. Defining the *ego* as the sense of self is one example; defining *effective teaching* as instruction that promotes learning is another. A conceptual definition establishes the meaning of a concept by reference to another concept rather than by reference to observable characteristics of reality, as an operational definition does. Conceptual definitions play important roles in the processes of logic associated with hypothesis formulation. However, they contribute little to efforts to bridge between the domain of the hypothetical and general and that of the real and specific. Instead, operational definitions perform this function. Ultimately, a concrete investigation requires operational definitions for the concepts it studies.

Another form of definition cites synonyms. Being *irate* is defined as being mad or angry. Being *aggressive* is defined as being forceful, pushy, or demanding. Being *intelligent* is defined as being smart. Such definitions do provide some information, but they cannot effectively link one thinker's concepts to observable phenomena. Finally, dictionary definitions cite many potential meanings in an attempt to clarify every word in a way that would be of some use to everyone. Again, although dictionary definitions offer useful and informative input, they are no substitute for formal operational definitions that clearly spell out the observable criteria associated exclusively with some object or state.

ALTERNATIVE WAYS OF GENERATING OPERATIONAL DEFINITIONS

Researchers employ three approaches for constructing operational definitions, theoretically allowing them to construct three operational definitions for any object or phenomenon. The three approaches are based on (1) manipulation, (2) dynamic properties, and (3) static properties.

Operational Definitions Based on Manipulation

The first type of operational definition can be constructed to correspond to the operations or manipulations that researchers must perform to cause the defined phenomenon or state to occur. In an experiment, a researcher causes the phenomenon being studied to occur by applying a certain procedure. The description of this procedure forms the first type of operational definition. (This type of operational definition is often more appropriate for defining a phenomenon or state than for characterizing an object.)

Consider some examples of operational definitions based on manipulation. *Frustration* may be operationally defined as the emotional state that results when an individual is blocked from reaching a highly desired goal that is close to attainment. A child may be shown a piece of candy that is held out of reach; this operation would fulfill the manipulation-based operational definition of frustration. A *drive* may be operationally defined as the mental state that results when a person is deprived of a needed substance or activity. *Hunger* may be operationally defined as the result of deprivation of food for 24 hours. Using this definition, observers would all agree on whether a person was hungry by determining when he or she had eaten last. Finally, a manipulation-based operational definition of *aggression* might cite the behavior of a person who has been repeatedly blocked from reaching a highly desired goal. Note that an operational definition for this term based on dynamic properties may be more appropriate for research, as the next section explains.

In an educational context, *individualized instruction* can be operationally defined as instruction that the researcher has designed to be delivered by a computer (or book) so that students can work on it by themselves at their own pace. This definition contrasts the term with *group instruction*, operationally defined as instruction designed to be delivered verbally by a live instructor to a number of students at the same time. As part of a study, the researcher would then create samples of these two kinds of instruction and impose them on different students. This creation and systematic imposition of different instructional conditions represents the research manipulation.

In each case, a manipulation-based operational definition is a statement of what manipulations or preconditions experimenters create or require as indicators of a certain phenomenon or state. Experimenters define that phenomenon operationally by stating the preceding operations or events that have reliably led to its occurrence. Although the label of the state or phenomenon may be somewhat arbitrary, the preconditions are quite concrete and observable activities, so they constitute an adequate definition for scientific purposes. Often, more than one operational definition can be constructed for a single variable, but each must be sufficiently operational to meet the criterion of exclusiveness, as discussed in a later section.

Review a few additional examples of manipulation-based operational definitions:

- *Fear* is the emotional state produced by exposing a person to an object that the person has indicated is highest in his or her hierarchy of objects to be avoided.
- *Conflict* is the state produced by placing two or more people in a situation where each pursues the same goal but only one can attain it.
- *Positive self-expectation of success* is the condition produced by telling students that the results of an intelligence test indicate they will likely achieve academic success.
- *Assertiveness training* is a program designed for women to (a) present them with model responses to apply in a variety of challenging and stressful social and job situations in order to stand up for their own interests, and (b) give them opportunities to practice these responses.

Because these operational definitions tell what manipulation a researcher will use to induce a particular observable state, they are useful for defining levels of independent variables; they function as prescriptions for the experimenter's actions. The same variable may, of course, be operationally defined by more than one type of definition, but someone seeking to define an independent variable to be manipulated by the experimenter must develop this type of operational definition.

Operational Definitions Based on Dynamic Properties

The second type of operational definition can be constructed by stating how the particular object or thing being defined *operates*, that is, what it *does* or what constitutes its observed properties. An *intelligent person* can be operationally defined as someone who gets high grades in school or someone who solves symbolic logic problems. Operationally defined, a *hungry person* might be considered any person who depresses a lever at the rate of 10 times a minute to get food. A *directive teacher* might be operationally defined as one who gives instructions, personalizes criticism or blame, and establishes formal relationships with students.

In educational research, operational definitions based on dynamic properties seem particularly appropriate for describing types of people (those that display certain qualities or particular states). Because the dynamic properties of people are manifested as behavior, this type of definition describes a particular type of person in terms of concrete and observable *behaviors* associated with the identified characteristics or state. While a manipulation-based operational definition of *aggression* might cite the behavior of a person blocked from attaining a goal, for example, *aggression* can also be operationally defined, based on dynamic properties, as speaking loudly or abusively or fighting. The definition based on dynamic properties may be more restricted or specific than its counterpart based on manipulation.

To clarify, review a few additional examples of operational definitions based on dynamic properties:

- *Subject matter preference* is the characteristic of reliably selecting to examine or use materials from one subject matter more frequently than from others available, given a room containing materials from different subject matter areas in equal numbers.
- *Motor activity* is any excursion by a student from his or her assigned seat.
- *Sensitivity* is the tendency of a teacher to smile at, touch, or exchange pleasantries with students during class.
- *Motivation* is the persistent attendance of students in school; alternatively, a *motivated person* is one who manifests persistent school attendance.
- *Arithmetic achievement* is demonstrated competency attainment in arithmetic, including mastery of basic skills (addition, subtraction, multiplication, and division), fractions, decimals, and whole numbers.[1]

Although researchers may construct them for other variables, definitions based on dynamic properties are particularly useful for characterizing dependent variables to be evaluated based on observations of the behavior of participants in the study.

---

[1] Actually, definitions of *achievement* fall between dynamic-property and static-property definitions, citing more behavioral characteristics than the latter and more static or internal ones than the former. *Achievement* has been classified here as a dynamic property, even though a test is typically used to measure it.

Operational Definitions Based on Static Properties

The third type of operational definition can be constructed by specifying what an object or phenomenon is *like*, that is, its *internal properties*. A sensitive person can be defined, for instance, as someone who *describes* himself or herself as having a strong concern for the feelings of others and who *reports* trying not to hurt or upset those feelings. Operational definitions based on static principles utilize reported structural properties of the objects.

In educational research, many operational definitions are based on the characteristics observable in or attributed to people or phenomena. To assess the internal characteristics and states of people, researchers often rely on self-reports from their subjects; the subjects might, for example, fill out questionnaires or attitude scales to report their own thoughts, perceptions, and emotions. Thus, one static-property operational definition of *course satisfaction* might be the perception—as reported by subjects on questionnaires—that a course has been an interesting and effective learning experience. In contrast, a dynamic-property operational definition of course satisfaction would be based on observable behaviors, such as recommending the course to friends, enrolling in related courses, or enrolling in other courses taught by the same teacher.

Note that static-property operational definitions describe the qualities, traits, or characteristics of people or things. Thus, researchers can construct them to define any type of variable, including independent, dependent, and moderator variables (those not manipulated by the researcher). When such a definition specifies a person's characteristic, it cites a static or internal quality rather than a behavior like that specified by a dynamic-property definition. Static-property operational definitions often lend themselves to measurement by tests, although feasibility of testing is not a requisite part of the definition. However, operational definitions are statements of observable properties—traits, appearances, behaviors—and statements of such properties are prerequisites to measuring them. For people, a static-property definition is measured based on data collected directly from the subjects of the study, representing their self-descriptions of inner states or performances.

To clarify, consider a few additional examples of static-property operational definitions:

- *Introversion* is the expression of a preference to engage in solitary rather than group activity (to view oneself as a "loner").
- *Attitudes toward school* are the self-reported receptiveness and acceptability of school activities, school rules, school requirements, and school work.
- *Subject matter preference* is the expressed choice of one subject matter over another in response to a request to rank order them.
- *Teacher enthusiasm* is the report by teachers of how excited they are by teaching and how much they look forward to doing it.

Many researchers refer to scores on tests or rating scales as static-property operational definitions. Such instruments do not themselves constitute operational definitions, but they must embody operational definitions. Thus, anxiety might be measured by a particular test according to a definition based on self-reported symptoms such as fearful thoughts and physically uncomfortable sensations like sweating and heart palpitations. Although the test itself measures these symptoms, the specifications that explicitly identify them constitute the operational definition. After settling on such an operational definition, the researcher would set out to uncover or develop a test or measurement procedure suitable for measuring the state, symptoms, or trait as operationally defined.

The typology of operational definitions is offered as an aid in constructing them, in recognizing them, and in understanding why a single state or object may be operationally defined in more than one way. Although the classification of an operational definition into the typology may reflect somewhat arbitrary distinctions, the construction of the operational definition is a definite process. The researcher uses the operational definition best-suited to bringing concepts and variables to a sufficiently concrete state for study and examination. Indeed, the notion of classifying an operational definition is often an after-the-fact consideration. The principal concern is the manner in which the defined object or state is examined in a research study.

THE CRITERION OF EXCLUSIVENESS

A researcher may operationally define an *aggressive child* as one who gets into a fight. Another might operationally define an *aggressive child* as one who habitually gets into fights. Still another might specify one who habitually gets into fights without provocation. Each of these operational definitions identifies an increasingly exclusive set of observable criteria associated with aggressiveness compared to the one preceding it. As an operational definition increases in exclusiveness, it gains usefulness, because it conveys progressively more information, allows the researcher to exclude undesired objects or states from consideration, and increases the possibility that others can replicate the sense of the variable. However, extreme exclusiveness restricts the generalizability of a concept by restricting its external validity. Researchers must try to strike a "happy medium" between the demands of internal validity, which call for increasing exclusiveness, and the demands of external validity, which call for relaxing exclusiveness.

Researchers would not be wrong to define school learning as presence in a classroom. However, many students present in a classroom are not learning, so the definition would lack exclusiveness. If the researchers were to enlarge the definition to include the appearance of enjoyment, its exclusiveness would increase, but it still would not exclude students who are happy but not learning. Thus, the operational definition would still offer only limited usefulness. It would have to specify some observable characteristic of the learners, such as their achievement, change in behavior, or gain in skills, to effectively distinguish the learners from the nonlearners. Thus, school learning might be defined as increase in ability to solve specific types of problems following presence in a classroom.

When formulating any operational definition, researchers should consider how completely the observable criteria it specifies distinguish the defined condition from everything else.

Examples

Tuckman (1996a) studied the different effects of a condition labeled *incentive motivation* to one labeled *learning strategy* on achievement in a course. (This is Example 1 on page 104.) The *incentive motivation* approach was operationally defined for the study as a method based on a weekly quiz on the information covered. The operation of giving a quiz was expected to yield incentive motivation to study, because the quiz would provoke the desire to demonstrate competency and to obtain a high grade or avoid a low one in the course. The *learning strategy* approach was operationally defined as a method based on completing a text-processing homework assignment on the information covered; students identified key terms, defined them, and elaborated on their definitions. These examples are manipulation-based operational definitions.

The study operationally defined *achievement* in the course as performance on two multiple-choice examinations. It defined another variable, *prior academic performance*, as grade point average for coursework in the upper division. Both are dynamic operational definitions.

For another example, Slavin and Karweit (1984) conducted a study of two instructional variables—mastery learning versus its absence and team learning versus its absence—each specified by manipulation-based operational definitions. This study was discussed as Example 2 in the last chapter's section on combining variable types. (Note that only one level of each variable is operationally defined: the presence of the experimental approach):

> In group-paced mastery learning initial instruction is followed by a formative test. Students who do not pass this test . . . receive corrective instruction, followed by a summative test. Students who fail the test may receive further instruction until all students finally pass, or the teacher may decide to move on when a specified portion of the class has demonstrated mastery of the unit. (p. 726)

> [Student team learning] refers to a set of instructional methods in which students study material initially presented by the teacher in four-member heterogeneous learning teams, and are rewarded based on average team performance on individually administered quizzes or other assessments. (p. 726)

The operational definition of the treatment that features neither mastery learning nor team learning, called *focused instruction,* is a "procedure consisting of teaching, individual worksheet work and tests" (p. 728). The operational definition of the combination of mastery and team learning simply joins the two separate operational definitions. In this way, the researchers set out operational definitions for each of the four instructional possibilities they wanted to study.

As a third example, consider a study by Prater and Padia (1983) of the effect of three modes of discourse on student writing performance. The researchers operationally defined three modes of discourse, or ways to categorize writing, as follows:

- *Expressive discourse:* Writing in which the writer is asked to tell the reader how the writer feels about or perceives something.
- *Explanatory discourse:* Writing in which the writer is asked to present actual information about something to the reader.
- *Persuasive discourse:* Writing in which the writer is asked to take and support a position and attempt to convince the reader to agree with it.

These examples illustrate manipulation-based operational definitions. Note that they cite the researchers' instructions to study participants.

Further consider a study of the relationship between teacher enthusiasm and pupil achievement. *Teacher enthusiasm* was operationally defined as the intensity of the following teacher behaviors: (1) vocal delivery, (2) eye movements, (3) gestures, (4) body movements, (5) facial expressions, (6) word selection, (7) acceptance of students' ideas and feelings, and (8) overall energy level.

Although this operational definition appears to emphasize dynamic properties in that it describes observable behaviors, it was actually a manipulation-based definition, since the researchers attempted to train teachers to carry out those behaviors. Were the behaviors merely observed, the definition would be a dynamic one, but when the researchers tried to cause the behaviors to occur, they utilized a manipulation-based operational definition.

OPERATIONAL DEFINITIONS AND THE RESEARCH PROCESS

Within the process of testing a hypothesis, the researcher must move repeatedly from the hypothetical to the concrete and back. To get the maximum value from data, he or she must make generalizations that apply to situations other than the experiment itself. Thus, the researcher often begins at the conceptual or hypothetical level to develop hypotheses that articulate possible linkages between concepts. A research study, however, operates in reality, requiring the investigator to transform the conceptual statements of the variables as they appear in the hypotheses to operational statements. For example, a researcher might construct a hypothesis such as, "Students prefer nondirective teachers to directive teachers."

To design a study to test this hypothesis, the researcher must pose the questions, "What do I mean by *prefer?*" and "What do I mean by *nondirective* and *directive* teachers?" The answers to these questions take the form of operational definitions.

Preference may be operationally defined as a student's expression of liking a specific teacher relative to other teachers. (This is a static-property definition.) Preference may be ultimately measured by asking students to rank order all their teachers according to how much they like each one. Using a dynamic-property operational definition, a *directive* teacher may be defined as a teacher who exhibits the following behaviors:

STRUCTURE

___ Formal planning and structuring of the course
___ Minimizing informal work and group work
___ Structuring group activity when it is used
___ Rigidly structuring individual and classroom activity
___ Requiring factual knowledge from students based on absolute sources

INTERPERSONAL

___ Enforcing absolute and justifiable punishment
___ Minimizing opportunities to make and learn from mistakes
___ Maintaining a formal classroom atmosphere
___ Maintaining formal relationships with students
___ Taking absolute responsibility for grades

In designing the study or experiment, operational definitions of all relevant variables must be transformed into a specific methodology and a specific set of measuring devices or techniques. In fact, the methods section of a research report is really a detailed set of measurement specifications based on operational definitions. However, the process of formulating operational definitions must be completed before deciding upon the details of measurement techniques. Thus, operational definitions of the concepts introduced in the hypotheses should appear in the introductory section of a report. (The organization of a report is considered in detail in Chapter 12.)

After completing a study, the researcher then relates back operational findings to the concepts included in the original hypotheses of the study, leading to generalizations from the results. Thus, the processes of conceptualizing and operationalizing have been combined and recombined in the total research process.

Testability

The testability of any hypothesis depends on whether researchers can construct suitable operational definitions for its variables. For example, a researcher might hypothesize that junior college deans trained in programs designed specifically

BOX 6

ILLUSTRATIONS FROM THE SAMPLE STUDIES

Sample Study I in Appendix A hypothesized that students who received encouragement would be persuaded to feel good about their own efforts and performance, so they would experience a concomitant increase in self-efficacy. The study also hypothesized that the encouraged students would produce more extensive task responses than would students who received neutral responses to their performance, reflecting stronger motivation due to the positive feedback.

The two levels of the independent variable, encouraging feedback and neutral feedback, were operationally defined based on a manipulation by the researchers, who created both kinds of feedback. *Encouraging feedback* was defined as teacher indications that a student turned in a qualitatively good performance ("You wrote good test items"), while *neutral* or *nonencouraging feedback* was defined as quantitative performance information alone ("Your items were acceptable for credit").

The first dependent variable, *self-efficacy*, was defined statically as the kind and number of test items that students *judged themselves* to be capable of writing, and their confidence in that judgment. The second dependent variable, *performance*, was defined dynamically as the sum of the points earned by writing test items based on the number written and their point value.

Consider also Sample Study II in Appendix A, a comparison of the classroom behaviors of good and poor readers. *Good readers* were operationally defined dynamically as students who scored among the three highest results in their class on a reading achievement test (which presumably measured vocabulary and reading comprehension skills, though this fact was not specified); *poor readers* were students who scored among the three worst results on this test. Seven dependent variables were studied, representing the nature and degree of involvement of students in the classroom learning process. Each was defined dynamically, under the heading *Procedure* in the Method section, by describing the behavior to be observed.

---

for administrators at that level will be more effective administrators than will those trained in programs designed for administrators in universities or secondary schools. He or she must then construct a useful operational definition for *effectiveness of a junior college administrator*. One possibility is to refer to perceptions of effectiveness by other administrators, but this approach leaves much room for error. Developing a dynamic-property definition might give more useful guidance to the study, beginning with the question: Which behaviors of effective administrators differentiate them from ineffective administrators? After compiling a list of such behaviors and tightening it to reduce overlap, the researcher could define effective administrators as those who can make decisions quickly, can delegate responsibility, are well liked by their superiors and subordinates, and receive reactions of confidence and trust from teachers and students.

The administrator's role can be operationalized in many ways, including individual task functions (or decision-making responsibilities), group task functions (or delegating responsibility), and sociability functions (or relations with teachers). Thus, an adequate operational definition of the effective administrator paves the way for testing hypotheses that include the concept.

Predictions

In defining the variables in a hypothesis to make it testable, a researcher constructs a prediction. A *prediction* is a statement of expectations, in which operational definitions have replaced the conceptual statements of the variables in the hypothesis. Thus, a prediction is a testable derivative of a hypothesis. In fact, to use terminology developed earlier, a prediction is a *specific hypothesis*. Because variables can have different operational definitions, alternative predictions (or alternative specific hypotheses) can be derived from any one general hypothesis.

Consider the following examples:

- **Hypothesis.** Attitudes toward school and aggressive behavior in school are inversely related.
  Prediction: Students who see the school as a place they enjoy and where they like to be will be less frequently cited for fighting or talking back to a teacher than those who see the school as a place they do not enjoy.
- **Hypothesis.** Programs offering stipends are more successful at retaining students than are programs without such payments.
  Prediction: The dropout rate among adults enrolled in training and retraining programs will be smaller in programs that pay stipends to students who attend than in comparable programs that do not pay stipends.
- **Hypothesis.** Performance in paired-associate tasks is inversely related to socioeconomic status.
  Prediction: Students whose parents earn more than $50,000 a year will require fewer trials to perfectly learn a paired-associate task than will students whose parents earn less than $20,000 a year.
- **Hypothesis.** In deciding on curricular innovations, authoritarian school superintendents will be less inclined to respond to rational pressures and more inclined to respond to expedience pressures than will nonauthoritarian school superintendents.
  Prediction: In judging curricular innovations, school superintendents who react to the world in terms of superordinate-subordinate role distinctions and power and toughness will less frequently acknowledge the opinions of

subject matter experts as sources of influence and more frequently acknowledge input from their superiors than will superintendents who do not react to the world in these terms.

THE RESEARCH SPECTRUM

The researcher has now developed operational definitions of the variables and restated the hypotheses in the operational form called *predictions*. He or she is now ready to conduct a study to test these predictions and thus the hypotheses. The next step requires a decision about how to control and/or manipulate the variables through a research design.

The schematic of the research process in Figure 6.1 places the steps and procedures already described in perspective relative to those covered in the remainder of this book. It also outlines the sequence of activities in research that form the basis for this book.

Note that research begins with a problem and applies both theories and findings of other studies, located in a thorough literature search, to arrive at hypotheses. (These points were covered in Chapters 2, 3, and 4.) These hypotheses contain variables that must be labeled and then operationally defined, as described in this

FIGURE 6.1   THE RESEARCH SPECTRUM

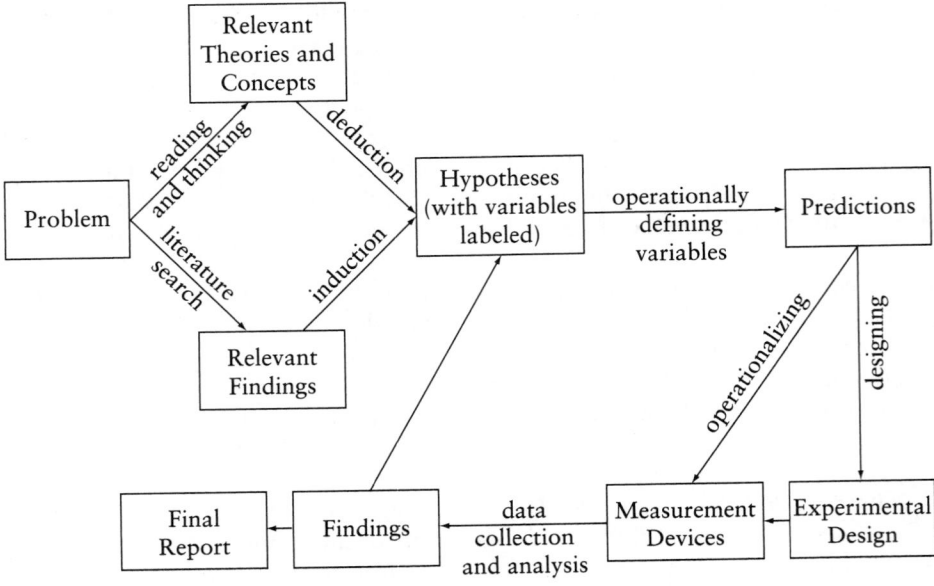

chapter, to construct predictions. These steps might be considered the *logical* stages of research. These stages are followed by the *methodological* stages, which include developing a research design and measurement devices. The final or *concluding* stages of the research process cover data analysis and write-up, culminating in the presentation of findings. The processes of designing a study or experiment and developing measures are the subjects of the chapters to follow: two on design and two on measurement. Following that material, two chapters (Chapters 11 and 12) deal with analyzing data and reporting results.

SUMMARY

1. Operational definitions refine variables to emphasize the observable characteristics of phenomena under study. These definitions enable researchers to convey the meanings of variables with sufficient precision that others can understand and replicate the work.
2. Researchers employ three types of operational definitions. The manipulation-based definitions, used only for independent variables, specify variables according to the operations or manipulations that the researchers apply to cause the phenomena to occur. For example, the variable *mastery learning* is operationally defined as an instructional method that gives students repeated opportunities to succeed.
3. The technique of dynamic-property operational definition defines a variable according to how it behaves or operates. For example, enthusiastic teachers are those who move around a lot and talk loud and fast to students.
4. The technique of static-property operational definition specifies a variable according to how people describe themselves based on self-reporting. For example, self-confidence is confirmed in your statement that you believe you will succeed.
5. Operational definitions can be evaluated based on exclusiveness, that is, the uniqueness of the variables that they define. An operational definition that simultaneously fits a number of variables lacks exclusiveness.
6. Although researchers begin at the conceptual level with broadly defined variables and hypotheses, to study those variables and test those hypotheses, they must operationalize them. Formulating operational definitions is an activity that occurs between conceptualizing a study and developing the methodology to carry it out. Operational definitions help researchers to make hypotheses into testable predictions.
7. A prediction (previously called a *specific hypothesis*) is a hypothesis in which the conceptual names of the variables have been replaced by their operational definitions. Predictions are then tested by the methods designed for research studies.
8. The research spectrum treats predictions as the bridge between the logical and conceptual stage described in previous chapters and the methodological stage described in subsequent chapters.

COMPETENCY TEST EXERCISES

1. Which of the following definitions is operational?
   a. Scientific occupation—Any occupation that falls under Category VI (science) of Roe's (1966) classification of occupations.
   b. Scientific occupation—Any occupation with activities in the field of science.
   c. Scientific occupation—Any occupation involving the use of the scientific method as a way of reasoning.

2. As stated, which of the following are observable characteristics of a teacher?
   a. A person who is confident
   b. A person who stands in front of a classroom
   c. A person who identifies himself or herself as a teacher
   d. A person who is liked by students

3. Below are three operational definitions. Identify the three types: A—manipulation-based; B—dynamic-property; and C—static-property.
   a. Scientist—A person trained in a doctoral program in biology, chemistry, physics, or a related field
   b. Scientist—A person who chooses "scientist" to describe herself or himself from a list of occupations that includes it
   c. Scientist—A person who engages in laboratory analyses and determinations involving live, chemical, or physical matter and then publishes the results

4. Below are three more operational definitions. Again, label the three types.
   a. Interest—A state evidenced by a person's own admission of concern for a subject
   b. Interest—A state provoked by showing someone something that he or she has said would appeal to him or her
   c. Interest—A state evidenced by increase of activity and attention to a new stimulus

5. Construct a manipulation-based operational definition of (a) achievement motivation and (b) cohesiveness (group solidarity).

6. Construct a dynamic-property operational definition of (a) achievement motivation and (b) cohesiveness.

7. Construct a static-property operational definition of (a) achievement motivation and (b) cohesiveness.

8. Hypothesis: Socioeconomic status and academic ability are positively related. Rewrite this hypothesis as a prediction.

9. Hypothesis: As classroom climate becomes progressively more unstructured, students demonstrate greater creativity. Rewrite this hypothesis as a prediction.

RECOMMENDED REFERENCES

Martin, D. W. (1991). *Doing psychology experiments* (3rd ed.). Monterey, CA: Brooks/Cole.

Part 3

METHODOLOGICAL STAGES

Designing and Measuring

Chapter 7

IDENTIFYING TECHNIQUES FOR MANIPULATING AND CONTROLLING VARIABLES

Objectives

▶ Identify the reasons for incorporating a control group into a research design.

▶ Identify and describe the sources of internal and external invalidity that induce researchers to rely on control groups.

▶ Describe the procedures for guarding against the various sources of invalidity.

▶ Identify procedures within a given study for controlling against the various sources of invalidity and evaluate the adequacy of these procedures.

▶ Describe procedures for gauging the success of an experimental manipulation.

THE CONTROL GROUP

The essence of experimental research is *control*. No researcher can make a valid assessment of the effect of a particular condition or treatment without eliminating or limiting other conditions that also influence the observed effect.

To eliminate those other factors, researchers incorporate control groups into the designs of their studies.[1] A *control group* is a group of subjects or participants in an experiment whose selection and experiences are identical in every way possible to the experimental group except that they do not receive the treatment. (See Table 7.1.)

To clarify this difference, suppose that a curriculum developer believes she has found an approach for teaching fourth and fifth graders who have never learned to read properly, causing them to read at grade level. In order to test the effectiveness of her instructional approach, she would design an experiment with that teaching method as the independent variable and the reading level of the subjects who experience this teaching as the dependent variable. If she were simply to try her approach on some group of students, perhaps 100 poor readers, and then measure their reading level a second time, she might have trouble interpreting data that showed a significant increase in reading level.

TABLE 7.1   **EXPERIMENTAL AND CONTROL GROUPS IN AN EXPERIMENT**

EXPERIMENTAL GROUP		CONTROL GROUP	
ENVIRONMENTAL STIMULI	SUBJECTS' RESPONSES	ENVIRONMENTAL STIMULI	SUBJECTS' RESPONSES
S_x	R_x	S_0	R_0
S_1	R_1	S_1	R_1
S_2	R_2	S_2	R_2
S_3	R_3	S_3	R_3
S_4	R_4	S_4	R_4

S_x: Independent variable (Level 1); S_0: Independent variable (Level 2)[a]

S_1, S_2, S_3, S_4: Control variables (arbitrary number)

R_x, R_0: Dependent variable (amounts)

---

[a]May be either absence of treatment or comparison treatment.

---

[1] Researchers often refer to control groups as *comparison groups* when different experiences are being compared.

The curriculum developer could not attribute the increase in reading level to her approach, because she would not know whether the reading levels of the subjects would have risen even without exposure to it. She might have found similar results if the subjects were more highly motivated the second time they took the reading test (the one given after experiencing the approach) than they were the first time. Further, the entire group might have received better instruction in school, more attention from their teachers, or more encouragement at home because they were known to be under observation as part of the research. Any of these possibilities, and many more, might have been responsible for the apparent increase in reading level.

To deal with this problem, the experimenter would form a control group also made up of poor readers in the fourth and fifth grades. These students would also experience an educational "treatment" at the same time as the first group, although the control group would undergo a neutral treatment. (This experience performs the same function in the research design as the *placebo* or salt tablet in a drug evaluation study.) None of the subjects would know whether they were receiving the real experimental approach or the neutral one (both of which would differ from their previous experience in school). They would be operating in the *blind*. Because the person administering the instruction to be evaluated, the "teacher," can subtly reveal the distinction between the approach under study and the neutral one, he or she also remains uninformed about which is which. The study presents each option as the new instructional approach being tested. Thus, the teacher also operates in the blind, creating what is referred to as a *double-blind* condition.

A control group allows a researcher to cancel or neutralize the effects of extraneous variables only if all conditions other than the independent and moderator variables remain constant for both experimental and control groups. (The moderator variable is controlled by treating it as an independent variable and systematically examining its effects.) To ensure this similarity between groups, researchers identify and classify variables that would prevent valid conclusions about the outcome of an experiment without adequate control. These variables can be organized into two broad categories: those that pose threats to internal validity and those that pose threats to external validity.

FACTORS AFFECTING INTERNAL VALIDITY OR CERTAINTY

To ensure internal validity or certainty for a study, the researcher must establish experimental controls to support the conclusion that differences occur as a result of the experimental treatment. In an experiment lacking internal validity, the researcher does not know whether the experimental treatment or uncontrolled factors produced the difference between groups. Campbell and Stanley (1966) identified classes of extraneous variables that can be sources of internal bias if not controlled.

This section reviews such factors, dividing them into three groups: (1) experience bias—based on what occurs within a research study as it progresses; (2) participant bias—based on the characteristics of the people on whom the study is conducted; (3) instrumentation bias—based on the way the data are collected.

Experience Bias Factors

HISTORY   In research, the term *history* refers to events occurring in the environment at the same time that a study tests the experimental variable. If a study tests a specific curriculum on a group of students who are simultaneously experiencing high stress due to an external event, then the measured outcomes of the experimental test may not reflect the effects of the experimental curriculum but rather those of the external, historical event. Researchers prevent limitations on internal validity due to history by comparing results for an experimental group to those for a control group with the same external or historical experiences during the course of the experiment.

In addition, experimental group participants and members of the control group must experience a comparable history *within* the experiment in all aspects other than the experiences being tested. Specifically, materials, conditions, and procedures within the experiment other than those specific to one of the variables being manipulated (that is, independent or moderator variables) must be identical for experimental and control subjects.

One common source of history bias, termed *teacher effect,* results from a comparison of results for Teacher A teaching by Method A to those for Teacher B teaching by Method B. In such cases, analysis cannot possibly separate the effect of the teacher from the effect of the instructional method.

TESTING   Invalidity due to *testing* results when experience of a pretest affects subsequent posttest performance. Many experiments apply pretests to subjects to determine their initial states with regard to variables of interest. The experience of taking such a pretest may increase the likelihood that the subjects will improve their performance on the subsequent posttest, particularly when it is identical to the pretest. The posttest, then, may not measure simply the effect of the experimental treatment. Indeed, its results may reflect the pretest experience more than the experimental treatment experience itself (or, in the case of the control group, the absence of treatment experience). A pretest can also blur differences between experimental and control groups by providing the control group with an experience relevant to the posttest.

Researchers often seek to avoid testing problems by advocating *unobtrusive measures*—measurement techniques that do not require acceptance or awareness by the experimental subjects. In this way, they hope to minimize the possibility that testing will jeopardize internal validity. (If subjects do not directly provide data by voluntarily responding to a test, they do not experience a test exposure that could benefit their performance.)

In more traditional experimental designs, the problem of testing can be avoided simply by avoiding pretests. (In fact, they are often unnecessary steps.) The next chapter presents research designs that avoid pretests. Apart from introducing possible bias, pretests are expensive and time-consuming activities.

EXPECTANCY   A treatment may appear to increase learning effectiveness as compared to that of a control or comparison group, not because it really boosts effectiveness, but because either the experimenter or the subjects believe that it does and behave according to this expectation. When a researcher is in a position to influence the outcome of an experiment, albeit unconsciously, he or she may behave in a way that improves the performance of one group and not the other, which alter results. So-called "smart" rats were found to outperform "dumb" ones when experimenters believed that the labels reflected genuine differences. Such *experimenter bias* has been well-documented by Rosenthal (1985).

Subjects may also form expectations about treatment outcomes. Referred to by some as *demand characteristics*, these self-imposed demands for performance by subjects, particularly by those experiencing an experimental condition, result from a respect for authority and a high regard for science. Motivated by these feelings, the subjects attempt to comply with their own expectations of appropriate results for the experiment. Expectancy effects can be controlled by use of the double-blind techniques described earlier in the chapter.

Participant Bias Factors

SELECTION   Many studies attempt to compare the effects of different experiences or treatments on different groups of individuals. Bias may result if the group experiencing one treatment includes members who are brighter, more receptive, or older than the group receiving either no treatment or some other treatment. Results for the first group may change, not because of the treatment itself, but because the group selected to receive the treatment differs from the other in some way. The personal reactions and behaviors of individuals within a group can influence research results. In other words, "people factors" can introduce a bias.

Random assignment minimizes the problems of selection by ensuring that any person in the subject pool has an equal probability of becoming a member of either the experimental group or the control group. Because experimental or control subjects assigned randomly should not differ in general characteristics, any treatment effects in the study should not result from the special characteristics of a particular group. In research designs that call for selection as a variable (for example, intelligence) under manipulation, subjects are separated systematically into different groups (for example, high and low) based on some individual difference measure, thus providing for control.

Obviously, if a researcher fails to control selection bias, he or she cannot say that the outcome of the study does not reflect initial differences between groups rather than the treatment being evaluated. Detailed procedures for minimizing selection bias are described in a later section of this chapter on equating experimental and control conditions.

MATURATION   *Maturation* refers to the processes of change that take place within subjects during the course of an experiment. Experiments that extend for long periods of time often lose validity because uncontrolled processes occurring simultaneously, such as developmental changes within the subjects, confound their results. Because people (especially students) are known to change through normal development, a study's final outcome could well result from this change rather than from any experimental treatment. To avoid such problems, an experimenter may form a control group composed of comparable persons who can be expected to have the same (or similar) maturational and developmental experiences. This precaution enables the experimenter to make conclusions about the experimental treatment independent of the confounding maturation effect.

STATISTICAL REGRESSION   When group members are chosen on the basis of extreme scores on a particular variable, problems of statistical regression occur. Say, for instance, that a group of students takes an IQ test, and only the highest third and the lowest third are selected for the experiment, eliminating the middle third. Statistical processes would create a tendency for the scores on any posttest measurement of the high-IQ students to decrease toward the mean, while the scores of the low-IQ students would increase toward the mean. Thus, the groups would differ less in their posttest results, *even without experiencing any experimental treatment.* This effect occurs because chance factors are more likely to contribute to extreme scores than to average scores, and such factors are unlikely to reappear during a second testing (or in testing on a different measure). The problem is controlled by avoiding the exclusive selection of extreme scorers and including average scorers.

EXPERIMENTAL MORTALITY   Researchers in any study should strive to obtain posttest data from *all* subjects originally included in the study. Otherwise, bias may result if subjects who withdraw from the study differ from those who remain. Such differences relevant to the dependent variable introduce posttest bias (or internal invalidity based on mortality). This bias also occurs when a study evaluates more than one condition, and subjects are lost differentially from the groups experiencing the different conditions.

As an example, consider a study to follow up and compare graduates of two different educational programs. The researchers may fail to reach some members of each group, for example, those who have joined the armed forces. Moreover, one of the two groups may have lost more members than the other. The original samples may now be biased by the selective loss of some individuals. Because the groups have not lost equally, the losses may not be random results; rather, they may reflect some bias in the group or program. If the purpose of the follow-up study were to assess attitudes toward authority, for example, graduates who had joined the armed services would differ systematically from other graduates on this variable. Failure to obtain data from these individuals, then, would bias the outcome and limit its effectiveness in assessing the attitudes produced by the educational program. Data from a representative sample of the graduates might support conclusions quite different from those indicated by the more limited input.

To avoid problems created by experimental mortality, researchers often must choose reasonably large groups, take steps to ensure their representativeness, and attempt to follow up subjects who leave their studies or for whom they lack initial results.

INTERACTIVE COMBINATIONS OF FACTORS   Of course, factors that affect validity may occur in combination. For example, one study might suffer from invalidity due to a selection-maturation interaction. Failure to equate experimental and control groups on age might create problems both of selection and maturation bias, because children at some ages mature or change more rapidly than do children at other ages. Moreover, the nature of the changes experienced at one age might be more systematically related to the experimental treatment than the changes experienced at another age. Thus, two sources of invalidity can combine to restrict the overall validity of the experiment.

Instrumentation Bias

Instrumentation is the measurement or observation procedures used during an experiment. Such procedures typically include tests, mechanical measuring instruments, and judgment by observers or scorers. Although mechanical measuring instruments seldom undergo changes during the course of a study, observers and scorers may well change their manner of collecting and recording data as the study proceeds. Because interviewers tend to gain proficiency (or perhaps become bored) as a study proceeds, they may inadvertently provide different cues to interviewees, take different amounts and kinds of notes, or even score or code protocols differently, thus introducing *instrumentation bias* into the results.

A related threat to validity results if the observers, scorers, or interviewers become aware of the purpose of the study. Consciously or unconsciously, they may attempt to increase the likelihood that results will support the desired hypotheses. Both the measuring instruments of a study and the data collectors should remain *constant across time* as well as *constant across groups* (or conditions).

Chapters 9 and 10 review ways in which researchers can minimize the potential bias from problems with subjects, raters, environment, and so on. Some of the major points covered in these chapters are itemized here to provide an overview in the context of internal validity.

Researchers employ many tactics to control instrumentation bias:

1. Establish the reliability or consistency of test scores over items and over time, thus showing that a test consistently measures some variable (see pages 198–200).
2. Use the same measure for both pretest and posttest, or use alternate forms of the same measure (see pages 198–200).
3. Establish the validity of a test measure, thus showing that it evaluates what you intended to measure (see pages 200–202).
4. Establish a relative scoring system for a test (norms) so that scores may be adapted to a common scale (see pages 202–205).
5. Gather input from more than one judge or observer, keep the same judges or observers throughout the course of study, and compare their judgments to establish an index of interjudge agreement (see pages 224–231).

Researchers can employ other techniques for controlling instrumentation bias, but these five are the most commonly encountered. The subspeciality called *psychometrics* focuses essentially on dealing with instrumentation bias in behavioral measurement.[2]

Factors Affecting External Validity or Generality

The term *external validity,* or *generality,* refers to the generalizability or representativeness of a study's findings. A researcher carries out an experiment hoping that the results can be applied to other people at other times and in other places. For findings to have any generality, which allows broader applications outside the experimental situation, the research design must give consideration

---

[2] Bias may also result from the effects of *stability*—the tendency for a finding or result to vary in unreliable ways, that is, to occur once but not thereafter. This whimsy in data can be examined through statistical tests. (See Chapter 11.) Such tests provide information on the probability that a finding was not a chance event.

to external validity.[3] At least four factors affect this question of generalizability: the reactive effects of testing, the interaction effects of selection bias, the reactive effects of experimental arrangements, and multiple-treatment interference.

Reactive Effects of Testing

If pretesting activity sensitizes the experimental subjects to the particular treatment, the effect of the treatment may be partially the result of the pretest. In another set of conditions without the pretest, the treatment would not have the same effects. For example, a study might seek to evaluate the effectiveness of a message intended to produce attitude change; if it were to begin with a pretest to gauge initial attitudes, the participants could become sensitized to the attitudes in question and therefore pay more attention to the message, leading them to show more attitude change when tested than they would have shown without experiencing the pretest. A design that presented the same message without a pretest would most likely produce different results, especially if the pretest were to act as a necessary precondition for effective change based on the message.

Also, subjects often try to "help" an experimenter by providing the result they think he or she is anticipating. Therefore, they may react differently to the treatment after a pretest because it indicates the experimenter's aim.[4]

Interaction Effects of Selection Bias

If the samples drawn for a study are not representative of the larger population, a researcher may encounter difficulty generalizing findings from their results. For instance, an experiment run with students in one part of the country might not yield results valid for students in another part of the country; a study run with urban dwellers as subjects might not apply to rural dwellers, if some unique characteristic of the urban population contributes to the effects found by the experiment. Thus, the desire to maintain external validity demands samples representative of the broadest possible population. The techniques for accomplishing this are described in Chapter 10.

---

[3] *External validity* here refers to the generalizability of a set of findings based on the design of the study. Recall that formulation of conceptual hypotheses and intervening variables can also contribute to generalizability, as described in Chapters 4 and 5.

[4] The work of Welch and Walberg (1970) tends to indicate that pretesting may threaten validity less seriously than previously assumed. The point bears reemphasizing, however: Pretesting is a costly and time-consuming process, and researchers may prefer to avoid it in certain situations (see Chapter 8).

Reactive Effects of Experimental Arrangements

The arrangements of the experiment or the experience of participating in it may create a sufficiently artificial situation to limit the generalizability of the results to a nonexperimental test of the treatment. An anecdote illustrates how subjects behave differently in experimental settings.

To study the effects of stress from near-drowning, two experimenters fastened a subject to the side of a swimming pool as it filled. They then forgot that they were carrying out the experiment for a time and returned to the pool just in time to turn off the water before the subject drowned. The experimenters, quite frightened by this experience and somewhat in a state of shock, pulled the subject from the pool and loosened him from the bonds. Upon being asked by the experimenters, "Weren't you frightened?" the subject calmly replied, "Oh, no. It was only an experiment."

Often a curriculum produces results on an experimental basis that differ from those in general application because of the *Hawthorne effect*. This effect was discovered and labeled by Mayo, Roethlisberger, and Dickson during performance studies at the Hawthorne works of the Western Electric Company in Chicago, Illinois, during the late 1920s (see Brown, 1954). The researchers wanted to determine the effects of changes in the physical characteristics of the work environment as well as in incentive rates and rest periods. They discovered, however, that production increased regardless of the conditions imposed, leading them to conclude that the workers were reacting to their role in the experiment and the importance placed on them by management. The term *Hawthorne effect* thus refers to performance increments prompted by mere inclusion in an experiment. This effect may lead participants, pleased by having been singled out to participate in an experimental project, to react more strongly to the pleasure of participation than to the treatment itself. However, the tested conditions often yield very different results when tried on a nonexperimental basis.[5]

Multiple-Treatment Interference

Research sometimes subjects participants to a number of treatments simultaneously, some of them experimental and others not. In such cases, the treatments often interact in ways that reduce the representativeness of the effects of any one of them. For example, if students serve as subjects, they experience a variety of other treatments as part of their normal school activity in addition to the experimental treatment. The treatments in combination may produce effects different from those produced by isolated application of the experimental treatment.

---

[5] Gephart and Antonoplos (1969) consider the Hawthorne effect to be a threat to internal validity rather than external validity. They contend that demand characteristics, affect external validity rather than internal validity. Of course, some arbitrariness complicates applications of these classifications, depending on the definitions and perspectives employed.

CONTROLLING FOR PARTICIPANT BIAS: EQUATING EXPERIMENTAL AND CONTROL GROUPS

By selecting a control group made up of people who share as nearly as possible all the idiosyncrasies of the experimental group subjects, the researcher minimizes *selection invalidity*—that is, the risk that the outcome of an experiment depends as much on uncontrolled individual differences (or more) as on the treatment.

Because selection problems are a common source of consternation for researchers, a number of approaches have been developed to deal with them.

Randomization

Randomization (also called *random assignment*) is a procedure for controlling selection variables without first explicitly identifying them. According to this method, a researcher avoids introducing a systematic basis of selection by reducing to chance the probability that the experimental in comparison to the control group includes more of one type of person than another.

A researcher randomizes by randomly assigning members of a subject pool to the experimental and control groups. Operationally, this may be accomplished by drawing names out of a hat or by arbitrarily assigning numbers to subjects (Ss) and using a table of random numbers (see Appendix C) to assign subjects to groups. With 50 Ss, for example, a researcher might alphabetize the list and number each person from 1 to 50. Then he or she would go down the random numbers list looking only at the first two digits in a column. If the first number began with 22, Subject 22 would be assigned to the experimental group. If the second number began with 09, Subject 9 would be assigned to the experimental group. The procedure would continue in this manner until half of the Ss were assigned to the experimental group. The remainder would then be assigned to the control group, to maintain the desirable goal of equal group sizes.

In a study designed to collect pretest data on the dependent variable, randomized assignment of Ss to conditions should be undertaken independently of pretest scores. That is, Ss should be assigned to conditions on the random basis described in the last paragraph rather than on the basis of pretest scores. Pretest scores may be subsequently examined, but it should not lead to group reassignments. Pretest scores could be used in analyzing of research data by designating them as a covariate in an analysis of covariance, by examining change scores (posttest minus pretest), or by comparing group pretest scores after the fact as a check on the distribution of selection factors across groups. In another method, Ss may be paired on pretest scores, and then one member of each pair, chosen randomly, would be assigned to the experimental group, the other to the control group. This procedure is described in a later section of the chapter on matched-pair technique.

To ensure random assignment, the researcher either must assign Ss to conditions or determine that no bias affected such an assignment, undertaken independently of the research.[6] Even when researchers believe that assignments were not undertaken on any systematic basis, they should often avoid relying on the expectation that groups have been randomly composed; the researchers themselves must find some objective basis for concluding that no bias affected assignments to conditions.

Designating *intact classes* (that is, classes to which students have been assigned by their school prior to an experiment) as experimental and control groups poses a particular problem. Although researchers often feel tempted to consider these classes as randomly assigned groups, they usually should treat them as nonrandom groups and proceed with specific designs for use with intact groups (described in Chapter 8). Researchers can sometimes demonstrate that random processes determined assignment to such intact groups, but when in doubt they should assume nonrandomness.

Researchers often carefully assign Ss randomly to groups and then double-check the distribution of control variables by comparing the groups to assess their equivalence on these variables. This comparison amounts to an after-the-fact check, though, rather than an assignment technique (such as matching groups).

Matched-Pair Technique

To form experimental and control groups according to the matched-pair technique, a researcher must first decide which individual difference variables present the most prominent sources of problems (that is, the most likely sources of internal invalidity due to selection) if left uncontrolled. Such a list often includes gender, age, socioeconomic status, race, IQ, prior school performance, pretest achievement, and various personality measures. To complete group assignments, the researcher identifies within the subject pool the pairs of Ss who most closely approach one another on the specific variable(s) for which control is desired. Thus, an 11-year-old male of low IQ (as defined operationally) would be paired with another 11-year-old male of low IQ. Through similar links, all Ss in the pool eventually would be paired with others. This process would reduce the pool of 50 individual Ss to 25 pairs of Ss matched on the chosen selection measures. One member of each pair, chosen *randomly* from among the two members, would be assigned to the experimental group and one to the control group until all of the

---

[6] This discussion concerns the procedure for assigning Ss to conditions to minimize internal invalidity due to selection bias. Random selection of a sample from a population, a procedure for increasing external validity, is described in Chapter 10.

pairs are split. The researcher can then consider the two resulting groups as reasonably equal on the measures in question, thus providing control over selection variables.[7]

Matches between individuals can also be based on a pretest measure of the dependent variable. If the dependent variable were, for instance, mathematics achievement, pairs could be matched according to their initial levels of mathematics achievement. Random assignment of pairs to separate groups would then control for initial level on the dependent variable. This procedure is an alternative to the randomization procedure described in the preceding section, which provides no specific matching or sorting on any measure. Of the two, random assignment by itself is preferred because it does not force the researcher to reject subjects who cannot be matched.

Matched-Group Technique

A similar but less extensive matching procedure calls for assigning individuals to groups in a way that gives equal mean scores for the groups on the critical selection variables. Thus, two groups might be composed to give the same mean age of 11.5, or between 11 and 12. Individuals might not form equivalent pairs across groups, but the groups on the average would be equivalent to one another. Groups can also be matched according to their average scores on a pretest measure of the dependent variable; this technique guarantees average equivalence of the groups at the start of the experiment.

Often, researchers must complete statistical comparisons to ensure that they have produced adequately matched groups. Note, however, that this technique, as the previous one, may lead to regression effects, as described earlier in the chapter; experimenters should avoid it in favor of random assignment in other than uncommon circumstances. (It is, however, appropriate to compare the composition of intact groups after the fact, to determine whether they match one another.)

Using Subjects as Their Own Controls[8]

If all subjects serve as members of both the experimental and control groups, then researchers can usually assume adequate control of selection variables. However, many situations do not allow this technique, because the experimental experience will affect performance in the control activity, or vice versa. In learning and teaching studies, for instance, after completing the experimental treatment, the subject no longer qualifies as a naive participant; performance on the control task

---

[7] It is important to avoid eliminating extreme scorers in this procedure as well as favoring certain combinations of scores for inclusion. Such actions would produce statistical regression effects, as explained earlier in the chapter.

[8] This procedure is labeled *repeated measurement* or *correlated measures* for statistical purposes.

will reflect the subject's experience on the experimental task. In other words, this technique controls adequately for selection bias, but it often creates insurmountable problems of *maturation* or *history bias*. *Ss* in the control and experimental groups may be the same individuals, but the relevant history of each person, and hence the present level of maturation, differs in completing the second task because of experience of the first.

In instances where *Ss* can serve as their own controls, careful researchers must control for order effects by counterbalancing. Half of the *Ss*, chosen at random, should receive the experimental treatment first, while the remainder first serve as controls. (A later section of the chapter discusses counterbalancing in more detail.)

Limiting the Population

The *population* is the entire group that a researcher sets out to study. The *sample* is the group of individuals chosen from that number to participate in the study. By narrowly restricting the population (for instance, to college sophomores in universities with graduate psychology departments), a researcher can control for a number of possibly confounding participant selection variables. In fact, most studies set some boundaries on their populations of subjects. However, overly restrictive boundaries may increase internal validity via selection at the price of greatly reduced external validity. Severely limiting a study's population may limit application of its conclusions to that restricted group, interfering with generalization of the conclusions.[9]

Moderator Variables as Selection Tools

If a particular individual difference measure is likely to influence the hypothesis that a study is designed to test, the researcher can both control it (as a source of confounding or bias) and study it (as it interacts with the independent variable). To accomplish these goals, the researcher uses the measure as a moderator variable within the study by comparing the results of participants whose scores on it fall into different levels. A factorial statistical design (described in Chapter 8) allows a researcher to control a variable in a study by making it a moderator variable. Such a design is an important means of dealing with selection variables, because it enables the researcher to examine interactions, that is, effects on the

---

[9] When a researcher describes variables in conceptual terms, that is, as intervening variables, their generality often extends applications beyond the specific sample studied. This process reinforces external validity—that is, it allows a broad delineation of the population of which the experimental group is a representative sample. Psychologists, for example, have conducted many studies on samples of college sophomores and then, because of their conceptualizations, often applied their findings to the population of all people.

dependent variable that result when the independent and moderator variables act in combination.

Using Control Variables as Covariates

Researchers can also apply a statistical procedure to eliminate the potential effect of a particular selection factor. This procedure, called *analysis of covariance,* is described in most statistics textbooks. It differs from the technique of selecting group members according to moderator variables; instead, it treats the potentially confounding variable as a control variable (one to be neutralized) rather than as a moderator variable (one to be studied).

Analysis of covariance separates out the effect on the dependent variable of potentially biasing characteristics of participants that may vary in an uncontrolled way from group to group by treating measures of these characteristics as covariates.

CONTROLLING FOR EXPERIENCE BIAS: EQUATING EXPERIMENTAL AND CONTROL CONDITIONS

Differing only in their experiences of the independent variable, the control and experimental groups should share as much as possible the same experiences or history in every other respect. Researchers face serious difficulty ensuring that the experiences of the two groups will be comparable outside the experimental setting; realistically, the maximum amount of control they can exercise comes from simply establishing a control group with members drawn from the same population as the experimental group. However, within the experiment itself, control efforts must also target many potentially confounding variables (that is, sources of internal invalidity due to history). A number of methods of such control are available.

Method of Removal

Where possible, extraneous influences should be entirely removed from the experiences in both the experimental and control conditions. Researchers should scrupulously avoid extraneous noises, interruptions, and changes in environmental conditions. For example, researchers may avoid possible confounding from subjects' questions and resulting answers during either the pretest or the posttest by disallowing questions. The double-blind technique described earlier is another way of preventing an administrator from influencing a subject's responses.

Method of Constancy

Experiences other than those resulting from the manipulation of the independent variable should remain *constant* across the experimental and control groups. If the manipulation includes instructions to subjects, these should be written in advance and then read to both groups to guarantee constancy across conditions. Tasks, experiences, or procedures not unique to the treatment should be identical for experimental and control groups. Experimental settings should also be the same in both cases. In an experiment that contrasts an experience with its absence, the researcher must not leave uncontrolled the factors of time, involvement in the experiment, and exposure to materials. To maintain constancy on these factors, the control group should experience an irrelevant treatment (rather than none at all) that takes as long as the experimental treatment and provides the same amount of exposure, thus providing the same amount of involvement. A design appropriate for controlling the Hawthorne effect, a risk if experimental Ss are treated and control Ss ignored, is discussed in Chapter 8.

Researchers encounter difficulty, not in deciding how to provide constancy, but in determining *what* experiences require constancy. If they fail to maintain constancy on potential confounding variables, their designs lack internal validity and fail to justify conclusions. Variables such as amount of material exposure, time spent in the experiment, and attention from the experimenter are occasionally overlooked as control variables.

Teacher effect can be controlled by keeping the teacher constant, that is, by assigning the same teacher to both treatment and control classes. (This approach does limit the generality of the study, however.)

Method of Counterbalancing

In experiments that require Ss to perform multiple tasks or take multiple tests, researchers often must control for the effects of *order*. They must account for apparent progressive shifts in Ss' responses as they continue to serve in the experiment. These shifts may result from practice or fatigue (so-called *constant errors*). This risk is particularly relevant when Ss serve as their own controls—that is, when the same Ss at different times form both the experimental and control groups, as previously explained. Order effects have equally serious implications when a study's design requires multiple treatments or multiple dependent measures.

Where a study utilizes two tasks (A and B) and Ss must perform each task once, counterbalancing is achieved by randomly dividing the group in half and giving each half the tasks in the opposite order:

Group I: A then B

Group II: B then A

When participants must take two tests, the same approach can prevent bias due to order of experiences.

When participants undergo each of two experiences twice or more, a counterbalanced order A B B A equalizes the constant errors across experiences. Where Ss are to react to pictures of dogs and cats, for example, the order can be DOG CAT CAT DOG.

A study that assigns a single, constant task order (A B) must independently assess the effect of this order as a potential source of history bias. Because such assessment requires difficult and burdensome analysis, a constant task order should be avoided. In counterbalancing task order, researchers gain input from which to assess task order effects within the experiment, allowing them to determine if such effects occur and how they affect the treatment. By randomizing task order, however, (that is, giving the tasks in a randomly chosen order) researchers can neutralize task order effects.

If task order effects interest researchers, they should practice counterbalancing to make task order a moderator variable. Most often, however, these effects are not of specific interest. Researchers can then control them most easily by randomizing the order of the tasks or tests across Ss. In this way, order effects are neutralized rather than systematized. Moreover, randomizing simplifies subsequent statistical analyses, reduces needed sample sizes, and avoids the need for assumptions by the researcher about order effects.

Method of Multiple Counterbalancing

The counterbalancing technique applies to research designs in which each subject completes *two* tasks two or more times. Some studies need to equate or order more than two tasks or experiences across Ss, however; the technique of multiple counterbalancing (also called *systematic randomization*) performs this function. This technique is merely a complex or multiple form of counterbalancing that simultaneously reorders many activities, as an example will illustrate.

Taylor and Samuels (1983) conducted an experiment in which Ss serving as their own controls read two passages each, and then were tested on their recall. The passages varied in each of two ways: (1) normal versus scrambled structure, and (2) Content A or B. Thus, the researchers had to control the following factors:

1. The number of times each passage structure was experienced
2. The number of times each passage content was experienced
3. The order in which the two passage structures were experienced
4. The order in which the two passage contents were experienced

TABLE 7.2   MULTIPLE COUNTERBALANCING OF PASSAGE STRUCTURE (NORMAL VERSUS SCRAMBLED) AND PASSAGE CONTENT (A VERSUS B) IN THE TAYLOR AND SAMUELS (1983) EXPERIMENT

	GROUP 1	GROUP 2	GROUP 3	GROUP 4
Time 1	Normal A	Normal B	Scrambled B	Scrambled A
Time 2	Scrambled B	Scrambled A	Normal A	Normal B

Table 7.2 shows that the study defined four groups and assigned two experiences per group to provide the required controls. Each group experienced each passage structure once and each passage content once, while each passage structure was paired with each passage content twice. This method produced four possible orders of the structure/content combination, and each group experienced one of these orders.

The experiment could not systematically control some combinations of experiences, because to do so would have required either too many groups or too many experiences per group. For instance, unique combinations of structure and content would ideally require that each group experience each of the four possible combinations rather than just two. For practical reasons, Taylor and Samuels could not include all possible structure-content-order combinations in their research design for each group. However, they developed a fully adequate approach.

Variations of this method allow for assigning teachers to instructional treatment conditions. Researchers can either randomly assign participating teachers, or designate multiple teachers, so that each one teaches one treatment class and one control class. Both approaches represent ways to control for teacher effect.

OVERALL CONTROL OF PARTICIPANT AND EXPERIENCE BIAS

Table 7.3 summarizes procedures for controlling both participant effects and experience effects as they affect the internal validity (certainty) and external validity (generality) of a study. To understand applications of these principles, consider a study of teacher enthusiasm and its effect on student achievement (McKinney et al., 1983).

The following quotations provide the necessary information:

TABLE 7.3

Maximizing Control of Participant and Experience Bias: Four "Windows"

IN DEALING WITH:	PRECAUTIONS TO ENSURE:	
	CERTAINTY	GENERALITY
Participants	Control all individual differences between groups on IQ, prior achievement, sex, age, etc., by: 1. Random assignment: group/group 2. Matching 3. Establishing equivalence statistically after the fact	Make the sample as representative as possible of population from which it is drawn by: 1. Random selection: sample/population 2. Stratified sampling (See Chapter 10)
Experiences	Control all differences in experiences between groups, other than the independent variable, by: 1. Employing a control group 2. Providing each group with comparable subject matter or tasks 3. Equalizing teacher effects across groups	Make experimental conditions as representative of real-life experiences as possible by: 1. Remaining as unobtrusive as possible 2. Minimizing the salience of the experiment and experimenter 3. Utilizing double-blind procedure

The students were randomly assigned to one of three treatment groups, defined by three levels of teacher enthusiasm—high, medium, and low. Teachers trained to exhibit the specified levels of enthusiasm administered the treatments, using scripted lessons covering three topics in social studies. (p. 249)

Treatments and lessons were rotated and counterbalanced to control for possible effects of time of day, order of treatment, and teacher effect. (p. 251)

The study included six teachers, each one teaching each of the three treatments (high, medium, and low enthusiasm) across three different social studies topics (cultural diffusion, arable land, and tertiary production), as shown in Table 7.4 (McKinney et al., 1983, p. 251).

This approach effectively controlled for history bias from sources such as content of lessons, order of treatment, teacher effect, and time of day. Such strict controls maximize internal validity, but they also raise other issues, as noted by the authors:

Although scripted lessons raise questions of external validity, we were more concerned with maintaining tight controls and establishing internal validity.

If teachers are allowed to develop individual lessons, several other variables, such as allocated time and degree of explanations are introduced. . . . The problem of external validity can be dealt with through replication. (p. 250)

TABLE 7.4

McKinney et al., 1983, p. 251.

ROTATION OF TREATMENTS, TEACHERS, AND LESSONS IN SCHOOL 1[a]

	TEACHER 1	TEACHER 2	TEACHER 3
Day 1	**Cultural Diffusion** High Medium Low	**Arable Land** Medium Low High	**Tertiary Production** Low High Medium
Day 2	**Arable Land** High Medium Low	**Tertiary Production** Medium Low High	**Cultural Diffusion** Low High Medium
Day 3	**Tertiary Production** High Medium Low	**Cultural Diffusion** Medium Low High	**Arable Land** Low High Medium

[a]Design repeated for School 2, Teachers 4 through 6.

Finally, the authors faced problems of experimental mortality: "68 of the original 228 subjects were dropped . . . because of absences on one or more days of the study or for lack of reading scores" (p. 251). However, analysis led the authors to discount this situation as a problem because "reading scores for the remaining 160 subjects indicated that pretreatment differences among experimental groups were small and nonsignificant" (p. 251).

APPRAISING THE SUCCESS OF THE MANIPULATION

Some experiments allow straightforward manipulation of the independent variable: Introduce a particular experience to the experimental group, and withhold it from the control group. If the independent variable is operationally defined by a dynamic-property or static-property definition (Chapter 6), a researcher can simply find an appropriate measuring device to detect the observable criteria associated with the levels of this variable. However, a study design that creates an independent variable (that is, one that forms an operational definition based on manipulation) usually requires a researcher to verify during the experiment that the created state displays the intended dynamic and static properties.

Suppose, for example, that you are interested in studying the effect of fear on behavior. You tell your experimental group a story intended to produce fear in them. At this point, a wise researcher would verify that the manipulation (the story) has produced the desired effect (fear). To accomplish this goal, you might give both your experimental and control groups an emotional symptomatology questionnaire or measure their palmar skin electrical conductivity to check for expected differences between the groups.

A study by Slavin and Karweit (1984), detailed in Chapter 6, compared mastery learning to team learning. It provides an example of methods to appraise the success of the manipulation, discussed under the heading "Implementation Checks." Trained observers monitored each of four treatments to determine whether the teachers followed the operational definitions of the variables. In the mastery-learning treatments, for example, minimum requirements included formative quizzes, corrective instruction, and summative quizzes; the team-learning treatments were expected to include heterogeneous teams, team scores, and team recognition. All treatments that included focused instruction (the control) were expected to follow regular schedules of teaching, worksheet completion, and quizzes. "All teachers were found to be using these major components of their assigned treatments adequately, although the quality of implementation varied widely."

If the independent variable requires that individuals, such as teachers, behave or perform in a specified way (that is, according to a manipulation-based operational definition), the study's outcome depends on how effectively their behavior or performance conforms to the instructions. Increasing deviation from required behavior standards reduces the likelihood that the treatment will yield the desired or anticipated effect on the dependent variable.

The study of mastery learning versus team learning, for instance, would have encountered problems if (a) a certain percentage of teachers who were assigned to use mastery instruction had failed to follow their instructions for implementing it, or if (b) a certain percentage of teachers who were not assigned to use mastery instruction implemented the method anyway. These occurrences would have prevented effective distinctions between the two levels of the independent variable—mastery versus nonmastery instruction. They would have overlapped, causing additional variability in any outcome associated specifically with one of the two levels. Such a lack of distinction between levels of the independent variable could have resulted in a failure to obtain differences on the dependent variable, even if it really were related to the independent variable.

Whenever a variable is defined by means of a manipulation-based operational definition, any researcher should carefully appraise and report the success of the manipulation.

For another example, reconsider the study of teacher enthusiasm and student achievement mentioned in the previous section. For control purposes, six teachers were trained to exhibit three levels of enthusiasm using a manipulation-based operational definition. The researchers specified descriptors for each level of each facet of enthusiasm to aid the participating teachers in accomplishing their appropriate performance:

BOX 7

ILLUSTRATIONS FROM THE SAMPLE STUDIES

Sample Study I utilized two comparison groups, one that received encouraging feedback and a second that received neutral feedback. One might designate participants who experienced the first condition as the experimental group and those who experienced the second, representing the "normal" method of feedback, as the control group. Aside from the difference in type of feedback, the two groups shared environments, procedures, and experiences as similar as possible.

An evaluation of the categories of internal validity or certainty begins with the participants. The study addressed problems of *selection* by randomly assigning students to feedback conditions. In addition, scores on measures of initial self-efficacy, initial outcome expectation, initial outcome importance, and procrastination tendency were used as covariates in the posttest analyses to adjust for any initial differences. Random assignment, inclusion of all students, and no losses of students helped the researcher to control for the other potential sources of participant bias. Given these procedures, the study appears to provide adequate control for participant bias.

To ensure internal validity of experiences, some important control variables were introduced to maintain equivalence among feedback groups. Both groups encountered the same curriculum materials, schedule of instruction, and teacher; indeed, they experienced these elements at the same time, since they were classmates. But each group was unaware that the other was receiving a different form of feedback. The use of comparison groups minimized the likelihood of an effect on performance due to individual histories of students outside the experiment but simultaneous to it. Within the experiment, *amount* of feed-

For instance, low enthusiasm in vocal delivery was defined as "monotone voice, minimum vocal inflection, little variations in speech, drones on and on and on, poor articulation." Medium enthusiasm on the same item was defined as "pleasant variations of pitch, volume, and speed, good articulation." High enthusiasm was defined as "great and sudden changes from rapid excited speech to a whisper. Varied lilting, uplifting intonation. Many changes in tone, pitch." (McKinney et al., 1983, p. 250)

Teachers were trained for 11 hours, working with four observers:

The four observers received additional training on the use of Collins' instrument. Samples of teaching were scored using the instrument and the ratings compared

back was equivalent for both groups. In fact, feedback was scripted to ensure its standardization. Expectancy bias was controlled by making sure that "the teacher was not aware of which students were given which response on the VHS task." Thus, experience bias was minimized.

In regard to external validity or generality based on participants, generalizations would have to be limited to the population studied. The study achieved broad generality based on experiences, since its treatments represented real-life experiences, both in terms of feedback condition and the classroom context of the study.

Sample Study II compared the classroom behavior of good and poor readers but encountered potential problems with participant bias. Since the study's sample included only "the three students with the highest and the three students with the lowest reading achievement scores," statistical regression errors may have resulted from the use of only extreme scorers. Moreover, because students could not be randomly assigned to good and poor reader groups—reading ability being an intrinsic characteristic—the research design risked difficulties in controlling for selection effects.

Controlling for experiences also proved difficult, since the study involved no manipulation of treatments by the researchers, and hence no control group. Overall, this type of study offers far less certainty than those that create treatments and assign students to them.

Few restrictions limit the study's generality other than population limitations. Since students were merely observed carrying out actual behaviors, reactive effects should be minimal, supporting high generality. Of course, observational measures raise questions of instrumentation bias, as Chapter 9 will explain.

across observers. Disagreements were discussed and resolved. Training continued until observers reached perfect agreement. (p. 250)

In the final task, the observers appraised the success of the manipulation, assuring themselves that teachers indeed manifested high, medium, and low enthusiasm as required in the design:

Observers were present during each treatment period in the course of the study to verify that the treatments were followed. They were not told at which level of enthusiasm the teachers would be teaching, and they were rotated each day so that each observer rated all of the teachers in the particular school. (p. 250)

TABLE 7.5

Intrateacher and Interteacher Observation Data

McKinney et al., 1983, p. 251.

	DAY 1			DAY 2			DAY 3		
TEACHER	HIGH[a]	MEDIUM[b]	LOW[c]	HIGH	MEDIUM	LOW	HIGH	MEDIUM	LOW
1	4.85	3.00	1.05	5.00	3.00	1.00	5.00	3.00	1.00
2	5.00	3.00	1.00	4.93	3.00	1.00	4.98	3.00	1.00
3	5.00	3.12	1.03	5.00	3.02	1.03	5.00	3.00	1.00
4	5.00	3.02	1.13	5.00	3.00	1.00	5.00	3.02	1.12
5	5.00	3.00	1.00	4.97	3.55	1.03	4.95	3.02	1.00
6	5.00	3.02	1.00	5.00	3.03	1.00	5.00	3.00	1.00

[a]5.00 = high level of enthusiasm.
[b]3.00 = medium level of enthusiasm.
[c]1.00 = low level of enthusiasm.

Based on these observer ratings, the researchers then evaluated the success of the manipulation. As Table 7.5 confirms, it clearly was a success.

Summary

1. Researchers try to eliminate factors other than their experimental treatments that may affect the dependent variable. As part of this effort, they define control groups, or groups of subjects whose selection and experiences are identical to those of the treatment group except that they do not receive the treatment.
2. Three categories of factors may affect the internal validity or certainty of a study: (1) those that come from the participants or subjects, (2) those that come from the experiences, and (3) those that come from the measurement process. (The third category is primarily covered in later chapters.)
3. Participants affect internal validity through selection or assignment effects (changes related to the characteristics of the individuals selected for or assigned to different groups or experiencing or displaying different levels of the independent variable), maturation (naturally occurring changes in study participants over time), statistical regression (changes caused by exclusion of middle-level scorers), and experimental mortality (changes caused by the characteristics of people who discontinue their participation in a study).
4. Experiences affect internal validity through history (changes caused by environmental variables other than the independent variable and operating at the same time), testing (changes caused by the sensitizing effects of a

pretest), and expectancy (changes caused by preexisting biases toward the outcome in the researcher or the participants).

5. External validity or generality is also affected by participant factors, such as bias in the selection of the sample, and experience factors, such as reactions by subjects to the experimental arrangements rather than to the basic character of the variables.

6. Threats to internal validity based on participant factors can be controlled by several techniques: random assignment of subjects to experimental and control groups, matching pairs of subjects on major control variables and then randomly assigning one member of each pair to a group, matching groups on major control variables, using subjects as their own controls, limiting the population, using the moderator variable as a selection device, and using control variables in analysis of covariance.

7. In addition to comparing results for an experimental group to those for a control group, researchers can control for threats to internal validity based on experience factors by removing extraneous influences, keeping extraneous influences constant across conditions, counterbalancing the order in which multiple tasks are experienced, and counterbalancing the combinations of task order and other extraneous variables.

8. Threats to external validity based on participants can be controlled by random or stratified random sampling from the broadest possible population. Similar threats based on experiences can be controlled by keeping the treatments and the measurements as unobtrusive as possible and ensuring that the data collector remains as unaware of the specifics as possible.

9. When manipulating the levels of an independent variable, a researcher should collect data to indicate whether the manipulation has successfully produced the intended conditions. He or she can perform this evaluation dynamically, by observing the results of the manipulation, or statically, by asking subjects what they are feeling or experiencing.

COMPETENCY TEST EXERCISES

1. A coach has given some youngsters training in swimming. Which of the listed distinctions would *not* be a valid indicator of the need for a control group to evaluate the effects of the training?
   a. Some youngsters might have began with superior potential for becoming good swimmers.
   b. The coach may not have sufficient free time to continue the training program.
   c. The experience in the water may have contributed more to success than the training per se.
   d. Normal physical development may have accounted for any improvement.

2. Youngsters initially showing highly aggressive behavior toward teachers and classmates have reduced this aggressiveness considerably after a special counseling program. Which of the listed distinctions would *not* be a valid indicator of the need for a control group to evaluate the effects of the counseling?

    a. Judgments of aggressive behavior following the program were biased by the judges' desire to see the program succeed.

    b. The oldest of the problem children never completed the program.

    c. People running the program were well-trained counselors.

    d. Special attention given to these students may have accounted for their change in behavior.

3. Six of the eight choices in Exercises 1 and 2 (1a, 1b, 1c, 1d, 2a, 2b, 2c, 2d) represent sources of internal invalidity. Label each choice according to its source of internal invalidity, leaving blank the two chosen as answers for Exercises 1 and 2. (Possible sources of internal validity are history, selection, maturation, testing, instrumentation, statistical regression, experimental mortality, stability, expectancy, and interactive combinations of factors.)

    1a: _____

    1b: _____

    1c: _____

    1d: _____

    2a: _____

    2b: _____

    2c: _____

    2d: _____

4. You are interested in determining the effect of programmed mathematics material on the level of mathematics achievement. What steps would you undertake to control for history, maturation, testing, instrumentation, selection, regression, and mortality biases?

5. In the study described in Exercise 4, what steps would you take to control for the various sources of external invalidity?

6. You are interested in determining whether a film about careers increases the tendency of students to make career decisions. What steps would you take to control for history, maturation, and selection biases?

7. You have designed an experiment to compare the effectiveness of directive and nondirective counseling. You are using the same counselors in both conditions, but have trained them to counsel differently for each condition.

How would you verify that your participating counselors were behaving directively and nondirectively in the appropriate conditions as instructed?

8. You are interested in studying the effects of anger on problem-solving. You attempt to make Ss angry by finding fault with their behavior and yelling at them. What can you do subsequent to this anger manipulation to determine whether the desired result has occurred?

RECOMMENDED REFERENCES

Cook, T. D. & Campbell, D. T. (1979). *Quasi-experimentation: Design and analysis issues for field settings.* Chicago: Rand McNally.

Mitchell, M., & Jolley, J. (1992). Research design explained (2nd ed.). Fort Worth, TX: Harcourt Brace.

Rosenthal, R. & Rosnow, R. L. (1969). Artifact in behavioral research. New York: Academic Press.

8 Chapter

Objectives

▶ Distinguish between pre-experimental designs, true experimental designs, and quasi-experimental designs based on how adequately they guard against different threats to validity.

▶ Construct true experimental designs (including factorial designs) given predictions.

▶ Identify circumstances that call for quasi-experimental designs.

▶ Identify the threats to validity that are not completely controlled by each of the quasi-experimental designs.

▶ Construct quasi-experimental designs given predictions and specific circumstances that preclude the use of true experimental designs.

▶ Describe the circumstances that call for criterion group or co-relational designs, and construct these designs to match specific situations.

▶ Construct designs to control for reactive effects, that is, the Hawthorne and expectancy effects, given predictions and situations in which such effects may operate.

A Shorthand for Displaying Designs

This section reviews the system of symbols used in the chapter to specify research designs.[1]

An *X* designates a *treatment* (the presence of an experimental manipulation) and a blank space designates a *control* (the absence of a manipulation). When treatments are compared, they are labeled X_1, X_2, and so on.

An *O* designates an *observation* or measurement. Each *O* carries an arbitrary subscript for ease of identification and referral (O_1, O_2, and so on).[2]

The letter *R* indicates that the design controls for participant bias factors (for example, selection) using *randomization* or some other technique described in Chapter 7. Finally, a dashed line shows that *intact groups* have been used, indicating incomplete control of selection bias.

Pre-Experimental Designs (Nondesigns)

Unfortunately, all too many researcher studies employ three common research procedures that do not qualify as legitimate experimental designs, because they do not control adequately against the sources of internal invalidity. These are referred to as *pre-experimental* designs, because they are component pieces or elements of true experimental designs. Because they are inadequate as they stand, they are also called *nondesigns*. Because students gain from knowledge of what they should not do as well as what they should do, this section reviews these unacceptable designs.

One-Shot Case Study

The one-shot case study can be diagrammed as follows:

$$X \quad O$$

Such a "study" tries some treatment *(X)* on a single group and then makes an observation *(O)* on the members of that group to assess the effects of the treatment. The lack of a control group (a group that does not experience *X*) and the lack of

---

[1] This system was originated by D. T. Campbell and J. C. Stanley (1966).

[2] These subscripts function solely for differentiation; they have no systematic meaning regarding sequence.

information about the Ss who do experience X violate most of the principles of internal validity in a design. Results of a one-shot case study provide no justification for concluding that X *caused* O.

Consider an example. Suppose that a school institutes a free lunch program (X). After the program has been in operation for 6 months, teachers report in interviews (O) that they have encountered only minimal instances of disruptive classroom activity. The school principal may then conclude that the school lunch program is reducing student tension and aggression. However, the principal does not know (1) whether specific experiences or occurrences other than the lunch program (history) have contributed to the observed behavior change, (2) whether current observations have detected a real change relative to past behavior, and, if such a change truly occurred, whether it is stable, or (3) whether students participating in the lunch program were likely to change anyway as a function of selection or maturation.

One-Group Pretest-Posttest Design

The one-group pretest-posttest design can be diagrammed as:

$$O_1 \quad X \quad O_2$$

Such a study differs from the one-shot case study design by beginning with a pretest, which provides some information about the sample. However, this design (or nondesign) fails to control for the effects of history, maturation, testing, or statistical regression, so it cannot be considered a legitimate experimental technique. Although it provides some information about selection, because the pretest describes the initial state of the selected Ss on the dependent variable, it falls far short of handling the other sources of internal invalidity.

Intact-Group Comparison

The intact-group comparison (also called *static-group comparison*) can be diagrammed as shown:

$$\begin{array}{cc} X & O_1 \\ \hline O_2 \end{array}$$

A control group that does not receive the treatment (X) acts as a source of comparison for the treatment-receiving group, helping to prevent bias from effects such as history and, to a lesser extent, maturation. Validity increases, because some coincidental event that affects the outcome will as likely affect O_2 as O_1.

However, the control group *S*s and the experimental group *S*s are neither selected or assigned to groups on a random basis (or on any of the bases required for the control of selection bias). The dashed line between the groups indicates that they are intact groups. Moreover, by failing to pretest the *S*s, the researchers lose the ability to confirm the essential equivalence of the control and experimental group *S*s. Thus, this approach is an unacceptable method, because it controls for neither selection invalidity or invalidity based on experimental mortality. That is, it gives no information about whether one group was already higher on *O* (or some related measure) before the treatment, which may have caused it to outperform the other group on the posttest.

Although differences between O_2 and O_1 probably do not result from different histories and rates of maturation during such an experiment, researchers should not simply assume that the observed outcomes are not based on differences that the *S*s bring with them to the experiment. Because the intact-group comparison does not satisfactorily control for all sources of invalidity, it is considered a pre-experimental design. By virtue of their shortcomings, this and the other nondesigns do not eliminate potential alternative explanations of their findings, so they are not acceptable or legitimate experimental designs.

TRUE EXPERIMENTAL DESIGNS

Several other research techniques qualify as *true* experimental designs, because they provide completely adequate controls for all sources of internal invalidity. They represent no compromise between experimental design requirements and the nature and reality of the situations in which studies are undertaken. Two of these true designs are described in this section.[3]

Posttest-Only Control Group Design

This experimental method offers potentially the most useful true design. It can be diagrammed as:

$$R \quad X \quad O_1$$
$$R \qquad\quad O_2$$

The posttest-only control group design provides ideal control over all threats to validity and all sources of bias. The design utilizes two groups, one that experiences the treatment while the other does not, so it controls for history and maturation bias. Random assignment to the experimental or control group prevents

---

[3] A third, the Solomon Four-Group Design, is not covered in this book because of its limited usefulness. The reader is referred to Campbell and Stanley (1966).

problems of selection and mortality. In addition, this design controls for a simple testing effect and the interaction between testing and treatment by giving no pretest to either group.

Data analysis for the posttest-only control group design centers on comparisons between the mean for O_1 and the mean for O_2.

Recall from the previous chapter the discussion of a study by McKinney et al. (1983) on the effects of teacher enthusiasm on student achievement. This research project illustrates the posttest-only control group design. It examined the independent variable teacher enthusiasm by establishing three levels: high, medium, and low enthusiasm. Subjects were randomly assigned to treatments, taught a prescribed unit, and tested to determine their achievement on the unit. The design would be diagrammed as:

$$R \quad X_1 \quad O_1 \quad \text{(high enthusiasm)}$$

$$R \quad X_2 \quad O_2 \quad \text{(medium enthusiasm)}$$

$$R \quad X_3 \quad O_3 \quad \text{(low enthusiasm)}$$

Another example of the useful posttest-only control group design comes from a study by Helm (1989, p. 362):

> The purpose of this study was to determine if selected students who were absent from school and who received calls to their homes from the principal via a computer message device, would have a better school attendance record than those students whose homes were not called.

This sentence gives the problem statement of the study. Subjects were randomly assigned to either the to-be-called or not-to-be-called conditions, and a "posttest" evaluated their attendance after the eighth month of the school year.

The researchers designated a control or comparison group and randomly assigned Ss to conditions, providing suitable control for internal validity. The posttest-only control group design may be used where such requirements can be met.

Pretest-Posttest Control Group Design

The pretest-posttest control group design can be diagrammed as:

$$R \quad O_1 \quad X \quad O_2$$

$$R \quad O_3 \quad \quad O_4$$

Two groups are employed in this design: The experimental group receives a treatment (X) while the control group does not. (Random assignment is used to place

Ss in both groups.)[4] Both groups are given a pretest (O_1 and O_3) and a posttest (O_2 and O_4). The use of a pretest is the only difference between this design and the previously discussed one.

By subjecting a control group to all the same experiences as the experimental group except the experience of the treatment itself, this design controls for history, maturation, and regression effects. By randomizing *Ss* across experimental and control conditions, it controls for both selection and mortality. This design, therefore, controls many threats to validity or sources of bias.

However, administration of a pretest does introduce slight design difficulties beyond those encountered in the posttest-only control group design. The pretest-posttest control group design allows the possibility of a *testing effect* (that is, a gain on the posttest due to experience on the pretest); this potential for bias may reduce internal validity. Also, the design lacks any control for the possibility that the pretest will sensitize *Ss* to the treatment, thus affecting external validity. In other words, the design does not control for a test-treatment interaction. Moreover, it lacks control for the artificiality of an experiment that may well be established through the use of a pretest.

In summary, then, an evaluation of the pretest-posttest control group design is that it incorporates effective controls for all the simple sources of invalidity. The pretest prevents control for sources of invalidity (both simple and interactive) associated with testing, and these influences may plague such studies. Still, the design offers a useful format when a researcher feels a strong need to collect pretest data on the dependent variable and has little fear that the pretest will provide a simple posttest gain or a differential sensitivity to the treatment. However, when the researcher has a reason to suspect that the pretest may introduce such bias, he or she should favor the posttest-only control group design. Indeed, under most circumstances the posttest-only control group design should be used, because random assignment of *Ss* to conditions is generally considered an adequate control for selection bias. Avoidance of a pretest also saves time and money. Obviously, however, an experimenter needs pretest data for a study intended to assess degree of change in the dependent variable.

In analyzing the data from the pretest-posttest control group design, the researcher can compare gain scores for the two groups. That is, a comparison of the mean of O_2 minus O_1 with the mean of O_4 minus O_3 indicates whether the treatment had a differential effect on the groups. Analysis may also compare means of the groups on the pretest (O_1 versus O_3). If the groups are equivalent, the posttest means (O_2 versus O_4) can be compared to evaluate the treatment.

A third possibility is to compare posttest scores of the groups (O_2 and O_4) through analysis of covariance using corresponding individual pretest scores (O_1 and O_3) as a covariate. This approach is illustrated in a study by Reiser, Tessmer, and Phelps (1984) to determine whether children would learn more from watching "Sesame Street" if the adults who watched with them asked

---

[4] Researchers may match individual subjects prior to random assignment, if desired.

questions and provided feedback than they would learn from watching the program without this adult interaction. Preschool children were randomly assigned to either an experimental condition, in which they were asked to name the letters and numbers shown on each of the three shows while they were watching, or a control condition, where they watched with adults but were not asked to perform. Children were both pretested and posttested on a measure designed to assess their ability to identify the letters and numbers presented on the shows.

The statistical procedure analysis of covariance, referred to above, allowed comparison of the two groups' posttest performance. This evaluation used the pretest scores as a control variable (or covariate) to control for initial group differences. This method gives results preferable to those of a direct comparison of gain scores (posttest minus pretest) for the two groups, because gains are limited in size by the difference between the test's ceiling and the magnitude of the pretest score. Children who experienced adult interaction while they watched were found to learn more than children who did not interact with adults.

FACTORIAL DESIGNS

Factorial research designs modify the true experimental designs described in the previous section. They incorporate further complications by adding independent variables (usually moderator variables) to supplement the treatment variable. One such design might modify the pretest-posttest control group design with one treatment variable into a factorial design with one treatment variable and one moderator variable. The moderator variable is indicated by the letter Y with two levels, Y_1 and Y_2, in the diagram:

$$R \quad O_1 \quad X \quad Y_1 \quad O_2$$
$$R \quad O_3 \quad \quad Y_1 \quad O_4$$
$$R \quad O_5 \quad X \quad Y_2 \quad O_6$$
$$R \quad O_7 \quad \quad Y_2 \quad O_8$$

In this example, two groups receive the experimental treatment and two groups do not. One group receiving the treatment and one group not receiving the treatment are simultaneously categorized as Y_1, while the remaining two groups, one receiving and one not receiving the treatment, are categorized as Y_2. Thus, if Y_1 represented a subgroup receiving oral instruction and Y_2 a subgroup receiving written instruction, only half of each subgroup would receive the treatment. Moreover, random assignment determines the halves of each subgroup to experience or not experience the treatment.

It is equally possible to create a factorial design by modifying the posttest-only control group design, as illustrated in the diagram, again for a two-factor situation:

$$R \quad X \quad Y_1 \quad O_1$$
$$R \qquad\;\; Y_1 \quad O_2$$
$$R \quad X \quad Y_2 \quad O_3$$
$$R \qquad\;\; Y_2 \quad O_4$$

Any design with an independent variable and a moderator variable must recognize that, when the moderator variable is an individual difference measure, Ss cannot be randomly assigned to the different levels of the moderator variable. However, Ss within each level on the moderator variable can be randomly assigned to each condition or level of the independent variable to ensure random distribution of all participant characteristics other than that indicated by the moderator variable across conditions within each level of independent variable experience. Figure 8.1 diagrams the design for a study of instructional effects using the factorial version of the posttest-only control group design. It incorporates two intact-group moderator variables.

FACTORIAL DESIGN ($4 \times 2 \times 2$) FOR AN INSTRUCTIONAL STUDY WITH TWO INTACT GROUP MODERATOR VARIABLES   FIGURE 8.1

$$R \quad X_1 \quad Y_1 \quad Z_1 \quad O_1$$
$$R \quad X_2 \quad Y_1 \quad Z_1 \quad O_2$$
$$R \quad X_3 \quad Y_1 \quad Z_1 \quad O_3$$
$$R \quad X_0 \quad Y_1 \quad Z_1 \quad O_4$$

$$R \quad X_1 \quad Y_2 \quad Z_1 \quad O_5$$
$$R \quad X_2 \quad Y_2 \quad Z_1 \quad O_6$$
$$R \quad X_3 \quad Y_2 \quad Z_1 \quad O_7$$
$$R \quad X_0 \quad Y_2 \quad Z_1 \quad O_8$$

$$R \quad X_1 \quad Y_1 \quad Z_2 \quad O_9$$
$$R \quad X_2 \quad Y_1 \quad Z_2 \quad O_{10}$$
$$R \quad X_3 \quad Y_1 \quad Z_2 \quad O_{11}$$
$$R \quad X_0 \quad Y_1 \quad Z_2 \quad O_{12}$$

$$R \quad X_1 \quad Y_2 \quad Z_2 \quad O_{13}$$
$$R \quad X_2 \quad Y_2 \quad Z_2 \quad O_{14}$$
$$R \quad X_3 \quad Y_2 \quad Z_2 \quad O_{15}$$
$$R \quad X_0 \quad Y_2 \quad Z_2 \quad O_{16}$$

TREATMENTS *(X)*
X_1 Computer-Assisted Instruction
X_2 Programmed Text
X_3 Televised Lecture
X_0 Lecture-Discussion

MODERATOR *(Y)*
Y_1 High-Motivation Students
Y_2 Low-Motivation Students

MODERATOR *(Z)*
Z_1 Females
Z_2 Males

All comments about the true experimental designs apply equally to related factorial designs. In addition, the factorial designs allow researchers to deal systematically with multiple independent variables. That is, within the factorial designs more than one variable can be manipulated and thus studied.

Within a factorial design, a researcher can assess the separate effect of each independent variable as well as their conjoint or simultaneous effects.[5] This approach shows how one of the variables might moderate the others. A diagram effectively illustrates the relationship between the various observations of the dependent variable and the levels of the two independent variables being studied. (One of these latter variables is typically called a *moderator variable*.)

$$
\begin{array}{c c c c}
 & X_1 & X_0 & \\
Y_1 & \boxed{\begin{array}{cc} O_1 & O_2 \end{array}} & & O_{Y_1} \\
Y_2 & \begin{array}{cc} O_3 & O_4 \end{array} & & O_{Y_2} \\
 & O_{X_1} & O_{X_0} &
\end{array}
$$

By comparing the observations under X_1 (that is, O_{X_1}) to the observations under X_0 (that is, O_{X_0}), a researcher can contrast the effects of the treatment with the control. By comparing the observations in the Y_1 row (that is, O_{Y_1}) to those in the Y_2 row (that is, O_{Y_2}), he or she can contrast the effects of Level 1 of the Y variable with those of Level 2 of the Y variable. Furthermore, by contrasting the individual cell effects, O_1 versus O_3 and O_2 versus O_4, the researcher can identify any simultaneous effects of the X and Y variables.[6]

Suppose, for example, that X_1 is an intensive program to improve memory, while X_0 is a control condition including reading but no memory training. The moderator variable (Y) might then be immediate memory span, with Y_1 designating subjects high on this measure and Y_2 designating subjects low on this measure. The findings might be something like those illustrated in Figure 8.2.

The data graphed in Figure 8.2 suggest that the training has an overall salutary effect (O_1 and O_3 are higher than O_2 and O_4, respectively). Further, subjects with high memory span values performed better than those with low memory span (O_1 is higher than O_3 and O_2 is higher than O_4). In addition, the Y variable seems to moderate the X variable. That is, training produces more pronounced effects for subjects with high memory spans than for those with low memory spans. Thus, the two independent variables seem to generate a conjoint effect as well as separate effects. (Of course, these conclusions would have to be substantiated by an analysis of variance.) The factorial research design allows the researcher to identify both simultaneous and separate effects of independent variables. That is, it allows a researcher to include one or more moderator variables.

---

[5] The appropriate statistical procedure for this determination is analysis of variance. The illustrated study would require a three-way analysis of variance. (See Chapter 11.)

[6] This simultaneous effect, called an interaction, is described in the discussion of analysis of variance in Chapter 11. (See particularly Figures 11.10 and 11.11.)

RESULTS OF A MEMORY EXPERIMENT

FIGURE 8.2

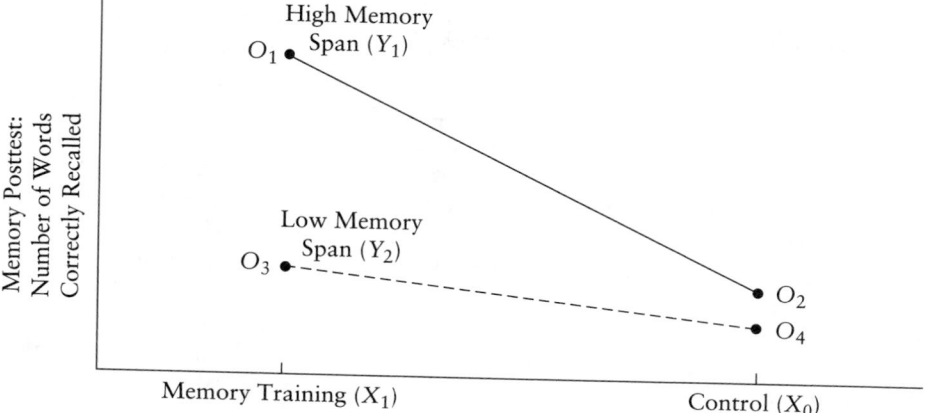

A study may incorporate multiple outcome measures but analyze each one in a separate evaluation. In such a case, time or trials function, not as moderator variables, but merely as multiple dependent variables. The research design is repeated for each dependent variable.

Sometimes, however, a study bases a moderator variable on repeated or multiple measurements of a single dependent variable, such as multiple performance trials or an immediate retention test followed by a delayed retention test. A design should explicitly indicate simultaneous analysis of data from multiple times or trials, but no common notation has been presented for this purpose. To represent repeated measurement of a dependent variable (also called a *within-subjects variable*), notation should include multiple Os following the representations of independent and moderator variables. For example, in a study, randomly assigned subjects might experience either real practice (X_1) or imaginary practice (X_2) in shooting foul shots. They would then complete five test trials of 20 shots each, and the researcher would evaluate the outcome as a moderator variable. The design would look like this:

$$R \quad X_1 \quad O_1 \quad O_2 \quad O_3 \quad O_4 \quad O_5$$
$$R \quad X_2 \quad O_6 \quad O_7 \quad O_8 \quad O_9 \quad O_{10}$$

QUASI-EXPERIMENTAL DESIGNS

Quasi-experimental designs are partly—but not fully—true experimental designs; they control some but not all sources of internal invalidity. Although they are not as adequate as true experimental designs (because the sources of bias are not completely controlled), they provide substantially better control of the threats to validity than do pre-experimental designs.

Quasi-experimental designs suit situations in which conditions complicate or prevent complete experimental control. The real world that confronts an educational researcher is fraught with practical limitations upon opportunities to select or assign Ss and manipulate conditions. School systems may not accept new programs for experimental testing; decision makers may not allow disruptions of intact classes or division into groups necessary to designate random or equivalent samples; policies may prohibit researchers from administering a treatment to some and withholding it from others; a situation may not provide an opportunity for pretesting in advance of the implementation of some program or change.

Researchers should not throw up their hands in despair or retreat to the laboratory. They should not advance upon the uncontrolled and uncontrollable variables of the educational milieu with only pre-experimental designs as their inadequate tools. They should instead employ quasi-experimental designs to carry experimental control to its reasonable limit within the realities of particular situations.

Time-Series Design

Some conditions prevent incorporation of comparison or control groups in experiments. When a change occurs throughout an entire school system, for example, identifying a control group might require the impossible step of finding a second school system that (1) is in most ways comparable to the first, (2) has not also incorporated a similar change, and (3) is willing to cooperate. Change often occurs without leaving an undisturbed control group for the comfort of the researcher. Faced with this predicament, she or he might consider the inferior one-shot case study or one-group pretest-posttest designs. However, a third solution, the time-series design, provides better control:

$$O_1 O_2 O_3 O_4 \quad X \quad O_5 O_6 O_7 O_8$$

The time-series design differs from the one-group pretest-posttest design by administering a series of pretests and posttests rather than a single administration of each. Over a period of time, such a series allows good control of maturation effects and some control of history—two important sources of internal invalidity left totally uncontrolled by the one-group pretest-posttest design. The time series also controls for testing effects, because repeated exposure to a single pretest is likely to lead to adaptation or desensitization, while any testing effects that do occur may not be expected to persevere through the series of posttests.

This design does not allow a researcher to rule out history as a source of invalidity, but its effect usually can be minimized. In general, any effects of extraneous events should occur across all of the observations, allowing researchers to infer these effects from an examination of O_1 to O_8. Historical bias would

SOME POSSIBLE OUTCOMES USING THE TIME-SERIES DESIGN

FIGURE 8.3

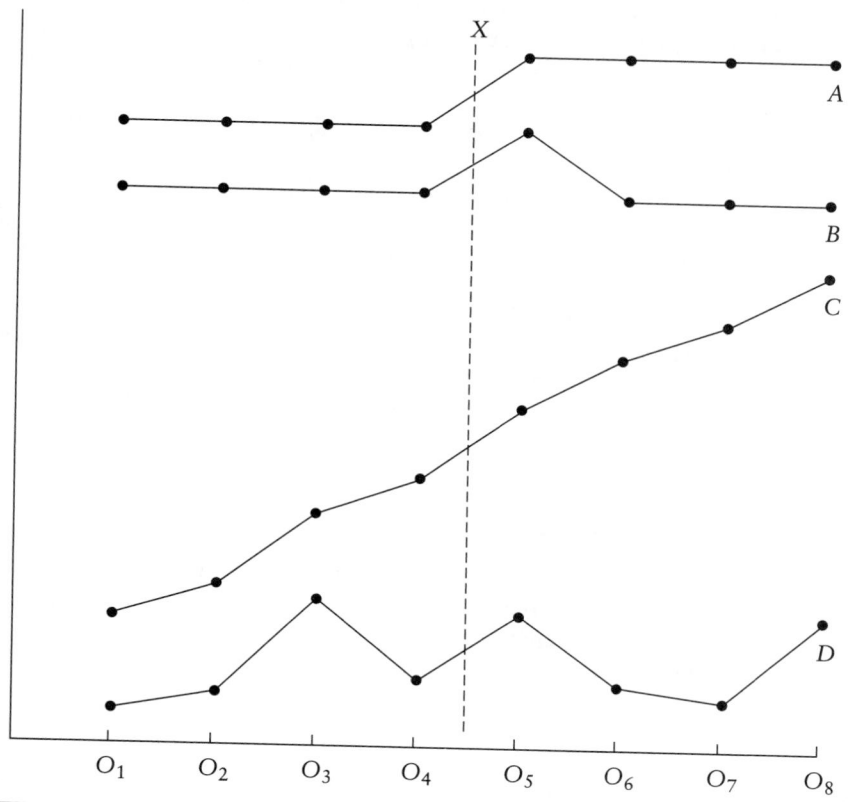

The data span measurements O_1 through O_8 with a treatment (X) occurring between O_4 and O_5. (While the gain from O_4 to O_5 is the same in each instance, the inference of an effect is most justified for Curves A and B; it is unjustified for C and D.)

invalidate conclusions from such a study in the possible (but improbable) event of an external event occurring simultaneously with the application of the treatment X (neither preceding it or following it, but falling just coincident with it). (See Figure 8.3.) Note that Chapter 1 illustrates the use of the time series design in Figure 1.2, which illustrates the example concerning violent incidents in schools.[7]

---

[7] Recall the conclusion that researchers should avoid simple statistical comparisons of O_4 and O_5 in analyzing the results of a time-series experiment. They can derive more reliable results through comparisons among all pairs of adjacent points or measures of the slope and intercept characteristics of the series.

Although the time-series design does not control for history as well as a true experimental design does, it helps a researcher to interpret the extent of historical bias. Thus it gives more adequate control than alternative single-group designs. In addition, the time-series design controls other threats to validity (except, perhaps, instrumentation bias).

One practical limitation in the use of this design is the unavailability of data for multiple pretest observations (O_1 through O_4). A researcher often depends on the school system to collect these data as a regular part of its assessment program. If such data represent achievement outcomes, they are usually available as a regular part of school records (perhaps standardized achievement test scores). However, if such data represent attitudes, the researcher would have to plan well in advance of the treatment to begin to collect these data.

If attitude data were regularly collected and made available, the time-series design would increase in practicality. Eliminating advance planning and testing would also reduce the likelihood that testing would function as a source of external invalidity by sensitizing participants to the treatment.

Equivalent Time-Samples Design[8]

Like the time-series design, the equivalent time-samples design suits situations when only a single group is available for study and the group requires a highly predetermined pattern of experience with the treatment. The second condition means that the researcher must expose the group to the treatment in some systematic way:

$$X_1 \quad O_1 \quad X_0 \quad O_2 \quad X_1 \quad O_3 \quad X_0 \quad O_4$$

This design, too, is a form of time-series. Rather than introducing the treatment (X_1) only a single time, however, the researcher introduces and reintroduces it, making some other experience (X_0) available in the absence of the treatment.

The equivalent time-samples design satisfies the requirements of internal validity, including controlling for historical bias. In this regard, it is superior to the time-series design, since it further reduces the likelihood that a compelling extraneous event will occur simultaneously with each presentation of the treatment (X_1). Thus, a comparison of the average of O_1 and O_3 with the average of O_2 and O_4 will yield a result unlikely to be invalidated by historical bias. Moreover, the analysis can be set up to determine order effects, as well:

	First Administration	Second Administration
X_1	O_1	O_3
X_0	O_2	O_4

---

[8] This design is also referred to as *using subjects as their own controls*.

Consider the following example application of this design. An art teacher wishes to determine the effect of a museum field trip on the attitudes and knowledge of students in a particular art class. The teacher takes this class to the local art museum (X_1) in lieu of the regularly scheduled art class for the week (X_0). Following the trip, the teacher administers a test of art knowledge and a measure of attitudes (O_1). The following week the teacher holds the regular art appreciation class (X_0) and subsequently measures knowledge and attitudes toward art (O_2). In the third week, the class again visits the local museum and concentrates on another portion of the collection (X_1). Knowledge and attitudes are again measured (O_3). The last week involves normal class activity (X_0) and measurement (O_4).

The analysis of the data from this study is set up as shown above. A comparison of O_1 and O_3 with O_2 and O_4 allows the teacher to contrast the results of the two experiences. The interaction between the four measurements provides a check on differential changes over time. Simple time effects can be determined by comparing O_1 and O_2 to O_3 and O_4. Selection and other participant factors are controlled by using the same Ss in both conditions (using the Ss as their own controls).[9] History bias is unlikely to affect the museum trips in ways different from the regular classes, particularly since the treatment is experienced on two separate occasions. Other sources of invalidity do not pose any major threat to this design.

As a second illustration of the equivalent time-samples design, consider a study comparing rewards for an individual's performance to those for the group's performance, where a single group of subjects serves as its own control. The control condition (X_0) involves an incentive system that distributes rewards and punishments to individual students; the experimental condition (X_1) distributes the same rewards and punishments according to group contingency criteria. The control (X_0) is administered in Phases I and III, whereas the experimental treatment (X_1) occurs in Phases II and IV. Observations (O_2, O_3, O_4, and O_5) are made following each phase, as well as prior to the start of the series (O_1). The result looks like this:

$$O_1 \quad X_0 \quad O_2 \quad X_1 \quad O_3 \quad X_0 \quad O_4 \quad X_1 \quad O_5$$

A third illustration of this design is a study by Taylor and Samuels (1983) that compared children's recall of normal and scrambled passages. The same children read both types of passage, but half, chosen at random, read the normal passage first and the scrambled passage second, while the other half read the passages in the reverse order: scrambled first and normal second. (Refer back to Table 7.2.) By reversing the sequence of the experiences, the researchers avoided possible bias due to order effects. Because the same subjects experienced both treatments, that is, read both types of passage, the study required two separate passages. If the same passage content were used twice, students might remember

---

[9] This procedure for controlling selection threats to validity was described in Chapter 7.

it the second time, thereby introducing history bias and reducing internal validity. Subjects read two passages, Passage A (about bird nests) and Passage B (about animal weapons). Both passages included the same number of words and were evaluated to be at the same reading level. Half of the subjects, randomly chosen, read a normal (N) version of Passage A and a scrambled (S) version of Passage B, while the other half reversed this arrangement: scrambled A and normal B. The treatment therefore required four test booklets, each with two passages as follows: SA/NB, NA/SB, SB/NA, NB/SA; one-quarter of the subjects received each test booklet. This precaution allowed researchers to avoid possible threats to internal validity while using subjects as their own controls.

The equivalent time-samples design shows some weakness in external validity. If the effect of the treatment differs in continuous application from its effect when dispersed, the results will not allow generalization beyond the experimental situation. That is, if the effect of X_1 when administered over time ($X_1 \rightarrow$) is different from the effect of X_1 when introduced and reintroduced (as it is in an equivalent time-samples design: $X_1 \; X_0 \; X_1 \; X_0$), then the results of such a study would not justify valid conclusions about the continuous effect of X_1. Moreover, some treatments lead to adaptation as a function of repeated presentation, again reducing the external validity of this design.

Thus, the equivalent time-samples design offers improved ability to control for history bias as compared with the time-series design, but it introduces certain problems of external validity that weaken its applicability, if particular conditions prevail. Like all quasi-experimental designs, this one has strengths and weaknesses, and researchers must match it to situations that maximize its strengths.

The equivalent time-samples design can also be used with a single subject or participant rather than a group, as discussed later in the chapter under the heading Single-Subject Design.

Nonequivalent Control Group Design

Educational researchers often find themselves unable to assign Ss randomly to treatments. Although school principals may be willing to make two math classes available for testing, they are not likely to permit researchers to break up the classes and reconstitute them; rather, administrators generally prefer to maintain intact groups. Although researchers may have no reason to believe that these classes were originally composed on some systematic basis (which would create a bias, invalidating research results), they still must be concerned about validity when working with such intact, possibly nonequivalent groups. They can deal with the problem of possible nonequivalence by implementing the nonequivalent control group design:

$$\begin{array}{ccc} O_1 & X & O_2 \\ \hline O_3 & & O_4 \end{array}$$

This design is identical to the pretest-posttest control group design in all respects except for the randomness of the assignment of Ss to conditions. If the experimenter does not make this assignment, then he or she cannot assume randomness without demonstrating satisfactorily that the school's scheduling staff employed randomizing methods. Any doubt or suspected bias creates conditions favoring this design rather than a true design. The procedures for this design are the same as those for a true design, except that intact groups rather than randomly assigned ones experience the treatments, creating a control problem for selection bias. This problem mandates the use of a pretest to demonstrate initial equivalence of the intact groups on the dependent variable.

The use of intact, nonequivalent classes rather than randomized or matched groups (shown by the dashed line between groups and the absence of the R designation) creates potential difficulty in controlling for selection and experimental mortality bias. To overcome the potential for selection bias in this design, the researcher can compare the intact groups on their pretest scores (O_1 versus O_3) and on their scores for any control variables that are both appropriate to selection and potentially relevant to the treatment; examples include IQ, gender, age, and so on.

Note that the pretest is an essential precautionary requirement here as compared to its optional role in a true experimental design. The recommended posttest-only control group design includes no pretest. In the pretest-posttest control group design, the pretest merely establishes a baseline, from which to evaluate changes that occur, or incorporates a further safeguard, beyond random assignment, to control for selection bias. The nonequivalent control group design *must* employ a pretest, however, as its only control for selection bias. Only through a pretest can such a study demonstrate initial group equivalence (in the absence of randomized assignment).

Lack of random assignment to groups necessitates some basis for initially comparing the groups; the pretest provides the basis. Thus, a researcher might begin working with two intact classes to compare the process approach to teaching science with the traditional textbook approach. At the outset of the experiment, she or he would compare the groups primarily on knowledge of that material they are about to be taught but also possibly on prior science achievement, age, and gender to ensure that the groups were equivalent. If the pretest establishes equivalence, the researcher can continue with diminished concern about threats to internal validity posed by selection or mortality bias. If the pretest shows that the groups are not equivalent on relevant measures, alternative designs must be sought (or special statistical procedures applied).

More often, however, pretesting uncovers (1) bias in group assignment on irrelevant variables but (2) equivalent pretest means on the study's dependent and control variables; such results confirm the nonequivalent control group design as a good choice. This design is not, therefore, as good a choice as the pretest-posttest control group design, but it is greatly superior to the one-group pretest-posttest design.

In one situation, however, researchers must exercise caution in implementing the nonequivalent control group design: where the experimental group is self-selected, that is, the participants are *volunteers*. Comparing a group of volunteers to a group of nonvolunteers does not control for selection bias, because the two groups differ—at least in their volunteering behavior and all the motivations associated with it. Where the researcher can exercise maximum control over group assignment, he or she should recruit twice as many volunteer subjects as the treatment can accommodate and randomly divide them into two groups—an experimental group that receives the treatment and a control group from which treatment is withheld. Effects of the treatment versus its absence on some dependent variable would then be evaluated using one of the two true experimental designs. When the volunteers cannot be split into two groups, the separate-sample pretest-posttest design (described later in this section) should be used. The nonequivalent control group design is usually inappropriate, however, where one intact group is composed of volunteers and the other is not. Although the design is intended for the situations that cause some suspicion of bias in the assignment of individuals to intact groups, it gives valid results only when this bias is not relevant to the dependent variable (demonstrated by equivalence of group pretest results). The bias imposed by comparing volunteers to nonvolunteers is typically relevant to almost any dependent variable.

A study conducted by a group of three students in a research methods course illustrates the use of the nonequivalent control group design. The researchers undertook the study to assess the effects of a program to improve handwriting among third graders. The school in their study made available two third-grade classes, but no evidence suggested that the classes had been composed without bias. The school principal was not willing to allow the researchers to alter the composition of the classes, and they could not undertake treatment and control conditions in the same classroom (that is, the treatment was a class activity). Consequently, the nonequivalent control group design was employed. A random choice (flipping a coin) determined which of the two classes would receive the treatment. A handwriting test to measure the dependent variable was administered both before and after the subjects experienced either the treatment or the comparison activity. Moreover, the researchers confirmed equivalence of the two intact classes on a number of control variables: gender, chronological age, standardized vocabulary test score, standardized reading comprehension test score, involvement in instrumental music lessons, and presence of physical disorders. Thus, the researchers satisfactorily established that the possible selection bias due to differences between the groups was not strongly relevant to the comparisons to be made in the study. The effect of the treatment was assessed by comparing the gain scores (that is, posttest minus pretest) of the two groups on the dependent variable. Analysis of covariance is another commonly used tool in such cases.

A study by Slavin and Karweit (1984) evaluating mastery learning versus team learning illustrates a factorialized (2 × 2) version of the nonequivalent control group design:[10]

---

[10] Addition of a moderator variable reflecting pretest achievement with three levels (high, middle, low), as mentioned in the last paragraph of the results section, would yield a 2 × 2 × 3 design with 12 conditions.

$$O_1 \quad X_1 \quad Y_1 \quad O_2 \quad \text{(mastery and teams)}$$

$$O_3 \quad X_2 \quad Y_1 \quad O_4 \quad \text{(teams alone)}$$

$$O_5 \quad X_1 \quad Y_2 \quad O_6 \quad \text{(mastery alone)}$$

$$O_7 \quad X_2 \quad Y_2 \quad O_8 \quad \text{(neither mastery or teams)}$$

In summary, the nonequivalent control group design gives researchers a capability to control for selection bias midway between those of the unacceptable intact-group comparison (a pre-experimental design) and the pretest-posttest control group design (a true experimental design). It offers less validity than the true design, because it fails to assign Ss randomly to groups; it gives stronger validity than the pre-experimental alternative by including a pretest that provides initial data on the equivalence of the intact groups on the study's dependent and control variables. Where intact groups (that is, groups whose members were not assigned by the researcher) serve as experimental and control groups, the researcher can partially control for selection bias by demonstrating their initial equivalence on relevant variables.

Systematically Assigned Control Group Design[11]

What happens to validity if the Ss in the group receiving an experimental treatment have been systematically preselected and assigned because they share some characteristic, and all of the preselected Ss experience the treatment? This situation occurs if, for example, the treatment is a remedial program required of all students who score below a certain point on an entry or screening test or who fail a course. Rather than haphazard selection bias influencing assignment, such a situation establishes systematic "selection bias" by assignment based on a preselection factor. Low scorers become participants, and high scorers are excluded. (Alternatively, if the treatment were appropriate for subjects with high capabilities, high scorers would participate, and low scorers would not.)

A chart might designate this design with a double-dashed line between groups to indicate that they were intentionally and systematically nonequivalent by assignment:

$$O_1 \quad X \quad O_2$$
$$O_3 \qquad\quad O_4$$

This alternative amounts to a variation of the nonequivalent control group design. However, it leaves no doubt about the basis for group assignments; the

[11] Cook and Campbell (1979) call this procedure the *regression-discontinuity design.*

researchers know initially that the groups differ on their pretest performance (O_1 versus O_3).

Evaluation of the treatment in this design should focus on determining whether the treatment group shows a stronger improvement in posttest performance relative to its own pretest performance than does the nontreatment group. The nontreatment group may still outperform (or underperform) the treatment group on the posttest, because it started higher (or lower), but its gain from its initial position of superiority (or inferiority) should not be nearly so great as the gain of the experimental group.[12]

This design allows researchers to compare a treatment to a control whenever assignment to groups has resulted from systematic evaluations of test or performance scores. When treatment Ss have been drawn exclusively from among those scoring on one side of a cutoff point and control Ss from among those scoring on the other side, this design can be usefully applied.

Separate-Sample Pretest-Posttest Design

In some research situations, studies cannot provide the experimental treatments to all subjects at the same time. For instance, a training program planned for 1,000 students may accommodate only 100 participants *at one time*. Thus, the program would have to run continuously, filling its ranks anew each time it started over again. (Many training and remedial treatment programs do, in fact, operate in this manner.) Because all students in a group experience the program at some time, they cannot be assigned to training and nontraining conditions; thus no true design fits this situation. Because each participant receives the treatment only once and then becomes unavailable for advance testing, the equivalent time-samples and time-series designs could not be used.

To deal with a situation that at first glance seems uncontrollable, researchers might gather valid results by taking an inadequate design, the one-group pretest-posttest design, and applying it twice:

$$O_1 \quad X \quad O_2$$
$$\overline{}$$
$$O_3 \quad X \quad O_4$$

By applying the one group pretest-posttest design ($O_1 \times O_2$) twice, researchers can overcome one of the major shortcomings of this pre-experimental design: its failure to control for history bias. Recall that the one-group pretest-posttest design fails to eliminate the possibility that some other event occurring

---

[12] The statistical test for this type of comparison is analysis of covariance of posttest scores, with pretest scores serving as the covariate or control variable. Regression analysis also allows researchers to compare the slopes of the lines relating posttest scores to pretest scores for the two groups.

simultaneously with X causes O_2. Using the separate-sample pretest-posttest design, if $O_2 > O_1$ and $O_4 > O_3$, researchers gain confidence due to the unlikelihood that some other event occurred simultaneously with X on *both administrations* of the treatment, lending validity to the conclusion that X caused O. Although the "other-event theory" (that is, history bias) remains a possibility, it is an unlikely one.

The separate-sample pretest-posttest design is vulnerable, however, to three sources of internal invalidity. The first of these is a simple *testing effect* brought on by the use of a pretest. Because a pretest is an essential element of this design, since it helps to control selection bias, the researcher must avoid the use of highly sensitizing pretest measures.

A second source of invalidity is *maturation*. The major control comparison in this design is O_3 versus O_2. However, the second group usually shows less maturation (that is, is younger) at the inception of the treatment than the first shows at its completion (is older). If a group of students begins a 1-year training program at an average age of 18, then O_2 occurs at an average age of 19 for the group, while O_3 occurs at an average age of 18. Comparing 19-year-olds to 18-year-olds creates the possibility that maturation will threaten validity. Researchers can compensate for this threat by converting measurements for one of the groups in the separate-sample design to a kind of time-series design as follows:

$$O_1 \quad X \quad O_2$$
$$\overline{ - - - - - - -}$$
$$O_5 \qquad\quad O_3 \quad X \quad O_4$$

Note the addition of O_5, which makes this version of the separate-sample design also a version of the nonequivalent control group design. However, researchers often cannot make such a change, because one of the conditions necessitating the use of the separate-sample design is restriction of opportunities to test subjects only immediately before and after the treatment.

The threat posed by maturation to the validity of a separate-sample pretest-posttest design is illustrated in a faculty study (mentioned early in Chapter 1) of the effects of student teaching on students' perceptions of the teaching profession. To control for the history bias encountered when this kind of study lacks a control group, the faculty researcher used this separate-sample design:

$$\overline{ - - - - \overset{\textstyle O_1}{} - - \overset{\textstyle O_2}{} - - -} \quad \text{(juniors)}$$
$$O_3 \qquad\quad O_4 \quad X \quad O_5 \qquad \text{(seniors)}$$

The *Ss* experienced student teaching in the spring of the senior year. The researcher recognized the difficulty of evaluating the effects of student teaching on students' perceptions of the profession without comparing it to a control group. Students not in the teacher education program would make poor control group members, because their perceptions of teaching as a profession would likely differ from those of students in the program. A longitudinal study, perhaps involving the time-series design, would have required more time than most research projects can be expected to take. The researcher solved the problem by designating juniors in the teacher education program as a control group, creating a variant of either the separate-sample or nonequivalent control group designs. Although this control group eliminated threats to internal validity without creating insurmountable bias based on selection, its design left maturation as a major threat. Seniors are older and have accumulated more educational experiences than juniors, so they might be expected to differ on perceptions of their chosen profession simply as a function of maturation. To check this possibility, the researcher added O_3. A finding of equivalence between O_4 minus O_3 and O_2 minus O_1 would indicate comparable maturation for juniors and seniors. In such a situation, juniors could serve as a valid comparison group for seniors. Therefore, a comparison of O_5 minus O_4 to O_2 minus O_1 would indicate the effect of X independent of maturation.

A third source of invalidity affects the separate-sample pretest-posttest design through the *interaction of selection and maturation*. Little can be done to offset this possibility.

Patched-Up Design

The separate-sample pretest-posttest design was essentially built on applying a pre-experimental design *(O X O)* twice. The patched-up design combines two *different* pre-experimental designs, neither of which gives valid results by itself, but which in combination can create an adequate design.[13] The hybrid is especially useful in situations like those previously described where a particular training program runs continuously with new participants as students graduate and enter, leaving the researcher no opportunity to withhold treatment from anyone. Moreover, the patched-up design shown here allows the study to begin in the middle of a training program rather than only at its inception.

Recall that the one-group pretest-posttest design *(O_1 X O_2)* provided some control over selection effects, but it totally failed to control for confounding due to history, maturation, and regression. Recall also the intact-group comparison:

$$\frac{X \quad O_1}{O_2}$$

It controlled for maturation and history effects but not at all for selection bias. The patched-up design shown below combines these two pre-experimental designs to merge their strengths and overcome their shortcomings:

---

[13] The two variants of the separate-sample pretest-posttest design illustrated in the preceding section can also be considered "patched-up" designs.

Class A X O_1
——————
Class B O_2 X O_3

The comparison O_2 versus O_1 contrasts results for intact groups, and it cannot be explained away by maturation or history. O_3 versus O_2 is the one-group pretest-posttest comparison, and it cannot be explained away by selection. Reasonably comparable superiority of O_1 over O_2 and O_3 over O_2 indicates that neither history, maturation, or selection account for the treatment effect.

This design illustrates the creative process of generating quasi-experimental designs, particularly from the building blocks of the pre-experimental designs, to deal with situations that prevent total experimental control (a prerequisite for true experimental designs). This patched-up design subjects all participants to the experimental treatment, a common requirement outside the control of the experimenter. However, the experimenter can control when and to whom the treatment is given at a particular point in time. Thus the groups get the treatment sequentially and their results are compared: The pretest score of the second group is compared to its own posttest score and to the posttest score of the first group.

Single-Subject Design

While most educational research studies involve groups of participants or subjects, primarily to maximize stability, in some situations researchers want or need to study individual subjects or to present data for one subject at a time. Studies in special education, for example, or those evaluating behavioral modification techniques often use single subjects, because of the participants' uniqueness or the nature of the data to be collected.

In the single-subject design, the subject must serve as his or her own control, since researchers can identify or have available no real equivalent. Observation methods involve repeated measurement of some behavior of the single subject under changes in some condition. Recall that this feature characterizes the equivalent time-samples design. In fact, the second study discussed in the section on that design (which alternated reward and punishment phases on an individual basis with control phases on a group basis and observed results) would serve as an illustration of the single-subject design if a researcher were to run it with an individual rather than a group of subjects.

A single-subject design incorporates two necessary phases. During the control or *baseline* phase, the researcher measures the subject's behavior under normal or typical conditions. During the experimental or *treatment* phase, he or she measures the subject's behavior under the special conditions targeted for investigation in the study. Normal versus experimental conditions represent the two levels of the independent variable in this design, and only one level can be studied at a time.

The single-subject design allows three variants. In the first, the subject experiences the control or baseline (A) and experimental (B) condition once each (creating the A-B design). In the second variant, the subject experiences the baseline condition twice and the experimental condition once (creating the A-B-A design). The third variant gives each experience twice (A-B-A-B design). Multiple repetitions enhance the internal validity of the design (which is already somewhat limited; as described earlier in the chapter) by increasing the stability of the findings. Results of repeated trials substitute for comparisons of results across subjects, an impossibility in the single-subject design.

An example of results using the A-B approach (also represented as $X_0 \, O_1 \, X_1 \, O_2$) are shown in Figure 8.4. The researcher monitored a single subject, a seventh-grade boy in a class for emotionally handicapped students, on two measures over a 16-week period: (1) rate of chair time out (the solid line), and (2) percentage of escalated chair time out (the dashed line). A chair time out (CTO) served as a punishment for three disruptive behaviors. A student disciplined in this way was required to sit in a chair at the back of the classroom for 5 minutes. If the recipient continued disruptive behavior, the consequence was an escalated CTO, which meant continuing to sit in the back of the classroom, with the added consequence of it being regarded as a more serious offense. If a student received more than one escalated CTO, he or she lost the privilege of participating in a special end-of-week activity.

FIGURE 8.4   **RESULTS OF A SINGLE-SUBJECT DESIGN: THE EFFECT OF A BEHAVIORAL INTERVENTION ON TWO MEASURES OF DISRUPTIVE BEHAVIOR**

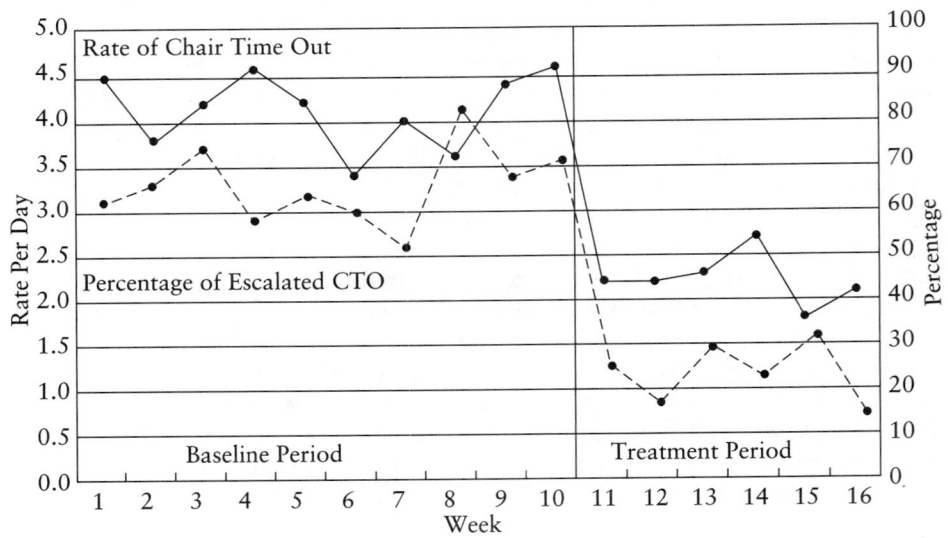

The researcher observed the subject for 10 weeks under normal conditions, termed the *baseline*, before the onset of a 6-week treatment. The treatment awarded bonus points to the subject for receiving no CTOs and no escalated CTOs for an entire day. The bonus points could be exchanged for prizes during the special end-of-week activity. The results clearly show that the treatment was accompanied by a reduction in disruptive behavior by the subject.

The single-subject design suffers from weak external validity. Many questions surround any effort to generalize to others results obtained on a single subject. To increase external validity, such a design should be repeated or replicated on other subjects to see if similar results are obtained. The results of each subject may be presented in individual reports. Adding subjects will ultimately render the design indistinguishable from the equivalent time-samples design.

Ex Post Facto Designs

The term *ex post facto* indicates a study in which the researcher is unable to cause a variable to occur by creating a treatment and must examine the effects of a naturalistically occurring treatment after it has occurred. The researcher attempts to relate this after-the-fact treatment to an outcome or dependent measure. Although the naturalistic or ex post facto research study may not always be diagrammed differently from other designs described so far in the chapter, it differs from them in that the treatment is included by selection rather than manipulation. For this reason, the researcher cannot always assume a simple causal relationship between independent and dependent variables. If observation fails to show a relationship, then probably no causal link joins the two variables. If a researcher does observe a predicted relationship, however, he or she cannot necessarily say that the variables studied are causally related. (Later discussion will address this point in more detail.) This section covers two types of ex post facto designs—the co-relational design and the criterion-group design.

Co-Relational Study

In a co-relational study[14] a researcher collects two or more sets of data from a group of subjects for analysis that attempts to determine the relationship between them:

$$O_1 \qquad O_2$$

Consider the study by McGarity and Butts (1984) that examined the relationship between the effectiveness of teacher management behavior and student

---

[14] This intentionally hyphenated designation suggests that the purpose of the design is simply to show a relationship between variables. Although correlation tests are the statistical methods typically employed in analyzing such data, they are by no means the exclusive tools of such research.

engagement in 30 high school science classes. Effective teacher management be-havior was operationally defined by observer judgments on a list of 10 behavioral indicators.[15] Student academic engagement was operationally defined by the number of students out of 10 observed per minute who were attending to in-struction, working on seatwork, or interacting on instructional content.

The study found a high correlation between the two measures. Note that the researchers did not assign teachers to management behavior conditions or other-wise directly affect any of the targeted variables. Hence, the high correlation does not indicate whether teachers who effectively manage their classes cause students to engage in learning, or whether classes of students likely to engage in learning cause teachers to be seen as especially effective managers.

Occasionally, a researcher who completes a co-relational study may suggest that the variable measured by O_1 has caused detected changes in the variable measured by O_2. However, a finding of a strong relationship between O_1 and O_2 allows three possible interpretations:

1. The variable measured by O_1 has caused O_2 (as the researcher has suggested).
2. The variable measured by O_2 has caused O_1.
3. Some third, unmeasured variable has caused both O_1 and O_2.

Because the researcher has not caused any variable to operate by his or her own manipulation or assignment, instead merely sampling naturally occurring characteristics, he or she cannot determine which of these three interpretations accounts for the observed relationship. A weak relationship or no relationship calls for rejection of all three interpretations, but a strong relationship does not help one to choose among the possibilities.

Still, co-relational studies serve useful purposes in determining the relation-ships among measures and *suggesting* possible causal links. Although co-relation does not necessarily imply causation, causation necessarily implies co-relation. As a next step, the researcher can design a study employing a treatment under direct experimental control.

Co-relational studies, then, are not adequate themselves for establishing causal relationships among variables. They may, however, be useful first steps in that direction.

Criterion-Group Design

When a researcher is working in an ongoing educational environment, particu-larly one focused on generating hypotheses about the causes of a specific state or

---

[15] These effective teacher management behaviors were (1) giving lesson-related directions, (2) pro-viding opportunities for participation, (3) maintaining learner involvement, (4) reinforcing learner involvement, (5) attending to routines, (6) being efficient, (7) being warm, (8) being sensitive to learner needs, (9) providing feedback, (10) promoting good relationships, (11) maintaining appro-priate behavior, and (12) managing disruptive behavior.

condition, it is often helpful to begin by contrasting the characteristics of one state with those of its opposite. The criterion-group design provides a format for such analysis. A *criterion group* is composed of people who display a certain characteristic that differentiates them from others, as determined by outside observation or judgment, or by self-description.

Suppose, for example, that a researcher were interested in studying the factors that contribute to teaching competence. Before conducting a true experiment intended to produce competent teachers by design, she or he would need some ideas about what factors separate competent and incompetent teaching. The criterion-group design requires the researcher to identify two criterion groups: competent teachers and incompetent teachers. This distinction might reflect students' or supervisors' judgments. The researcher would then observe and contrast the classroom behavior of these two groups of teachers in order to identify possible outcomes of teacher competence. The researcher could also examine the backgrounds and skills of these two teacher groups looking for ideas about factors that give rise to competence in some teachers.

Consider again the co-relational study of teacher management behavior and student engagement by McGarity and Butts (1984). These authors also divided the students into groups defined as those taught by teachers judged to be "competent" in teacher management behavior and those taught by teachers judged to be "incompetent" in that behavior. The study then compared these two criterion groups, competent and incompetent teachers, in terms of the amount of their engagement with students. The competent teachers' students were found to be more engaged in learning than were incompetent teachers' students.

Teachers judged competent in management behavior were found to engage in more interaction with students than were teachers judged incompetent in management behavior. However, because the association between competence in management behavior and student engagement was identified after the fact rather than through manipulation, the researchers could not reliably conclude that competent management behavior *causes* student engagement in learning; one could correctly conclude only that the two occur together.

To establish a causal relationship, further research would have to create a training program in competent management techniques. It would then compare the strength of student engagement in learning for pupils of teachers who have completed the program with that of students of teachers trained in some other manner.

The criterion-group design can be diagrammed as follows:[16]

$$
\begin{array}{ccc}
C \quad O_1 & O_1 \quad C \quad O_2 & C_1 \quad O_1 \\
\text{or} \; \overline{} & \overline{\;-\;-\;-\;-\;} \quad \text{or} \quad \overline{} \\
O_2 & O_3 \qquad O_4 & C_2 \quad O_2
\end{array}
$$

Rather than *X*, which stands for a manipulated experience or treatment, the diagram includes *C*, which stands for selection of an experience according to a

---

[16] Note the similarity between the third design and the co-relational design ($O_1 \; O_2$). This design resembles a nondesign, but it is not used primarily to establish cause-and-effect relationships.

criterion. Such an approach is used in instances where researchers randomly select Ss with criterion experiences from among larger groups of Ss who qualify on the criterion variable or in studies of intact groups of Ss, which include both criterion and noncriterion individuals. Similarly, the criterion-group approach can be used in a factorial design:

$$
\begin{array}{ccc}
C_1 & Y_1 & O_1 \\
\hline
C_2 & Y_1 & O_2 \\
\hline
C_1 & Y_2 & O_3 \\
\hline
C_2 & Y_2 & O_4
\end{array}
$$

To illustrate this approach, return again to the McGarity and Butts (1984) study of teacher management and student engagement. These authors were interested in determining whether the effect of competent versus incompetent teachers on student engagement depended on student aptitude. To accomplish this analysis, students were divided into three levels of aptitude: high, medium, and low (Y_1, Y_2, Y_3); they were then compared on engagement for competent (C_1) and noncompetent (C_2) teachers.

The criterion-group approach thus facilitates research in a number of contexts. In the first context, it helps researchers to identify characteristics associated with a criterion group that have presumably caused the criterion behavior; examples include previous training of people who display the criterion, other prior experiences they share, their common personality traits, and so on. Although the design gives ambiguous information about causality, it can help researchers to identify *potential* causes that often can then be tested more directly by manipulation.

Suppose, for example, that you want to determine the origins of creativity. To this end you might administer to a group of students a battery of tests designed to measure their creativity levels. On the basis of those test scores you would then identify a criterion group of students with high scores on these tests as well as students with low scores. You might then administer a questionnaire to the parents of both groups to identify particular experiences common among Ss in the high-creativity criterion group but lacking in their low-creativity counterparts. Without randomly assigning Ss to experiences, and because you have not created those experiences by manipulation, you could not conclude that those specific experiences have caused creativity differences. You might, however, generate some testable hypotheses from this criterion-group approach (some of which might be testable using additional criterion-group research and the others that would require a quasi-experimental or true experimental design).

The criterion-group design also works in a second context. Researchers identify one criterion group (for example, competent teachers) and its counterpart (incompetent teachers), then they assess the differential effects of these groups (criterion and noncriterion) on an entirely different group (for example, students).[17] In this context, the criterion-group approach analyzes a differential "treatment," but it too has limitations in the identification of causality. Because the experimenter does not create observed conditions, he or she cannot be sure whether the characteristics of the criterion group (that is, teachers) has caused the behavior of the other group (students) or whether observations have resulted from the reverse relationship. Although the former inference is often more likely than the latter one, the relationship is not beyond question.

In a third context, the criterion-group approach helps researchers to explore the behavioral implications of classification into different criterion groups. In other words, they employ the design to find out how members of different criterion groups behave in a situation. This approach is illustrated by Sample Study II from Appendix A, as reported in Box 8.

Another use of the criterion group design is to make inferences about development by comparing individuals of different ages or grade levels. When the criterion-group design serves this purpose, it is called a *cross-sectional design.* Suppose, for example, that you were interested in determining whether students felt an increasing need for independence as they progressed from elementary school to middle school to high school. As one way to accomplish this purpose, researchers could administer a measure of need for independence to randomly selected members of three groups: fifth graders, seventh graders, and ninth graders. This method would create a variation of the criterion-group design with three levels. If the ninth graders scored higher than the seventh graders, who in turn scored higher than the fifth graders, then the results would support the inference that need for independence increases with grade level (or age).

The cross-sectional version of the design could be factorialized, as well. Comparisons between genders, for example, could be included in the design by differentiating between boys and girls at each grade level as a moderator variable. The design, shown below, looks like one previously shown, except that it incorporates two more groups reflecting a third level of C:

$$
\begin{array}{ccc}
C_1 & Y_1 & O_1 \\
\hline
C_2 & Y_1 & O_2 \\
\hline
C_3 & Y_1 & O_3 \\
\hline
C_1 & Y_2 & O_4 \\
\hline
C_2 & Y_2 & O_5 \\
\hline
C_3 & Y_2 & O_6
\end{array}
$$

---

[17] In essence, the first use of this design seeks to identify the *antecedents* of the criterion characteristics, whereas the second seeks to identify their *concomitants.* Are relatively creative youngsters more intelligent than relatively uncreative ones? Are poor readers more easily distracted than good ones?

BOX 8

Illustrations From the Sample Studies

In Sample Study I (Appendix A) on the effect of encouragement on performance, subjects were randomly assigned to encouragement or no-encouragement groups. The study included no pretest for the dependent measure of performance (although pretests for four student characteristics were included to measure covariates). The resulting design fits the posttest-only control group type for the performance measure.

$$R \quad X_1 \quad O_1 \quad \text{(encouraging feedback)}$$
$$R \quad X_2 \quad O_2 \quad \text{(neutral feedback)}$$

This same sample study also illustrates the pretest-posttest control group design for the dependent variable of final self-efficacy:

$$R \quad O_1 \quad X_1 \quad O_3 \quad \text{(encouraging feedback)}$$
$$R \quad O_2 \quad X_2 \quad O_4 \quad \text{(neutral feedback)}$$

While performance allowed no pretest, self-efficacy did, and the result served as a covariate in the analysis of final self-efficacy, thus providing an additional control for selection bias. Analysis of covariance adjusts, and thereby eliminates, the influence of any initial differences between individuals on their final differences.

Because the study compares three different groups of students, rather than evaluating the same individuals at three points in time, this design shows some weakness in internal validity due to selection bias. This weakness can be somewhat reduced by including control variables such as socioeconomic status in selecting the samples. However, collecting data on all three groups at the same point in time would lessen the possible effect of history bias.

Longitudinal Designs

For making inferences about development, a longitudinal design offers an alternative to the cross-sectional design. A longitudinal design compares subjects at different points in time. For example, a longitudinal design might test the need for independence of fifth graders, then 2 years later test seventh graders, and two years after that test ninth graders.

Three versions of the longitudinal design would enable one to study different samples of students. If the students sampled each time come from the same

Sample Study II in Appendix A, a comparison of the classroom behaviors of good and poor readers, illustrates the third context for the criterion-group design: determining how members of different criterion groups behave in a given situation. Good readers (C_1) and poor readers (C_2) made up the criterion groups, identified on the basis of reading test scores. Initially, grade level was a moderator variable, but it was dropped from the analysis. The classroom behavior of each group (O_1 and O_2) was then observed for seven different measures, all related to what might be called the *distractibility* or *engagement* of the students in classroom learning activities. Each dependent variable was analyzed separately in seven runs of this design:

$$C_1 \quad O_1 \quad \text{(good readers)}$$

$$C_2 \quad O_2 \quad \text{(poor readers)}$$

The purpose of this analysis was to determine whether poor readers showed a stronger tendency toward distractibility than good readers showed, which would require additional or different classroom management strategies on the part of the teacher. Of course, this design does not support valid conclusions about cause and effect, because factors other than reading skill may have accounted for any observed differences. However, the design does provide a basis for establishing an association between variables, in this case reading ability and classroom distractibility.

general population, then the design is called a *trend study.* For example, a trend study might test different individuals in seventh grade 2 years after the initial assessment of fifth graders, as long as all participants came from the same general population (that is, they were students). Similarly, the ninth-grade group tested 2 years later would include another completely different sample from the same general population. In studying national issues such as public attitudes toward the quality of education, this approach achieves reasonable validity. For the example detailed, however, this approach would be strongly susceptible to both selection and history bias.

A better approach for the example study, called a *cohort study,* would follow students from the same specific population of students originally tested. If the original sample of fifth graders were drawn from a single school, then the seventh graders sampled 2 years later would be drawn from subjects who were fifth graders in the original school at the time the fifth-grade sample was drawn. After another 2 years, the study would draw a sample of ninth graders from the same original group. The three groups tested might include some, but probably not all, of the same students originally tested, but all three samples would be drawn from the same cohort or specific population. This precaution ensures that the students in each sample remain similar to one another, reducing selection bias.

A third longitudinal approach, called a *panel study,* tests exactly the same people each time as a way to minimize selection bias. However, all of the same people may not be available for each assessment, which would give rise to some selection bias due to experimental mortality. If some students' families moved after fifth grade, researchers might lose the possibility of collecting data from the same students each time. If those moving formed a random subset of the original group, then that activity would not create a problem. But if, for example, those who moved disproportionately represented children of military or upwardly mobile families, or families experiencing divorce, then the loss of their input may distort results by eliminating their systematic differences from the rest of the group on the dependent variable: need for independence. This effect would introduce considerable bias into the findings.

The cohort study offers the most practical way to control for various selection biases in a longitudinal design, since this method is less susceptible to selection bias than the trend study and less susceptible to experimental mortality than the panel study. However, researchers must recognize that all versions of the longitudinal design are susceptible to history (or experience) bias, since the passage of time brings not only naturally occurring developmental changes, which are the subject of study, but also changes in external circumstances for society at large, a source of confounding influences. For example, the nation could go to war, which might cause profound changes in independence strivings, particularly among older children. Therefore, as for all ex post facto designs, users should be careful to avoid making strong conclusions about cause (development) and effect (whatever dependent variables are studied) based on longitudinal studies.

DESIGNS TO CONTROL FOR EXTERNAL VALIDITY BASED ON REACTIVE EFFECTS[18]

Any study that tests an innovation or experimental intervention of any sort in a real environment such as an educational system may find an effect that results not from the specifics of the intervention but rather from the simple fact that the experiment is being conducted. This phenomenon has been termed the *reactive effect* of experimental arrangements, and it constitutes a common threat to external validity, as Chapter 7 explained. The Hawthorne effect, based on

---

[18] This section is based on material reported by Rosenthal (1985).

industrial studies completed in the late 1920s in the Western Electric Hawthorne works in Chicago, is a widely recognized reactive effect. The Hawthorne studies showed that workers' productivity increased during their participation in an experiment regardless of other experimental changes introduced. Apparently workers changed, because they knew that they were being observed and felt increasingly important by virtue of their participation in the experiment.

Many school-system studies compare results of experimental treatments to conditions of no-treatment or no-intervention. They risk recording differences based not on the specifics of the interventions, but on the fact that any interventions took place. That is, observed benefits may not accrue from the details of the interventions but from the fact that the subjects experienced some form of intervention. The effects may not be *true* but *reactive*—that is, a function of the experiment—which reduces external validity.

Similar problems in experiments can result from expectations by certain key figures in an experiment, such as teachers, about the likely effects of a treatment, creating another reactive effect. Such expectancies operate, for instance, in drug research. If someone administering an experimental drug knows what drug a subject receives, he or she may form certain expectancies regarding its potential effect. For this reason, such a study should ensure that the drug administrator operates in the blind, that is, remains unaware of the kind of drug administered to particular subjects in order to avoid the effects of those expectancies on the outcome of the experiment.

Designs to Control for the Hawthorne Effect

Rather than identifying the two familiar groups to test an intervention (the experimental group and the control group), researchers may gain validity by introducing a *second* control group that specifically controls for the Hawthorne effect. What is the difference between a no-treatment control and a Hawthorne control? A *no-treatment control group* like that typically employed in intervention studies involves no contact at all between the experimenter and the *S*s except for the collection of pretest data (where necessary) and posttest data. The *Hawthorne control group,* on the other hand, experiences a systematic intervention and interaction with the experimenter; this contact introduces some new procedure that is not anticipated to cause specific effects related to the effects of the experimental treatment or intervention. That is, the researcher deliberately introduces an *irrelevant, unrelated* intervention to the Hawthorne control group specifically in order to create the Hawthorne effect often associated with intervention. Thus the experimental and Hawthorne control groups experience partially comparable interventions, both of which are expected to produce a Hawthorne or facilitating effect. However, the Hawthorne control condition is unrelated and irrelevant to the dependent variables, so a comparison of its outcome with that for the treatment group indicates the differential effect of the experimental intervention.

For example, a study might seek to evaluate a technique for teaching first graders to read, identifying as the dependent variable a measure of reading achievement. The Hawthorne control intervention might take the form of playing games with the children while the experimental group experiences the reading training. The no-treatment control condition, on the other hand, would involve no contact whatever between experimenter and Ss.[19]

The Hawthorne control group contributes considerably to the external validity of an experiment. Because studies often involve some artificiality and confront subjects with novel experiences and people (or those they normally encounter in different contexts), any experiment will likely create some Hawthorne effect (a typical reactive effect) above and beyond the specific effects of the intervention. The Hawthorne control enables the experimenter to separate the "true" effects based on the specific experience of the intervention from reactive effects resulting from the Ss' participation in any experiment and their interaction with the experimental staff. Such assessment of the Hawthorne effect is impossible with only a no-treatment control group.

Designs to Control for Expectancy

An additional threat to external validity comes from the effect on a study's outcome produced by the agent of change, simply by virtue of his or her expectation regarding that outcome. Such an outcome would result, not only from the intervention alone, but in combination from the intervention *and* the expectation of the agent of change. This influence is another reactive effect. In a typical educational experiment, the agent of change is the teacher. If the teacher forms certain expectations for the outcome of a particular educational treatment, then, he or she can unconsciously and unintentionally affect the outcome of the experiment in the anticipated direction.[20]

To control for the invalidating effects of expectancy, a researcher could include four rather than two conditions in a study's design. Instead of the dual design including treatment and no-treatment conditions, she or he would designate two treatment and two no-treatment conditions. In one of the experimental treatment conditions, the teacher would believe that the experimental innovation would successfully produce the expected effect. The outcome then would be a combination of the treatment plus the teacher's expectation for success. In the alternative treatment condition, the teacher would be led to believe that the treatment was only a control condition; thus the design would gather results from a combination of a treatment expected to succeed and a neutral one without any

---

[19] Some studies use only the Hawthorne control group for comparison purposes and omit the regular, no-contact control group. In a study with a strong likelihood of a Hawthorne effect, the researcher may gain little from running a control group that does not control for the Hawthorne effect.

[20] Chapter 7 described these expectancies as *demand characteristics*. A somewhat arbitrary judgment determines whether they are considered to affect *external* or *internal* validity.

EXPERIMENTAL DESIGN WITH CONTROLS FOR REACTIVE EFFECTS: HAWTHORNE AND EXPECTANCY EFFECTS

FIGURE 8.5

$$R \quad X \quad E_p \quad O_1$$
$$R \quad X \quad E_n \quad O_2$$
$$R \quad H \quad E_p \quad O_3$$
$$R \quad H \quad E_n \quad O_4$$

X Experimental (relevant) treatment
H Hawthorne control (irrelevant experience)
E_p Positive teacher expectation created
E_n Neutral teacher expectation created

expectation of success. Similarly, the teacher administering one control condition would be led to believe that it served only control purposes, which, in fact, would be the truth. The teacher administering the other control condition, however, would be led to believe that it was actually an experimental intervention that should result in success or benefit to the experimental participants. This design appears in Figure 8.5.

Because the pure, no-treatment control would involve no interactions between experimenter and subject, this arrangement leaves little possibility of making teachers believe that they were participating in the experiment. (Teachers would certainly be hard pressed to believe that some benefit would accrue to *S*s who experienced no intervention.) However, as for a Hawthorne control group, a group designed to control for expectancies could experience an irrelevant interaction between *S*s and the experimenter. Such an arrangement would increase the likelihood of inducing teachers to believe that the students were participating in an experimental treatment (which, of course, they were not) in order to create positive teacher expectation in the absence of the experimental treatment.

Thus, the four conditions displayed in Figure 8.5 are (1) an experimental procedure with positive teacher expectations, (2) the same experimental procedure with a neutral or no teacher expectation, (3) a Hawthorne control with positive teacher expectation, and (4) a Hawthorne control with a neutral or no teacher expectation. These four conditions would allow a researcher to control for or systematically assess the effects of both the Hawthorne phenomenon and teacher expectancy. By using the statistical technique of analysis of variance (described in Chapter 11), he or she could determine independently the effect of the experimental procedure versus the control and the effect of teacher-positive expectation versus neutral or no expectation. Similar analysis could determine the interaction between the expectation phenomenon and the experimental procedure.

This design is particularly recommended for situations in which teachers function as agents of change in an experimental procedure, because such procedures often show some effects of teacher expectancy. To establish external validity that allows a researcher to generalize from the results of an experiment, the experimental design must separate the effects of the treatment from both kinds of reactive effects—teacher expectancy and Hawthorne effect. The design described in this section allows just this separation. In addition, this design helps with anticipation of effects expected from the experimental treatment in nonexperimental situations in the absence of both Hawthorne effect and positive teacher expectation, neither of which may apply in a nonexperimental setting.

SUMMARY

1. Pre-experimental designs or nondesigns do not control for threats to internal validity based on both participants and experiences. The one-shot case study $(X\ O)$ controls for neither source of bias; the one-group pretest-posttest design $(O_1\ X\ O_2)$ controls for participant bias, although it lacks a control group; it does not control for experience bias. The intact group comparison,

$$\left(\frac{X \quad O_1}{ \quad O_2} \right)$$

which lacks a pretest, controls for experience bias but not participant bias.

2. True experimental designs control for both types of threats to internal validity. This category includes two types of designs, the posttest-only control group design (on the left), and the pretest-posttest control group design (on the right).

$$R\ X\ O_1 \qquad\qquad R\ O_1\ X\ O_2$$
$$R\quad\ \ O_2 \qquad\qquad R\ O_3\ X\ O_4$$

3. Factorial designs include additional independent or moderator variables as part of true experimental designs. These designs allow researchers to evaluate the simultaneous or conjoint effects (called the *interactions*) of multiple variables on the dependent variable.

4. Some situations prevent researchers from satisfying either or both of the two basic requirements of a true design: freedom to give and withhold the treatment and freedom to assign subjects to conditions. In such circumstances, quasi-experimental or partly experimental designs may be used. In the time-series design $(O_1\ O_2\ O_3\ X\ O_4\ O_5\ O_6)$, multiple observations are made both before and after the treatment is administered. In the equivalent time-samples design $(X_1\ O_1\ X_0\ O_2\ X_1\ O_3\ X_0\ O_4)$, the treatment (X_1) is introduced and reintroduced, alternating with some other experience (X_0). In the commonly used nonequivalent control group design (shown below), the

comparison of intact groups requires pretests to partially control for potential participant bias.

$$\frac{O_1 \quad X \quad O_2}{O_3 \qquad O_4}$$

5. Other quasi-experimental designs include the systematically assigned control group design (same as the nonequivalent control group design, except that Ss are systematically assigned on the basis of some criterion to treatment and control groups). Researchers can also employ the separate-sample pretest-posttest design:

$$\frac{O_1 \quad X \quad O_2}{\qquad\qquad O_3 \quad X \quad O_4}$$

Also, a patched-up design resembles this one, but it omits O_1. The last three designs can be factorialized by the addition of one or more moderator variables.

6. In the single-subject design, a variation on the equivalent time-samples design, a single subject serves as his or her own control. Variations of baseline or control (A) and experimental treatment (B) include A-B, A-B-A, and A-B-A-B, depending on how many times the subject experiences each level of the independent variable.

7. When the independent variable is not manipulated, ex post facto designs are used. These designs lack the certainty of experimental designs since they cannot adequately control for experience bias. The co-relational design (O_1 O_2) simply looks at the relationship between two sets of scores. The criterion-group design compares two groups of participants who display a certain characteristic, as determined by observation, judgment, or self-description, that differentiates them from one another (for example, good readers and poor readers). The letter C replaces X, resulting in the design:

$$\frac{C_1 \quad O_1}{C_2 \quad O_2}$$

This design can also be factorialized.

8. The criterion-group design allows researchers to make inferences about development by comparing data for individuals of different ages or grade levels. This approach, called the *cross-sectional design*, can also be factorialized.

9. Longitudinal designs also support inferences about development by taking measurements over time on either (a) individuals from the same general

population (called a *trend study*), (b) individuals from the same specific population (called a *cohort study*), or (c) the same individuals (called a *panel study*). These three approaches vary in both practicality and ability to control for selection bias.

10. A research design may need provisions to control for external validity based on experiences (namely the Hawthorne effect and other reactive effects). In place of a normal control group, such a study would incorporate a Hawthorne control group whose members received a treatment other than the one being tested. This group would experience the same reactive effects as the treatment group, but would not experience the experimental treatment. A second approach, to control particularly for expectations, would include expectation as a moderator variable, with one level each of the treatment and control carrying positive expectations, and one level of each carrying neutral expectations.

COMPETENCY TEST EXERCISES

1. Rank order the three designs according to their adequacy for controlling for history bias:

   1. Most adequate   a. Time-series design
   2. Next most adequate   b. One-group pretest-posttest design
   3. Least adequate   c. Pretest-posttest control group design

2. Rank order the four designs according to their adequacy for controlling for selection bias:

   1. Most adequate   a. Patched-up design
   2. Next most adequate   b. Intact-group comparison
   3. Next least adequate   c. Posttest-only control group design
   4. Least adequate   d. Nonequivalent control group design

3. *Prediction:* Student teachers who are randomly assigned to urban schools to gain experience are more likely to choose urban schools for their first teaching assignments than student teachers who are randomly assigned to nonurban schools.
   Construct an experimental design to test this prediction.

4. *Prediction:* Students given programmed math instruction will show greater gains in math achievement than students not given this instruction, but this effect will be more pronounced among students with high math aptitude than among those with low aptitude.
   Construct an experimental design to test this prediction.

5. Which of the following circumstances create the need for a quasi-experimental design? (More than one may be a right answer.)

   a. Experimenter cannot assign *S*s to conditions.
   b. Experimenter must employ a pretest.
   c. Experimenter must collect the data himself or herself.
   d. The program to be evaluated has already begun.

6. Which of the following circumstances create the need for a quasi-experimental design? (More than one may be a right answer.)
   a. The study includes more than one independent variable.
   b. No control group is available for comparison.
   c. The pretest is sensitizing.
   d. Every member of the sample must receive the treatment.

7. A patched-up design has been created in which this year's first graders serve as the control group for a treatment experienced by this year's second graders. Which validity threat is not controlled?
   a. Selection
   b. History
   c. Maturation
   d. Mortality

8. *Prediction:* Student teachers who choose urban schools to gain experience are more likely to choose urban schools for their first teaching assignments than student teachers who choose nonurban schools.
   a. Why must researchers employ a quasi-experimental design to test this prediction?
   b. Construct one.

9. A school decides to implement a dental hygiene program for all students. It predicts a reduction in cavities among students as a result of this program.
   a. Why must researchers employ a quasi-experimental design to test this prediction?
   b. Construct one.

10. *Prediction:* Children from broken homes will create more extensive discipline problems in school (as evidenced by demerits) than will children from intact homes.
    a. Why must researchers employ a criterion-group design to test this prediction?
    b. Construct one.

11. *Prediction:* An after-school dance program will improve the physical and social skills of first graders.
    a. Why does a study to test this prediction call for a Hawthorne control?
    b. Construct a design for testing it.

12. A researcher has just designed a special program made up of a series of classroom lessons to increase verbal IQ scores She wants to try it out in some schools.

a. Why would a Hawthorne control be a good idea?
b. Why would teacher expectancy controls be a good idea?
c. Construct a design to test this program.

RECOMMENDED REFERENCES

Keppel, G. (1991). *Design and analysis: A researcher's handbook* (3rd ed.). Englewood Cliffs, NJ: Prentice-Hall.

Mitchell, M., & Jolley, J. (1992). *Research design explained* (2nd ed.). Fort Worth, TX: Harcourt Brace.

Trochim, W. M. K. (Ed.). (1986). *Advances in quasi-experimental design and analysis*. San Francisco: Jossey-Bass.

Chapter 9

IDENTIFYING AND DESCRIBING PROCEDURES FOR OBSERVATION AND MEASUREMENT

Objectives

- Identify and describe techniques for estimating test reliability.

- Identify and describe techniques for estimating test validity.

- Distinguish between four types of measurement scales: nominal, ordinal, interval, and ratio scales.

- Identify and describe different techniques for describing performance on tests, including percentiles, standard scores, and norms.

- Describe procedures for test identification using the *Mental Measurements Yearbook*.

- Identify different categories of standardized tests, and highlight specific tests in each category.

- Describe procedures for constructing a paper-and-pencil performance test and for performing item analysis on its contents.

- Describe procedures for constructing and using attitude scales of the Likert, semantic differential, and Thurstone types.

- Describe procedures for constructing and using recording devices such as rating scales, coding schemes, and behavioral sampling records.

TEST RELIABILITY

Test reliability means that a test gives *consistent* measurements. A ruler made of rubber would not give reliable measurements, because it could stretch or contract. Similarly unreliable would be an IQ test on which Johnny or Janie scored 135 on Monday and 100 on the following Friday, with no significant event or experience during the week to account for the discrepancy in scores. A test that does not give reliable measurements is not a good test regardless of its other characteristics.

Several factors contribute to unreliability in a test: (1) familiarity with the particular test form (such as multiple-choice questions), (2) subject fatigue, (3) emotional strain, (4) physical conditions of the room in which the test is given, (5) subject health, (6) fluctuations of human memory, (7) subject's practice or experience in the specific skill being measured, and (8) specific knowledge gained outside the experience evaluated by the test. A test that is overly sensitive to these unpredictable (and often uncontrollable) sources of error is not a reliable one. Test unreliability creates *instrumentation bias,* a source of internal invalidity in an experiment.

Before drawing any conclusions from a research study, a researcher should assess the reliability of his or her test instruments. Commercially available standardized tests have been checked for reliability; test manuals provide data relative to this evaluation. When using a self-made instrument, a researcher should assess its reliability either before or during the study. This section briefly discusses four approaches for determining reliability.

Test-Retest Reliability

One way to measure reliability is to give the same people the same test on more than one occasion and then compare individual performance on the two administrations. In this procedure, which measures *test-retest reliability,* each person's scores on the first administration of the test are related to his or her score on the second administration to provide a reliability coefficient.[1] This coefficient can vary from 0.00 (no relationship) to 1.00 (perfect relationship), but real evaluations rarely produce coefficients near zero. Because the coefficient is an indication of the extent to which the test measures stable and enduring characteristics of the test taker rather than variable and temporary ones, researchers hope for reasonably high coefficients.

The test-retest evaluation offers the advantage of requiring only one form of a test. It brings the disadvantage that later scores show the influence of practice and memory. They can also be influenced by events that occur between testing sessions.

---

[1] This relationship is usually computed by means of a correlation statistic, as described in Chapter 11.

Because the determination of test-retest reliability requires two test administrations it presents more challenges than do the other three reliability testing procedures (described in later subsections). However, it is the only one of the four that provides information about a test's consistency over time. This quality of a test is often important enough in an experiment to justify the effort to measure it, particularly when the research design involves both pretesting and posttesting.

Alternate-Form Reliability

Alternate-form reliability is determined by administering alternate forms of a test to the same people and computing the relationship between each person's score on the two forms. This approach requires two forms of a test that parallel one another in the content and required mental operations. The alternative test instruments must include carefully matched items so that corresponding items measure the same quality.

This approach allows a researcher to assess the reliability of either of the two test forms by comparison with the other. It also supports evaluation of the extent to which the two forms parallel one another. This second determination is particularly important if the study's design incorporates one form as a pretest and the other as a posttest.

Split-Half Reliability

The two approaches to reliability testing described so far seek to determine the consistency of a test's results over time and over forms. A researcher may also want to make a quick evaluation of a test's internal consistency. This judgment involves splitting a test into two halves, usually separating the odd-numbered items and the even-numbered items, and then correlating the scores obtained by each person on one half with those obtained by each person on the other. This procedure, which yields an estimate called *split-half reliability,* enables a researcher to determine whether the halves of a test measure the same quality or characteristic. The obtained correlation coefficient (r_1) is then entered into the Spearman-Brown formula to calculate the whole test reliability (r_2):

$$r_2 = \frac{nr_1}{1 + (n - 1)r_1}$$

r_2 = corrected reliability

r_1 = uncorrected reliability

n = number of parts (e.g., for halves, $n = 2$)

The actual test scores that will serve as data in a research study are based on the total test score rather than either half-test score. Therefore, the split-half reliability measure can be corrected by the formula to reflect the increase in reliability gained by combining the halves.

Kuder-Richardson Reliability

When a researcher uses an untimed test assumed to measure one characteristic or quality, she or he may want to evaluate the extent to which the test items all measure this same characteristic or quality. For a test with items scored with mutually exclusive categories *a* or *b* (for example, right or wrong), this judgment can examine individual item scores rather than part or total scores (as in the split-half method) followed by application of a *Kuder-Richardson formula*. This formula (known as *K-R formula 21*) is equivalent to the average of *all possible* split-half reliability coefficients:[2]

$$^rK\text{-R21} = \left(\frac{n}{n-1}\right)\left(1 - \frac{\overline{X}(n - \overline{X})}{ns^2}\right)$$

^rK-R21 = Kuder-Richardson reliability coefficient

n = number of items in the test

$\overline{X}$ = mean score on the test

s = standard deviation (a measure of variability)

TEST VALIDITY

The *validity* of a test is the extent to which the instrument measures what it purports to measure. In simple words, a researcher asks, "Does the test really measure the characteristic that I will use it to measure?" For example, a test of mathematical aptitude must yield a *true* indication of a student's mathematical aptitude. When you use a ruler to measure an object, you do not end up with a valid indication of that object's weight.

This section discusses four types of validity. A test's manual reports on these forms of validity, so that the potential user can assess whether the instrument measures what the title says it measures.

Predictive Validity

Validity can be established by relating a test to some actual behavior that it is supposed to predict. If a test's results can be expected to predict an outcome indi-

---

[2] The K-R20 formula on which this one is based, is:

$$^rK\text{-R20} = \left(\frac{n}{n-1}\right)\left(\frac{s^2 - \Sigma p_i q_i}{s^2}\right)$$

where p_i and q_i refer to the proportions of students responding correctly and incorrectly, respectively, to Item i.

cated by some performance or behavior criterion, then a researcher can evaluate its *predictive validity* by relating test performance to the appropriate behavioral criterion. For example, a test intended to predict student "staying power" in college could be validated by administering the instrument to students as they begin their freshman year and then measuring the percentage of high scorers who survive four years of college and the percentage of low scorers who drop out.

Concurrent Validity

Establishing predictive validity is a difficult challenge for some tests, particularly those that measure characteristics or qualities, because an analyst cannot easily identify specific performance outcomes related to that characteristic or quality. In this case, the judgment of validity usually tries to relate performance on the test with performance on another, well-reputed test (if any exists). This procedure gives an index termed *concurrent validity*. A new, experimental intelligence test, for example, is often validated concurrently by comparing a subject's performance on it with the same person's performance on an older, more established test.

Another procedure tries to establish the concurrent validity of a test by comparing qualities or performance as assessed by that test with those assessed by another procedure, such as human judges. For example, results of a test intending to measure the extent of a neurotic condition could be compared with judgments of the same sort made by a panel of clinical psychologists who are not aware of the test results (that is, working in the blind). Agreement between evaluations from the test and the judges would indicate the test's concurrent validity. (This last example is sometimes termed *criterion validity*.)

Construct Validity

A test builder might reason that a student with high self-esteem would be more inclined than one with low self-esteem to speak out when unjustly criticized by an authority figure; this reasoning suggests that such behavior can be explained by the construct (or concept) of self-esteem.[3] Such a proposed relationship between a construct and a derivative behavior might provide a basis for determining the *construct validity* of a test of self-esteem. Such an evaluation might seek to demonstrate the relationship of self-esteem test scores to a proposed derivative behavior (such as speaking out in self-defense).

Construct validity, therefore, is established by relating a presumed measure of a construct or hypothetical quality to some behavior or manifestation that it is hypothesized to underlie. Conversely, such a validity index might relate a behavior to a test of some construct that is an attempt to explain it.

---

[3] To relate the term *construct* to familiar language, this validity measure might indicate that some independent variable causes self-esteem—an *intervening variable* or construct—which in turn leads to the speaking-out behavior.

As another example, a test maker might expect that relatively sensitive teachers would express more positive feelings toward their students than would less sensitive teachers. An assessment of the construct validity of a test of sensitivity might compare the number of times that positive feelings toward students were expressed by teachers scoring high on a test of the construct sensitivity with the number observed for teachers with lower scores.

Content Validity

A researcher administers a test in an attempt to determine how a subject will function in a set of actual situations. Rather than placing individuals in each actual situation, a test offers a shortcut to determine their behaviors or performances in the total set of research situations. Thus, constructing the test involves selecting or sampling from situations in the total set. On the basis of the individual's performance on these sample situations, the researcher should be able to generalize regarding the full set of situations. A test has *content validity* if the sample of situations or performances it measures is representative of the set from which the sample was drawn (and about which the research will make generalizations).

For example, suppose a researcher constructed a performance test of secretarial skills to be used by companies for screening job applicants. The content validity of this test could be established by comparing (1) the skill areas it covers and the number of test items devoted to each with (2) the skill requirements of the job and the relative importance of each (for example, time generally spent on that task). If the sample on the test is representative of the set of real-life situations, then the test has content validity. Similarly, a final exam for an Algebra I class should be representative of the topics covered in the course and of the proportions of the total class time devoted to individual topics.[4]

TYPES OF MEASUREMENT SCALES

A *measurement scale* is a set of rules for quantifying a particular variable, or assigning numerical scores to it. Measurement scales (hereafter simply called *scales*) can quantify data by either nominal, ordinal, interval, or ratio criteria.

Nominal Scales

The term *nominal* means "named." Hence, a nominal scale does not measure variables, rather it names them. In other words, it simply classifies observations into categories with no necessary mathematical relationship between them.

---

[4] A further example of a method for establishing content validity appears in Chapter 13.

Suppose a researcher were interested in the number of happy and unhappy students in a class. If an interviewer were to classify each child as happy or unhappy based on classroom conversations, this classification system would represent a nominal scale. No mathematical relationship between happy and unhappy is implied; they simply are two different categories.[5] Thus, the happiness variable is measured by a nominal method.

When a study's independent variable includes two levels—a treatment condition and a no-treatment control condition (or two different treatments)—the independent variable is considered a nominal one, because measurement compares two discrete conditions. For example, splitting IQ scorers into high and low groups would make IQ into a two-category nominal variable. Although *high* and *low* denote an order, so they could be considered ordinal variables (as discussed in the next subsection), they can also be treated simply as category names and handled as nominal data. (For statistical purposes, two-category "orders" are usually best treated as nominal data, as Chapter 11 discusses.)

The behavioral sampling form later in the chapter in Figure 9.11 gives an example of a nominal scale. One discrete behavior is checked for each student observed.

Ordinal Scales

The term *ordinal* means "ordered." An ordinal scale rank orders things, categorizing individuals as more than or less than one another. (For two-level variables, the distinction between nominal and ordinal measurement is an arbitrary one, although nominal scaling, especially of independent variables, simplifies statistical analyses.)

Suppose the observer who wanted to measure student happiness were to interview every child in the class and then rank order them from highest to lowest happiness. Now each child's happiness level could be specified by the ranking. By specifying the rank order, the researcher has generated an ordinal scale. If you were to write down a list of your 10 favorite foods in order of preference, you would create an ordinal scale.

Although ordinal measurement may require more difficult processes than nominal measurement, it also gives more informative, precise data. Interval measurement, in turn, gives more precise results than come from ordinal measurement, and ratio measurement gives the most precise results of all.

Interval Scales

Interval scales tell not only the order of evaluative elements but also the intervals or distances between them. For instance, on a classroom test, one student scores

---

[5] These categories may be scored 0 and 1, implying the simplest sort of mathematical relationship, that is, presence versus absence.

95 while another scores 85. These measurements indicate not only that the first has performed better than the second but also that this performance was better by 10 points. If a third student has scored 80, the second student has outperformed the third by half as much as the first outperformed the second. Thus, on an interval scale, a distance stated in points may be considered a relative constant at any point on the scale where it occurs.

In contrast, on the ordinal measure of happiness, the observer can identify one child as more or less happy than another, but the data do not indicate *how much* more or less happy either child is compared to the other. The difference from any given child to the next on the rank order (ordinal) scale of happiness does not allow statements of constant quantities of happiness.

Rating scales and tests are considered to be interval scales. One unit on a rating scale or test is assumed to equal any other unit. Moreover, raw scores on tests can be converted to standard scores (as described in a later section) to maintain interval scale properties. As you will see, most behavioral measurement employs interval scales. The scales later in the chapter in Figures 9.3, 9.4, 9.5, and 9.9 all illustrate interval measurement.

Ratio Scales

Ratio scales are encountered much more frequently in the physical sciences than in the behavioral sciences. Because a ratio scale includes a true *zero value,* that is, a point on the scale that represents the complete absence of the measured characteristic, ratios are comparable at different points on the scale. Thus, 9 ohms indicates three times the resistance of 3 ohms, while 6 ohms stands in the same ratio to 2 ohms. On the other hand, because an IQ scale evaluates intelligence according to an interval scale, someone with an IQ of 120 is more comparable to someone with an IQ of 100 (they are 20 scale points apart) than is someone with a 144 IQ to someone with a 120 IQ (they are 24 scale points apart). The intervals indicate a larger difference in the second case, even though the ratios between the two sets of scores are equal ($120:100 = 144:120 = 6:5$). This result occurs because the IQ scale, as an interval scale, has no true zero point; intervals of equal size indicate equal differences regardless of where on the scale they occur. Were the IQ scale a ratio scale (which it is not), the two pairs of scores would be comparably related, because each pair holds the ratio $6:5$.

However, educational researchers rarely employ ratio scales, except for measures of time. Therefore, this book is not concerned with these measures as a category separate from interval scales.

Scale Conversion

If a researcher were interested in measuring the extent of happiness among a group of children, he or she might evaluate this variable in different ways:

1. Count categories (happy versus unhappy children)
2. Rank order children in terms of happiness
3. Rate each child on a happiness scale

If the researcher decides to rate each child on a happiness scale (Choice 3), and thus collect interval data, later data processing could always convert these interval data to rank orderings (ordinal data). Alternatively, the researcher could divide the children into the most happy half and the least happy half, creating nominal data. Educational researchers typically convert from higher to lower orders of measurement. They seldom convert from lower to higher orders of measurement.

To select the appropriate statistical tests, a researcher must identify the measurement scales—nominal, ordinal, or interval—for each of a study's variables. Chapter 11 gives a more detailed description of the process of converting data from one scale of measurement to another under the heading "Coding and Rostering Data."

DESCRIBING TEST PERFORMANCES

Interpretation of an individual's test score improves when a researcher places it in perspective by defining some standard or basis for comparison. Certain techniques allow such a comparison between one test score and others within a single group of test takers and between one score and others within a larger group of people who have previously taken the test. Explanation in depth of such approaches would exceed the scope of this book. However, this section briefly mentions some of these statistics or labels for describing and comparing test scores.

Percentiles

A single test score can be expressed as a percentile (an ordinal measure) by describing its relative standing among a group of scores. A percentile is a number that represents the percentage of obtained scores less than a particular raw score. It is computed by counting the number of obtained scores that fall below the score in question in a rank order, dividing this number by the total number of obtained scores, and multiplying by 100. Consider the following 20 test scores:

95	85	75	70
93	81	75	69
91	81	74	65
90	78	72	64
89	77	71	60

The score of 89 is higher than 15 of the 20 scores. Dividing 15 by 20 and multi-plying by 100 yields 75. Thus, the score of 89 is at the 75th percentile.

Although the scores themselves are interval measures, the percentile (in this case, 75) is an ordinal measure: It indicates rank order by reflecting that the score of 89 exceeds 75 percent of the scores in the group; in turn, 25 percent of the group's scores exceed 89. The percentile does not indicate by *how much* the score of 89 exceeds or is exceeded by the other scores.

Now, suppose another class of 20 achieved the following scores on the same test:

98	93	88	80
97	92	86	80
95	91	85	79
94	91	83	77
94	89	81	75

The same score of 89 exceeds only 10 of the 20 scores in this group, placing it at the 50th percentile. This illustration shows the benefits of interpreting scores rel-ative to other scores.[6]

Standard Scores

Standard scores express individual measurements as deviations or variations from the mean or average score for a group according to standard deviation units.[7] A *standard deviation unit* is a unit of magnitude equal to the standard deviation, a measure of the spread of a group of scores around their average score. This statistical device allows a researcher to adjust scores from absolute quantities to relative reflections of the relationship between all the scores in a group. Moreover, standard scores are interval scores, because the standard de-viation unit establishes a constant interval throughout the scale. An *absolute* raw score is converted to a *relative* standard score by (1) subtracting the group mean on the test from the raw score, (2) dividing the result by the standard deviation, and (3) adding a constant (usually 50) to avoid minus signs and multiplying by 10 to avoid decimals. (This procedure is described by Thorndike and Hagen, 1991.)

By converting raw test scores into standard scores, a researcher can compare scores within a group and between groups. She or he can also add the scores from

---

[6] Technically, a score of 88.5 would fall at the 75th percentile in the first example (with 5 scores above it and 15 below it) and at the 50th percentile in the second example (with 10 scores both above and below it). The actual score of 89 must be defined as the midpoint of a range of scores from 88.5 to 89.5.

[7] See Chapter 11 for a more complete description of these terms and their determination.

two or more tests to obtain a single score. Figure 9.1 illustrates the relationship between standard scores and the *normal distribution curve*.[8] Raw scores falling at the mean of the distribution are assigned the standard score of 50, scores falling 1 standard deviation above the mean are assigned the score of 50 plus 10, or 60, and so on. Each standard deviation defines a span of 10 points on the standard scale. This system gives scores a meaning in terms of their relationship to one another by fitting them within the distribution described by the total group of scores.

Norms

Interpretation according to norms describes a test score in relation to its location within a large body of previously collected scores. Rather than relating a

RELATIONSHIP BETWEEN THE NORMAL CURVE AND STANDARD SCORES

FIGURE 9.1

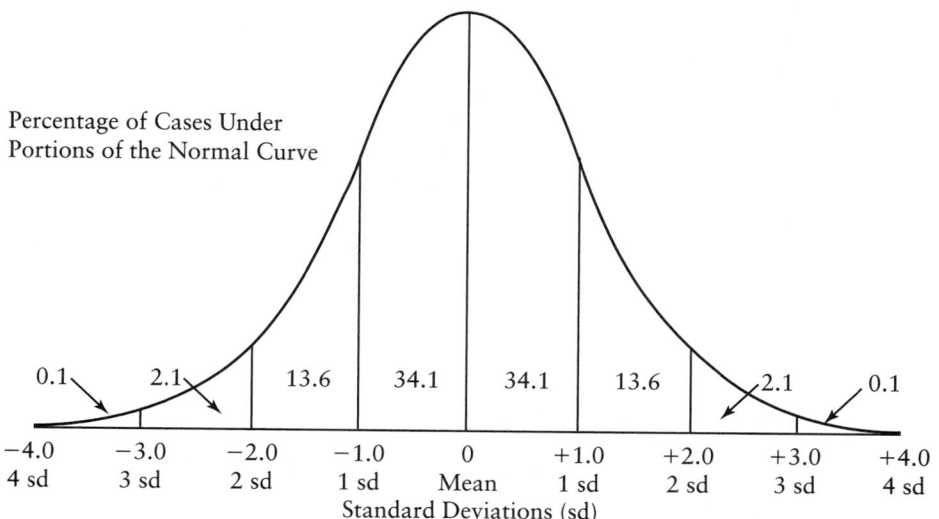

Percentage of Cases Under
Portions of the Normal Curve

| 0.1 | 2.1 | 13.6 | 34.1 | 34.1 | 13.6 | 2.1 | 0.1 |

| −4.0 | −3.0 | −2.0 | −1.0 | 0 | +1.0 | +2.0 | +3.0 | +4.0 |
| 4 sd | 3 sd | 2 sd | 1 sd | Mean | 1 sd | 2 sd | 3 sd | 4 sd |

Standard Deviations (sd)

T-score

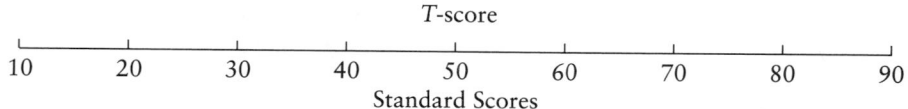

| 10 | 20 | 30 | 40 | 50 | 60 | 70 | 80 | 90 |

Standard Scores

---

[8] Again, Chapter 11 provides a more complete description of this term and its determination.

group of 10 scores only to one another, a researcher can relate them to a larger group of scores from other people who have previously taken the same test.

Table 9.1 shows a set of norms for the Piers-Harris Children's Self-Concept Scale as they appear in the test's manual. These norms, expressed in percentiles, stanines, and *T*-scores, apply to students in grades 4 through 12. They are based on data collected from 1,183 students, who represent the instrument's normative population. If a student taking the Piers-Harris scale obtained a score of 66, the norms would relate this single score to the 1,183 scores of the normative population, assigning it a percentile rank of 85. This rank indicates that a score of 66 exceeds 85 percent of the scores contained in the normative sample of 1,183. Note that on this scale, scores of 50 and 51 are farther apart on a relative basis (41st and 44th percentile, respectively) than scores of 76 and 80 (both of which fall at the 99th percentile). Thus, norms help researchers to assess the "meaning" of a score by comparing it to other scores.

Norm tables appear in the manuals for standardized tests. The terms *standardized test* and *norm-referenced test* indicate instruments for which norms are available, as is information on reliability and validity. The Piers-Harris test manual expresses norms as stanines and as percentile scores. A *stanine score* is a standard score with a mean of 5 and a standard deviation of 2, defining a range of nine scores. A comparison may utilize either stanines or percentiles, but the latter generally prove more advantageous because each percentile spans a narrower range.[9] When interpreting scores for a sample from a population on which no norms are available, researchers must test a sufficiently large number of individuals to generate their own norms, or they must utilize raw scores. Without norms, one may have trouble judging how high or low a particular score is.

STANDARDIZED, OR NORM-REFERENCED, TESTS

Instruments that refer to norms as standards for interpreting individual scores are called *norm-referenced* or *standardized tests*. The most complete guide to standardized tests, the *Mental Measurements Yearbook*, is generally found on library reference shelves. This volume is a compendium of more than 1,000 commercially available mental and educational tests. It has appeared regularly over the past 30 years, and new, updated versions are regularly published.

---

[9] Norms are also expressed as *T*-scores. A *T*-score is a standard score with a mean of 50 and a standard deviation of 10.

TABLE 9.1

SAMPLE NORMS: PERCENTILES, STANINES, AND *T*-SCORES FOR SCHOOL-AGE CHILDREN ON THE PIERS-HARRIS CHILDREN'S SELF-CONCEPT SCALE

Reproduced by permission. Copyright 1984 by Ellen V. Piers and Dale B. Harris and published by Western Psychological Services, Los Angeles, CA. All rights reserved.

PERCENTILE, STANINE, AND *T*-SCORE CONVERSIONS FOR TOTAL SCORES　　　PERCENTILE, STANINE, AND *T*-SCORE CONVERSIONS FOR TOTAL SCORES

Raw Score	Percentile	Stanine	T-Score	Raw Score	Percentile	Stanine	T-Score
80	99	9	81	49	38	4	47
79	99	9	79	48	36	4	46
78	99	9	79	47	33	4	46
77	99	9	77	46	31	4	45
76	99	9	74	45	29	4	45
75	98	9	70	44	27	4	44
74	97	9	69	43	24	4	43
73	96	8	68	42	23	3	43
72	95	8	67	41	21	3	42
71	94	8	66	40	20	3	42
70	93	8	65				
69	91	8	63	39	18	3	41
68	89	7	62	38	17	3	40
67	87	7	61	37	15	3	40
66	85	7	60	36	14	3	39
65	82	7	59	35	13	3	39
64	79	7	58	34	12	3	38
63	77	6	57	33	11	2	38
62	74	6	56	32	10	2	37
61	71	6	56	31	9	2	37
60	69	6	55	30	8	2	36
59	66	6	54	29	7	2	35
58	63	6	53	28	6	2	35
57	60	5	53	27	6	2	34
56	57	5	52	26	5	2	34
55	55	5	51	25	5	2	33
54	52	5	51	24	4	1	33
53	49	5	50	23	3	1	32
52	46	5	49	22	3	1	31
51	44	5	48	21	2	1	31
50	41	5	48	20	2	1	30
				19	2	1	29
				18	1	1	27
				17 or less	1	1	25

FIGURE 9.2   SAMPLE ENTRY FROM THE *MENTAL MEASUREMENTS YEARBOOK*

[30]

Anxiety Scales for Children and Adults.
Purpose: "To determine the presence and intensity of anxiety in adults and school-age children."
Population: Grade 2–adult.
Publication Date: 1993.
Acronym: ASCA.
Scores: Total score only.
Administration: Group.
Editions, 2: Youth, Adult.
Price Data, 1994: $84 per complete kit including examiner's manual (26 pages), 50 Forms Q, 50 Forms M, scoring acetate, and administration audiocassette; $31 per examiner's manual; $19 per 50 Form Q; $19 per 50 Form M; $6 per scoring acetate; $14 per administration audiocassette.
Time: (10–15) minutes.
Comments: Self-report; Form Q for children and Form M for adults.
Author: James Battle.
Publisher: PRO-ED, Inc.

A sample entry from the 12th edition of the *Yearbook* (Conoley and Impara, 1995) appears in Figure 9.2. The listing includes the name of the test (in bold type), the population for which it is intended, the publication date, and the test's acronym. Information about norms, forms, prices, and scoring is also given, as well as an estimate of the time required to complete the test and the names of the test's author and publisher. You can order specimen test kits for this and most other tests by contacting the publishers at the addresses listed in the back of the *Yearbook*. In addition, the compendium presents reviews of some of the tests by psychometricians and cites studies using them.

Achievement, Aptitude, and Intelligence Tests and Batteries

Achievement batteries are sets of tests designed to measure the knowledge that an individual has *acquired* in a number of discrete subject matter areas at one or more discrete grade levels. Widespread use of such standardized batteries facilitates comparisons of learning progress among students in different parts of the country. Because such batteries serve an important evaluative function, many elementary and secondary schools (as well as colleges) administer achievement batteries as built-in elements of their educational programs. The *Yearbook* describes such batteries as the California, Iowa, and Stanford achievement tests.

It also describes *multi-aptitude* batteries intended to measure students' potential for learning rather than what they have already learned. Whereas achievement tests measure acquired knowledge in specific areas (such as mathematics, science, and reading), aptitude tests measure potential for acquiring knowledge in broad underlying areas (for example, verbal and quantitative areas). Among the multi-aptitude batteries described in the *Yearbook* are the Differential Aptitude Test and SRA Primary Mental Abilities.

The concept of *intelligence* or *mental ability* resembles that of aptitude, each being a function of learning potential. *General intelligence* is typically taken to mean abstract intelligence—the ability to see relations in ideas represented in symbolic form, make generalizations from them, and relate and organize them. The *Yearbook* includes group, individual, and specific intelligence tests. Among the *group* tests, that is, those that can be administered to more than one person at the same time, are the Cognitive Abilities Test, Otis-Lennon Test of Mental Ability, and Short Form Test of Academic Aptitude. Among the *individually* administered intelligence tests are the Peabody Picture Vocabulary Test, Stanford-Binet Intelligence Scale, and Wechsler Intelligence Scale for Children. So-called *specific* intelligence tests measure specific traits thought to relate to intelligence (such as creativity)—for example, the Kit of Reference Tests for Cognitive Factors.

Other tests measure achievement or aptitudes in a variety of discrete and specified subject matter areas. The *Yearbook* lists tests in business education, English, fine arts, foreign languages, mathematics, reading, science, social studies, and many other areas.

Character, Personality, Sensory-Motor, and Vocational Tests

Character and *personality* tests measure subjects' characteristic ways of relating to the environment and the people in it, as well as their personal and interpersonal needs and ways of dealing with those needs. These tests can be subdivided into nonprojective and projective types. *Nonprojective* tests are typical paper-and-pencil instruments that require subjects to respond to written statements by choosing appropriate responses. *Projective* tests present either words or pictures intended to elicit free or unstructured responses. (One type, for example, invites a subject to look at an inkblot and tell what it represents; another asks one to look at a picture and make up a story about it.) Among the better-known nonprojective character and personality tests listed in the *Yearbook* are the California Psychological Inventory, Guilford-Zimmerman Temperament Survey, and Sixteen Personality Factor Questionnaire. Among the best-known projective character and personality tests covered there are the Bender-Gestalt Test, Rorschach test, and Thematic Apperception Test.

Also included in the *Yearbook* are *sensorimotor* tests, including tests of hearing, vision, and motor coordination. These tests are intended to measure an individual's sensory capacities and motor abilities. Some examples are the Granson-Stadler Audiometers and the Test for Color Blindness.

The *Yearbook* also includes *vocational* assessments, that is, tests of vocationally relevant skills and knowledge and those intended to determine a person's interests as an aid to making a vocational choice. (Such interest tests typically present sets of three activities, and the respondent must indicate his or her preference.) Tests of vocations include clerical, manual dexterity, mechanical ability, and specific vocation tests; selection and ratings forms; and interest inventories, including the Kuder General Interest Survey and the Strong-Campbell Interest Inventory.

CRITERION-REFERENCED TESTS

When scores on a test are interpreted on the basis of absolute criteria rather than relative ones, psychometricians refer to the process as *criterion referencing*. Rather than converting to standard scores or percentiles on the basis of norms or performances relative to that of all test takers, criterion-referenced interpretation refers only to the number of correctly answered items. This number may then be evaluated through comparison with a preset criterion (for example, 80 percent, 65 percent) or examined in light of the proportion of all test takers who correctly responded to a specific item (called the *p*-value).

Four principal features distinguish criterion-referenced tests: (1) They are constructed to measure specific sets of operationally or behaviorally stated objectives. (2) They attempt to maximize content validity based on that set of objectives. (They are often referred to as *objective-referenced* instruments.) (3) They are considered to represent samples of actual performance. (4) Performance on them can be interpreted by reference to predetermined cutoff scores.

Because most research involves comparisons of data between groups, even criterion-referenced test results can be evaluated through comparative analysis. Teacher-built or researcher-built tests, unless standardized, can be considered criterion-referenced instruments. Hence, the choice between norm-referenced and criterion-referenced tests may exert an important influence on individual student evaluation, but the distinction is less important for researchers.

CONSTRUCTING A PAPER-AND-PENCIL PERFORMANCE TEST

Construction of a performance test must begin, obviously, with the performance that it should measure. A test maker first constructs a list of instructional objectives for the course, program, treatment, or subject area the instrument will evaluate (if such a list does not already exist). The process then outlines all performance capabilities that students should display after successful instruction. Following this content outline, the test maker should write performance items and develop scoring keys. The content outline should establish content validity; that is, test items based on the outline should assess or sample the mastery of the content that they are intended to test. To ensure content validity, it is necessary to develop a content outline.[10]

This process should generate more items in each specific content area than the test will ultimately use. These items should modify the specific examples used in teaching the content to gauge the transfer of skills beyond rote learning. For example, if Shakespeare's *Macbeth* has been used in teaching iambic pentameter as a meter of writing, examples from *Hamlet* might be used in testing students' knowledge of this meter.

The items generated in this way should then be administered to a pilot group. The next step would be to calculate total subjects' scores on such measures as number of items passed. Performance on each item should then be compared to total scores using a procedure called *item analysis*.

Item Analysis

Item analysis is the analysis of responses on a multiple-choice test undertaken to judge the performance of each item on the test. Good items contribute to the reliability of the test, and item analysis can provide the information needed to revise items in order to improve a test's overall reliability.

This analysis yields four kinds of information about each item:

1. *Difficulty,* as represented by the difficulty index or the percentage of test-takers who gave correct answers;[11] a difficulty index between 50 and 75 is recommended.
2. *Discrimination,* as represented by the discrimination index, or the difference between the percentage of high performers on the total test and low performers on the total test who correctly answered a specific item; a discrimination index above 20 is recommended.
3. *Distractibility* of each distractor, as represented by the percentage of test-takers, particularly low performers, who chose each distractor; a distractibility of at least 10 for each distractor is recommended.
4. *Clues* about the reason for weakness in an item, represented by the distribution of responses across item choices.

Item analyses are usually accomplished by computer. Any item analysis, by computer or by hand, requires completion of some basic steps:

---

[10] Another illustration of this procedure appears in Chapter 13 on evaluation.

[11] The index of difficulty is computed as the number of subjects who *pass* an item, divided by the total number in both groups; computed in this way, it should actually be called the index of *easiness*.

1. Compute a total score on the test for each student in the sample.
2. Divide testing subjects into two groups based on total test scores: (a) an *upper* group of those who scored at or above the sample median, and (b) a *lower* group of those who scored below the sample median.
3. Array the results into the format shown in Table 9.2 to display the percentage of students in each group, upper and lower, who chose each potential answer on an item.
4. Compute the difficulty index, or the percentage of students who correctly answered each item.
5. Compute the discrimination index, or the difference between the percentage of upper group and lower group students who gave the right answer for each item.

The results of the item analysis for five items is shown in Table 9.2. Each item allows five answer choices (A, B, C, D, E), and the correct one is marked with an asterisk. Separate percentages are reported for the upper half and lower half of subjects taking the test, those designations based on their overall scores. The analysis presumes that upper-half students are the more knowledgeable ones, indicated by their high scores on the total test. The table also reports the percentage of students in each group who omit each item (that is, who do not answer it), as well as the percentage of all students choosing each option. Alongside data for each item, the table reports three summary statistics: the number of students responding to the item, the percentage correct or difficulty index, and the difference in performance by upper-half and lower-half students, or the discrimination index. From this display, judgments about each item's performance can be made.

Consider the data for Item 16 in Table 9.2. This item had a difficulty index of 65 and a discrimination index of 32. Despite the fact that two of the distractors lacked distractibility, the item would be considered a good one. Distractor B contributes to this quality level by distracting 42 percent of lower-half subjects.

Now look at data for Item 8. It was a very easy item; 93 percent of the subjects gave the correct answer. Such easy items always lack discrimination. This item will not contribute to the reliability of the test and should be rewritten. A good place to start would be to attempt to make the distractors more plausible in order to increase their distractibility.[12]

Item 4, the third one listed in the table, poses intermediate difficulty (56 percent gave the right answer) which is good, and its distractors all worked, another good trait. But the item lacked discrimination (only 5 percent), so it does not

---

[12] An item gotten right by a greater number of low scorers than high scorers receives a negative index of discrimination. These items should ordinarily be discarded. Sometimes an extremely easy item like Item 8 does no harm in a test. Because it is uniformly easy, it may have motivational value, and because of its uniform ease for both low and high scorers, it will not affect the relative distribution of scores.

TABLE 9.2

ITEM ANALYSIS

Item 16	A	B	C	D	*E	Omit	
Upper ½	0	17	0	0	79	4	43 students responded to the item
Lower ½	0	42	0	11	47	0	65 percent or 28 of 43 students taking the test responded correctly
All students	0	28	0	5	65	2	32 percentage points separate the upper and lower group on the correct answer

Item 8	A	*B	C	D	E	Omit	
Upper ½	9	91	0	0	0	0	43 students responded to the item
Lower ½	5	95	0	0	0	0	93 percent or 40 of 43 students taking the test responded correctly
All students	7	93	0	0	0	0	−4 percentage points separate the upper and lower group on the correct answer

Item 4	A	B	C	*D	E	Omit	
Upper ½	13	8	4	58	17	0	43 students responded to the item
Lower ½	0	26	5	53	16	0	56 percent or 24 of 43 students taking the test responded correctly
All students	7	16	5	56	16	0	5 percentage points separate the upper and lower group on the correct answer

Item 1	A	B	*C	D	E	Omit	
Upper ½	21	0	67	8	4	0	43 students responded to the item
Lower ½	21	16	42	0	21	0	56 percent or 24 of 43 students taking the test responded correctly
All students	21	7	56	5	12	0	25 percentage points separate the upper and lower group on the correct answer

Item 52	*A	B	C	D	E	Omit	
Upper ½	42	21	29	8	0	0	43 students responded to the item
Lower ½	42	21	26	11	0	0	42 percent or 18 of 43 students taking the test responded correctly
All students	42	21	28	9	0	0	0 percentage points separate the upper and lower group on the correct answer

*Indicates correct answer choice.

contribute to reliability. Choice A distracted upper-half subjects but not lower-half ones, so rewriting it may improve its discrimination.

Item 1, the fourth item in the table, has the same difficulty index as Item 4 (56) but a much higher discrimination index (25), and all of the distractors worked. This is another good item. Finally, Item 52, with a difficulty index of 42 and a discrimination index of 0, is the worst item of the five. It should be discarded and replaced by a new item.

Overall Summary for Test Construction

In summary, the process of building a performance test requires two essential activities:

1. Outline content areas to be covered to ensure content validity.
2. Try out the test on a pilot group to obtain data for item analysis to gauge item difficulty and discrimination.

You may also gather useful data by administering any other comparable or related test to your pilot group to see how your test relates to the other one. If this comparison shows a relationship between results from your test and those from another performance test, you have confirmed concurrent validity.[13] If your results relate to those of an aptitude test (as an example), this finding may contribute to construct validity. Finally, if classroom performance records are available, you can complete additional validity tests. For a performance test, however, the establishment of content validity (a nonstatistical concept) and the use of item analysis are usually sufficient to ensure effective test construction.

Attempts to establish forms of validity other than content validity are usually unnecessary for tests of performance, although efforts to establish their reliability give useful input. Although an item analysis contributes to the establishment of internal reliability, the Kuder-Richardson formula can also serve this purpose, as discussed earlier in the chapter.

CONSTRUCTING A SCALE

As explained earlier in the chapter, scales are devices constructed or employed by researchers to quantify subjects' responses on a particular variable. A scale can help researchers to obtain interval data concerning Ss' attitudes, judgments, or perceptions about almost any topic or object. The most commonly employed scales are:

1. Likert scale
2. Semantic differential
3. Thurstone scale

This section describes and illustrates each one in turn.

Likert Scale

A *Likert scale* lays out five points separated by intervals assumed to be equal distances.[14] It is formally termed an *equal-appearing interval scale*. This scale

---

[13] The relationship is usually tested by means of a correlation, a measure of the extent to which two sets of scores vary together. Correlation techniques are described in Chapter 11.

[14] Because analyses of data from Likert scales are usually based on summated scores over multiple items, the equal-interval assumption is a workable one. In the Thurstone scaling procedure, on the other hand, items are scaled by Ss and chosen to satisfy the equal-interval requirement. This procedure is considerably more complex than the Likert scale approach.

allows subjects to register the extent of their agreement or disagreement with a particular statement of an attitude, belief, or judgment. An example appears below:

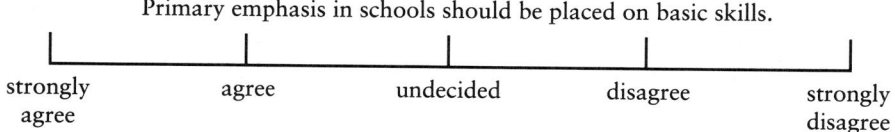

Primary emphasis in schools should be placed on basic skills.

strongly agree — agree — undecided — disagree — strongly disagree

The respondent indicates his or her opinion or attitude by making a mark on the scale above the appropriate word(s).

On the sample Likert-type attitude scale in Figure 9.3, the respondent is instructed to write in letter(s) indicating his or her self-description. This scale was built by first identifying the attitude areas (or subtopics) included within the topic of procrastination.

This initial exploration defined subtopics such as:

1. Tendency to delay or put off tasks (e.g., Item 3, When I have a deadline, I wait until the last minute).
2. Tendency to avoid or circumvent the unpleasantness of some task (e.g., Item 31, I look for a loophole or shortcut to get through a tough task).
3. Tendency to blame others for one's plight (e.g., Item 20, I believe that other people don't have the right to give me deadlines).

Following this content analysis, specific items were written for each subtopic. Some items were written as positive indications of procrastination (e.g., Item 1, I needlessly delay finishing jobs, even when they're important) so that agreement with them reflected a tendency toward procrastination. Some items were written as negative indications (e.g., Item 8, I get right to work, even on life's unpleasant chores) so that agreement with them reflected a tendency away from procrastination. An item phrased as a positive indication of procrastination was scored by the following key:

$$SA = 5, A = 4, U = 3, D = 2, SD = 1$$

An item reflecting a negative indication of procrastination was scored by the following key:

$$SA = 1, A = 2, U = 3, D = 4, SD = 5$$

The reason for writing items in both directions was to counteract the tendency for a respondent to automatically and unthinkingly give the same answer to all questions. By reversing the scoring of negative indications of procrastination, the scale provides a total score that reflects the degree of procrastination. A person with a tendency to procrastinate would agree with the positive indications

FIGURE 9.3

From Tuckman, 1990b.

SAMPLE LIKERT SCALE

PROCRASTINATION SCALE[a]   This scale has been prepared so that you can indicate how much each statement listed below describes you. Please write the letter(s) *SA* (strongly agree), *A* (agree), *U* (undecided), *D* (disagree), or *SD* (strongly disagree) on the left of each statement indicating how much each statement describes you. Please be as frank and honest as possible.

_____   1. **I needlessly delay finishing jobs, even when they're important.**
_____   2. **I postpone starting in on things I don't like to do.**
_____   3. **When I have a deadline, I wait until the the last minute.**
_____   4. **I delay making tough decisions.**
_____   5. I stall on initiating new activities.
_____   6. I'm on time for appointments.
_____   7. **I keep putting off improving my work habits.**
_____   8. I get right to work, even on life's unpleasant chores.
_____   9. **I manage to find an excuse for not doing something.**
_____ 10. I avoid doing those things which I expect to do poorly.
_____ 11. **I put the necessary time into even boring tasks, like studying.**
_____ 12. When I get tired of an unpleasant job, I stop.
_____ 13. I believe in "keeping my nose to the grindstone."
_____ 14. When something's not worth the trouble, I stop.
_____ 15. I believe that things I do not like doing should not exist.
_____ 16. I consider people who make me do unfair and difficult things to be rotten.
_____ 17. When it counts, I can manage to enjoy even studying.
_____ 18. **I am an incurable time waster.**
_____ 19. I feel that it's my absolute right to have other people treat me fairly.
_____ 20. I believe that other people don't have the right to give me deadlines.
_____ 21. Studying makes me feel entirely miserable.
_____ 22. **I'm a time waster now but I can't seem to do anything about it.**
_____ 23. **When something's too tough to tackle, I believe in postponing it.**
_____ 24. **I promise myself I'll do something and then drag my feet.**
_____ 25. **Whenever I make a plan of action, I follow it.**
_____ 26. I wish I could find an easy way to get myself moving.
_____ 27. When I have trouble with a task, it's usually my own fault.
_____ 28. **Even though I hate myself if I don't get started, it doesn't get me going.**
_____ 29. **I always finish important jobs with time to spare.**
_____ 30. When I'm done with my work, I check it over.
_____ 31. I look for a loophole or shortcut to get through a tough task.
_____ 32. **I get stuck in neutral even though I know how important it is to get started.**
_____ 33. I never met a job I couldn't "lick."
_____ 34. **Putting something off until tomorrow is not the way I do it.**
_____ 35. I feel that work burns me out.

[a]Note that the attitude topic or characteristic should not appear in the heading when the scale is administered, because an awareness of the topic may influence responses. Items in bold type represent a short form of the scale.

and disagree with the negative ones, whereas a nonprocrastinator would respond in exactly the opposite manner.

The total pool of 35 items was then administered to a pilot group of *Ss*. The responses they gave to each individual item were correlated (a statistical procedure described in Chapter 11) with the total scores they obtained on the whole scale. This item analysis procedure provides an indication of the degree of agreement or overlap between each individual item and the total test, that is, the extent to which each item measures what the total test measures. By identifying items that best agree with the overall scale, the designer achieves the greatest possible internal consistency. This procedure identified the 16 best items, that is, those items showing the greatest amount of agreement with the total score. (The choice to select 16 items was based on a determination that those items showed high agreement with the total score and would make up a scale that could be completed in a reasonably short time.)[15]

Note that a slightly altered version of the Procrastination Scale shown here was used in Sample Study I (Appendix A) as a measure of the control variable, tendency to procrastinate. Its reliability was reported to be quite high (0.75). It also showed a significant relationship (as a covariate) to performance (linking a low tendency to procrastinate to high performance). This observation provided an indication of the scale's construct validity.

The same procedure used to develop the Procrastination Scale was used to develop the Likert scale shown in Figure 9.4, which measures students' attitudes toward mathematics. In this case, the subtopics were (1) emotional reaction to math, (2) competence in math, and (3) preference for math.

Semantic Differential

The *semantic differential* scale is an attitude-measuring tool developed by Osgood, Suci, and Tannenbaum (1957). A sample semantic differential containing 30 bipolar adjective scales is shown in Figure 9.5. The scoring procedure for this instrument appears in Figure 9.6. This technique enables a researcher to measure judgments of the dimensions of a concept in a fairly circumspect way.[16] The respondent is instructed to rate the word or concept highlighted at the top of the page (in the example: "MY TEACHER IS") on each of the bipolar adjective scales by marking one of the seven points.

A researcher may want to measure attitudes toward some concept on a general, evaluative factor (rather than creating a new set of factors). He or she could consult Osgood et al. (1957) to find a list of evaluative adjective pairs and choose the number of them appropriate for the task at hand.

---

[15] These 16 items are shown in bold type in the figure; they may replace the 35-item complete scale if time limitations require an adjustment. These 16 items all measure the same topic area, namely the tendency to delay or put off tasks, and their selection as a single, short form of the scale was verified by a statistical procedure called *factor analysis*.

[16] These dimensions are also identified by the statistical process known as *factor analysis*.

FIGURE 9.4   **ANOTHER EXAMPLE OF A LIKERT SCALE**

MATH ATTITUDE SCALE   Each of the statements below expresses a feeling toward mathematics. Please indicate the extent of agreement between the feeling expressed in each statement and your own personal feeling by circling one of the letter choices next to each statement: *SA* = strongly agree, *A* = agree, *U* = undecided, *D* = disagree, or *SD* = strongly disagree.

SA A U D SD	1. Trying to do well in math class is awfully hard.
SA A U D SD	2. It scares me to have to take math.
SA A U D SD	3. I find math to be very interesting.
SA A U D SD	4. Math makes me feel secure.
SA A U D SD	5. My mind goes blank and I can't think when doing math.
SA A U D SD	6. Math is fascinating and fun.
SA A U D SD	7. Doing a math problem makes me nervous.
SA A U D SD	8. Studying math makes me feel uncomfortable and restless.
SA A U D SD	9. I look forward to going to math class.
SA A U D SD	10. Math makes me think I'm lost in a jungle of numbers and can't get out.
SA A U D SD	11. Math is something I'm good at.
SA A U D SD	12. When I hear the word *math,* I have a sense of dislike.
SA A U D SD	13. I like studying math better than studying other subjects.
SA A U D SD	14. I can't seem to do math very well.
SA A U D SD	15. I feel a definite positive reaction to math.
SA A U D SD	16. Studying math is a waste of time.
SA A U D SD	17. My mind is able to understand math.
SA A U D SD	18. I am happier in math class than in any other class.
SA A U D SD	19. Math is my most dreaded subject.
SA A U D SD	20. I seem to have a head for math.

Judgments on the semantic differential are quantified on a 1-to-7 scale (as described in Step I of the scoring procedure in Figure 9.6) with 7 representing the most positive judgment. Adjective pairs are phrased in both directions to minimize response bias.

Thurstone Scale

A *Thurstone scale* is a series of items ordered on a continuum from most positive to most negative. Items that appear to measure the quality of interest to a researcher are administered to a sample of "judges," who sort the items into 11 "piles" based on their judgments of the strength of positive or negative

A Sample Semantic Differential

FIGURE 9.5

Copyright 1980 by Bruce W. Tuckman and reproduced by permission. For further information, see Tuckman and Yates, 1980.

Person Observed _____ Observer _____

Date _____

TUCKMAN TEACHER FEEDBACK FORM (STUDENT EDITION)
MY TEACHER IS

#	Left	Scale	Right
1	DISORGANIZED	① ② ③ ④ ⑤ ⑥ ⑦	ORGANIZED
2	CLEAR	① ② ③ ④ ⑤ ⑥ ⑦	UNCLEAR
3	AGGRESSIVE	① ② ③ ④ ⑤ ⑥ ⑦	SOFT-SPOKEN
4	CONFIDENT	① ② ③ ④ ⑤ ⑥ ⑦	UNCERTAIN
5	COMMONPLACE	① ② ③ ④ ⑤ ⑥ ⑦	CLEVER
6	CREATIVE	① ② ③ ④ ⑤ ⑥ ⑦	ORDINARY
7	OLD FASHIONED	① ② ③ ④ ⑤ ⑥ ⑦	MODERN
8	LIKEABLE	① ② ③ ④ ⑤ ⑥ ⑦	"STUCK UP"
9	EXCITING	① ② ③ ④ ⑤ ⑥ ⑦	BORING
10	SENSITIVE	① ② ③ ④ ⑤ ⑥ ⑦	ROUGH
11	LIVELY	① ② ③ ④ ⑤ ⑥ ⑦	LIFELESS
12	ACCEPTS PEOPLE	① ② ③ ④ ⑤ ⑥ ⑦	CRITICAL
13	SNOBBY	① ② ③ ④ ⑤ ⑥ ⑦	MODEST
14	CONFUSED	① ② ③ ④ ⑤ ⑥ ⑦	ORDERLY
15	STRICT	① ② ③ ④ ⑤ ⑥ ⑦	LENIENT
16	IN CONTROL	① ② ③ ④ ⑤ ⑥ ⑦	ON THE RUN
17	TRADITIONAL	① ② ③ ④ ⑤ ⑥ ⑦	ORIGINAL
18	WARM	① ② ③ ④ ⑤ ⑥ ⑦	COLD
19	RUDE	① ② ③ ④ ⑤ ⑥ ⑦	POLITE
20	WITHDRAWN	① ② ③ ④ ⑤ ⑥ ⑦	OUTGOING
21	EASYGOING	① ② ③ ④ ⑤ ⑥ ⑦	DEMANDING
22	OUTSPOKEN	① ② ③ ④ ⑤ ⑥ ⑦	SHY
23	UNCHANGEABLE	① ② ③ ④ ⑤ ⑥ ⑦	FLEXIBLE
24	QUIET	① ② ③ ④ ⑤ ⑥ ⑦	BUBBLY
25	AWARE	① ② ③ ④ ⑤ ⑥ ⑦	FORGETFUL
26	"NEW IDEAS"	① ② ③ ④ ⑤ ⑥ ⑦	SAME OLD THING
27	IMPATIENT	① ② ③ ④ ⑤ ⑥ ⑦	PATIENT
28	UNCARING	① ② ③ ④ ⑤ ⑥ ⑦	CARING
29	DEPENDENT	① ② ③ ④ ⑤ ⑥ ⑦	INDEPENDENT
30	UNPLANNED	① ② ③ ④ ⑤ ⑥ ⑦	EFFICIENT

FIGURE 9.6   SCORING INSTRUCTIONS FOR THE SAMPLE SEMANTIC
DIFFERENTIAL SHOWN IN FIGURE 9.5

Person Observed _____   Observer _____
Date _____

TUCKMAN TEACHER FEEDBACK FORM SUMMARY SHEET

A. ITEM SCORING INSTRUCTIONS

I. Each response choice on the answer sheet contains one of the numbers
1-2-3-4-5-6-7.
This gives a number value to each of the seven spaces between the 30 pairs of
objectives.

II. Determine the number value for the first pair. Disorganized–Organized. Write it
into the formula given below on the appropriate line under Item I.
For example, if the student darkened in the first space next to "Organized" in
Item I, then write the number 7 on the dash under Item I in the summary
formula below.

III. Do the same for each of the 30 items. Plug each value into the formula.

IV. Compute the score for each of the 5 dimensions in the Summary formula.

B. SUMMARY FORMULA AND SCORE FOR THE FIVE DIMENSIONS

I. *Organized Demeanor*

Item   Item   Item   Item   Item   Item   Item
$$[(1 + 14 + 30) - (2 + 4 + 16 + 25) + 25] \div .42$$

II. *Dynamism*

Item   Item   Item   Item   Item
$$[(20 + 24 + 29) - (3 + 11 + 22) + 18] \div .36$$

III. *Flexibility*

Item   Item   Item   Item
$$[(15 + 23) - (10 + 21) + 12] \div .24$$

IV. *Warmth and Acceptance*

Item   Item   Item   Item   Item   Item   Item
$$[(13 + 19 + 27 + 28) - (8 + 12 + 18) + 17] \div .42$$

V. *Creativity*

Item   Item   Item   Item   Item   Item
$$[(5 + 7 + 17) - (6 + 9 + 26) + 18] \div .36$$

FIVE THURSTONE SCALES FOR MEASURING DIFFERENT ASPECTS OF MOOD

FIGURE 9.7

From Tuckman (1988).

The Mood Thermometers: Measuring Tension (or Anxiety), Confusion, Anger, Fatigue, and Depression.

HOW I FEEL RIGHT NOW

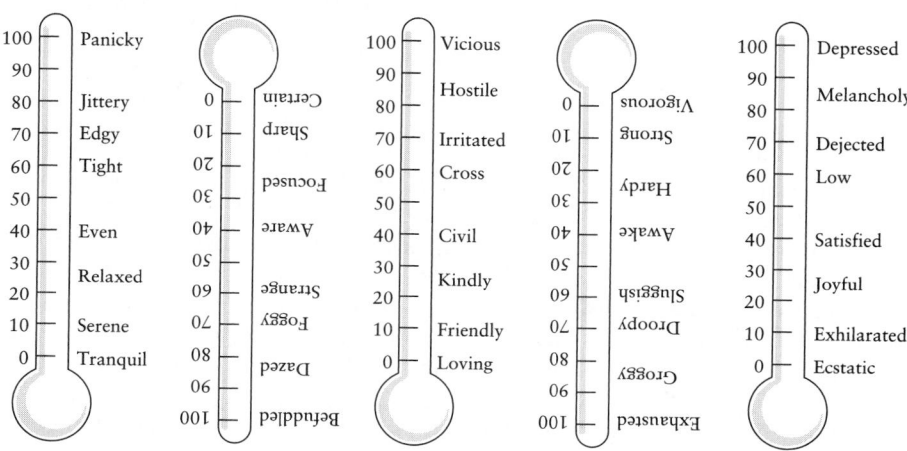

There are five thermometers to measure your feelings. Mark a line on each one to show how "high" or "low" you feel. Each one measures a different feeling. Don't just mark them all the same. For two of them you have to turn over the paper. Give your real, honest feeling. Don't just make up something.

Note: Some thermometers are inverted and out of line on the page to keep students from simply marking them all at the same level.

connotations. (Each pile carries a predetermined point value as follows: 0, 1, 2, 3, 4, 5, 6, 7, 8, 9, and 10.) After removing items whose placement varies extensively between judges, a *scale value* is computed for those that remain by determining the median point value of the judgments for each one. Thus, each item appears on the scale at a point determined by its median value assigned by the "judges." The final scale includes items whose medians are spaced equally along the continuum. This procedure, as well as those for constructing the other types of attitude scales, are described in more detail by Anderson (1981).

The final Thurstone scale presents the selected items in order of their scale values, and respondents are instructed to check one or more with which they agree. The scale or point values of those items (if subjects indicate more than one) can then be averaged to obtain individual attitude scores. An illustration of a Thurstone scale (actually five scales) appears in Figure 9.7.

CONSTRUCTING AN OBSERVATION RECORDING DEVICE

Researchers rely on basically three devices for recording observations: rating scales (or checklists), which summarize occurrences; coding systems, which collect occurrence-by-occurrence accounts; and behavior sampling, which selects some occurrences.

Rating Scales

A *rating scale* is a device used by an observer to summarize a judgment of an observed activity or behavior. Such a scale may lay out 3, 5, 7, 9, 100, or an infinite number of points on a line with descriptive statements on either end, and perhaps in the middle, as well. (Scales of 3, 5, and 7 points are the most common.) Following a selected period of time, an observer (often after completing pretraining) records his or her impressions on the scale, providing a quantitative estimate of observed events. Some examples are shown in Figure 9.8.

Figure 9.9 shows an example of an entire rating scale from Tuckman (1985). To apply this scale, observers—in this case, nonteaching personnel—worked independently and described teachers by filling out the 23 scale items. This scale was designed to assess a teacher's style on the directive-nondirective dimension, based on the operational definition given near the end of Chapter 6.

When human beings act as measuring instruments by completing rating scales, their perceptions are subject to many influences. One of these influences, the *halo effect,* reflects observers' tendency to rate people they like positively on all scales, so the scales measure simply how positive a general perception the observer has formed of the subjects. Any extremely strong relationship between a series of somewhat unrelated scales should raise a researcher's suspicions that the ratings are subject to the halo effect.

Because a rating scale reflects the judgments of human recorders whose perceptions are subject to influences, the scales themselves may reveal a number of inconsistencies or errors. Because these errors constitute threats to internal validity due to instrumentation bias, a researcher must determine the consistency or "accuracy" of such a rating procedure. Most accomplish this goal by employing two (or more) raters, each of whom completes the same scale, and then correlating the two ratings to obtain a coefficient of *interrater reliability.* (See Chapter 11 for a description of correlation procedures.) A sufficiently high correlation (arbitrarily, about 0.70 or better) usually indicates that individual differences in rater perceptions are within tolerable limits, thus reducing potential internal invalidity based on instrumentation.

As a further recommendation, a researcher should incorporate the average or mean of the two sets of rater judgments as data, if rating scale results become

SAMPLE RATING SCALES   **FIGURE 9.8**

	(5)	(4)	(3)	(2)	(1)
1.	___ :	_X_ :	___ :	___ :	___

Teacher talks
most of the time.   Students talk most
                                                          of the time.

	(7)	(6)	(5)	(4)	(3)	(2)	(1)
2.	___ :	___ :	_X_ :	___ :	___ :	___ :	___

Students often
ask questions.   Students rarely
                                                          ask questions.

	(9)	(8)	(7)	(6)	(5)	(4)	(3)	(2)	(1)
3.	___ :	___ :	_X_ :	___ :	___ :	___ :	___ :	___ :	___

Teacher makes   Teacher helps   No class-
all the class-   students make   room
room decisions.   classroom   decisions
                          decisions   are made

|←——————— x mm. ———————→|

4. _____ X _____

Teacher engages   Teacher rarely
in frequent   disciplines.
disciplinary
action.

5. Using any whole number from 0 to 100, indicate the amount of time the teacher talked (100 = all the time; 0 = none of the time). _30_

data for an actual study.[17] This precaution helps to ensure that conclusions reflect data more reliably than the independent ratings from either judge alone would provide. Because the mean is more reliable than either judgment alone, researchers who calculate mean ratings across judges may choose to modify reliability correlation coefficients using the Spearman-Brown correction formula presented early in this chapter. Many studies draw input from two or more raters specifically to increase the reliability of the data they analyze. Moreover, a comparison of the judgments made by the raters allows determination of interrater reliability to measure the accuracy of the ratings.

Although rating scales offer an efficient and ubiquitous recording technique, their results are highly subject to human error. Consequently, analysis must check for error by the humans who apply such a scale, and this error *must* be reported, thus helping both the researcher and the reader assess the threat that instrumentation poses to the validity of a study.

---

[17] Sometimes, reliability data are collected separately from a study itself. At other times, data analyzed for a study are also used to establish reliability.

FIGURE 9.9

A RATING SCALE TO MEASURE TEACHER DIRECTIVENESS

From Tuckman (1985.)

TEACHER DIRECTIVENESS OF TEACHER–STUDENT INTERACTION

Bruce W. Tuckman

Teacher directs.	1 2 3 4 5 6 7 8 9	Teacher uses structuring and suggesting.
Teacher reacts with personal criticism.	1 2 3 4 5 6 7 8 9	Teacher reacts with performance feedback.
Teacher reacts on a comparative basis.	1 2 3 4 5 6 7 8 9	Teacher reacts on an individual basis.
Teacher imposes values.	1 2 3 4 5 6 7 8 9	Teacher espouses value clarification.
Teacher espouses private, subjective values.	1 2 3 4 5 6 7 8 9	Teacher espouses cooperative values.
Teacher continually offers unsolicited remarks.	1 2 3 4 5 6 7 8 9	Other than when engaged in group or individual instruction or when giving feedback, teacher makes few unsolicited remarks.
Teacher is cold and critical.	1 2 3 4 5 6 7 8 9	Teacher is warm and accepting.
Teacher is conventional and noncreative.	1 2 3 4 5 6 7 8 9	Teacher is original and creative.
Teacher is passive.	1 2 3 4 5 6 7 8 9	Teacher is forceful and energetic.
Teacher is disorganized and preoccupied.	1 2 3 4 5 6 7 8 9	Teacher is organized and alert.
Teacher maximizes barriers between self and students.	1 2 3 4 5 6 7 8 9	Teacher minimizes barriers between self and students.
Teacher encourages students to revere her/him.	1 2 3 4 5 6 7 8 9	Teacher discourages students from revering him/her.
One activity at a time is pursued by all students.	1 2 3 4 5 6 7 8 9	A variety of activities occurs simultaneously.
Teacher does not monitor student progress.	1 2 3 4 5 6 7 8 9	Teacher uses a system for monitoring student progress.
Teacher does not encourage students to select their own activities.	1 2 3 4 5 6 7 8 9	Teacher encourages students to select activities within context.
Teacher does not prespecify goals.	1 2 3 4 5 6 7 8 9	Teacher prespecifies goals.
Teacher does not encourage students to organize their own work schedules.	1 2 3 4 5 6 7 8 9	Teacher encourages students to organize their own work schedules in ways that are consistent with goals.
Teacher limits activities to those that have been predesignated.	1 2 3 4 5 6 7 8 9	Teacher does not limit activities to those that have been predesignated.
Teacher does not provide vehicles whereby students can evaluate themselves.	1 2 3 4 5 6 7 8 9	Teacher provides vehicles whereby students can evaluate themselves.

(continued)

Teacher habitually uses one mode of imparting information.	1	2	3	4	5	6	7	8	9	Teacher makes use of a variety of means for imparting information.
Students work on activities in a single class unit.	1	2	3	4	5	6	7	8	9	A variety of student groupings occur simultaneously.
Space is used in an inflexible and single-purpose manner.	1	2	3	4	5	6	7	8	9	Space is used in a flexible and multipurpose manner.
Physical movement, talking, and groupings by students are not allowed.	1	2	3	4	5	6	7	8	9	Physical movement, talking, and grouping by students are allowed and encouraged.

A variation of the rating scale is an observer checklist, which simply presents a series of statements (such as might appear on a rating scale). An observer indicates which of two statements more accurately describes observed behavior. The checklist is a series of 2-point rating scales, where a check means that the named activity occurred, and no check means that it did not occur. A checklist limits an observer to describing what has or has not transpired (presence or absence of an event) rather than indicating the degree of the behaviors in question (as a rating scale would allow).

Coding Systems

A coding system offers a means for recording the occurrence of specific, preselected behaviors as they happen. Essentially, it specifies a set of categories into which an observer classifies ongoing behaviors.[18] Like rating procedures, coding techniques attempt to quantify behavior. If a researcher wants to determine the effect of class size on the number of question-asking behaviors in a class, such a system would code question-asking behavior during a designated block of time in large and small classes in order to establish a *measure* of this behavior as a dependent variable.

Rating and coding schemes convert behavior into measures. *Rating scales* are completed in retrospect and represent observers' memories of overall activities; *coding scales* are completed as coders observe (or hear) the behavior. A coding system records the frequency of specific (usually individual) acts predesignated for researcher attention, whereas rating scales summarize the occurrence of types of behavior in a more global fashion.

Researchers employ two kinds of coding systems. *Sign coding* establishes a set of behavioral categories; each time an observer detects one of these preselected, codeable behaviors, he or she codes the event in the appropriate category.

[18.] Coding may be done after the fact from tape recordings or video tapes.

For example, if a coding system included "suggesting" as a codeable act, the coder would code an event every time a subject made a suggestion.

An example of such a sign coding system for teacher behavior appears in Figure 9.10. The scheme lists 37 behaviors. Whenever a trained observer encounters one of these 37 behaviors, she or he records the occurrence by category. The behavior would be coded again only when it occurred again.

The second kind of coding, *time coding,* involves observer identification of all preselected behavior categories that occur during a given time period, such as 5 seconds. An act that occurs once but continues through a number of time periods is coded anew for each time period, rather than only once as in a sign coding system.

Compared with rating as a means of quantifying observations, coding has both advantages and disadvantages. On the negative side, it exposes a study to difficulties training coders and establishing intercoder reliability; coders must complete a difficult and time-consuming process to carry out coding activities (often based on tape recordings, which introduce other difficulties); at the completion of coding, a researcher may have little data besides a set of category tallies. However, on the positive side, data yielded from coding approaches more closely than that from other methods to what physical scientists call "hard data." Coding techniques may generate somewhat more objective pictures of true events than do rating-scale techniques.

Considering both sides of the issue, researchers may prefer to avoid coding in favor of rating unless well-developed coding systems are available, and unless they can call on the resources required to hire and train coders who will listen to lengthy tape recordings.

Behavior Sampling

In *behavior sampling,* actual behavior samples are collected by systematic observation. This technique requires a much lower level of concentration from an observer than that necessary for coding, and it demands much less extensive inference than rating methods require. An example of behavior sampling can illustrate its application to classroom research: A researcher develops a sampling plan that specifies the number, duration, and timing of samples or observations. He or she randomly selects a number of students (between four and six) from the class roster *before* each observation session. In any given session, the observer records a specific aspect of the behavior of each student on an appropriate form. A sample form to record the behaviors from Tuckman (1985) appears in Figure 9.11.

Over the period of time that the observations are made (for example, three 5-minute observations a day, every day for a week), the series of entries recorded should show a pattern across and within classrooms. Even though the pattern for

A Sample Instrument for Coding Teacher Performance FIGURE 9.10

DOMAIN	EFFECTIVE INDICATORS		Freq	Freq	INEFFECTIVE INDICATORS
ORGANI-ZATION AND DEVELOP-MENT OF INSTRUC-TION	1. Begins instruction promptly				Delays
	2. Handles materials in an orderly manner				Does not handle materials systematically
	3. Orients students to classwork/maintains academic focus				Allows talk/activity unrelated to subject
	4. Conducts beginning/ending review				
	5. Questions: academic comprehension/lesson development	asks single factual			Poses multiple questions asked as one
		requires analysis/reasons			Poses nonacademic questions/procedural questions
	6. Recognizes response/amplifies/gives corrective feedback				Ignores student or response/expresses sarcasm, disgust, harshness
	7. Gives specific academic praise				Uses general, nonspecific praise
	8. Provides for practice				Extends discourse, changes topic/no practice
	9. Gives directions/assigns/checks comprehension of assignment/gives feedback				Gives inadequate directions/no homework/no feedback
	10. Circulates and assists students				Remains at desk/circulates inadequately
PRESEN-TATION OF SUBJECT MATTER	11. Treats attributes/examples/nonexamples				Gives definition or examples only
	12. Discusses cause-effect/uses linking words/applies law or principle				Discusses either cause or effect only/uses no linking word(s)
	13. States and applies academic rule				Does not state or apply academic rule
	14. Develops criteria/evidence re: value judgment				States value judgment w/no criteria/evidence
VERBAL AND NON-VERBAL COMMUNI-CATION	15. Emphasizes important points				
	16. Expresses enthusiasm/challenges students				
	17.				Uses vague/scrambled discourse
	18.				Uses grating/monotone/inaudible talk
	19. Uses body behavior that shows interest/smiles/gestures				Frowns/deadpan/lethargic
MANAGE-MENT OF STUDENT CONDUCT	20. Stops misconduct				Doesn't stop misconduct/desists punitively
	21. Maintains instructional momentum				Loses momentum/fragments/overdwells

FIGURE 9.11 **INSTRUCTIONAL ACTIVITIES BEHAVIOR SAMPLING FORM**

From Tuckman (1985). Reproduced by permission.

CHILD OBSERVED

	1	2	3	4	5	6
Listening to teacher						
Listening to peer						
Reading assigned materials						
Reading reference materials						
Reading for pleasure						
Writing on programmed materials						
Writing in a workbook or worksheet						
Writing creatively (or on a report)						
Writing a test						
Talking (re: work) to teacher						
Talking (re: work) to peer						
Talking (socially) to teacher						
Talking (socially) to peer						
Drawing, painting, or coloring						
Constructing, experimenting, or manipulating						
Utilizing or attending to AV equipment						
Presenting a play or report to a group						
Presenting a play or report individually						
Playing or taking a break						
Distributing, monitoring, or in class routine						
Disturbing, bothering, interrupting						
Waiting, daydreaming, meditating						
Total	6	6	6	6	6	6

The user checks the box that indicates what each child being observed is doing.

each classroom will be unique in some ways, data may reveal an overall trend across all of the classrooms for a given condition or treatment.

Techniques for behavior sampling are described in more detail by Tuckman (1985). The relationship between behavior sampling, coding, and rating procedures is illustrated by a chart:

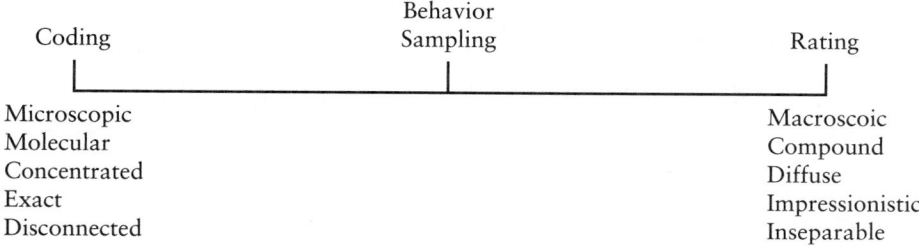

Coding	Behavior Sampling	Rating
Microscopic		Macroscoic
Molecular		Compound
Concentrated		Diffuse
Exact		Impressionistic
Disconnected		Inseparable

ILLUSTRATIONS FROM THE SAMPLE STUDIES   BOX 9

The Procrastination Scale, shown in Figure 9.3, was one of the measures used in Sample Study I (Appendix A). The other initial measures were one-item or two-item Likert Scales.

Note that time coding was used in Sample Study II to measure five dependent variables: *noise* (creating distracting noise), *out of place* (moving out of the appropriate work area), *physical contact* or destruction (kicking, hitting, etc.), *off task* (looking around, staring into space, etc.), and *volunteering* (willingly answering questions or participating in class activities). Initially, for every 20-second interval, independent observers marked any of the above behaviors they detected for each of six students (one mark per interval if the behavior occurred; no mark if it did not). Subsequently, 20-second observation intervals occurred only once during a 2-minute period, and apparently frequency counts were made (a combination of time and sign coding). Prior to observing students in the study, observers made pilot observations to achieve a reliability level of 90 percent agreement. During the study, observers were not told which of the six students were good readers and which poor ones. Both techniques were employed to minimize instrumentation bias in observer judgments.

SUMMARY

1. Test *reliability* refers to a test's consistency. Unreliability creates instrumentation bias.

2. Researchers can establish reliability in four ways: (1) a test-retest procedure, in which they give the same test twice to the same sample of people and comparing the results; (2) an alternate-form procedure, in which they prepare two forms of the test, giving both to the same people and comparing the results; (3) a split-half method, in which they compare the results on an instrument's odd-numbered items to those on its even-numbered items, eventually correcting the result to cover the whole test; (4) a Kuder-Richardson method, in which they apply the formula:

$$\text{Reliability} = \left(\frac{n}{n-1}\right)\left(1 - \frac{\overline{X}(n-\overline{X})}{ns^2}\right)$$

3. Test *validity* refers to the extent to which a test measures what it purports to measure. Invalidity creates instrumentation bias.

4. Researchers can establish validity in four ways: (1) predictive validity, established by comparing test scores to an actual performance that the test is supposed to predict; (2) concurrent validity, established by comparing test scores to scores on another test intended to measure the same characteristic; (3) construct validity, established by comparing test scores to a behavior to which it bears some hypothesized relationship; (4) content validity, established by comparing test content to the specifications of what the test is intended to cover.

5. Researchers rely on four types of measurement scales: (1) nominal scale, which represents scores as classification categories or "names" into which they are classified; (2) ordinal scale, which represents scores as rank orders; (3) interval scale, which represents scores as units of equal-appearing magnitude; (4) ratio scale, which represents scores as units of equal magnitude beginning at a true zero point. Scores can be converted from a higher-order scale (e.g., a ratio scale) to any lower order one (e.g., a nominal scale).

6. Test performances can be described in relative terms using norms, which detail the distribution of scores achieved by a representative sample. An ordinal score of relative standing is called a *percentile*. A score expressed in terms of standard deviation units is a *standard score*.

7. Commercially available tests for which researchers can obtain norms are called *norm-referenced* or *standardized tests*. They can be located by listings in the *Mental Measurement Yearbook*, which includes achievement and aptitude type tests as well as character and personality type tests.

8. A paper-and-pencil performance test should be constructed from a content outline; once developed, it should undergo pilot testing and item analysis to determine whether items display satisfactory difficulty and discrimination.

9. Three types of scales can be developed to quantify responses on a specific variable, such as an attitude toward a particular topic: (1) A Likert scale is a 5-point scale of equal-appearing intervals that covers specific subtopics within a topic, incorporating both positively and negatively phrased items. (2) A semantic differential is a 7-point bipolar adjective scale with alternating positive and negative poles that covers specific dimensions of the topic. (3) A Thurstone scale is a series of statements scaled from most positive to most negative based on the responses of a sample of "judges."

10. Three types of systems can be constructed to record observations of behavior. (1) A rating scale sets up an equal-appearing interval scale on which observers record their judgments. (2) A coding system defines a set of predetermined categories into which observations are categorized, based on individual occurrences (sign coding) or occurrences during a given time period (time coding). (3) Behavior sampling is a system of observing randomly preselected subjects and classifying their behavior using a category coding system. All three systems require that researchers establish interobserver reliability.

COMPETENCY TEST EXERCISES

1. Match up the items on the left with those on the right:
   a. Test-retest reliability
   b. Alternate-form reliability
   c. Split-half reliability
   d. Kuder-Richardson reliability

   1. Odd versus even items across test takers
   2. Scores at Time A versus scores at Time B
   3. Direct comparison of item scores by formula
   4. Scores on Form A versus scores on Form B

2. Describe procedures for determining test-retest reliability as compared to split-half reliability.

3. Match up the items on the left with those on the right:
   a. Predictive validity
   b. Concurrent validity
   c. Construct validity
   d. Content validity

   1. Test adequately samples from the total range of relevant behaviors
   2. Test of concept correlates with a hypothetically related behavior
   3. Test correlates with behavior it is presumed to predict
   4. Test correlates with another test of the same thing

4. Describe procedures for determining the concurrent validity of an IQ test as contrasted to its construct validity.

5. Match up the items on the left with those on the right:
   a. Nominal scale
   b. Ordinal scale
   c. Interval scale

   1. More apples, fewer apples
   2. Two apples, three apples
   3. Apples and oranges

6. Match up the items on the left with those on the right:
   a. Percentile score
   b. Standard score
   c. Norms
   d. Norm referencing
   e. Criterion referencing

   1. Deviation score from the mean
   2. Number of scores that a particular one exceeds
   3. Set of relative scores
   4. Absolute interpretation
   5. Relative interpretation

7. Look again at Table 9.1. A student obtained a raw score of 51 on the Piers-Harris Children's Self-Concept Scale.
   a. What would this student's percentile score be?
   b. If 1,000 students took the test, how many students would be expected to receive lower scores on this scale?
   c. If this score were calculated to fall exactly 1 standard deviation below the mean, what would the standard score be? (Use Figure 9.1.)

8. Go to the library and find the most recent *Mental Measurements Yearbook* available. Identify each of the following details for the "Pictorial Test of Bilingualism and Language Dominance":
   a. Test number
   b. Page number(s)
   c. Author(s)
   d. Publisher
   e. Time to complete the full test
   f. Age range
   g. Number of scores
   h. Number of forms
   i. Cost for the complete kit
   j. Date of publication

9. Recent *Mental Measurements Yearbooks* include tests of sex knowledge. Which of these tests would you use if you were doing a high school study of sex knowledge? Why?

10. Consider the following test scores of six people on a four-item test ($\checkmark$ = right, $\times$ = wrong):

	1	2	3	4	5	6
Item 1	$\checkmark$	$\times$	$\times$	$\checkmark$	$\times$	$\times$
Item 2	$\checkmark$	$\checkmark$	$\checkmark$	$\checkmark$	$\times$	$\checkmark$
Item 3	$\times$	$\times$	$\checkmark$	$\checkmark$	$\checkmark$	$\times$
Item 4	$\checkmark$	$\times$	$\times$	$\checkmark$	$\times$	$\checkmark$

Calculate the indexes of difficulty and discrimination for each item. Which item would you eliminate? (Do your calculations on only the two highest and two lowest scorers on the total test; eliminate the middle two scorers.)

11. In constructing a paper-and-pencil performance test, a researcher completes the following steps. List them in their proper order.
    a. Perform an item analysis
    b. Eliminate poor items
    c. Develop a content outline
    d. Collect pilot data
    e. Establish content validity
    f. Write test items

12. To test the items on a Likert-type attitude scale, the items are administered to a pilot group and then correlations are run between _____ .

13. The semantic differential, when used in a general way, measures the factor of _____ .

14. Two raters evaluating the same set of behaviors obtained an interrater reliability of 0.88. This can be converted to a corrected reliability of _____ by averaging their judgments.

RECOMMENDED REFERENCES

Conoley, J. C., & Impara, J. C. (Eds.). (1995). *The twelfth mental measurements yearbook*. Lincoln, NE: Buros Institute of Mental Measurements.

Oosterhof, A. (1994). *Classroom applications of educational measurement* (2nd ed.). New York: Macmillan.

Oosterhof, A. (1996). *Developing and using classroom assessments*. Englewood Cliffs, NJ: Prentice-Hall.

Wittrock, M. C., & Baker, E. L. (Eds.). (1991). *Testing and cognition*. Englewood Cliffs, NJ: Prentice-Hall.

10 Chapter

CONSTRUCTING AND USING QUESTIONNAIRES
AND INTERVIEW SCHEDULES

Objectives

▶ Identify the purposes served by questionnaires and interviews and the shortcomings of each.

▶ Identify different question formats and response modes, and describe their relative characteristics.

▶ Describe the bases for choosing between a questionnaire and an interview and for choosing a response mode for a specific set of conditions and purposes.

▶ Construct a series of items (for example, a questionnaire or interview) designed to answer specific research questions.

▶ Describe sampling procedures for questionnaire and interview studies.

▶ Lay out the process for administering a questionnaire, including the preparation of a cover letter.

▶ Describe procedures for conducting an interview.

▶ Describe the procedures for coding and scoring interview and questionnaire data.

WHAT DO QUESTIONNAIRES AND INTERVIEWS MEASURE?

Questionnaires and interviews help researchers to convert into data the information they receive directly from people (research subjects). By providing access to what is "inside a person's head," these approaches allow investigators to measure what someone knows (knowledge or information), what someone likes and dislikes (values and preferences), and what someone thinks (attitudes and beliefs). Questionnaires and interviews also provide tools for discovering what experiences have taken place in a person's life (biography) and what is occurring at the present. This information can be transformed into quantitative data by using the attitude or rating scales described in the previous chapter or by counting the number of respondents who give a particular response, which generates frequency data.

Questionnaires and interviews provide methods of gathering data about people by *asking* them rather than by observing and sampling their behavior. However, the self-report approach incorporated in questionnaires and interviews does present certain problems: (1) Respondents must cooperate to complete a questionnaire or interview. (2) They must tell what *is* rather than what they think ought to be or what they think the researcher would like to hear. (3) They must know what they feel and think in order to report it. In practice, these techniques measure not what people believe but what they *say* they believe, not what they like but what they *say* they like.

In preparing questionnaires and interviews, researchers should exercise caution. They must constantly consider:

- To what extent might a question influence respondents to show themselves in a good light?
- To what extent might a question influence respondents to attempt to anticipate what researchers want to hear or learn?
- To what extent might a question ask for information about respondents that they may not know about themselves?

The validity of questionnaire and interview items is limited by all three of these considerations. However, certain information can be obtained only by asking. Even when an alternative is available, simply asking subjects to respond may be (and often is) the most efficient one. Thus, the advantages and disadvantages of a questionnaire or interview as a source of data must be considered in each specific case before a decision can be made to use it or not to use it.

QUESTION FORMATS: HOW TO ASK THE QUESTIONS

Certain forms of questions and certain response modes are commonly used in questionnaires and interviews. This section deals with question formats and the following section addresses response modes.

Direct Versus Indirect Questions

The difference between direct and indirect questions lies in how obviously the questions solicit specific information. A direct question, for instance, might ask someone whether or not she likes her job. An indirect question might ask what she *thinks* of her job or selected aspects of it, supporting the researcher's attempt to build inferences from patterns of responses. By asking questions without obvious purposes, the indirect approach is the more likely of the two to engender frank and open responses. It may take a greater number of questions to collect information relevant to a single point, though. (Specific administrative procedures may help a researcher to engender frank responses to direct questions, as described later in the chapter.)

Specific Versus Nonspecific Questions

A set of specific questions focuses on a particular object, person, or idea about which a researcher desires input regarding an attitude, belief, or concept; nonspecific questions probe more general areas. For example, an interviewer can ask a factory worker (specifically) how he likes operating a lathe or (nonspecifically) how he likes operating machinery or working at manual tasks. An interviewer can ask a student (specifically) how much she likes a particular teacher versus (nonspecifically) how satisfied she feels with a particular class taught by the teacher. Specific questions, like direct ones, may cause respondents to become cautious or guarded and to give less-than-honest answers. Nonspecific questions may lead circuitously to the desired information while provoking less alarm by the respondent.

Questions of Fact Versus Opinion

An interviewer may also choose between questions that ask respondents to provide facts and those that request opinions. A factual question might ask a respondent the type of car he or she owns or to specify marital status. An opinion question might ask about preference for Ford or Chevrolet models or reasons why (or why not) a respondent thinks that marriage contributes to a meaningful relationship between a man and a woman. Because the respondent may have a faulty memory or a conscious desire to create a particular impression, factual questions do not always elicit factual answers. Nor do opinion questions necessarily elicit honest opinions, because they are subject to distortions based on *social desirability;* that is, respondents may reply in ways that show themselves in the most socially acceptable light. With both fact and opinion questions, questionnaires and interviews may be structured and administered to minimize these sources of bias.

Questions Versus Statements

To gather input on many topics, an interviewer can either ask a respondent a direct question or provide a statement and ask for a response. To a question, a respondent provides an appropriate answer. For a statement, the respondent indicates whether he or she agrees or disagrees (or whether the statement is true or false). Applied in this manner, statements offer an alternative to questions as a way of obtaining information. In fact, attitude measurement instruments more commonly present statements than ask questions. Consider an example:

- Do you think that the school day should   YES   NO
  be lengthened?
      versus
- The school day should be shortened.   AGREE   DISAGREE

These two formats are indistinguishable in their potential for eliciting honest responses. Usually, researchers choose between them on the basis of response mode, as discussed in the next section.

Predetermined Versus Response-Keyed Questions

Some questionnaires predetermine the number of questions to be answered; they require respondents to complete all items. Others are designed so that subsequent questions may or may not call for answers, depending upon responses to keyed questions. For example, a keyed item may ask a respondent if he is a college graduate. If the response is *no,* the respondent is instructed to skip the next question. The decision whether or not to answer the question is keyed to the response to the previous question.

Consider another example of response keying. An interviewer asks a school superintendent if her district is using a nationally known curriculum. Two possible questions are keyed to the response. If the superintendent says that the district is using the curriculum, the next question asks about its effectiveness; if the superintendent says the district is not using the curriculum, the next question asks why.

RESPONSE MODES: HOW TO ANSWER THE QUESTIONS

Besides asking questions in a variety of ways, responses can take a multiplicity of forms or modes. This section reviews a number of different response modes.

Unstructured Responses

An *unstructured response,* perhaps more commonly referred to by the term *open-ended question* (although the response, not the question, is open-ended), allows the subject to give a response in whatever form he or she chooses. Open-ended and nonopen-ended questions may target identical information. The difference between an unstructured (open-ended) question from a structured one centers on the type of response that the respondent is allowed to make. For instance, a question might ask if a respondent thinks that schools should not grade assigned work; if the respondent says *yes,* another question asks why he thinks so. The resulting unstructured response might take several minutes and include a series of arguments, facts, ramblings, and so on. A structured response format would offer, say, five reasons and ask the respondent to choose one.

Here are some examples of questions in the unstructured response mode:

- Why do you think you didn't try harder in high school?

  _____

  _____

  _____

- What led you to go to college?

  _____

  _____

  _____

- Describe your feelings as you think of your mother.

  _____

  _____

  _____

Items II and IV in Figure 10.1 provide additional examples of questions in the unstructured response mode.

Thus, the unstructured response mode is a responsive form over which the researcher attempts to exert little control other than by asking questions and limiting the amount of space (or time) provided for the answers. Once an unstructured question is asked, the response may be stated in the way the respondent chooses. Allowing the respondent such control over the response ensures that the

A Sample Questionnaire

FIGURE 10.1

I. Suppose you were offered an opportunity to make a substantial advance in a job or occupation. Place a check opposite each item in the following list to show how important it would be in stopping you from making that advance.

	Would stop me	Might stop me from making change	Would be a serious consideration but wouldn't stop me	Wouldn't matter at all
Endanger your health				
Leave your family for some time				
Move around the country a lot				
Leave your community				
Leave your friends				
Give up leisure time				
Keep quiet about political views				
Learn a new routine				
Work harder than you are now				
Take on more responsibility				

II. Looking at your present situation, what do you expect to be doing 5 years from now? _____

III. What are your chances of reaching this goal?
_____ excellent _____ good _____ fair _____ poor _____ very poor

IV. What would you like to be doing 5 years from now? _____

V. What are your chances of reaching this goal?
_____ excellent _____ good _____ fair _____ poor _____ very poor

respondent will give his or her own answers rather than simply agreeing with one provided by the researcher.

However, the unstructured mode does raise problems in quantification of data and ease of scoring (discussed in detail in the last section of the chapter, which covers coding and scoring procedures). In contrast, more structured response modes simplify quantification.

Fill-In Response

The fill-in response mode can be considered a transitional mode between un-structured and structured forms. Although it requires the subject to generate rather than choose a response, it typically limits the range of possible responses by limiting the answer to a single word or phrase. Consider the following examples:

- What is your father's occupation? _____
- In what school did you do your undergraduate work? _____
- Looking at the above picture, what word best describes the way it makes you feel? _____

Note that the unstructured response mode differs from the structured, fill-in mode in degree. The fill-in mode restricts respondents to a single word or phrase, usually in a request to report factual information (although the third example elicits a response beyond facts). The very wording of such a question restricts the number of possible responses the respondent can make and the number of words that can be used.

Tabular Response

The tabular response mode resembles the fill-in mode, although it imposes some-what more structure because respondents must fit their responses into a table. Here is an example:

Next Previous Job Title	Specify Type of Work Performed	Name of Employer	Annual Salary	Dates	
				From	To

Typically, a tabular response requires numbers, words, or phrases (often fac-tual information of a personal nature), but it may also allow respondents to re-flect their degree of endorsement or agreement along some scale, as shown in Item I in Figure 10.1. (This use of the tabular mode is described in more detail in the following section on scaled response.)

A table is a convenient way of organizing a complex response, that is, a re-sponse that includes a variety of information rather than a single element. How-ever, it is otherwise not a distinct response mode. The tabular form organizes either *fill-in* responses (as in the example) or *scaled* responses (as in Item I, Fig-ure 10.1).

Scaled Response

A commonly used structured response mode establishes a scale (that is, a series of gradations) on which respondents express endorsement or rejection of an attitude statement or describe some aspect of themselves. Item I in Figure 10.1 (which uses the tabular form of organization) illustrates the scaled response mode. Note that the question asks the respondent to consider each potential obstacle to job advancement and indicate on the scale the effect of that concern on his or her acceptance of a new job:

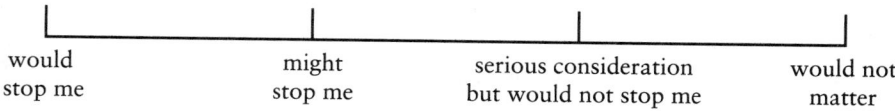

would	might	serious consideration	would not
stop me	stop me	but would not stop me	matter

This example illustrates a four-point scale of *degree* of influence, from total influence at the left to no influence at the right.

Consider also Items III and V in Figure 10.1. Identical in wording but referring to different goals, they ask the respondent to assess his or her likelihood of reaching a goal, using the following five-point scale:

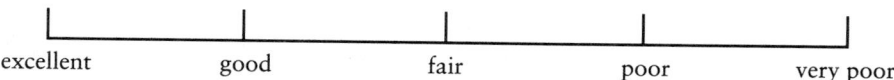

excellent	good	fair	poor	very poor

By choosing one of these five categories, the respondent indicates the *degree* to which he or she sees goal attainment as a likely prospect.

The Career Awareness Scale is an example of a questionnaire that uses a scale to indicate *frequency*. (See Figure 10.2.) The instrument presents a descriptive statement about career-seeking behavior to a respondent, a high school student, and asks for an indication of the frequency with which this behavior occurs, using the following four-point scale:

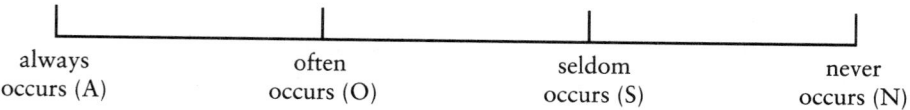

always	often	seldom	never
occurs (A)	occurs (O)	occurs (S)	occurs (N)

The scale is used primarily to assess whether a high school student has engaged in behaviors intended to learn about careers.

All scaled responses measure degree or frequency of agreement or occurrence (although a variety of response words may indicate these quantities). They all assume that a response on a scale is a quantitative measure of judgment or feeling. (Recall that Chapter 9 discussed priorities for constructing such a scale.) Unlike an unstructured response, which requires coding to generate useful data, a structured, scaled response collects data directly in a usable and analyzable form. Moreover, in some research situations, scaled responses can yield *interval* data.[1]

---

[1] See the early part of Chapter 9 for a discussion of the types of measurement scales.

FIGURE 10.2   **A FREQUENCY QUESTIONNAIRE: THE CAREER AWARENESS SCALE**

Instructions: All of the questions below are about what you actually do. If you "Always" do what the statement says, circle the 1 for *A*. If you "Often" do what the statement says, circle the 2 for *O*. If you "Seldom" do what the statement says, circle the 3 for *S*. If you "Never" do what the statement says, circle the 4 for *N*.

There are no right or wrong answers for these questions. We are interested only in what you *actually do.*

1. I think about what I will do when I finish school.	1. A	2. O	3. S	4. N
2. I read occupational information.	1. A	2. O	3. S	4. N
3. I visit my guidance counselor to talk about my future.	1. A	2. O	3. S	4. N
4. I attend "career days" held in school.	1. A	2. O	3. S	4. N
5. I think about what it will take to be successful in my occupation.	1. A	2. O	3. S	4. N
6. I talk to workers to learn about their jobs.	1. A	2. O	3. S	4. N
7. Before I go on a field trip, I read whatever information is available about the place I am going to visit.	1. A	2. O	3. S	4. N
8. I look at the "Want Ads" in order to find out about jobs.	1. A	2. O	3. S	4. N
9. I visit factories, offices, and other places of work to learn about different kinds of jobs.	1. A	2. O	3. S	4. N
10. I take advantage of opportunities to do different things so that I'll learn about my strengths and weaknesses.	1. A	2. O	3. S	4. N
11. I keep myself prepared for immediate employment should the necessity arise.	1. A	2. O	3. S	4. N
12. I talk with my parents about my choice of career.	1. A	2. O	3. S	4. N
13. I work at different kinds of part-time jobs.	1. A	2. O	3. S	4. N
14. When the school gives an interest or career aptitude test, I take it seriously.	1. A	2. O	3. S	4. N
15. I consider my own values, my own abilities, and the needs of the job market when I plan my career.	1. A	2. O	3. S	4. N

For example, the difference in frequency between *N* and *S* on the Career Awareness Scale would be considered equivalent to the differences between *S* and *O* and between *O* and *A*. Provided other requirements are met, such interval data can be analyzed using powerful parametric statistical tests. (These statistical procedures are described in Chapter 11.)

Ranking Response

If a researcher presents a series of statements and asks the respondent to rank order them in terms of a particular criterion, the question will generate ordinally arranged results. Consider an example:

- Rank the following activities in terms of their *usefulness* to you as you learn how to write behavioral objectives. (Assign the numbers 1 through 5, with 5 indicating the most useful activity and 1 indicating the least useful one. If any activity gave you no help at all, indicate this by a 0.)
  ___ Initial presentation by consultants
  ___ Initial small-group activity
  ___ Weekly faculty sessions
  ___ Mailed instructions and examples of behavioral objectives
  ___ Individual sessions with consultant

Ranking forces respondents to choose between alternatives. If respondents were asked to rate (that is, scale) each alternative or to accept or reject each one, they could assign them all equal value. A request for a ranking response forces them to give critical estimates of the values of the alternatives.

Typically, ranked data are analyzed by summing the ranks that subjects assign to each response, giving an overall or group rank order of alternatives. Such an overall ranking generated by one group (for example, teachers) can be compared to that generated by a second group (for example, administrators) using nonparametric statistical techniques. (See Chapter 11.)

Checklist Response

A respondent replies to a checklist item by selecting one of the possible choices offered. This form of response does not, however, represent a scale, because the answers do not represent points on a continuum; rather they are *nominal* categories. Consider two examples:

- The kind of job that I would most prefer would be:
  Check one:
  ___ (1) A job where I am almost always certain of my ability to perform well.
  ___ (2) A job where I am usually pressed to the limit of my abilities.
- I get most of my professional and intellectual stimulation from:
  Check *one* of the following blanks:
  ___ A. Teachers in the system
  ___ B. Principal
  ___ C. Superintendent
  ___ D. Other professional personnel in the system

___ E. Other professional personnel elsewhere
___ F. Periodicals, books, and other publications

Respondents often find the nominal judgments required by a checklist easier to make than scalar judgments, and they take less time to give such responses. At the same time, those responses yield less information for the researcher. Nominal data are usually analyzed by means of the chi-square statistical analysis (described in Chapter 11).

Categorical Response

The categorical response mode, similar to the checklist but simpler, offers a respondent only two possibilities for each item. (In practice, checklist items also usually offer only two responses: check or no check on each of a series of choices, but they may offer more possibilities.) However, the checklist evokes more complex responses, since the choices cannot be considered independently, as can categorical responses. Also, after checking a response, the remaining choices in the list leave no further option.)

A yes-no dichotomy is often used in the categorical response mode:

• Are you a veteran? Yes ____   No ____

Attitude-related items may give true-false alternatives:

• Guidance counseling does not begin early enough.
   True ____ False ____

Analysis can render true-false data into *interval* form by using the number of true responses (or the number of responses indicating a favorable attitude) as the respondent's score. The cumulative number of *true* responses by an individual *S* on a questionnaire then becomes an indication of the degree (or frequency) of agreement by that *S*—an interval measure. Counting the number of *S*s who indicate agreement on a single item provides a nominal measure. (See the section on coding and scoring at the end of this chapter to see how to score this and the other types of response modes.)

CONSTRUCTING A QUESTIONNAIRE OR INTERVIEW SCHEDULE

How do you construct a questionnaire or interview schedule? What questions should you ask and in what formats? What response modes should you employ? To answer, begin by asking, "What am I trying to find out?"

Specifying the Variables to Measure

The questions you should ask on a questionnaire or in an interview reflect the information you are trying to find, that is, your hypotheses or research questions. To determine what to measure, you need only write down the names of all the variables you are studying. One study might attempt to relate source of occupational training (that is, high school, junior college, or on-the-job instruction) to degree of geographic mobility; it would have to measure where respondents were trained for their jobs and the places where they have lived. A study might compare 8th graders and 12th graders to determine how favorably they perceive the high school climate; it would have to ask respondents to indicate their grade levels (8th or 12th) and to react to statements about the high school climate in a way that indicates whether they see it as favorable or not. A study concerned with the relative incomes of academic and vocational high school graduates 5 years after graduation would have to ask respondents to indicate whether they focused on academic or vocational subjects in high school and how much money they were presently earning.

Thus, the first step in constructing questionnaire or interview questions is to *specify your variables by name.* Your variables designate what you are trying to measure. They tell you where to begin.

Choosing the Question Format

The first decision you must make about question format is whether to present items in a written questionnaire or an oral interview. Because it is a more convenient and economical choice, the questionnaire is more commonly used, although it does limit the kinds of questions that can be asked and the kinds of answers that can be obtained. A questionnaire may present difficulties in obtaining personally sensitive and revealing information. Also, it may not yield useful answers to indirect, nonspecific questions. Further, preparation of a questionnaire must detail all questions in advance. Despite the possibility of including some limited response-keyed questions, you must ask all respondents the same questions. Interviews offer the best possibilities for gathering meaningful data from response-keyed questions.

Table 10.1 summarizes the relative merits of interviews and questionnaires. Ordinarily, a researcher opts for the additional cost and unreliability of interviewing only when the study addresses sensitive subjects and/or when personalized questioning is desired. (Interviews are subject to unreliability, because the researcher must depend on interviewers to elicit and record the responses and often to code them, as well.) In general, when a researcher chooses to use the unstructured response mode, interviewing tends to be the better choice because people find it easier to talk than write; consequently, interviews generate more information of this type.

The choice of question format depends on whether you are attempting to measure facts, attitudes, preferences, and so on. In constructing a questionnaire,

TABLE 10.1

Summary of the Relative Merits of Interviews Versus Questionnaires

CONSIDERATION	INTERVIEW	QUESTIONNAIRE
Personnel needed to collect data	Interviewers	Clerks
Major expense categories	Payments to interviewers	Postage and printing
Opportunities for response keying (personalization)	Extensive	Limited
Opportunities for asking	Extensive	Limited
Opportunities for probing (following leads)	Possible	Difficult
Relative magnitude of data reduction	Great (because of coding)	Mainly limited to rostering
Number of respondents typically reached	Limited	Extensive
Rate of return	Good	Poor
Sources of error	Interviewer, instrument, coding, sample	Limited to instrument and sample
Overall reliability	Quite limited	Fair
Emphasis on writing skill	Limited	Extensive

use direct, specific, clearly worded questions, and keep response keying to a minimum. In constructing an interview schedule, you may sacrifice specificity for depth and use indirect, subtle probes to work into an area of questioning. Response-keyed questions—those whose answers guide the choices of subsequent questions, if any, to ask—are also recommended as a labor-saving shortcut.

Choosing the Response Mode

No specific rules govern selection of response modes. In some cases, the kind of information you seek will determine the most suitable response mode, but often you must choose between equally acceptable forms. You can, for instance, provide respondents with a blank space and ask them to fill in their ages, or you can present a series of age groupings (for example, 20–29, 30–39, and so on) and ask them to check the one that fits them.

The choice of response mode should be based on the manner in which the data will be treated; unfortunately, however, researchers do not always make this decision before collecting data. It is recommended that data analysis decisions be made in conjunction with the selection of response modes. In this way, the researcher (1) gains assurance that the data will serve the intended purposes and (2) can begin to construct data rosters and to prepare for the analyses. (See Chapter 11.) If analytical procedures will group age data into ranges to provide nominal data for a chi-square statistical analysis, the researcher would want

Considerations in Selecting a Response Mode   TABLE 10.2

RESPONSE MODE	TYPE OF DATA	CHIEF ADVANTAGES	CHIEF DISADVANTAGES
Fill-in	Nominal	Limited bias; expanded response flexibility	Difficult to score
Scaled	Interval	Easy to score	Time-consuming; potential for bias
Ranking	Ordinal	Easy to score; forces discrimination	Difficult to complete
Checklist or categorical	Nominal (may be interval when totaled)	Easy to score; easy to respond	Limited data and options

Note: The tabular mode is just a way of organizing fill-in or scaled responses, so this table omits it as a distinct category.

to design the appropriate questionnaire item to collect these data in grouped form.

Scaled responses lend themselves most readily to parametric statistical analysis, because they often can be considered interval data. Ranking procedures may provide less information, because they generate ordinal data. Fill-in and checklist responses usually provide nominal data, suitable, unless otherwise coded, for chi-square analysis. Thus, the ultimate criterion in choosing a response mode is the nature of your variables and your intentions for statistically testing your hypotheses.[2] If the statistical tests for data analysis are not determined in advance, the best rule of thumb is to use the scaled response mode, because the interval data so collected can always be transformed into ordinal or nominal data. (See Chapter 11.)

Certain other practical considerations also influence the choice of response modes. Respondents may need more time to provide scaled responses than they would take to give true-false responses (and the researcher may spend more time scoring scaled responses). If your questionnaire is already lengthy, you may prefer the true-false response mode for additional questions in order to limit the burden upon the respondent. Fill-ins offer the advantage of not biasing the respondent's judgment as much as the other types, but they carry the disadvantage of difficulty in scoring or coding. Response-keyed questions provide respondents with response flexibility, but, like the fill-ins, they may be more difficult than other alternatives to score and do not provide parallel data for all respondents. Some of these considerations are summarized in Table 10.2.

Thus, selection between response modes requires consideration of several criteria:

---

[2] Conversely, should the response mode be specified first, it should be the criterion for choosing statistical tests.

1. *Type of data desired for analysis.* If you seek interval data to allow some type of statistical analysis, scaled and checklist responses are the best choices. (Checklist items must be coded to yield interval data, and responses must be pooled across items. An individual checklist item yields only nominal data.) Ranking provides ordinal data, and fill-in and some checklist responses provide nominal data.
2. *Response flexibility.* Fill-ins allow respondents the widest range of choice; yes-no and true-false items, the least.
3. *Time to complete.* Ranking procedures generally take the most time to complete, although scaled items may impose equally tedious burdens on respondents.
4. *Potential response bias.* Scaled responses and checklist responses offer the greatest potential for bias. Respondents may be biased not only by social desirability considerations but also by a variety of other factors, such as the tendencies to overuse the *true* or *yes* answer and to select one point on the scale as the standard response to every item. Other respondents may avoid the extremes of a rating scale, thus shrinking its range. These troublesome tendencies on the part of respondents are strongest on long questionnaires, which provoke fatigue and annoyance. Ranking and fill-in responses are less susceptible than other choices to such difficulties. In particular, ranking forces respondents to discriminate between response alternatives.
5. *Ease of scoring.* Fill-in responses usually must be coded, making them considerably more difficult than other response types to score. The other types of responses discussed in this chapter are approximately equally easy to score.

Preparing Interview Items

As pointed out earlier, the first step in preparing items for an interview schedule is to specify the variables that you want to measure; then construct questions that focus on these variables. If, for example, one variable in a study is openness of school climate, an obvious question might ask classroom teachers, "How open is the climate here?" Less direct but perhaps more concrete questions might ask, "Do you feel free to take your problems to the principal? Do you feel free to adopt new classroom practices and materials?" Note that the questions are based on the operational definition of the variable *openness,* which has been operationally defined as freedom to change, freedom to approach superiors, and so on. In writing questions, make sure they incorporate the properties set forth in the operational definitions of your variables. (Recall from Chapter 6 that these properties may be either dynamic or static, depending on which type of operational definition you employ.)

A single interview schedule or questionnaire may well employ more than one question format accommodating more than one response mode. The sample interview schedule in Figure 10.3 seeks to measure the attitudes of the general

A PORTION OF A TELEPHONE INTERVIEW SCHEDULE

FIGURE 10.3

Reprinted by permission of the Eagleton Institute of Politics, Rutgers University, New Brunswick, N.J.

Now, I've got a few questions about public education in New Jersey.

21. Students are often given the grades A, B, C, D, and FAIL to denote the quality of their work. Suppose the public schools, themselves, in your community were graded in the same way. What grade would you give the public schools in your community—A, B, C, D, or FAIL?

  135—1. A
    2. B
    3. C
    4. D
    5. FAIL
    9. DON'T KNOW

22. In your opinion, is enough money being spent on public schools in your community?

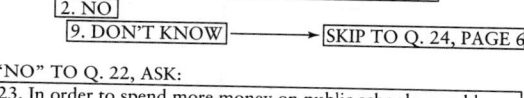

136—1. YES ⟶ SKIP TO Q. 24, PAGE 6
  2. NO
  9. DON'T KNOW ⟶ SKIP TO Q. 24, PAGE 6

(IF "NO" TO Q. 22, ASK:

  23. In order to spend more money on public schools, would you be willing to see an increase in local taxes?
    137—1. YES
      2. NO
      9. DON'T KNOW

24. At the present level of spending for public schools in your community, do you feel the citizens of your community are getting their money's worth?

  138—1. YES
    2. NO
    9. DON'T KNOW

25. Do you think that students should be required to pass a state examination in order to graduate from high school?

  139—1. YES
    2. NO
    9. DON'T KNOW

26. Which of the following three areas do you think is most important for the schools to concentrate on? [START AT DESIGNATED POINT AND READ CHOICES]

  140—1. TEACHING MATHEMATICS AND READING
    2. PREPARING STUDENTS FOR COLLEGE OR A CAREER
  OR 3. TEACHING A CODE OF VALUES AND MORAL BEHAVIOR
    9. DON'T KNOW

27. Which is second most important? [READ REMAINING TWO CHOICES]

  141—1. TEACHING MATHEMATICS AND READING
    2. PREPARING STUDENTS FOR COLLEGE OR A CAREER
  OR 3. TEACHING A CODE OF VALUES AND MORAL BEHAVIOR
    9. DON'T KNOW

28. How much attention do you think the schools pay to people like you when they decide what to teach—a great deal of attention, some attention, or no attention at all?

  142—1. A GREAT DEAL OF ATTENTION
    2. SOME ATTENTION
    3. NO ATTENTION AT ALL
    9. DON'T KNOW

29. Turning to the matter of discipline, are the schools in your community too strict, not strict enough, or just about right?

  143—1. TOO STRICT
    2. JUST ABOUT RIGHT
    3. NOT STRICT ENOUGH
    9. DON'T KNOW

public toward some current issues in public education such as cost, quality, curriculum emphasis, and standards. The interview schedule is highly structured to maximize information obtained in minimal telephone time. One of the questions is response keyed. All of them are specific, and all responses are precoded in scaled, categorical, or checklist form.

FIGURE 10.4

From Butler, 1977. Reprinted by permission of the author.

A FOLLOW-UP QUESTIONNAIRE

1. What is the title of your present job? _____
   From _____ To _____
2. What is the title of your next previous job?_____
   From _____ To _____
3. Check one of the following to show how you think you compare with other people.
   A _____ I like my work much better than most people like theirs.
   B _____ I like my work better than most people like theirs.
   C _____ I like my work about as well as most people like theirs.
   D _____ I dislike my work more than most people dislike theirs.
   E _____ I dislike my work much more than most people dislike theirs.
4. Check one of the following to show how much of the time you feel satisfied with your job.
   A _____ Most of the time   B _____ A good deal of the time
   C _____ About half of the time   D _____ Occasionally   E _____ Seldom
5. Put a check before the category which most accurately describes your total, personal income in 1975 before taxes.
   A _____ Less than $5,000.00   B _____ Less than $10,000.00
   C _____ Less than $15,000.00   D _____ Less than $20,000.00
   E _____ $20,000.00 or more
6. Was there anything unusual (e.g., sickness, layoffs, promotions, unemployment) about your income in 1975 as reported in question #5 above?
   CIRCLE ONE: YES   NO   If YES, please explain _____
   _____
7. If you answered YES to question 6 above, put a check before the category which most accurately describes your total, personal income in 1974 before taxes.
   A _____ Less than $5,000.00   D _____ Less than $20,000.00
   B _____ Less than $10,000.00   E _____ $20,000.00 or more
   C _____ Less than $15,000.00
8. Are you a high school graduate? CIRCLE ONE: YES   NO
   What high school? _____
9. Have you successfully completed one, two, or three college courses as   YES   NO
   a part-time student?
10. Have you successfully completed more than three college courses as a   YES   NO
    part-time student?
11. Have you attended a 2-year college as a full-time student without   YES   NO
    graduating?
12. Have you earned a 2-year college diploma?   YES   NO
    If YES to 9, 10, 11, or 12, what college? _____

Preparing Questionnaire Items

The procedures for preparing questionnaire items parallel those for preparing interview schedule items. Again, maintain the critical relationship between the items and the study's operationally defined variables. Constantly ask about your items: Is this what I want to measure? Three sample questionnaires appear in Figures 10.4, 10.5, and 10.6.

(continued)

13. Have you enrolled in a 4-year college and successfully completed one, two, or three years?   YES   NO
    If YES, how many years and what college? _____

14. Have you earned the bachelor's degree?   YES   NO
    If YES, what college? _____

15. Have you earned a degree beyond the bachelor's?   YES   NO
    If YES, what degree and what college? _____

16. What was your father's job title at the time you graduated from high school? _____

17. What was your mother's job title at the time you graduated from high school? _____

18. How many brothers and sisters do you have? CIRCLE ONE:
    1 2 3 4 5 6 7 8 9 10 11 12 13 14

19. How many brothers and sisters are older than you? CIRCLE ONE:
    1 2 3 4 5 6 7 8 9 10 11 12 13 14

20. Are you a veteran? CIRCLE ONE: YES   NO
    Dates of service: from _____ to _____

21. Describe your health since graduation from high school. CIRCLE ONE:
    EXCELLENT   GOOD   AVERAGE   FAIR   POOR

22. How many months have you been out of work because of illness since graduation from high school?
    CIRCLE ONE: 1 2 3 4 5 6 7 8 9 10 11 12 13 14 15 16
    17 18 19 NONE   OTHER _____

23. Did you receive your training for the job in which you are now employed:
    (CHECK ONE BELOW)
    _____ high school   armed forces _____
    _____ technical institute in-plant training _____
    _____ 2-year college   apprenticeship _____
    _____ 4-year college   other _____ please explain _____

24. Marital status. CHECK ONE (or more):
    _____ single   separated _____
    _____ married   remarried _____
    _____ divorced   other _____ please explain _____

25. Do you consider yourself a member of a minority group?
    CIRCLE ONE: YES   NO
    If YES, check one: Black _____ American Indian _____
    Chicano _____ other _____ please explain _____

The questionnaire in Figure 10.4 was used in a follow-up study of community college graduates and high school graduates who did not attend college. The researcher was interested in determining whether the community college graduates subsequently obtained higher socioeconomic status (that is, earnings and job status) and job satisfaction than a matched group of people who did not attend college. The items on the questionnaire were designed to determine (1) earnings, job title, and job satisfaction (the dependent variables) [Items 1–7]; (2) subsequent educational experiences, in order to eliminate or reclassify subjects pursuing additional education (a control variable) as well as to verify the educational status distinction of 2-year college students versus those who completed high school only (the independent variable) [Items 8–15, 23]; (3) background characteristics, in order to match samples [Items 16–20, 24, 25]; and (4) health, in order to eliminate those whose job success chances were impaired [Items 21, 22].

The researcher intended for all respondents to complete all of the items except Item 7, which was response keyed to the preceding item. (Items 12 to 15 also have response-keyed parts.) The result is a reasonably simple, easy-to-complete instrument.

The sample questionnaire in Figure 10.5 employs scaled responses in an attempt to measure students' attitudes toward school achievement based on the value they place on going to school and on their own achievement. This questionnaire actually measures the following six topics related to a student's perceived importance or value of school achievement:

1. Quality of school performance (Items 2, 3)
2. Importance of school (Items 1, 4, 8, 18)
3. Enjoyment of school (Items 5, 6, 7)
4. Pride taken in school performance (Items 9, 10, 14, 19)
5. Enjoyment of class participation (Items 11, 12, 13)
6. Importance of performing well (Items 15, 16, 17)

Note that for each of the 19 items, the questionnaire provides a 4-point scale for responses employing the statement format. (This sample resembles the standard Likert scale shown in Chapter 9, except that it omits the middle or "undecided" response.) Note further that some of the items have been *reversed* (Items 2, 5, 6, 9, 13, 14. These questions have been written so that *disagreement* or *strong disagreement* indicates an attitude favoring the importance of school achievement; on all the other items, *agreement* or *strong agreement* indicates such an attitude. *Agreement* with Item 10 for example, indicates that the respondent takes pride in school progress and performance, a reflection of a positive attitude toward school achievement. *Disagreement* with Item 9 indicates that the respondent does not feel that grades are unimportant, another reflection of a positive attitude toward school achievement.

Reversing direction in some items is a protection against the form of response bias caused when an individual simply selects exactly the same response choice for each item. This tendency to mark a single choice for all questions out of boredom, disinterest, or hostility is referred to as *acquiescence response bias*. Item reversal guards against respondents creating erroneous impressions of extremely positive or extremely negative attitudes, because responses to items written in one direction cancel out or neutralize items written in the other.

A QUESTIONNAIRE ON STUDENTS' ATTITUDES TOWARD SCHOOL ACHIEVEMENT

FIGURE 10.5

Instructions: All questions are statements to which we seek your agreement or disagreement. If you "Strongly Agree" with any statement, circle the 1. If you "Agree," but not strongly, with any statement, circle the 2. If you "Disagree," but not strongly, circle the 3. If you "Strongly Disagree" with any statement, circle the 4.

There are no right or wrong answers for these questions. We are interested only in *how* you *feel* about the statements.

1. I believe it is important for me to participate in school activities.	1. SA 2. A 3. D 4. SD
2. I do poorly in school.	1. SA 2. A 3. D 4. SD
3. I think I am a good student.	1. SA 2. A 3. D 4. SD
4. I believe education can offer many achievements.	1. SA 2. A 3. D 4. SD
5. Schoolwork is uninteresting.	1. SA 2. A 3. D 4. SD
6. Schoolwork bores me.	1. SA 2. A 3. D 4. SD
7. I am happy to be a student.	1. SA 2. A 3. D 4. SD
8. I believe school is challenging.	1. SA 2. A 3. D 4. SD
9. Grades are not important to me.	1. SA 2. A 3. D 4. SD
10. I take pride in my progress and performance in school.	1. SA 2. A 3. D 4. SD
11. I enjoy volunteering answers to teachers' questions.	1. SA 2. A 3. D 4. SD
12. I feel good when I give an oral report.	1. SA 2. A 3. D 4. SD
13. I dislike answering questions in school.	1. SA 2. A 3. D 4. SD
14. Success in extra-curricular activities means very little.	1. SA 2. A 3. D 4. SD
15. I feel depressed when I don't complete an assignment.	1. SA 2. A 3. D 4. SD
16. I feel good when I am able to finish my assigned homework.	1. SA 2. A 3. D 4. SD
17. I believe it is my responsibility to make the honor roll.	1. SA 2. A 3. D 4. SD
18. School offers me an opportunity to expand my knowledge.	1. SA 2. A 3. D 4. SD
19. I do well in school so that my parents can be proud of me.	1. SA 2. A 3. D 4. SD

To maximize the effectiveness of this safeguard, half of the items should be written in each direction. Note that in the sample questionnaire in Figure 10.5, only 6 of the 19 items have been reversed.

The likelihood of this form of response bias is lessened also by the elimination of the "undecided" response alternative from the basic Likert scale format. The possibility of noninvolvement or "fence sitting" is avoided by omitting the "undecided" response choice.

Note also that the sample questionnaire obscures its true purpose somewhat by measuring multiple features of the topic in question rather than a single one. As a questionnaire's purpose becomes more transparent or obvious, the likelihood increases that respondents will provide the answers they want others to hear about themselves rather than the truth. This tendency to respond in a way that shows oneself in the best possible light is referred to as *social desirability response bias*. It can be minimized by not revealing the true name or purpose of the questionnaire prior to its completion, by including items that measure a variety of topics or aspects of a single topic, or by including filler items—questions that deal with areas unrelated to the one being measured. The sample questionnaire combines the first approach (carrying the title "Questionnaire" when actually administered) and the second (including multiple topics). No filler items appear in this version of the questionnaire, but some may appear in longer versions. However, a questionnaire about attitudes toward school achievement may not benefit from efforts to disguise the nature of the attitude being measured, so some responses can be expected to reflect social desirability bias rather than true feelings.

A third sample questionnaire is shown in Figure 10.6. The Satisfaction Scale is used to determine the degree of students' satisfaction with a course. Items are scaled using a 5-point scale as the response mode. Note the format, which features a question followed by the response choices stated in both numbers and words.

No attempt has been made to counteract response bias by reversing the direction of some of the items or by disguising their meanings; each item has been written so that a *1* indicates a positive response on a single topic. Obviously, these items are susceptible to biased response based on considerations other than the respondent's judgment.

Pilot Testing and Evaluating a Questionnaire

Most studies benefit substantially from the precaution of running pilot tests on their questionnaires, leading to revisions based on the results of the tests. A pilot test administers a questionnaire to a group of respondents who are part of the intended test population but who will not be part of the sample. In this way, the researcher attempts to determine whether questionnaire items achieve the desired qualities of measurement and discrimination.

If a series of items is intended to measure the *same* variable (as the eight items in Figure 10.6 are), an evaluation should determine whether these items are mea-

A COURSE SATISFACTION QUESTIONNAIRE

FIGURE 10.6

Name _____   Course Name _____
Teacher _____

SATISFACTION SCALE

1. Do you ever feel like skipping this class?

1	2	3	4	5
never	rarely	sometimes	often	always

2. Do you like this class?

1	2	3	4	5
very much	quite a bit	it's all right	not much	hate it

3. How much do you feel you have learned in this class?

1	2	3	4	5
a great deal	quite a bit	a fair amount	not much	nothing

4. Are you glad you chose or were assigned to be in this class?

1	2	3	4	5
very glad	most of the time	sometimes	not too often	not at all

5. Do you always do your best in this class?

1	2	3	4	5
all the time	most of the time	sometimes	usually not	never

6. Do you like the way this class is taught?

1	2	3	4	5
very much	quite a bit	a fair amount	not much	not at all

7. Does the teacher give you help when you need it?

1	2	3	4	5
always	most of the time	usually	sometimes	never

8. Do you find the time you spend in this class to be interesting?

1	2	3	4	5
very much	quite	fairly	not too	not at all

suring something in common. Such an analysis would require administering the scale to a pilot sample and running correlations between response scores obtained by each person on each item and the scores obtained by each person across the whole scale. (See the discussion on item analysis in the previous chapter.) As the correlation between an item score and the total score rises, it indicates a stronger relationship between what the item is measuring and what the total scale is measuring. Following the completion of this item analysis, the researcher can select the items with the highest correlations with the total score and incorporate them in the final scale. For example, consider 10 items to measure a person's attitude toward some object, giving the following correlations between each item score and the mean score across all 10 items:

ITEM NUMBER	CORRELATION
1	.89
2	.75
3	.27
4	.81
5	.19
6	.53
7	.58
8	.72
9	.63
10	.60

Based on these data, the researcher should decide to eliminate Items 3 and 5 which fall below .50, and to place the other eight items in the final scale, confident that the remaining items measure something in common.

Item analysis of questions intended to measure the same variable in the same way is one important use of the data collected from a pilot test. However, item analyses are not as critical for refining questionnaires as they are for refining tests. Responses to questionnaire items are usually reviewed by eye for clarity and distribution without necessarily running an item analysis.

A pilot test can uncover a variety of failings in a questionnaire. For example, if all respondents reply identically to any one item, that item probably lacks discrimination. If you receive a preponderance of inappropriate responses to an item, examine it for ambiguity or otherwise poor wording. Poor instructions and other administration problems become apparent on a pilot test, as do areas of extreme sensitivity. If respondents refuse to answer certain items, try to desensitize them by rewording. Thus, pilot tests enable researchers to debug their questionnaires by diagnosing and correcting these failings.

SAMPLING PROCEDURES

Random Sampling

A researcher administers a questionnaire or interview to gain information about a particular group of respondents, such as high school graduates, school administrators in New England, or home economics teachers in New Jersey. This target group is the study's *population,* and the first step in sampling is to define the population. The researcher then selects a *sample* or representative group from this population to serve as respondents. As one way to ensure that this sample is representative of the larger population, a researcher might draw a *random* sample, because random selection limits the probability of choosing a biased sample.[3] For example, you are interested in obtaining information about presidents of 2-year colleges. The population is 2,800 presidents, from which you want a sample of 300. Which 300 should you choose? To draw a random sample, you might write the names of all the 2-year colleges in alphabetical order giving each a number in the sequence.[4] You could then select 300 numbers by matching schools' assigned numbers against a table of random numbers like the one in Appendix C. The resulting list of 300 colleges, each with one president, is a random sample of the population from which it was drawn. Systematic biases in selection or selectees can be minimized by this procedure.[5] However, when certain sample variables are of special interest to the researcher (for example, age) stratified sampling should be employed, defining variables of interest as *sampling parameters*. (See the section on stratified random sampling later in the chapter.)

Defining the Population

The *population* (or target group) for a questionnaire or interview study is the group about which the researcher wants to gain information and draw conclusions. A researcher interested in the educational aspirations of teachers, for example, would focus on teachers as the population of the study. The term *defining the population* refers to a process of establishing boundary conditions that specify who shall be included in or excluded from the population. In the example study, the population could be defined as elementary school teachers, or public school teachers, or all teachers, or some other choice.

Specifying the group that will constitute a study's population is an early step in the sampling process, and it affects the nature of the conclusions that may be drawn from a study. A broadly defined population (like "all teachers") maximizes external validity or generality, although such a broad definition may create difficulties in obtaining a representative sample, and it may require a large sample size. Conversely, defining the population narrowly (for example, as "female, elementary school teachers") may facilitate the selection of a suitable sample, but it will restrict conclusions and generalizations to the specific population used, which may be inconsistent with the intent of the study.

---

[3] The process for random assignment of subjects to groups was described in Chapter 7. The description here concerns the random selection of subjects from a population. Although random assignment is a strategy for controlling threats to internal validity, random selection is a strategy for controlling threats to external validity. A single study may combine both procedures to define experimental and control groups. Where groups are to be obtained only by sampling and not by assignment, random sampling or some variant would be used alone.

[4] Actually, you can write the names in any order. Alphabetizing is merely a convenience. Indeed, this example study might refer to a directory that lists the colleges in alphabetical order.

[5] A statistical test allows a researcher to determine how closely sample characteristics approximate population characteristics and thus the extent to which the sample is representative of the population from which it was drawn (as would be expected of a random sample). For a discussion of these statistics, see Ferguson (1981).

The most reasonable criteria for defining a study's target population reflect the independent, moderator, and control variables specified in the study design along with practical considerations such as availability of subjects or respondents. When a control variable in a study deals with a population characteristic, the researcher must systematically include or exclude individuals with this characteristic in defining the population. (Chapter 7 discusses priorities for limiting a study's population.) For example, a researcher might want to make a comparison between academic high school graduates and vocational high school graduates, but only for students who had attended one or the other school for 3 consecutive years; the population for this study would be defined to exclude all graduates who had switched from one school to the other. In studying school superintendents in urban and rural settings, a researcher might define the population to exclude all superintendents who have not yet completed their second year in their districts, thus controlling for longevity, a potentially important control variable. (Longevity might also be controlled through stratified sampling, as discussed later in the chapter.)

In addition to design considerations, practical considerations affect the definition of the population. In Slavin and Karweit's (1984) study of mastery learning, for example, the availability of inner-city children might have influenced the researchers to define their population as "urban" children. However, because of the variables of interest, both urban children and suburban children might have been included in the definition of the population, had both been available, allowing the researchers to evaluate residence as a moderator variable. In general, independent and moderator variables require that a population include individuals with certain characteristics, whereas control variables require exclusion of particular groups.

Thus, an early step in sampling is to define the population from which to draw the sample. By referring to the variables of interest and by taking into account practical considerations, the researcher chooses characteristics to be included in and excluded from the target population. A concrete sampling plan illustrating the process of exclusion in defining the population appears in Figure 10.7.

Establishing Specifications for Stratified Random Sampling

Techniques of *stratified* random sampling permit researchers to include parameters of special interest and to control for internal validity related to selection factors through applications of moderator or control variables. In addition, stratification represents a good operational strategy for screening members of the population into and out of the study and for reducing the variability of the sample.

The first step in stratified sampling is to identify the stratification parameters, or variables. Each stratification parameter represents a control variable, that is, a

A Sampling Plan for Sampling 2-Year Colleges

FIGURE 10.7

Population: All 2-year colleges in the U.S.A.

Variables controlled by exclusion:
  (1) College must have graduated a minimum of one class
  (2) President must have held position for a minimum of one year

Variables controlled by stratification:
  (1) Private–Public
    25% private   75% public
  (2) Urban–Rural
    15% urban   10% rural   60% urban   15% rural
  (3) Size of Student Body[a]

5%	1%	48%	3%
large	large	large	large
10%	9%	12%	12%
small	small	small	small

If the sample size were to be 300, it would be broken down as follows:

		Sample	Population
private, urban, large	5%	15	140
private, urban, small	10%	30	280
private, rural, large	1%	3	28
private, rural, small	9%	27	252
public, urban, large	48%	144	1,344
public, urban, small	12%	36	336
public, rural, large	3%	9	84
public, rural, small	12%	36	336
	100%	300	2,800

[a]Large = more than 2,000 students; small = fewer than 2,000 students.

potential source of error or extraneous influence that may provide an alternative explanation for a study's outcome. Assume that you want to contrast the teaching techniques of male and female elementary school teachers. The study would restrict the population to elementary school teachers, because that is a specified control variable, and it would sample across male and female teachers, because gender is the independent variable. You are concerned, however, that teaching experience may be an extraneous influence on your results. To offset this potential source of error, first you would determine the distribution of years of experience for male and for female elementary school teachers; then you would select the sample in proportion to these distributions. (The selection of specific subjects within each stratum or proportion would be done randomly.) The other control variables would be treated in a similar way.

Consider sampling procedures for national political polls. Results are usually reported separately for different age groups and for different sections of the country. The studies treat age and geography as moderator variables and define separate samples according to them. However, within each age and geographical group, such a study may control for gender, race, religion, socioeconomic status, and specific location by proportional stratification. If half of the young people in the northeastern United States are male, then males should constitute half of the sample of northeastern young people. If 65 percent of the southeastern middle-aged group is poor, then poor people should make up 65 percent of the sample of this group. (Of course, terms like *middle-aged* and *poor* must be operationally defined.) The pollsters then consider these subpopulation differences in evaluating the outcomes of their studies.

Consider the example on sampling 300 presidents of 2-year colleges. Some bias may still affect results in spite of this random selection due to overrepresentation of private colleges. To control for this factor, use it as a variable or parameter for stratified sampling. Suppose one-quarter of the 2-year colleges are private schools and three-quarters are public institutions. In proportional stratified sampling, you would embody these percentages in your sample. In a sample of 300 college presidents, you would want 75 from private, 2-year colleges and 225 from public ones (the specific individuals in each stratum being randomly chosen). These specifications ensure creation of a sample systematically representative of the population.

To accomplish this stratified sampling method, you would make two separate alphabetical lists, one of private colleges, the other of public schools. You would then use your table of random numbers to select 75 private and 225 public colleges from the two lists, respectively. Of course, you could go further and control also for factors such as urban versus rural setting or large versus small colleges. However, in considering stratification, remember that each additional control variable complicates the sampling procedure and reduces the population per category from which each part of the sample is drawn. The sampling plan for this study is shown in Figure 10.7.

Random choice is the key to overcoming selection bias in sampling; *stratification* adds precision in ensuring that the sample contains the same proportional distribution of respondents on selected parameters as the population. Where stratified sampling is used, *within each stratum, researchers must choose sample respondents by random methods* to increase the likelihood of eliminating sources of invalidity due to selection other than those controlled through stratification. The combination of stratification and random selection increases the likelihood that the sample will be representative of the population. Because it controls for selection invalidity based on preselected variables in a systematic way, stratification is recommended for use with the variables identified as representing the greatest potential sources of selection bias. For information about determining sample size, see Chapter 11.

Procedures for Administering a Questionnaire

This section focuses on procedures for mailing out a questionnaire, following it up, and sampling from among those in the sample who do not respond (hereafter called *nonrespondents*).

Initial Mailing

The initial mailing of a questionnaire to a sample of respondents typically includes a cover letter, the questionnaire itself, and a stamped, return-addressed envelope.

The cover letter is a critical part of the initial mailing, because it must establish the legitimacy of the study and the respectability of the researcher. The cover letter should briefly make its case for participation, focusing on the following points:

1. *The purpose of the study.* To satisfy the intellectual curiosity of potential respondents and to allay any doubts that participation will threaten their privacy or reputations, the researcher should disclose the ultimate uses of the data. Therefore, the cover letter should indicate the purposes and intentions of the study. It is often impossible, however, to give respondents complete details about the purposes of the study, because such knowledge might bias their responses.

2. *The protection afforded the respondent.* Respondents are entitled to know how a researcher will treat their privacy and confidentiality; thus the letter should indicate whether respondents must identify themselves and, if so, how their identities and responses will be protected. If questionnaires will be destroyed after rostering, and if rostering will be done by number rather than name (both recommended practices), the cover letter should include this information.

3. *Endorsements of the study.* Because respondents will feel secure about participating if they know that recognized institutions are behind the study, the cover letter should appear on university or agency letterhead. If a study will evaluate respondents as part of a professional group, then the cooperation and endorsement of this group should be obtained and mentioned in the letter. If the study is undertaken as a doctoral dissertation, mention the dissertation advisor by name and/or ask the dean of the school to sign or countersign the letter. If any agency or organization is providing financial support for the study, then this connection should be acknowledged.

4. *Legitimacy of the researcher.* Say who and what you are. Identify yourself by both name and position.

5. *Opportunities for debriefing.* If respondents can obtain the results of the study or additional explanations of its purpose at some later date, tell them so.

6. *Request for cooperation.* The letter constitutes an appeal from you for the respondent's help. If you have identified any special reasons why they should help (for example, the importance of the study for their profession) be sure to mention them.

7. *Special instructions.* The questionnaire should be self-administering and self-contained, although general instructions may be contained in the cover letter. Be sure to set a deadline for returning completed instruments, and caution against omitting answers to any items.

These seven points are important considerations in any research administration conducted by mail or in person. A personal interview should begin, in effect, with an *oral* cover letter. Figure 10.8 is an example of a cover letter.

The initial mailing may include more than one cover letter. For example, a letter of endorsement from a funding agency or from an organization to which the respondent belongs may help to gain the cooperation of prospective participants. A wise researcher does *not* print each respondent's name on his or her copy of the questionnaire to avoid causing alarm about the confidentiality of the study. Assignment of code numbers is a much better method of identification. Because filling out a questionnaire is, at the very least, an imposition on a respondent's time, both it and the cover letter should be as brief as possible.

Follow-Ups

After a period of about 2 weeks to a month has elapsed, a researcher should correspond with recipients who have not yet returned their questionnaires (that is, nonrespondents). This second mailing can consist simply of another letter soliciting cooperation. It should also include another questionnaire and another stamped, return-addressed envelope in case the respondent cannot find the original ones.

Ordinarily, about one-third to two-thirds of the questionnaires sent out will be returned during the month after the initial mailing. Beyond this period, about 10 to 25 percent can be stimulated to respond by additional urging. If the second mailing (the first follow-up letter) fails to stimulate a response, some researchers send a third mailing. This second follow-up typically takes the form of a postcard and follows the second mailing by about 2 to 3 weeks. Most researchers are unwilling to accept a return of less than 75 to 90 percent (and rightly so). Additional mailings, telephone calls, and a large sampling of nonrespondents (as discussed later) often help to elevate the return. Telegrams or telephone calls may be helpful in generating responses. If a study is worth doing, it is worth striving for the greatest return possible. An example of a follow-up letter is shown in Figure 10.9.

SAMPLE COVER LETTER

FIGURE 10.8

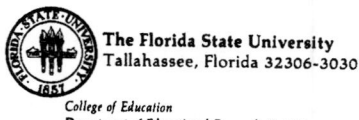

The Florida State University
Tallahassee, Florida 32306-3030

College of Education
Department of Educational Research, B-197

February 18, 1992

Dear Supervisor:

I am currently a doctoral candidate in the College of Education at Florida State University and am working with Dr. Bruce W. Tuckman on a project dealing with teacher feedback. The purpose of my study is to assist student teachers in developing their teaching skills through feedback from students.

I am asking you to have each of the student teachers you supervise administer the enclosed test instrument two times to one of the classes he or she teaches during the eight weeks of student teaching. The first time will be after two weeks of teaching, and the second time after the eighth week. I will provide each student teacher with all the necessary materials needed (pencils, questionnaires).

It should not take students more than five minutes to complete this form, which can be done after the student teacher has completed teaching the lesson. It is a form that is designed to describe the student teacher's style as seen by students.

The student teacher's name, the names of the students who respond, and the name of your school district will *not* be identified in my study. Instead, I will use a numerical coding process to label and identify my data. To assure the privacy of all involved, under no circumstances will I reveal the identity of the participants to either the school administration or the public.

I deeply appreciate your cooperation and support. Without you and the cooperation of your student teachers, I would not be able to conduct this research project, which hopefully will shed light on the improvement of teaching skills in preservice teachers. When the study is completed, I will provide you with a description of the results.

If you have any further questions, feel free to call me at 644-4592.

Sincerely,

Jane R. Richardson

P.S. Enclosed please find a copy of the feedback form.

FIGURE 10.9   SAMPLE FOLLOW-UP LETTER

From Forsyth,
1976. Reprinted
by permission of
the author.

RUTGERS
THE STATE UNIVERSITY
OF NEW JERSEY

GRADUATE SCHOOL OF EDUCATION • 10 SEMINARY PLACE • NEW BRUNSWICK • NEW JERSEY 08903

5/11/

School of Education
Old Ivy University
Hometown, U.S.A.

Dear Professor _____ :

The year's end approaches and soon many faculty will scatter for the summer in search of rest and/or individual pursuits. I, however, may sit "dataless" with perplexed and furrowed brow—contemplating for my dissertation Hamlet's immortal question. I need your assistance. The questionnaire I sent you a while back may be buried somewhere so here is another copy for your convenience.

If you were hesitant about completing a questionnaire asking you to list names of individuals, even though anonymously, let us address that issue briefly. The names as such are not significant to this researcher. However, they allow me to reconstruct interaction patterns in this and other academic organizations. The names, once received, are translated into symbols and the original data are destroyed.

A high response rate is essential to the success of this study. Your participation can make the difference. With it many long hours of work will all have been well spent. Again, let me assure you of the confidentiality of your response. The data will not be reported in any way which would allow the most astute student of interaction patterns at the School of Education to identify any individual or group. When you complete the instrument, send separately the signed postcard that will halt follow-up while protecting your anonymity.

If for some reason you still do not wish to participate, it would be greatly appreciated if you would indicate that decision on the return postcard and return it as addressed. In any case, thank you for your time and consideration. One last option: if you are reluctant to indicate names, I can conduct an interview with you which would allow you to do all the translating into numerical data. I can be reached at 201-932-7531.

Sincerely,

Patrick B. Forsyth

Sampling Nonrespondents

If fewer than about 80 percent of people who receive the questionnaire complete and return it, the researcher must try to reach a portion of the nonrespondents and obtain some data from them. Additional returns of all or critical portions of the questionnaire by 5 or 10 percent of the original nonrespondents is required for this purpose.

This additional procedure is necessary to establish that those who have not responded are not systematically different from those who have. Failure to check for potential bias based on nonresponse may introduce both external and internal invalidity based on experimental mortality (selective, nonrandom loss of subjects from a random sample) as well as a potential increase in sampling error.

Obtaining data from nonrespondents is not easy, since they have already ignored two or three attempts to include them in the study. The first step is to select at random 5 to 10 percent of these people from your list of nonrespondents, using the table of random numbers (Appendix C). Using their code numbers, go through the table of random numbers and pick those whose numbers appear first, then write or call them. About a 75-to-80-percent return from the nonrespondents' sample may be all that can be reasonably expected, but every effort should be made to achieve this goal.[6]

CONDUCTING AN INTERVIEW STUDY

Procedures for conducting an interview may differ from those involved in obtaining data by questionnaire, but the aim is the same: to obtain the desired data with maximum efficiency and minimum bias.

Selecting and Training Interviewers

Researchers would obviously prefer to select previously trained and experienced interviewers, but this is an elusive goal. Consequently, many studies employ graduate and undergraduate students. The necessary level of skill will depend on the nature of information you are trying to elicit: personal, sensitive material will require skilled interviewers.

The task of an interviewer is a responsible one, both in the manner of conducting an interview and in willingness to follow instructions. In training, a potential interviewer should observe interviews proceeding in the prescribed manner and then should have the opportunity to conduct practice interviews under observation. Some practice interviews should involve "live" respondents, that is, potential subjects from the study's sample. Practice sessions should also include

---

[6] One suggested alternative approach calls for comparing the responses of early returners and late returners to check for a response rate bias.

interviews that the researcher has arranged to present certain typical situations that the interviewer will encounter. These "rigged" interviews present trainees with a range of possible situations.

Training should also familiarize prospective interviewers with the forms that will be used in recording responses and keeping records of interviews. To control the sampling, the trainees must learn to determine whom they should interview. They also must know how to set up interview appointments, how to introduce themselves, how to begin interviews in a manner that will put the interviewees at ease, how to use response-keyed questions and other nonlinear approaches, how to record responses, and (if the job includes this task) how to code them.

All interviewers should receive similar training experiences where possible, for differences in interviewer style and approach represent a source of internal invalidity due to instrumentation bias. Interviewers are instruments for collecting data, and, as instruments, their own characteristics should affect the data as little as possible: Interviewers should reflect their respondents and not themselves. Of course, it is impossible to make perfect mirrors out of human interviewers, but if they are chosen from the same population and receive the same training and instructions, they should tend to become standardized against one another as a function of their training. Research may also benefit if the trainers divulge no more about the study to the interviewers than is absolutely necessary; training should not subtly make them confederates who may unconsciously bias the outcomes in the expected directions.

Conducting an Interview

The first task of an interviewer may be to select respondents, although some studies give interviewers lists of people to contact. Unless the interviewers are both highly trained and experienced, study directors should give them the names, addresses, and phone numbers of the people to be interviewed, along with a deadline for completion. The interviewer may then choose the interviewing order, or the researcher may recommend an order.

Typically, an interviewer proceeds by telephoning a potential respondent and, essentially, presenting a verbal cover letter. However, a phone conversation gives the interviewer the advantage of opportunities to alter or expand upon instructions and background information in reaction to specific concerns raised by potential respondents. During this first conversation, an interview appointment should also be made.

At the scheduled meeting, the interviewer should once again brief the respondent about the nature or purpose of the interview (being as candid as possible without biasing responses) and attempt to make the respondent feel at ease. This session should begin with an explanation of the manner of recording responses; if the interviewer will tape record the session, the respondent's assent should be obtained. At all times, interviewers must remember that they are data-collection instruments who must try to prevent their own biases, opinions, or curiosity from affecting their behavior. Interviewers must not deviate from their formats and interview schedules, although many schedules will permit some flexibility in choice of questions. The respondents should be kept from rambling, but not at the sacrifice of courtesy. (See Chapter 14 for additional information.)

CODING AND SCORING

Objectively Scored Items

Many questions, such as those presented in the form of rating scales or checklists, are precoded; that is, each response can be immediately and directly converted into an objective score. The researcher simply has to assign a score to each point on the list or scale. However, data obtained from interviews and questionnaires (often called *protocols*) may not contribute to the research in the exact form in which they are collected. Often further processing must convert them to different forms for analysis. This initial processing of information is called *scoring* or *coding*.

Consider Item 13 from the Career Awareness Scale, the sample questionnaire that appears in Figure 10.2:

13. I work at different kinds of part-time   1. A   2. O   3. S   4. N
    jobs.

You might assign *never* (N) a score of 1, *seldom* (S) a score of 2, *often* (O) a score of 3, and *always* (A) a score of 4. You could then add the scores on all the items to obtain a total score on the scale.[7]

Sometimes items are written in both positive and negative directions to avoid response bias. Consider the following two items on a questionnaire measuring attitudes toward school:

- I enjoy myself most of the time in school.
  strongly agree   agree   disagree   strongly disagree
- When I am in school I usually feel unhappy.
  strongly agree   agree   disagree   strongly disagree

If you were to score *strongly agree* for the first item as 4, then you would have to score the *strongly agree* response for the second item as 1, because strong agreement with the first item indicates that a respondent likes school whereas strong agreement with the second item indicates a dislike for school. To produce scores on these two items that you can sum to get a measure of how much a student likes school, you have to score them in opposite directions.

---

[7] Note that the numbers listed on the scale for the response choices have been reversed for scoring so that a higher score reflects more career awareness behavior.

Often a questionnaire or overall scale contains a number of subscales, each of which measures a different aspect of what the total scale measures. In analyzing subscale scores, a scoring key provides extremely helpful guidance. Typically, such a scoring key is a cardboard sheet or overlay with holes punched so that when it is placed over an answer sheet, it reveals only the responses to the items on a single subscale. One scoring key would be required for each subscale. Using answer sheets that can be read by optical scanners and scored by computers makes this process much easier.

Thus, in scoring objective items, such as rating scales and checklists, the first step is identification of the direction of items—separating reversed and nonreversed ones. The second step is assigning a numerical score to each point on the scale or list. Finally, subscale items should be grouped and scored.

By their very nature, ranking items carry associated scores, that is, the ranks for each item in the list. To determine the average across respondents for any particular item in the list, you can sum the ranks and divide by the number of respondents. All ranking items can be scored in this way. This set of averages can then be compared to that obtained from another group of respondents using the Spearman rank-order correlation procedure (described in the next chapter).

Some scales, such as those using the true-false and yes-no formats, lend themselves primarily to counting as a scoring procedure. Simply count the number of "true" or "yes" responses. However, you must still pay attention to reversed items. A "false" answer on a reversed item must be counted along with a "true" response on a nonreversed item. On a positively phrased item, for example, a "yes" would get a score of 1, and a "no" would get a score of 0. In contrast, on a negatively phrased item, a "yes" would get a score of 0, and a "no" would get a score of 1.

In another scoring procedure, a researcher can count people who fit into a particular category. For instance, if a questionnaire asks respondents to identify their gender, a scorer counts the number who indicate "male" and the number who indicate "female."

Generally speaking then, four scoring procedures apply to objective items:

1. *Scale scoring.* Where the item represents a scale, each point on the scale is assigned a score. After adjusting for reversal in phrasing, you can add a respondent's scores on the items within a total scale (or subscale) to get his or her overall score.
2. *Rank scoring.* A respondent assigns a rank to each item in a list. Here, typically, average ranks across all respondents are calculated for each item in the list.
3. *Response counting.* Where categorical or nominal responses are obtained on a scale (such as true-false), a scorer simply counts the number of agreeing responses by a respondent. This count becomes the total score on the scale for that respondent. Response counting works for a scale made up of more than one item, all presumably measuring the same thing.

4. *Respondent counting.* Where a questionnaire elicits categorical or nominal responses on single items, scoring can count the number of respondents who give a particular response to that item. By properly setting up the answer sheet in advance, mechanical procedures can complete respondent counts. Respondent counting enables a researcher to generate a *contingency* table (a four-cell table that displays the number of respondents simultaneously marking each of the two possible choices on two items) and to employ chi-square analysis (described in the next chapter). A contingency table is illustrated in Figure 10.10.

Fill-In and Free-Response Items

Although a scorer can apply any one of the four techniques described above to process fill-in and free-response items, the most common is respondent counting. However, before counting respondents, he or she must code their responses. Coding is a procedure for reducing data to a form that allows tabulation of response similarities and differences.

Suppose, for example, that an interviewer asks: Why did you leave school? Suppose, also, that the following potential responses to this question have been identified by the researcher:

___ Couldn't stand it (or some other indication of strong dislike)
___ Wasn't doing well
___ Waste of time
___ Better opportunities elsewhere
___ Other: _____

To maintain efficiency, researchers often establish such precoded response categories for fill-in and free-response items. Although respondents never see these

An Example of a Contingency Table

	Item 4: Sex		
	male	female	[For example, number of female high school graduates]
Item 5: high school graduate	47	59	106 (total high school graduates)
high school dropout	52	39	91 (total high school dropouts)
	99 (total males)	98 (total females)	197 (total number of respondents)

FIGURE 10.10

responses (if they did, the item would be a checklist), they appear on the interviewer's answer form; while the respondent is talking, she or he judges which one gives the best fit. Thus, these precoded response categories become a nominal checklist enabling the interviewer to code immediately the unstructured response into checklist form. As an alternative, the interviewer might indicate which of those reasons a respondent gave and rank their apparent importance to the respondent. Coding, therefore, represents a superimposition of a response format onto a free or unstructured response.

Often coding occurs before data collection by supplying interviewers with precoded interview schedules. While they ask open-ended questions and respondents give free responses, the interviewers attempt to catalog the responses into one or more category sets. Here are two examples to illustrate this point:

- *Question:* Whom do you consult when you have a problem in school?
  Answer: Mainly I go to my friends, especially my best buddy. Sometimes I talk to my rabbi.
  Coding: __ Parents   __X__ Friends
  __ Teacher(s)   __X__ Others: clergyman
  __ Counselor
- *Question:* What about school do you like least?
  Answer: I would say the work. I don't find my subjects interesting. They don't have anything to do with what I'm interested in.
  Coding: __ Teachers
  __ Organization
  __X__ Schoolwork
     __ boring
     __X__ irrelevant
     __ too easy
     __ too hard
  __ Other: _____

Of course, the coding scheme you employ in converting a response into analyzable data will be a function of the problem and the hypotheses with which you are working. Consider a hypothesis that youngsters in the upper third of the high school IQ distribution will be more likely to find their school work irrelevant than will youngsters in the middle or lower thirds. To test this hypothesis, you must find out how youngsters view their school work and then code their answers in terms of perceived relevance. The second example above represents an attempt to gather such information.

The extent to which precoding is possible is an indication of the extent to which the question is likely to yield relevant information. Precoding has the additional advantages of eliminating coding as a separate step in data reduction and providing the interviewer with an easy format for data collection.

Any attempt to design response-scoring codes must focus on the basic consideration of the information that you want to find out from the question. If you are testing to see whether tenured teachers are more or less interested in teaching effectiveness than nontenured teachers, you might ask: How interested are you in the objective determination of your teaching effectiveness? The interviewer could be provided with a rating scale such as:

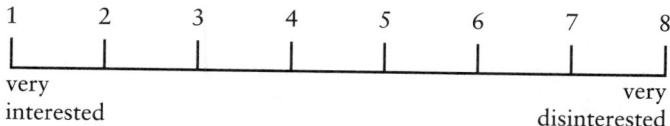

After listening to the teacher's free response to this question, the interviewer could summarize his or her opinion by placing a check on the rating scale. This method is an example of a *scale-scoring* approach to coding and scoring an open-ended response. An examination of the ratings indicated by the responses of the two groups of teachers would provide data to determine whether tenured or non-tenured teachers are more interested in teaching effectiveness. Alternatively, the response could be precoded as simply: _____ seems interested, _____ seems disinterested. This application represents the *respondent-counting* approach: Simply count the number of teachers in each group (tenured and nontenured) who were seen as interested as well as those seen as disinterested, and place the findings into a contingency table:

	interested in teaching effectiveness	disinterested in teaching effectiveness
tenured teachers		
nontenured teachers		

The discussion of coding so far has focused on applications of precoded categories. The same kinds of coding procedures can work in coding after data collections. Precoding has the advantage of greater efficiency than postcoding, which requires interviewers to record free responses verbatim (usually by tape recorder) or summarize them as respondents speak. These recordings are then transcribed by a typist and finally coded. However, coding after data collection has the advantage of careful preservation of coder reliability.

The reliability of coding judgments becomes an important issue here, just as the previous chapter considered the reliability of rating and coding techniques that describe behavior. If interviewers code every response, data analysts have no way to check the reliability of those coding decisions, because they lack any record of the responses. When interviewers do all the coding during the interviews rather than making verbatim records of responses, a researcher should be concerned about coding unreliability as a threat to instrumentation validity. To ensure this important priority, at least 20 percent of the responses should be recorded verbatim and then coded by at least two judges or interviewers, thus providing a sample of responses to assess intercoder reliability.

In postinterview coding, the response transcripts allow a second coder to code a sufficient number of protocols to establish reliability with the first coder, or for two coders to code all protocols to increase the reliability of the data.[8] Both first and second coders should be trained in the use of the coding system and complete practice trials under the scrutiny of the researcher. In such instances, reliabilities in the 0.70-to-0.90 range would be sufficient to prevent instrumentation bias in coding.

SUMMARY

1. Questionnaires and interviews provide self-reported data from respondents. Such data reflect what is inside a respondent's head, but they may be influenced by both self-awareness and the desire to create a favorable impression.
2. Questionnaire items represent five formats: (1) direct or obvious questions versus indirect or subtle questions; (2) specific or highly targeted questions versus nonspecific or relatively general questions; (3) fact versus opinion questions; (4) questions versus statements designed to stimulate agreement or disagreement; (5) predetermined questions versus response-keyed questions (those that depend on answers to previous questions).
3. Researchers employ seven response modes: (1) unstructured or open-ended responses; (2) fill-in responses; (3) tabular (table fill-in) responses; (4) scaled responses, in which respondents place themselves along a 5 (or more) point rating scale; (5) ranking responses, in which they rank order certain elements; (6) checklist responses, in which they check one or more selections that apply; (7) categorical responses, in which they check the one of two options that applies.
4. To construct a questionnaire or interview scale, a researcher completes the following five steps: (a) specifying the variables to be measured, or what she or he wants to find out; (b) choosing the question format(s) after considering the relative merits of each; (c) choosing the response modes depending on

---

[8] Where two coders code all protocols, their judgments can be averaged to obtain final scores. In such cases, the obtained reliability coefficients can be corrected by the Spearman-Brown formula (see Chapter 9), because the average is more reliable than either individual data set.

the type of data desired; (d) preparing either interview or questionnaire items; (e) pilot testing the instrument and evaluating the results using item analysis.

5. Sampling procedures begins with a definition of a study's population (setting its boundary characteristics). From this group, the researcher then draws a sample through simple random or stratified random sampling techniques, the latter requiring the establishment of sampling specifications. This careful process helps researchers to avoid subject selection bias that can affect external validity or generality.

6. Administration of a questionnaire requires (a) an initial mailing to a sample of respondents, accompanied by a cover letter to describe the study's purpose, protective measures for respondents, endorsements, legitimacy, debriefing, needed cooperation, and special instructions; (b) one or more follow-ups to those who do not respond; (c) a systematic attempt to get responses from 5 to 10 percent of the remaining nonrespondents (to evaluate the degree of potential mortality bias).

7. Conducting an interview study requires (a) selection and training of interviewers and (b) interviewing a sample of respondents.

8. Interview and questionnaire responses become usable data only after scoring or coding. For objectively scored items, scorers carry out four procedures: (1) scale scoring—totaling up scale points; (2) rank scoring—averaging ranks across respondents; (3) response counting—adding up the number of agreeing responses; (4) respondent counting—counting up the number of respondents who agree. Scoring for fill-in and free-response items requires a response-coding system that converts each response to quantitative data. The coded results may then be scored by any of the four procedures, most typically by respondent counting.

COMPETENCY TEST EXERCISES

1. Which of the following statements does *not* describe a purpose for which researchers use interviews and questionnaires?
   a. Finding out what a person thinks and believes
   b. Finding out what a person likes and dislikes
   c. Finding out how a person behaves
   d. Finding out what experiences a person has had

2. Which of the following limitations is *not* a shortcoming of a questionnaire or interview?
   a. The respondent may not know anything about the interviewer.
   b. The respondent may not know the information requested.
   c. The respondent may try to show himself or herself in a good light.
   d. The respondent may try to help by telling you what you expect to hear.

3. Match up the question types with the descriptions.
   a. Indirect question
   b. Specific question
   c. Question of opinion
   d. Statement
   e. Response-keyed question

   1. Declarative sentence form
   2. Requests reaction to a single object
   3. Next question depends on the response to this one
   4. Requests information for inferences
   5. Asks how the respondent feels about something

4. Match up the response types with the examples.
   a. Scaled response
   b. Fill-in response
   c. Ranking response
   d. Tabular response
   e. Checklist response
   f. Unstructured response
   g. Categorical response

   1. My favorite subject is (check one):
   English
   Chemistry
   Calculus
   2. My favorite subject is calculus. (yes, no).
   3. How do you feel about chemistry?
   4. English is a subject I (like a lot, like a little, dislike a little, dislike a lot).
   5. My favorite subject is _____ .
   6.

	English	Chem	Calc
Like			
Dislike			

   7. My order of preference of subjects is:
   English _____ (1,2,3)
   Chemistry _____ (1,2,3)
   Calculus _____ (1,2,3)

5. In the list of considerations, write *I* next to those suited to an interview and *Q* next to those suited to a questionnaire.
   a. I want to collect data from at least 90 percent of my sample. ___
   b. I want to keep my problems of data reduction to a minimum. ___
   c. I do not have very much money to conduct this project. ___
   d. I want to collect highly reliable data in this study. ___
   e. I'm not sure what questions respondents will likely answer. ___
   f. I have to ask some intensive questions, which may lead into sensitive areas. ___

6. In the list of considerations, write *F* next to those that support or describe the use of the fill-in response mode, *S* for those that support scaled response, *R* for ranking responses, and *C* for checklist or categorical responses.
   a. I do not have to anticipate potential responses. ___
   b. I want to gather ordinal data. ___
   c. This response mode does not provide for degrees of agreement, so it allows too few options. ___

d. I'll have a big scoring job. (Prescoring will be a difficult task.)___

e. I may get response bias away from the extremes.___

7. You are interested in finding out about the attitudes of teachers toward their school administration, particularly with regard to procedures for ordering classroom supplies. Construct three sequential interview questions.

8. You are interested in finding out about the attitudes of administrators toward teachers, particularly as regards their application of procedures for ordering classroom supplies. Construct three questionnaire items (using three different structured-response modes other than fill-in) to accomplish this goal.

9. You are planning to draw a stratified random sample of 200 from a high school population that contains 60 percent males and 40 percent females. Among the males, 40 percent are college prep majors, 10 percent business majors, 20 percent vocational majors, and 30 percent general majors. Among the females, 50 percent are college prep majors, 25 percent business majors, 5 percent vocational majors, and 20 percent general majors. How many respondents would you need in each of the eight categories?

10. You are going to interview 60 teachers in a school system of 200 teachers. The total includes 100 elementary school teachers—20 men and 80 women; 50 junior high school teachers—20 men and 30 women; and 50 high school teachers—30 men and 20 women. How many teachers in each of the six categories would you include in your sample of 60?

11. Which of the following subjects is *not* ordinarily discussed in a cover letter?

a. Protection afforded the respondent

b. Anticipated outcome of the study

c. Legitimacy of the researcher

d. Purpose of the study

12. You are planning to do a study of the relationship between a teacher's length of teaching experience and his or her attitudes toward discipline of students. You are sending out a questionnaire including an attitude scale and a biographical information sheet. Construct a sample cover letter to accompany this mailing.

RECOMMENDED REFERENCES

Berdie, D. R., Anderson, J. F., & Niebuhr, M. A. (1986). *Questionnaires: Design and use* (2nd ed.). Metuchen, NJ: Scarecrow Press.

Fowler, F. J. (1993). *Survey research methods* (2nd ed.). Beverly Hills, CA: Sage.

Lavrakas, P. J. (1987). *Telephone survey methods: Sampling, selection, and supervision.* Newbury Park, CA: Sage.

Part 4

CONCLUDING STAGES
Analyzing and Writing

Chapter 11

CARRYING OUT STATISTICAL ANALYSES

Objectives

▶ Choose a statistical test appropriate for different combinations of variables and different levels of measurement.

▶ Calculate a mean, median, and standard deviation.

▶ Code and roster data.

▶ Analyze data by computer and report statistical findings using (1) a t-test, (2) a Pearson product-moment correlation analysis and regression, (3) an analysis of variance, (4) a Mann-Whitney U-test, (5) a Spearman rank-order correlation, and (6) a chi-square test.

STATISTICAL CONCEPTS

Significance Testing

Statistical tests are major tools for data interpretation. By statistical testing, a researcher can compare groups of data to determine the probability that differences between them are based on chance, providing evidence for judging the validity of a hypothesis or inference.[1]

Imagine, for example, that you are comparing an experimental group to a control group on an achievement measure after collecting data from 50 students in each group. Now you want to ask, "Are the two groups equal in achievement, or is one group superior to the other?" If you calculate the mean or average achievement score (that is, the sum of the scores divided by the number of scores) for each group, the results may differ. But do they reflect real differences between the groups? How do you know that the differences are really due to the treatments you are comparing and not to chance fluctuations?

A statistical test can compare the means in this example relative to the degree of variation among scores in each group to determine the *probability* that the calculated differences between the means reflect real differences between subject groups and not chance occurrences. By considering the degree of variation within each group, statistical tests yield estimates of the probability or *stability* of particular findings. Thus, when a researcher reports that the difference between two means is significant at the .05 level (usually reported as $p < .05$), this information implies a probability less than 5 out of 100 that the difference is due to chance. (That is, the likelihood that the distribution of scores obtained in the study would occur simply as a function of chance is less than 5 percent.) On this basis, a researcher can conclude that the differences obtained were most likely the result of the treatment.

In statistical applications by behavioral scientists, the 5 percent level (that is, $p < .05$) often is considered an acceptable level of confidence to reject the null hypothesis (which implies equality between the means of the control and experimental groups). Nothing magic requires setting significance at the .05 level, though. It is simply an arbitrary level that many researchers have chosen as a decision point in either accepting a finding as reliable or rejecting it as sufficiently improbable to prevent confidence in its recurrence. Occasionally, research studies produce mean differences that are significant at the .01 confidence level. Differences at this level indicate a probability of only 1 out of 100 that chance alone would account for the differences.[2]

---

[1] Such statistical tests are referred to as *inferential statistics*. Statistics that describe a group of data (for example, a mean) are called *descriptive statistics*. This chapter deals with both, but primarily with the former.

[2] Although confidence levels are usually set at the 5 percent or 1 percent levels, findings that attain a degree of confidence between the .10 and .05 levels are often interpreted as indicators of trends.

Sampling Distribution

A *population* is the target group of a study, that is, the type of people the researcher is interested in studying. For example, one researcher might study a population of sixth-grade females. Since it is often impossible to test everyone in a population, unless that population is very narrowly defined, practicality requires selection of a small proportion of the population to test; that smaller number of subjects make up the study's *sample*. After testing the sample, the researcher draws conclusions about the population that the sample has been chosen to represent. The process of selecting a sample is called *sampling*.

A *distribution* is a set of scores arranged along some continuum. After computing the scores achieved by a sample of students on a test, data analysis might proceed by counting up the number of times or frequency with which each score appears. These counts become data in a plot of a frequency distribution of scores along the number line, as shown in the graph below.

If a researcher were to draw an infinite number of samples from a population, compute a mean score for each sample, and arrange these mean scores in the form of a distribution, these actions would produce a sampling distribution. This sampling distribution would more accurately represent characteristics of the population than any one sample could do. It would be an ideal version of the results. However, in reality, a typical researcher draws only a single sample, taken to be representative of the population. As the sample size increases, the match between the mean score and distribution of scores in the sample becomes a closer

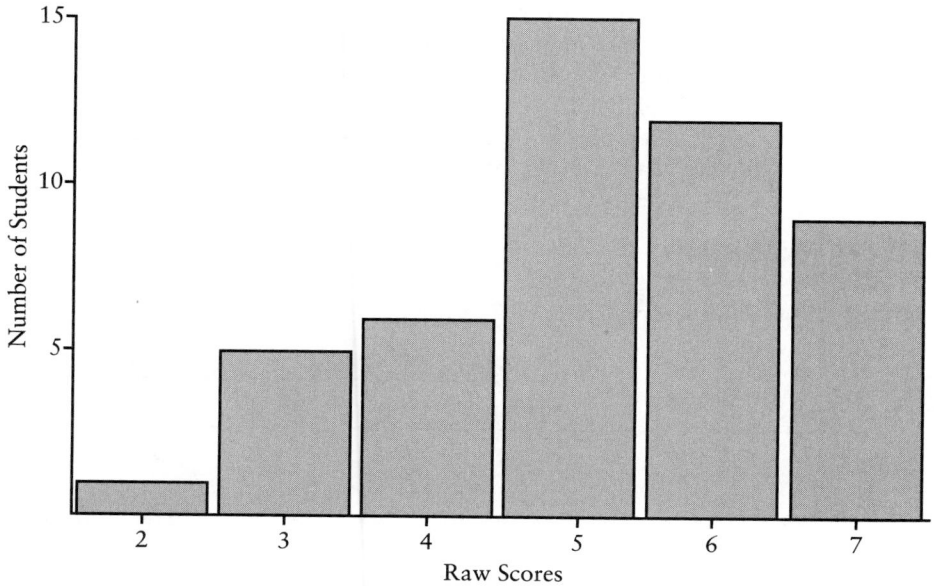

approximation of the sampling distribution. Since the sampling distribution is a theoretical representation of scores, statistical tests must establish probabilities about the extent to which the sample characteristics and sampling distribution characteristics correspond.

Types of Statistical Errors

Two kinds of hypotheses are important in using and understanding statistics: the null hypothesis and its alternative, the directional hypothesis. (See the last section of Chapter 4.) The null hypothesis, represented by H_0, predicts no differences between means for the experimental and control groups, while the directional hypothesis, represented by H_1, predicts a difference between means. The null hypothesis is held to be true unless evidence suggests another conclusion. In that case, researchers speak of "rejecting the null hypothesis." In the absence of such evidence, they accept the null hypothesis. Keep in mind that statistics allow a researcher to test the null hypothesis and determine whether evidence suggests rejecting or accepting it. If statistical results justify rejecting the null, then they provide support for the directional hypothesis.

However, such a conclusion can be affected by two types of statistical error. The first, called *alpha* or *Type I error,* is the risk of rejecting the null hypothesis (H_0) when it is, in fact, a true statement. This error represents a *false positive* result, the term for incorrectly attributing a difference to the means of two groups when they reflect the same value. In contrast, a *beta* or *Type II error* represents the risk of accepting the null hypothesis when it is, in fact, a false statement. This error represents a *false negative* result, the term for incorrectly believing the means of the two groups to be the same when they differ. The two types of errors are not independent of one another. A smaller Type I error corresponds to a larger potential Type II error, and vice versa. The definitions of the two types of errors are shown in Table 11.1.

If the two types of errors were considered to be equally serious, researchers would set equal significance levels for both. But Type I error is considered to be a more serious risk, because a false positive conclusion may lead people to rely

---

TABLE 11.1   **TWO TYPES OF STATISTICAL ERRORS**

	STATE OF AFFAIRS IN THE POPULATION	
DECISION	H_0 **True**	H_0 **False;** H_1 **True**
Reject H_0	Type I (α) error (false positive)	No error (power)
Do not reject H_0	No error	Type II (β) error (false negative)

on results that do not reflect true conditions. Because of the seriousness of a Type I error, it is ordinarily set at 5 percent, or the .05, level, meaning that researchers accept only 5 chances out of 100 of making such an error. If the Type I error were considered to be four times more serious than the Type II error, then Type II error would be represented by a significance level of .20.

One-Tailed and Two-Tailed Tests

A two-sided or two-tailed statistical test compares the null hypothesis that the means of two distributions are equal (H_0) against the alternative that they are not equal—meaning that the first may be either larger (H_1) or smaller (H_2) than the second. This term implies that the two tails or two sides of the normal distribution contribute to estimates of probabilities. A two-tailed test is concerned with the absolute magnitude of the difference regardless of sign or direction.

A researcher concerned with the direction of such a difference might employ a one-tailed or one-sided test. However, the one-tailed approach is a much less conservative evaluation than the two-tailed approach. A given degree of difference between means indicates half the likelihood that it resulted by chance in a one-tailed test as the same difference indicates in a two-tailed test. In other words, a difference that yields a p value at the .05 level in a one-tailed test will yield a p value at the .10 level in a two-tailed test. A one-tailed test thus doubles the probability of a Type I, or false positive, error. For this reason, two-tailed tests are recommended.

Sample Size

The primary issue in choosing a sample size requires a sufficiently large number of subjects to reveal the hypothesized difference, if it exists. Because of sampling errors and the other sources of internal invalidity described in Chapter 7, a study must test a number of cases in order to detect a hypothesized difference. The question of how many cases must be tested is the question of sample size.

Sample size depends on three factors: alpha level, power, and effect size. *Alpha level,* or magnitude of Type I error, has already been discussed. It is the probability of making a false positive conclusion or rejecting the null hypothesis when it is a true statement. It is usually set at .05.

The *power* of a statistical test of a null hypothesis is the probability of rejecting it when it is a false statement (Cohen, 1992). In other words, it is the probability of obtaining a statistically significant result. (In Table 11.1. the cell marked "power" indicates this possibility.) This value is the reciprocal of the Type II error (equal to 1.00 minus the Type II error level). Thus, if the Type II error is set at .20, power equals .80.

Finally, the *effect size* of a finding is its magnitude, generally regarded as an indication of its practical importance. In evaluating differences between groups, the effect size (*d*) is the degree of difference between treatment and control group means relative to, or divided by, the standard deviation of the control group (Cohen, 1992). According to Cohen (1988, 1992) a small effect size would be .2 (meaning that the mean difference was 20 percent as large as the standard deviation), a medium effect size is .5, and a large effect size is .8. As the effect size grows progressively larger, a study can more easily detect the effect (so it needs fewer cases).

Cohen (1988) provides tables for determining a sample size, given the alpha level, power, and effect size of a finding. He suggests (Cohen, 1992) a general strategy of setting alpha equal to .05, power equal to .80, and effect size equal to .2, .5, or .8, depending on your expectations. To carry out a two-tailed test between the means of two groups, a small effect size would require two groups of 393 subjects each, a medium effect size would require two groups of 64 each, and a large effect size would require two groups of 26 each. (For a one-tailed test at alpha = .05, the corresponding sample size numbers would be 310, 50, and 20.) If circumstances allowed you to test only a total of 100 subjects, you would likely obtain significant differences only for a relationship with a medium or larger effect size. Smaller effect sizes would be likely to result in acceptance of the null hypothesis.

Parametric and Nonparametric Statistical Tests

One group of statistical tests, called *parametric* tests, employs interval measurement of the dependent variable. That is, the dependent variable is a *parameter* or quantity characteristic of a population (Winer et al., 1991). The use of such a test requires conformance with certain assumptions:

1. *Normal distribution.* Parametric tests offer the most validity when they are performed on normally distributed data. A normal distribution (see Figure 11.1A) reflects data points that lie perfectly *symmetrically* about its mean, giving a bell-shaped curve. In contrast, the distributions of scores on the dependent variable for the different groups compared in a study (or on both variables in the case of a correlation) may reflect a *nonsymmetrical* or *skewed* distribution (see Figure 11.1B); a parametric statistical test of such data supports less valid conclusions than one performed on normally distributed data. As the skewness of a distribution increases, the validity of a parametric test on it falls.

2. *Homogeneity of variance.* Scores are easiest to compare parametrically when the data show an equal (homogeneous) variance or spread within the two groups. If two groups given an achievement test display equal means but different distributions, as shown in Figures 11.1C and 11.1D, respectively, a parametric test would be difficult to interpret, because of

GRAPHIC EXAMPLES OF DISTRIBUTION CURVES

FIGURE 11.1

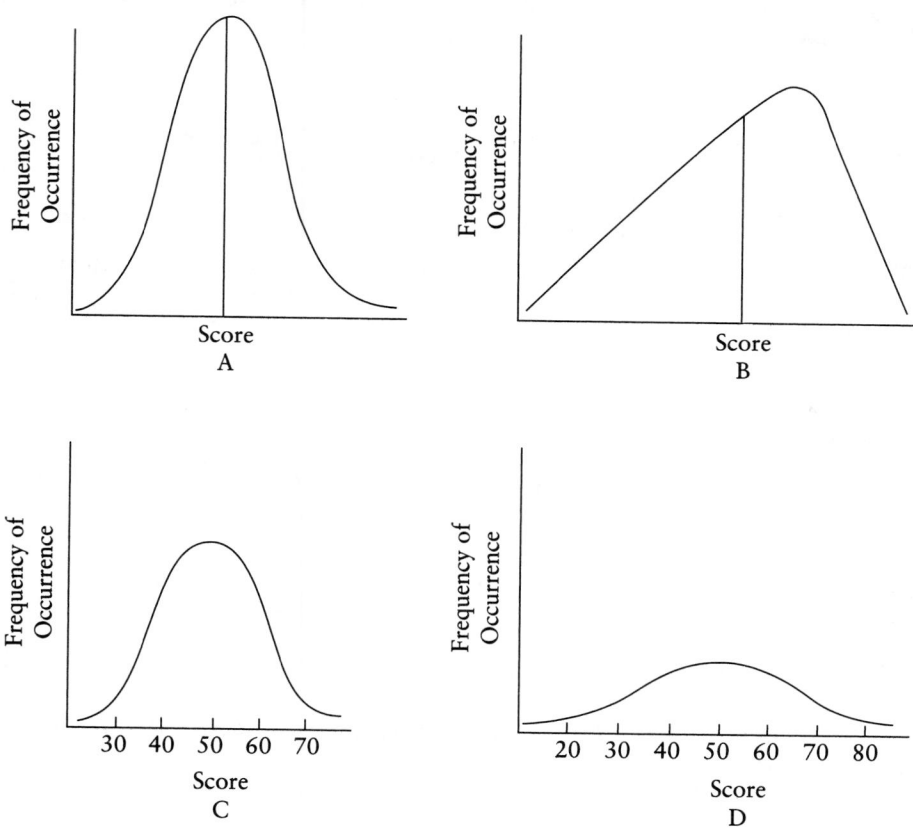

A, normal; B, skewed; C, low variance or spread in scores; and D, high variance or spread.

the differences in the spreads or variances within data for the two groups.

3. *Continuous equal interval measures.* Parametric tests, as conceived, can only accommodate scores (dependent measures) that represent interval scales; that is, the measurements must cover a continuous range of equal intervals. (This point is discussed more thoroughly in the next section.)

Compared to parametric tests, nonparametric tests make fewer assumptions about distributions; they require neither normal distributions or equal group variances. They are based on ordinal or nominal measurement techniques and allow some highly useful, quick calculations. They are also useful for large samples that do not satisfy the assumptions for parametric techniques, for very small samples, and for studies involving ordinal measuring devices.

MEASURES OF CENTRAL TENDENCY AND VARIABILITY

The two main measures of central tendency are the mean and the median. The principal statistical measure of variability is the standard deviation. Each is described in this section.

Mean

The *mean,* or average, is computed by adding a list of scores and then dividing by the number of scores. Its algebraic formula is:

$$\overline{X} = \frac{\Sigma X}{N}$$

where $\overline{X}$ is the mean, ΣX is the sum of the Xs, or individual scores, and N is the number of scores.

Consider an example. Fifteen students took a mathematics exam, earning the following scores:

98	89	78
97	89	73
95	84	70
93	82	60
90	82	50

To determine the mean score on this math test, add the 15 scores (that is, $\Sigma X =$ 1,230), then divide that sum by $N(15)$ to give $\overline{X} = 82.0$.

Median

The *median* is the score in the middle of a distribution: 50 percent of the scores fall above it, and 50 percent fall below it. In the table of 15 scores, the median score is 84. Seven scores are higher and seven are lower than that one. In a list containing an even number of scores, the middle two scores would be averaged to get the median.

The median is not as sensitive to extreme scores as is the mean. The mean defines the "middle" of a set of scores considered in terms of their *values,* whereas the median defines the "middle" of the distribution in terms of the *number* of scores. Note that the mean of the 15 scores is lower than the median, because two or three extremely low scores reduce the total.

Standard Deviation

The *standard deviation (s)* is a measure of the spread or dispersion of a set of scores. It can be calculated using the following formula:

$$s = \sqrt{\frac{\Sigma(X - \overline{X})^2}{N - 1}}$$

Note that the deviation of each score from the mean $X - \overline{X}$ is squared; these squared deviations are then summed, the result divided by $N - 1$, and the square root taken. This formula is offered, because it helps to illustrate the conceptual basis for a standard deviation calculation. For easier calculation, however, the following formula may be substituted.

$$s = \sqrt{\frac{N\Sigma X^2 - (\Sigma X)^2}{N(N - 1)}}$$

The term ΣX^2 indicates that you square each score and then sum the squares; first you square, then you sum. The term (ΣX^2) indicates that you add the scores together and then square the total; first you sum, then you square.

The scores in the preceding table would give the following calculation:

$$s = \sqrt{\frac{(15)(103,546) - (1,230)^2}{15(15 - 1)}}$$

$$s = \sqrt{\frac{1,553,190 - 1,512,900}{15(14)}}$$

$$s = \frac{40,290}{210} = \sqrt{191.9}$$

$$s = 13.8$$

Thus, the scores have a spread, or standard deviation, of 13.8, a value that reflects the range or difference between the highest and lowest score. Typically, increasing standard deviation reflects wider dispersion from the mean of the highest and lowest scores.

The square of the standard deviation is referred to as the *variance (s^2)* of a group of scores. In the example, the variance equals 191.9.

CHOOSING THE APPROPRIATE STATISTICAL TEST

Recall that the purpose of a statistical test is to evaluate the match between the data collected from two or more samples. Further, statistical tests help to determine the possibility that chance fluctuations have accounted for any differences between results from the samples.

To choose the appropriate statistic, first determine the number of independent and dependent variables in your study. (For statistical purposes, consider moderator variables as independent variables.) Next, distinguish nominal, ordinal, and interval variables. (These terms are explained in Chapter 9.) After making these determinations, refer to Table 11.2 for more specific information.

Notice in the table that if *both* independent and dependent variables are interval measures, correlation techniques (parametric correlations) may be employed. Ordinal measurement generally calls for nonparametric techniques.

Researchers rely on a basic tool kit of six commonly used statistical tests. If you are dealing with *two interval* variables, use a parametric correlation called the *Pearson product-moment correlation*. When dealing with *two ordinal* variables, most researchers use a Spearman rank-order correlation. With *two nominal* variables, they use the chi-square statistic. For a study with a *nominal independent* variable and an *interval dependent* variable with only two conditions or levels, use a *t*-test; use analysis of variance to evaluate more than two conditions or more than one independent variable. Finally, the combination of a *nominal independent* variable and an *ordinal dependent* variable requires a Mann-Whitney *U*-test (a nonparametric version of the *t*-test).[3]

Researchers often transform variables to render the data they collect suitable to specific statistical tests (which may differ from those originally anticipated for the studies). For instance, if interval performance data are available in a two-condition study, but they do not satisfy the conditions for a *t*-test (normal distribution, equal sample variance), you could transform the interval dependent variable into an ordinal measure and use a Mann-Whitney *U*-test.

Consider another example. Suppose you are studying the effect of programmed science materials on learning, with student IQ as a moderator variable. One of the independent variables is a nominal variable—programmed learning versus traditional teaching—whereas the second, IQ, is an interval variable. The dependent variables, you decide, are subsequent performance on an achievement test (interval) and attitudes as measured by an attitude scale (interval). How should you proceed? The first step is to convert the second independent variable (IQ) from an interval variable to a nominal variable. (Recall from Chapter 9 that you can always convert from a *higher* order of measurement to a *lower* order—from interval to ordinal or nominal, or from ordinal to

---

[3] These tests are described in more detail in the subsequent pages.

TABLE 11.2

BASIS FOR SELECTING A STATISTICAL TEST

Type and Number of Independent Variables

Type and Number of Dependent Variables		Interval (Column A)		Ordinal (Column B)		Nominal (Column C)	
		1	More than 1	1	More than 1	1	More than 1
Interval (Row 1)	0		Factor analysis				
	1	Correlation	Multiple correlation	Transform ordinal variable into nominal and use C-1, or transform the interval variable into ordinal and use B-2, or transform both variables into nominal and use C-3		Analysis of variance (or t-test)	Analysis of variance
	More than 1	Multiple correlation					
Ordinal (Row 2)	0				Coefficient of concordance (W)		
	1	Transform ordinal variable into nominal and use C-1, or transform the interval variable into ordinal and use B-2, or transform the interval variable into nominal and use C-2		Spearman correlation, Kendall's τ		Sign test, median test, U-test, Kruskal-Wallis	Friedman's two-way analysis of variance
	More than 1						
Nominal (Row 3)	0						
	1	Analysis of variance (see C-1)		Sign test, median test, U-test, Kruskal-Wallis (see C-2)		Phi Coeff. (ϕ), Fisher exact test, chi-square	Chi-square
	More than 1	Analysis of variance (see C-1)		Friedman's two-way analysis of variance			

nominal—but that converting from a *lower* to a *higher* order of measurement is not advised.)

To convert an interval variable to a nominal variable, separate the students into groups based on their scores on the interval measure. Place the scores on IQ (or another interval variable) in numerical order (that is, essentially, recast the interval data in ordinal form) and locate the median score. You can then label everyone above the median as high IQ and everyone below the median as low IQ, thus assigning Ss to a high category or a low category. As an alternative, the students could be broken into three groups—high, medium, and low—by dividing the total group into equal thirds, or *tertiles*. Categorical assignment to groups represents nominal measurement.

Next draw a diagram of the design and enter the data into it, as shown in Figure 11.2. Because the dependent variables will be analyzed separately, draw one diagram for each variable.

Now that you have two nominal independent variables and an interval dependent variable, the analysis of variance technique allows for evaluation of the data.[4] Be sure to keep in mind the three conditions discussed in the previous section that must be met to justify the use of parametric statistical techniques.

FIGURE 11.2   DEPENDENT VARIABLE SCORES IN A DESIGN WITH TWO NOMINAL INDEPENDENT VARIABLES[a]

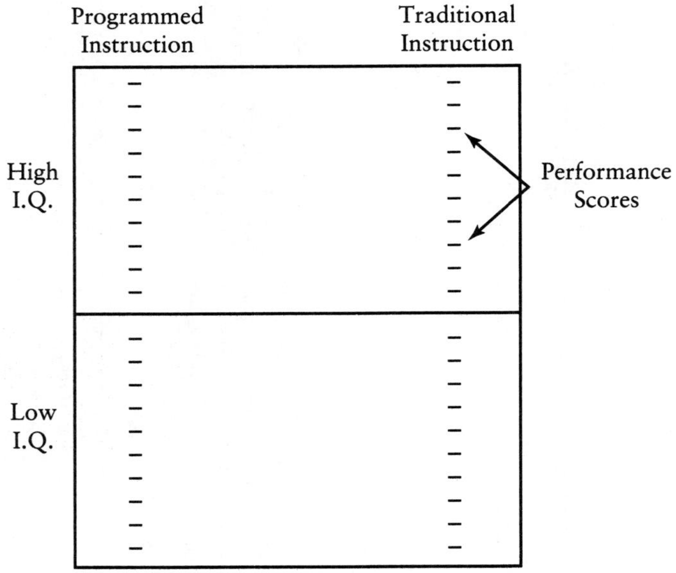

[a]Actually an independent variable plus a moderator.

---

[4] You could also conduct an analysis of covariance prior to converting IQ scores to nominal form.

CODING AND ROSTERING DATA

Ordinarily, a researcher does not analyze data in word form. For instance, a data-processing device cannot conveniently record the fact that a subject was male or female through the use of those words. The solution is to assign a numerical *code:* Perhaps each male subject would be coded as 1 and each female subject as 2. The numerical code gives another name to a datum, but one that is shorter than its word name and therefore easier to record, store, process, and retrieve.

Such codes are used regularly in data processing. Similar techniques allow you to code characteristics like the subject's name, gender, socioeconomic status, years of education completed, and so on. Consider the simple data codes shown in Table 11.3.

TABLE 11.3

SIMPLE DATA CODES

EXAMPLE 1	EXAMPLE 2	EXAMPLE 3
Gender	**Marital Status**	**Hair Color**
1 = male	1 = single	1 = brown
2 = female	2 = married	2 = black
	3 = divorced	3 = blonde
	4 = widowed	4 = red
		5 = other

EXAMPLE 4	EXAMPLE 5	EXAMPLE 6
Years of Education	**Occupational Categories**[a]	**Subject Matter**
1 = some high school	1 = professional, technical, and managerial	1 = English
2 = high school graduate	2 = clerical and sales	2 = Social studies
3 = some college	3 = service	3 = Mathematics
4 = college graduate	4 = farming, fishery, forestry, and others related	4 = Science
5 = professional or graduate training	5 = processing	
	6 = machine trades	
	7 = bench work	
	8 = structural work	
	9 = miscellaneous	

[a]From the *Dictionary of Occupational Titles.*

Note that the data are collected in nominal categories designated by word name (for example, single, married, divorced) and that the word name of each category is then replaced by a number. The researcher makes an arbitrary choice of which number represents which word. Typically, however, consecutive numbers are chosen; when appropriate, one number (usually the last in the series) is reserved for a category labeled "other" or "miscellaneous."

Numerical data codes are essential for nominal data, which are typically collected in word form and must therefore be coded to obtain numerical indicators of categories. These codes can also be assigned to interval data (or ordinal data) if, to facilitate data storage or analysis, you desire to replace a long series of numbers with a shorter one, or if you choose to convert these data to nominal form. (Coding produces nominal data, because it groups scores into categories.) For instance, if your subjects' ages run from a low of 16 years old to a high of 60 years old, you can replace an interval scale of 45 possible scores (individual ages) with a compressed scale of five categories (which would then be considered nominal categories for computations): Ages 11 to 20 receive the code 1; ages 21 to 30 receive 2; ages 31 to 40 receive 3; ages 41 to 50 receive 4; and ages 51 to 60 receive 5.[5]

To summarize, researchers have several options with interval data. They can retain them in interval form and use the two-digit numbers collected for subjects' ages, or they can treat the data as classes or categories by coding them into nominal form. If they choose to use a statistic requiring nominal data, such as chi-square analysis, they would have to adopt the second option.

Coding can also define ordinal categories within a series of scores. Thus, 1 might represent scores in the high 20 percent of a series, 2 those in the second highest 20 percent, and so on, down to 5 for those in the lowest 20 percent. Consider an example of scores from a class of 25 students:

	98	84	79	70	60
	96	84	78	69	58
	94	84	77	68	53
	92	80	77	68	42
	87	80	71	65	30
Code	1	2	3	4	5

This coding system ensures that an equal number of scores will fall into each coding category; it offers an attractive system for a study that requires equal numbers of scores in a category. (It can also be used to compare the distributions of two independent samples using chi-square analysis.)

Some examples of more complex coding systems for converting interval scores to ordered categories appear in Table 11.4. Computations based on

---

[5] Technically, age is a *ratio* scale; that is, it has a true zero point, which occurs at birth. Also, the years of education scale shown as Example 4 in Table 11.3 could be treated as an *ordinal* scale, because each number represents a numerically higher degree of education.

COMPLEX DATA CODES

TABLE 11.4

EXAMPLE 1	EXAMPLE 2
Weight in Pounds	**Number of Correct Responses**
1 = under 121	01 = 0–5
2 = 121–140	02 = 6–10
3 = 141–160	03 = 11–15
4 = 161–180	04 = 16–20
5 = 181–200	05 = 21–25
6 = 201–220	06 = 26–30
7 = over 220	07 = 31–35
	08 = 36–40
	09 = 41–45
	10 = 46–50

EXAMPLE 3	EXAMPLE 4
Grade	**Grade**
1 = 90 and above	1 = top 10% (percentile 91–100)
2 = 80–89	2 = next to top 20% (percentile 71–90)
3 = 70–79	3 = middle 40% (percentile 31–70)
4 = 60–69	4 = next to lowest 20% (percentile 11–30)
5 = 59 and below	5 = lowest 10% (percentile 1–10)

such categories are still likely to treat them as nominal variables. Note that the coding schemes avoid labeling any category as 0. It is recommended that a coding category begin with 1 or 01 and that 0 be used only to designate *no data*. Note also that in each case, the number of digits in the code must be the same as the number of digits in the last category of the coded data. Because the number 10 in Example 2 has two digits, a two-digit code must be used from the beginning. A coding scheme for 350 categories would require three-digit codes, because the number 350 has three digits.

It is important to emphasize that all data should not be automatically coded. Actual data values may be rostered and analyzed. Data codes are assigned (1) when interval or ordinal data have been collected but discrete data categories (nominal data) are desired for analysis purposes, or (2) when the data themselves come in nominal form (that is, as words).

The step between data collection and data analysis, *data rostering,* is the procedure by which data are recorded for use in a statistical analysis. In fact, the following discussion of data rostering is predicated on the expectation that the next step will be analysis.

TABLE 11.5

DATA CODES FOR THE READING STUDY

SUBJECT NUMBER	TREATMENT	SEX	IQ	PARENT'S INCOME
01 = Johnny J.	1 = Readiness and sight reading	1 = male	1 = high	1 = under $12,000
02 = George T.	2 = Sight reading only	2 = female	2 = low	2 = $12,000–$25,000
03 = Nancy R.	3 = Readiness only			3 = over $25,000
•	4 = Phonics approach			
•				
•				
32 = Blair Z.				

Suppose that children participating in a study concerning reading methods were grouped as follows: (1) eight children were given readiness instruction and then sight reading training, (2) eight children received sight reading training only, (3) eight children received readiness instruction only, and (4) eight children received reading training using a phonics approach. Type of treatment represents the major independent variable in this study. As a moderator variable, half of the children in each treatment group were boys. As a second moderator variable, half of the boys and half of the girls in each treatment group had scored above the group mean on the Stanford-Binet IQ test. The parents' income served as a control variable. Codes necessary for rostering these data appear in Table 11.5.

Once you have prepared the coding scheme, the next step is to either prepare a data sheet or enter the data into a computer. It is helpful to indicate on a separate piece of paper which are the independent, moderator, control, and dependent variables for each analysis.

The dependent variables in this study include rate, accuracy, and comprehension scores on the school's own reading test and scores on the Picture Reading Test. In addition, the number of days absent from school were rostered, as well as the scores on a group IQ test administered at the end of the experiment. The sample roster sheet appears in Table 11.6.

Note that the first five items on the roster have been designated by codes, while the remaining six are actual scores. Decimal points can be eliminated when they are in a constant position for each variable and add nothing to the data. However, maintaining them, as in the grade equivalency scores on the Picture Reading Test in Table 11.6 (next to last column), often aids interpretation of the data roster and subsequent results.

TABLE 11.6

DATA ROSTER FOR THE READING STUDY

SUBJECT NUMBER	TREATMENT	SEX	IQ	PARENTS' INCOME	DAYS ABSENT	SCHOOL READING TEST				GROUP IQ
						RATE	ACCURACY	COMPREHENSION	PICTURE READING TEST	
01	1	1	1	2	00	21	07	18	2.4	115
02	1	1	1	3	01	19	10	16	3.1	095
03	1	1	2	3	01	09	04	17	0.9	101
04	1	1	2	1	05	17	02	10	1.6	097
05	1	2	1	2	00	22	14	04	1.8	122
06	1	2	1	2	11	14	06	11	2.0	124
07	1	2	2	1	08	13	12	18	1.1	110
08	1	2	2	1	07	16	03	16	1.2	104
09	2	1	1	1	01	11	04	17	0.3	122
10	2	1	1	2	04	18	09	12	0.9	100
11	2	1	2	1	01	25	02	14	2.9	101
12	2	1	2	2	03	23	12	15	1.0	099
13	2	2	1	3	06	11	08	10	2.1	133
14	2	2	1	3	09	17	11	14	2.1	130
15	2	2	2	2	06	29	14	11	1.0	129
16	2	2	2	1	00	13	08	16	2.0	103
17	3	1	1	3	02	15	10	12	3.0	092
18	3	1	1	1	06	17	10	09	2.8	104
19	3	1	2	2	08	27	06	23	2.0	101
20	3	1	2	2	10	25	14	17	1.7	093
21	3	2	1	1	01	13	12	16	2.2	109
22	3	2	1	1	02	24	09	21	2.7	131
23	3	2	2	2	06	31	10	14	2.5	105
24	3	2	2	3	03	15	15	18	2.9	108
25	4	1	1	2	05	19	10	17	1.8	111
26	4	1	1	1	11	13	12	18	0.6	130
27	4	1	2	2	01	25	08	12	1.5	090
28	4	1	2	1	10	30	09	13	1.9	100
29	4	2	1	3	07	19	19	24	2.6	119
30	4	2	1	1	03	11	15	23	2.0	124
31	4	2	2	2	03	18	10	20	3.5	101
32	4	2	2	3	09	24	15	15	2.1	095

INPUTTING DATA

Later sections of this chapter describe procedures for conducting data analyses using six different statistical tests in the popular software package SPSS (SPSS, 1997). The tests include a *t*-test, parametric correlation/regression, analysis of variance, Mann-Whitney *U*-test, Spearman rank-order correlation, and chi-square test. Running SPSS on a personal computer provides a much more practical and convenient method of data analysis than either hand computation or using a mainframe computer. While other software packages are available, SPSS appears to be the most widely used, especially on college campuses. To use SPSS (or any other computer package), a researcher must input data in a preestablished format. This section reviews the procedure for inputting data into SPSS, taking as an example a second version of the reading study described in the previous section. (The instructions assume that you have loaded the software for SPSS, either the Windows or Macintosh version, onto your personal computer.)

When you open the SPSS software, you see a grid for entering data. Each column represents a variable and each row represents a subject. The variable columns are numbered, but numbers can be replaced by names by double clicking on each variable number and entering a shorthand name for the variable in the dialog box that appears. You can read and interpret printouts more easily when they show variable names than when they show only column numbers. After labeling columns, enter data for each subject on each variable.

The SPSS data roster in Table 11.7 (readexp2) will provide values for all the data analyses in the following sections. Variable names have been shortened to fit the software format, and all entries have been carried out to two decimal places. Variables entered (and shown in Table 11.7) are as follows: (1) treatment, (2) sex, (3) IQ, (4) reading rate, (5) reading accuracy, (6) reading comprehension, and (7) picture reading score. The first three variables—treatment, sex, and IQ—represent nominal data coded into levels as shown earlier in Table 11.5. Treatment has four levels and sex and IQ two each. Reading rate is a time measure, so comparatively low scores represent fast and hence effective readers. Reading accuracy is an error measure, so comparatively low scores represent few errors, hence effective readers. Reading comprehension and picture reading represent proficiency test scores, so high scores represent good readers.

Once the data are entered, they can be saved with the filename "readexp2" (see Table 11.7).[6] You are now ready for high-speed data analysis. These data will be analyzed seven different ways to illustrate different statistical tests.

---

[6] The specific software used in the examples is SPSS, Version 6.1, for the Macintosh. It is stored on the hard drive (HD) of the computer. The same procedures can be employed for the Windows version of SPSS.

TABLE 11.7

DATA INPUT FOR **READEXP2**

	TREATMNT	SEX	IQ	READRATE	READACCU	READCOMP	PICREAD
1	1.00	1.00	1.00	21.00	7.00	18.00	2.40
2	1.00	1.00	1.00	19.00	4.00	17.00	3.10
3	1.00	1.00	2.00	9.00	10.00	12.00	.90
4	1.00	1.00	2.00	17.00	9.00	15.00	1.60
5	1.00	2.00	1.00	22.00	2.00	23.00	1.80
6	1.00	2.00	1.00	14.00	6.00	20.00	2.00
7	1.00	2.00	2.00	13.00	6.00	19.00	1.10
8	1.00	2.00	2.00	16.00	12.00	17.00	1.20
9	2.00	1.00	1.00	11.00	8.00	17.00	1.00
10	2.00	1.00	1.00	18.00	11.00	12.00	2.90
11	2.00	1.00	2.00	25.00	14.00	15.00	.30
12	2.00	1.00	2.00	23.00	11.00	14.00	.90
13	2.00	2.00	1.00	11.00	8.00	21.00	2.10
14	2.00	2.00	1.00	17.00	9.00	14.00	2.10
15	2.00	2.00	2.00	29.00	10.00	9.00	1.00
16	2.00	2.00	2.00	13.00	10.00	12.00	2.00
17	3.00	1.00	1.00	15.00	8.00	17.00	3.00
18	3.00	1.00	1.00	17.00	12.00	16.00	2.80
19	3.00	1.00	2.00	27.00	19.00	14.00	2.00
20	3.00	1.00	2.00	25.00	15.00	18.00	1.70
21	3.00	2.00	1.00	13.00	10.00	18.00	2.20
22	3.00	2.00	1.00	24.00	12.00	13.00	2.70
23	3.00	2.00	2.00	31.00	19.00	12.00	1.80
24	3.00	2.00	2.00	15.00	15.00	13.00	.60
25	4.00	1.00	1.00	19.00	14.00	15.00	2.50
26	4.00	1.00	1.00	13.00	9.00	20.00	2.90
27	4.00	1.00	2.00	25.00	15.00	10.00	1.50
28	4.00	1.00	2.00	30.00	16.00	11.00	1.90
29	4.00	2.00	1.00	19.00	12.00	20.00	2.60
30	4.00	2.00	1.00	11.00	10.00	23.00	2.00
31	4.00	2.00	2.00	18.00	12.00	12.00	1.80
32	4.00	2.00	2.00	24.00	14.00	13.00	.60

Carrying Out Parametric Statistical Tests

The t-Test

A *t*-test is a statistical test that allows you to compare two means to determine the probability that the difference between them reflects a real difference between the groups of subjects rather than a chance variation in data. To run the *t*-test using SPSS, go to the menu labeled STATISTICS, pull it down to reveal the choices, and click on INDEPENDENT SAMPLES t-TEST. (The program offers other *t*-tests, as well, but this example requires comparing two different groups, each made up of different subjects, so this is the appropriate form of the test.)

This illustration of the *t*-test will treat picture reading as the dependent (or test) variable and IQ as the independent (or grouping) variable, in order to determine whether students of high IQ read at a higher rate (that is, faster or in less time) than do students of low IQ. In SPSS, choose picture reading as the test variable and IQ as the grouping variable. Because IQ is a nominal or grouped variable, it is necessary to designate group makeup. To do this, choose "Define Groups," and designate the high IQ group (Group 1) as 1 and the low IQ group (Group 2) as 2, as shown in Table 11.5 under IQ. These designations will enable the computer to divide subjects into the proper IQ groups. Now click on "Continue" and then "OK," and the computer will do the analysis and report the results, as shown in Table 11.8.

Picture reading is actually a measure of reading proficiency, and the results show that the high-IQ students (IQ 1) are more proficient readers than are the

TABLE 11.8   *T*-Tests for Independent Samples of IQ on Picture Reading

VARIABLE	NUMBER OF CASES	MEAN	SD	SE OF MEAN
PICREAD				
IQ 1	16	2.3813	.548	.137
IQ 2	16	1.3063	.552	.138

Mean Difference = 1.0750
Leverne's Test for Equality of Variances: F = .231 p = .634

	t-TEST FOR EQUALITY OF MEANS				95% CI
VARIANCES	*t*-VALUE	DF	2-TAIL SIG	SE OF DIFF	FOR DIFF
Equal	5.53	30	.000	.194	(.678, 1.472)
Unequal	5.53	30.00	.000	.194	(.678, 1.472)

low-IQ students (IQ 2), with means of 2.3813 and 1.3063 respectively. The resulting *t* value of 5.53 (positive because the second mean was subtracted from the first), with 30 degrees of freedom (df = N − 2), is significant at *p* = .000.[7] You can look in Table II in Appendix C under df = 30 and see that for *p* < .01 (for a two-tailed test), a *t* value of 3.646 or higher indicates a significant result; the calculated *t* of 5.53 greatly exceeds that level of significance.

(To see the exact computational procedures for calculating the value of *t,* go to Figure I in Appendix E. An examination of this figure shows the steps undertaken in carrying out this statistical test.)

Parametric (Pearson) Correlation and Regression

The parametric (Pearson) correlation helps researchers to deal with pairs of interval variables, each of which is normally distributed. A correlation is an indication of the predictability of one variable, given the other. It is an indication of covariation.

The relationship between two variables can be examined by plotting the paired measurements on graph paper. (It can also be done, considerably more quickly, using SPSS or other statistical software packages.) Such a plot, which represents each pair of observations by a single point, is called a *scatter diagram.* Some examples appear in Figure 11.3. A scatter diagram enables you to see the degree of relationship between two variables.

CORRELATION SCATTER DIAGRAMS FIGURE 11.3

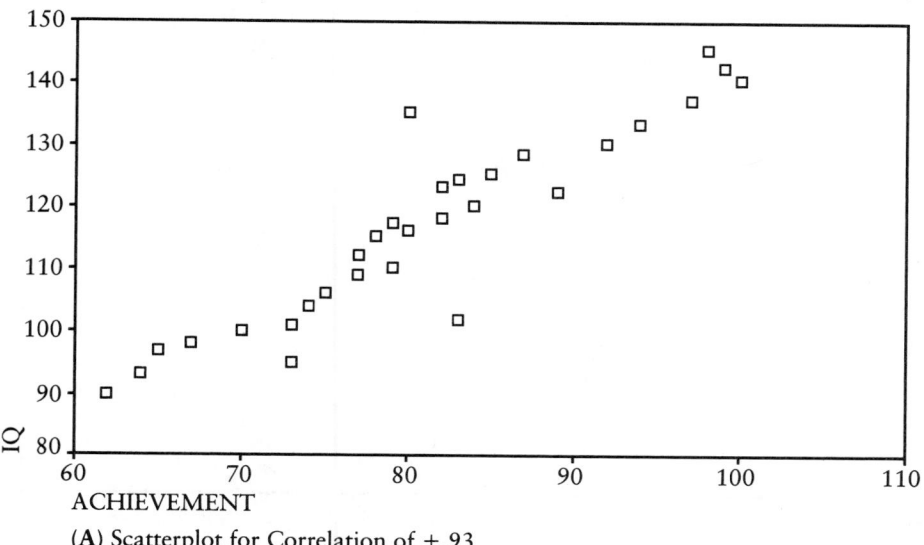

(A) Scatterplot for Correlation of +.93

---

[7] This means *p* < .0001, because the program carries the significance value only to three decimal places.

FIGURE 11.3   **Correlation Scatter Diagrams–*continued***

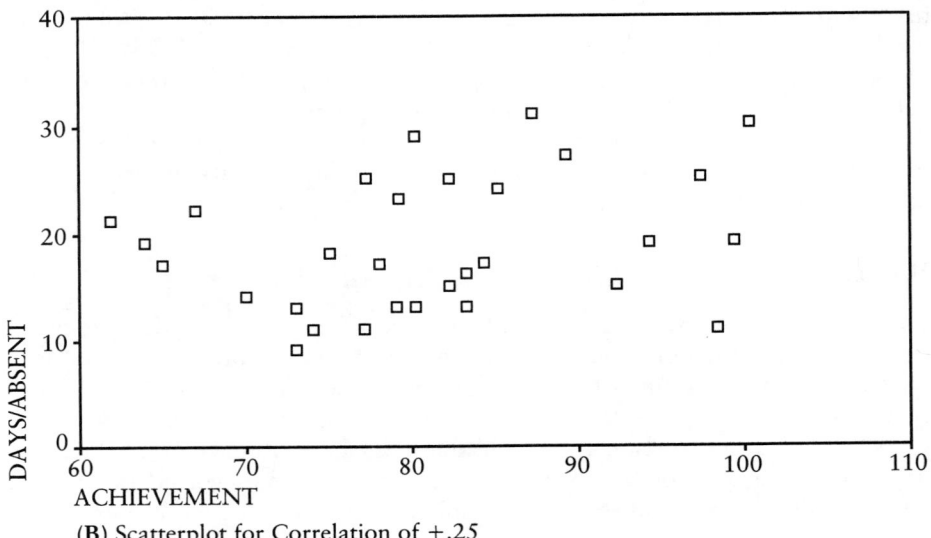

(**B**) Scatterplot for Correlation of +.25

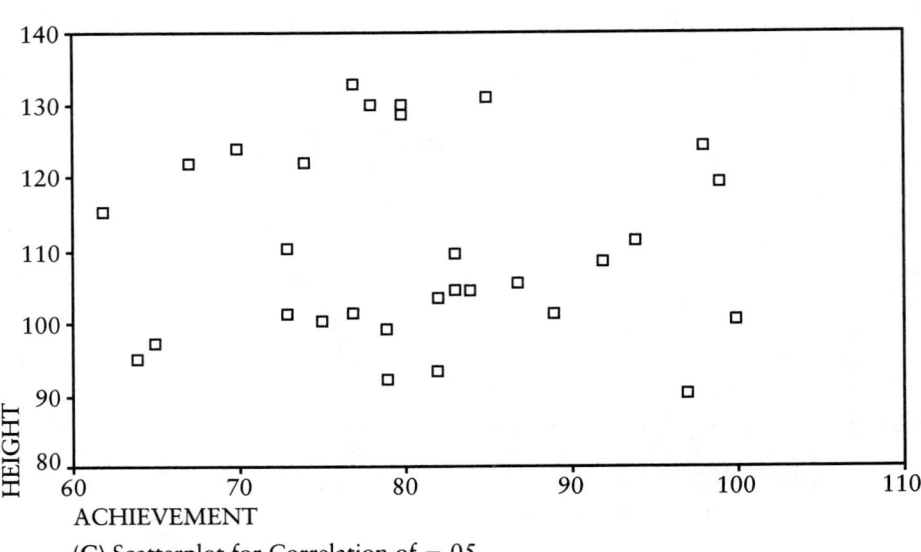

(**C**) Scatterplot for Correlation of −.05

CORRELATION SCATTER DIAGRAMS–*continued*

FIGURE 11.3

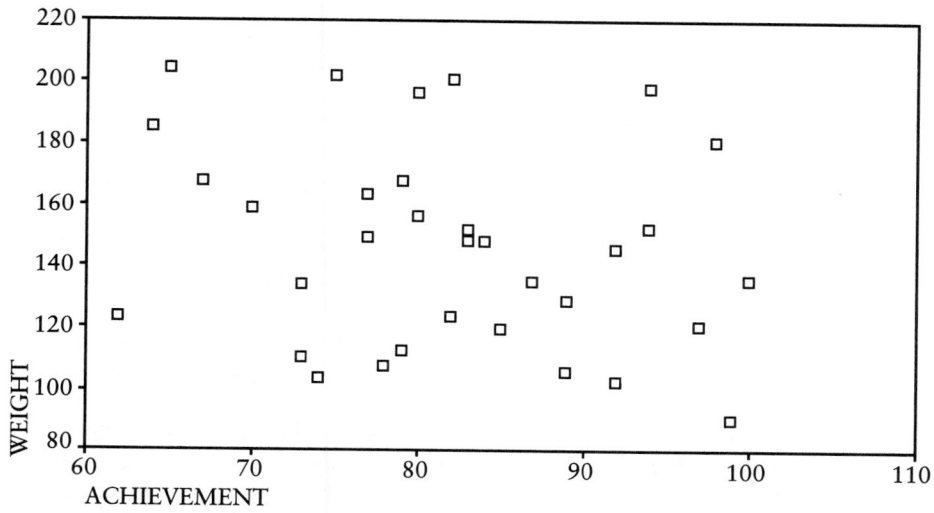

(D) Scatterplot for Correlation of −.25

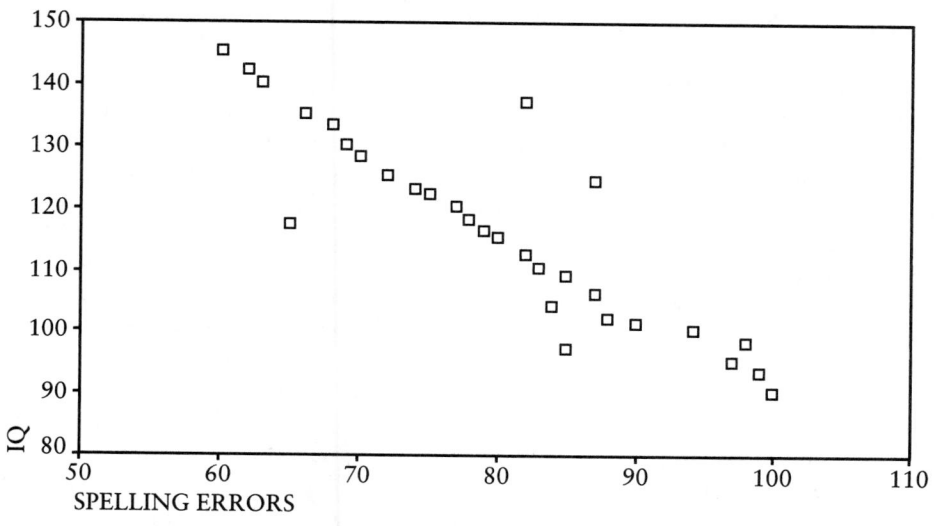

(E) Scatterplot for Correlation of −.90

To illustrate this analysis, consider the correlations between pairs of variables in the example reading experiment. Using a computer, it is easy to compute a matrix of correlations between each pair of variables in a set. The data from Table 11.7 (read exp2) cover seven variables, so analysis requires a 7×7 matrix to represent 49 correlation values.

To compute the matrix of correlations using SPSS, go to the STATISTICS menu, pull down to CORRELATIONS, and choose BIVARIATE. (This test gives correlations between two variables.) From the box on the left, transfer all seven of the variables to the variable box. Then choose CORRELATION COEFFICIENT (Pearson) and TWO-TAILED TEST OF SIGNIFICANCE. Click on "OK," and you will see the matrix of correlations shown in Table 11.9.

The matrix (Table 11.9) shows all 49 correlations. Note that the correlation between each variable and itself is given as 1.0000. Each correlation appears twice; if you were to fold the matrix in half along the diagonal of 1.0000 values, each side would be a mirror-image of the other. The number of subjects is given (in parentheses) as well as the *p*-value or level of significance. Discounting the correlation of each score with itself (a correlation of 1.0000), which occurs seven times, the remaining correlations number 42. Since each correlation is given twice, the table lists 21 unique correlations. Three of these are 0.0000 (those between the three coded variables: treatment, sex, and IQ) because the data include equal numbers of each gender and IQ group members in each treatment. Eliminating the zero correlations leaves 18 correlations, about half of which turned out to be significant ones. The largest correlations indicate links between IQ and the four reading measures, and between treatment and reading accuracy.

(To see the exact computational procedures for calculating the value of the Pearson correlation, go to Figure II in Appendix E. This figure shows the steps undertaken in carrying out this statistical test.)

A variation of correlational analysis is called *regression* analysis. This approach combines a number of independent variables to predict or explain one dependent variable. Regression analysis of the data from Table 11.7 might seek an answer to the question whether three variables—treatment, sex, and IQ—can account for reading comprehension (READCOMP) scores. To answer this question using regression analysis in SPSS, select REGRESSION from the STATISTICS menu and go to LINEAR. For the dependent variable (DV), choose READCOMP; for the independent variable (IV), choose TREATMNT, SEX, and IQ; for "Statistics Needed," choose "estimates, confidence intervals, and model fit." Click on "OK" to get the printout shown in Table 11.10. It shows that the three independent variables together do explain the dependent variable, producing a multiple R (R stands for correlation) of .58413. However, only one of the three variables in the equation is a significant predictor, namely IQ (as shown in the bottom part of the table).

TABLE 11.9
MATRIX OF PARAMETRIC (PEARSON) CORRELATION COEFFICIENTS

	IQ	PICREAD	READACCU	READCOMP	READRATE	SEX	TREATMNT
IQ	1.0000 (32) P=.	-.7104 (32) P=.000	.5285 (32) P=.002	-.5841 (32) P=.000	.3994 (32) P=.024	.0000 (32) P=1.000	.0000 (32) P=1.000
PICREAD	-.7104 (32) P=.000	1.0000 (32) P=.	-.2221 (32) P=.222	.2750 (32) P=.128	-.1217 (32) P=.507	-.1569 (32) P=.391	.1773 (32) P=.332
READACCU	.5285 (32) P=.002	-.2221 (32) P=.222	1.0000 (32) P=.	-.5568 (32) P=.001	.5450 (32) P=.001	-.1220 (32) P=.506	.6072 (32) P=.000
READCOMP	-.5841 (32) P=.000	.2750 (32) P=.128	-.5568 (32) P=.001	1.0000 (32) P=.	-.4745 (32) P=.006	.1546 (32) P=.398	-.1690 (32) P=.355
READRATE	.3994 (32) P=.024	-.1217 (32) P=.507	.5450 (32) P=.001	-.4745 (32) P=.006	1.0000 (32) P=.	-.1261 (32) P=.492	.2444 (32) P=.178
SEX	.0000 (32) P=1.000	-.1569 (32) P=.391	-.1220 (32) P=.506	.1546 (32) P=.398	-.1261 (32) P=.492	1.0000 (32) P=.	.0000 (32) P=1.000
TREATMNT	.0000 (32) P=1.000	.1773 (32) P=.332	.6072 (32) P=.000	-.1690 (32) P=.355	.2444 (32) P=.178	.0000 (32) P=1.000	1.0000 (32) P=.

(Coefficient / (Cases) / 2-tailed Significance)
" . " is printed if a coefficient cannot be computed.

TABLE 11.10   MULTIPLE REGRESSION

LISTWISE DELETION OF MISSING DATA

Equation Number 1   Dependent Variable. .   READCOMP
Block Number 1.   Method: Stepwise   Criteria   PIN   .0500   POUT   .1000

IQ   SEX   TREATMNT

Variable(s) Entered on Step Number
1..   IQ

Multiple R	.58413
R Square	.34120
Adjusted R Square	.31924
Standard Error	3.04959

Analysis of Variance

	DF	Sum of Squares	Mean Square
Regression	1	144.50000	144.50000
Residual	30	279.00000	9.30000

F = 15.53763   Signif F = .0004

Variables in the Equation

Variable	B	SE B	Beta	T	Sig T
IQ	−4.250000	1.078193	−.584127	−3.942	.0004
(Constant)	22.000000	1.704773		12.905	.0000

Variables not in the Equation

Variable	Beta In	Partial	Min Toler	T	Sig T
SEX	.154622	.190500	1.000000	1.045	.3047
TREATMNT	−.169031	−.208253	1.000000	−1.147	.20609

End Block Number   1   PIN = .050 Limits reached.

Analysis of Variance (ANOVA)

A statistical technique is most useful when it can accommodate more than two variables at a time. Analysis of variance allows a researcher to study the simultaneous effect of almost any number of independent variables, but its typical applications include two, three, or four. When using a *factorial research design* that includes an independent variable, moderator variable, and dependent variable, the size of the analysis of variance equals the number of independent and moderator variables, called *factors*.[8] For a study with one independent variable and one moderator variable, a researcher would conduct a two-factor analysis of variance.

Suppose the independent variable from the second reading experiment, reported in Table 11.7, is the experimental treatment, that is, the method of teaching reading (readiness and sight reading, sight reading only, readiness only, and phonics). This independent variable represents one factor with four *levels* (or variations). Suppose the moderator variable is IQ, and the interval IQ measure has been split at the median to give two levels: high and low IQ. These conditions call for a 4×2 analysis of variance. The two digits indicate two factors, one with four levels and the other with two. Because the independent and moderator variables must be nominal measures to work within an analysis of variance, the median-split technique or another equal *n*-split, is a useful data preparation step. The dependent variable should be an interval measure to work in the parametric analysis of variance. Only one dependent variable can be analyzed at a time using the kind of analysis of variance to be illustrated.

Assume that reading rate is the dependent variable, and call the independent variable *A* and the moderator variable *B*. Analysis of variance will indicate the effect of the independent variable (the *A* effect), the effect of the moderator variable (the *B* effect), and the effect of both variables in *interaction* (the *AB* interaction). The concept of interaction is explored more fully later in this chapter.

Figure III in Appendix E is a worksheet for performing a two-way or two-factor analysis of variance. In this design, the number of levels of the independent variable is *p* (equal to the number of columns in the design), and the number of levels of the moderator variable is *q* (equal to the number of rows in the design).

Once the analysis of variance calculations are completed, the results are displayed in an analysis of variance *source table*:

ANALYSIS OF VARIANCE OF DEPENDENT VARIABLE BY INDEPENDENT VARIABLE (A) AND MODERATOR VARIABLE (B)

SOURCE	df	MS	F
A	$p - 1$	MS_A	F_A[a]
B	$q - 1$	MS_B	F_B[b]
AB	$(p - 1)(q - 1)$	MS_{AB}	F_{AB}[a]
Error	(total of *n*'s $- pq$)	MS_W	

[a] $p < .05$; [b] $p < .01$.

To run the ANOVA on reading experiment 2 data from Table 11.7 using SPSS, pull down the STATISTICS menu and choose ANOVA MODELS. From the four models offered, choose SIMPLE FACTORIAL. Then transfer

---

[8] The terms *variable* and *factor* are synonyms here. Variables or factors are further subdivided into levels, treatments, or conditions—another set of interchangeable words. In explanations of statistical operations, variables will be called *factors,* and their subdivisions will be called *levels.*

(1) READRATE to the Dependent Variable box, (2) TREATMNT to the Factors box, and (3) IQ to the Factors box. For TREATMNT, click on "Define Range" and enter a *minimum* of 1 and a *maximum* of 4 to reflect its four possible levels. For IQ, click on "Define Range" and enter a *minimum* of 1 and a *maximum* of 2 to reflect its two possible levels. Then click on "Options," and (1) under "Method," click on "Hierarchical," and (2) under "Statistics," click on "Means and counts." Then click on "OK" to get the printout shown in Table 11.11.

Part A of Table 11.11 shows the means and sample sizes for (1) all the subjects in each of the four levels of the treatment, (2) all the subjects in each of the two IQ levels, and (3) high-IQ and low-IQ subjects separately in each of the four levels of the treatment. This data is followed by the source table (Part B), which shows two significant effects: (a) the main effect of IQ (that is, the effect of IQ by itself; $p = .012$), and (b) the effect of the interaction (that is, the combined effect of treatment and IQ; $p = .017$). The main effect of treatment (that is, the effect of treatment by itself) is not significant ($p = .315$). An examination of the means suggests that the main effect of IQ is based on the fact that high-IQ students read at a more rapid rate than do low-IQ students (16.50 versus 21.25, respectively). The significant interaction effect between the treatment and IQ factors appears to result from the facts that high-IQ students read at a more rapid rate than do low-IQ students in three of the four treatment levels, but in the first treatment level low-IQ students read at a more rapid rate than do high-IQ students.

One of the most valuable features of analysis of variance is its potential for statistical identification of interactions, the combined effects of two or more independent variables on a dependent variable. To aid interpretation of the significant interaction between treatment and IQ on reading rate, revealed in Table 11.11B, a researcher could graph the means from Part A of the table, as shown in Figure 11.4.

The top graph (A) displays reading program along the x-axis and presents a separate curve for each level of IQ. The bottom graph (B) measures IQ along the x-axis and presents a separate curve for each treatment level. Both graphs display reading rate along their y-axes. The interaction is reflected on both graphs in Figure 11.4 by the divergence from parallel of the separate curves; indeed in both graphs, one curve crosses the other(s). The graph confirms that low-IQ students outperform high-IQ students in Treatment 1, the combination of readiness and sight reading instruction. (Remember that lower scores represent better performance.) In contrast, high-IQ students outperform low-IQ students in all the other treatments; in this way, the graphs reveal the basis for the significant interaction. When graph lines cross researchers describe the effect as a *disordinal* interaction, while distinctly nonparallel lines that do not cross demonstrate an *ordinal* interaction (Glass & Hopkins, 1996). When a significant interaction is found, particularly a disordinal one like that shown in Figure 11.4, a researcher should undertake additional post-hoc analyses to determine the significance of differences between the various combinations, such as treatment level and IQ level.

Consider another example, a study comparing the independent variable team teaching against traditional teaching and self-teaching for high-IQ and low-IQ

ANALYSIS OF VARIANCE: READING RATE BY TREATMENT AND IQ   TABLE 11.11

A. CELL MEANS

READRATE
by TREATMNT
IQ

Total Population
18.88
(32)

TREATMNT

1	2	3	4
16.38	18.38	20.88	19.88
(8)	(8)	(8)	(8)

IQ

1	2
16.50	21.25
(16)	(16)

	IQ	
	1	2
TREATMNT		
1	19.00	13.75
	(4)	(4)
2	14.25	22.50
	(4)	(4)
3	17.25	24.50
	(4)	(4)
4	15.50	24.25
	(4)	(4)

B: ANALYSIS OF VARIANCE

READRATE
by TREATMNT
IQ

HIERARCHICAL sums of squares
Covariates entered FIRST

Source of Variation	Sum of Squares	DF	Mean Square	F	Sig of F
Main Effects	272.5002	4	68.125	2.771	.050
TREATMNT	92.000	3	30.667	1.247	.315
IQ	180.500	1	180.500	7.342	.012
2-Way Interactions	269.000	3	89.667	3.647	.027
TREATMNT IQ	269.000	3	89.667	3.647	.027
Explained	541.500	7	77.357	3.147	.017
Residual	590.000	24	24.583		
Total	1131.500	31	36.500		

32 cases were processed.
0 cases (.0 pct) were missing.

<u>FIGURE 11.4</u>   GRAPHS OF THE INTERACTION BETWEEN TREATMENT
AND IQ ON READING RATE

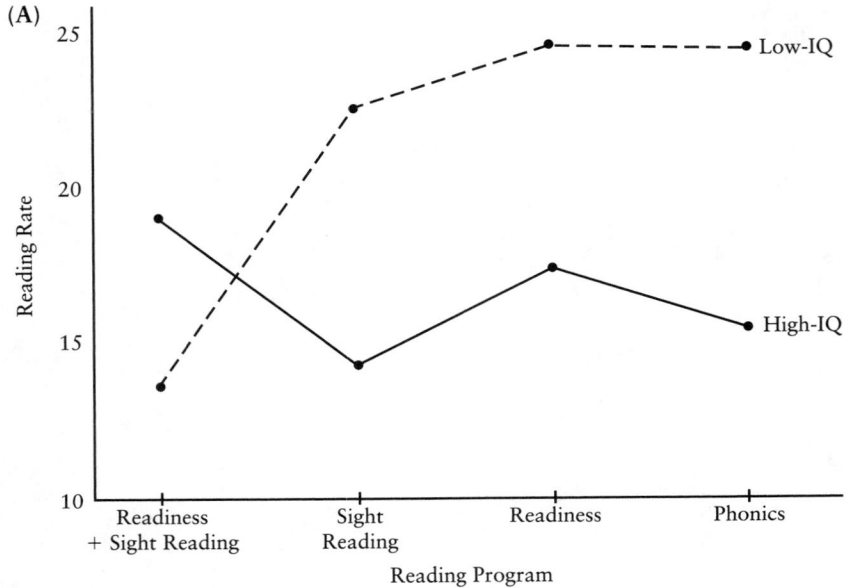

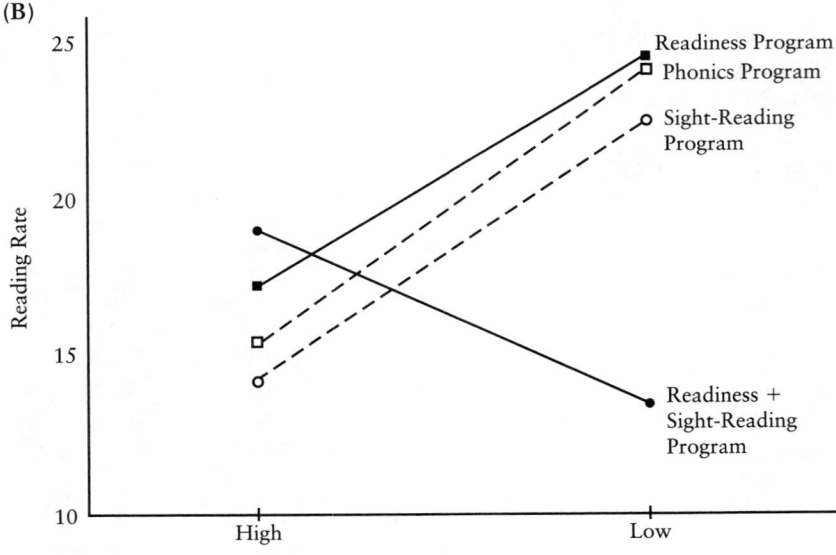

SAMPLE GRAPHS ILLUSTRATING STATISTICAL INTERACTIONS OR THEIR ABSENCE

FIGURE 11.5

Graph 1
No Interaction

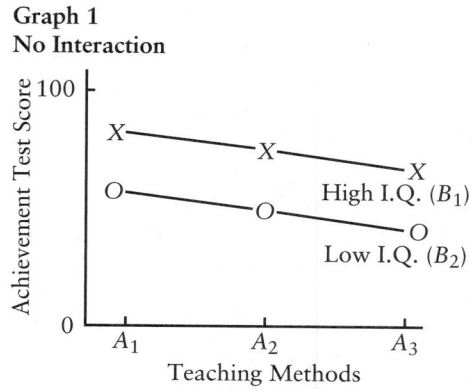

Graph 2
Moderate Interaction

Graph 3
Strong Interaction

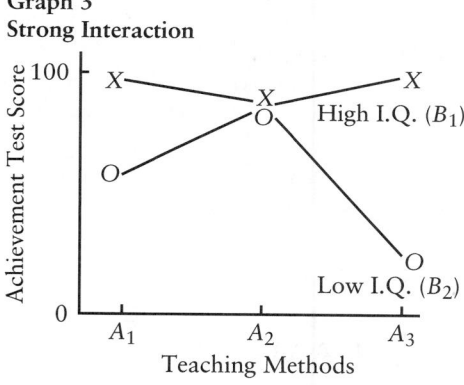

KEY
A_1: Team Teaching
A_2: Traditional Teaching
A_3: Self-Teaching

students (the moderator variable). The dependent variable is performance on an achievement test. Some sample graphs appear in Figure 11.5.

Notice in Graph 1 that team teaching produces higher achievement than traditional teaching, which in turn produces higher achievement than self-teaching for both IQ groups. Considering teaching technique as the *A* variable, the overall superiority of this approach (or inferiority of the self-teaching approach) would show up in the analysis of variance as a significant *A* effect. Similar analysis would reveal a significant *B* effect, because the high-IQ group outperforms the low-IQ group. In fact, the data in all three graphs would probably produce significant *B* effects (as well as significant *A* effects, although these results seem less dramatic than the *B* effects). Notice in Graph 1 that the IQ curves parallel one another, indicating that the three teaching methods do not produce differential effects on subjects in the two IQ groups. The superiority of the high-IQ group over the other group remains constant from one teaching technique to the other. Thus, Graph 1 demonstrates *no interaction* between the independent variable and the moderator variable.

Graph 2 shows, however, that the superiority of the high-IQ subjects over the others increases from one teaching technique to the next. If students had not been separated by IQ level, the researcher could not determine that team teaching produces very similar achievement among high-IQ and low-IQ students, but low-IQ students fare very poorly in a self-teaching situation when compared to their high-IQ counterparts. Thus, Graph 2 shows an *interaction* between teaching technique and IQ.

Graph 3 indicates that high-IQ and low-IQ students benefit equally from traditional teaching; however, high-IQ students achieve more with team teaching and even more with self-teaching. Thus, the effects of the teaching techniques *strongly interact* with IQ in Graph 3. Had the effects of the three teaching techniques not been separated for the two IQ levels, only a slight tendency for inferiority of self-teaching (a small possible *A* effect) would be apparent in these graphs. However, introduction of the moderator variable (IQ) reveals an interaction effect that reflects differences in the effects of the treatments for different IQ groups.

When group means are graphed and the lines between points for the different moderator variables depart from parallel, you can usually expect to find an interaction effect. At least, these conditions alert a researcher to the possibility for one. As the tendency away from parallel increases, so does the likelihood that an interaction effect is a statistically significant part of the results. When an analysis of variance yields both a significant main effect and a significant interaction, it is useful to plot the results two ways, once with a moderator or *B* variable inside the graph (as shown in Figure 11.4A) and once with the independent or *A* variable inside the graph (as shown in Figure 11.4B).

CARRYING OUT NONPARAMETRIC STATISTICAL TESTS

Mann-Whitney U-Test

The Mann-Whitney *U*-test is a nonparametric test that compares two samples for possible significant differences. The *U*-test is not bound by the same restrictions as the *t*-test (its parametric counterpart). Like all other nonparametric tests, it eliminates the requirement for parametric statistics for normally distributed data with equal sample variances.

The *U*-test calls for a nominal independent variable (such as a distinction between treatment and control groups) and an ordinal dependent variable. If the dependent variable is an interval measure, it is easily transformed to an ordinal measure by casting the scores into ranks and then analyzing the ranks.[9]

---

[9] Note, however, that data lose some of their information value when they are transformed to a lower order of measurement.

An example could look at the same variables used to illustrate the *t*-test. The independent variable will be IQ, with two levels, and the dependent variable will be the picture reading score. In the Mann-Whitney test, however, the picture reading score will be analyzed as ordinal data (ranks) rather than interval data, as it was in the *t*-test. The two tests should yield approximately the same results.

To run the Mann-Whitney *U*-test in SPSS, pull down the STATISTICS menu, and choose NONPARAMETRICS. Go to TWO INDEPENDENT SAMPLES (as for running the *t*-test, since the groups incorporate different subjects), and choose MANN-WHITNEY U. For test variable, choose READRATE; for grouping variable, choose IQ. Under grouping variable, click on "Define Groups," and indicate a minimum of 1 and maximum of 2 to represent the levels (the same procedure for running the *t*-test). The software automatically converts the test scores to ranks and yields the printout shown in Table 11.12. (The software actually

---

> ### ILLUSTRATIONS FROM THE SAMPLE STUDIES   BOX 11
>
> Sample Study I uses analysis of covariance (ANCOVA), a variation of analysis of variance. Two ANCOVAs are run, one for each dependent variable. Four student characteristic measures are used as covariates. The statistical procedure adjusts for their effect on the dependent variables. Sample Study II uses two-way analysis of variance, as described in this chapter. The factors are reading level (good versus poor) and grade level (1, 3, 5, 7, 9, and 11). Seven dependent variables are each analyzed separately by two-way ANOVA.

MANN-WHITNEY *U*—WILCOXON RANK SUM *W* TEST   TABLE 11.12

PICREAD
by IQ

Mean Rank	Cases	
23.47	16	IQ = 1.00
9.53	16	IQ = 2.00
	32 Total	

		Exact	Corrected for Ties	
U	W	2-Tailed P	Z	2-Tailed P
16.5	375.5	.0000	−4.2097	.0000

performs two nonparametric statistical tests on the data, the Mann-Whitney *U* and the Wilcoxon Rank Sum *W* Test.)

The results in Table 11.12 show a significant difference between high-IQ and low-IQ subjects on the picture reading score (just as the *t*-test indicated). High-IQ subjects (Level 1 of that variable) differed significantly in their PICREAD rankings from low-IQ subjects (Level 2) with $p = .0000$.

A worksheet for the *U*-test appears as Figure IV in Appendix E. This worksheet has been set up for experiments involving fewer than 20 and more than 8 observations in the larger of two samples. For larger sample sizes, use techniques described in Siegel (1956).

Spearman Rank-Order Correlation

A researcher applies the Spearman rank-order correlation *(r_s)* test to compare two sets of ranks to determine their degree of equivalence. (Remember that data arranged in ranks represent ordinal data; therefore, the rank-order correlation describes the relationship between two sets of ordinal data.) Analysis can convert data collected in interval form to ordinal form to allow analysis by Spearman correlation (rather than a Pearson product-moment correlation, as would be used to compare sets of interval data).[10]

The most common use of the Spearman rank-order correlation is to compare judgments by a group of judges of two objects or the scores of a group of subjects on two measures. (See Siegel, 1956, for an example of this use.) A second valuable but less frequent use of the test is to compare judgments by two judges of a group of objects or items. (See Hays, 1973, for an example of this use.) The second use is essentially a technique for assessing equivalence between judges' tendencies over a set of items or objects. To evaluate multiple judges' rankings on two measures, *N* is equal to the number of judges or subjects. To evaluate two judges ranking multiple objects, *N* is equal to the number of objects. In the case of multiple subjects, the Spearman rank-order correlation answers the question, "Do the measures tend to agree; are they measuring the same thing or a related thing?" Such analysis would be applicable, for example, in assessing concurrent test validity or test-retest reliability. In the case of multiple objects, the Spearman rank-order correlation answers the question, "Do the judges tend to agree?" This analysis would be applicable, for example, in assessing interrater reliability.[11]

As an example, consider a rerun of the matrix of parametric (Pearson) correlations shown in Table 11.9 as nonparametric (Spearman) correlations. This test will include all seven variables that appeared in Table 11.9. To run this

---

[10] Such a conversion might prove helpful, for one example, when judges using the same scale display different response tendencies—one rates observations toward the ends of the scale and the other rates them near the middle.

[11] In the case of multiple judges and multiple objects, a Friedman two-way analysis of variance by ranks or a Kendall coefficient of concordance would be used (see Siegel, 1956).

TABLE 11.13

A MATRIX OF SPEARMAN CORRELATION COEFFICIENTS

	IQ	PICREAD	READACCU	READCOMP	READRATE	SEX
PICREAD	−.7561 N (32) Sig .000					
READACCU	.5309 N (32) Sig .002	−.2632 N (32) Sig .145				
READCOMP	−.5815 N (32) Sig .000	.3003 N (32) Sig .095	−.5529 N (32) Sig .001			
READRATE	.3631 N (32) Sig .041	−.1295 N (32) Sig .480	.5702 N (32) Sig .001	−.4440 N (32) Sig .011		
SEX	.0000 N (32) Sig 1.000	−.1288 N (32) Sig .482	−.0987 N (32) Sig .591	.1190 N (32) Sig .516	−.1663 N (32) Sig .363	
TREATMNT	.0000 N (32) Sig 1.000	.1638 N (32) Sig .370	.6270 N (32) Sig .000	−.1886 N (32) Sig .301	.2383 N (32) Sig .189	.0000 N (32) Sig 1.000

(Coefficient / (Cases) / 2-tailed Significance)
" . " is printed if a coefficient cannot be computed

analysis on SPSS, go to the STATISTICS menu, and choose CORRELATE and then BIVARIATE CORRELATION. Transfer all seven variables to the variable box. (This is the same procedure for running the Pearson correlation.) Then, under the variable box, you will see three choices: Pearson, Kendall's tau-b, and Spearman. Pearson is the type run in Table 11.9, and Kendall's tau-b is another type of nonparametric correlation, so choose Spearman. Then, choose two-tailed test. Click on OK, and you will get the printout shown in Table 11.13.

Table 11.13 is less cluttered than the Pearson correlation table (Table 11.9), because each correlation appears only once. If you disregard the three correlations of .0000 between the nominal or coded variables, this analysis presents 18 correlations to consider. As you would expect, these 18 correlations are very similar in magnitude to the corresponding Pearson correlations.

A worksheet for the Spearman rank-order correlation (r_s) appears in Appendix E in Figure V. This worksheet can be used where multiple subjects are providing rankings on two measures as well as where two judges are providing rankings of multiple objects.

Chi-Square (χ^2) Test

The χ^2 test allows analysis of one, two, or more nominal variables, but researchers commonly apply it to situations with two.[12] Data in the two-variable case are cast into a *contingency table:* [13]

	College	Noncollege	
Firstborns	75	30	105
Later-borns	23	80	103
	98	110	208

The numbers in the contingency table represent the *frequencies* of cases that jointly satisfy a particular set of conditions specified by the variables. (In the example, these numbers represent the distributions of the two samples—firstborns and later-borns—across two categories—went to college and did not go to college.) For instance, 75 students out of a graduating class of 208 meet the contingency of being firstborn children going on to college.

The values obtained by summing the frequencies across rows and columns are called the *marginals* (for example, 98 and 105). They are so named because they appear in the margins of the table.

The χ^2 test tells you whether the two independent samples (firstborns and later-borns) show significantly different distributions across the two categories (college and noncollege), allowing you to consider them as having been drawn from different populations. That is, the test indicates whether the frequencies obtained in the cells of the table differ from the frequencies you might expect based on chance variation alone. Thus, the χ^2 test compares *obtained* frequencies to *expected* frequencies and indicates the probability that they will differ from one another.

The basic formula for computing χ^2 is:

$$\chi^2 = \Sigma\Sigma\frac{(o - e)^2}{e}$$

where o is the obtained frequency in a cell and e is the expected frequency. The double summation sign ($\Sigma\Sigma$) indicates that the calculation sums across both the rows and columns of the contingency table. In calculating the expected frequency for each cell, if all the marginal values for a contingency table were the same, you would simply divide the total frequency by the number of cells. However, because the marginals are rarely the same, you calculate the expected frequencies for a cell by dividing the product of its marginals by the total frequency. In the example,

---

[12] For information about the use of the chi-square test for one variable (called the *one-sample case*) or for two variables with more than two levels per variable (called the *K Independent sample case*), see Siegel (1956). The version described here is for two independent samples (firstborn and later-born subjects). However, all three computations follow highly similar methods.

[13] Contingency tables were described in Chapter 10.

the cell showing an *obtained* frequency of 75 would have an *expected* frequency of (98 × 105) ÷ 208, or 49.4.

Occasionally, chi-square analysis requires transforming a variable from an interval measurement to a nominal measurement to make both variables nominal ones.[14] This is usually best accomplished by splitting the interval measure at the median to obtain a high half and a low half. Considering students as high or low on a measure, rather than working with their actual scores, allows you to apply a χ^2 test. However, it is preferable to retain the variable in interval form and employ a parametric test to avoid losing information.

In order to use the chi-square test on data from reading experiment 2 reported in Table 11.7, it is necessary to transform one of the test scores (for the current analysis, the READCOMP score) from an interval measurement to a nominal one. To do this, the median split procedure will be applied. The first step will obtain the median or middle score on READCOMP. To obtain the median using SPSS, pull down the STATISTICS menu and choose SUMMARIZE, and then choose FREQUENCY. Move READCOMP to the dialog box. Then click on "Statistics," and, under "Central Tendency," click on "Median." Click on "Continue" and then "OK." You will get the printout in Table 11.14, which shows the

FREQUENCIES OF VALUES OF **READCOMP**

TABLE 11.14

VALUE LABEL	VALUE	FREQUENCY	PERCENT	VALID PERCENT	CUM PERCENT
	9.00	1	3.1	3.1	3.1
	10.00	1	3.1	3.1	6.3
	11.00	1	3.1	3.1	9.4
	12.00	5	15.6	15.6	25.0
	13.00	3	9.4	9.4	34.4
	14.00	3	9.4	9.4	43.8
	15.00	3	9.4	9.4	53.1
	16.00	1	3.1	3.1	56.3
	17.00	4	12.5	12.5	68.8
	18.00	3	9.4	9.4	78.1
	19.00	1	3.1	3.1	81.3
	20.00	3	9.4	9.4	90.6
	21.00	1	3.1	3.1	93.8
	23.00	2	6.3	6.3	100.0
	Total	32	100.0	100.0	

Median   15.000

Valid cases   32   Missing cases   0

---

[14] An alternative strategy may be to use a *t*-test or else a point biserial correlation, that is, a correlation between a biserial nominal variable (one with two levels) and an interval variable (one that designates points on a scale or continuum). See Glass and Hopkins (1984).

frequency of occurrence for each value or score on READCOMP. It also shows the median READCOMP score of 15.

The next step is to create a new variable that is a nominal version of READ-COMP with two levels, labeled 1 for values below and including the median, and 2 for values above the median. To make this change in SPSS, pull down the TRANSFORM menu, and choose RECODE. Then choose INTO DIFFERENT VARIABLES (because you want to transform READCOMP interval scores into new, nominal scores). Move READCOMP to the dialog box, and click on "Old and New Values." Now you must provide instructions for the transformation. Click on "Range Lowest Thru," and enter the median value, 15, in the box. This specification indicates that scores from the lowest through the median on the old variable, READCOMP, will be coded as one value on the new variable. To indicate what this value will be, click on "New Value," enter "1," and click on "Add." This specification indicates that the lowest half of the scores will be coded as 1. Now for the highest half of the scores, click on "Range Thru Highest," and enter the score immediately above the median—which is 16. Then, click on "New Value," enter "2," and click on "Add." The highest half of the scores will be coded as 2. Now click Continue. Now you have to name the new variable. Under "Output variable" enter "RCGROUP." Then click "Change" and then "OK." A new variable, RCGROUP, has now been added to the data set. It is shown in Table 11.15.

TABLE 11.15   THE NEW VARIABLE IN THE **READEXP2** DATA SET

	RCGROUP		RCGROUP
1	2.00	17	2.00
2	2.00	18	2.00
3	1.00	19	1.00
4	1.00	20	2.00
5	2.00	21	2.00
6	2.00	22	1.00
7	2.00	23	1.00
8	2.00	24	1.00
9	2.00	25	1.00
10	1.00	26	2.00
11	1.00	27	1.00
12	1.00	28	1.00
13	2.00	29	2.00
14	1.00	30	2.00
15	1.00	31	1.00
16	1.00	32	1.00

We are now ready to run a chi-square test to check for a significant relationship between IQ and the new variable, RCGROUP (which is a really high or low classification on reading comprehension score). To run the chi-square test, pull down the STATISTICS menu, choose SUMMARIZE, and then choose CROSSTABS. Move the two variables to the dialog boxes, RCGROUP to rows and IQ to columns. Then click on "Statistics," choose "Chi-square," and click on "OK." You will get the printout shown in Table 11.16.

The printout shows the contingency table and a number of versions of chi-square. The first, the Pearson chi-square, has a value of 10.16471, which is significant at the .00143 level. Clearly, high-IQ subjects (those coded 1 on IQ) are much more likely to achieve high scores on the reading comprehension test (results coded 2 on RCGROUP) than are low-IQ subjects (those coded 2 on IQ). The low-IQ students are much more likely to achieve low scores on the test (results coded 1 on RCGROUP).

A worksheet for a 2×2 χ^2 test appears in Appendix E, Figure VI. This worksheet employs a different formula that is easier to apply than the one presented earlier, so this version is recommended for computation purposes. Note, however,

CHI-SQUARE TEST OF **RCGROUP** BY **IQ**   TABLE 11.16

Count		IQ		
RCGROUP		1.00	2.00	Row Total
1.00		4	13	17 53.1
2.00		12	3	15 46.9
Column Total		16 50.0	16 50.0	32 100.0

Chi-Square	Value	DF	Significance
Pearson	10.16471	1	.00143
Continuity Correction	8.03137	1	.00460
Likelihood Ratio	10.79913	1	.00102
Mantel-Haenszel test for linear association	9.84706	1	.00170

Minimum Expected Frequency—7.500

Number of Missing Observations: 0

that the worksheet formula can accommodate only a 2×2 contingency table. In other than the 2×2 case (that is, with more than 2 independent samples or more than 2 categories), the first formula should be used.[15]

SUMMARY

1. Statistical tests enable a researcher to compare groups of data to determine the probability that chance variations have produced any differences between them.

2. Type I (or alpha) error is the probability of rejecting the null or no difference hypothesis when it is a true statement. It represents a false positive result, and researchers usually set the possibility of making such an error at .05. Type II (or beta) error is the probability of accepting the null hypothesis when it is a false statement. It represents a false negative result, and researchers usually tolerate a .20 chance of making such an error. Power, or the probability of getting a significant difference, equals 1 minus the Type II error.

3. A two-tailed test, the most common type of statistical evaluation, includes scores from both ends or tails of the normal distribution. A one-tailed test includes scores from only the tail of the distribution covered by a hypothesis. The same statistical outcome that yields a .05 alpha error on a one-tailed test will yield a .10 alpha error on a two-tailed test.

4. The mean of a distribution is determined by the formula:

$$\overline{X} = \frac{\Sigma X}{N}$$

The standard deviation, or dispersion of scores in a sample, is determined by the formula:

$$s = \sqrt{\frac{\Sigma(X - \overline{X})^2}{N - 1}}$$

5. Sample size is based on alpha level, power (the reciprocal of beta level), and effect size (the ratio of mean differences to standard deviation). Alpha level is usually set at .05, power at .80, and effect size at .2 (small), .5 (medium), or .8 (large). A medium effect size requires two groups of 64 subjects each.

---

[15] A point about the use of the chi-square test itself: Its value diminishes for extremely small frequencies in each cell. If the smallest expected frequency is less than 5, the Fisher exact test should be used. (See Siegel, 1956.) Moreover, in all instances with sample sizes (Ns) less than 20, the Fisher exact test should also be employed.

6. Parametric statistics assume interval measurement of, and a normal distribution of scores on, the dependent variable. Nonparametric tests are appropriate for ordinal and nominal measures.
7. With a nominal variable and an interval variable, use a *t*-test or analysis of variance; where both variables are interval measures, use correlation; where one is interval, conduct a nonparametric test; where both variables are nominal measures, use a chi-square test. (See Table 11.2 for a summary.)
8. Nominal data should be coded numerically and all data rostered, either by hand or electronically, prior to analysis.
9. A *t*-test is computed as the difference between the means of two distributions divided by their pooled standard deviations. (See Table 11.8.)
10. A parametric correlation shows the relationship between variables (see Table 11.9), and regression is used to show the relationship between predictor variables and an outcome variable. (See Table 11.10.)
11. Analysis of variance provides a statistical tool for partitioning the variance within a set of scores according to its various sources in order to determine the effects of variables individually (main effects) and in combination (interactions). See Table 11.11.
12. The Mann-Whitney *U*-test compares the relative rank orders of two sets of scores. (See Table 11.12.)
13. The Spearman rank-order correlation compares two sets of ranks to determine their degree of equivalence. (See Table 11.13.)
14. The chi-square (χ^2) test uses contingency tables to identify differences between two distributions of nominal scores. (See Table 11.16.)

COMPETENCY TEST EXERCISES

1. You have designed a study with an independent variable (experimental treatment versus control), a moderator variable (IQ), and a dependent variable (performance on a criterion test). Which statistical test should you employ to analyze your data?
    a. *t*-test
    b. correlation
    c. analysis of variance
    d. chi-square

2. You are analyzing the results of an experiment comparing the performance of *S*s assigned to experimental and control groups. Your dependent measure is a score that, for purposes of analysis, has been converted to a rank assignment relative to the scores of other *S*s. To statistically compare such experimental and control group scores, you should conduct a:
    a. Mann-Whitney *U*-test
    b. Spearman rank-order correlation

  c. chi-square
  d. *t*-test

3. The following data have been collected:

36	92	74	85	39
98	41	40	90	45
47	73	58	70	22
49	62	67	71	52
54	68	81	78	50

   Develop a five-category coding scheme, and assign each score to a category.

4. Prepare 20 sets of data, each including a subject identification number, gender code (1 or 2), age, experimental condition code (1 or 2), and two-digit scores on each of 10 dependent variables. Roster these data on a roster sheet or by computer.

5. For the remaining exercises, refer to the following scores of two groups of Ss ($N = 20$ in each) on a performance measure:

Group 1		Group 2	
a. 75	k. 81	a. 72	k. 79
b. 88	l. 89	b. 81	l. 83
c. 80	m. 77	c. 70	m. 73
d. 85	n. 84	d. 80	n. 85
e. 78	o. 88	e. 70	o. 82
f. 90	p. 93	f. 85	p. 90
g. 82	q. 91	g. 73	q. 80
h. 88	r. 81	h. 82	r. 78
i. 76	s. 85	i. 72	s. 81
j. 82	t. 87	j. 78	t. 74

   Calculate the mean, median, and standard deviation of the scores in Group 1.

6. Calculate the mean, median, and standard deviation of the scores in Group 2.

7. Compare the means for Groups 1 and 2 using a *t*-test. Report the *t* value and its level of significance (if any).

8. Compare the scores for Groups 1 and 2 using a Mann-Whitney *U*-test. Report the smaller *U* value and its level of significance (if any).

9. Compare the scores for Groups 1 and 2 using a chi-square (χ^2) test. (Split the scores into two categories.) Report the χ^2 value and its level of significance (if any).

10. Consider the data from Exercise 5. Assume that Group 1 is the experimental group, Group 2 is the control group, and together they constitute *Variable A* (the independent variable). In addition, assume you have a moderator variable, *Variable B* (high versus low IQ, for example). Alternating members of each group (a, c, e, g, . . . s) are low on Variable B; the remaining members (b, d, f, h, . . . t) are high on that variable. Run a two-way analysis of variance and report mean squares and *F* ratios for each source of variance (*A, B, AB,* error). Also report levels of significance (if any). (*Note:* If you do it by hand rather than by computer, you can use the forms for unequal *n*s even though this analysis has equal *n*s.)

11. Now use the data given in Exercise 5 in a slightly different way. Instead of thinking of Groups 1 and 2 as they are labeled, think of them as Tests 1 and 2, administered to a single group of *S*s. The letter appearing alongside each score is now the subject identification code. Compute a Spearman rank-order correlation between the scores for the 20 *S*s on Test 1 (the Group 1 data) and the scores for these same *S*s on Test 2 (the Group 2 data). Report the r_s and the level of significance (if any).

12. Again, consider Groups 1 and 2 to be Tests 1 and 2, respectively, as you did in Exercise 11. But this time only consider the first 10 *S*s. (Again use the letters alongside the scores as identification codes.) Compute a Pearson product-moment correlation between the Test 1 and Test 2 scores for the first 10 *S*s. Report the *r* value and the level of significance (if any).

RECOMMENDED REFERENCES

Glass, G. V., & Hopkins, K. D. (1996). *Statistical methods in education and psychology* (3rd ed.). Englewood Cliffs, NJ: Prentice-Hall.

Linn, R. L. (1986). Quantitative methods in research on teaching. In M. C. Wittrock (Ed.). *Handbook of research on teaching* (3rd ed.). New York: Macmillan.

Tatsuoka, M. M. (1988). *Multivariate analysis: Techniques for educational and psychological research* (2nd ed.). New York: Macmillan.

Winer, B. J., Brown, D. R., & Michels, K. M. (1991). *Statistical principles of experimental design* (3rd ed.). New York: McGraw-Hill.

12 Chapter

Writing a Research Report

Objectives

▶ Write a research proposal including an introductory section and a method section.

▶ Write a final report including the following sections: introduction, method, results, discussion, references, and abstract.

▶ Prepare tables to illustrate experimental designs and results of data analysis.

▶ Prepare graphs to illustrate the results of data analysis.

The Research Proposal

Proposal preparation is a significant part of the development and pursuit of a research project. In fact, whether a planned research project is accepted by a dissertation committee or funding agency often depends on the quality of the proposal.

A research proposal consists of two parts: an introduction and a method section. Because these sections appear in both the proposal and the final project report in virtually identical form, this explanation would gain little from separate descriptions of proposals and final reports. Consequently, the remainder of this chapter is devoted to preparation of a final research report.

Note that the parts of research proposals and reports discussed here, and their order of presentation, are guidelines, not absolute requirements. Different types of studies and different writing styles may yield somewhat different parts in somewhat different arrangements.

The Introduction Section

This and the next five sections deal with the preparation of the parts of an educational research report in the form of either a dissertation or a journal article manuscript.[1]

This section describes the preparation of the introductory section. Depending upon the length of the section, subsection headings may or may not appear (for example, "Context of the Problem," "Statement of the Problem," "Review of the Literature," "Statement of the Hypotheses," "Rationale for the Hypotheses," and so on).

Context of the Problem

The first paragraph or two of the introduction should acquaint the reader with the problem addressed by the study. This orientation is best accomplished by providing its background. One accepted way to establish a frame of reference for the problem is to quote authoritative sources. Consider the following opening paragraphs of introductions from each of two articles in the *American Educational Research Journal*:

---

[1] The research reports in Appendix A may be used as models for preparing reports. They have all been taken from journal sources. Readers are also referred to *The Publication Manual of the American Psychological Association* (4th edition, 1994) which is the most frequently used source for journal article form and style.

Context of the Problem[2]

The number of children in special classrooms is likely to be approximately one-half to one-third the number in regular classrooms. This is likewise true for mentally retarded children who are placed in resource rooms, at least for that part of their school day that is spent in direct resource room instruction (Sargent, 1981). Research on effects of class size, done primarily in regular classrooms, has frequently been inconclusive, but recent meta-analysis suggests generally positive effects for smaller classes in both learning (Glass & Smith, 1979) and behavior (Smith & Glass, 1980). The mean size of most special classrooms, however, tends to be generally smaller than that of most regular classrooms studied. That fact, coupled with the arguably different nature of instruction of special classrooms, raises questions as to the validity of the "smaller is better" theory applied to special classes for the mentally retarded. [Forness & Kavale, 1985, pp. 403–404]

Context of the Problem

Mathematics is a subject in which males continue to outperform females. Although controversy exists as to both the size and antecedents of the differences, male superiority in mathematics is seen in upper elementary years and increases throughout high school. Male superiority increases as the difficulty level of mathematics increases and is evident even when the number of mathematics courses taken by girls and boys in high school is held constant (Fennema, 1984). The Second and Third National Assessments of Educational Progress (NAEP) have provided specific information about these sex-related differences (Fennema & Carpenter, 1981; NAEP, 1983). The largest differences exist, as early as fourth grade, in tasks of high level cognitive complexity, that is, those tasks defined by NAEP that can be classified as requiring understanding (which "refers to explanation and interpretation of mathematical knowledge") or application (which "relies on processes of memory, algorithm, translation, and judgment"). [Carpenter, Corbitt, Kepner, & Reys, 1981, p. 6]

While there is an increasing body of knowledge about variables associated with sex-related differences in mathematics (Fox, 1981), little is known about characteristics of classrooms or teachers that contribute to these differences. [Peterson & Fennema, 1985, pp. 309–310]

Note that each introduction identifies the area in which the researchers find their problem. Additionally, they state their reasons for undertaking the projects; the introductions point out that the problems have not been fully studied or that the current studies promise useful contributions to understanding. These illustrations are short because each was drawn from a journal that emphasizes brevity of exposition. In other forms of research reports (and in some journal articles, as well), context statements may run somewhat longer than these examples. However, three paragraphs is recommended as a maximum.

---

[2] Because the use of headings is optional, the original material cited as examples often lacks these headings. When missing from the original, the appropriate headings have been added for clarity.

Statement of the Problem

The next element of an introduction is a statement of the research problem. Although some writers prefer to state their problems late in the introductions, a writer may gain an advantage by stating it early as a way to provide readers with an immediate basis from which to interpret subsequent statements (especially the review of the literature). Placing the statement of the problem near the beginning of the introduction helps readers to determine quickly the purpose of the study; they need not search through the introduction to discover what problem the study examines.

The statement of the problem should identify, if possible, all independent, moderator, and dependent variables, and it should ask, in question form, about their relationships. At this point in the exposition, it has given no operational definitions of the variables, so the problem statement should identify the variables in their conceptual form rather than in operational form. The variables should be named, but no description of measurement techniques is necessary at this point.

One or two sentences will normally suffice to state a research problem. Often the statement begins: "The purpose of this study was to examine the relationship between . . ." or "The present study explored. . . ."[3] Here are problem statements for the two previously quoted studies:

Problem

The purpose of the present study was to determine if any differential effects occur in the behavior of mildly mentally retarded children in EMR classrooms as a result of variations in class size. Does class size make a difference in the relative frequency of significant classroom behaviors such as attention, communication, and disruption? [Forness & Kavale, 1985, p. 404]

Problem

We addressed these issues by asking the following questions:

1. Do fourth grade girls and boys differ significantly in mathematics achievement on low level and high level items, and do they differ significantly in their achievement gains over a 6-month period?
2. Do fourth grade boys and girls differ significantly in the percentage of time that they are engaged in various types of activities during mathematics class?
3. Do significant relationships exist between the type of mathematics classroom activity in which girls and boys are engaged and their low level and high level achievement, and do these relationships differ significantly for boys and girls?

---

[3] In a research proposal, *is* or *will be* would be substituted for *was*, and *explores* or *will explore* would replace *explored*. A proposal is written in the present or future tense and a final report in the past tense.

4. Are there significant sex-related differences in engagement in classroom activities between classes that show low level and high level mathematics achievement gains that are greater for boys than girls, greater for girls than boys, and do not differ for boys and girls? [Peterson & Fennema, 1985, p. 311]

As additional examples, consider some problem statements taken from students' research projects:

Problem

The purpose of this study was threefold. An attempt was made to test the differential effects of the verbal praise of an adult (the type of reinforcement most often utilized by classroom teachers) (1) on a "culturally disadvantaged" as opposed to a white middle-class sample, (2) as a function of the sex of the agent, and (3) as a function of the race of agent and recipient of this reinforcement.

Problem

The purpose of this study was to determine whether girls who plan to pursue careers in science are more aggressive, more domineering, less conforming, more independent, and have a greater need for achievement than girls who do not plan such careers.

Problem

It was the purpose of this study to determine what differences, if any, existed in the way principals of large and small schools and principals (collectively) and presidents of teacher organizations viewed the level of involvement of the principal in a variety of administrative tasks.

Review of the Literature

The purpose of the literature review is to expand upon the context and background of the study, to refine the problem definition, and to provide an empirical basis for subsequent development of hypotheses. The length of the review may vary depending upon the number of relevant articles available and the purpose of the research report. Dissertations are usually expected to provide more exhaustive literature reviews than journal articles. Although some dissertation style manuals recommend devoting an entire chapter (typically the second) to a review of the literature, building the review into the introductory chapter has the advantage of forcing the writer to keep the review relevant to the problem statement and the hypotheses that surround it. This section examines the task of writing a literature review according to the procedures described in Chapter 3.

A good guideline for selecting the literature to cover in the review section is to cite references dealing with each of the variables in the study, paying special attention to articles that deal with both variables. Literature concerning conceptually similar or conceptually related variables should likewise be cited.

Subheadings should reflect the major variables (key words) of the literature review. The review should expand its descriptions of articles as their relevance to the study increases. Remember the purpose of the literature review—is to provide a basis for formulating hypotheses. In other words, review articles not for their own sake but as a basis for generalizing from them to your own study.

Consider the following organization of subheadings for the literature review section in a study of the relationship between teacher attitudes and teaching style:

Teacher Attitudes

Overview and Definitions
Open-Minded versus Closed-Minded: General Studies
Open-Minded versus Closed-Minded: Relation to Teaching
Humanistic versus Custodial: General Studies
Humanistic versus Custodial: Relation to Teaching

Teaching Style

Overview and Definitions
Directive versus Nondirective: General Studies
Directive versus Nondirective: Relation to Teacher Attitudes

Organizing the literature review section by subheadings helps readers to follow this information. Consequently, a lengthy review benefits from frequent subheadings to facilitate organization and meaning. To be most meaningful, these subheadings should reflect the study's variables and the general research problem (that is, their relationship). The subheadings should also be your guide to the searching process as well as to the reviewing process. The organization of the literature review section to support the problem statement enables you to work toward establishing hypotheses, thus providing a logic for both the reader and yourself. Consider an example:

An alternative approach to improve academic achievement is to enhance cognitive engagement by assuring that a particular learning strategy is used. One such strategy is the identification of key terms, along with their definitions, listed in outline form, which then can serve as an advance organizer for subsequent text processing (Mayer, 1987), or as a means of constructing meaning from text (Cook & Mayer, 1983). This approach has been shown to enhance recall and understanding (Weinstein & Mayer, 1986; Wilhite, 1988). Another learning strategy is elaboration, which involves having learners generate their own images or examples for main ideas. This strategy, too, has been shown to enhance recall and understanding (Gagne, Weidemann, Bell, & Anders, 1984; Gagne, Yekovich, & Yekovich, 1993; King, 1992). Elaboration also improves near- and far-transfer (Donnelly & McDaniel, 1993) and academic achievement

(Wittrock, 1986). In a synthesis of research on elaboration conducted over 2 decades, Levin (1988) concluded that it is an effective learning strategy because it prompts active information processing on the part of the learner. In other words, it activates processes required for knowledge construction. [Tuckman, 1996a; pp. 198–199]

It is also recommended that the subsection under each subheading begin with a sentence introducing the purpose, content, or relevance of the literature to be reviewed in the subsection. Each subsection should end with a sentence summarizing the conclusions or trends evident from the literature it reviews.

Statement of the Hypotheses

Repeated recommendations throughout this book (particularly in Chapter 4) have urged development of hypotheses that describe the anticipated relationships between variables. Hypotheses help to focus a study and to give it direction. Statements of these expectations often help readers to follow the report of a study. The introduction need not state hypotheses operationally, but it should articulate them clearly and concisely in conceptual terms for greatest generality. They may also be underlined or italicized for emphasis and to help readers locate them.

Although examples of hypotheses have been given in Chapter 4, here are two more examples:

Hypotheses

The specific hypotheses investigated were:

H_1: 1. There will be a difference in cognitive achievement between agents using paired/cooperative CAI and agents using CAI individually which will be influenced by agents' prior CAI experience and familiarity with the topic.

H_2: 2. There will be a difference in time spent on the lesson between agents using paired/cooperative CAI and agents using CAI individually which will be influenced by agents' prior CAI experience and familiarity with the topic. [Makuch, Robillard, & Yoder, 1992, p. 201]

Hypotheses

Thus, in the case of computers, we expected individuals' attributions about how much they enjoy using computers to decline significantly over time. We also expected gender to play a significant role with girls' assessments of computer enjoyment being significantly lower than boys' over time. In addition, based on previous work on the relationship between grade level and computer attitudes, we predicted that younger students' enjoyment of computers would be significantly higher than older students' enjoyment over time. That is, we anticipated a negative relationship between grade level and computer enjoyment. [Krendl & Broihier, 1992, p. 218]

Rationale for the Hypotheses

Hypotheses may be justified on two grounds—logical and empirical arguments. Logical justification requires a researcher to develop arguments based on concepts or theories related to the hypotheses; empirical justification requires reference to other research. A research report's introduction must provide justification for each hypothesis to assure the reader of its reasonableness and soundness. (Justification is especially critical in a proposal for a study that requires approval.) To provide logical arguments in support of hypotheses, describe or allude to appropriate premises, concepts, or theories. For empirical justification, you may refer to literature cited in the review section, although perhaps omitting some detail from the first description.

Inexperienced researchers often neglect to provide clear rationales for their hypotheses. All too often, they assume that the reasoning behind a hypothesis is obvious, an assumption that leads to confusion on the part of readers. Some may react by saying to themselves, "Whatever led you to expect that," or "I don't believe it." After reading the results, some may scoff, "You must have made this one up after you collected the data!" A strong rationale with logical and empirical support, contiguous to the statement of the hypothesis, minimizes the likelihood of such reactions.

Construct your hypotheses and establish their logical and empirical support *prior* to data collection and analysis, not after. Hypotheses are tools for helping researchers see the relationships between their theories and the work to be done; writing hypotheses after seeing the data makes hypothesizing a sterile activity (although such a review may identify hypotheses for future study).

Consider an example:

Hypotheses

Accordingly, the specific purpose of the present training study was to examine the role of knowledge of information sources in children's question-answering abilities through the examination of an instructional program designed to heighten their awareness of information sources. It was predicted that as a result of training, (a) students' awareness of appropriate sources of information for answering comprehension questions would be heightened, (b) students' strategies for providing answer information would be consistent with their identification of question-answer relationships, and (c) the quality of their answers would improve. Finally, it was predicted that these outcomes would vary with the students' reading levels, given the differential performance of students of varying levels in both the Raphael et al. (1980) and the Wonnacott and Raphael (1982) studies.

Rationale

Although the studies by Raphael et al. (1980) and by Wonnacott and Raphael (1982) suggested that knowledge about the question-answering process and sources of information for answering comprehension questions is important, both studies were essentially descriptive. Thus, they cannot provide causal explanations of the relationship between students' strategic (i.e., meta-cognitive) knowledge and actual performance. Belmont and Butterfield (1977) suggested that training studies can provide such information about cognitive processes. They proposed that successful intervention implies a causal relationship between the means trained and the goal to be reached; that is, one can learn if a component of a process is related to a goal, or cognitive outcome, by manipulating the process. Similar suggestions were proposed by Brown, Campione, and Day (1981) in their discussion of "informed" training studies where students are taught about a strategy and induced to use it and are given some indication of the significance of the strategy. Finally, Sternberg (1981) provided an extensive discussion of prerequisites for general programs that attempt to train cognitive skills, including suggestions such as the need to link such training to "real-world behavior" as well as to theoretical issues. [Raphael & Pearson, 1985, p. 219]

Operational Definitions of the Variables

A useful element of a study's introduction is a brief statement of operational definitions of the independent, moderator, and dependent variables. Although the method section that follows provides a detailed operational statement specifying exactly how the study will manipulate or measure variables, a reader may benefit from an early idea of what the variables mean. It is not considered necessary to operationally define all terms, just the principal variables.

Many examples of operational definitions are offered in Chapter 6. Two additional examples may add to that material:

Operational Definitions

Rhetorical Questions: Questions that do not expect some participation by the reader. Such questions never require the student to do anything, mentally or otherwise. Example: "But when a single cell enlarges, what then?"

Factual Questions: Questions that ask the reader to recall or recognize specific information (facts, concepts, laws) which were read previously in the text. Example: "What are some organisms that have a thin, thread-like body?"

Valuing Questions: Questions that ask the reader to make a cognitive or affective judgment or to explain the criteria used in an evaluation. Example: "How tolerable would life be under these conditions?"

Hypothesizing Questions: Questions that ask the reader to predict the outcome of or give a specific explanation for a question, problem, or situation. Example: "With the emergence of predatory organisms, would increased size and complexity result in traits with real survival advantage?" [Leonard & Lowery, 1984, pp. 378–379]

Operational Definitions

One of the most promising of these methodologies is the method of repeated readings (Dowhower, 1989; Samuels, 1979). In this approach, readers practice reading one text until some predetermined level of fluency is achieved. . . .

A related technique used to improve reading fluency is repeated listening-while-reading texts. This method differs from repeated readings in that the reader reads the text while simultaneously listening to a fluent rendition of the same text. [Rasinski, 1990, p. 147]

Operational Restatement of the Hypotheses (Predictions)

Although not absolutely essential, an introduction may aid reader understanding by restating hypotheses in operational form to provide a concrete picture of the aims of the study.[4] Because the hypotheses have already been stated conceptually and operational definitions of all the variables have been provided, this section of the introduction can easily restate the hypotheses in operational terms. Such operationalized hypotheses are often referred to as *predictions*. Consider these examples, which restate general expectations (hypotheses) as specific predictions about expected behaviors or performances:

Predictions

It was therefore predicted that teachers labelled as innovative by virtue of their applying for funds to develop an innovative classroom program would perceive their working environment to be more open as characterized by greater participation by teachers and students in the decision process, greater control by teachers over their own classroom behavior, and greater tolerance for dissent.

Predictions

Specifically, teachers displaying more liberal political attitudes as measured by the Opinionation Scale and the Dogmatism Scale (both developed by Rokeach) were expected to show more liberal tendencies toward the treatment of students as evidenced by a greater emphasis on autonomy for students and allowing students to set their own rules and regulations and enforce them.

Predictions

1. There would be a significant change in Vocational Identity, Occupational Information, and Barriers scores from pre- to post-course administrations of the *My Vocational Situation* (the outcome measure described in the method section).
2. There would be a greater change in Vocational Identity, Occupational Information, and Barriers scores over the first half of the course than over the last half.
3. There would be interactions between instructor and student characteristics and increases in Vocational Identity, Occupational Information, and Barrier scale scores (i.e., student and instructor characteristics would have an

---

[4] Restatement is more appropriate in dissertations than in journal articles, because space is at a premium in the latter.

impact on the effects achieved). [Rayman, Bernard, Holland, & Barnett, 1983, p. 347]

Significance of the Study

Readers of a research proposal or report are usually concerned with the relevance of the problem it addresses both to practice and to theory. Many people highly value research that makes primary or secondary contributions to the solutions of practically oriented educational problems. The field of education also needs research that establishes and verifies theories or models. To these ends, a report introduction benefits by indicating the value or potential significance of the problem area and hypothesized findings to educational practice, educational theory, or both. Again, some examples are offered:

Significance of the Study

Thus, the purpose of the present study was to explore the effect of examiner familiarity on handicapped and nonhandicapped preschool and school-age children. In doing so, this investigation extends previous research (a) by determining whether examiner unfamiliarity affects handicapped and nonhandicapped children similarly, or biases test results against handicapped populations, and (b) by exploring whether handicapped preschoolers' poorer performance with strange testers primarily is a developmental issue or whether it is more consistently related to the nature of being handicapped. [Fuchs, Fuchs, Power, & Dailey, 1985, p. 186]

Significance of the Study

Finally, the relations between motivation, self-regulated learning, and student performance on classroom academic tasks were examined. The focus on classroom assessments of student performance reflects a concern for ecologically valid indicators of the actual academic work that students are asked to complete in junior high classrooms (Doyle, 1983). Most students spend a great deal of classroom time on seatwork assignments, quizzes, teacher-made tests, lab problems, essays, and reports rather than on standardized achievement tests (Stiggins & Bridgeford, 1985). These assignments may not be the most psychometrically sound assessments of student academic performance, but they are closely related to the realities of instruction and learning in most classrooms (Calfee, 1985). If we are to develop models of student motivation and self-regulated learning that are relevant for much of the academic work in classrooms, then it is important to examine student performance on these types of academic tasks (cf., Doyle, 1983; Pintrich et al., 1986). [Pintrich & De Groot, 1990, p. 34]

THE METHOD SECTION

This section discusses a recommended set of categories for describing the methods and procedures of a study. Each category may correspond to a subheading in the research report. Such a high degree of structure for the method section is recommended, because this section contains detailed statements of the actual steps undertaken in the research.

Subjects

The purpose of the proposal or report section entitled "Subjects" is to indicate *who* participated in the study and *how many* it involved. Where relevant, this section should also indicate whether or not the subjects were volunteers (that is, how their participation was arranged), how they were selected, and what characteristics they displayed. Characteristics typically reported include gender, age, grade, and IQ (median and/or range). All potential sources of selection bias covered by control variables should be identified in this section.

Providing such information allows another researcher to select a virtually identical sample if he or she chooses to replicate the study. In fact, the entire method section should be written in a way that provides another researcher with the possibility of replicating your methodology.

Consider some examples:

Participants

The participants were 109 juniors and seniors in college, all preparing to be teachers. They were enrolled in three sections of an educational psychology course required for teacher certification during the summer term. The course lasted 15 weeks. All three sections met once a week (on consecutive days) at the same time of day, covered the same content (learning theories), used the same textbook, and were taught by the same instructor (the researcher). For the students in each section, the average age was between 20 and 22, the average percentage of females was between 65% and 70%, and the average score on the reading subtest of the College Level Academic Skills Test (CLAST) was between 315 and 320. A comparison of the three classes on age, gender, and CLAST scores showed them to be equivalent (F < 1 in all three cases), thus satisfying the requirements for a quasi-experimental design. Correlations between CLAST reading scores and achievement in this course have been found to be about .5 (Tuckman, 1993). [Tuckman, 1996a, p. 200]

Subjects

The sample consisted of 53 eighth-grade subjects (34 girls, 19 boys) attending a public middle school. Subjects were judged most likely to be from middle-class families and were predominantly white (87%). The subjects were classified into two groups: good and poor readers. Subjects were primarily classified on the basis of stanine scores obtained on a reading subtest of the Comprehensive Test of Basic Skills (CTBS), which had been administered in the spring of the previous school year. Subjects were classified as poor readers ($n = 27$) if their stanine score on the vocabulary and comprehension reading subtest of the CTBS was 3 or below. Subjects were classified as good readers ($n = 26$) if they had stanine scores of 6 or above. Subjects with stanine scores in the 4 to 5 range were thought of as average readers and unsuited for this investigation. Subjects were also rated by their teachers as either good or poor readers according to such criteria as fluency, oral reading errors, and comprehension. Ages for the subjects ranged from 12 years, 4 months to 14 years, 11 months. No emphasis was placed on sex because similar studies in the past generally reported a nonsignificant difference between the sexes in points gained due to answer changing. [Casteel, 1991, pp. 301–302]

Tasks and Materials

Some studies (but definitely not all) incorporate certain activities in which all subjects participate or certain materials that all subjects use. These tasks and materials represent neither dependent or independent variables; rather than being treatments themselves, they are vehicles for introducing treatments. In a study comparing multiple-choice and completion-type response modes for a self-instructional learning program, for example, the content of the learning program would constitute the task, because Ss in both groups would experience this content. Apart from the content that remained constant across conditions, one group would experience multiple-choice questions in its program, while the second would experience completion-type questions. Program question format is thus the independent variable, and it would be described in the next report section (on "Independent Variables"). Program content is the task and would be described in this section. Activities experienced by all groups are described in this section; thus, if the content of a program or presentation were constant for both groups, it would be described under "Tasks." Activities experienced by one or some but not all of the groups are described in the "Independent Variable" section. Frequently, however, studies include no common activity or task, and the report on such a study would entirely omit this section.

Some examples suggest the information appropriate to this section:

Tasks and Materials

Instructional program. Two computer-based lessons developed by Carrier and her associates were used (Carrier, Davidson, Higson, & Williams, 1984; Carrier et al., 1985; Carrier & Williams, 1988). Both lessons teach four defined concepts in advertising—bandwagon, testimonial, transfer, and uniqueness. According to Carrier et al. (1984), the definition for each concept was based on an assessment of its critical attributes, and an instance pool for each concept was generated. Each instance pool was tested with a group of 35 sixth graders to test difficulty level and to eliminate confusing instances. [Klein & Keller, 1990, p. 142]

In this study, all Ss received the same instructional material; the only difference consisted in the conditions under which it was used. In the study exerpted in the next quote, all *S*s received the same tasks but with differing instructions, allowing the researchers to solicit the dependent variable measures:

Tasks and Materials

Three paired-associate lists, each consisting of 10 concrete noun pairs, were constructed. Within each condition, seven subjects each received a given list as the first, second, or third list presented. Two additional lists, one consisting of 5 pairs and one of 10 pairs, were used to assess long-term maintenance of the effective strategy. A practice list of 3 pairs was also constructed. [Ghatala, Levin, Pressley, & Lodico, 1985, p. 202]

In another study, each student learned the subject matter described in the next excerpt. However, in the different conditions of the independent variable, the instruction was controlled in different ways. This process is described in detail in the first example in the later section of this chapter on "Independent Variables."

Tasks and Materials

The instructional task selected for this study was a mathematics rule lesson concerning divisibility by two, three, and five. This content had not yet been taught to the target students. Each treatment consisted of the same basic tutorial CAI program, designed to teach the rules for divisibility by two, three, and five, and the application of these rules to five and six digit numbers. The lesson structure was based on the "Events of Instruction" and adapted to CAI (Gagne, Wager, & Rojas, 1981). Three versions representing different CAI design strategies were developed. [Goetzfried & Hannafin, 1985, p. 274]

Independent Variables

In this section, the researcher report should describe independent (and moderator) variables, each under a separate heading.[5] Researchers generally must explain two types of independent variables—manipulated and measured variables. The description of a manipulated variable (often referred to as a *treatment*) should explain the manipulation or materials that constituted the treatment (such as, what you did or what you gave). Be specific enough so that someone else can replicate your manipulation. Identify each level of the manipulation or treatment, itemizing each for emphasis.

---

[5] Recall from Chapter 5 that a moderator variable is a secondary type of independent variable, one that is included in a study to determine whether it affects or moderates the relationship between the primary independent variable(s) and the dependent variable. A moderator variable is, therefore, a special type of independent variable, and the write-up treats it as an independent variable but labels it differently, for purposes of clarity.

This example describes a manipulated independent variable with three levels or conditions:

Treatments

Incentive motivation condition. One class ($n = 36$) took a seven-item, completion-type quiz at the beginning of each class period. A sample item is: "A consequence of a response that increases the strength of the response or the probability of the response's reoccurrence is called a (an) _____" (ans.: reinforcer). The quiz covered the textbook chapter assigned for that week. It was projected via an overhead projector, and 15 min were allowed for its completion. No instruction on the chapter had been provided before the quiz. The only information resource for the student was the textbook itself. Following the quiz, students exchanged papers and the instructor discussed the answers so that students could grade one another's tests. Students were informed that the average of their quiz grades would count for one half of their grade for that segment, the same as the end-of-segment achievement test. Each segment of the course involved 5 weeks of instruction and covered from four to five textbook chapters.

Learning strategy condition. One class ($n = 35$) was given the homework assignment of identifying the 21 most important terms in the assigned chapter and preparing a definition of each term and a one-sentence elaboration of each definition. A list of approximately 28 terms was predetermined by the instructor for each chapter, and students' choices had to fit this list. The text included many signals so that it was not difficult for students to identify each term and information about it. The text did not include a list of major terms in each chapter or a glossary, so students had to identify the important terms on their own. For example, in the chapter on reinforcement theory, *reinforcer* was identified as a key term. An example of a student definition would be "something that increases the likelihood of occurrence of the response it follows," and the student's elaboration might be "getting something good to eat after doing my homework."

Students were given 1 hr of training, including examples and practice, before they started and another hour after having done two assignments. They were also given feedback on all aspects of each assignment so their proficiency would improve. Each assignment was graded (A, B, or C) based on number of correct terms included, correctness of definitions, and appropriateness of elaborations. The grades were averaged and counted for half of the segment grade, the same as the average of quiz grades in the incentive motivation condition.

Control condition. One class ($n = 38$) heard only lectures in class on the chapters. No quizzes were given, and no homework was assigned. This is the manner in which the course is typically taught. [Tuckman, 1996a, pp. 200–201]

The second form of independent variable is a *measured* variable, that is, a variable based on test scores or observational data. A study may include such measured variables in addition to or instead of a treatment variable. In describing the measured independent variable (such as intelligence, personality, aptitude), the research report must indicate what instrument the researcher used to measure it. If a standardized test was used, provide a published reference source for it, such as the test manual, and indicate the test's reliability and validity. If the assessment used a homemade instrument, indicate whatever psychometric properties were determined and place a copy of the homemade test instrument in an appendix to the report.

Consider a description of a measured independent variable, in this case a moderator variable:

Moderator Variable

Formal Operational Reasoning Test (FORT). This paper-and-pencil test constructed by Roberge and Flexer (1982) was used to evaluate subjects' logical thinking abilities. It contains subtests that can be used to assess subjects' level of reasoning for three essential components of formal operational thought: combinations, propositional logic, and proportionality (cf. Greenbowe et al., 1981).

Roberge and Flexner illustrated the content validity of the FORT by describing the relationship between each of the FORT subtests and the corresponding Inhelder and Piaget (1958) formal operations scheme, and they presented factor analytic evidence of the construct validity of the FORT. Furthermore, Roberge and Flexner reported test-retest reliability coefficients (2-week interval) of .81 and .80 for samples of seventh and eighth graders, respectively, on the combinations subtest. They also reported internal consistency reliability coefficients (K-R Formula 20) of .75 and .74 for samples of seventh and eighth graders, respectively, on the logic subtest; and internal consistency coefficients of .52 and .60 for seventh and eighth graders, respectively, on the proportionality subtest.

Subjects also were classified as high operational or low operational on the basis of their performance on the FORT. To be classified as high operational, the subjects had to correctly answer at least 60% of the items on two (or more) of the FORT subtests. Subjects whose scores did not meet this criterion were classified as low operational. [Roberge & Flexner, 1984, pp. 230–231]

This example might have given more detail about the measure than was required. The amount of detail reported varies as a function of the familiarity of the instrument, the requirements of the readers, and the report's space allocation.

Dependent Variables

Each dependent variable should also be described. Because a dependent variable is typically a measured variable, it is necessary to describe the behavior measured, the instrument for measuring it, and the scoring procedure. Review two examples:

Dependent Variables

1. *Mathematics Achievement.* The Mathematics Computations and Concepts and Applications subscales of the Comprehensive Test of Basic Skills (CTBS) were the achievement criterion measures. Fourth graders took Level 2, Form S, while fifth and sixth graders took Level H, Form U. Standardized rather

than curriculum-specific tests were used to be sure that the learning of students in all treatments was equally likely to be registered on the tests. The CTBS Computations scales covered whole number operations, fractions, and decimals, objectives common to virtually all texts and school districts, and the Concepts and Applications scales focused on measurement, geometry, sets, word problems, and concepts, also common to most texts and school districts.

District-administered California Achievement Test (CAT) scores were used as covariates for their respective CTBS scores. That is, CAT Computations was used as a covariate for CTBS Computations, and CAT Concepts and Applications was a covariate for CTBS Concepts and Applications. Because of the different tests used at different grade levels, all scores were transformed to T scores (mean = 50, SD = 10), and then CTBS scores were adjusted for their corresponding CAT scores using separate linear regressions for each grade. These adjusted scores were used in all subsequent analyses. Note that this adjustment removes any effect of grade level, as the mean for all tests was constrained to be 50 at each grade level.

2. *Attitudes.* Two eight-item attitude scales were given as pre- and posttests. They were Liking of Math Class (e.g., "this math class is the best part of my school day") and Self-Concept in Math (e.g., "I'm proud of my math work in this class"; "I worry a lot when I have to take a math test"). For each item, students marked either YES!, yes, no, or NO! Coefficient alpha reliability estimates on these scales were computed in an earlier study (Slavin et al., 1984) and found to be .86 and .77, respectively. [Slavin & Karweit, 1985, pp. 355–356]

Dependent Variable

A 50-multiple-choice-item test, matched to instructional content, was given to measure end-of-segment achievement. The test had a K-R reliability of .82. Virtually all the test questions related to key terms, a central feature of the assignments in the learning strategy condition; however, they measured comprehension rather than factual recall. In other words, the test questions represented a higher order cognitive task than the homework assignment did. Students typically were asked to identify the concept that fit a given example or the example that fit a given concept. For instance, "According to the PREMACK PRINCIPLE, which of the following reinforcers would be most appropriate for the given group? a. Money for adults; b. Tokens for inner city children; c. Playing for third graders; d. Praise for teenagers." (The answer is c. because the Premack principle applies only to activity reinforcers and playing is the only activity among the four choices.)

The test questions were equally unlikely to favor the incentive motivation group because the quiz questions assessed factual recall using a completion-type format. Moreover, the quiz questions focused on details and specific points in the chapter such as illustrations and activities. Thus, there was minimal overlap between test questions and quiz questions. [Tuckman, 1996a, pp. 201–202]

Procedures

The procedures section should describe any operational details that have not yet been described and that another researcher would need to know to replicate the method. Such details usually include (1) the specific order in which steps were undertaken, (2) the timing of the study (for example, time allowed for different procedures and time elapsed between procedures), (3) instructions given to subjects, and (4) briefings, debriefings, and safeguards.

Consider some illustrations:

Procedures

Standardized mathematics scores were gathered for each student before the study. The 20th percentile was the median score for the 47 students and was used to classify students as "below average" or "low" in prior mathematics achievement. Those students below the 20th percentile were classified as low achievement, and those above the 20th percentile were classified as below average achievement for purposes of this study.

The students were randomly assigned to one of the three treatment groups, stratified to ensure [that] approximately equal numbers of males and females with low and below average achievement were assigned to each treatment. Each student received a brief review of computer operation and was instructed to proceed with the lesson. At the conclusion of the lesson the elapsed time was noted and the immediate posttest was administered. One week later students were given the parallel retention test in their classroom. [Goetzfried & Hannafin, 1985, p. 275]

Procedure

Students participated in research sessions lasting 55 minutes a day for 11 days. Each condition was assigned a separate classroom comparable in size. The curriculum unit used for instruction was a science unit on the ecology of the wolf. Each day the teachers would explain the day's task to the students, distribute the appropriate materials, and review the condition's nature. The teachers followed a daily script detailing what they were to say and do each day. [Johnson & Johnson, 1985, p. 245]

Procedures

After permission to conduct the study was granted, we searched school records to obtain student-ability scores for each subject. All subjects were given the IAR questionnaire to measure their beliefs in internal versus external control over academic responsibility (Crandall et al., 1965). This measure was given to subjects in their English classes several days prior to receiving the treatment.

Subjects were randomly assigned to one of the two treatment conditions. One half of the subjects completed the learner-controlled lesson, and the other one half completed the program-controlled lesson. To receive the treatment, we brought subjects in groups of 14 to an Apple computer lab for 1 hour on 3 consecutive days. Seven subjects using the learner-controlled lesson and 7 using the program-controlled lesson were represented in each group.

On the 1st day, we told the subjects that they would be using a computer lesson to learn about some ideas used in advertising. On each day, subjects were asked to work through the lesson until they were finished and to raise their hands to indicate when they were done. At the end of the lesson on the 3rd day, all the subjects completed the confidence measure and then took the posttest. A formative evaluation of these procedures was conducted prior to the actual study. No problems were found at that time, and none occurred during the study. [Klein & Keller, 1990, p. 142]

Data Analysis

The data analysis section of a research report describes the statistical design used and the statistical analyses undertaken. It is usually not necessary to describe these procedures step by step. If the study relied on common statistical tests (such as, analysis of variance, *t*-tests, chi-square analysis, correlation), the test may simply be named and its source referenced. More unusual approaches require more detail.

These points are illustrated in some examples:

Design and Data Analysis

This study used a $3 \times 2 \times 2$ between-subject factorial design with two additional within-subject factors. The between-subject factors included three levels of CAI strategy (adaptive control, learner control with advisement, and linear control), two levels of achievement (low and below average), and sex of student. The within-subject factors included test scale (rule recall and rule application) and test interval (immediate and retention). Rule recall and application data, as well as learning efficiency data, were analyzed using MANOVA procedures for repeated measures designs. ANOVA procedures were used to examine effects for differences in time on task. Comparisons among treatment means were accomplished using Newman-Keuls pairwise contrast procedures. [Goetzfried & Hannafin, 1985, pp. 275–276]

Research Design and Statistical Analysis

The proposed study compared the effectiveness of two stress reduction methods in interaction with the locus of control of the participating teachers. The independent variables in the study were (a) treatments—an LDW and SDT, and (b) locus of control—internal and external. The dependent variables were scores on stress posttests after a 5-week treatment program. The fundamental research design was a 2×2 factorial, however, with an attached control group. Analysis of covariance was used to test the hypotheses. Those pretest measures that correlated significantly with the posttest measures were used as covariates. Hypothesis 1 was tested at the .05 level of significance, whereas hypothesis 2 was tested at the .10 level of significance. A more liberal alpha level was adopted for testing the interaction hypothesis in order to improve the probability of detecting (i.e., power) the interaction effect. [Friedman et al., 1983, p. 570]

Analysis

For purposes of interpretive clarity, scores on the memory tests were converted into percentages. Means and standard deviations for each test (i.e., FR, FIB, and

MC) as a function of role group (teacher vs. learner) and verbal ability (high vs. low) are presented in Table 1.

To assess performance differences between groups, a $2 \times 2 \times 3$ within-subjects analysis of variance (ANOVA) was performed on test scores using type of test (FR, FIB, and MC) as the within-subjects measure. Role condition (teacher vs. learner and verbal ability (high vs. low) were the between-groups factors. [Wiegmann, Dansereau, & Patterson, 1992, pp. 113–114]

A proposal or final research report (such as a dissertation) may need to provide more detail in each category of the method section than is evident in the examples. (The examples chosen for this text were selected in part for their brevity. Moreover, the examples were drawn from journal sources, which place a premium on space, thus resulting in a terse style.) To obtain some idea of length and level of detail, read research reports of the same form that you are about to prepare (that is, dissertations, master's theses, journal articles), paying particular attention to form. Occasions will undoubtedly arise when a particular study will require more or fewer categories or a different order of presentation than that shown in this section.

THE RESULTS SECTION

The purpose of the results section in a research report is to present the outcomes of the statistical tests that were conducted on the data, particularly as they relate to the hypotheses tested in the study. However, the results section omits discussion, explanation, or interpretation of the results. These functions are carried out in the discussion section, which follows. Tables and figures are usually essential to a results section, with the text briefly describing the contents of those visual displays in words.

The best structure for the results section relates its information to the hypotheses the study set out to test. The first heading announces results for Hypothesis 1, the second for Hypothesis 2, and so on. (Such subdivisions would not be necessary, of course, in a study with only a single hypothesis.) In general, each heading would then be followed by several elements:

1. A brief restatement of the hypothesis, with a clear indication of the dependent variable
2. An indication of descriptive statistics (usually means and standard deviations on the dependent variable for each treatment group) with a reference to a specific table, if the number of means is sufficient to warrant a table
3. An indication of the statistical tests employed to evaluate the hypothesis (for example, analysis of variance, t-tests, correlations)
4. The alpha level set for testing the hypothesis (usually $p < .05$)

5. A brief statement identifying the statistical assumptions examined (for example, normality of the score distribution, homogeneity of variance in the treatment groups on the dependent variable)
6. The anticipated effect size, if desired, including the number of subjects per condition, and the power of the statistical test used
7. The results of the statistical tests, including a verbal description of their findings along with actual results of the statistical tests (for example, *F*-ratios, *t*-values, correlations, degrees of freedom, and probability values, paralleling, in brief, the table in which these data are listed)
8. The magnitude of the effect obtained, if it proves significant and the researcher desires to report it, expressed as an effect size or proportion of variance in the dependent variable accounted for by the independent variable
9. An indication of whether the data justified acceptance or rejection of the hypothesis

Following the report of results bearing directly on the hypotheses, incidental results should be reported, using a format similar to that just described for reporting results of hypothesis tests. The general order for presenting results would be first, tests of major hypotheses, second, tests of minor hypotheses; and third, incidental results or research questions for which no hypotheses were formulated.

A general rule calls for providing sufficient detail so that the reader can comprehend the results by reading the text without consulting the tables or figures. Similarly, tables and figures should be prepared so that they can stand alone as descriptions of the outcomes of the study.

The following seven examples were drawn from the results sections included in journal articles. Each example represents only a portion of a report's section, typically pertaining to a single finding or cluster of related findings. Each refers to a table or figure or both, and each illustration proceeds to identify the relevant statistical findings as set forth in the table or figure with little explanation or embellishment.

Declarative Knowledge

On the pretest, no differences on the declarative knowledge variables were found between subjects. On the immediate posttest, there was an effect of the dispersion of the examples on the number of characteristics of windflowers mentioned on the declarative knowledge test, $F(1, 45) = 4.62$, $p < .03$. Subjects in the narrow-dispersion conditions remembered more characteristics than did subjects in the wide-dispersion conditions (see Table 4). On the delayed posttest, no effects were noticed. [Ranzijn, 1991, p. 326]

Results

Table I shows the means and standard deviations for rule recall and application. A significant difference for prior achievement was found, $F(1, 34) = 16.74$, $p < .0005$. A prior achievement-by-scale interaction was also detected, $(1, 34) =$

6.63, $p < .01$. Below average students scored higher across both the rule and application scales, but proportionally higher on application items.

A significant difference in instructional time was found for CAI strategy, $F(2, 38) = 15.80$, $p < .001$. As shown in Table II, the linear strategy averaged less time to complete than both the externally controlled adaptive strategy, $p < .05$, and the learner advisement strategy, $p < .01$. The time differences between the adaptive and advisement strategies were also significant, $p < .01$. A significant effect was again detected for prior achievement, $F(1, 38) = 4.88$, $p < .05$. Below average students used less time to complete treatments than low achievement students. [Goetzfried & Hannafin, 1985, p. 276]

Results

Table II presents the mean learning scores, rote and conceptual, for the experimental and control groups (maximum scores on each part were 24). Subjects who learned in order to teach evidenced significantly greater conceptual learning than subjects who learned in order to be tested ($t = 5.42$; $df = 38$; $p < .001$), although the two groups did not differ on rote learning ($t = 1.39$).

As indicated earlier, subjects were asked to keep track of how long they spent learning the material, after it was suggested that they spend approximately 3 hours. Results revealed no difference in the amount of time spent ($t = .69$); the experimental group reported spending an average of 2.55 hours working on the material, and the control group reported spending an average of 2.71 hours. [Benware & Deci, 1984, p. 762]

Procedural Knowledge

A multivariate analysis of variance (MANOVA) and subsequent univariate analysis of variance (ANOVA) revealed no significant effects on the pretest nor on the immediate posttest. On the delayed posttest, there was a significant effect of the dispersion of the examples on the number of correctly classified color pictures of windflowers (COL.WIND), $F(1, 45) = 8.14$, $p < .006$, on the number of correctly classified windflowers (WIND.TOT), $F(1, 45) = 4.81$, $p < .03$, and on the total number of correctly classified flowers (TOTAL), $F(1, 45) = 3.52$, $p < .06$. This means that subjects who were presented with the widely dispersed video examples classified more flowers correctly than did subjects who were presented with the narrowly dispersed examples (see Tables 2 and 3).

The analysis also showed an interaction between the number and dispersion of the examples, $F(1, 45) = 3.86$, $p < .05$. This means that subjects in the Narrow-4 condition performed less well than did subjects in the Narrow-1 condition on the delayed posttest. However, subjects in the Wide-4 condition performed better than did subjects in the Wide-1 condition. [Ranzijn, 1991, pp. 325–326]

Results

The results of the analysis revealed a significant three-way interaction, $F(2, 72) = 3.48$, $p \leq .05$. Analyses of simple effects (Kirk, 1982) revealed that high verbal ability participants in the learner-role condition outperformed both high ability participants in the teacher-role condition, FR: $F(1, 72) = 4.76$, $p \leq .05$; FIB: $F(1, 72) = 16.90$, $p \leq .01$; MC: $F(1, 72) = 6.33$, $p \leq .05$. High verbal ability participants also outperformed low ability participants in the learner-role condition, FR: $F(1, 72) = 7.29$, $p \le .05$: FIB: $F(1, 72) = 45.07$, $p \le .05$; MC: $F(1, 72) = 17.05$. $p \le .05$. In contrast, low verbal ability participants in the teacher-role condition outperformed low verbal participants in the learner-role condition on the FR test, $F(1, 72) = 3.37$, $p = .07$, and the FIB test, $F(1, 72) = 19.30$, $p \le .01$, but not on the MC test. ($MS_e = 60.81$ for all interactions.) There were no significant differences between high and low ability participants in the teacher-role condition. No other comparisons were made. [Wiegmann et al., 1992, p. 114]

Results

The achievement test performance of each experimental group was as follows: (a) incentive motivation group mean = 82.8% ($SD = 9.3$), (b) learning strategy group mean = 71.6% ($SD = 9.4$), and (c) control group mean = 66.9% ($SD = 12.6$). The analysis of variance (ANOVA) for the difference between the three group means yielded $F(2, 106) = 21.69$, $p < .001$. The Newman-Keuls test revealed that the incentive motivation group earned a significantly higher test score ($p < .001$) than did either of the groups in the other two conditions. The effect size was near or above 1.00 for each comparison with the incentive motivation group. The mean score of the learning strategies group exceeded that of the control group ($p < .10$). [Tuckman, 1996a, p. 202]

Additional Results

The number, percentage, and type of revised answers made by the two levels of readers on the multiple-choice test are presented in Table 4. Among the 53 students in the investigation, 652 revisions were made in answers on the 76-item test, of which 415 or 64% represented changes from wrong to right answers, resulting in a net gain in the scores. On the other hand, 139 or 19% of those revisions made were from right to wrong answers, which lowered scores accordingly. There were 4,028 total responses. Group differences with respect to the three types of response changes were small. Poor readers were more likely than good readers to make a revision of wrong to right.

Ninety-eight percent of all subjects (96% good and 100% poor readers) changed at least 1 answer; almost two-thirds of the subjects changed responses to at least 11% of the 76 items. The ratio of subjects gaining to subjects losing points was 10:3 for poor readers and 5:1 for good readers. Moreover, the ratio of changes for gains to changes for losses was about 2:1 for both good and poor readers. Simply stated, when subjects of both groups made revisions, their changes resulted in a net gain in points twice that of points lost through revision. [Casteel, 1991, p. 306]

THE DISCUSSION SECTION

The discussion section of a research report considers the nuances and shades of the findings; finally, this material gives scope for displaying the perceptiveness and creativity of the researcher and writer. A critical part of the research report, this section is often the most difficult to write, because it is the least structured. The details of the research dictate content in the introduction, method, and results sections, but not in the discussion section.

The discussion section, however, does have a frame of reference: It follows the introduction section. Elements of this discussion must address the points raised in the introduction. But within this frame of reference, the writer is free to use whatever art and imagination he or she commands to show the range and depth of significance of the study. The discussion section ties the results of the study to both theory and application by pulling together the theoretical background, literature reviews, potential significance for application, and results of the study.

Because a research report's discussion section is such a personalized expression of a particular study by a particular researcher, it would be unwise to recommend definite categories for this section like those provided for previous sections. It may be helpful, however, to identify and describe the various functions of the discussion section.

Discussion to Conclude or Summarize

One very straightforward function of the discussion section is to summarize the findings of the study in the form of conclusions. If the study has been set up to test specific hypotheses, the discussion section must report the outcome on each hypothesis, along with ancillary findings. A useful discussion section often begins with a summary of the main findings (numbered as the original hypotheses when reports articulate multiple, numbered hypotheses) under the heading "Conclusions." As a starting point, this presentation enables readers to get the total picture of the findings in encapsulated form, and it also helps to orient them to the discussion that follows. Three examples of conclusion summaries appear below:

Conclusions

Classroom behavior appears to differ as a function of size of EMR classrooms. These differences are most apparent in communication of EMR pupils and are furthermore in the direction that might be expected, that is, more verbalization or gestures in smaller classrooms, less in medium-size classrooms, and least in the largest classrooms. In attending or nonattending behavior, subjects apparently tended to be more attentive in either large or small classrooms, as compared to medium-size classes. In classroom disruption, post hoc differences suggested significantly less misbehavior by subjects in smaller classes compared to subjects in medium-size classrooms, when such behavior involves teachers; but, when it involves peers, misbehavior appeared significantly less often in medium-size classrooms but only when these are compared to larger classrooms. [Forness & Kavale, 1985, p. 409]

Conclusions

The results of this study show, as expected, that presenting subjects broadly dispersed examples in an instruction for natural concepts had a positive effect on the development of procedural knowledge. Subjects who received broadly dispersed examples classified more objects correctly on a delayed posttest than did subjects who received examples that were centered around the prototype. Further, it was shown that the number of visually presented examples in the instruction did not significantly influence classification skill. [Ranzijn, 1991, pp. 326–327]

Conclusions

The results indicate that enhancing incentive motivation by giving quizzes helps students, primarily those with low GPAs, perform better on regular achievement tests than a prescribed learning strategy that is aimed at improving text processing. This finding suggests that poorly performing students do not necessarily lack text-processing skills. Rather, they lack the motivation to process the text. [Tuckman, 1996a, p. 206]

Discussion to Interpret

What do the study's findings mean? What might have been happening within the conduct of the study to account for the findings? Why did the results turn out differently from those hypothesized or expected? What circumstances accounted for the unexpected outcomes? What were some of the shortcomings of the study? What were some of its limitations? The discussion section must address these kinds of questions.

It must offer reasoned speculation. It may even include additional analyses of the data, referred to as *post-hoc analyses,* because they are done after the main findings are seen. Such analyses are introduced into the discussion section to support the interpretation and to account further for findings that on the surface appear inconsistent or negative with respect to the researcher's intentions.

For example, in one study, a researcher hypothesized that, among students whose parents work in scientific occupations, males are more likely to choose an elective science course than females. No mention was made of students whose parents do *not* work in scientific occupations. The hypothesis was not supported, however; students whose parents worked in scientific occupations were as likely to choose a science elective whether they were male or female. This finding contradicted other researchers' prior findings of gender differences. To try for clarification, the researcher ran a post-hoc analysis of students whose parents were not employed in science fields and presented the results in the discussion section. As in the prior studies, the researcher found that males chose science more frequently than did females. Because this analysis was not planned in advance but occurred after and as a result of seeing the planned analyses, it was considered post hoc and placed in the discussion section.

Review some further examples:

The results of this study showed that working in groups increased the performance of middle self-efficacy subjects whereas the performance of high and low self-efficacy subjects decreased. Why should shared outcomes or shared fate have the effect of helping those subjects average in self-efficacy while hindering those either high or low in self-efficacy? It is not uncommon for groups to have an averaging or leveling effect on the performance of individual group members. High believers are discouraged from working up to their level of expectation because their extra effort may bear no fruit if their teammates perform at a lower level. Low believers may feel that their effort is unnecessary because their teammates will "carry them." Only those in the middle may see the benefits of having partners and the benefits of performing at a level higher than they might if they were working alone. [Tuckman, 1990a, pp. 295–296]

There is at least one alternative explanation for the handicapped students' differential performance: Examiners may have been prejudiced in favor of their familiar examinees, awarding them more credit than their performance was due. Such an explanation receives some support from a large and enduring literature on rater bias (e.g., Guilford, 1936; Kazdin, 1977; Rosenthal, 1980). However, two points reduce the plausibility of this notion. First, previous research (Fuchs & Fuchs, 1984), conducted with a comprehensive language test requiring similar types of examiner judgments as the test instrument employed in the present study, indicates handicapped children performed better in the familiar examiner condition, regardless of whether examiners or independent observers of the test sessions completed subjects' protocols. [Fuchs et al., 1985, p. 194]

An alternative explanation for the present findings is that low ability students benefited from assuming the teacher role simply because the role allowed them to be more of a leader or more in charge of the sequence of activities during the interaction. Therefore, the teacher role simply served to disinhibit low ability students from contributing to the interaction and motivated them to learn the material. On the other hand, high ability students benefited more from assuming the learner role because the role not only removed the burden of teaching lower ability students but also provided them with a partner who was more likely to contribute to the interaction. [Weigmann et al., 1992, p. 114]

Another issue that affects the interpretation of the results is whether the quizzes functioned as a direct training aid or targeted study guide for the achievement tests rather than as an incentive to study. Unavoidably, some quiz items covered content also covered on one of the exams, as did terms that were studied in the homework assignments in the learning strategy condition. However, the nature of the items was quite different in the two experimental conditions. In the quizzes, students were given the definition of a conditioned stimulus and asked to supply the term *conditioned stimulus* as the correct answer. In the homework assignments, the students were asked to both define and elaborate on the term *conditioned stimulus*. On the achievement test, students were given one actual, unfamiliar example of conditioning in a natural environment and asked to identify one of its elements, namely, the conditioned stimulus. If the quizzes were merely study guides, they should have helped students at all three GPA levels, particularly those at the middle and low levels. Although they did help the low-GPA students substantially, they had no effect at all on the middle-GPA students. [Tuckman, 1996a, pp. 208–209]

How can the differences between these findings and previous research be explained? It might be that at least some of the differences lie in the measure of the dependent variable, departmental quality. Almost all previous studies have measured quality on the basis of departments identified in reputational peer ratings. Since most faculty raters of departmental quality in reputational studies probably had little knowledge about the overall quality of the programs they were evaluating, it seems likely that their assessment of the quality of various departments was based principally on their judgment of faculty scholarly reputation and productivity. In turn, it does not seem surprising that previous studies have been able to isolate a small number of correlates—many related to faculty scholarly productivity and reputation—that explain much of the variation in quality.

In this study, however, the measure of departmental quality was extracted from the comprehensive reports of reviewers that were clearly aimed at judging overall departmental quality. Since these peer judgments were based on a broad base of information, it does not seem unusual that when factors previously found highly correlated with departmental quality were correlated with those peer judgments they did not have the same strength of association found in previous research. The fact that other important correlates and dimensions of quality were identified here may be due in part to the measure of the dependent variable as well as to the fact that these correlates had not been previously investigated. [Conrad & Blackburn, 1985, pp. 292–293]

Discussion to Integrate

Not only must the discussion section of a research report unravel findings and inconsistencies, as part of its interpretation function, but it must also attempt to put the pieces together to achieve meaningful conclusions and generalizations. Studies often generate disparate results that do not seem to "hang together." A report's discussion section should include an attempt to bring together the findings—expected and unexpected, major and ancillary—to extract meaning and principles. Some brief examples illustrate this kind of material:

These findings may be contrasted with those of Johnson and Johnson (1975) and Slavin (1983), who found an advantage for cooperative conditions over competitive and individualistic ones. In work by these authors, students were not differentiated in terms of self-beliefs so that reactions of students who differed in self-efficacy may have been obscured by the averaging process. Another possible difference is that in the "traditional" cooperative learning paradigm, students actually work together under conditions imposed by the teacher, whereas in this study students who shared a common fate did not necessarily work cooperatively. Hence, the ability of students to influence one another may have been weaker than in past cooperative learning studies. [Tuckman, 1990a, p. 296]

Although theoretical statements about strategy-monitoring metamemory relationships abound in the literature, there are few studies that include unconfounded examinations of strategy instruction and monitoring instruction (e.g., Lodico et al., 1983). When the data presented here are combined with the Lodico et al. (1983) results, there is solid evidence that monitoring training per se makes an important contribution to efficient strategy instruction. This evidence bolsters the case for including monitoring instructions in multicomponent strategy training packages aimed at producing durable strategy use (e.g., Brown, Campione, & Barclay, 1979; Day, 1983; Palinesar & Brown, 1983; Schleser, Meyers, & Cohen, 1981). [Ghatala et al., 1985, p. 212]

Discussion to Theorize

When a study generates a number of related findings, it occasionally becomes possible not only to integrate them into some superordinate point or principle but to integrate them into an already existing theory or to use them to formulate an original theory. The goal is to make your findings part of a comprehensive body of theory, either by working within an existing theory or by generating original theory. (In the former case, you should state in the introductory section the existing theory that will serve as the study's frame of reference.) Some examples show the introduction of theory to the discussion section:

More theoretically, results seriously question the fundamental and still popular Galtonian view that a test is no more or less than a sample of the examinee's responses to a standard nonpersonal stimulus. Although the present study required examiners to administer the CELF in accordance with the user's manual, the dissimilar performance of handicapped, but not nonhandicapped, children across familiar and unfamiliar tester conditions suggests that the two groups attributed different meanings to the tester and test situation. This suggestion that the "standard" test condition was perceived differently by the handicapped and nonhandicapped seems reasonable if it is appreciated that, by requiring the speech- and/or language-impaired children to respond to the CELF, handicapped subjects were asked to reveal their disabilities. In contrast, nonhandicapped subjects, by definition, were presented with an opportunity to demonstrate competence. Such a conceptualization is consonant with Cole and Bruner's (1972) theoretical work, which argued that, despite efforts to objectify tests, select subgroups of the population will subjectivize them in ways that reflect their unique experiential backgrounds. [Fuchs et al., 1985, pp. 195–196]

If poorly performing students lack the motivation to process the text, why would regular quizzes activate motivation? Overmier and Lawry's (1979) theory of incentive motivation states that incentives can motivate performance by mediating between a stimulus situation and a specific response. Assuming that students in the incentive motivation condition value doing well on quizzes (and based on informal discussions with students following Experiment 1, it would appear that they do), they would be motivated to apply their existing text-processing skills and thereby learn more. The text-processing homework assignments, although performed well by the students in the learning strategy condition, apparently had less incentive value to motivate students to achieve success or avoid failure. The goal of completing homework was primarily its completion. It was not associated with the same consequences for success and failure as quizzes. [Tuckman, 1996a, pp. 206–207]

The affective variable of locus of control, which was used to represent an aspect of motivation, also had a positive relationship with performance and confidence. Regression analysis indicated that locus of control accounted for approximately 5% of the variance in posttest performance and about 6.7% of the variance in confidence scores. The canonical analysis indicated that locus of control and the linear combination of performance and confidence were positively related. These findings provide support for the assumption that the motivation to learn, including expectancies for control, makes a difference in performance and motivation (Keller, 1979, 1983). Social learning theorists (Phares, 1976; Rotter 1966) suggested that locus of control will influence student performance in unfamiliar environments. Subjects may have viewed the task used in the present study as unfamiliar, thus the relationship between locus of control and performance. In addition, the positive relationship between locus of control and confidence supports attribution theorists who contend that locus is related to affective outcomes (Weiner, 1979, 1980, 1985). [Klein & Keller, 1990, p. 145]

Discussion to Recommend or Apply

Because education is essentially an applied field, research in education should yield some recommendations for alterations in educational practices.[6] In the discussion section, typically toward the end, you should examine your findings in the light of suggested applications, as these examples illustrate:

> From an applied perspective, the findings of this study leave the potential motivator of students in a quandary. How does one tailor-make or customize motivational conditions to the needs of students differing in levels of self-efficacy? If using groups helps those in the middle self-efficacy level, using goal-setting helps those at the low level, and leaving them to their own devices helps those at the top, how then can all three techniques be employed at the same time? The answer may lie in not trying to affect all students in the same manner.
>
> One suggestion is to identify those students who are low in academic self-efficacy based on their past lack of self-regulated performance and work with them separately, possibly after class, to engage them in the goal-setting process. Such efforts should focus on helping these students to set attainable goals and to

---

[6] Dissertation writers often choose to follow the "Discussion" section with a separate "Conclusions and Recommendations" section, highlighting their conclusions and recommendations based on the results their studies produced.

specify when and where they will engage in necessary goal-related performance. As the students least likely to perform on their own, these would be the ones on which to expend one's primary effort.

Cooperative group assignments on self-regulated tasks should perhaps be used on a voluntary basis so students can choose whether or not they wish to bind their fate to others or to work alone. This would enable students of average self-efficacy to gain the support of group members without simultaneously hampering those at either high or low self-efficacy levels. The recommendation, therefore, is to personalize or individualize motivational enhancement efforts to the greatest degree possible. [Tuckman, 1990a, pp. 297–298]

Based on the results of this study, it is recommended that the expository examples in the first phase of concept teaching should be selected in such a way that they closely resemble the best example and each other. In the second phase of concept teaching, the selected interrogatory examples should form a widely dispersed set in order to focus attention on the range of the variable attributes and to allow the students to elaborate their knowledge base (Christensen & Tennyson, 1988). Further, because it is suggested that the number of expository examples should at least be equal to the number of defining characteristics of the concept (Merrill & Tennyson, 1977), it seems that the number of interrogatory examples should at least be the same as the number of expository examples to prevent undergeneralization. More research needs to be performed on the ratio between the two types of examples. [Ramzijn, 1991, p. 328]

The results of the two experiments suggest that achievement among students of college age, particularly those who tend to perform poorly, can be enhanced by increasing their incentive motivation to study the text on a regular basis and that frequently occurring quizzes, as used in this study, may be an effective technique for enhancing incentive motivation. Because quiz grades appear to constitute a strong study incentive for college students, frequent testing may be a better inducement for effective and timely processing of textbook content than using homework assignments as a required strategy for this purpose. [Tuckman, 1996a, p. 209]

Discussion to Suggest Extensions

Often the discussion section of a research report concludes with suggestions for further research, replications, or refinements, thus indicating directions that future research in the area might take. Such suggested extensions can be offered in general or more specific forms:

The findings of this study have some implications for researchers of learner-control questions. Future research into learner control should attempt to determine student perceptions toward their feelings of control over instruction and should investigate the relationship between these perceptions and motivation and performance in actual instructional settings. Future studies also should continue to delineate specific aspects of control, using them individually and in combination, to determine the critical features of control that influence performance and motivation. The effects of instructions should be investigated. In both real world and in studies of expectations, people are sometimes told what to expect in regard to personal control. The effects of these instructions in conjunction with actual variations in learner control should be studied. [Klein & Keller, 1990, p. 145]

Finally, further work may help in understanding the areas discussed here. One important project would be applying the analyses used here to data from earlier years. It could also be important to look at underachievement in specific courses, to determine other variables that influence variations in underachievement, and to examine the long-range implications of adolescent underachievement, especially its relation to educational and occupational attainment. [Stockard & Wood, 1984, pp. 835–836]

Second, if it is assumed that findings can be attributed to examiners awarding spuriously high scores to familiar examinees, why was differential performance obtained for handicapped, but not nonhandicapped, subjects? Future research might explore whether examiner familiarity and the handicapped status of examinees interact so that examiners inflate handicapped students' test scores more than those of nonhandicapped pupils. Since the current study employed only speech- and/or language-impaired subjects and a single language test, further research also might attempt operational replications of present findings on subjects with different handicapping conditions and with diverse test instruments. [Fuchs et al., 1985, pp. 194–195]

THE REFERENCES

Research reports display a variety of different formats for their references, only one of which is covered here. The one used in this book is the style used in the psychological journals, such as the *Journal of Educational Psychology*. This format is described in detail in *The Publication Manual of the American Psychological Association* (4th ed., 1994, pp. 174–222).[7] This format does not cite references in footnotes. Rather, references are cited in the text by author's surname and year of publication. A section headed "References," appearing at the end of the report, includes the full publication information for each citation in alphabetical order according to the senior author's surname. A journal reference would appear as follows:

> Casteel, C. A. (1991). Answer changing on multiple-choice test items among eighth-grade readers. *Journal of Experimental Education, 59,* 300–309.

---

[7] This book may be ordered from APA Order Dept., P.O. Box 2710, Hyattsville, MD 20784.

A book would be referenced as follows:

Tuckman, B. W. (1997). *Theories and applications of educational psychology*
  (2nd ed.). New York: McGraw-Hill.

Every item in the reference list must be specifically cited in the text and vice versa.
To see how this format treats other types of references (for example, dissertations, government reports, convention papers), obtain a copy of *The Publication Manual of the APA* or examine references for articles appearing in the *Journal of Educational Psychology*. Many journals outside of psychology now use *The Publication Manual of the APA* as a stylistic guide (for example, *American Educational Research Journal*).[8]

THE ABSTRACT

Journal articles and other research reports typically require accompanying abstracts written according to well-delineated standards. An abstract usually must fit within a limited number of words. A dissertation typically requires a summary or what may be called a *long abstract*—often between 600 and 1,000 words. The rules for writing such a long abstract are essentially the same as those for writing a short one, as Campbell and Ballou (1990) explain.[9]

A short abstract for a journal article or research paper should run between 100 and 175 words. It should be written in block form (that is, without indentations) and in complete sentences. The abstract should contain statements of the study's (1) problem, (2) method, (3) results, and (4) conclusions. Results are vitally important to readers, so every abstract should state at least the trend of the results a study has generated. Another recommended component is a statement of the number and kind of *Ss*, the type of research design, and the significance levels of the results. Results and conclusions may be itemized for brevity. Standard abbreviations and acronyms should be used where possible. An example helps to illustrate the priorities for writing an abstract. The Sample Studies in Appendix A also provide instructive examples.

> **Abstract.** Two experiments were conducted to determine the relative effectiveness of increasing students' incentive motivation for studying and prescribing a text-processing strategy for them to use in studying. The incentive motivation condition involved administering a weekly quiz, and the learning strategy condition involved homework assignments that required students to identify key terms

---

[8] Additional information about referencing as well as about preparing research reports can be found in Campbell and Ballou (1990).

[9] An example of a long abstract or research summary appears as a sample evaluation report at the end of Chapter 13.

in their textbook chapters, write definitions of them, and generate elaborations of their definitions. The 1st experiment spanned a 5-week period in an educational psychology course and included a control group. On the achievement posttest, students in the incentive motivation condition substantially outscored the learning strategy group and the control group. The 2nd experiment involved the same course in a subsequent term, but this time over a 15-week period. Also, students were divided into high, medium, and low groups on the basis of prior grade point average (GPA). As in the 1st experiment, the incentive motivation condition was generally more effective than the learning strategy condition, but the advantage accrued primarily to low-GPA students. The findings were interpreted to mean that college students generally have acquired learning strategies that are suitable for studying textbook content, but their use of these strategies depends on their motivational level. [Tuckman, 1996a, p. 197]

PREPARING TABLES

Tables are extremely useful tools for presenting the results of statistical tests as well as mean and standard deviation data. The results of analyses of variance and correlations (when sufficient in number) are typically reported in tabular form.

Table 12.1, an analysis of variance table, indicates the source of variance along with many supporting data: degrees of freedom (df) associated with each source, sums of squares of the variance, mean squares of the variance for effects and error terms, F ratios for both main effects and interactions, and p values. The study from which this table came evaluated two treatment methods (reader type and response type) as they affected the number of test answers revised by students. The same author also prepared Table 12.2, an example of a table of means, and a statistical comparison of results combined into a single table. Similarly, Table 12.3 combines means and statistical results but also includes standard deviations. Table 12.4 displays analysis of variance results, while Table 12.5 provides accompanying means and standard deviations. Table 12.6 is an example of a tabular display of correlations.

TABLE 12.1

From Casteel (1991). Reprinted by permission.

ANALYSIS OF VARIANCE FOR READER TYPE AND RESPONSE TYPE

SOURCE	df	SS	MS	F	p
Reader type	1	2.02	2.0	0.14	.71
Response type	2	832.96	416.4	28.43	.05
Interaction (reader type × response type)	2	6.45	3.2	0.22	.80
Within-subject (error)	153	2241.0	14.6		
Total score	158	3082.5			

Tukey (HSD) Pair-wise Comparisons of Mean Number of Revisions by Response Type of Good and Poor Readers

TABLE 12.2

From Casteel (1991). Reprinted by permission.

RESPONSE TYPE	M	GOOD	POOR
Wrong to right	7.8[a]	7.4	8.2
Right to wrong	2.6[b]	2.2	3.0
Wrong to wrong	1.8[b]	1.7	2.0

Notes: Group means sharing common notation within are not significantly different from one another. Critical Q value = 3.314, rejection level = 0.05; critical value for comparison = 1.7261; standard error for comparison = 0.736; error term used: Reader × Response × Subject, 153 *df*.

Univariate Tests for Six Academic Performance Tasks

TABLE 12.3

From Mahn & Greenwood (1990). Reprinted by permission.

TASK	EXPERIMENTAL ($n = 29$)		CONTROL ($n = 27$)		F[a]	p[b]
	M	SD	M	SD		
1	20.55	0.91	18.89	3.65	6.33	.04
2	14.79	0.67	14.00	1.41	7.26	.03
3	13.45	1.18	11.26	2.61	12.06	.01
4	9.62	0.62	8.00	1.17	36.01	.0005
5	15.10	1.01	12.33	1.92	50.42	.0002
6	8.97	0.18	7.85	1.51	4.31	.07

[a]F statistics from nested ANOVA; [b]Significance probabilities for F statistics.

TABLE 12.4

Tuckman (1996a).

ANOVA RESULTS FOR EACH ACHIEVEMENT TEST AND THE COMBINED ACHIEVEMENT TESTS, BY CONDITION AND GPA LEVEL

TEST	CONDITION ($df = 1$)	GPA LEVEL ($df = 2$)	INTERACTION ($df = 2$)	ERROR ($df = 109$)
Test 1				
MS	4.82	56.23	41.31	11.95
F	0.04	4.71[b]	3.46[b]	
Test 2				
MS	32.54	82.94	24.61	7.58
F	4.29[b]	10.94[c]	3.25[b]	
Test 3				
MS	51.91	91.40	17.21	12.88
F	4.03[b]	7.10[c]	1.34	
Combined				
MS	185.05	667.29	213.65	65.64
F	2.82[a]	10.16[c]	3.25[b]	

[a]$p < .10$; [b]$p < 05$; [c]$p < .01$.

TABLE 12.5

From Tuckman (1996a). Reprinted by permission of the author and publisher.

MEANS AND STANDARD DEVIATIONS FOR THE INCENTIVE MOTIVATION AND LEARNING STRATEGY GROUPS ON THE THREE ACHIEVEMENT TESTS AND THE COMBINED ACHIEVEMENT TESTS

CONDITION	TEST 1	TEST 2	TEST 3	COMBINED ACHIEVEMENT TESTS
Incentive motivation ($n = 56$)				
M	73.0	79.6	76.9	76.5
SD	11.0	8.5	9.7	9.7
Learning strategy ($n = 59$)				
M	73.0	75.7	72.0	73.6
SD	11.9	10.5	13.9	12.1

Two additional examples illustrate tabular presentations of other kinds of results. (The samples shown in this chapter do not necessarily illustrate all possible kinds of tables.) Table 12.7 shows a contingency table used in conjunction with a chi-square analysis, and Table 12.8 shows a table of frequency counts.

TABLE 12.6

ZERO-ORDER CORRELATIONS BETWEEN MOTIVATION AND SELF-REGULATED LEARNING VARIABLES AND PERFORMANCE

From Pintrich & De Groot (1990). Reprinted by permission.

VARIABLE	GRADE 1	SEAT-WORK	EXAMS/QUIZZES	ESSAYS/REPORTS	GRADE 2
Motivation components					
Intrinsic value	.25[b]	.21[b]	.20[b]	.27[b]	.30[c]
Self-efficacy	.34[b]	.19[a]	.24[b]	.25[b]	.36[c]
Test anxiety	−.24[b]	−.14	−.24[b]	−.14	−.23[b]
Self-regulated learning components					
Strategy use	.18[a]	.07	.20[b]	.19[a]	.20[b]
Self-regulation	.32[c]	.22[b]	.28[b]	.36[c]	.36[c]

Note. $N = 173$.
[a]$p < .05$; [b]$p < .01$; [c]$p < .001$.

PERCENTAGES OF MENTORSHIPS AS A FUNCTION OF SEX OF PROFESSORS AND STUDENTS AND THE RESULTANT CHI-SQUARE

TABLE 12.7

From Busch (1985). Reprinted by permission of the author and publisher.

	STUDENTS		
	FEMALE	MALE	TOTAL
Professors			
Female	39.46%	10.54%	50.00%
Male	24.74	25.26	50.00
Total	64.20	35.80	

$\chi^2(1) = 9.43, p < .01$

For further information on preparing tables, see *The Publication Manual of the American Psychological Association* (4th ed., 1994). This source also gives instructive guidance for preparing figures. For further input, examine tables and figures that appear in journal articles.

Tables often play a useful role in a research report's method section by depicting a complex arrangement among conditions, an experimental design, a sequence of procedures, or numbers and characteristics of subjects in a complex study. Table 12.9 illustrates an application of a table to display the number of

TABLE 12.8

From Mark & Anderson (1985). Reprinted by permission of the authors and publisher.

Number of Pupils and Teachers in the St. Louis Metropolitan Area, 1969–1982

YEAR	PUPILS	TEACHERS	PUPILS PER TEACHER
1969	378,682	17,873	21.19
1970	380,705	18,443	20.64
1971	366,631	19,282	19.01
1972	371,226	19,941	18.62
1973	367,687	19,890	18.49
1974	360,459	20,084	17.95
1975	350,878	19,909	17.62
1976	336,893	19,998	16.85
1977	328,420	19,704	16.67
1978	315,120	19,643	16.04
1979	324,003	19,411	16.69
1980	316,018	19,605	16.12
1981	272,438	20,642	13.20
1982	263,353	18,970	13.88

TABLE 12.9

From Marsh, Parker, & Barnes (1985). Reprinted by permission of the authors and publisher.

Characteristics of Students at Each Grade Level and for the Total Sample

	GRADE					
	7	8	9	10	11/12	TOTAL
Sample size	236	223	181	189	77	901
Age						
Mean	12.3	13.4	14.4	15.3	16.7	
SD	.5	.5	.6	.5	.8	
% females	50	44	41	47	57	47
IQ						
Mean	99.6	100.7	101.3	102.2	110.6	101.6
SD	13.9	14.3	12.9	11.4	11.4	13.4
Valid N	225	219	161	180	66	851
Number of ability streams	10	10	10	73	3	

subjects by grade taking part in a large, complex study as well as the means and standard deviations for the separate groups on a number of control variables. This type of table should appear in the method section under the heading "Subjects" to help clarify the details of complex studies.

ILLUSTRATIONS FROM THE SAMPLE STUDIES   BOX 12

Sample Study I supports its results with one table, an analysis of covariance source table, and one figure, a graph of the means on the performance and self-efficacy measures (the dependent variables) for the encouragement and no encouragement groups (the levels of the independent variable) over time. The graph shows (1) the stronger effect, over time, of encouragement in comparison to no encouragement, and (2) the relative correspondence or parallel relationship between effects on self-efficacy and effects on performance.

The discussion contains five paragraphs. The first paragraph *summarizes*: ". . . the intuitive expectation that students will be motivated or persuaded to perform more when they are encouraged by receiving positive feedback was borne out by the data." The second paragraph *theorizes* that self-efficacy functioned as a mediator based on its stronger correlation with performance at the end of 10 weeks than at the beginning. The third paragraph provides further *interpretation* of the point made in the preceding paragraph by presenting additional data showing that ". . . when performance is held constant, encouragement can be seen to affect self-efficacy, but when final self-efficacy is held constant, encouragement has no effect on performance." The fourth paragraph *integrates* the findings on performance outcomes with and without the covariates included in the analysis, yielding the conclusion that ". . . For those students who are inclined to procrastinate or who have little regard for a grade bonus, it may take considerably more than encouragement from teachers to increase their motivation." The fifth paragraph makes *recommendations* to teachers about using encouragement to enhance their students' performance.

Sample Study II supports its results by two tables of means on the seven dependent measures, one for poor and good readers (the levels of the independent variable) and one for each of six grade levels (the levels of the moderator variable).

The discussion contains six short paragraphs. The first two paragraphs *summarize* the results, while the third paragraph draws *conclusions* based on them. The fourth, fifth, and sixth paragraphs make *recommendations* to teachers for dealing with poor and good readers, based partly on the results of the study and partly on previous work by others.

Preparing Figures and Graphs

Figures often provide useful tools for presenting research results, as well. Data collected over time are often amenable to graphic presentation, as are data displaying statistical interactions, means, and so on.

Figure 12.1 illustrates the use of a bar graph to display means in a way that highlights an interaction between an independent variable (*condition:* incentive motivation versus learning strategy) and a moderator variable (*grade point average:* high versus medium versus low). The figure shows how these variables affected the study's dependent variables (scores on three achievement tests). Representing three variables simultaneously can be a difficult job, but it is done with great clarity in this illustration.

FIGURE 12.1

Tuckman (1996a). Reprinted by permission of the author and publisher.

Mean Test Scores for the Two Treatment Groups on Each of the Three Tests Across Three Levels of Grade Point Average (GPA)

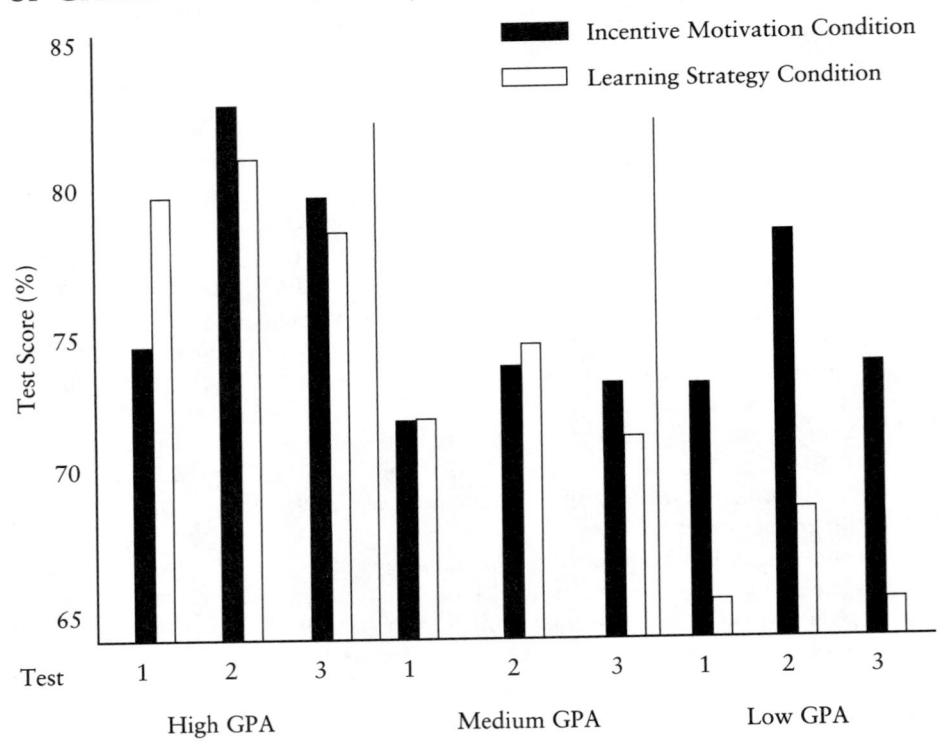

Figure 12.2 shows another complex interaction of variables. The graph clearly illustrates the interaction between the two variables in question (that is, *handicapped* versus *nonhandicapped* and *familiar* versus *unfamiliar* testing conditions) on the dependent measure (*CELF score*). Certainly, a report writer might struggle to say in words what this graph depicts with relative ease.

Figures can also be used effectively in the method section to illustrate tasks or other aspects of methodology. Figure 12.3 illustrates the types of test items used to measure each of two dependent variables, *high-level mathematics achievement* and *low-level mathematics achievement*.

DISPLAY OF INTERACTION: CELF SCORES OF HANDICAPPED (DASHED LINE) AND NONHANDICAPPED (SOLID LINE) CHILDREN IN FAMILIAR (*F*) AND UNFAMILIAR (*U*) TESTING CONDITIONS

FIGURE 12.2

From Fuchs et al. (1985). Reprinted by permission of the authors and publishers.

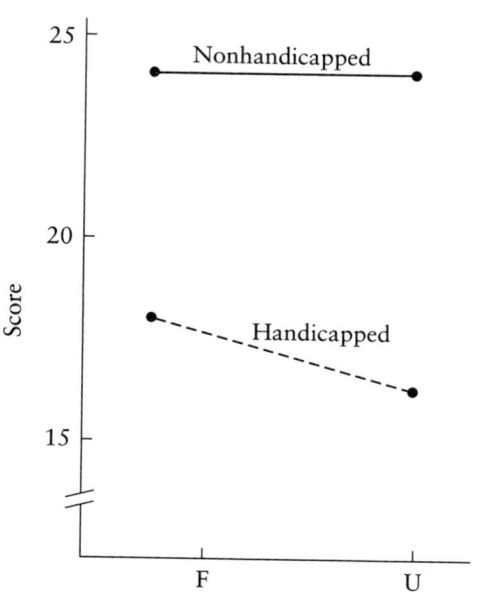

FIGURE 12.3

From Peterson & Fennema (1985). Reprinted by permission of the authors and publishers.

EXAMPLES OF LOW-LEVEL AND HIGH-LEVEL MATHEMATICS PROBLEMS

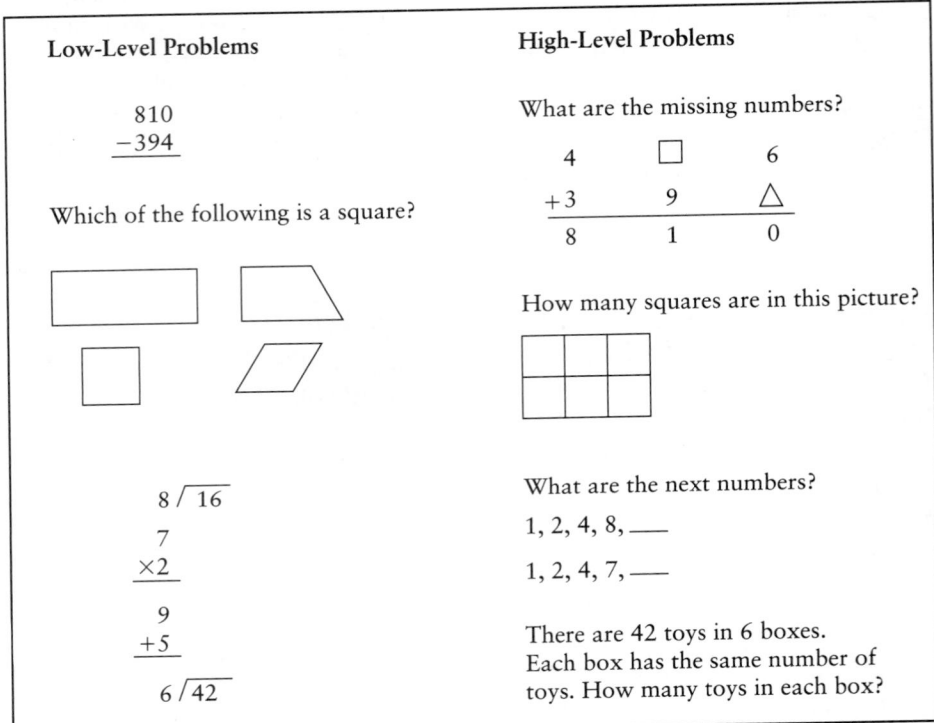

GETTING AN ARTICLE PUBLISHED

Most journals print sections called "guidelines for contributors" or "instructions to authors" in each issue, usually on an inside cover or a page near the end. Look for a listing in the issue's table of contents. These guidelines or instructions often describe the purpose of the journal and the kinds of articles it publishes, the length limits of manuscripts, the desired format (typically that set forth in *The Publication Manual of the American Psychological Association* (4th ed.). They also specify the length limit of the abstract (usually 120 words), the number of paper copies that must be submitted (usually between three and five), whether or not the author is required to include a copy on disk as well, and to whom these materials should be sent. This information indicates whether the journal reviews articles blind (that is, without identifying the author) and how authors should prepare manuscripts to facilitate this process. It also states an expectation that authors will not submit the same manuscripts to more than one journal at the same time. In addition, specific journals may set specific requirements of their own, such as requiring authors to calculate and report effect sizes for all significant results. (For additional details, see Chapters 5 and 6 of the *APA Publication Manual.*)

To prepare a manuscript for publication, follow the general rules described in this chapter and adhere closely to the format set forth in Chapter 4 (pp. 235–272) of the *APA Publication Manual.* (See also Appendix B of that manual, which contains a Checklist for Manuscript Submission.) Try to keep the manuscript to a maximum of 25 pages from start to end, make sure the abstract is no longer than 120 words, and keep the title to 10 words, if possible.

The *APA Publication Manual* also contains a section about converting a dissertation into a journal article (Appendix A, pages 336–339). An expanded version of this information can be found in Calfee and Valencia (1991).

To find a suitable journal, first consider those in the specific content area in which the manuscript would most likely fit (for example, reading, teaching English, educational administration, physical education, special education). To reach a wider, more general audience, consider submitting your article to journals that cover a wide range of topics such as the *Journal of Educational Psychology, American Educational Research Journal, Journal of Experimental Education, Journal of Educational Research,* or *Contemporary Educational Psychology.* If you are not very familiar with the journal, get a recent copy and skim through it to get an idea of the types of articles it publishes.

Much research has a limited shelf life; a study's currency becomes questionable within a short time of its completion. Therefore, you should not wait too long after finishing a research project to write it up and submit the report for publication. You may want to test its appeal by first submitting it to a convention or annual meeting for presentation before submitting it to a journal. This process may also provide some useful feedback.

Journals evaluate submitted manuscripts according to the criteria described in Chapter 15. Most reviewers judge a research report according to a few major concerns: (a) the theoretical base of the study, (b) the adequacy and validity of the methodology for meeting the purposes of the study, (c) the quality and applicability of the findings, and (d) how well the manuscript is written, particularly its clarity. As a general rule, journals rarely publish articles that do not report significant and important findings. Part of the author's responsibility is to establish the importance and relevance of the findings, but if they include no significant effects, this is exceedingly difficult to do.

Typically, journals require about 3 months to respond to a manuscript submission. The authors are notified of whether the manuscript is accepted for publication (with or without revisions), rejected, or whether a revised manuscript may be submitted without guarantee of acceptance. Regardless of the decision, authors are supplied with a list of reasons, usually in the form of comments from two reviewers (and, sometimes, by the editor as well). If the article is accepted pending revision or recommendations for revision are provided with an invitation to resubmit, the author should closely follow the reviewers' and editor's recommendations in preparing a revision. If the article is rejected, the author is advised to use the criticisms offered by the editor, where possible, to make revisions, and then to submit it to another journal.

SUMMARY

1. A research proposal consists of (a) introduction and (b) method sections, following the same guidelines as for preparing a research report.
2. The introduction section contains parts covering several topics: (a) context of the problem (acquainting the reader with the study's frame of reference); (b) problem statement (identifying all variables); (c) literature review (expanding on the problem and providing an empirical basis for hypotheses); (d) statement of hypotheses (anticipated relationships between variables); (e) rationales for hypotheses (logical and empirical justifications for these expectations); (f) operational definitions (brief statements of how variables were manipulated or measured); (g) predictions (operational restatements of the hypotheses); (h) significance of the study (potential relevance to theory and practice).
3. The method section contains parts covering additional topics: (a) subjects (description of the participants in the study); (b) tasks and materials (experiences in which all the subjects participate); (c) independent (and moderator) variables (techniques for manipulating or measuring them); (d) dependent variables (techniques for measuring them, including validity and reliability); (e) procedures (any operational details not yet described); (f) data analysis (design and statistical analyses).
4. The results section is best structured in terms of the study's hypotheses. Statistical results for each hypothesis should be described, and tables and figures provided where needed.
5. The discussion section should fulfill the following functions: (a) to conclude or summarize, based on the study's findings; (b) to interpret those findings, that is, to explain or account for them, especially the unexpected ones; (c) to integrate the findings to produce generalizations; (d) to theorize about what the findings mean; (e) to apply the findings or make recommendations for their use; (f) to suggest extensions or possible future studies.
6. The references should be consistent with a recommended format such as American Psychological Association style.
7. The abstract, between 100 and 175 words long, should summarize the study's problem, method, results, and conclusions.
8. Tables are useful tools for presenting statistical results such as means, standard deviations, and analysis of variance outcomes.
9. Figures and graphs are also useful ways to present results such as group means.

10. To get an article published, prepare the manuscript in accordance with the style defined in the *APA Publication Manual* (4th ed.) and with specific instructions given in the journal to which you submit it. Consider the evaluative criteria set forth in Chapter 15 of this text.

COMPETENCY TEST EXERCISES

1. Write a brief paragraph illustrating the significance of a study to relate teaching style to the degree to which children learn self-control and internal motivation.

2. You have hypothesized a positive relationship between ratings of a youngster's aggressiveness by the school psychologist and the number of demerits each youngster has accumulated in school. A study found a correlation of .875 for 10 students; write a brief paragraph describing these results.

3. A study has shown that youngsters in high-ability groups have better school attendance records than youngsters in low-ability groups. Write a brief paragraph interpreting this finding.

4. A study evaluated the teaching styles of 24 teachers, 12 who taught vocational subjects and 12 who taught academic subjects. Based on a personality test, half of each group of teachers was classified as abstract personalities and half as concrete personalities. Students then completed a questionnaire describing how directive they perceived their teachers' teaching styles. Means were computed on directiveness for each group of teachers (a higher mean corresponding to a more nondirective teacher). Among the vocational teachers, those with abstract personalities had a mean directiveness rating of 53.8 compared to 55.3 for concrete-personality teachers. Among the academic teachers, those with abstract personalities had a mean directiveness rating of 44.5 compared to 46.3 for concrete-personality teachers. Analysis of variance of directiveness scores as a function of teachers' subject area and personality yielded a significant result for subject area ($MS = 504.17$, $df = 1,20$, $F = 45.22$, $p < .01$), but not for personality ($MS = 16.67$, $df = 1,20$, $F = 1.49$). The interaction also failed to achieve significance ($MS = 0.17$, $df = 1,20$, $F = 0.01$), relative to an error mean square of 11.15 ($df = 20$). Construct an analysis of variance source table to shows these results. Make sure to give your table the proper title.

5. Construct a table to display the cell and marginal means for the analysis in Exercise 4 (and for which the analysis of variance source table was constructed). Make sure to assign a proper title to your table. Indicate significant mean differences that you know from the analysis of variance.

6. Draw a graph to illustrate the cell means listed in the table you created in Exercise 5. (Be sure to title it and label the axes.)

7. Draw a graph of the scores given in Competency Test Exercise 3 of Chapter 11. Do not distinguish between groups. Plot all the data together in bar graph form, showing the frequency distribution of each score or group of scores.

RECOMMENDED REFERENCES

American Psychological Association. (1994). *Publication manual* (4th ed.). Washington DC: American Psychological Association.

Calfee, R. C., & Valencia, R. R. (1991). *APA guide to preparing manuscripts for journal publication.* Washington DC: American Psychological Association.

Campbell, W. G., & Ballou, S. V. (1990). *Form and style: Theses, reports, term papers* (8th ed.). Boston: Houghton Mifflin.

Dees, R. (1993). *Writing the modern research paper.* Boston: Allyn & Bacon.

Henson, K. T. (1995). *The art of writing for publication.* Boston: Allyn & Bacon.

Locke, L. F., Spirduso, W. W., & Silverman, S. J. (1993). *Proposals that work: A guide for planning dissertations and grant proposals* (3rd ed.). Newbury Park, CA: Sage.

Turabian, K. L., & Honigsblum, B. B. (1987). *A manual for writers of term papers, theses, and dissertations* (5th ed.). Chicago: University of Chicago Press.

Part 5

ADDITIONAL APPROACHES

Chapter 13

CONDUCTING EVALUATION STUDIES

Objectives

▶ Distinguish between formative and summative evaluation.

▶ Design a study to evaluate a treatment or intervention utilizing the concepts of identification and operational definition of variables, research design, and observation and measurement.

▶ Analyze and interpret the data from an evaluation study, and draw appropriate conclusions.

FORMATIVE VERSUS SUMMATIVE EVALUATION

The labels *formative* and *summative* describe two types of evaluation. *Formative evaluation* refers to an internal evaluation of a program, usually undertaken as part of the development process, that compares the performance of participating students to the objectives of the program. Such analysis attempts to debug learning materials or some other form of program under development by trying them out on a test group. Such tryouts enable the developers to tell whether the materials work as expected and to suggest changes. Formative evaluation often leads a program developer "back to the drawing board."

Summative evaluation—demonstration[1] is a systematic attempt to determine whether a fully developed program is meeting its objectives more successfully than might be obtained from alternative programs (or no program). Summative evaluation uses the comparison process to evaluate a fully implemented program, whereas formative evaluation is part of the development process and thus precedes summative evaluation.

The varied techniques that researchers employ for formative evaluation are less systematic than those for summative evaluation. Because the purpose of formative evaluation is to help program developers to judge the adequacy of the materials under development, it often incorporates questionnaires or performance tests completed by pilot subjects. The developer then evaluates the success or failure of the materials and makes appropriate revisions. By comparison, summative evaluation should proceed in a more systematic fashion, conforming to some model and providing a basis for comparison between programs or products.

This process accommodates a variety of summative evaluation methods. The one described in detail in this chapter conforms to the logical research process described in this book, and yet it is general enough to be applied in a variety of situations.

A MODEL FOR SUMMATIVE EVALUATION

The model presented here for evaluating an intervention or program is based on the model of experimental design described in detail throughout the preceding

---

[1] When Chapter 1 linked the terms *evaluation* and *demonstration,* it was referring to summative evaluation.

chapters of this book.[2] This model includes the techniques of formulating a hypothesis, identifying variables, constructing operational definitions, building a design, developing measuring instruments, and conducting statistical analyses. The research design model supports summative evaluation in three ways: (1) It offers a logical and consistent approach. (2) It allows a researcher to establish cause-and-effect relationships (or at least, to make inferences about cause and effect). (3) It provides the conditions conducive to systematic comparisons.

The overall evaluation model illustrated in Figure 13.1 includes five steps, each described in detail in the preceding chapters. The first step *identifies the dependent variables* of the evaluation study, namely, the aims of the intervention or experimental program. The second step *transforms these aims into operational definitions* by stating them in behavioral terms. The third then *develops tests or measuring devices for the dependent variables* that ensure content validity. The fourth step *establishes an independent variable* that distinguishes an experimental group (the group receiving the intervention) and a comparison or control group. In addition, establishing experimental and comparison groups requires a researcher to ensure or demonstrate the equivalence of both groups on selection factors. Finally, in the fifth step, the researcher undertakes *data collection and statistical analyses* to provide a basis for drawing conclusions. Each of these steps is described in detail in the next section of this chapter.

Note that omitting Step 4 transforms this model into a procedure for formative evaluation. Because formative evaluation attempts to determine whether a program is successfully meeting its own objectives, it may be carried out by specifying these objectives, operationalizing them, building a test to measure them, and then administering this test to a group of subjects that are completing the program. This streamlined process differs from summative evaluation in its lack of a control or comparison group (defined in Step 4). This difference will also be reflected in the fifth step: design, data collection, and statistical analyses.

An Evaluation Model

FIGURE 13.1

Step 1   Identification of the program's aims and objectives (the dependent variable)

Step 2   Restatement of these aims and objectives in behavioral terms (an operational definition)

Step 3   Construction of a content valid (or appropriate) test to measure the behaviorally stated aims and objectives (measurement of the dependent variable)

Step 4   Identification and selection of a control, comparison, or criterion group against which to contrast the test group (establishing the independent variable)

Step 5   Data collection and analysis

---

[2] This chapter makes no attempt to survey the literature on evaluation and describe all possible evaluation models. Rather, it explains one model for evaluating educational programs. Of course, a researcher might choose to implement alternative models described by Tuckman (1985).

DEFINING THE GOALS OF A PROGRAM

Identifying the Aims of the Intervention: The Dependent Variable

People who introduce an intervention[3] in a school system—whether it is a specific course of study, a new facility, or some special piece of equipment—usually launch the project with the goal of achieving certain aims or objectives, or at least with expectations for certain outcomes. These objectives or anticipated outcomes differ for different specific interventions. Some educational programs aim to help students master the content of certain courses of study, whereas others aim to produce very specific influences on students' future lives. Vocational programs, for example, often set objectives related to specific trade competencies and skills for entry-level jobs or potential advancement.

The decision concerning aims and objectives should rest with people who implement an intervention. Those who decide to try the interventions must determine their expectations for it. They must ask themselves, "What do we expect of students who have completed the experience that we do not expect of students who have not?" They may look to the developer of the intervention to help them answer this question.

Thus, the first step in the summative evaluation process is to approach the people who will implement the intervention and ask, "What aims and objectives should this intervention accomplish? What abilities do you expect students to gain by experiencing the program?" In response to such questions, they may respond in several ways; examples include: (1) The program will help the students develop an appreciation of art. (2) It will help them to enhance their understanding of themselves. (3) It will provide them with the skills they need to enter the carpentry trade. (4) It will increase their chances of becoming constructive citizens. (5) They will know more American history than they did before they started. (6) They will increase their interest in science.[4]

Each of these statements is an example of the kinds of aims that program implementers identify and their likely ways of expressing their intentions. Thus, Step 1 identifies the dependent variable of the evaluation, but largely in conceptual (vague and ambiguous) terms that are difficult to measure.

Operationally Defining the Dependent Variable: Behavioral Objectification

In completing the first step, the researcher has *identified* the dependent variable for the evaluation. He or she has also made substantial progress toward

---

[3] The terms *program* and *intervention* are used interchangeably, although an educational program is only one form of intervention.

[4] The subsequent measurement stage should also look for unintended or unanticipated outcomes, because these often occur, and information about them helps in the evaluation process.

formulating a hypothesis about the dependent variable stating that it should attain a certain magnitude after the subjects experience the intervention exceeding that for comparable subjects who have experienced some other or no other intervention. The next step is to *produce an operational definition* of this dependent variable, which will move the evaluator one step closer to the concrete terms and dimensions on which he or she can base the development or selection of valid measures.

In completing this second step, the evaluator asks some questions of himself or herself and the program's implementers (and occasionally of its developers): How can we tell whether the aims and objectives of the intervention, outlined previously, have been achieved? What observable and measurable behaviors will the students exhibit if these aims and objectives have been achieved that they will not exhibit if these aims and objectives have not been achieved? At this stage, the evaluator does not ask, "How will they be different after the intervention?" Instead, she or he asks, "What difference can we *see* in them?"

Unfortunately, no one can look inside the heads of the students to determine whether they appreciate, understand, are interested in, or are motivated by the program under evaluation. Judgments are limited to their overt actions and self-reports—that is, an evaluator can only study their behavior. Any conclusions about thoughts, fears, and the like can only be inferred from some study of behavior. Thus, the aims and objectives of the intervention must be operationally defined in behavioral terms. The conceptual (vague and ambiguous) statements of aims and objectives must be replaced by statements of behavior.

In practice, an intervention of any size will likely have many aims or objectives, rather than just one. Moreover, in transforming these objectives into statements of behaviors that define them or imply their presence, evaluators often must deal with a number of behaviors associated with each aim and objective rather than with one behavior per objective. For this reason, evaluation requires that they articulate a *series* of behavioral objectives that will represent the identified dependent variables.

The first criterion for such an operational definition requires an explicit statement in specific behavioral terms. That is, the definition must include an *action verb*, as in the following example: "Upon completion of the program, the student will be able to (1) *identify* or point to something with specified properties; (2) *describe* or tell about those properties; (3) *construct* or make something with those properties; or (4) *demonstrate* or use a procedure of a particular nature. Words like *identify, describe, construct, demonstrate,* and so on are action verbs that indicate behavior. They are required elements of operationally defined behavioral objectives. To specify something in behavioral terms, use behavioral words that specify doing rather than knowing. Words such as *know, appreciate,* and *understand* are not action verbs for behaviors, so they should not appear in operational definitions.

Figure 13.2 lists some suggested action verbs originally compiled by the American Association for the Advancement of Science. (The specific illustrations

FIGURE 13.2 A LIST OF ACTION VERBS FOR CONSTRUCTING BEHAVIORAL OBJECTIVES

Identify
Given a list of eight statements, the student shall identify all that are instances of hypotheses.

Distinguish
Given a list of eight statements, the student shall distinguish between those that are hypotheses and those that are inferences.

Describe
The student shall describe two characteristics that distinguish a hypothesis from an inference.

Name
The student shall name four statistical tests for comparing two treatments with small n's and outcomes that are not normally distributed.

State a Rule
The student shall state a rule limiting the transformation of interval, ordinal, and nominal measurements, one to the other.

Order
Given a list of ten statements, the student shall order them in the correct sequence to represent the research process.

Demonstrate
Given a set of data, the student shall demonstrate the procedure for their analysis using analysis of variance procedures and a worksheet.

Construct
Given the following set of data for processing by analysis of variance, the student shall construct computer instructions for an ANOVA program.

Apply a Rule
Given the following set of interval data, the student shall convert them to nominal measures (high, middle, and low) using the rule of the tertile split.

Interpret
Given the following set of analyzed data and hypothesis, the student shall interpret the outcome of the experiment and the support it provides for the hypothesis.

of the use of each one have been added by the author.) By basing operational definitions on these action verbs, researchers can be sure they are writing behavioral objectives. In addition, this standardization enables researchers to compare objectives with a degree of certainty that a specific word has the same meaning in various experimental situations.

The second element of a behavioral objective is the specific *content* in which students will show mastery or competence. What should a student be able to identify after completing the program under evaluation? What should a student be able to describe? What should a student be able to construct?

The third element of the objective is a specification of the *exact conditions* under which the student will exhibit the expected behavior: "Given a list of 20 items, the student shall identify . . ." or "Using the following pieces of equipment, the student shall construct or demonstrate . . ." These examples illustrate how an operational definition must specify conditions.

Finally, if possible, a behavioral objective should specify the *criterion* for judging satisfactory performance, such as the amount of time allowed for a student to complete a task and how many correct responses he or she should make in that amount of time. However, at this stage of behavioral objectification, an acceptable operational definition may include only an action verb, a statement of content, and any specific conditions.

Evaluators should not discourage those who implement a program from stating creative and imaginative goals for the evaluation simply to avoid the difficulty in restating them in behavioral terms. For instance, an objective for a program intended to heighten students' awareness of form in art should emerge from identified behaviors that would indicate attainment of this goal. ("Given a painting, a student will describe it in part by identifying its form.") Because the program implementers often look for subjective evidence of the attainment of these creative or imaginative goals, the evaluator must work with them or other experts to identify behaviors associated with these outcomes.

Thus, the second step in the suggested evaluation model is to convert the aims and objectives that represent the dependent variable into concrete and observable statements of behavior—that is, to transform the dependent variable statement into operational definitions or behavioral objectives.

MEASURING THE GOALS OF A PROGRAM (THE DEPENDENT VARIABLE)

Now that the program's goals—the dependent variable—have been transformed into operational definitions stating behavioral objectives, the next step in evaluation is to devise an instrument to measure those behaviors. Building a test from behavioral objectives is a relatively straightforward process.[5] Figure 13.3 illustrates a few behavioral objectives and test items that measure them.

---

[5] Researchers ordinarily think of tests as tools for evaluating individuals and their performance. However, when a group of individuals who have commonly experienced an intervention or training program take a test, one can pool their test data and examine them as group indicators. Analysis with proper comparisons (as discussed in the next section) allow such test data to contribute to an evaluation of the intervention or program.

FIGURE 13.3   SAMPLE BEHAVIORAL OBJECTIVES AND CONTENT-VALID TEST ITEMS FOR EACH

1. *Demonstrating a Procedure for Expressing Mixed Numbers as Improper Fractions.*
   Express $1\frac{1}{16}$ as an improper fraction.

2. *Describing the Function of Information Conveyed in a Purchase Order.*
   Circle the letter next to the correct answer.
   A purchase order is used when:
      A. A retailer orders merchandise from a wholesaler.
      B. A retailer orders services from a consumer.
      C. A wholesaler orders merchandise from a retailer.
      D. A foreman orders stock from inventory.

3. *Demonstrating an Interest in the Study of Science.*
   List any books or articles you have read on your own that concern science.
   Do you own a chemistry set? A microscope?
   Did you get these things before or after beginning your new science program?

4. *Demonstrating a Procedure for Preparing Permanent Microscope Slides.*
   Below is a sequence of steps for making a permanent microscope slide of a tissue specimen. Arrange the steps in their proper order.
      A. Soak in baths of progressively lower alcohol content
      B. Fix and mount
      C. Section
      D. Stain
      E. Soak in baths of progressively higher alcohol content

5. *Constructing a Magnetic Field Using Electrical Current.*
   Identify the materials you would need to construct a magnetic field using electrical current, and describe the procedure you would use.

Some program objectives appear to require evaluations based on physical performances by students. Effective evaluations may still employ paper-and-pencil tests that accurately and efficiently, albeit less directly, measure attainment of objectives that involve physical performances. However, in attempting to replace performance items with paper-and-pencil items, one must carefully preserve the essential characteristic that the item intends to measure. Items 4 and 5 in Figure 13.3 illustrate how an evaluation can accomplish performance judgments appropriate for objectives that call for demonstrations and constructions using paper-and-pencil instruments with identifications and descriptions.

The critical quality that an instrument for testing a program's behavioral objectives must possess is content validity. (See Chapter 9.) The test must reflect accurately upon the intervention or program, and it must evaluate the skills,

A Schematic Representation of Content Validity[a]   FIGURE 13.4

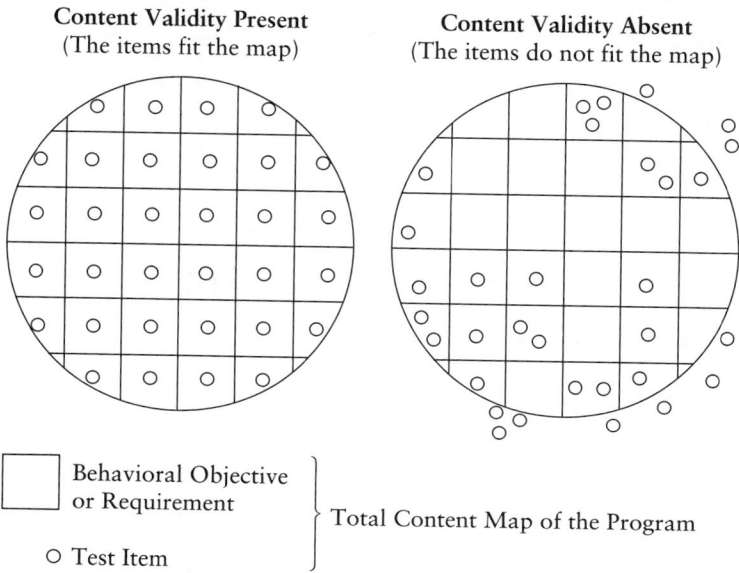

Content Validity Present
(The items fit the map)

Content Validity Absent
(The items do not fit the map)

☐ Behavioral Objective
or Requirement

○ Test Item

} Total Content Map of the Program

[a]Achieved when the items testing the achievement of content fit, or are appropriate for measuring, the objectives making up that content.

competencies, aims, and objectives previously set for the program. By systematically delineating each program objective and then mapping out measurement items for each objective, an evaluator can guarantee that such test items, taken together, will accurately represent the program's outcome and thus achieve content validity. This concept is illustrated in Figure 13.4.

As the figure illustrates, the process of developing a test that represents the program content begins by breaking down the program into its separate units. The evaluator then identifies the competencies and skills to be obtained from each unit and develops test items to measure each competency or skill. As a test more accurately represents the program content, its content validity rises. Without a content outline or breakdown, it is difficult to identify areas that the test must cover or to determine that completed test items accurately represent the program's content or objectives. The content outline and its objectives guide construction of test items that accurately reflect the effect of exposure to that content. A test so written will have content validity. That is, the test is appropriate for measuring the objectives.

To evaluate an instructional intervention, the major dependent variable usually represents the amount of student achievement resulting from instruction.

Often, however, evaluators are interested in assessing the effect of the intervention on students' attitudes toward the subject taught or on students' satisfaction with the instructional experience; these are typical goals of instructional developers. To accomplish these purposes, refer to four instruments that have appeared in previous chapters: (1) Math Attitude Scale (Figure 9.4), (2) Mood Thermometers (Figure 9.7), (3) Attitudes Toward School Achievement (Figure 10.5), and (4) Satisfaction Scale (Figure 10.6).

ASSESSING ATTAINMENT OF A PROGRAM'S GOALS

Identifying a Comparison Group: The Independent Variable

Up to this point, the chapter has explained a process that in and of itself could serve as a formative evaluation. The next step, the comparison process, truly distinguishes formative from summative evaluation. The important difference is that summative evaluation is more than an attempt to describe behaviors that a student has acquired as a result of specific program experiences but further to judge the level of performance of these acquired behaviors against some standard of success or effective performance. Thus, unlike formative evaluation, summative evaluation distinctly implies comparison of some sort.

Evaluators can contrast results for three kinds of groups with those of the experimental group to assess the effect of the treatment or intervention: control, comparison, and criterion groups. A *control* group is a group of Ss who have not experienced the treatment or any similar or related treatment. A contrast between a treatment and a control group attempts to answer questions like, "Would the behavioral objectives of the program have been met even if the program had not occurred? Can these objectives be expected to occur spontaneously or to be produced by some unspecified means other than the program under evaluation?" Students who complete a program may show more abilities than they showed before they completed the program due to the effects of history or maturation—sources of internal invalidity. To ensure that neither history or maturation is responsible for the change and pin down responsibility to the intervention or program, an evaluator can compare results for an equivalent group of individuals who have not experienced the program against results for those who have experienced it. This is control group contrast.

Very often, however, problems in evaluation take a somewhat different form, posing the question, "Is the treatment or program producing stronger behaviors or the same behaviors more efficiently than would be possible with alternative programs or interventions?" When stated in this way, the problem moves beyond control to involve *comparison*. Thus, the evaluator could compare results for an intervention or program group to those for a group of students who have presumably been trained to attain the same behavioral objectives in a different (and in many cases more traditional) way. A comparison of performance results for the two groups would answer the question, "Is the new way better than the old way?"

Occasionally, evaluation questions take even a third form in which the standard for judgment refers to some ideal state that students should attain. Such a question might ask, "Have vocational students developed job skills sufficient for reasonable success in the occupations for which they were trained?" If the objective of a program is to develop enough competence in calculus to allow students to solve specific problems in physics and aerodynamics, an evaluator might ask, "How does the students' knowledge of calculus compare to that of people who succeed at solving physics and aerodynamics problems?" Questions like these ask for contrasts, not with results for a comparison group that has completed an alternative experience, but with results for a *criterion* group that displays the behavior in another context, namely, applications of the knowledge to be acquired in the treatment (that is, calculus) to physics and aerodynamics problems.

Very often evaluations of vocational or professional programs seek to evaluate progress toward objectives of preparing individuals for on-the-job competence. To make this judgment, the evaluator chooses a criterion group from among workers who demonstrate such competence in practice. Of course, he or she must identify these individuals as a criterion group using a measuring instrument other than the one developed to evaluate the intervention. Typically this group is chosen on the basis of criteria such as supervisors' judgments, promotion rates, salaries, or indications of mastery other than direct measurement of competence and skill.

Questions of Certainty

An important consideration in assessing goal-attainment is the degree of certainty provided by selecting participants. In selecting a control, comparison, or criterion group, an evaluator must control for individual differences in potentially relevant characteristics to avoid participant bias. Evaluation studies often cannot use random assignment for this purpose, because individuals have come to participate in the procedure or its alternatives on a voluntary basis or on some basis other than assignment by the evaluator. The evaluator arrives after completion of these assignments and loses the opportunity to randomly assign half of a pool of subjects to the treatment and half to the control. More often, the evaluator begins with an intact group of subjects, possibly volunteers, who are already experiencing the treatment (or will soon begin it). Beginning with an intact group, the evaluation study thus calls for the nonequivalent control group design. However, sometimes the evaluator does not arrive on the scene before the program starts and thus cannot give the posttest instrument as a pretest (as is typically done in this design). She or he must then select a control or comparison group that is as similar as possible to the treatment group.

When you begin evaluation with an experimental group that has already been composed, you should attempt to select control Ss by random methods from the same population as the experimental Ss. As an alternative, you could select them systematically to establish a group reasonably equivalent to the experimentals. Where you have reason to believe that experimental group assignment has been essentially unbiased (although completed prior to your arrival as the evaluator), control group assignment should be random where the situation allows. Where either, or both, treatment and comparison groups have been preassigned, you can compare the groups on selection factors after the fact to determine their equivalence. Age, for instance, is an important variable for comparison, as are gender, IQ (or some other measure of ability or aptitude), socioeconomic status, and prior achievement. Effective evaluation requires treatment and control groups, treatment and comparison groups, or treatment and criterion groups as equivalent as possible on all potentially relevant individual difference measures. In addition, where possible, all groups should be pretested on the dependent variable measure developed in the preceding step.

Ideally, of course, potential Ss should be assigned randomly by the evaluator to experimental and control (or comparison or criterion) groups; however, this procedure often proves an impossibility. Thus, when conditions prevent use of a true experimental design (or pretesting to measure the dependent variable), the evaluator must make every effort to show that experimental and control groups are equivalent on all potentially relevant individual difference measures to minimize selection threats to certainty or internal validity. This goal is best accomplished by random selection of control Ss from the same population as experimental ones and after-the-fact comparisons of the presumably equivalent groups. This process is discussed in expanded detail under the section heading "Sampling," on the following page.

Determining That the Independent Variable Was Implemented

An evaluator cannot assume that one or more classes received a set of experiences while others did not. Simply because teachers are told to teach in a certain way, for example, or are even trained to teach that way, one cannot automatically state that they did in fact teach that way. Nor does it assure that teachers not so trained will not themselves manifest the same teaching behaviors as the trained teachers out of habit or previous experience.

Evaluators must assure themselves that the independent variable has indeed been fully implemented. To accomplish this goal, they must observe or otherwise measure the characteristics that represent the essentials of the intervention or treatment to ensure that those characteristics were always present in the treatment condition and always absent in the control or comparison condition. (Refer again to the last section of Chapter 7 for a discussion of this procedure.)

DESIGN, DATA COLLECTION, AND STATISTICAL ANALYSIS

The method of summative evaluation involves methods described in preceding chapters for selecting a sample and tasks; deciding how to measure or manipulate independent, moderator, and dependent variables; selecting a design; and choosing suitable statistics.

This section focuses on sampling, establishing reliability, choosing designs, collecting data, and choosing and interpreting statistical tests. The discussion focuses on applying these familiar processes to summative evaluation of instructional approaches in a classroom setting.

Sampling

A researcher who has access to a single class often chooses to test an instructional intervention on that class. This situation would be a convenient setting for naturalistic observation and exploratory work, but summative evaluation requires the opportunity to control variables, which is difficult with a single class. Some researchers may identify two sections of the same class and apply the intervention in one while teaching the second by conventional methods. This is another difficult situation to treat fairly; the researcher's biases may be showing by the time he or she gathers final results. Comparing one's own class taught experimentally to a colleague's taught conventionally does not permit the separation of treatment effects from teacher effects or student selection effects. A better evaluation method would randomly assign two pairs of classes to the experimental and control conditions:

	INNOVATION	COMPARISON
Teacher A	Class 1	Class 2
Teacher B	Class 3	Class 4

However, this procedure for assigning classes to conditions is not the best to control for invalidity due to student selection. In effect, it uses the class as the unit of analysis, because that is the unit of assignment, and reduces the total number of observations to four. A better procedure would pool all the students and then randomly assign each to one of the four groups. This random assignment adequately controls for student selection effects:

	INNOVATION	COMPARISON
Teacher A	Randomly assigned Group 1	Randomly assigned Group 2
Teacher B	Randomly assigned Group 3	Randomly assigned Group 4

A compromise between the two methods starts with intact classes, but it randomly divides each class in half and then exposes one-half of each to the control condition. Normal classroom circumstances often create difficulties, however, for teaching each half of a class in a different way.

	INNOVATION	COMPARISON
Teacher A	Random half of Classes 1 and 2	Random half of Classes 1 and 2
Teacher B	Random half of Classes 3 and 4	Random half of Classes 3 and 4

Reliability

All measuring instruments contain errors that affect their accuracy. Error is quantified as a reliability coefficient, as explained in Chapter 9. Evaluation, in particular, involves observational variables and instruments. To establish reliability of judgment on these observational instruments, follow these rules:

1. Combine observations by more than one observer (preferably not yourself, if possible).
2. Train all observers to use the instruments in live situations with the maximum possible agreement.
3. Assign at least two observers *together* to make at least 20 percent of the observations as the basis for the reliability calculation.
4. Ensure that observers do not know whether any teacher or classroom they observe is part of the experimental or control group. (Have them observe "blind.")

Sample Designs for Evaluation Studies: (A) Posttest-Only Control Group Design, (B) Nonequivalent Control Group Design

FIGURE 13.5

A

R	X_1	Y_1	O_1
R	X_2	Y_1	O_2

R	X_1	Y_2	O_3
R	X_2	Y_2	O_4

B

O_1	X_1	Y_1	O_2

O_3	X_2	Y_1	O_4

O_5	X_1	Y_2	O_6

O_7	X_2	Y_2	O_8

R = randomly assigned students; dashed line = intact groups; $X_1 X_2$ = innovation and comparison treatments; $Y_1 Y_2$ = levels of moderator variable.

5. Prepare an observation schedule that distributes the assignments of each observer over all teachers in both experimental and control groups.
6. Revise your instruments and train your observers until adequate reliability is obtained in a pilot study.

Design and Data Collection

The recommended research design for an evaluation study is a factorialized version of a true design or nonequivalent control group design. Although other designs may fit specific situations, the two shown in Figure 13.5 are best for summative evaluation of instructional approaches.

An evaluation study using this design might involve four classrooms with students assigned randomly to each. One teacher (Y_1) would teach one section experimentally (X_1) and the other as a control (X_2), and the other teacher (Y_2) would do the same. Dependent measures would be taken at the end of the term. This description fits Design A in Figure 13.5.

A second design might evaluate audiovisual aids by contrasting results for a group that experiences them (X_1) with those of a group that does not (X_2) in each of two intact classrooms, both taught by the same teacher. (This study treats the teacher assignment as a control variable, not a moderator. That is, it neutralizes or equalizes teacher effects across treatments instead of systematically varying and studying them. For a discussion of control variables, refer to Chapter 5.) All the students in the evaluation might take a standardized achievement test in reading, with results defining two subgroups—better readers (Y_1) and poorer readers (Y_2)—with each class likely to include approximately half of each. To control for prior achievement in the topic taught with and without audiovisual aids, a pretest would be administered (O_1, O_3, O_5, O_7). At the conclusion of the evaluation, a posttest for achievement and an attitude measure would be given (O_2, O_4, O_6, O_8). During the evaluation, data would be collected indicating whether students experienced the audiovisual aids and attended to them. This description fits Design B in Figure 13.5.

Statistical Analysis

The type of design advocated above suits an analysis of variance (ANOVA) statistical approach.[6] Both designs in Figure 13.5 can be diagrammed to fit a 2×2 ANOVA layout:

	X_1	X_2
Y_1	$X_1 Y_1$	$X_2 Y_1$
Y_2	$X_1 Y_2$	$X_2 Y_2$

This analysis would yield information on three effects: (1) the main effect of X—that is, whether the innovation (X_2) was more effective overall than the comparison (X_1); (2) the main effect of Y—that is, whether the high group on the moderator variable (Y_2) overall outperformed the low group (Y_1); and (3) the interaction of X and Y—that is, whether the group high in the moderator variable experiencing the innovation ($X_2 Y_2$) differed as much from the group high in the moderator variable receiving the comparison condition ($X_1 Y_2$) as the group low in the moderator group experiencing the innovation ($X_2 Y_1$) differed from group low in the moderator variable experiencing the comparison ($X_1 Y_1$). When an interaction effect occurs, the result looks like Graph A or B in Figure 13.6; when it does not occur, it looks like Graph C.[7]

The method for summative evaluation described in this chapter is an application of the research approach described and advocated in this book. The consistent and systematic research model often allows the researcher to attribute cause and effect or to make inferences. Because decision makers must determine cause and effect, this information provides invaluable assistance to them. Where

---

[6] Where after-the-fact comparisons show nonequivalence between the groups on relevant selection factors, a researcher can adjust somewhat for differences by analysis of covariance procedures.

[7] Following the analysis of variance, it would be possible to do multiple range tests such as the Newman-Keuls Multiple Range test or the Scheffé test in order to compare the three means simultaneously using the error term from the analysis of variance. These techniques are aptly described in Winer, Brown, and Michels (1991) and other statistics books. Where pretest data are available, a researcher may conduct analysis of covariance of the posttest scores with pretest scores as the covariate.

GRAPHS OF SAMPLE INTERACTION EFFECTS

FIGURE 13.6

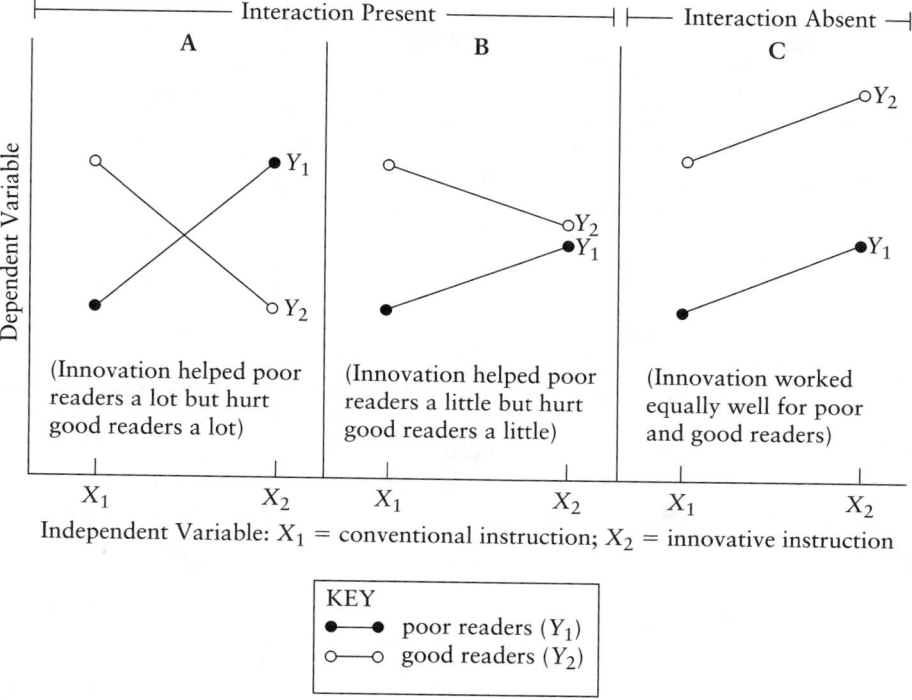

Independent Variable: X_1 = conventional instruction; X_2 = innovative instruction

KEY
●———● poor readers (Y_1)
○———○ good readers (Y_2)

necessary, quasi-experimental designs may be employed for evaluation purposes. Although alternative evaluation models (which do not include the many requirements of research design) are probably more efficient and easier to use, they are also further removed from cause and effect and thus rely more heavily on judgment or intuition. The purpose of this chapter has not been to contrast these approaches but to develop an approach that is a natural outgrowth of the rest of the book. In that sense, this chapter summarizes and illustrates the research approach developed in the book.

BOX 13 ____

ILLUSTRATION OF A SUMMATIVE EVALUATION STUDY

Evaluating an Individualized Science Program

Suppose that you designed an individualized, community-college-level course to teach basic science, consisting of chemistry and physics. Furthermore, you put this course into operation with a group of 40 freshmen and were now interested in evaluating the outcome.[8]

The first step in evaluation would be to identify the aims and objectives of the course. Broadly speaking, the course sought to enable students to master the content of basic science. A more specific objective would be to enable students to perform and apply the course content in physics and chemistry. A second objective might be to develop positive attitudes toward science in community college freshmen.

The second step in implementing the evaluation model would be to construct an operational definition of the dependent variables. For example, the dependent variable, "mastery of course content" might be defined operationally as "constructing answers to questions requiring knowledge of basic chemistry and physics with 70 percent accuracy." This particular behavioral objective could then be broken down into 10 components:

1. Constructing answers to questions about the structure of chemical substances with 70 percent accuracy.
2. Constructing answers to questions about the periodic table of elements with 70 percent accuracy.
3. Constructing answers to questions about chemical bonding with 70 percent accuracy.
4. Constructing answers to questions about writing chemical formulas with 70 percent accuracy.
5. Constructing answers to questions about balancing chemical equations with 70 percent accuracy.
6. Constructing answers to questions about scientific notation with 70 percent accuracy.
7. Constructing answers to questions about the principles of motion with 70 percent accuracy.
8. Constructing answers to questions about the principles of energy with 70 percent accuracy.
9. Constructing answers to questions about the principles of light and sound with 70 percent accuracy.
10. Constructing answers to questions about electricity with 70 percent accuracy.

---

[8] This illustration represents an actual evaluation. (See Tuckman and Waheed, 1981.)

The second aim of the study might be stated operationally as student agreement with 70 percent of the positive statements about the study of science and disagreement with 70 percent of negative ones.

A third evaluative step would require building tests to measure the dependent variables. A paper-and-pencil achievement test could be constructed to measure knowledge in the 10 content areas and an attitude scale could be constructed to measure attitudes toward science. Both tests could be tried out to establish their reliabilities using techniques described in Chapter 9.

The fourth step, the identification of comparison groups, might involve the following approach: Teach some basic science (chemistry and physics) classes using the conventional method of lecture and discussion, and compare the results with those of a class that experiences individualized instruction, in which students complete unitized modules at their own pace before taking a self-assessment test to determine whether they can move on or require additional instruction. Another possibility would be to teach half of the basic science course the traditional way and half the individualized way, with the chemistry half of the course taught one way and the physics half taught the other. In addition, the order in which the two types of instruction are experienced should be alternated between classes. Alternating both the content and order of each instructional method is necessary to control for various effects of history (or experience) bias.

By exposing each class to both types of instruction, you would equalize selection factors as well as potential Hawthorne and expectancy effects. In this way, you would use subjects as their own controls or comparisons. The only potential shortcoming is in history bias, which can be overcome by alternating the content and order of the two instructional methods across classes.

The fifth and last step in the evaluation would be to collect and analyze data. Administer the achievement and attitude tests developed in the third step to the students in the basic science classes after each half of the course, and compare the results following individualized instruction to those following conventional instruction. For these comparisons, you would conduct *t*-tests unless more complex designs across the two content areas or various orders of instructional method make analysis of variance the more suitable statistical test. If, for example, (1) content area were treated as a moderator variable, (2) some classes were taught the chemistry portion the conventional way and the physics portion the individualized way, and (3) the other classes were taught physics the conventional way and chemistry the individualized way, comparisons might look like this:

(Continued)

BOX 13

(continued)

	TYPE OF INSTRUCTION	
	INDIVIDUALIZED	CONVENTIONAL
Content Area — Physics		
Chemistry		

Suppose your results revealed that the main effect for type of instruction was significant for both knowledge and attitude, and that it was based on superior performance following individualized instruction in contrast to conventional instruction. You could then conclude that the individualized basic science course was more effective in improving science knowledge and attitudes in community-college students than was the conventionally taught version.

SUMMARY

1. *Formative evaluation* refers to the internal evaluation of a program, accomplished by comparing student performance outcomes to the program's own objectives. *Summative evaluation,* or *demonstration,* refers to an external evaluation of a program, accomplished by comparing performance outcomes of students experiencing the program to those of students experiencing an alternative or comparison program.

2. The experimental model for summative evaluation begins with a definition of the program's goals. The first step is identifying its aims or objectives as dependent variables, often accomplished by asking its designers and implementers. The second step is operationally defining each aim by writing it in behavioral or measurable terms using action verbs such as *identify, describe,* and *demonstrate.* The behavioral objective should include, in addition to an action verb and an indication of content, the conditions under which the behavior will be performed and the criteria for evaluating it.

3. The next stage in evaluation is to devise a way of measuring the program's goals, that is, a test. Basing test items on the program's behavioral objectives helps to ensure content validity.

4. Assessing attainment of a program's goals comes next. This process begins by identifying a comparison group to represent the second level of the inde-

pendent variable (the program under evaluation defining the first level). The comparison group should include subjects trained in some fashion other than the evaluated program to achieve the same goals as those of its subjects. Occasionally, the program group may be compared to students receiving no training (a control group) or to people who already display proficiency on the relevant skills (a criterion group).

5. In selecting a comparison group, an evaluator must carefully control threats to certainty that may result from selection of participants. To accomplish this goal, volunteers should be avoided; groups should be equated on control variables such as gender, age, aptitude, and socioeconomic status; and subjects should be pretested on the dependent variable. It is also important to complete a manipulation check to ensure that program subjects have received the program and comparison subjects have not.

6. Design, data collection, and statistical analysis constitute the final stage of evaluation. Where possible, classes and/or students should be randomly assigned to conditions . Teachers should also be assigned in such a way as to minimize the bias of teacher effects. Reliability between observers must also be established for observational instruments. Where true designs cannot be used, evaluators should try to use quasi-experimental designs (rather than nondesigns). Statistical comparisons can often employ analysis of variance.

COMPETENCY TEST EXERCISES

All but the last question below are to be answered on the basis of the sample evaluation report, "Evaluating Developmental Instruction," which appears below.

1. What dependent variables did the evaluation include, and how closely did they fit the goals of the program under evaluation?

2. How accurately were the dependent variables measured?

3. What treatment was evaluated, and to what was it compared?

4. What evidence, if any, was offered that the treatment operated as intended?

5. What experimental design did the evaluation implement? How well did it suit the situation, that is, how adequate were the controls?

6. Did the evaluation include a moderator variable? If so, name it.

7. What statistical test would you have used for this design?

8. Design an evaluation study to evaluate this book. Describe each step in the process, being as concrete as possible.

Sample Evaluation Report: "Evaluating Developmental Instruction"

The project, modeled on the British infant school approach, was tested in two elementary schools and included Grades 1 through 3 in one and Grades 1 through 5 in the other. For comparison purposes, the evaluator identified regular classrooms in Grades 1 through 5 of a matched control school in the same community. The study was aimed at comparing developmental classrooms to regular classrooms in terms of both *process*, that is, the behavior of teachers presumably resulting from training, and *product*, the behavior of students presumably resulting from the behavior of teachers.

The study attempted "conversion" of teachers to the developmental approach by means of in-service training and ongoing supervision. An initial trip to England was followed up by visitations, and regular evening programs throughout the year. Teachers so trained were expected to foster more diversity and flexibility in their classrooms than would regular classroom teachers. Hence, their teaching was expected to yield more positive student attitudes and higher achievement.

Two classrooms at each grade level (1 through 5) in each school were randomly selected from among available classrooms. Subsequently, comparisons were made for grade levels 1 through 3, with two experimental schools and one control, and grade levels 4 and 5, with one experimental school and two controls. (Grades 4 and 5 in one of the experimental schools served as a second control in the Grade 4 and 5 comparison.) The table summarizes the experimental design:

		SCHOOL 1	SCHOOL 2	SCHOOL 3	
	1	Expt.	Expt.	Control	
	2	Expt.	Expt.	Control	Expt. 1
Grade	3	Expt.	Expt.	Control	
Level					
	4	Expt.	Control	Control	Expt. 2
	5	Expt.	Control	Control	

The behavior of teachers was examined by means of systematic classroom observations conducted by trained observers using (1) the Flexible Use of Space Scale to measure flexibility in use of space, (2) simultaneous Activity and Grouping Measures to measure diversity of student classroom activities, and (3) the Tuckman Teacher Feedback Form to measure teacher style. These rating forms and behavior sampling procedures were designed specifically to measure space, organization, and teacher characteristics. Interrater reliabilities on all measures centered around 0.85. Student outcomes studied included problem-solving ability on a Bruner-type concept identification task, attitudes toward self as measured by the Self-Appraisal Inventory, attitudes toward school as measured by the

School Sentiment Index, and standardized achievement as measured by the California Achievement Tests given as both pretests and posttests. The preexisting tests provided adequate reliabilities, as reported in their manuals.

Findings reflected clear differences between developmental classrooms and regular classrooms in some areas. Developmental classroom teachers were more flexible in their use of space and made greater use of small-group instruction, but they relied as much as regular classroom teachers on workbook-type activities as a mode of "individualization." Developmental classroom teachers were rated by observers as more creative and more warm and accepting than their control counterparts, but they received equal ratings as organized and dominant. Students in both developmental classrooms and control classrooms manifested equal problem-solving skills, but developmental classroom students' results on the self-appraisal and school sentiment measures demonstrated significantly more positive attitudes toward both themselves and school than did control students. Analyses of achievement data showed only slight, scattered differences with no clear trends in either direction.

Project goals focused on changing teacher behavior and consequently on improving student achievement and attitudes. Considering the limited amount of time and teacher training offered, teachers made significant changes in some of their organizational and personal qualities to help children develop positive views of themselves and their school experiences. That is, no doubt, an important beginning. Unfortunately, the goal of superior achievement was not attained in the evaluation time frame.

RECOMMENDED REFERENCES

Gredler, M. E. (1996). *Program evaluation.* Englewood Cliffs, NJ: Prentice-Hall.
Worthen, B. R., & Sanders, J. R. (1987). *Educational evaluation: Alternative approaches and practical guidelines.* New York: Longman.
Sanders, J. R. (1992). *Evaluating school programs: An educators guide.* Newbury Park, CA: Corwin.

14 Chapter

QUALITATIVE RESEARCH: CASE STUDY OR ETHNOGRAPHY

Objectives

▶ Identify the characteristics of qualitative research, including research problems and questions suited to this method.

▶ Describe the qualitative research methodology, including various data sources.

▶ Describe procedures for conducting case studies or ethnographic research, including data analysis and report preparation.

This book has so far focused on methods for systematic, objective, and quantitative measurement of variables and their relationships. Although no researcher can ever carry out a totally systematic or totally objective study, the procedures described have aimed at mirroring variables as objectively as possible by representing them as numbers or quantities. In some situations, however, researchers choose to rely on their own judgment rather than quantitative measuring instruments to accurately identify and depict existing variables and their relationships. This chapter discusses such qualitative research.

CHARACTERISTICS OF QUALITATIVE RESEARCH

Bogdan and Biklen (1992) ascribe five features to *qualitative research:* (1) The natural setting is the data source, and the researcher is the key data-collection instrument. (2) Such a study attempts primarily to describe and only secondarily to analyze. (3) Researchers concern themselves with process, that is, with events that transpire, as much as with product or outcome. (4) Data analysis emphasizes inductive methods comparable to putting together the parts of a puzzle. (5) The researcher focuses essentially on what things mean, that is, *why* events occur as well as *what* happens.

This type of research methodology, also called *ethnography,* is said by Wilson (1977) to be based on two fundamental beliefs: (1) Events must be studied in natural settings; that is, understanding requires field-based research. (2) A researcher cannot understand events without understanding how they are perceived and interpreted by the people who participate in them. Thus, participant observation is one of the method's major data-collection devices.

Ethnography relies on observations of interactions and interviews with participants to discover patterns and their meanings. These patterns and meanings form the basis for generalizations, which are then tested through further observation and questioning.

The application of the qualitative or ethnographic approach to the field of evaluation has been termed *responsive evaluation* (Stake, 1975) and *naturalistic evaluation* (Guba & Lincoln, 1981).[1] In such an evaluation, the researcher visits a site or field location to observe—perhaps as participant observer—the phenomena that occur in that setting. The researcher also interviews people in and around the setting. These activities focus on identifying the chief concerns of the various participants and audiences and assessing the merit, worth, or meanings of the phenomena to the participants. To accomplish these goals, the researcher must determine the effects of the setting, the participants, and the observed phenomena on each other.

---

[1] Both labels aptly describe the case study or ethnographic research methodology described in detail later in this chapter.

FIGURE 14.1

THEMES OF QUALITATIVE RESEARCH

1. *Naturalistic inquiry*	Studying real-world situations as they unfold naturally: nonmanipulative, unobtrusive, and noncontrolling; openness to whatever emerges—lack of predetermined constraints on outcomes
2. *Inductive analysis*	Immersion sin the details and specifics of the data to discover important categories, dimensions, and interrelationships; begin by exploring genuinely open questions rather than testing theoretically derived (deductive) hypotheses
3. *Holistic perspective*	The *whole* phenomenon under study is understood as a complex system that is more than the sum of its parts: focus on complex interdependencies not meaningfully reduced to a few discrete variables and linear, cause-effect relationships
4. *Qualitative data*	Detailed, thick description: inquiry in depth: direct quotations capturing people's personal perspectives and experiences
5. *Personal contact and insight*	The researcher has direct contact with and gets close to the people, situation, and phenomenon under study: researcher's personal experiences and insights are an important part of the inquiry and critical to understanding the phenomenon
6. *Dynamic systems*	Attention to process: assumes change is constant and ongoing whether the focus if on an individual or an entire culture
7. *Unique case orientation*	Assumes each case is special and unique: the first level of inquiry is being true to, respecting, and capturing the details of the individual cases being studies: cross-case analysis follows from and depends on the quality of individual case studies
8. *Context sensitivity*	Places findings in a social, historical, and temporal context: dubious of the possibility or meaningfulness of generalizations across time and space
9. *Empathic neutrality*	Complete objectivity is impossible: pure subjectivity undermines credibility; the researcher's passion is understanding the world in all its complexity—not proving something, not advocating, not advancing personal agendas, but understanding; the researcher includes personal experience and empathic insight as part of the relevant data, while taking a neutral nonjudgmental stance toward whatever content may emerge
10. *Design flexibility*	Open to adapting inquiry as understanding deepens and/or situations change; avoids getting locked into rigid designs that eliminate responsiveness; pursues new pathos of discovery as they emerge

Source: M. Q. Patton. Qualitative Evaluation and Research Methods *(Newbury Park, Calif.: Sage Publications. © 1990), Table 2.1, pp. 40–41. Used with permission of Sage Publications.*

Patton (1990) identifies ten themes of qualitative research, shown in Figure 14.1. These themes reflect a rather sharp contrast between qualitative and quantitative approaches.

Guba and Lincoln (1981) point out some methodological concerns associated with the qualitative approach, including the need to set boundaries and the importance of finding a focus to ensure a credible, appropriate, consistent, confirmable, and neutral process. In an attempt to meet these criteria, which collectively provide rigor in qualitative research, the case study or ethnographic approach described here is structured as much as possible within certain governing principles described in the following subsections of the chapter.

Phenomenological Emphasis

An ethnographic research project involves a study of phenomena or occurrences as seen through the eyes of those experiencing them, rather than through the eyes of outside observers. While the study's observers record what people say and do, they attempt to do so through the perspective of the participants they observe. Hence, they try to capture the subjective or felt aspect of experience. To accomplish this goal, ethnographic researchers attempt to follow some general rules:

1. Avoid beginning observations with a priori assumptions about the phenomena under study. (That is, do not attempt to explain them before observing them.)
2. Do not attempt to reduce a situation of great complexity to a few variables.
3. Do not allow the methods used for collecting data to influence or change what you are trying to study.
4. Consider alternative explanations for what you observe; in other words, allow theory to spring from observations rather than allowing predetermined theory to influence what you observe.

Naturalistic Setting

Ethnographers carry out their research in naturally occurring situations, such as classrooms, schoolyards, and board rooms; such a setting constitutes the study's "field." They observe and interview rather than manipulating variables or measuring variables by externally introduced instruments. An ethnographer examines the behavior under study in the context in which it occurs through description, rather than attempting to abstract it from the context through the use of tests, surveys, or questionnaires. For this reason, ethnographic research findings must be considered in reference to their contexts, and generalization to other contexts requires caution.

Emergent Theory

Ethnographic research does set out to test hypotheses. Rather than formulating specific hypotheses on the basis of prior research or preconceived theories, the ethnographic approach calls for theories and explanations to emerge from, and therefore remain grounded in, the data themselves (hence the term *grounded theory*). Data, taken in context, come first; then the explanations emerge from intensive examination of the data, providing a natural basis for interpretation rather than an a priori one. Such an approach is also termed *holistic*, research, since the data are examined as a whole to find a basis for explanation for observed phenomena. To support appropriate explanations, data must incorporate "heavy" or detailed description of observations and events from multiple perspectives so that situations can be reconstructed and reexamined by the researcher after they have occurred.

IDENTIFYING GENERAL RESEARCH PROBLEMS

Listed below are a number of research problems that constitute a cross-cultural outline of education as identified by Jules Henry (1960). Qualitative study would expand insights into these general issues:

1. On what activity does the educational process focus? (For example, on social manipulation? On use of the mind?)
2. By what teaching methods is information communicated?
3. What are the characteristics of the people who do the educating (status, expected rewards, relationships to learners)?
4. How does the person being educated participate? (For example, are students accepting, defiant, competitive, cooperative during the process?)
5. How does the educator participate, and what attitude does he or she display?
6. What is taught to some people and not to others?
7. Does the educational process include any discontinuities?
8. What limits the quality and quantity of information a child receives from the teacher? (For example, teaching methods? Time? Equipment? Stereotyping?)
9. What forms of conduct control (discipline) are used?
10. What is the relationship between the intent and result of the child's education?
11. What self-conceptions are reinforced in the students?
12. What is the duration of formal education?

Wiersma (1995, p. 253) suggests a number of typical ethnographic studies in education:

1. A study of life in an urban classroom
2. A study of decision making in an inner-city high school
3. A study of student life in law school
4. A study of student relations in an integrated school
5. A study of peer interactions in racially mixed classrooms of a suburban high school
6. A study of racial attitudes of children in a desegregated elementary school
7. A study of interaction patterns among faculty in a private prep school

FIGURE 14.2

TYPES OF QUALITATIVE STUDIES

PERSPECTIVE	DISCIPLINARY ROOTS	CENTRAL QUESTIONS
1. Ethnography	Anthropology	What is the culture of this group of people?
2. Phenomenology	Philosophy	What is the structure and essence of experience of this phenomenon for these people?
3. Heuristics	Humanistic psychology	What is *my* experience of this phenomenon and the essential experience of others who also experience this phenomenon intensely?
4. Ethnomethodology	Sociology	How do people make sense of their everyday activities so as to behave in socially acceptable ways?
5. Symbolic interactionism	Social psychology	What common set of symbols and understandings have emerged to give meaning to people's interactions?
6. Ecological psychology	Ecology, psychology	How do individuals attempt to accomplish their goals through specific behaviors in specific environments?
7. Systems theory	Interdisciplinary	How and why does this system function as a whole?
8. Chaos theory: nonlinear dynamics	Theoretical physics, natural sciences	What is the underlying order, if any, of disorderly phenomenon?
9. Hermeneutics	Theology, philosophy, literary criticism	What are the conditions under which a human act took place or a product was produced that makes it possible to interpret its meanings?
10. Orientational, qualitative	Ideologies, political economy	How is *x* ideological perspective manifest in this phenomenon?

Source: Patton, Qualitative Evaluation and Research Methods *(© 1990), Table 3.2, p. 88. Used with permission of Sage Publications.*

8. A study of writing instruction in an elementary school
9. A study of socialization in a rural high school

Patton (1990) identifies the central research questions raised in the 10 qualitative research perspectives shown in Figure 14.2. They range from description of a culture (that is, "the acquired knowledge people use to interpret experience and generate behavior," Spradley, 1980, p. 6) to the manifestations of an ideology or way of thinking.

SPECIFYING THE QUESTIONS TO ANSWER

A case study or ethnographic research project may seek to answer specific questions about occurrences and their explanations similar to those answered by the quantitative research methods previously described in this book. The differences between the methods reflect the kinds of data needed to answer those questions and techniques for collecting and analyzing those data. Even though the researcher serves as the data collector and analyst, the process is not entirely without structure. To maintain neutrality and to use limited time in the most efficient possible way, the process is structured to some degree. This principle suggests that some of the questions to be answered should be specified in advance, as should the general data-collection procedures employed to answer those questions.

Building some structure into the case study or ethnographic research process enhances its confirmability. *Confirmability*, in this instance, means that other researchers using essentially the same procedures to examine the same phenomena in the same setting would likely arrive at similar conclusions.

The questions that a qualitative study sets out to answer must relate to the data-collection procedures described later in this chapter. These questions help to determine (1) what specific events constitute the observed phenomena and (2) to what extent these events are related to one another. In a classroom setting, for example, it may be helpful to think of outcomes in terms of the four categories discussed in Chapter 2—specific knowledge and comprehension, thinking and problem solving, attitudes and values, and learning-related behavior.

Qualitative researchers also gain important clarification by trying to determine what events are influencing observed outcomes, including not only the details of observed behavior but also the reasons behind or causes of such behavior. In a classroom setting, again, an ethnographer might consider both input and process (that is, the implementation of input) within the categories of Chapter 2: instructional approach, teacher behavior, environment, subject matter, and student input.

Analysis of inputs and processes should consider both their intentions and their actuality. In other words, a researcher should examine and report not only the behavior that took place but also the reasons or plans behind the behavior. Thus, she or he may want to ask:

- Did some plan (or intention) shape the observed behavior?
- What specific intentions exerted influence?
- What was the likelihood that the behavior would achieve the intentions?
- To what specific extent was the behavior carried out as intended?

A qualitative researcher should explore these questions in addition to basic ones such as: Who was present in the setting? What did they do? What happened next? How do these aspects relate to one another? Thus, the questions basically take this form:

- Who were the participants?
- What was the setting?
- What roles did the participants play?

- What intentions motivated participants in the different roles?
- What behavior did participants in the different roles actually display?
- What results or effects did this behavior produce?
- What were the relationships between roles, intentions, behaviors, and effects among the different participants?

RESEARCH METHODOLOGY

Dobbert (1982) identifies a particular sequence of steps as the methodology of ethnographic research:

1. Statement of research questions
2. Situations and problems that led to those questions
3. Background research and theory that helped to refine the questions
4. Study design
   a. Knowledge of the setting before the researcher's entry
   b. How initial entry was accomplished
   c. How the researcher acquired a feel for the setting
   d. How the researcher's presence was explained to the participants (explanation of the researcher's role)
   e. Specification of each research technique used (sample, sequence, timing)
   f. Relations between the researcher and setting members (for example, volunteers, paid, willing)
   g. Problems encountered, their eventual disposition, and their effects on validity and reliability
5. Presentation of data
6. Conclusions

Another qualitative research methodology, termed *ethnoscience,* is designed to uncover and interpret the mental maps that groups of people follow in navigating through daily life. Ethnoscience is oriented toward answering questions such as:

- What do people see themselves and others doing?
- How do they see and interpret the world around them?

Ethnoscience addresses these questions in four steps:

1. *Description:* Conduct open-ended interviews of informants to ask about the whole situation.
2. *Discovery:* Learn what categories informants use in making their mental maps.

3. *Classification:* Determine the principles for classifying phenomena in each category. (Seek the definitions of categories and their boundaries.)
4. *Comparison:* Uncover the relationships between categories.

Consider, for example, the culture of the college classroom and, in particular, the behavior and performance of the professor toward the students. In the *description* step, an ethnoscience researcher would ask students to describe their teachers: how they teach, how they react to students, what they are like. Students are also asked to give their opinions of their teachers. The researcher also attempts, through interviews, to *discover* what categories students use in determining what teachers are like and in formulating opinions of them. For example, students may describe their teachers as using handouts, course outlines, and schedules, leading to the discovery that students categorize the behavior of teachers as organized or disorganized; a professor described as soft-spoken and noncritical may be categorized by students as accepting, and so on.

In the *classification* step, the researcher would refer to these categories in drafting direct, probing questions to determine all the cues and characteristics that students consider in deciding whether a particular professor is or is not organized, is or is not accepting, is or is not flexible, and so on. Students would be asked to classify their professors in terms of the categories discovered in the previous step.

Finally, the researcher would make *comparisons* between classifications. For example, connections might become evident between how organized a professor is and how much he is liked by his students, or between how dynamic a professor is and how much students feel they have learned from her or him. Professors who differ in popularity can be compared in terms of students' classifications of them on dimensions such as organization, flexibility, and so on. In this way, the study would seek to learn not only how students think about or categorize their professors but also about the connections between the qualities that students perceive in their professors. Thus, it would reveal the mental representations or maps that college students form of professors.

Bogdan and Biklen (1992) describe the *constant comparative method* as a search by a researcher for key issues, recurrent events, or activities that then become categories of focus. Further observation looks for incidents that reflect the categories of focus to determine the diversity of the dimensions under the categories. Such incidents are continually sought and described, guided by the categories, in an effort to discover basic social processes and relationships.

In the example of the college classroom, the categories of focus may be different kinds of interactions between professor and students, such as asking questions, offering explanations, building relationships, and maintaining barriers. Interactive incidents would be observed and related to each of the categories to build a "theory" of the social processes through which professors and students build relationships.

Glaser (1978) lists the following steps for implementing the constant comparative method:

1. Begin collecting data.
2. Look for key issues, recurrent events, or activities in the data that become categories of focus.
3. Collect data that provide many incidents of the categories of focus with an eye toward the diversity of the dimensions under the categories.
4. Write about the categories you are exploring, attempting to describe and account for all the incidents detailed in your data while continually searching for new incidents.
5. Work with the data and the emerging model to discover the bases for social processes and relationships.
6. Engage in sampling, coding, and writing as the analysis focuses on the core categories.

Of course, not all qualitative designs are so open-ended that the problem of study emerges entirely from the data. Many researchers identify problems they want to study and seek to obtain qualitative data that bear on those issues.

DATA SOURCES

Case study research usually gathers data from three types of sources: (1) interviews of various people or participants in the setting who are involved in the phenomena of study; (2) documents such as minutes of meetings, newspaper accounts, autobiographies, and depositions; and (3) direct observation of the phenomena in action. The researcher collects data in any of these three ways to acquire information related to the questions posed in Figure 14.2. This section discusses each of these data sources in turn.

Interviews

One direct way to find out about a phenomenon is to ask questions of the people who are involved in it in some way. Each person's answers will reflect his or her perceptions and interests. Because different people experience situations from different perspectives, a reasonably representative picture of the occurrence and absence of a phenomenon may emerge and provide a basis for interpreting it.

To maximize the neutrality of a study's methods and the consistency of its findings, the researcher often follows an interview schedule. To gather varying perspectives on the same questions, she or he often asks the same questions of different people. These prepared questions are embodied in the interview schedule (described in detail in Chapter 10).

TYPES OF INTERVIEWS   Researchers conduct four types of interviews, described by Patton (1990) in Figure 14.3. They range from totally informal, conversational exchanges to highly structured sessions asking closed-end, fixed-response questions. The type of interview chosen depends on the context of the study and the kinds of questions to be asked.

SPECIFIC QUESTIONS   In selecting questions, an interviewer should ask not only about intentions but about actual occurrences. Information about occurrences and outcomes can also be obtained from source documents, as described later in this section. However, interviews often prove the major sources of information about people's intentions and other subjective elements of observed phenomena. Consider a sample list of such interview questions and directives:

1. Describe the behavior that is going on here. Describe your own behavior. Describe the behavior of other participants.
2. Describe the reasons behind the behavior that is going on here. Why are you behaving the way you are? Why do you suppose others are behaving the way they are? How are these reasons interrelated? How are they affected by the setting?
3. Describe the effects of the behavior that is going on here. Describe the effects of your behavior. Describe the effects of the behavior of other participants. Are these effects interrelated?

These questions are posed in generalized form as illustrations. An actual case study would tailor them to fit the specifics of the phenomena in question.

Suppose, for example, that a study in a high school classroom uncovers an incident in which a student had apparently verbally threatened a teacher and then stormed out of the room. The researcher interviews some of the students in the class, first asking them to *describe* the incident. Later questions elicit their suggestions about the *reasons* behind the incident; in response, students detail previous in-class encounters between the teacher and the particular student in which the teacher ridiculed the student in front of classmates for lack of preparation. The *effect* of that ridicule on the students being interviewed was, by their own admission, to be sure to prepare for class. However, this ridicule did not have the same effect on the student who talked back. Rather, the ridicule affected him by causing him to behave toward the teacher as the teacher had behaved toward him. The researcher has gathered information that the effect of ridicule as a motivational device is not uniform across all students but depends on their reactions to it.

This line of questioning would be suitable for participants in a given phenomenon. Their answers may suggest further lines of related questions, perhaps increasingly standardized ones, that the researcher could ask. These additional questions need not be preplanned in specific form; the topics would emerge from answers to preplanned questions. Experience in interview situations teaches a researcher to recognize worthwhile but unanticipated lines of questioning.

FIGURE 14.3

Types of Interviews

TYPE OF INTERVIEW	CHARACTERISTICS	STRENGTHS	WEAKNESSES
(1) Informal conversational interview	Questions emerge from the immediate context and are asked in the natural course of things; there is no predetermination of question topics or wording.	Increases the salience and relevance of questions; interviews are built on and emerge from observations; the interview can be matched to individuals and circumstances.	Different information collected from different people with different questions. Less systematic and comprehensive if certain questions do not arise "naturally." Data organization and analysis can be quite difficult.
(2) Interview guide approach	Topics and issues to be covered are specified in advance, in outline form; interviewer decides sequence and working of questions in the course of the interview.	The outline increases the comprehensiveness of the data and makes data collection somewhat systematic for each respondent. Logical gaps in data can be anticipated and closed. Interviews remain fairly conversations and situational.	Important and salient topics may be inadvertently omitted. Interviewer flexibility in sequencing and working questions can result in substantially different responses from different perspectives, thus reducing the comparability of responses.
(3) Standardized open-ended interview	The exact working and sequence of questions are determined in advance. All interviewees are asked the same basic questions in the same order. Questions are worded in a *completely* open-ended format.	Respondents answer the same questions, thus increasing comparability of responses; data are complete for each person on the topics addressed in the interview. Reduces interviewer effects and bias when several interviewers are used. Permits evaluation users to see and review the instrumentation used in the evaluation. Facilitates organization and analysis of the data.	Little flexibility in relating the interview to particular individuals and circumstances; standardized working of questions may constrain and limit naturalness and relevance of questions and answers.
(4) Closed, fixed response interview	Questions and response categories are determined in advance. Responses are fixed; respondent chooses from among these fixed responses.	Data analysis is simple; responses can be directly compared and easily aggregated; many questions can be asked in a short time.	Respondents must fit their experiences and feelings into the researcher's categories; may be perceived as impersonal, irrelevant, and mechanistic. Can distort what respondents really mean or experienced by so completely limiting their response choices.

Source: Patton, Qualitative Evaluation and Research Methods *(© 1990), Table 7.1, p. 288–289. Used with permission of Sage Publications.*

The specific questions posed to participants in a phenomenon may not be suitable for other respondents, such as observers. Incomplete awareness of the reasons behind the participants' behavior would limit outsiders' efforts to contrast intentions and actual events. However, observers could describe actual events from their own perspectives, allowing the researcher to make the contrasts in later analysis. Moreover, although outside interpretations of intent give only speculative suggestions, and evaluation must treat them as such, the interpretations of other observers might help a researcher formulate an understanding of the intentions that underlie the observed behaviors of participants. Again, a list of examples must state them in extremely general language. Real situations call for the most specific possible questions.

1. How did you come to observe the phenomena in question? What is your role in these events? Under what conditions and circumstances did you observe the phenomena?
2. Describe what is going on here. Identify the participants and the behavior of each one.
3. Why do the participants behave as they do?
4. What effect does the behavior of the participants produce on one another and on future events or outcomes?

Because each observer views phenomena from a different perspective, all of these questions could reasonably be preceded by the phrase, "In your opinion . . ." However, interviews questioning a number of observers may reveal a pattern in apparently diverse responses.

It is important to recognize that participants in a set of phenomena might occupy distinctly different roles. Often, roles can be differentiated into two levels: providers and recipients, or agents and clients, or authority figures and followers, or adults and children. In dealing with the latter group (often students, in a classroom study) useful questions might ask:

1. Describe your experiences. Tell about what actually happened. How did the teacher behave? How did you behave? How did the other students behave? What was the sequence of events?
2. What caused things to happen as they did? Why did you behave the way you did? Why did the teacher behave the way he or she did? Why did the other students behave the way they did?
3. Did any incidents, either good or bad, occur that stand out in your mind?
4. Did you enjoy the experience? Was it an interesting one? Did you learn from it?

The first set of questions deals with actual behavior, so it parallels the questions asked of other participants and observers. The second set of questions concerns the reasons behind behavior, again in a parallel pattern. The third question represents the *critical incident technique,* in which respondents are asked to recall critical or outstanding incidents that can guide researchers, either in forming hypotheses about outcomes or in illustrating generalizations of results or conclusions.

A fourth set of questions represents a way of evaluating outcomes or phenomena based on the subjective reactions of the participants. This set of questions aims to identify three levels of evaluation from their perspective:

I. Did the intended or expected experience occur? (Did you get what you expected?)
II. Were you satisfied with what you received? (Was it what you wanted?)
III. Did you change as a result of the experience? (For example, did your knowledge and/or competence improve?)

This fourth set of questions attempts to reveal whether the participants felt satisfied with their experiences. Even when an interviewer asks participants whether they have learned or improved, these questions really only ask for their *opinions* of an experience's worth, which essentially reflect their satisfaction. Any attempt to actually test whether their knowledge and/or competence improved would require some measurement of their level of relevant knowledge or competence at the conclusion of the experience. The researcher would then have to compare current levels to the levels prior to the experience, and to contrast the difference with that of a group who did not have the same experiences. But that analysis is a quantitative approach quite different from qualitative research. Satisfaction and self-estimates of change are by definition subjective evaluations "measured" by asking participants for their self-assessments.

Finally, useful further interviews might seek input from people who are neither participants or direct observers, but who are aware of a set of experiences through second-hand information. In school research, such secondary sources could be parents, for example. If a phenomenon is having an effect of great enough magnitude, parents will be aware of it. Their impressions are worth gathering, because subsequent experiences (that is, whether or not a program is continued) may depend on them. Also, some studies may lack opportunities to locate people who either participated in or observed events. Those researchers must rely on secondary sources for answers to certain questions:

1. Are you aware of a particular event (or experience or phenomenon)? If so, how did you find out about it? (If not, it is pointless to ask further questions.)
2. What are your impressions of what actually transpired? How did you arrive at this information (stated in the most specific possible terms)?
3. What are your impressions of why events happened as they did? How did you arrive at these judgments (stated in the most specific possible terms)?
4. What was the result or outcome of the event? How did you determine that this was, in fact, the result?

INTERVIEWING CHILDREN   Qualitative researchers often must implement some special procedures for conducting successful interviews with children. Questioning must accommodate the limited verbal repertoires of children from preschool age through adolescence. It must also anticipate the paradox that children seldom give responses as socially controlled as the statements of adults, but on occasion they do strictly censor their responses according to rigid rules. Moreover, because other, more structured approaches like questionnaires are often impractical for research with children, the interview becomes the data collection device of choice.

A primary goal in interviewing a child is to establish rapport, that is, a positive relationship between the interviewer and the child. Exchanges based on feelings of warmth, trust, and safety help to increase both the amount and accuracy of the information that young subjects provide. Boggs and Eyberg (1990) provide the comprehensive list of communication skills to guide the adult interviewer, as shown in Table 14.1.

The purpose of *acknowledgement* is to provide feedback to assure the subject that the interviewer is listening and understanding. This input influences children to continue talking. The level of subtlety of the acknowledging response must be matched to the child's social development.

Descriptive statements of what the child is doing show the child that the interviewer is accepting of the child's behavior. This input also helps to focus the child's attention on the current topic and encourages the child to offer further elaboration. Descriptive statements such as "That's a hard question to answer, isn't it," can be particularly helpful when a child responds to a question only with silence. *Reflective statements,* when delivered with the proper inflection, demonstrate acceptance and interest in what the child says and convey understanding. They can also prompt additional, clarifying statements by the child. To avoid being seen as insincere, especially with adolescents, *praise statements* should be offered only after establishing rapport, and then they should be "labeled" to specify exactly what the interviewer is encouraging. Properly introduced, especially in age-appropriate language, praise can greatly increase a child's information-giving on a particular topic.

Questions make explicit demands upon a child. Interviewers may ask open-ended or closed-ended questions, but open-ended ones are preferred, because they yield more information than the typical "yes" or "no" response to a closed-ended question. Children often respond especially readily to indirect questions, that is, declarative statements preceded by "I wonder . . . ," because they perceive these invitations to speculate as less demanding than direct questions. A reflective question, that is repeating a child's statement with an interrogative inflection, may help to clarify the statement. "Why" questions are typically counterproductive, because they call for justification rather than description. Questioning children about moods often yields little information, as well. Questions should be kept simple and deal with individual points.

The most direct way of requesting information from a child is to give a *command,* but this method should be used sparingly, and then only to elicit a

TABLE 14.1

Communication Skills

SKILL	DEFINITION	EXAMPLE
Acknowledgment	A verbal or nonverbal behavior that has little or no manifest content.	"Mm-hmm," head nod.
Descriptive statement	A nonevaluative comment that describes the present situation.	"You look like you're thinking hard about that question."
Reflective statement	A statement that repeats what the child has said.	"You sound pretty happy that she kept her promise."
Praise statement	A statement that expresses explicit positive evaluation.	"You're doing a nice job of explaining this to me."
Question	An expression of inquiry made to elicit information.	"What chores do your parents want you to do?"
Command	An instruction in declarative form.	"Tell me more about that."
Summary statement	A condensed reiteration of preceding content.	"We've talked about everyone who lives at your house."
Critical statement (to be avoided)	A statement that expresses disapproval.	"That isn't very nice."

Source: Boggs & Eyberg. In La Greca (ed.), Through the Eyes of the Child (© 1990), Table 4.1, p. 88. Used with permission of Allyn & Bacon.

response that the child is developmentally able to provide. Responses to commands should be praised. *Summary statements* can effectively prompt a child to elaborate upon or continue talking about a particular area of content. They can also introduce entirely new topics. Finally, *critical statements* should be carefully avoided. When a child displays inappropriate behavior during an interview, an interviewer should ignore it in order to preserve rapport.

Boggs and Eyberg (1990) also describe five stages or steps of a child interview, and the strategies employed within each, as shown in Table 14.2. While these stages correspond most closely to the clinical interview setting, they can be generalized to any data-collection situation. The interviewer should come to the interview with a prepared set of questions (see Chapter 10 for more information on preparing interview questions) and an understanding of the kinds of behaviors and response patterns typical for the child's age group. The setting should also be prearranged to ensure comfort and to minimize distractions, especially if the interview takes place in a classroom in the presence of other children. In nonclinical interview settings, especially in schools, a child interviewee will not be alone, so arrangements should maintain privacy. A familiar playroom or classroom offers the advantage of putting the child at ease, but the interviewer must arrange for separation between the child interviewee and classmates. At the onset of the meeting, the interviewer should practice the kinds of behaviors described earlier to establish rapport with the child.

TABLE 14.2
 	
 Source: Boggs & Eyberg. In La Greca, Through the Eyes of the Child (© 1990), Table 4.2, p. 97. Used with permission of Allyn & Bacon.
	STAGES OF THE CHILD INTERVIEW
	
	 Preparing for the interview
	      Gather initial information about the child and the reasons for referral.
	      Review relevant literature about presenting the problem.
	      Arrange a conducive interview setting.
	
	 Meeting the child and family
	      Observe the child and family prior to introduction.
	      Formally introduce yourself.
	      Describe the structure of the interview.
	
	 Beginning the interview
	      Explain the purpose of interview to the child.
	      Ask the child to express any concerns.
	      Discuss confidentiality, if appropriate.
	      Discuss playroom rules, if appropriate.
	
	 Obtaining the child's report
	      Move from least to most distressing topics.
	      Deal sensitively with child resistance.
	      Minimize parent interruption.
	
	 Closing the interview
	      Express appreciation for cooperation.
	      Summarize the major topics discussed.
	      Solicit additional concerns.
	      Inform the child of follow-up plans.

The interview is likely to be a new experience for the child. At the outset, the purpose should be explained and the child given an opportunity to ask questions. Any rules to be followed during the interview (e.g., no playing with toys) should be made explicit at this time, and confidentiality should be assured. The interview itself should move from least to most potentially distressing or difficult topics; when and if the child shows resistance, the interviewer should move to another topic and attempt to return to the more difficult one later in the interview. The interviewer should respect the child's ultimate decision not to answer a particular question.

When the interview is complete, the interviewer should express appreciation for the child's cooperation and give the child an opportunity to add any unsolicited information. Successfully engaging a child in the interview process requires good planning and skillful communication of an interviewer. The interviewer must often be prepared to follow a less direct route in acquiring information from a child than from an adult.

Documents

In addition to conducting interviews, a qualitative researcher may also gather information about an event or phenomenon from documents that participants or observers have prepared, usually in the form of minutes or reports.

Minutes are written descriptions of the actions considered and taken during a meeting. They are usually official records of all transactions and proceedings by the members of the organization holding the meeting. They state all discussion items and motions for action and the dispositions of those motions. They also indicate which of a meeting's participants offered specific discussion and motions. Minutes can give an accurate picture of official events, but these records usually lack the detail to help you understand why.

Reports of events may also be written by either participants or observers. The most common observers' reports are newspaper accounts. If an event is deemed important or newsworthy enough, a newspaper prints an account, usually written by an observer. This account may be both descriptive and interpretive, although its principal intent is description. Groups also sometimes issue reports, recommendations, or proceedings of their own that describe processes, results, or both. This information may vary depending on the formality of the group and its task.

Reports may take other forms, usually incorporating additional detail. One form, which is prompted by the motivation of an eyewitness, is an *autobiography*. An eyewitness account may describe events with more limited scope. This is a description of an event by one in attendance as either a participant or an observer. A researcher reading this kind of information receives no absolute assurance about its accuracy.

Another form of report, prompted by forces other than the observer's motivation, is a *deposition*. In such a statement, given under oath, a person answers a set of questions usually describing an event or occurrence in which he or she was a participant or observer.

All of these written accounts attempt to describe and occasionally to explain events or phenomena that have taken place. In no instance, however, can the researcher confidently assume that such an account accurately portrays events or conditions. Any such conclusions should rest on information from accounts by multiple sources.

Observations

Observations, the third qualitative data source, can also provide quantitative data, depending upon the techniques for recording observational data. If observers record events on formal instruments such as coding or counting systems or rating scales, the observation will generate numerical data; hence they form part of quantitative research. If an observer simply watches guided only by a general scheme, then the product of such observation is fieldnotes, and the research is a qualitative study.

The target for observation is the event or phenomenon in action. In qualitative educational research, this process often means sitting in classrooms in the most unobtrusive manner possible and watching teachers deliver instructional programs to students. Such an observer does not ask questions as part of this role, because that is interviewing. (Questions can be asked either before or after observing.) An observer just watches. But the watching need not totally lack structure. She or he usually watches for something, primarily (1) relationships between the behaviors of the various participants (Do students work together or alone?) (2) motives or intentions behind the behavior (Is the behavior spontaneous or directed by the teacher?) and (3) the effect of the behavior on outcomes or subsequent events (Do students play together later on the playground or work together in other classes?). Observers may also watch to confirm or disconfirm various interpretations that have emerged from the interviews or reports and to identify striking occurrences about which to ask questions during subsequent interviewing.

The critical aspect of observation is watching, taking in as much as you can without influencing what you watch. Be forewarned, however, that what goes on in front of you, the researcher, will represent—at least in part—a performance intended to influence your judgments. This is an inevitable element of observation. Increasingly frequent and unobtrusive observations reduce the likelihood that they will influence what occurs before you.

Transcribed Conversations

Interactive events may also be tape recorded to provide exact evidence of each participant's statements. Tape recordings can then be transcribed into typed copy, and transcriptions can be subjected to conversation analysis. A sample transcription notation appears in Figure 14.4, and a transcribed interview fragment appears in Figure 14.5. (Analysis of this fragment appears later in the chapter.)

FIGURE 14.4   TRANSCRIPTION NOTATION FORMAT

Note: This protocol was derived from work initially done by Gail Jefferson and reported in "Explanation of Transcript Notation," in J. Schenkein (Ed.) (1978), Studies in the organization of conversational interaction (pp. xi–xvi). New York: Academic Press.

–	a dash signals a slight pause, generally of less than .2 seconds
(0.0)	parentheses show longer pauses, timed in tenths of seconds
∧	a caret shows rising intonation
∧	a subscripted caret shows falling intonation
° °	superscripted *o*s enclose passages which are quieter than the surrounding talk
[ ]	brackets enclose simultaneous talk, marking onset and resolution
____	words underlined are given stress by the speaker
( )	parentheses show transcriber's doubt, or inaudible passages
(( ))	double parentheses note occurrences in the setting, not necessarily part of the talk
> <	arrows show passages spoken at a much quicker rate than surrounding talk
=	latches show where one speaker begins immediately after the preceding speaker with no pause
:	colons show elongated sounds; generally, each colon represents a beat
CAPS	show talk which is louder than surrounding talk
·h	shows an audible in-breath
h	shows an audible exhalation

TRANSCRIPT FRAGMENT

FIGURE 14.5

Source: From Waite, D. (1993). Teachers in conference: A qualitative study of teacher-supervisor face-to-face interactions. American Educational Research Journal, 30, page 683.

```
 1 Vern:    um, but once again if you were going to have them up
 2          there, you might've taken a more proactive role in seating
 3          them. (0.8) I don't know if y- a boy girl boy girl
 4          pattern will be better, or the ones who you know are going
 5          to interact here, you do that. It's like a seating chart=
 6 Doug:    = um hum um ⌈hum        yeah
 7 Vern:              ⌊you kn⌋ow?    AND um, um (1.0) I did it with
 8          ninth graders so the likelihood that you'd have to do it
 9          with first graders would be great.
10 Doug:    um hum
11 Vern:    OK?
12 Doug:    yeah, that would be a good idea hhh ((nervous laugh))
13 Vern:    WHAT, WHAT YOU NEED is to expand the repertoire of
14          skills that you can use to ensure classroom management.
15          and ⌈whatchu h̲ ̲a̲d going on
16 Doug:        ⌊um hum                  ⌋
17 Vern:    up front was less than productive classroom management
18          because there were a number of times you had to
19          go Tim (0.8), you know, Zack, um m-m-m, you know,
20          whatever the names were or wha- whatever. u- w-
21          yo⌈u h̲a̲ ̲d to go on with
22 Doug:      ⌊um:               ⌋
23 Vern:    that a few times. So that w- would be of something
24          you really need to focus on. The second thing that I
25          would mention here is is (3.0) °and in an art lesson, I
26          might add, there there isn't an easy way of doing this,
27          but it's something for you to think about.° (0.8) UM (2.3)
28          THE OLD, we've talked about this before, the old (0.7)
29          never give more than three directions to k- anybody at one
30          time=
31 Doug:    =um hum=
```

CONDUCTING A CASE STUDY

The next section of this chapter deals with specific procedures for conducting a qualitative case study.

Obtaining Needed Documents

The first step in conducting a qualitative study is to obtain copies of all available documents describing the event or phenomenon (or its background) and carefully study them. This preparation is the best and most objective way to orient yourself to the situation that you are about to research. In reading the documents, take particular note of (1) the setting, (2) the participants and their respective roles, (3) the behaviors displayed by the various participants, (4) your perceptions of the participants' motivations or intentions, (5) the relationships between intentions and behaviors, and (6) the results or consequences of the behavior.

The information that you glean from background documents will help you to prepare your own plan for direct information-gathering as part of your case study.

Conducting a Site Visit

To collect some data for a qualitative or case study, you will have to accomplish *fieldwork* during a *site visit*. This is ordinarily a period of time during which the researcher enters the setting in which the event under study has occurred or is occurring. Of course, a particular study may incorporate more than a single visit, and the research may be conducted by more than a single researcher. To use the time on site most efficiently and effectively, a researcher should plan as specifically as possible how the time there will be spent. This planning should include developing a visitation schedule and interview instruments.

A *visitation schedule* includes a list of all the people the researcher wants to see and the amount of time intended to spend with each. Efficient use of limited time calls for a visitation schedule made up of specific arrangements to see specific people, such as teachers involved in a particular project. It should also set aside time to make observations or to see people without specific appointments.

A visitation schedule also helps with advance preparation of interview questions, although you need not attempt to write in advance every question you might ask. (Recall the guidelines in Figure 14.3.)

After reading the documents and reviewing this chapter's earlier discussion about interview questions, you should be able to prepare a general line of interview questions. Each scheduled interview may require a separate set of questions, in which case each session should be sketched out in advance.

Preparation should also include development of a mechanism for recording responses to interview questions. You may want to tape record each interview to prevent the need for taking notes. If you choose to tape record, you must request in advance permission from each interviewee, and you may record only when this permission is granted. In place of or in addition to tape recording, you should prepare a notebook for taking fieldnotes. Systematic prior marking of the notebook pages with interview questions or question numbers will aid in taking and interpreting fieldnotes. A notebook should allow a page for each observation's fieldnotes by listing the date, time, teacher, and other, more specific entries for the phenomena you will be observing. A sample page of fieldnotes appears in Figure 14.6.

Good planning also should allow for observation. This preparation may include a set of questions that you hope to answer as a result of the observation, or it may list critical incidents. You may simply prepare to describe the activities of students and teachers during your visit.

The site visit merits important emphasis, because it is the data-collection phase of a case study. It requires effective preparation and organization. Helpful planning tools include (1) a specific, preset list of appointments and (2) a procedure or mechanism for taking the fieldnotes that constitute your observation and interview data.

A SAMPLE PAGE OF FIELDNOTES   **FIGURE 14.6**

Date: November 24, 1992
Time: 10:20–11:20 AM
Teacher: Mrs. Hitchcock
Class: 4th grade (Wynn School, Room 112)
Program: Developmental
Subject of observation: classroom management

① Class returned to classroom after P.E. Mrs. H. had set up room for project work and greeted children upon return by reminding them that they would now work on their projects.

② Without further direction, children dispersed to desks after taking project "books" out of their regular storage area. (Projects were nature "books" done on an individual basis, to relate personal experience, interest, and natural science theme.)

③ Some children work alone, quietly, drawing or writing or pasting. Some talk in pairs about project work. Some show work to teacher and ask for help. Some scurry around looking for materials. [It is amazing to see how many things are going on at once in an orderly yet comfortable fashion without the teacher exerting overt management behavior. It is a stark contrast to children seated in rows listening—or at least being quiet.]

④ At 10:55 teacher interrupts by striking gong and without any further instructions children gather around her for reading. Teacher proceeded to read a story to entire class punctuated often by teacher asking questions and students answering enthusiastically.

Also, prepare to answer the kinds of questions that the people you visit and observe may ask regarding your data-collection activity. Bogdan and Biklen (1992) list five of the most frequently asked questions: (1) What are you actually going to do? (2) Will you disrupt the activities you study? (3) What will you do with your findings? (4) Why us? (5) What will we get out of this? Those authors suggest honesty as a general rule to follow in answering all questions. They also offer the following suggestions regarding your behavior: (1) Do not take personally what happens. (2) Set up your first visit so someone present can introduce you. (3) Don't try to accomplish too much the first few days (a rule that cannot be followed if you have only that much time or less). (4) Remain relatively a noncontroversial presence. (5) Adopt a friendly attitude.

An Illustration

A study of teacher-supervisor conferences (Waite, 1993) followed this methodology:

1. Conducted three interviews with each of three supervisors
2. Shadowed supervisors as they interacted with teachers
3. Conducted informal ethnographic interviews with each of four teachers
4. Recorded five supervisory conferences (each lasting from 5 to 28 minutes)
5. Made nonparticipant observations in the schools
6. Made participant observations at the university
7. Accompanied each of the three supervisors on at least one classroom visit
8. Met with the teachers in district seminars and at university program seminars
9. Transcribed and analyzed conference tapes using a conversation analysis notation protocol (See Figure 14.4.)

ANALYZING THE DATA AND PREPARING THE REPORT

The data for the qualitative research project includes the fieldnotes that you bring back in your notebook and in your head, interview transcripts, plus any information gleaned from program documents. Analysis of these data means using the data to answer the questions the research set out to answer.

Analyzing the Data

Fieldnotes contain both descriptions and reflections. Descriptions, say Bogdan and Biklen (1992), may include: (1) portraits of subjects, (2) reconstructions of dialogue, (3) descriptions of physical settings, (4) accounts of particular events, (5) depictions of activities, and (6) notes about the observer's behavior. Reflections may deal with (1) analysis, (2) method, (3) ethical dilemmas and conflicts, (4) the observer's frame of mind, and (5) points of clarification. Hence, fieldnotes serve both descriptive and interpretative or analytical purposes. They relate not only what happened, but often why and wherefore, as well. They also may include conclusions based on descriptions and reflections.

Turner (1981) identifies eight stages of development for organizing data:

1. Review the data you have collected and *develop category labels* for classifying them.
2. Identify enough specific examples of each category in the data to completely define or *saturate each category,* clearly indicating how to classify future instances into the same categories.
3. Based on the examples, *create an abstract definition* of each category by stating the criteria for classifying subsequent instances.
4. *Apply the definitions* you have created as a guide to both data collection and theoretical reflection.
5. Attempt to *identify additional categories* that suggest themselves on the basis of those already identified (e.g., opposites, more specific ones, more general ones).
6. *Look for relationships between categories,* develop hypotheses about these links, and follow up on them.
7. Try to *determine and specify the conditions under which relationships between categories occur.*
8. Where appropriate, *make connections* between categorized data and previously articulated theories.

Figure 14.7 illustrates the process of analyzing qualitative data. The researchers were attempting to study the role of school peer groups in the transmission of gender identities. As a data-generating device, they interviewed 10 fifth and sixth grade students in a single public school using an approach called the "talking diary," and tape recorded the responses.

From the stream of responses, they identified a number of "facts" (some of which have been italicized in Figure 14.7 for illustrative purposes) as well as some of the data on which these facts are based. These facts are conclusions or generalizations based on the specific answers students gave to the researchers' questions. Based on these facts and others, the authors concluded that "gender identities and relations were the primary focus of the peer groups. . . . In a sense, a world of female students and a world of male students existed [and] cross-gender

FIGURE 14.7

From Eisenhart & Holland (1985). Reproduced by permission.

AN ILLUSTRATION OF QUALITATIVE DATA AND INTERPRETATION

Data from the talking diary interviews revealed that in addition to engaging in gender-segregated activities and indicating friendship depending on gender, boys and girls made differing judgments in their normative statements. *Girls, especially, were prone to comment on the interpersonal styles of other girls.* For white girls, it was important to be seen as "nice," "cute," "sweet," and "popular." Positive remarks referred to a girl who did not act stuck up, overevaluate her assets, or flaunt her attractive features in front of her friends. Among black girls, it was also important to be "nice" and "popular," although the meanings of these terms were somewhat different. For blacks, these terms referred to a girl who demonstrated the ability to stand up for herself and who assisted others when they were having difficulty or were in trouble. For them, girls who did not demonstrate an intention to stand firm and help friends in the face of verbal or nonverbal challenges were criticized.

Girls, both black and white, also spent a great deal of time talking about their appearance. They advised each other on such things as how often to wash one's hair, how to get rid of pimples, and how to dress in order to look good and be in style.

Especially by the sixth grade, a large proportion of what girls talked about to each other concerned romantic relationships with boys. Almost every lunch and breakfast conversation included at least some mention of who was "going with" whom, how to get boys to like you, how to get someone to "go with" you, what to do if someone was trying to break up with you, how to steal someone else's boyfriend, what to wear on a date, where to go and how to get there, and who was attractive or ugly and why. In the following examples taken from the notes, girls advise one another on their romantic ventures. In the first example, Tricia describes how she coaches one of her girlfriends to get a boy to take her to the end-of-the-year banquet held for sixth graders.

> I tell her what to say, how to do, how to dress . . . like how to fix her hair in the morning, how to talk, how to laugh . . . just culture . . . everything culture tells you to do, you do it. Then she'll turn around and coach me back, with Jackson.

Another example concerns Jackie and her efforts to get Bob to take her to the banquet.

> Jackie frequently called Bob at night, arranged to run into him in the hall, and sent notes to him via her friends. Bob was not particularly responsive to these overtures. Finally, in desperation when he appeared on the verge of asking someone else, Jackie discussed her problem with some of her girlfriends. One friend suggested that Jackie had been too pushy and, as a result, Bob did not like her anymore, though he had at one time. The friend suggested that the way to catch a boy was to let him think that you are shy. The friend pointed out that all the girls who had steady boyfriends were shy at school [Clement et al. 1978: 191].

In this context, girls who were not interested in romantic relationships were considered strange. Ruth, for example, expressed her feelings of being "weird" as follows:

> I like boys, but I don't like to go with anybody. Most girls are crazy about boys, but I'm a little on the funny side. I like this boy who lives near me: I like to play with him, but I don't like to *do* anything with him [i.e., I don't want him to be my boyfriend].

(continued)   **FIGURE 14.7**

Boys' talk also revealed a concern with being liked by girls. For example, at a skating party given by the researchers for the students, Joseph was overheard telling Edward how to be successful in dealing with women: "You have to be cool."

Although boys gave attention to their interpersonal styles, boys also talked frequently about their abilities in sports and in getting away with things at school.

Boys also wished to be seen as strong. As with some of the girls, a boy's ability to defend himself, especially in contests with equals, was highly valued. One of the girls, for example, made the following criticism of a male classmate:

> I don't want nobody to see me if I was a boy . . . wouldn't want nobody seeing me fighting a girl, but won't fight a boy.

Another expression of this value came from a boy who was shorter than most of his classmates:

> Like if a big boy comes messing with me, Vernon'll take him, but if a little shrimp-o comes messing with Vernon, I take care of 'em. If one a little taller comes messing with me, Joseph takes care of 'em. . . .

Boasting about their proficiencies in these areas competed with romantic relationships and being well liked as topics among the boys at Grandin. These male/female differences in conversational interests were reflected in a comment made by one sixth-grade boy about girls:

> I like 'em, but not as much as I like boys . . . I just can't talk to them the way I can boys . . . they don't like sports, they don't like to do nothing fun . . . I be nice to 'em because my mom says you're spose to be polite.

These differences in the valued identities of girls and boys are reminiscent of the findings of Coleman (1965). He reports that in the context of adolescent peer groups, girls learn to want to make themselves attractive to others, especially boys. Boys, on the other hand, develop interests in task-oriented activities, such as sports, as well as learning the importance of being well liked.

---

contact . . . was interpreted in romantic terms only" [Eisenhart & Holland, 1983, p. 329].

In an ethnographic study of teacher-supervisor conferences, Waite (1993) relied most heavily on analysis of transcriptions of a number of such conferences with four teachers. An example of one transcript fragment appeared earlier in Figure 14.5. In this fragment, the teacher (Doug) meets with his supervisor (Vern). As the transcript shows, he always agreed with, or at least never disagreed with, the advice he received. (See Lines 6, 10, 12, 16, 22, and 31 of the figure.)

Based on his analysis, Waite (1993, p. 696) summarized his findings as follows:

> Analysis of the conferences here presented concerned at least three distinctive teacher roles in supervision conferences: the passive, the collaborative, and the adversarial. The teacher who enacted a passive conference role, Doug, mainly acknowledged the supervisor's remarks, encouraging the supervisor to speak more. Due to his passivity, he was unable or unwilling to forcefully counter the supervisor's direct and indirect criticisms. The teachers who enacted the collaborative conference role, Kari and Ed, did so by timing and phrasing their utterances so as not to appear confrontational. This requires a high level of active listening and communicative competence. Still, these two teachers successfully advanced their agendas. The teacher who enacted an adversarial conference role, Bea, did so through marked competition for the floor and actions that demonstrated her reluctance to accept either what her supervisor, Faye, had to say or her role as her evaluator. She broke the frame of the conference and enlisted tenets of teacher culture and other, absent teachers in her defense.

Protocol Analysis

In order to study the thinking process students apply to learn or solve problems, researchers have developed a technique that asks students engaged in the learning or problem-solving process to *think aloud,* that is, to say out loud what they are thinking as they progress. These statements are tape recorded and transcribed, representing what is called a *protocol.* These protocols are then examined and coded to identify characteristics of the thinking process. This technique, called *protocol analysis,* has been described in detail by Ericcson and Simon (1993).

The coding scheme for a set of protocols can vary, depending upon what a particular researcher is interested in determining. For example, Chi, DeLeeuw, Chiu, and LaVancher (1994) were interested in finding out whether a special form of mental construction, called a *self-explanation,* would improve acquisition of problem-solving skills. Self-explanations were defined as spontaneously generated explanations that one makes to oneself as one studies worked-out examples from a text. While such an example provides a sequence of action statements, it lacks explanations or justifications for the actions chosen. The researchers were interested in determining whether the number of self-explanations students generated while studying the examples would be related to the amounts they learned.

After reading each sentence of a 101-sentence text passage about the functions of the human circulatory system, students were asked to think aloud about the meaning of the particular sentence. Students' statements about their thinking were coded using protocol analysis. A statement was coded as a self-explanation if it went beyond the information given in the sentence, that is, if it inferred new knowledge. For example, students read, "These substances (including vitamins, minerals, amino acids, and glucose) are absorbed from the digestive system and transported to the cells"; expressions of thoughts like "the purpose of hepatic portal circulation is to pick up nutrients from the digestive system" or "eating a balanced diet is important for your cells" would be coded as self-explanations. For another example, students read the sentence, "During strenuous exercise, tissues need more oxygen"; a self-explanatory thought might be "the purpose of the blood is to transport oxygen and nutrients to the tissues."

The findings of the study showed that generating self-explanations did indeed contribute to superior learning.

Another study using protocol analysis was done by Wineburg (1991). He was interested in identifying differences, if any, in the ways that experts and novices reasoned about historical evidence. He asked a group of working historians and a group of high school seniors to think aloud as they reviewed a series of written and pictorial documents about the Battle of Lexington. He analyzed their protocols of the pictures using the following coding categories:

1. *Description:* Included descriptive statements that made no reference to the purpose or function of the feature being described.
2. *Reference:* Included statements that related some aspect to the subjects' overall impressions or that referred pictures to one another.
3. *Analysis:* Included statements that related to the point of view, intentions, goals, or purposes of the pictures.
4. *Qualification:* Included statements that qualified other statements (e.g., judged them, stated their limitations).

For the protocol analysis based on the subjects' processing of the documents, Wineburg applied three "heuristics" for coding: (a) corroboration—comparing documents with one another; (b) sourcing—looking at the document's source before reading it; (c) contextualization—placing the document in a concrete context with regard to time and place. Wineburg found that historians' employed much more sophisticated thinking processes than those of students, making much greater use, in general, of qualification and contextualization. These historians also used the other coding categories differently than did the students. Protocol analysis enabled Wineburg to get a picture of the differences in information processing by the two groups of people he studied.

Preparing the Report

The last step in qualitative research, as in any type of research, is preparing the research report. Examples of report forms appear in Figure 14.8. The format of the qualitative research report should follow essentially the same patterns as the research reports described in Chapter 12.

FIGURE 14.8

REPORT FORMS

EMPHASIS	REPORT TYPE	CHARACTERISTIC OF REPORT	USE
Insider's view	Typical biography or career	Centers on one person treated as typical or representative; individual's development is carefully related to the entire sociocultural system so as to create a holistic picture.	Very appropriate for an educational or a training emphasis.
	Ethos	Organized around the culturally standardized system of emotions. The emotional system is treated as primary and the remainder of the sociocultural system is related to it. Culture expresses ethos.	For reports where a group's feelings are central to research.
	Modal personality	Individual emotional structure typical for a group is the core of this form. An individual, or a small group of individuals, is shown as representative of the culture. Culture is presented as personality writ large.	Excellent where a cross-cultural understanding is needed.
	World view	Emphasizes cognitive organization of a group; delineates underlying rules and concepts that guide perceptions, judgments, and actions in all areas of life. Culture is visioned as a guiding map.	Is good for a cross-cultural understanding.
Outsider's scientific view	Ecological	Description centers on consecutive important features of the environment, showing how each shapes the social situation studied. Relations between the internal and external are treated as critical linkages.	Useful where outside influences are critical in answering research question.
	Social-structural	Subgroups, status differences, intergroup relations, including norms and expectations, are explored. Reports in this genre usually focus on how the subgroups make up harmonious whole or on conflict between groups.	For research problems that center on the internal workings of an organization.
	Comparison-contrast	Compares a case at hand with a well-known case of a similar type or contrasts with a known case, usually on a point-by-point basis. May be combined with other report types.	Useful in restudies or studies closely related and designed to confirm or refute earlier work.
	Central event	Uses a critical event as diagnostic and illustrative of the entire social scene; the event is taken as typical and the report details the way that it is representative.	For process-oriented studies or for groups where ritual is important.
Either insider's or outsider's view	Community within a community	Reports on a larger social group by centering on one subgroup and looking out. The small group is often treated as representative of the larger, though the whole may be constructed via contrasts.	Where a study question asks about a particular group.
	Historical	Events are reported chronologically, usually as seen by an omniscient observer.	Where development and/or process are central.

(From Dobbert, 1982. Reproduced by permission of author and publisher.)

SUMMARY

1. Qualitative research takes place in the natural setting with the researcher as the data-collection instrument. It attempts primarily to describe, focuses on process, analyzes its data inductively, and seeks the meanings in events.

2. This category of research methods includes ethnography, responsive or naturalistic evaluation, and case study research, to cover a variety of themes dealing with unique, whole events in context. The researcher's experience and insight form part of the data.

3. Qualitative research (a) displays a *phenomenological emphasis*, focusing on how people who are experiencing an event perceive it; (b) occurs in a *naturalistic setting* based on field observations and interviews; (c) accommodates *emergent theory*, since explanations come from the observations themselves.

4. Research questions typical in qualitative studies focus on culture, experience, symbols, understandings, systems, underlying order, meaning, and ideological perspective. Problems studied in this way include plans, intentions, roles, behaviors, and relationships of participants.

5. Qualitative methodology involves a set of research questions, a natural setting, and people behaving in that setting. Data collection focuses on describing, discovering, classifying, and comparing through a process often referred to as the *constant comparative method*.

6. Data sources include interviews, documents, observations, and transcribed conversations. Interviews range from highly informal and conversational exchanges to highly structured sessions that elicit fixed responses. Participants may be asked to describe behavior (their own and others'), reasons behind or causes of behavior, and effects of behavior on subsequent events. Participants or direct observers can also report on critical incidents, as well as offer their opinions. Secondhand information can also be solicited.

7. Interviews with children require special skills regarding the following communication actions: acknowledgment; descriptive, reflective, and praise statements; questions; commands; and summary and critical statements. The child interview itself includes the following stages: preparation, initial meeting, beginning, obtaining the child's report, and closing.

8. Transcribed conversations are tape recordings of interviews or conferences.

9. Qualitative researchers often review documents, including minutes, reports, autobiographies, and depositions. Formal or informal observations provide additional data.

10. A qualitative study involves obtaining documents, conducting interviews, and making observations. The data typically take the form of fieldnotes, or transcripts of interviews, made during site visits. While on site, a qualitative researcher should be prepared to answer questions (honestly) about the study activities and to remain as passive, noncontroversial, and friendly as possible.

11. Fieldnotes contain both descriptions and reflections, thus representing both the data and its analysis. Conclusions and generalizations are also often included. Interviews are typically transcribed, leading to transcript analysis.

12. Another method of collecting qualitative data asks students to "think aloud" as they solve problems. Their spoken thoughts are transcribed to produce *protocols,* which are then analyzed to look for the kinds of mental constructions the researcher is interested in studying.

13. The last step in qualitative research is preparation of a report. The types and focuses of these reports vary depending on their intended uses.

COMPETENCY TEST EXERCISES

1. Write an *L* next to each characteristic below that describes qualitative research and a *T* next to each one that describes quantitative research.
   a. Data are analyzed inductively
   b. Focuses on input-output relationship
   c. Concerned with explanations
   d. Descriptive
   e. Data are analyzed statistically
   f. Primarily concerned with process
   g. Concerned with outcomes
   h. Causal
   i. Naturalistic
   j. Uses measuring instruments
   k. Uses subjective observation
   l. Manipulated

2. Which of these questions states a qualitative research problem?
   a. Do suburban teachers earn higher salaries than urban teachers?
   b. How does a teacher in an urban classroom control the behavior of students?
   c. Does some relationship link school socioeconomic status and school attendance?

3. One approach to qualitative research is to try to uncover and interpret the mental maps that people use. This approach uses four steps: description, discovery, classification, and comparison. Give a one-sentence description of each step.

4. You have just heard of an incident in a classroom involving the behavior of a student and the response of a teacher, which culminated in the student's expulsion from the classroom. You are now interviewing the teacher. State three questions that you might ask.

5. Following the incident mentioned in Exercise 4, state three questions that you might ask a student in the class who observed the incident.

6. A group of teachers has just completed a 6-week, after-school, in-service workshop on using questioning as part of the teaching process. You are conducting an exit interview of the teachers to evaluate the workshop. State three questions that you might ask each teacher.

7. What are four elements of the necessary preparation for a site visit?

8. "Students in classrooms using the developmental teaching approach were seldom alone, seldom in their seats, and seldom quiet. They were usually clustered in small groups around some object of inquiry, talking away fast and furiously." State one conclusion about developmental teaching that you might draw from this observation.

RECOMMENDED REFERENCES

Bogdan, R. C., & Biklen, S. K. (1992). *Qualitative research for education: An introduction to theory and methods* (2nd ed.). Boston: Allyn & Bacon.

Eisner, E. W. (1991). *The enlightened eye: Qualitative inquiry and the enhancement of educational practice.* New York: Macmillan.

Fontana, A., & Frey, J. H. (1994). Interviewing: The art of science. In N. K. Denzin & Y. S. Lincoln (Eds.). *Handbook of qualitative research* (pp. 361–376). Thousand Oaks, CA: Sage.

Glesne, C., & Peshkin, A. (1992). *Becoming qualitative researchers.* New York: Longman.

Part 6

THE RESEARCHER AS "CONSUMER"

Chapter 15

ANALYZING AND CRITIQUING A RESEARCH STUDY

Objectives

▶ Analyze and critique the following parts of a research study: problem, problem statement, literature review, hypotheses, variables, operational definitions, methods for manipulating and controlling variables, research design, methods for observing and measuring variables, statistical analysis, presentation of results, and discussion.

All of the chapters preceding this one have discussed designing and conducting a research study as preparation for carrying out that activity. However, researchers (and nonresearchers, as well) are also "consumers" of research when they read and attempt to understand research articles appearing in journals. In fact, even a dedicated researcher typically spends more time reading studies done by others than designing and conducting new research. Particularly in planning a research study, one needs to find and read relevant literature.

When reading a research study, it is necessary to understand it, comprehending its problem, methodology, and results, in order to interpret and use its findings. This understanding requires knowledge of what problem the study investigated, what variables and operational definitions it articulated, how it controlled for potentially confounding variables and measured or manipulated variables of interest, what research design it employed, how it analyzed data, what those data indicated, and what meaning the researcher found in the results. These determinations require *analysis* of the study into all of its component parts and elements.

Additional helpful input comes from careful judgment of the effectiveness with which the researcher implemented the various steps and aspects of the study. This judgment provides particularly important help in deciding how much confidence to place in the results and the conclusions drawn from those results. Before incorporating a prior study into a literature review or using it as a basis for formulating a new hypothesis, a *critique* of that study must be made. Hence, an intelligent reading of the literature requires both analytical and critical evaluation processes.

Analysis and critical evaluation of a research study require applications of many principles already presented in this book—but from the slant of the reader rather than the researcher. The reader of a research study applies almost all the knowledge learned so far in this book. Such analysis provides the designer of a research study with a set of skills to apply to that process, as well, by playing the role of analyst and evaluator of his or her own work. The result should be a better study than one designed without a critical eye on both analysis and evaluation. In other words, self-analysis and self-evaluation can only improve a developing piece of research. In fact, Tuckman (1990c) advocated providing researchers with analysis and critical evaluation skills in order to improve the quality of published research.

A word now about how this chapter will proceed. For purposes of analysis and critique, a research article will be divided into three parts: (1) the *introductory section,* (2) the *methods section,* and (3) the *results and discussion sections.* (However, the reader is encouraged to read an entire article before attempting to analyze and critique any part of it, because "clues" that clarify the beginning of the article may appear in the middle or end, and vice versa.) Successive sections of the chapter will discuss criteria for analysis and critical evaluation of these sections of a research report in turn. In the introductory section, an analyst/evaluator examines the problem and problem statement, literature review, hypotheses, variables, and operational definitions. In the method section, she or he examines the processes of manipulation and control, research design, and measurement. In the

FIGURE 15.1

QUESTIONS TO ANSWER IN ANALYZING AND CRITICALLY EVALUATING A RESEARCH STUDY

1. (a) Does the research report articulate a **problem statement?** If so, (b) what does it say? (c) Is it a clear statement? (d) Is it introduced prior to the literature review?

2. Does the **problem statement** give a complete and accurate statement of the problem actually studied, or does it leave out something?

3. Does the study's **problem** offer sufficient (a) workability, (b) critical mass, and (c) interest?

4. (a) Does the **problem** studied offer theoretical and practical value? (b) Does the report establish these criteria?

5. Does the **literature review** present a high-quality overview? Does it achieve adequate (a) clarity, (b) flow, (c) relevance, (d) recency, (e) empirical focus, and (f) independence?

6. Does the **literature review** include technically accurate citations and references?

7. (a) Does the introduction offer **hypotheses?** If so, (b) what are they? Are they (c) directional, (d) clear, (e) consistent with the problem, and (f) supported by effective arguments?

8. What actual **variables** does the study examine; identify: (a) independent, (b) moderator (if any), (c) dependent, and (d) control variables (only the most important two or three)?

9. (a) What intervening **variable** might the study be evaluating? (b) Was it suggested in the research report?

10. What **operational definitions** did the researcher develop for the variables listed in answering Question 8?

11. (a) What type of **operational definition** was used for each variable? (b) Was each definition sufficiently exclusive to the corresponding variable?

12. In **controlling** for extraneous effects, (a) how did the study prevent possible bias to **certainty** introduced by the **participants** it employed, and (b) did these precautions completely and adequately control for those effects?

13. In **controlling** for extraneous effects, (a) how did the study prevent possible bias to **certainty** introduced by the **experiences** it presented, and (b) did these precautions completely and adequately control for those effects?

14. In **controlling** for extraneous effects, (a) how did the study prevent possible bias to **generality** introduced by the **participants** it employed and, (b) did these precautions completely and adequately control for those effects?

15. In **controlling** for extraneous effects, (a) how did the study prevent possible bias to **generality** introduced by the **experiences** it presented, and (b) did these precautions completely and adequately control for those effects?

16. (a) Which variables did the study **manipulate?** (b) How successfully did the researcher carry out the manipulation?

17. (a) What **design** did the study employ, and (b) how adequately did it ensure certainty?

18. For each **measurement** procedure in the study, (a) what evidence of validity does the research report provide, and (b) does this information indicate adequate validity?

19. For each **measurement** procedure (including observation) in the study, (a) what evidence of reliability does the research report provide, and (b) does this information indicate adequate reliability?

20. (a) Which **statistics** did the study employ, (b) were they the right choices (or should it have used different ones or additional ones), and (c) were the procedures and calculations correctly completed?

21. (a) What **findings** did the study produce, and (b) do they fit the problem statement?

22. Did the research report adequately support the study's **findings** with text, tables, and figures?

23. How significant and important were the study's **findings?**

24. Did the **discussion** section of the research report draw conclusions, and were they consistent with the study's results?

25. (a) Did the **discussion** section offer reasonable interpretations of why results did and did not match expectations, and (b) did it suggest reasonable implications about what readers should do with the results?

results and discussion sections, the analysis focuses on the statistical tests, nature and presentation of findings, and functions of the discussion.

In discussing each topic, the chapter will pose a series of questions to guide analysis and critical evaluation of a research study or article. These questions will be numbered sequentially, section after section. The resulting set of questions, combined in Figure 15.1, provide an overall model or approach for the analysis and critique. These questions, each one covering an aspect of a research study, are closely patterned after those posed in the 11 Performance Evaluation Worksheets that appear in Appendix B.

Following the description of the analysis and critical evaluation process, the chapter presents a study to be analyzed and critiqued in its entirety. The remaining segment of the chapter offers an analysis and critique of this study using the questions in Figure 15.1 to illustrate the process. Readers are encouraged to attempt an analysis and critical evaluation of the study prior to reading the explanations that follow.

Further practice can be obtained by reading Sample Studies III and IV in Appendix A and then analyzing and critiquing them using the worksheets in Appendix B. After completing the process, readers can check their answers against those in Appendix D.

THE INTRODUCTORY SECTION

The introductory section is the first section of an article. It usually does not follow a heading because none is needed to tell the reader where the section starts. The abstract, which precedes the introduction, is a condensed version of the entire article rather than a part of any of its sections. The introductory section typically introduces the reader to the problem and presents a literature review. It may also offer hypotheses.

Problem and Problem Statement

The *problem* is the question that the study seeks to answer. The introduction presents or communicates it as a *problem statement*. The two are separated here, because the statement of the problem does not always correspond to the problem actually studied. Four criteria govern an evaluation of the problem statement: location, clarity, completeness, and accuracy. The first step in analyzing and evaluating a problem statement is to read through the entire article and locate every version of this statement. Such a sentence generally begins: "The purpose of this study was . . ." or words to that effect. After identifying the problem statement, analysis seeks to answer some questions about it.

1. (a) Does the research report articulate a **problem statement?** If so, (b) what does it say? (c) Is it a clear statement? (d) Is it introduced prior to the literature review?

A study should explicitly enunciate a problem statement, and the reader should be able to find it and underline it as a major point of reference. After all, the problem statement tells the reader what subject the study addresses. Also, if the report presents multiple versions of the problem statement, they all should state equivalent problems.

Clarity is an important criterion for a problem statement. If readers cannot understand the problem statement, they may not understand much else about the study. *A good general test of clarity is rewriting a statement in one's own words.* When this revision requires some guessing, then the problem statement has achieved unacceptably low clarity. When it can be done easily, then the researcher has achieved high clarity.

Analysis should also consider the location of the problem statement. Since this statement orients readers to the study by telling them what subject it investigates, after the abstract, the statement should appear initially in the introductory section, preferably prior to the literature review. A less effective arrangement places the problem statement as the last sentence of the introductory section; an ineffective format places it in the middle or final sections.

2. Does the **problem statement** give a complete and accurate statement of the problem actually studied, or does it leave out something?

The first issue to consider here is completeness. A researcher may leave introductions of questions to study or variables to include until the middle of the methods section, or even the results section, without ever mentioning them in the problem statement. Such late additions appear to represent omissions or afterthoughts. Unprepared for these late introductions, readers may miss them. For example, data might be analyzed by gender or by grade level (as moderator variables), although the problem statement indicated that the study was designed merely to compare a treatment condition to a control condition. The problem statement might list achievement as the dependent variable and then analyze four different kinds of achievement never previously mentioned or enumerated.

Any introduction of new variables or new comparisons not initially mentioned in the problem statement is a delicate matter. Accepted practices for legitimate research allow addition of what are called *post hoc*, or after-the-fact, analyses only with a strong written justification. Simply adding elements to a study after delineating the problem statement is not generally considered an acceptable practice.

After looking for possible incompleteness, the analytical reader determines whether and to what degree the problem statement fits the problem. This question concerns the problem statement's accuracy. If a researcher gives a name to the variables that does not represent the variables actually studied, then the problem statement is not an accurate one. Occasionally, researchers name their independent variable in a way that better represents a possible intervening variable (for example, calling "exercise" by the name "physical fitness" or "choosing to continue a task" by the name "motivation"). This practice diminishes the accuracy of the problem statement. Sometimes researchers talk about the moderating effect of a variable and then do not apply statistical analysis that tests for that effect, creating problems with inaccuracy of the problem statement.

Often, the true problem of a study is revealed only in the description of data analysis techniques and results. These representations list the actual variables and reveal the relationships actually tested. Tables, in particular, can reveal a great deal about the problem actually studied.

The criteria for evaluating a research problem itself have already been mentioned in Chapter 2, so this discussion will only briefly review them.

3. Does the study's **problem** offer sufficient (a) workability, (b) critical mass, and (c) interest?

Minor considerations to a reader (as opposed to a researcher) are workability, critical mass, and interest value. If the study has been completed, then it must be a workable one. (Readers may consider the amount of work done in typical research studies as a guide for their own research choices.) If the study is in print, then it must have sufficient critical mass. (On occasion, however, readers may wonder how a journal or thesis committee could have accepted such a "thin" or "skimpy" project.) If researchers have chosen to complete a study, then it must interest them as well as others who have chosen to read the report, although individual readers might assess the study's degree of general interest.

4. (a) Does the **problem** studied offer theoretical and practical value?
   (b) Does the report establish these criteria?

The two most important criteria for evaluating a problem from the reader's or reviewer's perspective are its *theoretical* and *practical value*. Theoretical value reflects a study's contribution to a field's understanding of a phenomenon. It addresses the question: Why did it happen? Then it attempts to answer this question by articulating a theoretically based intervening variable. If no one has studied the problem before or others have recommended that someone study it, these facts do not provide a study with theoretical value. This value comes from the study's contribution to efforts to choose between alternative explanations or to settle on one developed on the basis of prior theoretical work. References to a theory in the study's literature review and citations often indicate that it builds on an established theoretical base. The study's author should explicitly demonstrate that base, rather than expecting readers to do this on their own, to establish the study's theoretical value. This background should preferably be laid down in the introductory section of the article.

Practical value reflects the study's contribution to subsequent practical applications. Do the results of this study have the potential to change practice? In an applied field like education, this value may result in potential changes in the way people teach or study or administer institutions or counsel.

Theoretical and practical value represent the significance of a study, the justification for undertaking it prior to seeing the results. Therefore, the author should explicitly establish a study's anticipated value or significance in the Introductory section, so that the reader need not guess at or imagine potential benefits. Studies in education and other applied fields often promise practical value, but considerably fewer aspire to theoretical value. However, the link between research and theory gives research its explanatory power. Therefore, theoretical value should not be overlooked.

Literature Review

The literature review represents the bulk of a research report's introductory section, although it may run only 12 paragraphs or less, given the overall brevity of journal articles. Analysts refer to two major criteria to evaluate a literature review: quality and technical accuracy.

>   5. Does the **literature review** present a high-quality overview? Does it achieve adequate (a) clarity, (b) flow, (c) relevance, (d) recency, (e) empirical focus, and (f) independence?

The *quality* of a literature review depends primarily on its *clarity* and *flow*. It should lead the reader through relevant prior research by first establishing the context of the problem, then reviewing studies that bear on the problem, and ultimately providing a rationale for any hypotheses that the new study might offer. One way to determine the sequence and flow of the literature review, indeed of the entire introductory section, is to number its paragraphs and then, on a separate sheet of paper, write a single summary sentence that states the essence of each paragraph's content. If a researcher can adequately summarize information in this way, the process provides evidence of the *clarity* of the literature review. Then by reading over these summary sentences in order, she or he can evaluate the degree to which the literature review presents a reasonable, logical, and convincing *flow*.

The quality of the literature review also depends on the degree of *relevance* of all studies reviewed or cited, that is, how closely their topics are related to the current study's problem. "Name dropping" or "padding" by including irrelevant citations reduces quality rather than enhancing it. Another useful analysis tries to determine whether a literature review omits any relevant work, but this determination of *omissions* is challenging for any reader not intimately familiar with the field.

Finally, quality also depends on the *recency* of the work cited. Except for "classic" studies in the field, a literature review should cite research completed within 10 years of the study itself. An analyst evaluates the *empirical focus* of the work cited in a literature review by determining whether most of it is data-based as opposed to discursive. Judgments of the *independence* of the work cited reflect the common expectation that a substantial portion of the citations refer to studies by researchers other than the current study's own author(s).

6. Does the **literature review** include technically accurate citations and references?

This evaluation is based on three considerations: (1) that the reference list includes all articles cited in the text, (2) that the text cites all articles in the references list, and (3) that all text citations and references display proper forms according to some accepted format such as that in the *Publication Manual of the American Psychological Association* (APA, 1994). Despite the usual editing, surprising numbers of errors in these three areas come to the attention of careful readers. These errors may cause difficulties in following up on particular studies cited in an article's literature review.

Hypotheses

7. (a) Does the introduction offer **hypotheses?** If so, (b) what are they? Are they (c) directional, (d) clear, (e) consistent with the problem, and (f) supported by effective arguments?

Hypotheses serve a useful purpose in justifying a study and giving it direction. For this reason, analysts hold a study that explicitly states one or more hypotheses in higher regard than one that requires the reader to "read between the lines" to figure out what relationships its authors expect. Explicitly stated hypotheses usually are introduced by the phrase: "It was expected that . . ." or words to that effect. Analysts and evaluators should look through the introductory section to locate a hypothesis statement and, if one is found, underline it. Some research reports offer statements of hypotheses only in the results sections, but a more appropriate structure introduces them in the introduction (usually toward or at the end of this section).

Analysis of a study's hypothesis, if the report offers one, may then determine whether it is directional, clear, consistent with the problem, and sufficiently supported by evidence and reasoned arguments. A *directional* hypothesis specifies the direction of an expected difference between the experimental and control groups. (For example, "Treatment A will result in *greater* achievement than Treatment B.") By specifying an anticipated outcome, a directional hypothesis offers infinitely more informative value and utility than either a positive hypothesis (one that predicts a difference without specifying its direction) or a null hypothesis (one that accommodates statistical testing by predicting no difference). The hypothesis statement should, moreover, articulate the study's focus *clearly* enough that readers can easily restate it in their own words. It should remain *consistent* with the problem by positing an expected answer to the problem actually studied. The statement should provide sufficient *support* from logic and literature that it represents more than a seeming guess by the study's authors (or a conclusion written after examining the study's results).

Variables

Identifying a study's variables is an entirely analytic effort rather than an evaluative one, but this process helps the reader considerably to understanding the subject of a study.

> 8. What actual **variables** does the study examine; identify: (a) independent, (b) moderator (if any), (c) dependent, and (d) control variables (only the most important two or three)?

Independent, moderator, and dependent variables should be evident in the problem statement, although an ex post facto study may apply arbitrary labels to variables treated as independent and dependent. Most studies refer to moderator variables as additional independent variables, so the reader must judge their individual status (secondary to the major independent variable) and the researcher's reasons for including them (to see if they mediate or moderate the relationship between the main independent variable and the dependent variable).

Inspection of the method of analysis, tables, and results can often help a reader to identify variables. The number of variables (or factors) in an analysis of variance, for example, reveals the number of independent plus moderator variables, while the numerical value of each factor reveals the number of levels it contains. Thus, a 2×3 analysis of variance would include a two-level independent variable and a three-level moderator variable. Variable names can often be determined from analysis of variance source tables (when they are provided) or from tables of means. The number of analyses that a study runs often provide a clue to the number of dependent variables. Sample Study II, for example, involved seven analysis of variance tests, because it measured seven dependent variables. Sample Study I conducted two analyses, and hence included two dependent variables.

Analysis usually requires information from the method section of a research report to determine the important control variables. Baseline or pretest score on the dependent variable is often a study's most important control variable. Also, pay particular attention to gender, grade level, socioeconomic status, race or ethnicity, intelligence or ability, time, and order.

Analysis to identify variables must avoid confusing variables and levels. A *categorical* or *discrete* variable divides conditions or characteristics into levels. A treatment versus a control condition would be two levels of a single variable rather than two variables. High expectations versus low expectations would be two levels of a single variable rather than two variables. Encouraging feedback versus neutral feedback, as in Sample Study I, represent two levels of a single variable, as do good versus poor readers in Sample Study II. In order to vary, a variable must contain at least two levels.

Continuous variables are not divided into levels. They contain numbers of scores. Most studies include continuous dependent variables, while many (but not all) include categorical or discrete independent and moderator variables.

A reader must also recognize the distinction between variables a study *measures* and those it *manipulates*, a distinction clarified in the operational definitions. Dependent variables are never manipulated, while other types can be either measured or manipulated.

9. (a) What intervening **variable** might the study be evaluating? (b) Was it suggested in the research report?

To determine the intervening variable, examine the independent variable closely and try to imagine what kind of internal process the subjects might experience as a result of its various levels. For example, Sample Study I compared encouraging feedback, an experience likely to stimulate the subjects' internal process of self-confidence, to neutral feedback, an experience unlikely to have the same effect. (Reports that they did something well should enhance the confidence of subjects in the encouraging feedback condition in their ability to perform.) Hence, degree of self-confidence would be a plausible, even likely, intervening variable for that study. Remember, determination of intervening variables is based on judgment rather than fact, but some judgments fit specific circumstances better than do others. Moreover, the study's authors may suggest some possible intervening variables if they speculate on possible reasons to explain anticipated or observed changes in the dependent variable.

Operational Definitions

Analysis of a research report's introductory section may benefit by determining operational definitions of the independent, moderator, dependent, and important control variables. However, journal articles seldom provide formal operational definitions, particularly in their introductory sections. Therefore, even though this discussion of that section considers operational definitions, readers usually identify them from information given in the method section.

10. What **operational definitions** did the researcher develop for the variables listed in answering Question 8?

Analysis of an article should not seek to provide a complete description of methodology for testing each variable, but to provide a *one-sentence* statement of how the researcher operationalized each variable (that is, what she or he did to manipulate or measure it). This sentence provides a concrete statement of what the variable "means." For example, in Sample Study I, *encouragement* or *encouraging feedback* means feedback that tells students what tasks they performed well, while neutral feedback simply tells them how many tasks they completed. A research report should give information necessary for constructing an operational definition for the variables studied.

11. (a) What type of **operational definition** was used for each variable?
    (b) Was each definition sufficiently exclusive to the corresponding variable?

Another useful analytical step tries to classify each operational definition by type. Did the researcher manipulate the independent variable rather than measuring it? If so, then the study utilizes an experimental approach. If the operational definition specifies a dynamic or static independent variable, operationalized by measurement, then the study follows an ex post facto approach. A study that employs static independent and dependent variables (that is, all measures are self-reported), provides no external or behavioral referent, requiring caution in judging the accuracy of its results. Remember that dependent variables can never be manipulated; manipulation can produce only independent variables. Also, moderators are usually dynamic or static variables.

Finally, analysis should evaluate the exclusiveness of each operational definition. How well does the operational definition fit the related variable as opposed to some other variable? Could the authors of Sample Study I apply the term *encouraging* to any feedback praising success, for example, or would a more exclusive operational definition restrict the term to feedback that explicitly stated in words the specific aspect of the performance that made it an outstanding example? As an operational definition becomes more exclusive, it supports a stronger conclusion that a researcher studied the intended phenomenon and not something else.

THE METHOD SECTION

The method section is the middle section of a research article, typically preceded by the heading "Method." It describes subjects, subject selection processes, methods for manipulating or measuring variables, procedures followed, and the research design. (This section sometimes describes statistical tests, but we will defer the discussion of evaluating statistical procedures until the next section.) Rather than analyzing and evaluating each of the topics described in this section, a more meaningful analysis and evaluation would judge methodology in terms of its adequacy for controlling any sources of bias that threaten internal validity (certainty) and external validity (generality). Hence, the subsequent presentation will be organized along these lines.

Manipulation and Control

Remember that a study can either manipulate or measure its variables. Consider, first, the issue of variable manipulation. Researchers manipulate variables for two purposes: (1) to control extraneous variables (influences called *control variables* in this book) in order to maximize certainty and generality, or (2) to create independent variables that represent the results of a manipulation. An evaluation of the first purpose for manipulation follows the model defined in the four windows shown in Table 7.3. The first two questions asked in analyzing this aspect of a study deal with certainty.

> 12. In **controlling** for extraneous effects, (a) how did the study prevent possible bias to **certainty** introduced by the **participants** it employed, and (b) did these precautions completely and adequately control for those effects?

This question corresponds to the first window of Table 7.3, CERTAINTY/ PARTICIPANTS. This part of the analysis asks for a description of the procedures used in the study; evaluation then asks about their adequacy and completeness. One might restate this evaluation question: Did the study control for all possible sources of participant or subject bias, and were the methods of control sufficient to prevent a confounding influence on the results from these sources?

Remember the sources of potential participant bias described in Chapter 7: selection, maturation, experimental mortality, and statistical regression. These biases are affected by the manner in which subjects are selected and assigned to conditions and by losses of members from the different groups studied. These biases are generally controlled by avoiding systematic elimination of a portion of the sample, by random assignment to conditions, or, for studies that deal with intact groups, by either establishing pretest equivalence or using subjects as their own controls.

These techniques work for studies that manipulate their independent variables, as Sample Study I (encouraging feedback versus neutral feedback) does. (Sample Study I *randomly assigned* Ss to conditions. Hence, it would rate highly in the upper-left window of Table 7.3.) Studies that measure their independent variables, such as in Sample Study II (good readers versus poor readers), can control for participant bias only through sampling or selection, and with imperfect results at best. How can Sample Study II assure, for example, that good and poor readers are otherwise equivalent in physical development, motivation, and other internal characteristics without the possibility of random assignment to groups, that is, without arbitrarily deciding who is a good reader and who is a poor reader? Students cannot be assigned to reading abilities; the study can only sample from students of given reading abilities. In fact, the study provides no assurance even of gender equivalence across reading ability samples. Moreover, readers sampled were either the best or the worst in the population, creating potential bias due to regression toward the mean. Hence, Sample Study II would be rated somewhat low in the upper-left quadrant of Table 7.3.

13. In **controlling** for extraneous effects, (a) how did the study prevent possible bias to **certainty** introduced by the **experiences** it presented, and (b) did these precautions completely and adequately control for those effects?

This question corresponds to the second or lower-left window of Table 7.3, CERTAINTY/EXPERIENCES. This part of the analysis asks for a description of the procedures used in the study; evaluation then asks about their adequacy and completeness. One might restate this evaluation question: Did the study control all possible sources of experience bias, and were the methods of control sufficient to prevent a confounding influence on the results from these sources?

Experience bias is often introduced by the order of experiences presented to subjects, the time periods provided for them, the manners of their presentation (for example, who presents them), and the conditions under which they are presented. Experience bias reflects the possibility that some experience other than the one evaluated in the study may account for the results. Techniques to control experience bias focus primarily on contrasting results for the experimental group with those of a control or comparison group. In addition, a researcher may try to remove variables, hold them constant, or counterbalance them across conditions.

Sample Study I established a comparison condition (neutral feedback) as a contrast to the experimental condition (encouraging feedback). Moreover, students in both encouraging and neutral feedback conditions experienced the same instruction from the same instructor, and all students received some form of written feedback. Sample Study I seems to have ensured adequate control of possible experience bias by comparing two feedback conditions and providing the same experiences other than the content of feedback to both groups. Sample Study II, on the other hand, lacking a manipulated independent variable, could not ensure that reading ability alone, rather than some other variable such as the way these students were treated by their teachers, was responsible for observed differences in classroom conduct. However, it controlled for expectancy bias by keeping observers unaware of which students were the good readers and which the poor ones. Hence, Sample Study II would be evaluated lower than Sample Study I in this window of Table 7.3.

The second two questions about the study deal with generality.

14. In **controlling** for extraneous effects, (a) how did the study prevent possible bias to **generality** introduced by the **participants** it employed

and, (b) did these precautions completely and adequately control for those effects?

This question corresponds to the third or upper-right window in Table 7.3, GENERALITY/PARTICIPANTS. Effects related to participants or subjects can bias or limit generality when a study draws its sample from a narrow population. The description of the sample of subjects reflects upon the population of which it is representative. Most studies use samples of convenience made up of available participants, thus limiting generality. Many research reports give insufficient information about samples to accurately determine the populations they represent.

Sample Study I sampled college students, juniors and seniors, mostly white, mostly women, all prospective teachers. The high specificity of this sample clearly limits the study's generality. Sample Study II tells nothing more than the size of the city and geographical region from which the sample came. Such limited information also limits a reader's confidence in the study's generality.

15. In **controlling** for extraneous effects, (a) how did the study prevent possible bias to **generality** introduced by the **experiences** it presented, and (b) did these precautions completely and adequately control for those effects?

This question corresponds to the fourth or lower-right window of Table 7.3, GENERALITY/EXPERIENCES. Generality of experiences depends on unobtrusive operationalizing of variables, data collection, and researcher interactions with the sample, which give assurance that the same outcome would be likely to occur in the "real world." Manipulation-based studies often lack this kind of generality. Readers must judge this quality after reading the descriptions of the manipulation in the methods section of a research article. Like generality based on subjects, lack of information often limits this judgment.

Both sample studies appear to achieve reasonable generality based on experiences. Both involved real classrooms and reasonably unobtrusive methods. Sample Study I's principal weakness is the possibility that students in the two different feedback conditions would "compare notes" and conclude that some arbitrary condition was influencing the feedback they received. The report allows no way to evaluate this possibility, other than to note that it is not supported by the findings of the study.

Readers typically face a more challenging task in evaluating the generality of a study than in evaluating its certainty based on the information and descriptions that authors provide. Descriptions of methods for manipulating variables and procedures employed in conducting a study generally cover internal conditions far more extensively than relationships to external ones.

16. (a) Which variables did the study **manipulate?** (b) How successfully did the researcher carry out the manipulation?

The final issue under manipulation and control deals with the effectiveness of manipulations in creating the states or conditions required by the variables being manipulated. Such a so-called *manipulation check* is a recommended part of conducting a research study that employs a manipulation-based variable. In the study of teacher enthusiasm described near the end of Chapter 7, teachers were trained to display three different levels of enthusiasm. To determine whether they did, in fact, create the intended levels as instructed, the researchers observed and rated the levels of teaching enthusiasm. (Table 7.5 reported the results.) Data like this help readers to appraise the success of the manipulation. Without any such evidence, readers are left guessing about the manipulation's success; they can only form critical opinions regarding the absence of such important information.

In evaluating Sample Study I, the reader must judge whether the so-called *encouraging* feedback truly encouraged the students who received it. If it seemed a transparent attempt that did not effectively promote feelings of encouragement, then the study could not truly be said to measure the effects of "encouraging" feedback. The fact that students' beliefs in their own ability to perform the task steadily increased in the encouraging feedback condition while remaining the same in the neutral feedback condition strongly suggests that the feedback did indeed encourage students.

Research Design

Identifying the research design implemented in a study helps with the task of evaluating its certainty, while also clarifying its procedures. This analytical task resembles that of identifying the different types of variables in a study, both of which help to clarify its subject and how the researcher proceeded with the investigation. Since the research report seldom names the design model implemented in a study, the reader must figure it out from available information.

17. (a) What **design** did the study employ, and (b) how adequately did it ensure certainty?

The first clue for identifying the design is whether the independent variable was manipulated or measured. If the independent variable was manipulated, then the study employed an experimental design; if the independent variable was measured, then it implemented an ex post facto design. Assume that the independent variable was manipulated. Then the next clue is whether or not the researcher presented a pretest, followed by whether subjects were randomly assigned to levels of the independent variable, intact groups served as samples, or subjects served as their own controls. The combination of these determinations differentiates pre-experimental, true experimental, and quasi-experimental designs and their specific variations. A final determination checks for inclusion of moderator variables, and if so, how many the design accommodated and how many levels each one contained. This information helps a reader to identify factorial designs.

If the independent variable was measured, then the analytic reader seeks to distinguish between co-relational and criterion-group designs by determining whether or not this variable was divided into levels. (Only criterion-group designs divide independent variables into levels.) If a perceptive reader finds levels, then she or he must search further for moderator variables (a step presumably completed earlier) to determine whether the criterion-group design was factorialized.

After determining all of these details, a useful additional step is to attempt to draw the design, representing its exact particulars using the notation provided in Chapter 8. (The designs for Sample Studies I and II appear in Box 8 near the end of that chapter.)

As a way of evaluating a design, a reader can judge the degree to which it contributes to or detracts from the study's certainty. Additional speculation could ask how the design might be improved. Occasionally, adding a pretest or a moderator variable could provide such an improvement. For example, Sample Study I treated procrastination tendency (PRO) as a control variable, but the researcher could have divided up that variable into two or three levels and used it as a moderator variable. In other words, the experimental design could have been factorialized. (Chapter 5 discusses considerations affecting the choice of whether to simply control a variable or to study it as a moderator variable.)

Measurement of Variables

After considering manipulated variables, should a study include any, the analysis next step considers measured variables, examining the quality of that measurement as a way of evaluating instrumentation bias. Measurement devices to be evaluated include not only tests, but any sort of observation system that produces systematic data. The analyst should look for a description of the procedures used to measure or observe each variable (other than the manipulated ones) in the method section of the research report. Note that any one study may incorporate many measured variables. (Sample Study I has six, and Sample Study II has eight.) The analyst must find descriptions of all such measurement procedures. Finding and noting these descriptions constitutes the analysis portion of the task.

The evaluation portion of the task focuses on two characteristics or qualities of all measurement techniques, validity and reliability, both of which were described in Chapter 9. After determining the measurement procedure for each measured variable, check to see whether the authors provided evidence or information about the technique's validity and reliability. In other words, try to answer Questions 18 and 19.

> 18. For each **measurement** procedure in the study, (a) what evidence of validity does the research report provide, and (b) does this information indicate adequate validity?

Validity requires a comparison of test results to some independent criterion, such as another test, or actual behavior. Articles often describe the measures that studies employ without discussing their validity. Without evidence, a critical reader may have trouble concluding that the tests used actually measured the variables they were intended to measure.

19. For each **measurement** procedure (including observation) in the study,
    (a) what evidence of reliability does the research report provide, and
    (b) does this information indicate adequate reliability?

This characteristic of measuring devices is reflected in their reliability coefficients. Reliability of observations results from agreement between observers. Reliability of tests results from their internal consistency or consistency over time. A critical reader should look for these reliability coefficients and then evaluate their magnitude. Observational reliabilities should be at .75 or above; test reliabilities should be at .75 or above for achievement tests and .50 or above for attitude tests.

THE RESULTS AND DISCUSSION SECTIONS

Because evaluations of these sections of a research report must consider fewer criteria than those of other sections, this chapter will deal with them together. Concerns in these sections will focus on statistical tests, the nature and presentation of results, and functions of discussion.

Statistical Tests

Analysis and evaluation of a study's statistical techniques focuses on three questions.

20. (a) Which **statistics** did the study employ, (b) were they the right choices (or should it have used different ones or additional ones), and (c) were the procedures and calculations correctly completed?

Part a is the analysis element of Question 20. It simply determines the statistical tests that the study applied to its data. This information usually appears in the results section of a research report. For example, Sample Study I details the choice of analysis of covariance (ANCOVA) in both the methods and results sections, and in Table 1. Sample Study II used two-way analysis of variance (ANOVA), as mentioned in the results section. The name *two-way* ANOVA means that the analysis included one independent variable and one moderator variable.

To answer Part b, first refer to the problem statement to see if it specifies statistical tests to answer the question or questions it poses. If this statement specifies a moderator variable, for example, then statistical tests should have analyzed that variable together with the independent variable. Next, refer to Table 11.2 to see if the statistical tests used in the study fit the way it measured its variables. As a further step, look for some typical examples of questionable practices: continuing to perform additional, subordinate statistical tests despite failure by initial, superordinate ones to yield significant results; using parametric tests without evidence of normally distributed data or with categorical data; not including both levels of a moderator variable in the same analysis.

Check to see whether data bearing on all of the problems posed were actually subjected to statistical analysis in order to provide adequate answers. See whether statistical tests actually completed the comparisons specified in the problem statement. A researcher may, for example, test whether differences in the independent variable affect the dependent variable but fail to follow up this analysis by making direct comparisons between levels of the independent variable.

The question of whether the study correctly carried out its statistical tests (Part c) requires a difficult judgment; often a reader cannot answer this question from available information. A definitive answer requires sufficient tables to allow confirmation of various aspects of the statistical approach. This evaluative judgment also requires a reasonably strong background in statistics. When a study provides analysis of variance source tables, for example, check the entries to confirm that sources have not been overlooked (that is, determine that the variance has been correctly partitioned), and that mistakes have not been made in computing degrees of freedom and sums of squares.

Nature and Presentation of Results

A critical reader must answer a number of questions about the results of a study.

21. (a) What **findings** did the study produce, and (b) do they fit the problem statement?

Answering Part a requires both analysis and evaluation. First, the findings must be found and summarized, an analytical task. The research report must state them clearly enough to tell the reader what the study determined. Hence, the reader must evaluate its clarity of presentation. A study is not very useful if its readers cannot tell what the researchers found.

The question about the fit between the results and the problem statement (Part b) was asked earlier as a way of evaluating the accuracy and completeness of the problem statement. It can be turned around and repeated as a way of evaluating the results.

22. Did the research report adequately support the study's **findings** with text, tables, and figures?

Readers find explicit numbers to be very helpful elements of research reports, and these numbers are far easier to follow when they appear in tables or figures than when they are only quoted in text. Tables and figures also provide clues to help readers answer many other questions posed earlier in this process (such as the names and types of variables). An adequate presentation of findings usually requires tables, and figures can give helpful support, as well. In many studies, readers particularly appreciate tables of means and standard deviations, so they can see the basis for differences. Inferential statistics, particularly analysis of variance and covariance, are easiest to understand and interpret when a report provides source tables. At a minimum, means tables and source tables should appear, and both should give complete information. Other kinds of statistical results, as well, are most easily understood when a report presents various types of summary tables.

23. How significant and important were the study's **findings**?

This is the key question. Did the research discover anything of substance? Did it reveal any significant differences? To find nothing is to prove nothing. The quality of the methodology becomes relatively unimportant if the report cannot present significant results. To check significance, review the text and tables to find whether they report differences that equal or exceed the preset alpha level, usually .05. If any are reported, check to see if they represent the major question that the study investigated, or some subsidiary question, perhaps even one posed after discovering that results did not match expectations. Authors sometimes change directions after the fact when tests of their original hypotheses yield insubstantial results. Such post hoc procedures and results call for close evaluation.

Beyond the question of significance of a study's findings is the question of their importance. In studies with large sample sizes, even seemingly trivial differences can achieve statistical significance. A second test of a study's results utilizes a measure called *effect size*. Effect size is represented by the ratio of the size of a difference between the means of two distributions to their averaged standard deviations (or the larger of the two). According to Cohen (1992), mean differences that amount to 80 percent of the average of the relevant standard deviations qualify as large differences, those that amount to 50 percent are moderate differences, and those that amount to 20 percent are small differences. Others have suggested that a ratio of two-thirds (67 percent) indicates an important difference. In other words, the difference in the relative effects of two procedures must be at least two-thirds as large as the average of the variability within each one before an evaluation can conclude that they really produced different impacts. Authors seldom report effect sizes: The reader must approximate them, and the research report must give information necessary for this purpose.

Functions of the Discussion

The discussion section of a research report performs three major functions: to draw conclusions, to interpret the study's results, and to present implications of the results. These considerations combine in two relevant questions.

24. Did the **discussion** section of the research report draw conclusions, and were they consistent with the study's results?
25. (a) Did the **discussion** section offer reasonable interpretations of why results did and did not match expectations, and (b) did it suggest reasonable implications about what readers should do with the results?

Chapter 12 provided a number of examples of conclusions, interpretations, and implications. A critical reader should look for all three functions in the discussion section of an article, noting their presence or absence. For a report that provides this discussion, each should be evaluated. Evaluation of conclusions looks for consistency with the study's findings. Occasionally, authors draw conclusions that lack support in their findings. Evaluation of a researcher's interpretations looks for reasonable elaborations. Readers must judge whether an interpretation offered in a research report is likely to apply. An author may say that an uncontrolled variable would not likely have affected the results and then offer some reason in support of this statement. The reader may judge that the reason is not sufficient, however, and that the uncontrolled variable may indeed have influenced the study's outcome. Evaluation of a researcher's implications also focuses on reasonableness. An author may assert that a technique to teach reading will work in the public schools, but the reader may feel that the study's methodology has not achieved sufficient generality to justify the author's implication.

A SAMPLE RESEARCH REPORT: ANALYSIS AND CRITIQUE

Read the study reprinted in this section. The remainder of this chapter will analyze and critique this study as an example.

The Effect of Student Planning and Self-Competence on Self-Motivated Performance

BRUCE W. TUCKMAN
Florida State University

This study evaluated the self-regulated performance of 130 collegiate teacher education majors assigned to either the condition of being given forms to plan their performance on a specific task or to the condition of being given no planning forms. The task enabled students to earn various exam grade point bonuses for writing test items related to weekly reading assignments in a required educational psychology course. Students were divided into high and medium + low perceived self-competence groups based on their self-rated capability for writing test items before the task began. Planning form users earned significantly more grade bonuses than did students not given the form, but this finding was true only for students of medium + low perceived self-competence. Planning appeared to provide those unsure of their own capability with the strategy necessary to perform well on the task.

THE PURPOSE of this study was to determine the effect of planning on student motivation—in this case, the amount of effort put forth by college students on a voluntary, course-related task. A second purpose was to determine whether planning effects varied for students whose beliefs in their own level of initial competence at the task varied from high to low.

Student motivation becomes an increasingly important influence on teaching and learning outcomes as students progress through the grades. As students get older, school requires them to exercise far greater control over their own learning and performance if they are to succeed. Tuckman and Sexton (1990) labeled the amount or level of performance *self-regulated performance* and used it as an indication of motivation. In contrast to quality of performance, which depends on ability, quantity of performance can be assumed to represent the amount of effort students are willing to apply to their assignments and school responsibilities. Because students are not able to modify their ability levels in the short term, effort becomes the prime causal attribute to modify if school outcomes are to be successful (Weiner, 1980).

Self-regulated performance is posited to be different from self-regulated learning, the latter being comprised of both competence and choice, whereas the former primarily reflects choice. McCombs and Marzano (1990) define self-regulated learning as a combination of will—a state of motivation based on "an internal self-generated desire resulting in an intentional choice," which is primary in initiating self-regulation—and skill—"an acquired cognitive or metacognitive competency" (p. 52). Self-regulated performance is viewed as the result of a state of motivation that is based considerably more on will than on skill (Tuckman & Sexton, 1990).

Self-regulated performance is largely a function of students' self-beliefs in their competence to perform (Bandura, 1977). However, it is affected by external forces such as informational feedback and working in groups, both of which tend to enhance self-regulated performance but primarily among persons who believe themselves to be average in self-competence (Tuckman & Sexton, 1989). Goal setting tends to motivate those low in perceived self-competence (Tuckman, 1990), whereas encouragement influences students at all self-competency levels to perform (Tuckman & Sexton, 1991).

An important variable that would seem to affect self-regulated performance is *planning*, yet little attention has been paid to it in research on student motivation. The focus instead has been on goal setting, which is only one aspect of planning. Other features of planning for goal-directed performance include (a) where and how performing will be done, (b) the reasons for performing, (c) the manner of dealing with potential obstacles and unexpected events, and (d) the specification of incentives, if any, that one will provide oneself for goal attainment (Tuckman, 1991a).

Some studies of goal setting have included some of the above features (Gaa, 1979; Locke, Shaw, Saari, & Latham, 1981; Mento, Steel, & Karren, 1987; Schunk, 1990; Tuckman, 1990), but not systematically, and have found positive effects on self-regulated performance. There have been, however, no findings about the combined effect of all of the above aspects of planning on motivation. There has also been no research on whether planning is differentially effective for students varying in perceived ability.

Because research has shown a positive effect of goal setting on performance, planning, which incorporates goal setting, was expected to enhance the amount of performance of students in this experiment. This enhancement effect was expected primarily for students whose perceptions of their own competence to perform the task was low to average. This prediction is based on prior findings that external influences minimally affect students who perceive themselves to be high in competence (Tuckman, 1991a).

Method

Subjects were 130 junior and senior teacher education majors in a large state university. The majority were women, and the mean age was 21 years. All were enrolled in one of four sections of a required course in educational psychology, which covered the topics of test construction and learning theory. All sections were taught by the same instructor.

The course included a procedure for allowing students to earn extra credit toward their final grade. The procedure was called the Voluntary Homework System or VHS (Tuckman & Sexton, 1989, 1990), and it served as the performance task for this study. Subjects were given the opportunity to write test items on work covered in that week's instruction. Completion items were worth 1 point each; multiple-choice items, 2 points each; and multiple-choice comprehension items, 3 points each. Point values reflected the effort required to produce each type of item. Submitted items were loosely screened for quality and returned for corrections where necessary.

VHS extended over the first 4 weeks of a 15-week course, and the points earned each week were cumulative. Subjects who earned 350 points or more received a full-grade bonus for the first third of the course (e.g., a B became an A); subjects who earned between 225 and 349 points received a two-thirds grade bonus (e.g., a B became an A−); subjects who earned between 112 and 224 points received a one-third grade bonus (e.g., a B became a B+); and subjects who earned fewer than 112 points earned no bonus (nor were they penalized). *Bonus received,* a reflection of the amount of self-regulated perfor-mance, served as the dependent variable in this study.

Students in two of the sections, chosen at random, were given a form called the VHS Weekly Performance Plan (see Appendix) at the beginning of each week and were asked to complete it. They were also asked to return all four forms at the end of the 4 weeks. The form provided planning instructions by giving places for students to indicate the number of items they planned to write each day along with the daily time, location, and self-reward for item writing that day. The form also asked students to identify their reason for item writing, the obstacles they might encounter, how they would overcome them, their bonus goal, their self-assessment of progress toward that goal, any changes in procedure from their last plan, and to whom and why they assigned the responsibility for item writing. Students in the remaining two sections were not given the form to com-plete. *Using the planning form* versus *not given the planning form,* therefore, was the independent variable in this study.

Students were asked to complete a VHS form at the start of the course be-fore attempting to write any items. On this form, they used 9-point scales to judge (a) their own capability or competence to write test items and (b) their cer-tainty in this judgment. The product of judged capability times certainty was used as a measure of perceived self-competence. This computational procedure was recommended by Bandura (1977) based on his view of self-efficacy as a combination of judgments of its level and strength.

Scores on the perceived self-competence scale were used to rank subjects into high, medium, and low groups. Medium and low groups were subsequently combined because the limited sample size made the use of three levels im-practical. This combining of groups is supported by prior research that showed that the performance of high self-competence subjects was largely unaffected by external conditions, whereas the performance of medium and low self-competence subjects was similarly enhanced by external facilitation (Tuckman, 1990; Tuckman & Sexton, 1989).

Subjects also used the VHS form to rate the importance to them of earning a bonus. They also completed the Procrastination Scale (Tuckman, 1991b) and the Advanced Vocabulary Test II (French, 1963) at the start of the course. The former has been shown to be a valid and reliable measure of the tendency to delay starting or completing a task, and the latter has been linked to mental ability. Both have been shown to measure variables that affect self-regulated performance (Tuckman & Sexton, 1991) and hence were used to provide mea-sures that could be used to test the initial equivalence of the classes.

Results

The initial equivalence of the four classes was determined by comparing them on self-competence level, outcome importance, procrastination tendency, and advanced vocabulary. None of the differences approached signifi-cance ($F = 0.34, 1.00, 0.17, 0.33$; $df = 3/129$, respectively), leading to the conclusion that the classes were equivalent. Hence, the design of the study can be regarded as quasi-experimental with adequate control for potential selection bias.

Eighteen subjects from the two sections that were given the planning forms either failed to return them at the end of the 4 weeks or returned them with little or nothing written on them. Their reasons for not doing the planning, when asked, ranged from "no time" to "not necessary." Therefore, they were not included in the data analysis for the planning form group. They were compared on perceived self-competence and on all of the control variables with subjects who used the planning form and with subjects who were not given forms; they were found not to differ significantly from either. None of these 18 subjects earned double or triple performance bonuses.

Of the 54 subjects who used the planning form, 27 (50%) earned either double or triple performance bonuses, compared with 16 (27.5%) of the 58 subjects not given the planning form. This comparison yielded a chi-square value of 5.03 ($df = 1$, $p < .05$).

The effects of planning forms for subjects at two levels of perceived self-competence (high and medium + low) were compared. Slightly more than one-third of the high self-competence subjects in the planning form group and the no planning form group earned double and triple bonuses. Among the medium + low self-competence subjects, 21 of 37 subjects (57%) in the group that used the planning form received double or triple bonuses, compared with 9 of 38 subjects (24%) who did not use planning forms. This comparison yielded a chi-square value of 7.24 ($df = 1$, $p < .01$). The results for the different self-competence groups are shown in Figure 1.

Discussion

It can be concluded from the results of this study that using the planning form had a strong positive effect on the self-regulated performance of students to perform, particularly among students who believed that their own performance capability was low to average. In fact, the use of the planning form resulted in a greater percentage of students of medium and low self-competence obtaining item-writing bonuses than students high in self-competence.

Even when the planning form was used, it was surprising to see students with low and medium perceived item-writing self-competence writing more items than students whose perceived self-competence was high. Some insight into this finding is provided by examining self-competence judgments for exam performance. At the outset of the study, students were asked to judge the level of their anticipated exam grade and the certainty with which this judgment was made. Because the reward for item writing was a bonus to be added to the exam grade, the value of this reward would be contingent on whether or not students felt they would need it. Two-thirds of students who judged themselves to be high in item-writing competence anticipated getting a high exam grade, whereas only one-quarter of students who judged themselves to be low or medium in

ITEM-WRITING PERFORMANCE FOR STUDENTS OF HIGH VERSUS   FIGURE 1
MEDIUM + LOW SELF-COMPETENCE WHO USED A PLANNING
FORM AND WHO DID NOT USE A PLANNING FORM

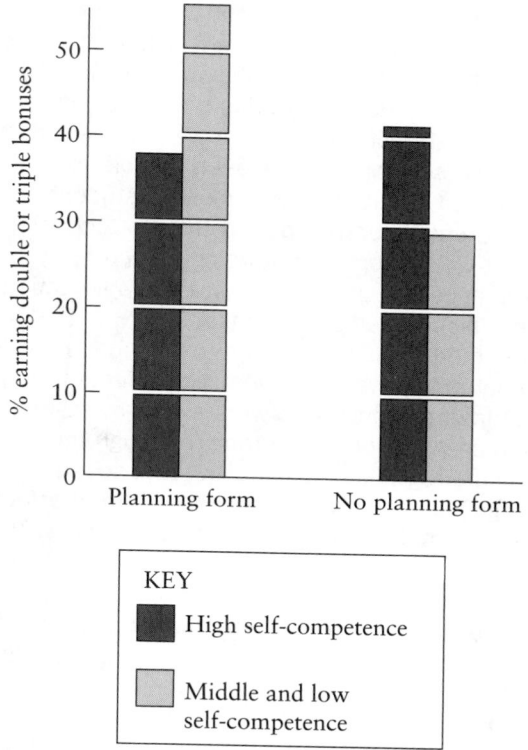

KEY

■ High self-competence

▨ Middle and low
self-competence

item-writing competence anticipated getting a high exam grade. Hence, the poorer self-judged item writers could be expected to have a greater interest in writing items than those who judged their item-writing competence to be high.

The observed effects of planning forms are remarkably consistent with past findings on the effects of other external variables on students at the different self-competence levels. Students who view themselves as competent seem least affected by performance conditions (Tuckman, 1991a). They appear to be "internally programmed" to regulate their own performance and do so under a variety of conditions (Bandura, 1986). It is possible that many of these highly self-competent students planned out their own task performance, regardless of whether a form was provided for this purpose. By contrast, students of medium and low perceived self-competence required a formal, external process to plan their performance.

The findings also can be explained in terms of various theories of human agency in the self-regulation process. Bandura (1989) argued that the belief in one's capability to perform is key to the initiation of self-regulated performance, and that motivation can be enhanced through the exercise of forethought and self-regulating activities such as goal setting. McCombs and Marzano (1990) offered the self-system as the basis for a real-time processing framework in which self-goals, self-beliefs, and self-evaluations mediate between the self and the external world. They argue that students need to be taught metacognitive and affective strategies to activate and use this framework. In this study, students of high perceived self-competence seemed able to activate their own self-systems for purposes of self-regulation, whereas students of low and medium perceived self-competence clearly required the strategic elements provided by the planning form. It would appear that being helped to systematically plan for subsequent performance can overcome a student's limitations in motivation to perform based on a lack of self-competence.

There are some methodological issues to consider in evaluating the results of this study. To what extent was the enhancing effect of the planning form created by its goal-setting function and to what extent by other planning functions? It is hard to do planning without goal setting (although the reverse can be done) so that planning can be regarded as a strategy that subsumes goal setting. Prior work on goal setting (Tuckman, 1990) has shown that it affects students low in self-competence substantially more than average students. The addition of planning to goal setting may have been the critical element in this study that extended its effect to the average group.

There is also the question of the students who failed to use the planning form despite the fact that it was provided. Regarding the initial level of motivation of these students, comparisons of their procrastination tendency, judged importance of getting the bonus, and perceived self-competence with students who used the form suggest that they were not initially different. Yet none of these nonusers put forth the effort to earn large bonuses, whereas half of the form users did. As in past studies (cf. Tuckman & Sexton, 1991), it appears that a small percentage of students resist external efforts to facilitate their self-regulated performance.

Finally, there is the question of the degree to which students' ability to write items may affect the amount of effort required. More skilled item writers may be able to write items that are worth more points than less skilled item writers with the same amount of effort. Although the groups were shown to be initially equivalent on a measure of verbal ability, this may not necessarily equate to item-writing ability. In future research, it may be useful to have students indicate on the planning form the type of items they intend to write, since comprehension items require more effort to write than knowledge items. However, the fact that more than three-quarters of the students wrote exclusively multiple-choice items to measure knowledge would mitigate against the importance of this factor.

Appendix: VHS Weekly Performance Plan

Name _____ Date _____ Class: M T W Th

	No. of items I will write	Time of day I will write	Place I will write	Reward for writing
MON				
TUE				
WED				
THU				
FRI				
SAT				
SUN				

Total _____

I am writing items because _____

_____

_____

To do so I will have to overcome _____

_____

_____

I will be able to follow my plan because _____

_____

_____

I will make it easier for myself to write by _____

_____

_____

My final bonus goal, as of today, is: triple   double   single   none _____

So far, relative to my final goal, I am doing _____

What I have changed from my last plan is _____

_____

because _____

The responsibility for writing items is _____

The findings of this study suggest that teachers should provide their students with formal assistance in planning their self-regulated performance, for example, in planning for doing their homework, reading assignments, and other studying tasks. This assistance is likely to be most helpful for students who doubt their own competence to perform.

Author's Note

This study was reported on at the annual meeting of the American Educational Research Association, Chicago, IL, 1991.

References

Bandura, A. (1977). Self-efficacy: Toward a unifying theory of behavior change. *Psychological Review, 84,* 191–215.

Bandura, A. (1986). *Social foundations of thought and action: A social cognitive theory.* Englewood Cliffs, NJ: Prentice-Hall.

Bandura, A. (1989). Human agency in social cognitive theory. *American Psychologist, 44,* 1,175–1,184.

French, E. P. F. (1963). *Test kit of cognitive factors.* Princeton, NJ: Educational Testing Service.

Gaa, J. P. (1979). The effect of individual goal-setting conferences on academic achievement and modification of locus of control orientation. *Psychology in the Schools, 16,* 591–597.

Locke, E. A., Shaw, K. N., Saari, L. M., & Latham, G. P. (1981). Goal setting and task performance: 1969–1980. *Psychological Bulletin, 90,* 125–152.

McCombs, B. L., & Marzano, R. J. (1990). Putting the self in self-regulated learning: The self as agent in integrating will and skill. *Educational Psychologist, 25,* 51–69.

Mento, A. J., Steel, R. P., & Karren, R. J. (1987). A meta-analytic study of the effects of goal-setting on task performance: 1966–1984. *Organizational Behavior and Human Decision Processes, 39,* 52–83.

Schunk, D. H. (1990). Goal setting and self-efficacy during self-regulated learning. *Educational Psychologist, 25,* 71–86.

Tuckman, B. W. (1990). Group versus goal-setting effects on the self-regulated performance of students differing in self-efficacy. *Journal of Experimental Education, 58,* 291–298.

Tuckman, B. W. (1991a). Motivating college students: A model based on empirical evidence. *Innovative Higher Education, 15,* 167–176.

Tuckman, B. W. (1991b). The development and concurrent validity of the Procrastination Scale. *Educational and Psychological Measurement, 51,* 473–480.

Tuckman, B. W., & Sexton, T. L. (1989). *The effects of relative feedback and self-efficacy in overcoming procrastination on an academic task.* Paper presented at the meeting of the American Psychological Association, New Orleans, LA.

Tuckman, B. W., & Sexton, T. L. (1990). The relation between self-beliefs and self-regulated performance. *Journal of Social Behavior and Personality, 5,* 465–472.

Tuckman, B. W., & Sexton, T. L. (1991). The effect of teacher encouragement on student self-efficacy and motivation for self-regulated performance. *Journal of Social Behavior and Personality, 6,* 137–146.

Weiner, B. (1980). *Human motivation.* New York: Holt, Rinehart and Winston.

Reprinted from the *Journal of Experimental Education, 60,* (1992) 119–127, by permission.

AN EXAMPLE EVALUATION

This section presents an analysis and evaluation of the preceding study in order to illustrate the process. Readers should attempt the process themselves before reading further, and then check their "answers" against the information in this section. Each of the 25 questions in Figure 15.1 will be considered in turn.

1. (a) Does the research report articulate a problem statement? If so, (b) what does it say? (c) Is it a clear statement? (d) Is it introduced prior to the literature review? Yes, the article gives a clear problem statement in the first paragraph.

> The purpose of this study was to determine the effect of planning on student motivation—in this case, the amount of effort put forth by college students on a voluntary, course-related task. A second purpose was to determine whether planning effects varied for students whose beliefs in their own level of initial competence at the task varied from high to low.

The study is quite satisfactory on this question.

2. Does the problem statement give a complete and accurate statement of the problem actually studied, or does it leave out something? Assessing accuracy raises some question about the use of the term *planning* to describe one level of the independent variable. Can "use of a planning form" and "planning" be equated? Although researchers commonly label variables in such broad conceptual terms, often seeming to represent intervening variables rather than actually manipulated ones, this practice can lead readers to overgeneralize the findings.

An assessment of completeness determines that the problem statement is a good one, since it reflects both questions of interest, and therefore includes all variables. It fails, however, to specifically mention the other level of the independent variable, "not planning" (or more accurately, "not given a form on which to plan"). This comment may be more than a minor criticism, since most readers will infer a comparison of "planning" to "not planning," when in fact the study compares it to lack of a formal opportunity to plan.

In addition, no single analysis compared performances by students at the different levels of self-competence; the study conducted separate analyses. Hence, the study achieved its second purpose only indirectly (i.e., by "eye-balling" the results).

The study falls somewhat short of satisfactory on this question.

3. Does the study's problem offer sufficient (a) workability, (b) critical mass, and (c) interest? The study employs a sufficiently large sample and enough variables, yet it remains workable due to the researcher's access to the necessary number of classes from which to draw subjects. (Without this access, such a study would be a relatively unworkable project.) The topic studied is also of considerable current interest. The study is satisfactory on this question.

4. (a) Does the problem studied offer theoretical and practical value? (b) Does the report establish these criteria? The study promises some theoretical value, which the article attempts to establish in the fourth paragraph of the discussion section by relating planning to self-beliefs, self-system, and metacognitive strategies. A better arrangement would have mentioned this theoretical base in the introduction. The study has obvious practical value, demonstrating that planning is a highly practical strategy, but no mention of this value appears until the last paragraph of the discussion section. The study seems to offer satisfactory value, but the report does not clearly establish its importance in the introduction.

5. Does the literature review present a high-quality summary? Does it achieve adequate (a) clarity, (b) flow, (c) relevance, (d) recency, (e) empirical focus, and (f) independence? Of the introduction's seven paragraphs, the middle five constitute the literature review. (Literature is also cited in the discussion section, but these references do not constitute part of the literature review.) The first paragraph of the literature review (the second paragraph of the introduction, the first being the problem statement) attempts to show that the study focused on motivation, as reflected in self-regulated performance. The next paragraph distinguishes between self-regulated learning and performance, while the following one cites studies relating various external conditions and one internal propensity to self-regulated performance. The next paragraph introduces and describes planning, the focus of the study, but cites no reference directly related to it. The final paragraph of the literature review discusses the impact of goal setting on motivation to perform.

An evaluation detects a striking absence of cited research on planning, a failure to establish a theoretical base for the study, and a preponderance of citations of work done by the study's author. While the literature review is reasonably clear and flows well, it shows substantial weakness in its omissions. It must be evaluated as a considerably less than satisfactory element.

6. Does the literature include technically accurate citations and references? The literature review follows a technically accurate format, except perhaps for citing and referencing a paper presented at a professional meeting by year as opposed to year and month (Tuckman & Sexton, 1989, August) as required by the American Psychological Association (1994) reference format. However, the procedure used was appropriate at the time the article was published, under guidelines provided in an earlier edition of the publication manual.

7. (a) Does the introduction offer hypotheses? If so, (b) what are they? Are they (c) directional, (d) clear, (e) consistent with the problem, and (f) supported by effective arguments? The last paragraph of the introduction states two directional hypotheses:

. . . planning was expected to enhance the amount of performance of students. . . . This enhancement effect was expected primarily for students whose
perceptions of their own competence to perform the task was low to average.

Paraphrasing the first hypothesis, it expects that students who plan will outperform those who do not plan. The second hypothesis asserts that students low
to average in self-competence will gain a greater benefit of planning than will
students high in self-competence. The introduction supports the first hypothesis
with statements that "research has shown a positive effect of goal setting on
performance," and "planning . . . incorporates goal setting." It supports the second hypothesis by noting "prior findings that external influences minimally affect
students who perceive themselves to be high in competence"; planning is one
such external influence.

The study rates as excellent on this question.

*8. What actual variables does the study examine; identify: (a) independent,
(b) moderator (if any), (c) dependent, and (d) control variables (only the most important two or three)?* The independent variable is planning versus no planning,
a manipulated variable with two discrete levels.

The moderator variable is self-competence, a measured variable initially continuous, that is subsequently divided into two levels: high and medium plus low.
Note, however, that the levels changed from the original formulation (from three
to two), and that the levels were not compared in the same analysis, a requirement for testing a variable's moderating effect.

The dependent variable is performance, a measured variable, but one that is
cast into discrete categories as the number of bonuses a student earns.

One major control variable is initial self-competence level. (In addition to serving as a moderator variable, it served as a control variable to establish the equivalence of the classes.) Other control variables included outcome importance, procrastination tendency, and mental ability. All are measured, continuous variables.

*9. (a) What intervening variable might the study be evaluating? (b) Was it
suggested in the research report?* The use of a system or metacognitive strategy, particularly one that might not otherwise have been self-initiated or self-
regulated, is a possible intervening variable. In other words, the planning form
may have caused students to use a strategy they may not have implemented on
their own. This possibility is suggested in the discussion section.

*10. What operational definitions did the researcher develop for the variables
listed in answering Question 8?*

*11. (a) What type of operational definition was used for each variable? (b)
Was each definition sufficiently exclusive to the corresponding variable?* Planning
versus no planning was operationally defined as receiving and using a planning
form versus not receiving the form. It was a manipulation-based variable. Self-
competence level was operationally defined as subjects' judgments of their own
task performance capability times their self-ratings of confidence in those judgments. It was a static variable. The dependent variable, performance, was operationally defined dynamically as number of performance bonuses earned on an
item-writing task. Outcome performance and procrastination tendency were

static judgments without explicit operational definitions. Mental ability was a dynamic measure of vocabulary skill.

In evaluating exclusivity, one might question whether not receiving a planning form equates to not planning, and whether vocabulary skill equates to mental ability. However, the use of a manipulation-based independent variable and dynamic dependent variable gives the study a strong operational base.

12. In controlling for extraneous effects, (a) how did the study prevent possible bias to certainty introduced by the subjects it employed, and (b) did these precautions completely and adequately control for these effects? The study controlled possible subject bias affecting certainty by establishing the equivalence of the four intact classes on initial self-competence level, outcome importance, procrastination tendency, and mental ability, all of which were presumably related to performance on the task, the dependent variable. The best possible design would have randomly assigned students to planning and no-planning conditions, but apparently the researcher was not in a position to alter the composition of the classes, and both treatment levels could not possibly have been carried out in the same class. Pretesting students on actual task performance would have given stronger control than pretesting them on the other control variables, but the researcher could not have done this, since the planning forms were given out prior to the introduction of the task. A better procedure would have started the task 1 week prior to the introduction of the forms in order to obtain a pretest measure of task performance. Lacking a direct pretest measure of the dependent variable, the author resorted to establishing initial equivalence on possible performance-related measures, but this precaution does not ensure equivalence between the groups. The control efforts gave better assurance than doing nothing, however.

A second problem is introduced by the elimination of subjects, creating possible mortality bias. Data analysis eliminated 18 students from the planning group, because they did not fill out and return the forms as instructed. To assess possible mortality bias, the researcher determined their reasons for failing to comply and compared them to the students who did comply on the four control variables, finding no differences. (See the second paragraph of the results section and the sixth paragraph of the discussion section.) However, none of those 18 subjects earned double or triple performance bonuses, while 50 percent of those that complied with instructions did earn such bonuses. In eliminating those 18 noncompliers, did the researcher introduce a major bias into the results, because they were motivationally different from the remaining 54 students who actually filled out and returned the forms? Does their equivalence with the larger group on the four measures ensure that they were motivationally the same? The study gives no way to answer these questions with certainty.

A third possible certainty/participant bias is introduced by possible differences in the academic capabilities and related grade expectations of the participating students, particularly as related to the moderator variable, task self-competence. The motivation for writing test items was to obtain grade bonuses. Students who expected, based on their past academic performance, to get high grades would be less motivated to write items than students who expected lower grades. If self-competence for item writing equated to self-competence for grades, then the difference in performance of self-competence groups on the task would relate less to planning than to characteristic motivation. The author speaks to this issue in the second paragraph of the discussion section, indicating recognition of a relationship between self-competence for item writing and self-competence for grades. Because of this link, a critical reader must seriously question the certainty of the moderating effect being a function of item-writing self-competence, as opposed to a function of task motivation.

Finally, an evaluation must consider the question of students' actual item-writing capability (in contrast to their self-judged capability), which the study did not assess as a control variable. Without random assignment, the researcher cannot assure equal distribution of this capacity across groups. (The author raises this question himself in the next-to-last paragraph of the discussion section.)

These criticisms reveal a weakness in the study in its control for threats to certainty, because it failed to control adequately for participant or subject bias.

13. In controlling for extraneous effects, (a) how did the study prevent possible bias to certainty introduced by the experiences it presented, and (b) did these precautions completely and adequately control for those effects? The researcher controlled for experience bias as a threat to certainty by including a control group whose members did not receive the planning form in order to assess the impact of planning on performance. The combination of a manipulation-based independent variable with a control group makes a considerable contribution to certainty. However, "not receiving the planning form" does not necessarily equate to "not planning." Even without the form, students may have conducted some planning as part of their normal practice. Therefore, the reader cannot be certain that group differences are based entirely on the planning form. However, planning by students not given the form would have reduced the differences between the two conditions, increasing the possibility of a false negative error rather than a false positive one. Since the study found significant differences, the reader can effectively conclude that students using the form were more likely to plan than those not using it. Hence, the possibility of planning without the form did not adversely affect certainty, and the study can be deemed quite satisfactory on this question.

14. In controlling for extraneous effects, (a) how did the study prevent possible bias to generality introduced by the participants it employed, and (b) did these precautions completely and adequately control for those effects? "Subjects were 130 junior and senior teacher education majors in a large state university. The majority were women, and the mean age was 21 years." The sample, young college women preparing to become teachers, is clearly not representative of a broad population. It is highly selective in terms of age, gender, education, and career plans. For this reason, the study must be considered very limited in its generality, at least as regards subjects.

15. In controlling for extraneous effects, (a) how did the study prevent possible bias to generality introduced by the experiences it presented, and (b) did these precautions completely and adequately control for those effects? The study was conducted within the setting of a regular college class and was introduced as a normal part of that class. In comparison to the typical laboratory experiment, or one that pulls students out of classes to help someone carry out some "experiment," this study must be considered much less obtrusive, and hence much higher in generality. Although college courses generally did not involve the practices that defined the study's dynamic dependent variable (that is, writing test items to get grade bonuses), it also constituted a normal part of the course used in the study. This integration of research manipulations with normal course expectations also contributes to generality. The only procedure that may limit the study's generality was the requirement that subjects return the planning forms. Any generalization about the potential effectiveness of using planning forms to enhance performance would have to include some accountability procedure, such as this study's requirement that students return the completed forms.

With this sole limitation, an evaluation finds satisfactory generality in the study based on its experiences.

16. (a) *Which variables did the study manipulate? (b) How successfully did the researcher carry out the manipulation?* The study manipulated its independent variable, planning versus no planning, by giving a planning form to one group but not the other. It confirmed that the planning group actually used the form by collecting returned, completed forms at the conclusion of the study period. The researcher apparently made a reasonable assumption that filling out the planning form constituted planning. (This variable was further operationalized by eliminating data for students who did not return filled-out forms.) For this level of the independent variable, the manipulation must be considered a success.

The control group members received no planning forms, but the study made no attempt to determine whether and to what extent they engaged in planning without the forms. It might have gained useful insight by surveying students at the end of the study period to determine the degree to which they planned their item-writing activity.

17. (a) *What design did the study employ, and (b) how adequately did it ensure certainty?* Based on the author's description, this study followed the non-equivalent control group design, diagrammed as:

$$\frac{O_1 \quad X_1 \quad O_3}{O_2 \quad X_2 \quad O_4}$$

However, since O_1 and O_2 were not pretest measures in the strict sense of the term (that is, they measured, not the dependent variable, but other, presumably performance-related variables), then the design can be considered to be an intact group comparison:

$$\frac{X_1 \quad O_1}{X_2 \quad O_2}$$

If the reader as evaluator settles on the second design, then he or she attributes low certainty to the study; if the reader accepts the first design as the correct one, then it achieves adequate certainty. The decision hinges on the question of threats to certainty imposed by subjects. Clearly, this question points out a major weakness of the study.

The design ran tests three times: (1) for all students, (2) for students high in self-competence, and (3) for students medium and low in self-competence. Since no single analysis compared students at the high versus medium plus low self-competence levels, the design cannot be considered a factorial one.

18. For each measurement procedure in the study, (a) what evidence of validity does the research report provide, and (b) does this information indicate adequate validity? The dynamic dependent variable, level of bonus earned, was based on performance on the item-writing task. The measure, number of points earned, translated directly into bonus level based on preset criteria. This measure must be considered a highly valid indicator of performance, since it varies directly with behavior and requires relatively little judgment for its assessment. (The only judgment concerns the acceptability of the written items which, the author explains, were "loosely screened for quality and returned for corrections where necessary.")

Self-competence and outcome importance, both static variables, were measured by answers to direct questions, ensuring validity as long as students give reasonably frank and self-aware responses. Procrastination (another static variable) was measured by a scale that the author confirms as valid by quoting a reference. Mental ability (a dynamic variable) was measured by a vocabulary test to which it has been "linked," according to the author, citing another reference.

The measures are judged to be valid ones, with possible questions about aspects of mental ability other than just vocabulary.

19. For each measurement procedure (including observation) in the study, (a) what evidence of reliability does the research report provide and (b) does this information indicate adequate reliability? The research report gives no specific evidence of the reliability of any measure. However, the dependent measure of bonus earned is based on an objective measure of points that students earned by writing items, so its reliability is not at issue (except perhaps if judgment influenced item screening). The report characterizes the procrastination measure as a reliable measure without giving any specific numbers. That leaves the measures of self-competence and outcome importance, the first apparently based on two items, the second on one item, without any mention of reliability. The article should have provided some indication of reliability for these two measures.

20. (a) Which statistics did the study employ, (b) were they the right choices (or should it have used different ones or additional ones), and (c) were the procedures and calculations correctly completed? Initial class equivalence was established by four one-way ANOVAs across the four classes, one for each control variable. The study tested the overall effect of planning versus no planning by means of a chi-square test, the same test it applied to gauge the effect of planning versus no planning on subjects low and medium in self-competence. The researcher completed no statistical comparison among students high in self-competence, presumably because the same approximate number in planning and no planning conditions earned double or triple bonuses.

The chi-square test requires nominal variables as both independent and dependent variables. The independent variable was inherently so: planning versus no planning. The dependent variable was apparently recast into two levels: (1) double or triple bonus; (2) single bonus or none. The intended moderator variable was recast into two levels: (1) high and (2) medium plus low. The article indicates that the measure of self-competence was divided into two rather than three levels because of limited sample size. Presumably the same reason led the researcher to combine the four levels of the dependent variable into two, but the article does not say so. The chi-square test does require a reasonable number of entries in each cell, so collapsing cells in this way is not an uncommon practice.

Some question remains about whether chi-square analysis was the best way to test the hypotheses. Since the study measured performance on a continuous or interval point scale, and the second hypothesis expected results to reveal a moderating relationship or interaction, a better statistical approach would have employed two-way analysis of variance. In this way, the study could have directly tested the hypothesized interaction between planning/no planning and levels of self-competence on performance (indicating the moderating effect of student self-competence), rather than evaluating this relationship indirectly, as it did.

Although the statistical tests applied in the study appeared correctly completed, the reader must question the choice of the statistics by which it tested the hypotheses.

21. (a) What findings did the study produce, and (b) do they fit the problem statement? 22. Did the research report adequately support the study's findings with text, tables, and figures? The research report explains the findings: (1) Overall, 50.0 percent of subjects who used the planning form earned big performance bonuses compared to 27.5 percent of those not given the form. (2) Among subjects high in self-competence, the same amount (about 33 percent) in both planning and no-planning groups earned big bonuses. (3) Among subjects middle or low in self-competence, 57 percent of form users earned big bonuses compared to 24 percent of those not given the form.

These findings fit the problem statement, with two reservations: (1) Did access to the planning form or lack of access constitute a good indicator of planning or no planning? (The discussion of Question 2 raised this issue earlier in the evaluation.) (2) Did the study effectively test student self-competence as a moderator variable?

The article presented no tables, and none seemed necessary since the findings were well-described in the text. It did include a figure—a bar graph that clearly showed the findings.

23. How significant and important were the study's findings? The overall difference between the planning-form condition and the no-form condition was significant at the .05 level. The difference for medium plus low self-competence students was significant at the .01 level. Two facts suggest that the findings were not only significant but important, as well: Almost twice as many planning-form students earned big bonuses as those not given the form, and among subjects medium and low in self-competence, more than twice as many form users as nonusers earned big bonuses.

24. Did the discussion section of the research report draw conclusions, and were they consistent with the study's results? The article presents the researcher's conclusions in the first paragraph of the discussion section. This material restates the findings more than articulating broad conclusions. The author restricted his conclusions to the effect of the planning form rather than extending them to the effect of planning. These conclusions were indeed consistent with the study's results, but they might have drawn inferences somewhat broader than the results.

25. (a) Did the discussion section offer reasonable interpretations of why results did and did not match expectations, and (b) did it suggest reasonable implications about what readers should do with the results? Much of the discussion was devoted to interpretations, with particular emphasis on methodological issues. (This evaluation has already referred to most of the issues, particularly in answering the questions on control.) All interpretations seemed to offer quite reasonable suggestions.

Although identified as a "methodological issue" in the fifth paragraph of the discussion, a substantial and important question arises about the specific way in which the planning form affected performance. Since use of the form apparently involved subjects in a number of processes, among which was goal setting, the article leaves difficult if not impossible questions about the critical activities that affected performance. Perhaps more interpretation could have been provided on this point.

Only one clear implication was offered in the discussion section's last paragraph. More detailed treatment of that one reasonable implication would have improved the article.

Despite the potential for improvement, the discussion section seemed adequate for the study's results.

Overall

Evaluation of the study has found the most important weaknesses in two areas: the accuracy and completeness of the problem statement (based on the confusion between planning and using the planning form), and methods of controlling for participant or subject bias, which might have affected certainty. Changes in statistical methods might have strengthened the study (although many readers value simplicity). The reader must consider the serious possibility that the results may have been unduly affected by subject bias.

On the positive side, the study used a manipulation-based independent variable and a dynamic dependent variable, both contributing to its validity. It also included a moderator variable, offered hypotheses, and obtained strong findings. Unfortunately, stronger steps might have more effectively controlled for potential subject bias.

SUMMARY

1. The first step in evaluating a study focuses on its problem statement. A reader identifies this component, notes its location, tries to rewrite it (to develop evidence of its clarity), and compares it to the rest of the study to determine its accuracy and completeness.
2. Evaluation of the problem itself considers its workability, critical mass, interest, theoretical value, and practical value.
3. The literature review, which occupies most of the introductory section, is then evaluated for its quality (primarily clarity and flow) and technical accuracy (agreement between citations and references).
4. Next, the reader looks for hypotheses and determines whether any found are directional, clear, consistent with the problem, and supported by effective arguments.
5. The variables studied are noted and labeled as independent, moderator, dependent, control, and intervening variables.
6. Operational definitions of variables are then identified, classified by type, and evaluated for their exclusiveness to the variables they define.
7. An important part of the evaluation reviews the methods or techniques used in the study to control for potential threats to certainty that result from bias in selection of participants and the experiences presented to them. A critical reader pays particular attention to judgments about the adequacy of these control methods and the degree of certainty that they provide to the study.
8. A similar review evaluates control methods for potential participant and experience biases affecting the study's generality.
9. For a study that manipulates any variables, evaluation must assess the nature and success of that manipulation.
10. Techniques for measuring variables must be evaluated to judge both their validity and reliability.
11. A reader identifies statistical tests employed in the study and evaluates their appropriateness and correctness.
12. After determining what findings the study produced, an evaluating reader compares them to the problem statement, checks for needed tables and figures, and assesses their significance and importance.
13. Finally, the discussion section of the report must be evaluated for reasonable conclusions, interpretations, and implications.

14. A study on planning provided a sample for evaluation. Consideration of this study revealed principal weaknesses related to the accuracy and completeness of the problem statement and the effectiveness of controls for potential subject bias affecting certainty.

COMPETENCY TEST EXERCISES

In lieu of completing exercises for Chapter 15, the reader is encouraged to analyze and evaluate Sample Studies III and IV in Appendix A using the worksheets in Appendix B, checking the results against the answers given in Appendix D.

RECOMMENDED REFERENCES

Hittleman, D. R., & Simon, A. J. (1997). *Interpreting educational research* (2nd ed.). Columbus, OH: Merrill.

Katzer, J., Cook, J. H., & Crouch, W. W. (1991). *Evaluating information: A guide for users of social science research* (3rd ed.). New York: McGraw-Hill.

Part 7

APPENDIXES

Sample Studies

SAMPLE STUDY I

The Effect of Teacher Encouragement on Student Self-Efficacy and Motivation for Self-Regulated Performance

BRUCE W. TUCKMAN
Florida State University

THOMAS L. SEXTON
University of Nevada, Las Vegas

Encouragement was defined as feedback designed to make college students feel better about their own performance capability on a given educational task. This study was undertaken to see if encouragement would (1) increase Ss' self-efficacy and (2) motivate them to increase performance of a task (i.e., their self-regulated performance). Sixty-four junior and senior teacher education majors earned grade bonuses in a course by voluntarily writing test items to measure course content as part of the Voluntary Homework System (VHS). Half of the Ss received statements praising their items on the back of their feedback forms while the other half did not. ANCOVAs showed that recipients of encouragement (1) were significantly higher in final self-efficacy levels, and (2) earned significantly more performance points, than non-recipients.

THIS STUDY examined encouragement as a factor that motivates students to engage in, or to persist in, performance on a task where they could choose for themselves how much or how long to perform. Tuckman and Sexton (1989, 1990) have coined the term *self-regulated performance* to describe performance in such task situations. Self-regulated performance differs from self-regulated learning in that self-regulated learning is based on both will and skill (McCombs & Marzano, 1990) while self-regulated performance is based just on will. Sticking to a diet or an exercise plan, spending time studying, and writing test items for extra credit (the task used in this study) are examples of self-regulated performance. Self-regulated performance is offered as a manifestation of *motivation* because of its primary reliance on will alone.

What causes a person to be motivated or to engage in self-regulated performance? Bandura (1977) has contended that *self-efficacy,* or the belief in one's capability to perform the task successfully, is a primary source of influence on motivation. He cites a considerable body of work by himself and others that supports this contention (cf., Bandura, 1986). What can be done then to increase a person's belief in his or her capability to perform a given task successfully? Bandura (1977) suggests that the most effective influence is the direct experience of success, with other factors such as vicarious experience and verbal persuasion also having substantial influence (cf., Bandura, 1986).

But what is it about the direct experience of success that increases motivation? While there is undoubtedly some effect based on the mere sense of having performed a behavior, the most critical component would seem to be the *response* to that performance by an expert or judge. The response has the potential for producing the strongest sense of self-efficacy and, hence, of motivating someone to continue to perform. If the response is positive, it may also have the power to persuade someone that he or she is good enough to succeed since "attempts to boost perceived self-efficacy persuasively often take the form of evaluative feedback about ongoing performances" (Bandura, 1986, p. 406).

Schunk (1982, 1983) has shown that feedback to children *crediting* the amount of effort they were perceived to have expended in their performance or the amount of talent they possessed caused them to increase both self-efficacy and task achievement. Relich et al. (1986), as well, showed that effort and ability feedback both affected achievement. However, in these studies, feedback did not affect persistence (or self-regulated performance), the essential manifestation of motivation. Moreover, these studies provided feedback only about how hard the children worked and how smart they were (i.e., the attributes that caused them to succeed). No feedback was provided directly about the quality of their performance.

The purpose of the present study was to see if *encouragement* or feedback praising the quality of college students' performance on a given educational task would (1) increase their self-efficacy and (2) motivate them to increase the extent to which they performed that task, or their self-regulated performance.

Deci and Porac (1978) and Deci and Ryan (1985) distinguish between *information* feedback, or telling people how good their performance was, and *controlling* feedback, or telling them what they have to do to succeed. The former provides choice, thereby producing intrinsic motivation, while the latter pushes someone to think or act in a specific way, thereby producing extrinsic motivation. Encouragement, as used in the present study, would seem to be an instance of "informational feedback." However, the term "encouragement" seems a more apt label for a positive, and thus persuasory, response to performance.

Other findings support the contention that knowing of one's success enhances subsequent performance. Becker (1978) found that informational feedback improved task performance but only if a difficult performance goal was set. Bandura and Cervone (1983) proposed that the magnitude or amount of performance varied as a function of (1) the distance between one's performance and one's goal, and (2) informational feedback regarding progress toward goal attainment.

Tuckman and Sexton (1989), using the same test-item writing task as in the present study, found that amount of self-regulated performance, a measure of motivation, was increased by factual feedback about relative standing in a competitive situation, but only for students whose beliefs in their own capabilities placed them in the middle and bottom thirds of the class. Perhaps these are the very students the work cited above identified as those with the furthest to go to meet their goals. However, the feedback in this study was not necessarily encouraging, particularly for those ranking low in the relative standings.

Given Kazdin's (1974) dictum that to be effective, feedback must support the desired behavior change, it may be argued that feedback in the form of knowledge of results is not necessarily supportive, encouraging, or persuasive, but merely factual. Such information only tells students how far they have to go to meet their goal, not necessarily how likely they are to have the required capability. For students far from their goal, such factual feedback would actually be discouraging. It would seem that prior work on feedback as a motivator has concentrated on knowledge of results rather than examining the effect of direct attempts to encourage students to perform, thus providing a rationale for the current study.

The distinction between the approach here and prior work is, first of all, that the response to performance was oriented toward the quality of the performance rather than to the amount of effort expended. Secondly, the task was part of a real-world experience with real payoffs rather than a laboratory task. A third difference is that the response to performance was designed to provide encouragement, thereby having a persuasive effect based on the likelihood of subsequent success (what Bandura, 1986, called a "persuasory efficacy appraisal"), rather than merely confirming the level of that performance. Finally, college students were the participants rather than younger children.

In the present study, a type of feedback or response that might more accurately be called *encouragement* was employed. This type of feedback indicated that the student's performance was qualitatively good and, hence, went beyond mere quantitative performance information which might be good or bad, and which was provided to all students automatically within the task. It was expected that those students who received encouragement would be persuaded to feel good about their own effort and performance and to experience a concomitant increase in self-efficacy. They were also expected to produce a more extensive task response than students who received a neutral response to their performance, reflecting a greater degree of motivation.

Method

Subjects

*S*s were 65 undergraduate students in their junior and senior years studying in a teacher education program and currently enrolled in a State-mandated

Educational Psychology course. The course covered the topics of learning theory applied to teaching and test construction and interpretation. *Ss'* ages ranged from 19 to 30 with a mean age of 21. All but four of the *Ss* were female and all but three were white.

Task

The self-regulated performance task was called Voluntary Homework System or VHS (Tuckman & Sexton, 1989, 1990). *Ss* were given the opportunity to write test items covering the content of the course on a weekly basis up to a maximum of 25 items per week for 10 weeks. Items had to cover the topic taught that week. *Ss* could choose to write multiple-choice items measuring comprehension (worth 3 points each), multiple-choice items measuring knowledge (worth 2 points each), completion items (worth 1 point each), or no items at all. Points for the three item types reflected the amount of effort that writing each required. In any given week, only one type of item could be turned in.

Over the course of 10 weeks, all items were loosely screened and *Ss* received points for acceptable items written—a measure of self-regulated performance. *Ss* were told that the top third cumulative point scores would get a double grade bonus (e.g., from a C to a B−), the middle third a single grade bonus (e.g., from a C to a C+), and the bottom third no grade bonus. Each week *Ss* received a feedback form indicating their cumulative point totals, their current class rank, and the current point totals separating high, middle, and low thirds. Thus, quantitative or factual feedback was a standard part of the procedure for all *Ss*.

Treatments

Half of the *Ss* (32), randomly chosen, received a positive statement of encouragement on the back of their feedback form each week. These statements were written in hand by a teaching assistant, and alternated from week to week. Examples of encouraging feedback include: "Your items are well-constructed and to the point." "Your items show good imagination and cleverness." "You did a good job of constructing very plausible distractors for your items." "You did a good job of writing items to cover the material in the text." And, in the few cases of *Ss* who submitted no items that week, the response was: "I'll bet you could write good items if you tried," or "You've done fine up until now—keep trying!"

The second half of the *Ss*, chosen at random, received no encouragement on the back of their feedback forms. They all received the handwritten message that their items were acceptable, that they were OK, or that they had written no items. Thus, all *Ss* received a message each week but only for the treatment half were the messages encouraging in content. The teacher was not aware of which students were given which response on the VHS task.

Measures

Four measures were used to control for individual differences in motivation at the start of the study. At the beginning of each week, *Ss* completed a questionnaire where they indicated the kind and number of items they felt capable of writing that week and the confidence they had (on a 9-point scale) of that judgment. Following Bandura (1977), self-efficacy was determined by multiplying expected performance (in this case, point value of the items they felt capable of writing times number of items they felt capable of writing) by confidence. *Initial self-efficacy* (SE1) was determined at the start of the experiment prior to the submission of items and, hence, prior to experiencing any feedback or encouragement. Prior work (Sexton & Tuckman, in press) has shown that initial self-efficacy and subsequent performance on VHS are independent. In addition, a correlation of .70 between the self-efficacy score at the beginning of week one and that at the beginning of week two was found in the current study, indicating an acceptable degree of reliability for this judgment.

Outcome expectation (OE1) was also measured in the manner prescribed by Bandura (1977). Ss were asked to indicate, on a 9-point scale, their likelihood of obtaining a bonus for VHS performance. Data were used only from the initial measurement taken prior to the start of the study. *Outcome importance* (OI1) was measured by asking Ss at the start how important the bonus was to them, on a 9-point scale. Correlations between week 1 and week 2 scores on each of these measures were .69 and .75 respectively, acceptable degrees of reliability.

Ss were also given a test prior to the start of the study to measure and control for inherent differences between them in the *tendency to procrastinate* (PRO) or to delay starting or completing a task. This test was the *Procrastination Scale* (Tuckman, in press), a 32 item Likert Scale for which an alpha coefficient of .75 is reported. Items included: "I needlessly delay finishing jobs, even when they're important," "I manage to find an excuse for not doing something," and "I always finish important jobs with time to spare."

The two dependent measures were as follows: (1) *total points* accumulated, a measure of self-regulated or self-motivated performance, which was the sum of the points earned over the 10 weeks; (2) *final self-efficacy* (SE10) which was the self-efficacy score based on capability judgments of item-type, number of items to be written, and confidence at the start of the final week.

Analyses

One-way analyses of covariance were run on each of the dependent measures with treatment versus no treatment as the independent variable. The four individual difference measures: SE1, OE1, OI1, and PRO were used as covariates.

Results

The results of the analysis of covariance of final self-efficacy (SE10) by treatment condition with initial self-efficacy (SE1), initial outcome expectation (OE1), initial outcome importance (OI1), and procrastination (PRO) as covariates are shown in Table 1. As the table shows, the effect of treatment condition was significant at the .01 level ($F = 9.73$, $df = 1, 58$).

TABLE 1   Analyses of Covariance of Final Self-Efficacy (SE10) and Performance Points by Treatment Conditions With Initial Self-Efficacy (SE1), Initial Outcome Expectation (OE1), Initial Outcome Importance (OI1), and Procrastination (PRO) as Covariates

SOURCE	df	FINAL SELF-EFFICIENCY		PERFORMANCE POINTS	
		MS	F	MS	F
Condition	1	296145	9.73[c]	107716	4.04[b]
SE1	1	43214	1.42	21835	0.82
OE1	1	11707	0.38	49646	1.86
OI1	1	67233	2.21	79469	2.98[a]
PRO	1	17720	0.58	104011	3.90[a]
Error	58	30450		26662	

[a]$p < .10$; [b]$p < .05$; [c]$p < .01$.

Although they started at about the same level (means of 25 and 26 respectively), Ss in the encouragement condition gained 12 points in self-efficacy from SE1 to SE10 while Ss in the no encouragement condition gained none during the same period (see Figure 1). The expectation that encouragement would result in increased self-efficacy was confirmed by these results.

The results of the parallel analysis of covariance of performance points by treatment condition using the same covariates also appears in Table 1. Again, the effect of treatment condition was significant ($F = 4.04$, $df = 1, 58$, $p < .05$). Ss in the encouragement condition earned an average of 300 points in comparison to the 231 averaged by Ss in the no encouragement condition. The effects of encouragement and no-encouragement on self-efficacy and item-writing performance over the 10-week period are shown in Figure 1. Encouragement Ss went from 17 performance points in week 1 to 37 in week 10 while no-encouragement Ss went from 7 points to 28. These findings confirmed the prediction that encouragement would enhance performance.

Figure 1 also shows that over time self-efficacy and performance parallel one another.

Discussion

As expected, encouragement was related to increases in perception of capability to perform a task. This increase in perceived self-efficacy was accompanied

SELF-EFFICACY AND PERFORMANCE POINTS OVER TIME FOR
ENCOURAGEMENT AND NO-ENCOURAGEMENT GROUPS

FIGURE 1

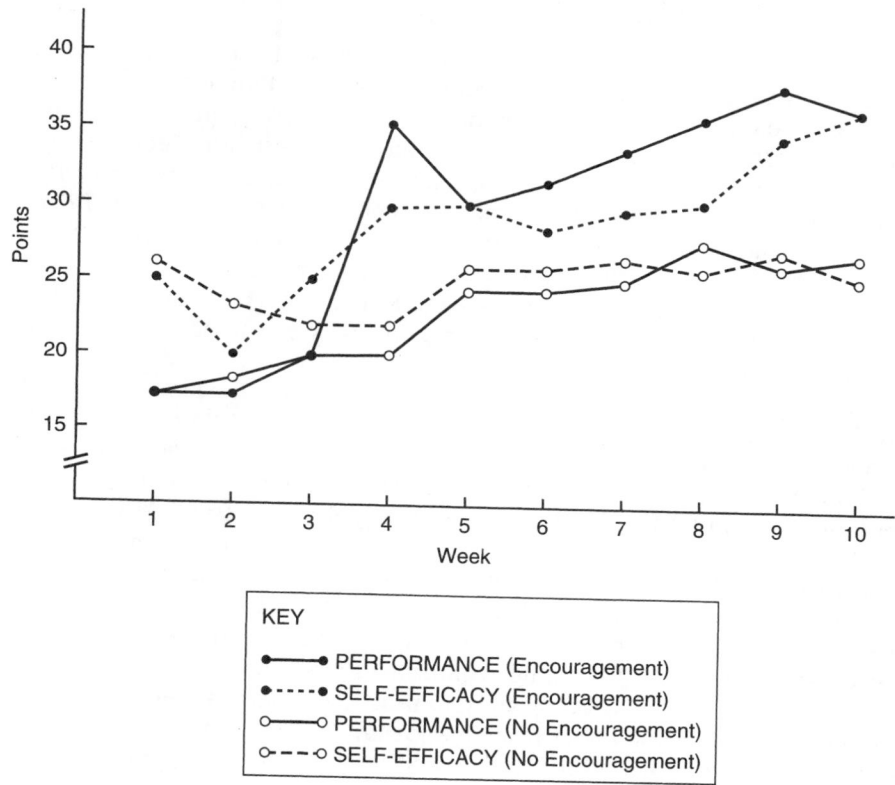

by an increase in motivation as evidenced by an increase in voluntary task
performance. Hence, the intuitive expectation that students will be motivated or
persuaded to perform more when they are encouraged by receiving positive
feedback was borne out by the data.

The findings do not suggest that mere knowledge of results has a motivational effect because all *S*s received knowledge of results. Rather, it would appear to be the *positive* judgments about performance capability that were persuasively motivating, and that led to the observed increase in the level of
performance. Further support is lent to this conclusion by the finding that *S*s'
perceptions of their own levels of self-efficacy were affected by encouragement.
Self-efficacy may be functioning as a mediator between environmental conditions and performance, as proposed by Bandura (1977). In fact, self-efficacy
data, collected prior to performance data each week, mirrored performance
results quite closely over time (as seen in Figure 1). In addition, self-efficacy at

time 1 correlated .20 with total performance points while self-efficacy at time 10 correlated .80 with total performance points, suggesting that as people believe more in themselves they perform better, and as they perform better they believe more in themselves.

To provide additional evidence for the conclusion that self-efficacy functioned as a mediator between encouragement and performance, two analyses of covariance were run: (1) the effect of feedback condition on final self-efficacy with total performance points as a covariate; (2) the effect of feedback condition on total performance points with final self-efficacy as a covariate. In the first, significant effects were found for both feedback condition ($F = 5.77$, $df = 1/61$, $p < .02$) and total performance ($F = 102.80$, $df = 1/61$, $p < .001$). In the second, the only significant effect found was for final self-efficacy. Hence, when performance is held constant, encouragement can be seen to affect self-efficacy, but when final self-efficacy is held constant, encouragement has no effect on performance.

The statistical demonstration of the effect of encouragement on performance required that *initial* individual differences in motivation be controlled. Without the covariates, the treatment effect yielded an insignificant F value of 2.65 ($df = 1, 62$) in comparison to the significant F value of 4.04 obtained with the covariates. In particular, tendencies among Ss to procrastinate (PRO) and initial value or importance placed on earning the grade bonus contingent upon performance (OI1) limited or enhanced the impact of encouragement received upon performance. One is reminded of the old adage that "you can lead a horse to water but you cannot make him drink." For those students who are inclined to procrastinate or who have little regard for a grade bonus, it may take considerably more than encouragement from teachers to increase their motivation to the point where it will affect performance levels. Teachers must presumably satisfy themselves with the realization that they can only motivate by encouragement those students who are receptive to it.

Bandura (1977) has listed enactive attainment—defined as the direct experience of success—as the major influence on self-efficacy and, hence, on self-regulated performance. To be effective, enactive attainment must yield a sense of one's performance capability or, put another way, it must also be persuasory. Simply "grinding out" the work may not provide this sense to a sufficient degree. Based on the findings of this study, it would appear that qualitatively encouraging feedback, or being told that one's work is indeed of good quality, is part of what persuades a person that the experience was a successful one. Authority figures such as teachers should be admonished by these results to provide students with qualitatively encouraging feedback (telling them what they did right) rather than focusing on either negative feedback (telling them what they did wrong) or straight factual feedback (telling them what they did) if they hope to motivate them to increase the amount of their performance.

References

Bandura, A. (1977). Self-efficacy: Toward a unifying theory of behavior change. *Psychological Review, 84,* 191–215.

Bandura, A. (1986). *Social foundations of thought and action: A social cognitive theory.* Englewood Cliffs, NJ: Prentice-Hall.

Bandura, A., & Cervone, D. (1983). Self-evaluative and self-efficacy mechanisms governing the motivational effects of goal systems. *Journal of Personality and Social Psychology, 45,* 1,017–1,028.

Becker, L. J. (1978). Joint effect of feedback and goal setting on performance: A field study of residential energy conservation. *Journal of Applied Psychology, 65,* 428–433.

Deci, E. L., & Porac, J. (1978). Cognitive evaluation theory and the study of human motivation. In M. R. Lepper & D. Greene (Eds.). *The hidden costs of reward: New perspectives on the psychology of human motivation.* Hillsdale, NJ: Lawrence Erlbaum.

Deci, E. L., & Ryan, R. M. (1985). *Intrinsic motivation and self-determination in human behavior.* New York: Plenum.

Kazdin, A. E. (1974). Reactive self-monitoring: The effects of response desirability, goal-setting, and feedback. *Journal of Counseling and Clinical Psychology, 42,* 704–716.

McCombs, B. L., & Marzano, R. J. (1990). Putting the self in self-regulated learning: The self as agent in integrating will and skill. *Educational Psychologist, 25,* 51–69.

Relich, J. D., Debus, R. L., & Walker, R. (1986). The mediating role of attribution and self-efficacy variables for treatment effects on achievement outcomes. *Contemporary Educational Psychology, 11,* 195–216.

Schunk, D. H. (1982). Effects of effort attributional feedback on children's perceived self-efficacy and achievement. *Journal of Educational Psychology, 75,* 548–556.

Schunk, D. H. (1983). Ability versus effort attributional feedback: Different effects on self-efficacy and achievement. *Journal of Educational Psychology, 75,* 848–856.

Sexton, T. L., & Tuckman, B. W. (in press). Self-beliefs and behavior: The role of self-efficacy and outcome expectation over time. *Personality and Individual Differences.*

Tuckman, B. W. (in press). The development and concurrent validity of the Procrastination Scale. *Educational and Psychological Measurement.*

Tuckman, B. W., & Sexton, T. L. (1989, August). *The effects of relative feedback and self-efficacy in overcoming procrastination on an academic task.* Paper presented at the meeting of American Psychological Association, New Orleans, LA.

Tuckman, B. W., & Sexton, T. L. (1990). The relation between self-beliefs and self-regulated performance. *Journal of Social Behavior and Personality, 5,* 465–472.

Reprinted from the *Journal of Social Behavior and Personality,* 1991, 6(1):137–146. © Select Press.

SAMPLE STUDY II
Classroom Behavior of Good and Poor Readers

BARBARA B. WASSON, PAUL L. BEARE, AND JOHN B. WASSON
Moorhead State University

The purpose of this study was to investigate objectively observable categories of behavior for good and poor readers in classroom settings. Seven specific observable behaviors of 3 good and 3 poor readers from each of three regular classrooms at each of six grade levels were viewed under natural classroom conditions. Trained observers recorded student behavior for 30 min a day for 10 days. A two-way analysis of variance procedure was used in data analysis. Results indicated that poor readers did not differ from good readers in starting to work on assignments, having necessary materials available, making unacceptable noise, being out of place, or making unacceptable contact with other persons or their property. Poor readers, however, were off task more and volunteered less than good readers did. The results were interpreted to suggest that poor readers could be viewed as uninvolved students. Instructional suggestions are given.

RESEARCHERS HAVE written that poor readers and good readers behave differently. In an early review of clinically observed characteristics of poor readers, Robinson (1946) included restlessness, introversive or withdrawal tendencies, inadequate school relations, and conscious self-control bordering on rigidity. Harris and Sipay (1985) cited expressed hostility, negative emotional response to reading, lack of effort, passivity, distractibility or restlessness, and lack of attentive concentration as characteristics of poor readers.

Poor readers, in general, although not in every case, have been characterized as tending to demonstrate maladaptive behavior (Gentile & McMillan, 1987; Jorm, Share, Matthews, & MacClean, 1985). Based on a substantial review of research, Gentile and McMillan characterized the behavior of poor readers as ranging from anger and aggression to avoidance and apprehension.

Classroom behavior has been shown to be highly related to reading achievement among first- and second-grade children (Jorm et al., 1985; McMichael, 1979; Swanson, 1984). On the other hand, Zigmond, Kerr, and Schaeffer (1988) found that the classroom behavior of learning-disabled adolescents enrolled in Grades 1 through 11 is not significantly different from the behavior of their non-learning-disabled peers. Among the behaviors studied were on-task behavior, disruptive behavior, and volunteering comments.

Confusion arises about behavioral characteristics of good and poor readers when clinically derived subjective descriptions are compared with objectively measured classroom behavior and when the behavior of primary children is compared with that of adolescents.

The present research attempts to provide consistency by investigating a single set of objectively observable behaviors of both good and poor readers in classroom settings from Grades 1 through 11.

Method

Subjects

The subjects were 108 students enrolled in regular classes from Grades 1, 3, 5, 7, 9, and 11. Classrooms were selected from public schools in a midsized (population 65,000) city in the north central United States.

We chose subjects who were the 3 best and the 3 worst readers in each of three classrooms at each of six grade levels. The relative standing of students was determined by examining the latest standardized reading achievement test scores for each student in each class, except for first-grade students, for whom kindergarten teachers' ratings were used as the basis for selection. The 3 students with the highest and the 3 students with the lowest reading achievement scores became subjects. The fourth highest and the fourth lowest students became alternates if any of the original choices were absent on the first day of observation.

At each of six grade levels, we chose a total of 9 good readers and 9 poor readers from three classrooms. Selection thus resulted in the total of 108 students from 18 classrooms, 54 categorized as good and 54 categorized as poor readers. The final sample was composed of 106 originally chosen subjects and 2 alternates.

Procedure

Based on a review of literature that specified classroom behaviors associated with good as opposed to poor readers (Gentile & McMillan, 1987; Jorm et al., 1985; McMichael, 1979; Zigmond, Kerr, & Schaeffer, 1988), discussion with classroom teachers, and review of methods for objectively observing student behavior in classroom settings (Deno, 1980; Grambrell, Wilson, & Gantt, 1981; Hoge, 1985; Hoge & Luce, 1979), we chose specific behaviors that seemed likely to differentiate good from poor readers. We observed these specific behaviors in classrooms on a trial basis to ensure that they could be consistently identified. From the original set of specific behaviors, we chose seven that could be consistently identified and precisely defined. Behavioral definitions were refined through pilot sessions performed in classrooms not used in the actual research. Pilot sessions continued until a reliability of 90% was attained by independent observers recording the behavior of the same students at the same time. The behaviors and definitions used in the research follow:

1. *Seconds to start*—number of seconds from the beginning of an activity, as indicated by the teacher, until the student is first on task. Duration recording, 5-min. maximum. *First on task*—materials are out and the student is in

place, listening to the teacher, making eye contact with the appropriate stimuli, and writing, or has pencil poised, ready to write. The student is not on task when looking for materials.

2. *Material missing*—number of materials needed for instruction that a student is missing, based on a list obtained from the teacher prior to the observation.

The following five behaviors were recorded using an interval method—one mark for 20-s interval during which the behavior occurred.

3. *Noise*—any sounds created by the student that may distract either another student (or students) or the teacher from the business at hand. The noise may be generated vocally (including talk outs or unintelligible sounds) or nonvocally (tapping a pencil or snapping fingers). Incidentally produced noises (chair squeaks, etc.) are excluded.

4. *Out of place*—any movement beyond the either explicitly or implicitly defined boundaries in which the student is allowed movement. If the student is doing desk work, then movement of any sort out of the seat is out of place. If the student is working with a group, then leaving the group is out of place.

5. *Physical contact or destruction*—any unacceptable contact with another person or another person's property. Kicking, hitting, pushing, tearing, breaking, and taking are categorized as physical contact or destruction.

6. *Off task*—any movement off a prescribed activity that does not fall into one of the three previously defined categories. Looking around, staring into space, doodling, or any observable movement off the task at hand is included.

7. *Volunteering*—deliberately volunteering to answer questions or verbally participate in class, including raising a hand to answer or speaking out to answer, even without permission.

We gathered research data by observing each classroom for 30 min a day for 10 days. To prevent experimenter bias, we were not told which students were poor readers, but only which 6 students to observe.

We did not observe reading classes because of a lack of secondary-level reading classes and because the behavior that characterizes poor readers, according to the literature, is more general than a simple reaction to a reading class. Instead, social studies classes, which require students to apply reading skills, were selected for observation. When certain elementary classroom teachers did not teach clearly defined social studies lessons, we substituted language arts lessons.

Behavioral observation began at the start of each day's lesson. Prior to the start of the lesson, the classroom teacher supplied the trained observer with a list of materials that the children needed for the lesson. The teacher also indicated to the observer when the lesson began. The observer then measured the length of time until each student was first on task. The maximum time allotted was 5 min. After 5 min elapsed, the observer recorded materials missing, that is, materials the student did not have that were required for the lesson. Length of time until each student was first on task and materials missing were recorded for each student each day.

The remaining five categories of behavior listed above as numbers 3 through 7 were measured on a rotating interval basis. We observed each student, in turn, for 20 s, and he or she could receive a mark any time during the 20-s interval. Following this procedure, we observed each student for 20 s every 2 min, and he or she could receive a score of from 0 to 15 for noise, out of place, physical contact, off task, or volunteering each day.

Results

We analyzed the data by using a two-way analysis of variance (ANOVA) procedure. Rate of behavior was the dependent variable, and good versus poor reader groups and grade level were the two independent variables.

The mean scores for each of the seven measured behaviors are reported by reader group in Table 1 and by grade level in Table 2. Table 2 does not break

TABLE 1

MEAN SCORES FOR SEVEN BEHAVIORS EXHIBITED BY 54 GOOD AND 54 POOR READERS OVER 10 DAYS OF OBSERVATION

			BEHAVIOR				
GROUP	SECONDS TO START	MATERIALS MISSING[a]	NOISE[b]	OUT OF PLACE[b]	PHYSICAL CONTACT[b]	OFF TASK[b]	VOLUNTEERS[b]
Poor reader	51	.00	1.67	.31	.02	6.63	1.45
Good reader	43	.02	1.50	.32	.00	5.51	2.47

Note. $p < .05$ pertains to both off-task and volunteering behavior.
[a]Number of missing objects. [b]Number of intervals during which behavior occurs (out of 15 possible).

TABLE 2

MEAN SCORES FOR SEVEN BEHAVIORS EXHIBITED BY 18 SUBJECTS AT EACH OF SIX GRADE LEVELS OVER 10 DAYS OF OBSERVATION

			BEHAVIOR TOTALS				
GRADE	SECONDS TO START	MATERIALS MISSING[a]	NOISE[b]	OUT OF PLACE[b]	PHYSICAL CONTACT[b]	OFF TASK[b]	VOLUNTEERS[b]
1	42	.0	2.1	.7	0	4.8	3.6
3	63	.0	0.9	.7	0	7.3	2.8
5	68	.0	1.3	.1	0	8.5	1.7
7	26	.0	1.0	.1	0	2.8	1.9
9	25	.1	1.9	.3	0	5.8	1.0
11	59	.0	2.3	.1	0	7.3	0.8

[a]Number of missing objects. [b]Number of intervals during which behavior occurs (out of 15 possible).

down grade level by good and poor readers because no significant interactions were found by grade level and reading achievement. Analysis of variance for each of the behaviors yielded the following results:

1. *Seconds to start*—No difference was found between good and poor readers. Although significant differences were found between grade levels, $F(5,107) = 6.337$, $p < .05$, they made little practical difference, because most students at every grade level started from $\frac{1}{2}$ to 1 min after the beginning of the lesson.

2. *Materials missing*—No differences were found between good and poor readers or between grade levels. There were almost no missing materials throughout the duration of the study.

3. *Noise*—Incidents of unacceptable distracting noise were infrequent. No difference was found between good and poor readers or between grade levels.

4. *Out of place*—No difference was found between good and poor readers. There were significant grade level differences, $F(5, 107) = 5.851$, $p < .05$. Post hoc analysis indicated that 1st- and 3rd-grade children were out of place significantly more often than were 5th-, 7th-, 9th-, and 11th-grade students.

5. *Physical contact or destruction*—Incidents of physical contact or destruction were infrequent. No difference was found between good and poor readers or between grade levels.

6. *Off task*—Much off-task behavior was observed, almost 6 min (median) for the entire group of 108 students per 30-min observation. Poor readers were off task significantly more often than good readers, $F(1, 107) = 7.925$, $p < .05$. Seventh-grade students were significantly less off task, $F(5, 107) = 18.01$, $p < .05$, than were students from other grades.

7. *Volunteering*—Significant differences were found between good and poor readers in deliberately volunteering information, $F(1, 107) = 14.99$, $p < .05$. Students from Grade 5 and above volunteered less than those from Grades 1 and 3.

Discussion

We found no differences between good and poor readers in starting to work on assignments, having necessary materials available, making unacceptable noise, being out of place, or making unacceptable contact with other persons or their property. In these respects, poor readers did not differ from good readers when they were systematically observed in regular classroom situations that involved application of reading, but not direct instruction in reading.

On the other hand, we found significant differences between good and poor readers in attending to instructional tasks. Similar to findings reported by Grambrell, Wilson, and Gantt (1981), poor readers attended less. Significant differences also were found in volunteering to participate verbally in class. Poor readers volunteered less.

This research suggests that in the regular classroom, at all grade levels observed, poor readers did not demonstrate disruptive or noncompliant behaviors that interfered with learning any more than did good readers. In terms of active participation in learning, however, a difference did appear to exist. The poor readers were less engaged and involved than good readers and also inferior in responsiveness and attentive learning.

Gentile and McMillan (1987) made suggestions specifically for poor readers who are uninvolved in learning. The authors suggested that the teachers should emphasize drawing these students out and focusing them on instructional tasks. The teachers should directly prompt and cue unengaged, inattentive learners, guiding them back to academic tasks. Unresponsive learners should be, in a supportive manner, directly requested to respond. The teachers should provide emotional and instructional support designed to generate students' willingness to try.

Students will be more willing to respond when teachers do not embarrass them over incorrect responses and do not give them text materials that are too difficult (Wilson, 1985, pp. 183–198). Bristow (1985) recommended that, to encourage active participation, poor readers must encounter instructional situations in which their efforts can make a difference. In addition, because poor readers tend to perceive themselves as less successful than they are, teachers should honestly and accurately expose the readers' successes.

Teachers who want to help poor readers participate more actively in the classroom should directly, but supportively, ask them to respond, ensure that the classroom learning environment permits participation to result in success, and commend poor readers directly and specifically for their responses and for their successes.

References

Bristow, P. S. (1985). Are poor readers passive readers? Some evidence, possible explanations, and potential solutions. *The Reading Teacher, 39,* 318–325.

Dezo, S. L. (1980). Direct observation approach to measuring classroom behavior. *Exceptional Children, 47,* 396–399.

Gentile, L. M., & McMillan, M. M. (1987). *Stress and reading difficulties: Research, assessment, intervention.* Newark, DE: International Reading Association.

Grambrell, L. B., Wilson, R. M., & Gantt, W. N. (1981). Classroom observations of task-attending behaviors of good and poor readers. *Journal of Educational Research, 74,* 400–404.

Harris, A. J., & Sipay, E. R. (1985). *How to increase reading ability* (8th ed.). New York: Longman.

Hoge, R. D. (1985). The validity of direct observation measures of pupil classroom behavior. *Review of Educational Research, 55,* 469–483.

Hoge, R. D., & Luce, S. (1979). Predicting academic achievement from classroom behavior. *Review of Educational Research, 49,* 479–496.

Jorm, A. F., Share, D. L., Matthews, R., & MacClean, R. (1985). Behavior problems in specific reading retarded and general reading backward children: A longitudinal study. *Journal of Child Psychology & Psychiatry & Allied Disciplines, 27,* 33–43.

McMichael, P. (1979). The hen or the egg? Which comes first—Antisocial emotional disorders or reading ability? *British Journal of Educational Psychology, 49,* 226–238.

Robinson, H. M. (1946). *Why pupils fail in reading.* Chicago: University of Chicago Press.

Swanson, B. B. (1984). The relationship of first graders' self-report and direct observational attitude scores to reading achievement. *Reading Improvement, 21,* 170.

Wilson, R. M. (1985). *Diagnostic reading for classroom and clinic* (5th ed.). Columbus, OH: Merrill.

Zigmond, N., Kerr, M. M., & Schaeffer, A. (1988). Behavior patterns of learning disabled and non-learning-disabled adolescents in high school academic classes. *Remedial and Special Education, 9* (2), 6–11.

Reprinted from the *Journal of Educational Research,* 1990, 83(3), 162–165, by permission.

SAMPLE STUDY III

Acquisition and Retention of Written Words by Kindergarten Children Under Varying Learning Conditions

JUDY RASH
Coquitlam School District

TERRY D. JOHNSON AND NORMAN GLEADOW
University of Victoria

Investigates the effect of word acquisition by kindergarten children under two conditions of instruction: an isolated-word condition and a word-sentence condition. A review of the literature reveals inconclusive and contradictory findings. Previous studies in the area tend to introduce a teach/test bias, use oral rather than written contexts, and measure only immediate learning. The original contribution made by this study is that all words presented to the subjects were target words in written forms. In addition the teach/test bias was eliminated and the long-term retention period extended considerably. Results indicate that kindergarten children learn words in significantly fewer trials when the target words are presented in a meaningful sentence. When short-term retention was tested in a sentence condition, children learning via this method were significantly superior to children learning via an isolated word method. When tested in an isolated word condition, in new context, and on word designation tasks, no significant differences where noted between the two groups. The same pattern of results was obtained in tests of long-term retention.

THE QUESTION of the cues children employ when learning to read and the effective presentation of new words to beginning readers has been a topic of debate for more than three decades. Two reading theorists who represent extreme positions in the discussion are Samuels and Goodman.

Samuels states that the student will try to get the meaning of a sentence using the easiest means possible. If prompts in the form of accompanying pictures or sentence context are present and represent an easier route to meaning then the reader will use them and thus be distracted from the word to be learned (Singer, Samuels, & Spiroff, 1974). Samuels's focal attention hypothesis states that for a word to be learned it must be the focus of the reader's attention. Anything that distracts attention from the word, such as pictorial aids or strong sentence context, will interfere with learning the word. It seems reasonable to assume that a teacher adopting Samuels's hypothesis would teach new vocabulary in isolation. Goodman (1969) argues that syntactic and semantic cues provided by the context are vital sources of information in reading. The reader is said to sample the visual information available, combine this with the contextual information and his/her intuitive knowledge of how language is composed and make tentative hypotheses as to the meaning of the text. Further reading involves the testing of these hypotheses and the formation of new ones. Forcing the reader to rely on visual cues alone makes his/her task more difficult. A teacher adopting Goodman's hypothesis might reasonably assume that new vocabulary should be introduced in a meaningful context (Goodman, 1971).

Investigations into acquisition and retention of new words under varying conditions of presentation are plentiful. Prominent in the literature are Samuels's two studies (1966, 1974) comparing word and picture methods with beginning readers which led him to accept his focal attention hypothesis: that any stimuli other than the target word disrupts the learning of the word and "less capable students (are) more distracted by the stimuli than the more capable students" (Samuels, 1967, p. 341).

Controversial studies by Montare, Elman, and Cohen (1977), Dollinger and Walker (1978), and Arlin, Scott, and Webster (1978–1979), led these investigators to reach conclusions that contradict Samuels's position. However, since 1978–1979 Arlin et al. have failed to replicate their original findings and reported support for the focal attention hypothesis.

Introducing oral context to the issue, Hartley (1970) concluded that different presentation methods are suitable for different list types; word-oral context was most successful with maximal contrast words and word-alone was most successful with minimal contrast words. Singer, Samuels, and Spiroff (1974) found that Grade 1 students learned words printed in an artificial alphabet more readily when presented in isolation than when presented with a picture cue or in a sentence printed in standard orthography with or without a picture cue. Wood (1976) reported that Grade 1 subjects in a sentence-context group learned eight new words in significantly fewer trials than subjects taught by a word-alone or a word-picture method. No significant differences were found on word-picture or story-context tests of retention but a teach-test bias was revealed in that both the isolated-word group and the sentence-context group performed significantly better in the condition that matched their instructional mode.

Ehri and Roberts (1979) found that context-trained subjects remembered more about the syntactic/semantic qualities of printed words, whereas isolation-trained subjects remembered more about the orthographic identities of words. Ehri and Wilce (1980) reported these same results with first-grade students learning function words. However, their subjects had previous knowledge of the reading process in that only 6 of the 40 subjects recognized none of the target words on the pretest; both groups were given access to target word meaning; and post-testing time varied for the subjects.

Several studies, however, support the conclusion that even young readers do use context to aid in word identification. Samuels (1966) found that Grade 1 students were significantly better at a word recognition task when the word presented was expected than when an unexpected word was shown. Pearson and Studt (1975) reported that, for both high and low frequency words, fewer letter clues were needed by first-grade and third-grade children as the sentence context increased in richness. Juel (1979) reported that, regardless of ability, all subjects in the second and third grades utilized context; however, more skilled readers relied on context only where internal word cues were minimal (low frequency, hard to decode words).

The key issues in this controversy are the use of an isolated word list as an indicator of reading ability, and the nature of the relationship between reading words in isolation and reading connected text. Studies by Shankweiler and Liberman (1972), and Perfetti and Hogaboam (1975) support the view that there is a strong relationship between identifying words on isolated lists and reading performance in contextual conditions. Dahl (1975–1976) recommends that, by beginning with word training in isolation and advancing towards sentence processing, improvements can be made in reading connected text. Research by Oaken, Wiener, and Cromer (1971), and Fleisher and Jenkins (1977) reveals that training in reading isolated words had no significant effect upon success in contextual reading. However, Blanchard (1980) found that training poor sixth-grade readers in single-word decoding of vocabulary to be encountered in context had a beneficial effect on their subsequent comprehension. Goodman (1965) and Levitt (1970) suggest that words are more successfully identified when encountered in the flow of meaningful written discourse; word recognition scores were significantly higher on story context tests than on isolated word tests. Analyses of errors made by young children reading orally led Clay (1968, 1969) and Weber (1970a, 1970b) to conclude that beginning readers make heavy use of syntactic and semantic information.

The purpose of this study was to try to disentangle some of the controversy about the effect of teaching the initial acquisition of written words in isolation and in context. This work differed from previous studies in several ways: (a) subjects who recognized one or more of the target words on the preliminary screening test were excluded, thereby eliminating those subjects who had already synthesized some knowledge of the reading process; (b) written contexts are used rather than oral contexts; (c) all subjects were tested in both isolated and context conditions in order to minimize the effects of teach/test bias; (d) transfer of word recognition from one condition to a different contextual condition was tested by presenting target words, underlined, in new sentence context, and by a designation task whereby target words were embedded in new contexts and subjects indicated words they recognized; (e) long-term retention testing was extended to 3 weeks. Thus, in the present research study, there were nine dependent measures, as illustrated in the following diagram.

ACQUISITION	TRIALS TO CRITERION			
Short-term retention	isolation test	sentence test	new context test	word designation test
Long-term retention	isolation test	sentence test	new context test	word designaation test

Method

Subjects

The subjects were 115 kindergarten children in six kindergarten classrooms selected from schools in middleclass areas of a Greater Vancouver school district, British Columbia, Canada. Prior to the experiment, all subjects were randomly assigned to one of the two treatment groups, word-alone (WA) or word-sentence (WS), or to a control group. Forty-three subjects were eliminated because of illness, holidays, transfer, little understanding of English, or recognition of one or more of the target words during the preliminary screening. The remaining 72 children were distributed equally among the three experimental groups, resulting in 24 subjects per treatment.

Materials

Eight target words were chosen. They were: television, Our, fixing, tooth, fell, out, Nicki's, needs. These words were formed into two sentences that commented upon events of interest to children:

Nicki's tooth fell out.
Our television needs fixing.

All words except "Nicki's" and "television" appear on the Grade 1 list in Rinsland's basic vocabulary scale (Rinsland, 1947). It was our conjecture that "Nicki" was a reasonably common name among the children in the population samples and that "television" was in their aural vocabulary.

Procedure

Each subject met individually with the senior author on three separate occasions in a room available for the experiment.

Occasion 1: *The treatment: Step 1—Preliminary screening.* Each target word was presented on a white 5" × 8" (12.70 × 20.32 cm) index card in large type. The subject was given 7 seconds to respond. If he/she did not recognize any of the words, the treatment was administered. Twenty-eight children were eliminated because they recognized one or more target words. A control group participated in this initial step.

Step 2—Training trials. Treatment 1 was the Word Alone (WA) treatment. The target words had been previously arranged into two sets; Set A contained the words "needs," "tooth," "fell," "Our," and Set B contained the words "out," "television," "Nicki's," and "fixing." The words were typed in large print on white 2½" × 5" (6.35 × 12.70 cm) index cards. Each set of word cards was laid out in a column in the first randomly predetermined non-meaningful order. The words in Set B were covered, leaving exposed only the four words in Set A. The examiner pointed to each word and said its name. Then, separating the first word in the scheduled order by placing it in front of the subject, the examiner said, "This word is _____. What is this word?" The word was then returned to its position in the column. This procedure was repeated for each of the other words in Set A. Then the examiner covered the words and followed the same procedure for the words in Set B. This cycle was repeated for a total of three training trials, with a different non-meaningful word order for each trial. Each time, four words were visible to the subject but each word in turn was isolated from the others in the group.

Treatment 2 was the Word Sentence (WS) treatment. The eight target words used in the WA treatment were used in the WS treatment. However, they were arranged in two meaningful sentences: "Nicki's tooth fell out." (Sentence A) and "Our television needs fixing." (Sentence B). Each sentence was typed in large print on 5" × 8" (12.70 × 20.32 cm) index cards. Covering Sentence B card and placing Sentence A card in front of the subject, the researcher read the sentence while pointing to the words. The researcher then pointed to the first word in the sentence, covered it with a small piece of colored transparent acetate, and said, "This word is _____. What is this word?" This procedure was repeated for the other words in the sentence. Then, covering Sentence A, the same procedure was followed with the words in Sentence B. The researcher repeated the cycle for a total of three trials. Each time, four words were visible but each word in turn was indicated with a piece of colored acetate.

Step 3—Teach/test trials. Following the three trials, each target word was tested in the random order specified by the predetermined list. For both treatment groups, the same procedure was followed. The examiner covered the words in Set B, and pointing to the first word listed for Trial #1, said "What is this word?" Subjects were given 7 seconds to respond. If a correct response was given, the examiner repeated it. If an incorrect response or no response was given, the examiner supplied the correct response for the subject, who repeated it. This was continued until all four words in Set A were tested. The examiner then read all four words in the order in which they were arranged, before repeating the testing procedure with the words in Set B. When a target word had been correctly identified on two consecutive teach/test trials, the subject was considered to have achieved criterion for that target word. The teach test cycle was continued, excluding that specific word from the testing procedure.

No target words were tested consecutively; when only one word was left to be learned an intervening task was used. This task involved the subject reading his/her own name. Teach/testing continued until each target word had been correctly identified twice on consecutive trials at some point in the session. If 20 teach/test trials had been administered and criterion had not been reached, that target word was designated "unmastered" and the subject was allowed to stop. Thus a range of 16 to 160 trials to criterion for the eight target words was possible.

Throughout this session, four words were visible to the subject at all times; however, as each target word was tested in the word-alone treatment, it was separated from the others and presented in an isolated condition or, in the word-sentence treatment, it was indicated by a small piece of colored transparent acetate.

Occasion 2: *Short-term retention.* Twenty-four hours after the treatment, each subject was individually tested using the following procedures:

1. *Test of Word Recognition in Treatment Condition.* Four cards with Sentence A and four with Sentence B were alternated with the eight isolated target words. The subject was shown one card at a time. If the target word was in isolation he/she was asked, "What is this word?" If it was a sentence card, the researcher pointed to the underlined target word and asked the subject, "What is this word?" No target word was tested on two successive trials. Each response was recorded. This test yielded two scores for separate analysis: word recognition in isolation and word recognition in treatment sentences.

2. *Test of Word Recognition in New Context.* The eight target words were embedded in eight new sentences (see Appendix). As each sentence was presented, the researcher pointed to the underlined target word and said, "What is this word?"

3. *Test of Word Designation in New Context.* Four sentences, each containing two target words, were placed one at a time in front of the child. The examiner asked, "Are there any words here that you know?" The student was asked to point to the word (if he/she knew any) and read it aloud. After each response the question was repeated until the subject replied, "No." This procedure was included to counteract the possible assumption that each sentence contained only one target word; on previous tests, only one word per sentence had been tested. At no time was verbal feedback given on correctness of the subjects' responses.

Occasion 3: *Long-term retention.* The researcher returned 3 weeks after the treatments. The procedure used for short-term retention was followed. The preliminary screening test was re-administered to the control group.

Results

Table 1 gives the means and standard deviations for the number of trials required to learn the eight words, and for the number of words retained on the

<table>
<tr><td rowspan="3">TABLE 1</td><td colspan="5">SUMMARY OF PERFORMANCE OF EXPERIMENTAL GROUPS ON THE DEPENDENT VARIABLES OF TRIALS TO CRITERION AND RETENTION OF TARGET WORDS</td></tr>
</table>

DEPENDENT VARIABLE	WORD-ALONE GROUP $n = 24$		WORD-SENTENCE GROUP $n = 24$	
	M	*SD*	*M*	*SD*
Total Trials to Criterion	56.50	25.22	26.42	10.23
Total Retention Score (24 hours)	11.33	7.64	15.33	7.12
Isolation test	2.96	1.83	3.00	1.82
Sentence test	2.88	1.99	6.42	1.86
New Context test	3.04	2.16	3.00	2.25
Word Designation test	2.46	2.17	2.92	2.28
Total Retention Score (3 weeks)	10.29	8.34	15.96	7.83
Isolation test	2.46	2.04	3.21	2.17
Sentence test	2.33	2.12	6.13	2.38
New Context test	2.88	2.29	3.46	2.04
Word Designation test	2.63	2.16	3.17	2.16

short-term and long-term retention tests. The control group ($n = 24$) did not learn any of the words over the 3-week period, and was excluded from further analysis.

Acquisition of Target Words

A two-way analysis of variance (Treatment × Sex) computed on the total trials to criterion indicated a statistically significant difference between the two treatment methods, $F(1,44) = 29.27$, $p < .001$. The word sentence group learned the eight target words in significantly fewer trials. All subjects in the WS group reached criterion with all target words whereas six subjects in the WA group did not reach criterion on at least one word. There were no significant Sex or Treatment by Sex effects.

Retention

A three-way analysis of variance (Test × Treatment × Sex) with repeated measures across all levels of the test factor was computed on the short-term retention data. Although the main effect of treatment was not significant, $F(1,44) = 3.33$, $.05 < p < .075$, there was a significant difference among the tests, $F(3,132) = 34.46$, $p < .0001$, and a significant interaction between tests and treatment, $F(3,132) = 32.42$, $p < .0001$. Tukey HSD comparisons showed that the mean score on the words-in-treatment-sentence test was significantly different ($p < .01$) from the means of each of the other three retention tests. This difference was caused by the high scores of the WS treatment group on the words-in-treatment-sentence test (see Table 1). No other pairs of tests were significantly different. A repeated measures analysis of variance conducted on long-term retention data indicated a significant main effect of treatment, $F(1, 44) = 5.66$, $p < .05$, a significant difference among the tests, $F(3, 132) = 22.87$, $p < .0001$ and a significant interaction between tests and treatment, $F(3, 132) = 34.79$, $p < .0001$. Tukey HSD comparisons revealed that, once again only the mean score on the words-in-treatment-sentences test was significantly different ($p < .01$) from the means of each of the other three retention tests and that this difference was due to the WS group's high score on the words-in-treatment-sentences test (see Table 1).

An analysis of variance on the gain (loss) scores between the 24-hour and 3-week testing periods showed no significant difference between treatment groups for total retention. All analyses conducted on retention data revealed no significant sex or treatment by sex effects.

Discussion

In this study children who were taught words in sentences learned them with significantly fewer trials than children who were taught the same words in isolation. These results are at variance with those of Singer, Samuels, and Spiroff (1974). Possible explanation for the discrepancy may center around differences in the orthography employed, the semantic richness of the training sentences, or the strength of syntactic and semantic links formed among the target words, or the fact that in this study each word in the sentence condition had to be learned whereas in the Singer et al. study only one word per sentence had to be learned.

In the present study, the ease with which the WS subjects acquired the words gives support to the theoretical formulations of Goodman (1965) and provides experimental support for the observational data of Clay (1968, 1969) and Weber (1970a, 1970b).

When the children were tested in a sentence condition the word-sentence group did significantly better than the word-alone group. At face value this finding could be taken to mean that the word-sentence group had learned the words to greater degree than the word-alone group. However, our findings on the other tests contradict this interpretation.

It should be noted that when the two groups were tested with words in isolation they were not significantly different in their performance. It seems reasonable to conclude that the word-sentence group learned what it was taught significantly better than the word-alone group and learned what the word-alone group was taught about as well as that group.

The lack of significant difference between the two treatments on new context and word designation tasks suggest, at first glance, that the treatments were equally effective. Recall, however, that the word-sentence group learned what they knew in significantly fewer trials than the word-alone group. Thus while equal in their ability to transfer acquired knowledge to new situations, the word-sentence group acquired this ability much more economically.

The results of tests of long-term retention given 3-weeks after initial instruction exhibit the same pattern of results as the tests of short-term retention, indicating a reasonably durable effect.

The small amount of forgetting by all subjects in the 3-week period between the initial instruction and the long-term retention tests is surprising. Some retention may be an artifact of the experimental situation. The senior author, who conducted the teaching and testing interviews, was a stranger to the children. The visit to the testing room represented a break from normal classroom routines. It may well be that these extraneous aspects contributed to the memorability of the material.

In interpreting the findings from this study it is important to note the extremely carefully controlled equivalence of instruction. Both groups of children were exposed to exactly the same material in exactly the same manner. The amount of visual information confronting the children at any one time was precisely the same in quantity and content. The type of verbal reinforcement for right or wrong responses was held constant. The single difference in the training procedures was that for the word-sentence group the words were arranged into meaningful sentences, whereas for the word-alone group they were presented in meaningless strings.

In order to pinpoint processing strategies responsible for observed differences, we looked, informally, at the kinds of errors made by each group on the test/training trials.

The WA group confused words with the same initial letter more frequently than the WS group suggesting that they were paying closer attention to the visual aspects of the test. The WS group tended to make positional and semantically linked errors suggesting that they were attending to the structure and meaning of the sentence in which target words occurred.

The results, while providing some support for the contextual position, should be viewed within the limitations of the study. It is possible to interpret the results by a simple chunking hypothesis: the word-alone group was given eight items to learn and the word-sentence group only two. However, contextualists might justifiably say that that is their point. Human beings seem quite capable of processing at least simple sentences as units. The greater degree of meaningfulness in sentences as compared with words renders the task of learning to read easier to accomplish.

Our research paradigm was not a strong test, for example, of the language-experience position since the language used was generated by adults. It would be useful to compose, for example, adult versus child generated contexts for word-learning. Replication needs to be done with larger groups, different word lists and varying populations before definitive conclusions are drawn. However, the results do suggest, at the very least, that context renders word learning both efficient and durable, as long as key words are tested in context.

References

Arlin, M., Scott, M., & Webster, J. (1978–1979). Effects of pictures on rate of learning sight words: A critique of the focal attention hypothesis. *Reading Research Quarterly, 4,* 645–660.

Blanchard, J. S. (1980). Preliminary investigation of transfer between single-word decoding ability and contextual reading comprehension by poor readers in grade six. *Perceptual and Motor Skills, 51,* 1,271–1,281.

Clay, M. M. (1968). A syntactic analysis of reading errors. *Journal of Verbal Learning and Verbal Behavior, 7,* 434–438.

Clay, M. M. (1969). Reading errors and self-correction behavior. *British Journal and Educational Psychology, 39,* 47–56.

Dahl, P. R. (1975–1976). Mastery-based experimental program for teaching high speed word recognition skills. *Reading Research Quarterly, 11,* 203–211.

Dollinger, R. A., & Walker, D. N. (1978). The effect of three methods of presentation and socio-economic class on recognition performance in presentation of low-frequency words to kindergarteners. *Journal of Reading Behavior, 10,* 303–307.

Ehri, L., & Roberts, K. T. (1979). Do beginners learn printed words better in context or in isolation? *Child Development, 50,* 675–685.

Ehri, L. C., & Wilce, L. (1980). Do beginners learn to read function words better in sentences or in lists? *Reading Research Quarterly, 15* (4), 451–476.

Fleisher, L. S., & Jenkins, J. R. (1977). *Effects of contextualized and decontextualized practice conditions on word recognition.* (Technical Report No. 54). Cambridge, MA. (ERIC Document Reproduction Service No. ED 144 043).

Goodman, K. (1965). A linguistic study of cues and miscues in reading. *Elementary English, 42,* 639–643.

Goodman, K. (1969). Analysis of oral reading miscues: Applied psycholinguistics. *Reading Research Quarterly, 5,* 9–30.

Goodman, K. (1971). Decoding—from code to what? *Journal of Reading, 14,* 455–462, 498.

Hartley, R. N. (1970). Effects of list types and cues on learning word lists. *Reading Research Quarterly, 6,* 97–121.

Juel, C. (1979). *Comparison of word identification strategies with varying context, word type, and reader skill.* Paper presented at the Annual Meeting of the American Educational Research Association, San Francisco, California. (ERIC Document Reproduction Service No. ED 169 494).

Levitt, E. (1970). The effect of context on the reading of mentally retarded and normal children at the first grade level. *Journal of Special Education, 4,* 425–429.

Montare, A., Elman, E., & Cohen, J. (1977). Words and pictures: A test of Samuels's findings. *Journal of Reading Behavior, 9,* 269–285.

Oaken, R., Wiener, M., & Cromer, W. (1971). Identification, organization, and reading comprehension for good and poor readers. *Journal of Educational Psychology, 62,* 71–78.

Pearson, P. D., & Studt, A. (1975). Effects of word frequency and contextual richness on children's word identification abilities. *Journal of Educational Psychology, 67,* 89–95.

Perfetti, C. A., & Hogaboam, T. (1975). Relationship between the single-word decoding and reading comprehension skill. *Journal of Educational Psychology, 67,* 461–469.

Rinsland, H. D. (1947). *A basic vocabulary of elementary school children.* New York: Macmillan.

Samuels, S. J. (1966). Effect of experimentally learned word associations on the acquisition of reading responses. *Journal of Educational Psychology, 57,* 159–163.

Samuels, S. J. (1967). Attentional processes in reading: The effect of pictures on the acquisition of reading responses. *Journal of Educational Psychology, 58,* 337–342.

Shankweiler, D., & Liberman, I. (1972). Misreading: A search for causes. In J. F. Kavanagh & I. G. Mattingly (Eds.). *Language by ear and by eye* (pp. 293–317). Cambridge, MA: MIT Press.

Singer, H., Samuels, S. J., & Spiroff, J. (1974). Effects of pictures and contextual conditions on learning responses to printed words. *Reading Research Quarterly, 9,* 555–567.

Weber, R. (1970a). A linguistic analysis of first grade reading errors. *Reading Research Quarterly, 5,* 427–451.

Weber, R. (1970b). First graders' use of grammatical context in reading. In H. Levin & J. Williams (Eds.). *Basic studies in reading* (pp. 147–163). New York: Basic Books.

Wood, M. (1976). *Multivariate analysis of beginning readers' recognition of taught words in four contextual settings.* Unpublished doctoral dissertation, Texas Women's University.

Appendix: Sentences for Retention Tests

NEW CONTEXT SENTENCES

1. Can you come <u>out</u> and play?
2. This is <u>Nicki's</u> bike.
3. I am watching <u>television</u>.
4. The book is <u>Our</u> Family.
5. I <u>fell</u> off the swing.
6. He <u>needs</u> some more paint.
7. Mom is <u>fixing</u> my sweater.
8. I lost a <u>tooth</u> today.

WORD DESIGNATION SENTENCES

1. My tooth needs pulling.
2. Our lights went out.
3. Dad's fixing the television.
4. Nicki's thermos fell over.

Reprinted from *Reading Research Quarterly,* 1984, Summer 1984, XIX: 452–460, by permission of the authors and publisher.

SAMPLE STUDY IV

Effects of Computer-Assisted Mathematics Instruction on Disadvantaged Pupils' Cognitive and Affective Development

ZEMIRA R. MEVARECH AND YISRAEL RICH
Bar Ilan University, Ramat Gan, Israel

Schofield (1981) demonstrated a degree of incompatibility in simultaneously maximizing pupils' cognitive and affective outcomes in elementary school mathematics. In contrast, computer-assisted instruction (CAI) incorporates elements that should facilitate accomplishing both goals. This study was conducted to investigate the impact of CAI on the mathematical achievement and self-concept as well as the perception of the quality of school life among disadvantaged boys and girls in third, fourth, and fifth grades ($N = 376$). Results indicated that in a combined CAI-traditional program, as opposed to only traditional instruction, students consistently scored higher on both cognitive and affective measures while grade level and gender were generally nonsignificant. Differences between this study and previous research are discussed as well as the differential influence of CAI and traditional instruction on disadvantaged pupils.

SCHOFIELD (1981) reported research findings demonstrating an inverse relationship between mathematics achievement and pupil attitudes toward mathematics. This evidence was interpreted as "consistent with the contention that there is a degree of incompatibility in maximizing both cognitive and affective outcomes in children (Bennett, 1976; Good, Biddle, & Brophy, 1975) at least in the grades 4–6 level in the area of mathematics" (p. 470). The explanation suggested for this lack of compatibility was based on the assumption that the attainment of high pupil achievement requires "adherence to a well-organized curriculum and the exertion of pressure on children to apply themselves continually during class periods to tasks leading to content mastery; it does not entail commensurate concern for the pupil's enjoyment of classroom activities and intrinsic interest in learning or for the pupil's feelings of self esteem and emotional adjustment" (Schofield, 1981, p. 462).

Positive pupil outcomes in the cognitive and affective domains do seem quite incompatible when considering teacher-centered, whole-class instruction in classrooms with 30 or more disadvantaged children. It is probably a particularly unlikely contingency for elementary school subjects such as mathematics, which demand frequent drill and practice to achieve mastery. It seems that most teachers are simply incapable of exerting pressure on children to master content and, at the same time, demonstrating genuine active concern for their personal development and attitudes toward school-related activities. Thus, for many teachers employing standard instructional techniques in mathematics, the assertion regarding the incompatibility of furthering pupils' cognitive and affective development is definitely relevant.

It is possible, however, that this incompatibility results from classroom conditions arising from the teacher-centered, whole-class method of instruction and is not necessarily characteristic of classrooms where other instructional methods are employed. This argument receives indirect support from research on cooperative small-group instruction (e.g., Johnson, Maruyama, Johnson, Nelson, & Skon, 1981; Slavin, 1980). Findings from this body of research indicate that when pupils study cooperatively in heterogeneous small groups for several hours per week, their cognitive and affective development is frequently enhanced. Although we cannot be certain at this stage of research on cooperative small groups, it is possible that the interdependence among pupils in the small group generated by a cooperative task or reward structure serves as a powerful motivational stimulus within the group. Thus, the pupils themselves become the primary source for exerting pressure on one another to attain high levels of achievement (Slavin, 1978) while the teacher is freed from virtually exclusive concern with academic progress and is able to invest concurrent efforts in the enhancement of pupils' affective outcomes.

Computer-assisted instruction (CAI) is another instructional practice that seems to hold promise for the simultaneous enhancement of disadvantaged pupils' cognitive and affective development. The most basic usage of computers in mathematics instruction is in the area of drill and practice as a supplement to the regular curriculum. Characteristics of CAI, such as a curriculum specially tailored to the individual pupil's level and rate of achievement, immediacy and accuracy of feedback-correctives, and multisensory modes of informational input and output, create more positive conditions for drill and practice than is possible in the typical classroom. Several educational psychologists (e.g., Bloom, 1976) have argued that these characteristics are particularly relevant to the academic success of low-achieving children. The sense of success and progress engendered by these characteristics of CAI should foster pupils' willingness to invest efforts to master the subject matter. Furthermore, teachers may be partially freed from the perceived need to exert constant pressure on the pupil to master content since interaction with the computer should provide the pupil with the necessary drill and practice to achieve mastery. The reduction in perceived need to exert academic pressure on pupils may allow teachers to invest greater efforts in classroom processes which foster enhanced affective development of pupils.

Recent studies demonstrated the efficacy of CAI for the mathematics achievement of elementary (Burns & Bozeman, 1981), secondary (Kulik, Bangert, Williams, 1983), and college students (Kulik, Kulik, & Cohen, 1980), and another report claims that CAI benefits the children of disadvantaged migrant workers (Saracho, 1982). However, research on CAI effects for pupils' affective development has been more limited in scope focusing almost exclusively on attitudinal measures of components of schooling directly related to CAI (e.g.,

Kulik et al., 1983). Broader measures of CAI effects for pupils' affective development have not been carefully examined.

This study was initiated to determine whether CAI as a supplement to traditional mathematics instruction (hereafter referred to as CATI) fosters gains for disadvantaged elementary school pupils in the affective as well as academic domains. Pupil gender was included as an independent variable to provide further empirical data on differences between boys and girls in schooling outcomes related to mathematics and CATI. In addition to mathematics achievement, we investigated CATI effects on pupils' mathematical self-concept and perceptions of school life, two important measures of children's affective development directly related to schooling but not narrowly focused on the computer. These variables are also parallel to those mentioned by Schofield (1981) as being somewhat incompatible with meaningful growth in mathematics achievement.

Following Shavelson and Bolus (1982), self-concept was conceptualized as a relatively stable multi-faceted construct comprising descriptive and evaluative dimensions of a person's self-perceptions. Subject-matter of facets of self-concept, such as mathematical self-concept, were viewed as distinct but correlated with one another and with academic and general self-concept as well as with academic achievement. Since CATI emphasizes components considered critical for the positive development of academic self-concept including successful learning experiences and positive feedback (see Bloom, 1976; Wylie, 1979), it was predicted that CAI as a supplement to traditional mathematics instruction would enhance pupils' mathematical self-concept.

We also predicted that use of CATI would improve pupils' perceptions of school life. Since Jackson's (1968) seminal work on this topic, several researchers demonstrated relationships between pupils' affective reactions to school and a host of pupil variables in the affective and cognitive domains, such as school anxiety (Epstein & McPartland, 1976), student self-concept (Darom & Rich, 1981), and report card grades (Epstein & McPartland, 1976). CAI should foster students' positive perceptions of school because the individualized program enables pupils to make clear academic progress and achieve positive feedback without the harmful social comparison characteristic of traditional classrooms that threatens the pupil's feelings of security and status (Pepitone, 1964). Again, this aspect of CAI should be especially beneficial to the disadvantaged, low-achieving child who is particularly vulnerable in this area.

Method

Subjects

Participants were 376 elementary school students. Intact classes of pupils drawn from three schools in different Israeli development towns served as subjects in the CATI treatment. Each school was represented by one third, one fourth, and one fifth grade (third grade $N = 67$; fourth grade $N = 66$; fifth grade

N = 65). In each of these schools, CATI was practiced for at least three years and was implemented beginning in second grade. A comparable group of children (third grade *N* = 67; fourth grade *N* = 52; fifth grade *N* = 59), similarly drawn from three schools in three development towns, were exposed to traditional mathematics instruction only. In one relatively large development town, one school was assigned to the CATI condition, while another school served in the contrast group.

Because reliable pretreatment test data were unavailable, considerable efforts were made to equate the CATI and traditional instruction groups on a series of relevant variables. Schools in both conditions were from similar development towns and were categorized by the Israeli Ministry of Education as disadvantaged based on the low achievement level of the pupils. In each instructional group, approximately 80% of the children's families were of Middle Eastern origin and the remainder were of Western origin. Boys constituted 53% of the CATI sample and 55% of the contrast group. All mathematics teachers were fully certified and had at least 5 years of teaching experience.

Dependent Measures

Three instruments were employed to assess educational outcomes: a national Arithmetic Achievement Test (Israeli Ministry of Education, 1977), the Mathematical Self-Concept questionnaire developed specially for this study, and the Quality of School Life scale (Epstein & McPartland, 1976). All instruments were administered in the spring term.

Arithmetic Achievement Test (AAT)

This test was developed by the Israeli Ministry of Education to assess the achievement of elementary school pupils in basic mathematical operations, concept comprehension, and application. Based on data gathered in this study, the reliability of the AAT calculated by the Kuder-Richardson (21) formula was .93 in third grade, .81 in fourth grade, and .87 in fifth grade.

Mathematical Self-Concept (MSC) Questionnaire

A 21-item questionnaire was developed to assess pupils' self-concept of mathematical achievement, ability, and affect. These dimensions were chosen because in previous research (Aiken, 1976; Sandman, 1980) they were demonstrated as particularly important aspects of mathematical self-concept. A relatively indirect technique less susceptible to faking desirable responses than direct measures was employed to tap attitudes toward self. Each item described a hypothetical child's attitude towards mathematics or behavior in a math classroom. The student responded to the item on a 3-point Likert scale by noting the respondent's similarity to the hypothetical child. For example,

Q. He/She is proud of his/her grades in math.
    a. I am very proud of my grades in math.
    b. I am similar to him/her.
    c. I'm not so proud of my grades in math.

Several earlier studies of self-concept in Israel have successfully utilized this method (Eshel & Klein, 1981; Glantz, 1978; Minkovich, Davis, & Bashi, 1977).

Pupils' MSC scores were factor analyzed to examine the construct validity of the measure. Five common factors were extracted accounting for 50% of the variance. These factors were subjected to a varimax rotation resulting in five independent factors: two regarding self-concept of mathematics achievement, two related to affective aspects of self and mathematics, and one factor reflecting self-concept of ability in mathematics. Based upon content considerations, the two achievement factors were combined as were the two affective factors resulting in 18 MSC items and 3 factors: achievement (9 items), affect (5 items), and ability (4 items). The coefficient alpha score for the MSC scale was .83.

Quality of School Life (QSL) Scale

Epstein and McPartland (1976) developed this 27-item scale as a measure of pupils' perceptions of three dimensions of school life—satisfaction with school, commitment to schoolwork, and attitudes towards teachers. After translation and adaptation to the Israeli classroom, the three-factor structure was generally confirmed (Darom & Rich, 1981). Previous research on the QSL demonstrated respectable levels of reliability and validity (see Darom & Rich, 1981; Epstein & McPartland, 1976). For this sample the alpha internal consistency score was .84.

Procedure

Pupils in the contrast group received four class periods of traditional mathematics instruction weekly, while the CATI group was taught three periods weekly by means of traditional instruction and one class period (two 20-minute sessions) with a CAI package called TOAM. Developed in 1977 by the Centre for Educational Technology in Israel, TOAM is the Hebrew acronym for "computer-assisted testing and practice." Instead of the standard CRT terminal, a 10-inch black-and-white video monitor with a minimal keyboard (20 keys) was employed (for more details see Osin, 1981).

The first 12 lessons (10 minutes each) of the year for the CATI group were devoted to the computer-based diagnosis of pupils' achievement on 14 mathematical skill areas. Thereafter, each pupil was exposed to an individualized curriculum with the aid of the computer, which generated problems for drill and practice in each of the 14 skill areas including horizontal and vertical operations with whole numbers, equations, measures and weights, fractions and decimals, negative numbers, and word problems. In addition to feedback-correctives for each task, all children regularly received information regarding their progress relative to the expected level of achievement. For example, a child who successfully solved problems at level 4/5 knew that he or she had developed competency in a particular skill area expected of a pupil halfway through fifth grade. Teachers were similarly provided with period reports of each child's progress in the various skill areas.

Results

Three factors were included in this study: instruction (CATI or traditional), grade level (third, fourth, or fifth), and pupil gender. The arithmetic achievement data were subjected to a three-way univariate ANOVA, while multiple analysis of variance followed by separate univariate ANOVAs were employed with the MSC and QSL scales, respectively.

Means and standard deviations of the AAT results expressed in z scores are presented in Table 1, and ANOVA F values appear in Table 2. A significant difference was found between the CATI and traditional instruction groups. At all three grades, CATI pupils scored higher on arithmetic achievement than did pupils receiving traditional instruction only. An instruction by grade interaction indicates that this difference was particularly large in fourth grade where CATI pupils reached an achievement level approximately one standard deviation higher than traditional instruction children. The achievement of boys and girls did not significantly differ nor were there any other significant interaction effects.

Means and standard deviations of the MSC scores appear in Table 3, while MANOVA and univariate ANOVA F values are summarized in Table 4. These analyses demonstrate that CATI pupils rated themselves significantly higher than

TABLE 1   **MEANS AND STANDARD DEVIATIONS (IN z SCORES) OF AAT SCORES FOR INSTRUCTIONAL METHOD AND GENDER AT THIRD, FOURTH AND FIFTH GRADES**

		CATI		TRADITIONAL	
		BOYS	GIRLS	BOYS	GIRLS
Third grade	$\overline{X}$	0.24	−0.21	−0.12	0.03
	SD	0.89	1.34	0.90	0.89
Fourth grade	$\overline{X}$	0.54	0.43	−0.39	−0.92
	SD	0.70	0.82	1.01	0.80
Fifth grade	$\overline{X}$	−0.04	0.16	−0.03	−0.16
	SD	0.67	0.91	1.25	1.05

ANALYSIS OF VARIANCE OF AAT SCORES FOR INSTRUCTIONAL METHOD AND GENDER AT THIRD, FOURTH AND FIFTH GRADES

TABLE 2

SOURCE	df	MS	F
Instruction	1	18.561	<20.475[a]
Grade	2	0.177	<1.0
Sex	1	1.941	<2.141
Instruction × grade	2	10.680	<11.782[a]
Instruction × sex	1	0.056	<1.0
Grade × sex	2	0.898	<1.0
Instruction × sex × grade	2	2.517	<2.775

[a]$p < .0001$.

MEANS AND STANDARD DEVIATIONS OF MSC SCORES FOR INSTRUCTIONAL METHOD AND GENDER AT GRADES THREE, FOUR AND FIVE

TABLE 3

			3RD GRADE		4TH GRADE		5TH GRADE	
			BOYS	GIRLS	BOYS	GIRLS	BOYS	GIRLS
CATI	Achievement	$\overline{X}$	2.00	2.22	2.19	2.06	2.07	2.00
		SD	0.44	0.34	0.54	0.53	0.41	0.43
	Affect	$\overline{X}$	2.56	2.73	2.52	2.50	2.59	2.56
		SD	0.44	0.41	0.41	0.39	0.38	0.39
	Ability	$\overline{X}$	2.55	2.57	2.66	2.54	2.67	2.54
		SD	0.41	0.31	0.39	0.45	0.35	0.46
Traditional	Achievement	$\overline{X}$	1.99	2.05	2.17	2.07	1.80	1.77
		SD	0.54	0.66	0.58	0.53	0.45	0.42
	Affect	$\overline{X}$	2.22	2.44	2.45	2.58	2.22	2.38
		SD	0.62	0.53	0.48	0.43	0.48	0.55
	Ability	$\overline{X}$	2.30	2.41	2.46	2.56	2.42	2.35
		SD	0.46	0.37	0.43	0.47	0.44	0.42

Note: Range = 1–3: The higher the score, the more positive is the respondent's MSC.

TABLE 4

SUMMARY OF MULTIVARIATE AND UNIVARIATE Fs OF MSC SCORES AND GENDER AT THIRD, FOURTH, AND FIFTH GRADES

SOURCE	df	MULTIVARIATE F	UNIVARIATE Fs ACHIEVEMENT	AFFECT	ABILITY
Instruction	1	<6.54[c]	<4.9[a]	<18.0[c]	<8.0[c]
Grade	2	<2.60[a]	<6.1[c]	<1.0	<1.9
Sex	1	<1.82	<1.0	<4.3[a]	<1.0
Instruction × grade	2	<1.93	<1.9	<4.1[b]	<1.0
Instruction × sex	1	<1.03	<1.0	<1.8	<1.0
Grade × sex	2	<1.04	<2.2	<1.0	<1.3
Instruction × grade × sex	2	<1.0	<1.0	<1.0	<1.0

[a] $p < .05$; [b] $p < .01$; [c] $p < .001$.

traditional instruction pupils on self-concept of arithmetic achievement, ability, and liking of mathematics. Examination of the cells relevant to the multivariate main effect for grade on the MSC achievement scale indicates that fourth graders rated themselves highest on MSC while fifth graders had the lowest MSC scores, especially in the traditional instruction group. The remaining multivariate F's were not significant.

Table 5 presents the means and standard deviations of the QSL scores, while MANOVA and univariate ANOVA F values appear in Table 6. Pupils exposed to CATI in mathematics expressed significantly more positive evaluations of their schooling experience than did traditional instruction pupils on all three school life scales. Also, in contrast to most earlier research (e.g., Darom & Rich, 1981), fifth graders were more satisfied with school than were younger pupils. Other multivariate analyses for gender and interaction effects proved insignificant.

Discussion

Results from this study supported the general hypothesis that computer-assisted mathematics instruction positively affects the cognitive and affective development of disadvantaged elementary school pupils. At all three grade levels (third, fourth, fifth), pupils in the CATI condition reported more positive perceptions of school life and scored higher on mathematics achievement than did

MEANS AND STANDARD DEVIATIONS OF QSL SCORES FOR INSTRUCTIONAL METHOD AND GENDER AT THIRD, FOURTH, AND FIFTH GRADE

TABLE 5

			3RD GRADE		4TH GRADE		5TH GRADE	
			BOYS	GIRLS	BOYS	GIRLS	BOYS	GIRLS
CATI	SAT	$\overline{X}$	1.62	1.71	1.64	1.68	1.74	1.69
		SD	0.18	0.17	0.23	0.28	0.19	0.22
	COM	$\overline{X}$	2.16	2.31	2.20	2.28	2.24	2.22
		SD	0.18	0.17	0.23	0.28	0.19	0.22
	TCH	$\overline{X}$	4.00	4.17	3.98	4.13	4.05	4.14
		SD	0.52	0.37	0.61	0.47	0.49	0.24
Traditional	SAT	$\overline{X}$	1.55	1.57	1.49	1.56	1.59	1.72
		SD	0.24	0.23	0.26	0.27	0.19	0.22
	COM	$\overline{X}$	2.14	2.06	2.10	2.07	1.99	2.12
		SD	0.32	0.29	0.34	0.43	0.30	0.20
	TCH	$\overline{X}$	3.83	3.79	3.64	3.69	3.79	3.86
		SD	0.64	0.62	0.65	0.73	0.52	0.54

Note: SAT = satisfaction with school; COM = commitment to schoolwork; TCH = relations with teachers.

TABLE 6

SUMMARY TABLE OF *F* VALUES OF QSL SCORES FOR INSTRUCTIONAL METHOD AND GENDER AT THIRD, FOURTH, AND FIFTH GRADES

			UNIVARIATE *F*s		
SOURCE	df	MULTIVARIATE *F*	SAT	COM	TCH
Instruction	1	$<11.97^c$	$<16.9^c$	$<28.2^c$	$<28.6^b$
Grade	2	$<3.61^b$	$<5.9^b$	<1.0	<1.1
Sex	1	<1.48	$<4.38^a$	<2.0	<1.9
Instruction × grade	2	<1.0	<1.0	<1.0	<1.0
Instruction × sex	1	<1.64	<1.0	<1.4	<1.0
Grade × sex	2	<1.0	<1.0	<1.0	<1.0
Instruction × grade × sex	2	<2.1	<2.2	<4.3	<1.0

Note: SAT = satisfaction with school; COM = commitment to school work; TCH = relations with teachers.
[a]$p < .05$; [b]$p < .01$; [c]$p < .001$.

their peers in the traditional instruction classes. Furthermore, the mathematical self-concept of children exposed to CATI was higher than that of pupils receiving traditional instruction in the third and fifth grades. In light of the ongoing controversy on gender differences for mathematics achievement (e.g., Benbow & Stanley, 1980; Pallas & Alexander, 1983), it is of particular interest to note the lack of significant differences between boys and girls on virtually all analyses suggesting that approximately equal levels of arithmetic achievement, mathematical self-concept, and attitudes toward school prevailed for both boys and girls.

These results reaffirm previous research (see Kulik et al., 1983) reporting positive effects of CAI on mathematics achievement. They are also congruent with the hypothesis posited earlier that the reported incompatibility of simultaneously maximizing cognitive and affective development (e.g., Schofield, 1981) may well be a function of the teacher-centered, whole-class method of instruction and is not an inherent characteristic of mathematics instruction. Since this study did not focus on process variables, it is impossible to know which specific components of CATI were critical to pupil gains in mathematics achievement and self-concept as well as perceptions of school life. However, it is clear that the computer facilitates uniquely positive conditions for drill and practice for disadvantaged children. Accordingly, teachers are enabled to alter their usual instructional practices with the whole class and may behave in ways more conducive to improved affective pupil growth. Future studies on CAI may be especially productive if researchers pay attention to teacher-pupil interactions during traditional instruction hours as well as focusing on computer-pupil interactions.

Three characteristics of this study allow us to further generalize the previously reported effects of CAI on pupil outcomes in mathematics achievement. First, subjects in this sample—low-achieving, disadvantaged children in Israeli schools—differ in many ways from subjects in much reported research on CAI. Second, CATI and traditional instruction pupils in this study were exposed to an equal number of mathematics instruction hours weekly, while in much of earlier research (e.g., Saracho, 1982) CAI pupils received more instructional hours than did their non-CAI peers. Despite this equality of input, CATI pupils demonstrated greater academic proficiency and more positive affective growth. Third, CAI in these schools was not a recent innovation thereby eliminating the possibility of a Hawthorne Effect. Pupils were exposed to CAI for at least two years, while teachers implemented CAI for at least three years prior to this study.

However, one aspect of this study leads us to view the results with caution. All analyses were conducted on posttreatment data only because reliable achievement or ability scores were not available from the period prior to the use of CAI. One could argue that the positive results of the CATI pupils were a function of their initial higher level on the dependent variables. This seems to be a spurious contention because both groups were comparable on a series of socioeconomic and educational indicators including overall level of achievement, class composition, teacher qualifications, and community characteristics. Thus, the possibility of significantly different initial levels of mathematics achievement, self-concept, and perceptions of school life seems a less likely explanation for the results than the positive impact of CATI. Nevertheless, it would be advisable in future research to control for pretreatment levels of the dependent variables while assuring that the Hawthorne Effect is not operating and equal hours of instruction are provided for the traditional and CAI groups.

Results from this study lend considerable support to the assertion that CAI provides significant mathematics achievement gains for disadvantaged pupils. Furthermore, it has been demonstrated that the computer does not serve to alienate children from the school but leads disadvantaged pupils to improved perceptions of self and schooling. We concur with Saracho (1982) that CAI is not a panacea for the educational problems of disadvantaged populations, however its potency as an instructional tool for the disadvantaged should not be minimized.

References

Aiken, L. R. (1976). Update on attitudes and other affective variables in learning mathematics. *Review of Educational Research, 46,* 193–211.

Benbow, C. P., & Stanley, J. C. (1980). Sex differences in mathematical ability: Fact or artifact? *Science, 210,* 1,262–1,264.

Bloom, B. S. (1976). *Human characteristics and school learning.* New York: McGraw-Hill.

Burns, P. K., & Bozeman, W. C. (1981). Computer-assisted instruction in mathematics achievement: Is there a relationship? *Educational Technology, 21,* 32–39.

Darom, E., & Rich, Y. (1981). Development and validation of the Israeli quality of school life scale. In J. L. Epstein (Ed.). *The quality of school life* (pp. 179–195). Lexington, MA: Lexington Books.

Epstein, J. L., & McPartland, J. M. (1976). The concept and measurement of quality of school life. *American Educational Research Journal, 50,* 13–30.

Eschel, Y., & Klein, Z. (1981). Development of academic self-concept of lower-class and middle-class primary school children. *Journal of Educational Psychology, 75,* 287–293.

Glantz, Y. (1978). *"He is so—I am so" self-concept inventory and user's manual.* Ramat Gan, Israel: Bar Ilan University Press (Hebrew).

Israeli Ministry of Education. (1977). *Arithmetic achievement test.* Jerusalem (Hebrew).

Jackson, P. (1968). *Life in classrooms.* New York: Holt.

Johnson, D. W., Maruyama, G., Johnson, R., Nelson, D., & Skon, L. (1981). The effects of cooperative, competitive and individualistic goal structures on achievement: A meta-analysis. *Psychgological Bulletin, 89,* 47–62.

Kulik, J. A., Bangert, R. L., & Williams, D. W. (1983). Effects of computer-based teaching on secondary school students. *Journal of Educational Psychology, 75,* 19–26.

Kulik, J. A., Kulik, C.-L. C., & Cohen, P. A. (1980). Effectiveness of computer-based college teaching: A meta-analysis of findings. *Review of Educational Research, 50,* 525–544.

Minkovich, A., Davis, D., & Bashi, J. (1977). *An evaluation study of Israeli elementary schools.* Jerusalem: Hebrew University.

Osin, L. (1981). Computer-assisted instruction in arithmetic in Israeli disadvantaged elementary schools. In R. Lewis & D. Tagg (Eds.). *Computers in education* (pp. 469–475). Amsterdam: North-Holland Publishing Company, IFIP.

Pallas, A. M., & Alexander, K. L. (1983). Sex differences in quantitative SAT performance: New evidence on the differential coursework hypothesis. *American Educational Research Journal, 20,* 165–182.

Pepitone, A. (1964). *Attraction and hostility.* New York: Atherton Press.

Sandman, R. S. (1980). The mathematics attitude inventory: Instrument and user's manual. *Journal for Research in Mathematics Education, 11,* 148–149.

Saracho, O. N. (1982). The effects of a computer-assisted instruction program on basic skills achievement and attitudes toward instruction of Spanish-speaking migrant children. *American Educational Research Journal, 19,* 201–219.

Schofield, H. L. (1981). Teacher effects on cognitive and affective pupil outcomes in elementary school mathematics. *Journal of Educational Psychology, 75,* 462–471.

Shavelson, R. J., & Bolus, R. (1982). Self-concept: The interplay of theory and methods. *Journal of Educational Psychology, 74,* 3–17.

Slavin, R. E. (1978). Student teams and achievement divisions. *Journal of Research and Development in Education, 12,* 39–49.

Slavin, R. E. (1980). Cooperative learning. *Review of Educational Research, 50,* 315–342.

Wylie, R. C. (1979). *The self concept: Theory and research on selected topics.* Lincoln, NE: University of Nebraska Press.

Reprinted from the *Journal of Educational Research*, 1985, 79: 5–11, by permission of the authors and publisher.

Performance Evaluation Worksheets

Unlike many disciplines, research methodology is not a collection of facts to be understood and remembered. Rather, it represents a set of skills that are applied to a large variety of situations. The art of research is to use these skills to solve researchable problems. Mastery of these skills requires opportunities for active engagement in both critical evaluations of completed research and the design of new studies. To facilitate this process, the performance evaluation worksheets in this appendix provide materials that require active responses and offer prompt feedback.

Note a distinction between the analytical aspect of research methodology (analysis and evaluation of research already completed) and the design aspect (construction of a new research study). The performance evaluation worksheets focus on the first aspect as a prerequisite for the second. Appendix A contains four sample research studies; boxed text in each chapter discusses elements of the first two, while the last two (Sample Studies III and IV) offer opportunities for student analysis and criticism that address concepts ranging across the categories of design considerations.

The performance evaluation worksheets cover the aspects of research discussed in the chapters. Remember, however, that analysis cannot identify any one set of correct answers to a research problem. Appendix D gives one set of appropriate answers for each sample study to provide feedback about the student's own analysis and hence facilitate inductive learning—that is, learning by doing.[1]

The process of analyzing and critiquing a research study has been broken down into 11 steps, and a worksheet in this appendix corresponds to each step:

Worksheet A: Problem statement
Worksheet B: Supportive literature
Worksheet C: Hypotheses
Worksheet D: Variables
Worksheet E: Operational definitions
Worksheet F: Manipulation and control
Worksheet G: Research design

---

[1]Instructors may wish to supply additional feedback for the case studies in order to increase the range of viewpoints with which students become acquainted and perhaps even to provoke critiques of the given answers. Instructors may also wish to assign additional sample studies for their students to analyze and critique using the worksheets. Students can then compare their answers to one another or to a set prepared by the instructor.

Worksheet H: Observation and measurement of independent and dependent variables

Worksheet I: Observation and measurement of moderator and control variables

Worksheet J: Statistical analysis

Worksheet K: Presentation and discussion of results

Each worksheet asks you to carry out both an analysis and a critique. The analysis requires a description of a particular feature of the research report, primarily to increase your skill in identifying, labeling, and writing about each element of the research process. The critique requires that you rate the components or elements of a study on a five-point scale, described below. This informed, judgmental process helps you to evaluate the quality of a piece of research. Where you assign low ratings (3 or lower), you should offer a specific criticism and/or a specific suggestion for improvement as a way to sharpen your skills of critical evaluation.

The five-point rating scale is in the form 5 4 3 2 1 NA. To apply it to a sample research study, you should judge the article's merit on the criterion under consideration, according to these standards:

5   *Outstanding:* The element or aspect is as good or as clear as possible; it could not be improved.

4   *Good:* The element or aspect is certainly well done but leaves a little room for improvement.

3   *Adequate:* The element or aspect is marginal but acceptable, leaving clear room for improvement.

2   *Substandard:* The element or aspect fails to meet the standard of clarity for acceptability; it leaves much room for improvement.

1   *Inadequate:* The element or aspect is unacceptable and would require considerable revision to reach minimum acceptability.

NA   *Not applicable:* The criterion cannot be applied, either because it is irrelevant or because the study does not incorporate the appropriate element or aspect.

Learning is often an inductive process; people often learn by trying things out and learning from mistakes. However, this process requires feedback or knowledge of results. For this reason, Appendix D provides a detailed set of "answers" or suggested responses for each question as applied to Sample Studies III and IV. After you have completed each worksheet twice, once for each sample study (III and IV), check your answers against those provided in Appendix D.

Worksheet A
Problem Statement

1. Cite the **problem statement** as stated in study.

Does it appear on the first page?[2]　　　　　　　Yes (5)　No (1)

2. Rewrite the **problem statement** in your own words.

Was the authors' version clear enough to make this task an easy one?

5　4　3　2　1　NA

(continued)

---

[2]In evaluating typed manuscripts (in contrast to printed ones), the placement of the problem statement is acceptable if it appears somewhere within the first *two* pages. (Score 3 points for second page.)

3. Evaluate the **problem** in terms of Criteria a through e. Give both a verbal description, particularly of shortcomings, and a numerical rating.

   a. Workability   5   4   3   2   1   NA

   b. Critical mass   5   4   3   2   1   NA

   c. Interest[3]

   d. Theoretical value   5   4   3   2   1   NA

   e. Practical value   5   4   3   2   1   NA

[3]Not rated because interest reflects personal values.

WORKSHEET B
Supportive Literature

1. What, in a sentence, is the **context** of the problem?

Is the context clear and sufficiently established?   5 4 3 2 1 NA

---

2. a. What is the magnitude of the **literature** review?   5 4 3 2 1 NA

---

   b. How empirical and up-to-date is it?   5 4 3 2 1 NA

---

   c. Does it bear on the problem(s) of the study?   5 4 3 2 1 NA

---

   d. Is it well-organized (introduction, subheadings, summary)?
                                            5 4 3 2 1 NA

---

   e. Try to summarize it in a sentence or two.

(continued)

3. a. Do the researchers attempt to establish **significance** of the study
    using argument and/or supportive literature?   Yes (5)   No (1)

---

b. Is the attempt convincing?   5   4   3   2   1   NA

---

c. Summarize it in a sentence or two.

---

d. Suggest a point of significance that might be added.

WORKSHEET C
Hypotheses

1. Were **hypotheses** cited in the study?   Yes (5)   No (1)
   If yes, cite them. If no, construct one that might have been offered.

2. Rewrite any **hypotheses** in your own words.

Was the authors' version clear enough to make this task an easy one?

                           5   4   3   2   1   NA

(continued)

3. For each **hypothesis** answer these questions:

a. Is it directional (5), positive (4), null (3), or absent (1)?[4]

b. Is it supported by clear and understandable logic? (If you rated 3 or lower, indicate how you think it might have been improved.)

5 4 3 2 1 NA

c. Is it consistent with the problem statement?
(If you rated 3 or lower, indicate specific inconsistencies.)

5 4 3 2 1 NA

d. Is it supported by sufficient literature or arguments?
(If 3 or lower, offer specific criticism.)

5 4 3 2 1 NA

---

[4]A directional hypothesis calls for differences and specifies their direction; a positive hypothesis calls for differences but does not specify their direction; a null hypothesis calls for no differences.

WORKSHEET D
Variables

1. What is (are) the **independent variable(s)?**

2. What is (are) the **moderator variable(s),** if any?

3. What is (are) the **dependent variable(s)?**

(continued)

4. What are the important **control variables?**

5. What are two possible **intervening variables?**

6. Did the study omit any important variables that it might have included? If so, list them and label them by type.

WORKSHEET E
Operational Definitions

1. How did the researchers operationalize each of the study's **independent variables?**[5]

Does each operational definition (OD) seem sufficiently operational and exclusive? (If you rate 3 or lower, give specific criticisms.)

 5   4   3   2   1   NA

2. How did the researchers operationalize each of the **moderator variables,** if any?

Does each OD seem sufficiently operational and exclusive? (If you rate 3 or lower, give specific criticisms.)

 5   4   3   2   1   NA

(continued)

[5]Where operational definitions are lacking, try to write them yourself based on the methods described.

3. How did the researchers operationalize each of the **dependent variables**?

Does each OD seem sufficiently operational and exclusive? (If you rate 3 or lower, give specific criticisms.)

5   4   3   2   1   NA

4. How did the researchers operationalize each of the important **control variables**?

Does each OD seem sufficiently operational and exclusive? (If you rate 3 or lower, give specific criticisms.)

5   4   3   2   1   NA

WORKSHEET F
Manipulation and Control

1. Internal validity (certainty):
   a. How did the researchers control for **participant bias?** Cite specific precautions. What sources were uncontrolled?

   How **certain** are the study's results?   5 4 3 2 1 NA

   b. How did the researchers control for **experience bias?** Cite specific procedures. What sources were uncontrolled?

   How **certain** are the results?   5 4 3 2 1 NA

2. External validity (generality):
   a. What participant **selection** procedures limit the study's generality? Cite specific procedures.

   How **generalizable** are the results?   5 4 3 2 1 NA

   b. What **experience** procedures limited the study's generality? Cite specific procedures.

   How **generalizable** are the results?   5 4 3 2 1 NA

3. For each independent or moderator variable manipulated by the researchers:
   a. Describe briefly how the variable was manipulated.

   b. How successful was the manipulation?   5 4 3 2 1 NA

WORKSHEET G

Research Design

1. a. Diagram the study's **design** and give its name.

   b. Was the design a true experimental one (4), or was it quasi-experimental (3), ex post facto (2), or a nondesign (1)? Was it a factorial design? If yes, add 1 point.

2. Consider a (or an additional) moderator variable that might have been added to the design. Name that variable, and draw the revised design, with that variable added.

3. How else could the design be improved?

4. Describe the population to which the study's results can be generalized.

WORKSHEET H

Observation and Measurement of Independent and Dependent Variables

1. For each **independent variable** answer each of the following questions:
   a. Was it measured?

   b. If so, describe briefly how the researchers accomplished this measurement.

   c. How suitable (or valid and reliable) was the measurement, on the basis of both face validity and documentation?   5   4   3   2   1   NA

   (If you rated 3 or lower, make a suggestion for improvement.)

2. For each **dependent variable** answer each of the following questions:
   a. Describe briefly how it was measured.

   b. How valid and reliable was its measurement as documented?
                                                                  5   4   3   2   1   NA

   (If 3 or lower, give specific suggestions for improvement.)

WORKSHEET I

Observation and Measurement of Moderator and Control Variables

1. For each **moderator variable** answer each of these questions:
   a. Was it measured? (If the research included no moderator variable, write *none* and omit this section.)

   b. Describe briefly how the study accomplished this measurement.

   c. How suitable (or valid and reliable) was the measurement, on the basis of validity and documentation?   5 4 3 2 1 NA

   (If you rated 3 or lower, make a suggestion for improvement.)

2. For each of the major **control variables** (up to three) answer each of these questions:
   a. Was it measured?

   b. Describe briefly how the study accomplished this measurement.

   c. How suitable (or valid and reliable) was the measurement, on the basis of both face validity and documentation? (If you rate 3 or lower, make a suggestion for improvement.)   5 4 3 2 1 NA

WORKSHEET J
Statistical Analysis

1. Did the study apply **statistical tests** to collected data?   Yes   No
   If yes, name them.

2. Did the researchers conduct the proper **statistical tests** or the most suitable
   ones for the design?   5   4   3   2   1   NA
   (If you rate 3 or lower, suggest another.)

3. Did the research report clearly describe the applications of these tests, and
   were they correctly completed?   5   4   3   2   1   NA
   (If you rate 3 or lower, describe the source of confusion.)

4. Should the researchers have carried out additional **statistical tests** or
   presented additional **statistical results?**   Yes   No
   If yes, name them.

5. Did the research report include a **presentation of statistical results** in graphic
   or tabular form?   Yes   No
   If yes, could it (they) be understood and interpreted?

   5   4   3   2   1   NA

   (If you rate 3 or lower, describe the source of confusion and suggest how the
   problematic aspects might be overcome.)

WORKSHEET K

Presentation and Discussion of Results

1. a. Briefly describe the **findings** of the study.

___

b. Does the article include an adequate and clear **summary** of the authors' findings?   5 4 3 2 1 NA

(If you rate 3 or lower, offer a specific criticism.)

___

c. Does it clearly relate the **findings** to the study's problem and hypotheses?   5 4 3 2 1 NA

(If you rate 3 or lower, offer a criticism.)

___

2. a. Give a brief **interpretation** of the findings to indicate why they came out as they did or what they mean.

___

b. Did the authors offer and support a meaningful and convincing **interpretation** of the study's findings that helped you to understand those results?   5 4 3 2 1 NA

(If you rate 3 or lower, offer a specific criticism or a useful interpretation.)

___

3. a. Briefly state a **conclusion** that could be drawn from the study and a **recommendation** based on that conclusion.

___

b. Did the study's findings support meaningful **conclusions** and **recommendations**, and did the research report offer any?   5 4 3 2 1 NA

(If you rate 3 or lower, offer a suggestion for improvement.)

___

Tables

RANDOM NUMBERS[a]

```
22 17 68 65 84    68 95 23 92 35    87 02 22 57 51    61 09 43 95 06    58 24 82 03 47
19 36 27 59 46    13 79 93 37 55    39 77 32 77 09    85 52 05 30 62    47 83 51 62 74
16 77 23 02 77    09 61 87 25 21    28 06 24 25 93    16 71 13 59 78    23 05 47 47 25
78 43 76 71 61    20 44 90 32 64    97 67 63 99 61    46 38 03 93 22    69 81 21 99 21
03 28 28 26 08    73 37 32 04 05    69 30 16 09 05    88 69 58 28 99    35 07 44 75 47

93 22 53 64 39    07 10 63 76 35    87 03 04 79 88    08 13 13 85 51    55 34 57 72 69
78 76 58 54 74    92 38 70 96 92    52 06 79 79 45    82 63 18 27 44    69 66 92 19 09
23 68 35 26 00    99 53 93 61 28    52 70 05 48 34    56 65 05 61 86    90 92 10 70 80
15 39 25 70 99    93 86 52 77 65    15 33 59 05 28    22 87 26 07 47    86 96 98 29 06
58 71 96 30 24    18 46 23 34 27    85 13 99 24 44    49 18 09 79 49    74 16 32 23 02

57 35 27 33 72    24 53 63 94 09    41 10 76 47 91    44 04 95 49 66    39 60 04 59 81
48 50 86 54 48    22 06 34 72 52    82 21 15 65 20    33 29 94 71 11    15 91 29 12 03
61 96 48 95 03    07 16 39 33 66    98 56 10 56 79    77 21 30 27 12    90 49 22 23 62
36 93 89 41 26    29 70 83 63 51    99 74 20 52 36    87 09 41 15 09    98 60 16 03 03
18 87 00 42 31    57 90 12 02 07    23 47 37 17 31    54 08 01 88 63    39 41 88 92 10

88 56 53 27 59    33 35 72 67 47    77 34 55 45 70    08 18 27 38 90    16 95 86 70 75
09 72 95 84 29    49 41 31 06 70    42 38 06 45 18    64 84 73 31 65    52 53 37 97 15
12 96 88 17 31    65 19 69 02 83    60 75 86 90 68    24 64 19 35 51    56 61 87 39 12
85 94 57 24 16    92 09 84 38 76    22 00 27 69 85    29 81 94 78 70    21 94 47 90 12
38 64 43 59 98    98 77 87 68 07    91 51 67 62 44    40 98 05 93 78    23 32 65 41 18

53 44 09 42 72    00 41 86 79 79    68 47 22 00 20    35 55 31 51 51    00 83 63 22 55
40 76 66 26 84    57 99 99 90 37    36 63 32 08 58    37 40 13 68 97    87 64 81 07 83
02 17 79 18 05    12 59 52 57 02    22 07 90 47 03    28 14 11 30 79    20 69 22 40 98
95 17 82 06 53    31 51 10 96 46    92 06 88 07 77    56 11 50 81 69    40 23 72 51 39
35 76 22 42 92    96 11 83 44 80    34 68 35 48 77    33 42 40 90 60    73 96 53 97 86

26 29 13 56 41    85 47 04 66 08    34 72 57 59 13    82 43 80 46 15    38 26 61 70 04
77 80 20 75 82    72 82 32 99 90    63 95 73 76 63    89 73 44 99 05    48 67 26 43 18
46 40 66 44 52    91 36 74 43 53    30 82 13 54 00    78 45 63 98 35    55 03 36 67 68
37 56 08 18 09    77 53 84 46 47    31 91 18 95 58    24 16 74 11 53    44 10 13 85 57
61 65 61 68 66    37 27 47 39 19    84 83 70 07 48    53 21 40 06 71    95 06 79 88 54

93 43 69 64 07    34 18 04 52 35    56 27 09 24 86    61 85 53 83 45    19 90 70 99 00
21 96 60 12 99    11 20 99 45 18    48 13 93 55 34    18 37 79 49 90    65 97 38 20 46
95 20 47 97 97    27 37 83 28 71    00 06 41 41 74    45 89 09 39 84    51 67 11 52 49
97 86 21 78 73    10 65 81 92 59    58 76 17 14 97    04 76 62 16 17    17 95 70 45 80
69 92 06 34 13    59 71 74 17 32    27 55 10 24 19    23 71 82 13 74    63 52 52 01 41

04 31 17 21 56    33 73 99 19 87    26 72 39 27 67    53 77 57 68 93    60 61 97 22 61
61 06 98 03 91    87 14 77 43 96    43 00 65 98 50    45 60 33 01 07    98 99 46 50 47
85 93 85 86 88    72 87 08 62 40    16 06 10 89 20    23 21 34 74 97    76 38 03 29 63
21 74 32 47 45    73 96 07 94 52    09 65 90 77 47    25 76 16 19 33    53 05 70 53 30
15 69 53 82 80    79 96 23 53 10    65 39 07 16 29    45 33 02 43 70    02 87 40 41 45

02 89 08 04 49    20 21 14 68 86    87 63 93 95 17    11 29 01 95 80    35 14 97 35 33
87 18 15 89 79    85 43 01 72 73    08 61 74 51 69    89 74 39 82 15    94 51 33 41 67
98 83 71 94 22    59 97 50 99 52    08 52 85 08 40    87 80 61 65 31    91 51 80 32 44
10 08 58 21 66    72 68 49 29 31    89 85 84 46 06    59 73 19 85 23    65 09 29 75 63
47 90 56 10 08    88 02 84 27 83    42 29 72 23 19    66 56 45 65 79    20 71 53 20 25

22 85 61 68 90    49 64 92 85 44    16 40 12 89 88    50 14 49 81 06    01 82 77 45 12
67 80 43 79 33    12 83 11 41 16    25 58 19 68 70    77 02 54 00 52    53 43 37 15 26
27 62 50 96 72    79 44 61 40 15    14 53 40 65 39    27 31 58 50 28    11 39 03 34 25
33 78 80 87 15    38 30 06 38 21    14 47 47 07 26    54 96 87 53 32    40 36 40 96 76
13 13 92 66 99    47 24 49 57 74    32 25 43 62 17    10 97 11 69 84    99 63 22 32 98
```

(continued)

10 27 53 96 23	71 50 54 36 23	54 31 04 82 98	04 14 12 15 09	26 78 25 47 47
28 41 50 61 88	64 85 27 20 18	83 36 36 05 56	39 71 65 09 62	94 76 62 11 89
34 21 42 57 02	59 19 18 97 48	80 30 03 30 98	05 24 67 70 07	84 97 50 87 46
61 81 77 23 23	82 82 11 54 08	53 28 70 58 96	44 07 39 55 43	42 34 43 39 28
61 15 18 13 54	16 86 20 26 88	90 74 80 55 09	14 53 90 51 17	52 01 63 01 59
91 76 21 64 64	44 91 13 32 97	75 31 62 66 54	84 80 32 75 77	56 08 25 70 29
00 97 79 08 06	37 30 28 59 85	53 56 68 53 40	01 74 39 59 73	30 19 99 85 48
36 46 18 34 94	75 20 80 27 77	78 91 69 16 00	08 43 18 73 68	67 69 61 34 25
88 98 99 60 50	65 95 79 42 94	93 62 40 89 96	43 56 47 71 66	46 76 29 67 02
04 37 59 87 21	05 02 03 24 17	47 97 81 56 51	92 34 86 01 82	55 51 33 12 91
63 62 06 34 41	94 21 78 55 09	72 76 45 16 94	29 95 81 83 83	79 88 01 97 30
78 47 23 53 90	34 41 92 45 71	09 23 70 70 07	12 38 92 79 43	14 85 11 47 23
87 68 62 15 43	53 14 36 59 25	54 47 33 70 15	59 24 48 40 35	50 03 42 99 36
47 60 92 10 77	88 59 53 11 52	66 25 69 07 04	48 68 64 71 06	61 65 70 22 12
56 88 87 59 41	65 28 04 67 53	95 79 88 37 31	50 41 06 94 76	81 83 17 16 33
02 57 45 86 67	73 43 07 34 48	44 26 87 93 29	77 09 61 67 84	06 69 44 77 75
31 54 14 13 17	48 62 11 90 60	68 12 93 64 28	46 24 79 16 76	14 60 25 51 01
28 50 16 43 36	28 97 85 58 99	67 22 52 76 23	24 70 36 54 54	59 28 61 71 96
63 29 62 66 50	02 63 45 52 38	67 63 47 54 75	83 24 78 43 20	92 63 13 47 48
45 65 58 26 51	76 96 59 38 72	86 57 45 71 46	44 67 76 14 55	44 88 01 62 12
39 65 36 63 70	77 45 85 50 51	74 13 39 35 22	30 53 36 02 95	49 34 88 73 61
73 71 98 16 04	29 18 94 51 23	76 51 94 84 86	79 93 96 38 63	08 58 25 58 94
72 20 56 20 11	72 65 71 08 86	79 57 95 13 91	97 48 72 66 48	09 71 17 24 89
75 17 26 99 76	89 37 20 70 01	77 31 61 95 46	26 97 05 73 51	53 33 18 72 87
37 48 60 82 29	81 30 15 39 14	48 38 75 93 29	06 87 37 78 48	45 56 00 84 47
68 08 02 80 72	83 71 46 30 49	89 17 95 88 29	02 39 56 03 46	97 74 06 56 17
14 23 98 61 67	70 52 85 01 50	01 84 02 78 43	10 62 98 19 41	18 83 99 47 99
49 08 96 21 44	25 27 99 41 28	07 41 08 34 66	19 42 74 39 91	41 96 53 78 72
78 37 06 08 43	63 61 62 42 29	39 68 95 10 96	09 24 23 00 62	56 12 80 73 16
37 21 34 17 68	68 96 83 23 56	32 84 60 15 31	44 73 67 34 77	91 15 79 74 58
14 29 09 34 04	87 83 07 55 07	76 58 30 83 64	87 29 25 58 84	86 50 60 00 25
58 43 28 06 36	49 52 83 51 14	47 56 91 29 34	05 87 31 06 95	12 45 57 09 09
10 43 67 29 70	80 62 80 03 42	10 80 21 38 84	90 56 35 03 09	43 12 74 49 14
44 38 88 39 54	86 97 37 44 22	00 95 01 31 76	17 16 29 56 63	38 78 94 49 81
90 69 59 19 51	85 39 52 85 13	07 28 37 07 61	11 16 36 27 03	78 86 72 04 95
41 47 10 25 62	97 05 31 03 61	20 26 36 31 62	68 69 86 95 44	84 95 48 46 45
91 94 14 63 19	75 89 11 47 11	31 56 34 19 09	79 57 92 36 59	14 93 87 81 40
80 06 54 18 66	09 18 94 06 19	98 40 07 17 81	22 45 44 84 11	24 62 20 42 31
67 72 77 63 48	84 08 31 55 58	24 33 45 77 58	80 45 67 93 82	75 70 16 08 24
59 40 24 13 27	79 26 88 86 30	01 31 60 10 39	53 58 47 70 93	85 81 56 39 38
05 90 35 89 95	01 61 16 96 94	50 78 13 69 36	37 68 53 37 31	71 26 35 03 71
44 43 80 69 98	46 68 05 14 82	90 78 50 05 62	77 79 13 57 44	59 60 10 39 66
61 81 31 96 82	00 57 25 60 59	46 72 60 18 77	55 66 12 62 11	08 99 55 64 57
42 88 07 10 05	24 98 65 63 21	47 21 61 88 32	27 80 30 21 60	10 92 35 36 12
77 94 30 05 39	28 10 99 00 27	12 73 73 99 12	49 99 57 94 82	96 88 57 17 91
78 83 19 76 16	94 11 68 84 26	23 54 20 86 85	23 86 66 99 07	36 37 34 92 09
87 76 59 61 81	43 63 64 61 61	65 76 36 95 90	18 48 27 45 68	27 23 65 30 72
91 43 05 96 47	55 78 99 95 24	37 55 85 78 78	01 48 41 19 10	35 19 54 07 73
84 97 77 72 73	09 62 06 65 72	87 12 49 03 60	41 15 20 76 27	50 47 02 29 16
87 41 60 76 83	44 88 96 07 80	83 05 83 38 96	73 70 66 81 90	30 56 10 48 59

TABLE II

[a]Table II is abridged from Table III of Fisher, Statistical Methods for Research Workers, published by Oliver and Boyd, Ltd., Edinburgh, and by permission of the author and the publisher.

CRITICAL VALUES OF t[a]

df	Level of significance for one-tailed test					
	.10	.05	.025	.01	.005	.0005
	Level of significance for two-tailed test					
	.20	.10	.05	.02	.01	.001
1	3.078	6.314	12.706	31.821	63.657	636.619
2	1.886	2.920	4.303	6.965	9.925	31.598
3	1.638	2.353	3.182	4.541	5.841	12.941
4	1.533	2.132	2.776	3.747	4.604	8.610
5	1.476	2.015	2.571	3.365	4.032	6.859
6	1.440	1.943	2.447	3.143	3.707	5.959
7	1.415	1.895	2.365	2.998	3.499	5.405
8	1.397	1.860	2.306	2.896	3.355	5.041
9	1.383	1.833	2.262	2.821	3.250	4.781
10	1.372	1.812	2.228	2.764	3.169	4.587
11	1.363	1.796	2.201	2.718	3.106	4.437
12	1.356	1.782	2.179	2.681	3.055	4.318
13	1.350	1.771	2.160	2.650	3.012	4.221
14	1.345	1.761	2.145	2.624	2.977	4.140
15	1.341	1.753	2.131	2.602	2.947	4.073
16	1.337	1.746	2.120	2.583	2.921	4.015
17	1.333	1.740	2.110	2.567	2.898	3.965
18	1.330	1.734	2.101	2.552	2.878	3.922
19	1.328	1.729	2.093	2.539	2.861	3.883
20	1.325	1.725	2.086	2.528	2.845	3.850
21	1.323	1.721	2.080	2.518	2.831	3.819
22	1.321	1.717	2.074	2.508	2.819	3.792
23	1.319	1.714	2.069	2.500	2.807	3.767
24	1.318	1.711	2.064	2.492	2.797	3.745
25	1.316	1.708	2.060	2.485	2.787	3.725
26	1.315	1.706	2.056	2.479	2.779	3.707
27	1.314	1.703	2.052	2.473	2.771	3.690
28	1.313	1.701	2.048	2.467	2.763	3.674
29	1.311	1.699	2.045	2.462	2.756	3.659
30	1.310	1.697	2.042	2.457	2.750	3.646
40	1.303	1.684	2.021	2.423	2.704	3.551
60	1.296	1.671	2.000	2.390	2.660	3.460
120	1.289	1.658	1.980	2.358	2.617	3.373
∞	1.282	1.645	1.960	2.326	2.576	3.291

CRITICAL VALUES OF THE PEARSON PRODUCT MOMENT CORRELATION COEFFICIENT[a]

TABLE III

[a]Table III is taken from Table VII of Fisher, Statistical Methods for Research Workers, published by Oliver and Boyd, Ltd., Edinburgh, and by permission of the author and the publisher.

	Level of significance for one-tailed test				
	.05	.025	.01	.005	.0005
	Level of significance for two-tailed test				
$df = N-2$	.10	.05	.02	.01	.001
1	.9877	.9969	.9995	.9999	1.0000
2	.9000	.9500	.9800	.9900	.9990
3	.8054	.8783	.9343	.9587	.9912
4	.7293	.8114	.8822	.9172	.9741
5	.6694	.7545	.8329	.8745	.9507
6	.6215	.7067	.7887	.8343	.9249
7	.5822	.6664	.7498	.7977	.8982
8	.5494	.6319	.7155	.7646	.8721
9	.5214	.6021	.6851	.7348	.8471
10	.4973	.5760	.6581	.7079	.8233
11	.4762	.5529	.6339	.6835	.8010
12	.4575	.5324	.6120	.6614	.7800
13	.4409	.5139	.5923	.6411	.7603
14	.4259	.4973	.5742	.6226	.7420
15	.4124	.4821	.5577	.6055	.7246
16	.4000	.4683	.5425	.5897	.7084
17	.3887	.4555	.5285	.5751	.6932
18	.3783	.4438	.5155	.5614	.6787
19	.3687	.4329	.5034	.5487	.6652
20	.3598	.4227	.4921	.5368	.6524
25	.3233	.3809	.4451	.4869	.5974
30	.2960	.3494	.4093	.4487	.5541
35	.2746	.3246	.3810	.4182	.5189
40	.2573	.3044	.3578	.3932	.4896
45	.2428	.2875	.3384	.3721	.4648
50	.2306	.2732	.3218	.3541	.4433
60	.2108	.2500	.2948	.3248	.4078
70	.1954	.2319	.2737	.3017	.3799
80	.1829	.2172	.2565	.2830	.3568
90	.1726	.2050	.2422	.2673	.3375
100	.1638	.1946	.2301	.2540	.3211

TABLE IV

CRITICAL VALUES OF F[a]

[a]Reprinted by permission from *Statistical Method* by George W. Snedecor and William G. Cochran, sixth edition © 1967 by Iowa State University Press, Ames, Iowa.

n_1 degrees of freedom (for greater mean square)

Each cell shows the 5% value (top) and 1% value (bottom).

n_2	1	2	3	4	5	6	7	8	9	10	11	12	14	16	20	24	30	40	50	75	100	200	500	∞
1	161 / 4,052	200 / 4,999	216 / 5,403	225 / 5,625	230 / 5,764	234 / 5,859	237 / 5,928	239 / 5,981	241 / 6,022	242 / 6,056	243 / 6,082	244 / 6,106	245 / 6,142	246 / 6,169	248 / 6,208	249 / 6,234	250 / 6,258	251 / 6,286	252 / 6,302	253 / 6,323	253 / 6,334	254 / 6,352	254 / 6,361	254 / 6,366
2	18.51 / 98.49	19.00 / 99.00	19.16 / 99.17	19.25 / 99.25	19.30 / 99.30	19.33 / 99.33	19.36 / 99.34	19.37 / 99.36	19.38 / 99.38	19.39 / 99.40	19.40 / 99.41	19.41 / 99.42	19.42 / 99.43	19.43 / 99.44	19.44 / 99.45	19.45 / 99.46	19.46 / 99.47	19.47 / 99.48	19.47 / 99.48	19.48 / 99.49	19.49 / 99.49	19.49 / 99.49	19.50 / 99.50	19.50 / 99.50
3	10.13 / 34.12	9.55 / 30.82	9.28 / 29.46	9.12 / 28.71	9.01 / 28.24	8.94 / 27.91	8.88 / 27.67	8.84 / 27.49	8.81 / 27.34	8.78 / 27.23	8.76 / 27.13	8.74 / 27.05	8.71 / 26.92	8.69 / 26.83	8.66 / 26.69	8.64 / 26.60	8.62 / 26.50	8.60 / 26.41	8.58 / 26.35	8.57 / 26.27	8.56 / 26.23	8.54 / 26.18	8.54 / 26.14	8.53 / 26.12
4	7.71 / 21.20	6.94 / 18.00	6.59 / 16.69	6.39 / 15.98	6.26 / 15.52	6.16 / 15.21	6.09 / 14.98	6.04 / 14.80	6.00 / 14.66	5.96 / 14.54	5.93 / 14.45	5.91 / 14.37	5.87 / 14.24	5.84 / 14.15	5.80 / 14.02	5.77 / 13.93	5.74 / 13.83	5.71 / 13.74	5.70 / 13.69	5.68 / 13.61	5.66 / 13.57	5.65 / 13.52	5.64 / 13.48	5.63 / 13.46
5	6.61 / 16.26	5.79 / 13.27	5.41 / 12.06	5.19 / 11.39	5.05 / 10.97	4.95 / 10.67	4.88 / 10.45	4.82 / 10.27	4.78 / 10.15	4.74 / 10.05	4.70 / 9.96	4.68 / 9.89	4.64 / 9.77	4.60 / 9.68	4.56 / 9.55	4.53 / 9.47	4.50 / 9.38	4.46 / 9.29	4.44 / 9.24	4.42 / 9.17	4.40 / 9.13	4.38 / 9.07	4.37 / 9.04	4.36 / 9.02
6	5.99 / 13.74	5.14 / 10.92	4.76 / 9.78	4.53 / 9.15	4.39 / 8.75	4.28 / 8.47	4.21 / 8.26	4.15 / 8.10	4.10 / 7.98	4.06 / 7.87	4.03 / 7.79	4.00 / 7.72	3.96 / 7.60	3.92 / 7.52	3.87 / 7.39	3.84 / 7.31	3.81 / 7.23	3.77 / 7.14	3.75 / 7.09	3.72 / 7.02	3.71 / 6.99	3.69 / 6.94	3.68 / 6.90	3.67 / 6.88
7	5.59 / 12.25	4.74 / 9.55	4.35 / 8.45	4.12 / 7.85	3.97 / 7.46	3.87 / 7.19	3.79 / 7.00	3.73 / 6.84	3.68 / 6.71	3.63 / 6.62	3.60 / 6.54	3.57 / 6.47	3.52 / 6.35	3.49 / 6.27	3.44 / 6.15	3.41 / 6.07	3.38 / 5.98	3.34 / 5.90	3.32 / 5.85	3.29 / 5.78	3.28 / 5.75	3.25 / 5.70	3.24 / 5.67	3.23 / 5.65
8	5.32 / 11.26	4.46 / 8.65	4.07 / 7.59	3.84 / 7.01	3.69 / 6.63	3.58 / 6.37	3.50 / 6.19	3.44 / 6.03	3.39 / 5.91	3.34 / 5.82	3.31 / 5.74	3.28 / 5.67	3.23 / 5.56	3.20 / 5.48	3.15 / 5.36	3.12 / 5.28	3.08 / 5.20	3.05 / 5.11	3.03 / 5.06	3.00 / 5.00	2.98 / 4.96	2.96 / 4.91	2.94 / 4.88	2.93 / 4.86
9	5.12 / 10.56	4.26 / 8.02	3.86 / 6.99	3.63 / 6.42	3.48 / 6.06	3.37 / 5.80	3.29 / 5.62	3.23 / 5.47	3.18 / 5.35	3.13 / 5.26	3.10 / 5.18	3.07 / 5.11	3.02 / 5.00	2.98 / 4.92	2.93 / 4.80	2.90 / 4.73	2.86 / 4.64	2.82 / 4.56	2.80 / 4.51	2.77 / 4.45	2.76 / 4.41	2.73 / 4.36	2.72 / 4.33	2.71 / 4.31
10	4.96 / 10.04	4.10 / 7.56	3.71 / 6.55	3.48 / 5.99	3.33 / 5.64	3.22 / 5.39	3.14 / 5.21	3.07 / 5.06	3.02 / 4.95	2.97 / 4.85	2.94 / 4.78	2.91 / 4.71	2.86 / 4.60	2.82 / 4.52	2.77 / 4.41	2.74 / 4.33	2.70 / 4.25	2.67 / 4.17	2.64 / 4.12	2.61 / 4.05	2.59 / 4.01	2.56 / 3.96	2.55 / 3.93	2.54 / 3.91
11	4.84 / 9.65	3.98 / 7.20	3.59 / 6.22	3.36 / 5.67	3.20 / 5.32	3.09 / 5.07	3.01 / 4.88	2.95 / 4.74	2.90 / 4.63	2.86 / 4.54	2.82 / 4.46	2.79 / 4.40	2.74 / 4.29	2.70 / 4.21	2.65 / 4.10	2.61 / 4.02	2.57 / 3.94	2.53 / 3.86	2.50 / 3.80	2.47 / 3.74	2.45 / 3.70	2.42 / 3.66	2.41 / 3.62	2.40 / 3.60
12	4.75 / 9.33	3.88 / 6.93	3.49 / 5.95	3.26 / 5.41	3.11 / 5.06	3.00 / 4.82	2.92 / 4.65	2.85 / 4.50	2.80 / 4.39	2.76 / 4.30	2.72 / 4.22	2.69 / 4.16	2.64 / 4.05	2.60 / 3.98	2.54 / 3.86	2.50 / 3.78	2.46 / 3.70	2.42 / 3.61	2.40 / 3.56	2.36 / 3.49	2.35 / 3.46	2.32 / 3.41	2.31 / 3.38	2.30 / 3.36
13	4.67 / 9.07	3.80 / 6.70	3.41 / 5.74	3.18 / 5.20	3.02 / 4.86	2.92 / 4.62	2.84 / 4.44	2.77 / 4.30	2.72 / 4.19	2.67 / 4.10	2.63 / 4.02	2.60 / 3.96	2.55 / 3.85	2.51 / 3.78	2.46 / 3.67	2.42 / 3.59	2.38 / 3.51	2.34 / 3.42	2.32 / 3.37	2.28 / 3.30	2.26 / 3.27	2.24 / 3.21	2.22 / 3.18	2.21 / 3.16

n₁ degrees of freedom (for greater mean square)

n_2	1	2	3	4	5	6	7	8	9	10	11	12	14	16	20	24	30	40	50	75	100	200	500	∞
14	4.60 / 8.86	3.74 / 6.51	3.34 / 5.56	3.11 / 5.03	2.96 / 4.69	2.85 / 4.46	2.77 / 4.28	2.70 / 4.14	2.65 / 4.03	2.60 / 3.94	2.56 / 3.86	2.53 / 3.80	2.48 / 3.70	2.44 / 3.62	2.39 / 3.51	2.35 / 3.43	2.31 / 3.34	2.27 / 3.26	2.24 / 3.21	2.21 / 3.14	2.19 / 3.11	2.16 / 3.06	2.14 / 3.02	2.13 / 3.00
15	4.54 / 8.68	3.68 / 6.36	3.29 / 5.42	3.06 / 4.89	2.90 / 4.56	2.79 / 4.32	2.70 / 4.14	2.64 / 4.00	2.59 / 3.89	2.55 / 3.80	2.51 / 3.73	2.48 / 3.67	2.43 / 3.56	2.39 / 3.48	2.33 / 3.36	2.29 / 3.29	2.25 / 3.20	2.21 / 3.12	2.18 / 3.07	2.15 / 3.00	2.12 / 2.97	2.10 / 2.92	2.08 / 2.89	2.07 / 2.87
16	4.49 / 8.53	3.63 / 6.23	3.24 / 5.29	3.01 / 4.77	2.85 / 4.44	2.74 / 4.20	2.66 / 4.03	2.59 / 3.89	2.54 / 3.78	2.49 / 3.69	2.45 / 3.61	2.42 / 3.55	2.37 / 3.45	2.33 / 3.37	2.28 / 3.25	2.24 / 3.18	2.20 / 3.10	2.16 / 3.01	2.13 / 2.96	2.09 / 2.89	2.07 / 2.86	2.04 / 2.80	2.02 / 2.77	2.01 / 2.75
17	4.45 / 8.40	3.59 / 6.11	3.20 / 5.18	2.96 / 4.67	2.81 / 4.34	2.70 / 4.10	2.62 / 3.93	2.55 / 3.79	2.50 / 3.68	2.45 / 3.59	2.41 / 3.52	2.38 / 3.45	2.33 / 3.35	2.29 / 3.27	2.23 / 3.16	2.19 / 3.08	2.15 / 3.00	2.11 / 2.92	2.08 / 2.86	2.04 / 2.79	2.02 / 2.76	1.99 / 2.70	1.97 / 2.67	1.96 / 2.65
18	4.41 / 8.28	3.55 / 6.01	3.16 / 5.09	2.93 / 4.58	2.77 / 4.25	2.66 / 4.01	2.58 / 3.85	2.51 / 3.71	2.46 / 3.60	2.41 / 3.51	2.37 / 3.44	2.34 / 3.37	2.29 / 3.27	2.25 / 3.19	2.19 / 3.07	2.15 / 3.00	2.11 / 2.91	2.07 / 2.83	2.04 / 2.78	2.00 / 2.71	1.98 / 2.68	1.95 / 2.62	1.93 / 2.59	1.92 / 2.57
19	4.38 / 8.18	3.52 / 5.93	3.13 / 5.01	2.90 / 4.50	2.74 / 4.17	2.63 / 3.94	2.55 / 3.77	2.48 / 3.63	2.43 / 3.52	2.38 / 3.43	2.34 / 3.36	2.31 / 3.30	2.26 / 3.19	2.21 / 3.12	2.15 / 3.00	2.11 / 2.92	2.07 / 2.84	2.02 / 2.76	2.00 / 2.70	1.96 / 2.63	1.94 / 2.60	1.91 / 2.54	1.90 / 2.51	1.88 / 2.49
20	4.35 / 8.10	3.49 / 5.85	3.10 / 4.94	2.87 / 4.43	2.71 / 4.10	2.60 / 3.87	2.52 / 3.71	2.45 / 3.56	2.40 / 3.45	2.35 / 3.37	2.31 / 3.30	2.28 / 3.23	2.23 / 3.13	2.18 / 3.05	2.12 / 2.94	2.08 / 2.86	2.04 / 2.77	1.99 / 2.69	1.96 / 2.63	1.92 / 2.56	1.90 / 2.53	1.87 / 2.47	1.85 / 2.44	1.84 / 2.42
21	4.32 / 8.02	3.47 / 5.78	3.07 / 4.87	2.84 / 4.37	2.68 / 4.04	2.57 / 3.81	2.49 / 3.65	2.42 / 3.51	2.37 / 3.40	2.32 / 3.31	2.28 / 3.24	2.25 / 3.17	2.20 / 3.07	2.15 / 2.99	2.09 / 2.88	2.05 / 2.80	2.00 / 2.72	1.96 / 2.63	1.93 / 2.58	1.89 / 2.51	1.87 / 2.47	1.84 / 2.42	1.82 / 2.38	1.81 / 2.36
22	4.30 / 7.94	3.44 / 5.72	3.05 / 4.82	2.82 / 4.31	2.66 / 3.99	2.55 / 3.76	2.47 / 3.59	2.40 / 3.45	2.35 / 3.35	2.30 / 3.26	2.26 / 3.18	2.23 / 3.12	2.18 / 3.02	2.13 / 2.94	2.07 / 2.83	2.03 / 2.75	1.98 / 2.67	1.93 / 2.58	1.91 / 2.53	1.87 / 2.46	1.84 / 2.42	1.81 / 2.37	1.80 / 2.33	1.78 / 2.31
23	4.28 / 7.88	3.42 / 5.66	3.03 / 4.76	2.80 / 4.26	2.64 / 3.94	2.53 / 3.71	2.45 / 3.54	2.38 / 3.41	2.32 / 3.30	2.28 / 3.21	2.24 / 3.14	2.20 / 3.07	2.14 / 2.97	2.10 / 2.89	2.04 / 2.78	2.00 / 2.70	1.96 / 2.62	1.91 / 2.53	1.88 / 2.48	1.84 / 2.41	1.82 / 2.37	1.79 / 2.32	1.77 / 2.28	1.76 / 2.26
24	4.26 / 7.82	3.40 / 5.61	3.01 / 4.72	2.78 / 4.22	2.62 / 3.90	2.51 / 3.67	2.43 / 3.50	2.36 / 3.36	2.30 / 3.25	2.26 / 3.17	2.22 / 3.09	2.18 / 3.03	2.13 / 2.93	2.09 / 2.85	2.02 / 2.74	1.98 / 2.66	1.94 / 2.58	1.89 / 2.49	1.86 / 2.44	1.82 / 2.36	1.80 / 2.33	1.76 / 2.27	1.74 / 2.23	1.73 / 2.21
25	4.24 / 7.77	3.38 / 5.57	2.99 / 4.68	2.76 / 4.18	2.60 / 3.86	2.49 / 3.63	2.41 / 3.46	2.34 / 3.32	2.28 / 3.21	2.24 / 3.13	2.20 / 3.05	2.16 / 2.99	2.11 / 2.89	2.06 / 2.81	2.00 / 2.70	1.96 / 2.62	1.92 / 2.54	1.87 / 2.45	1.84 / 2.40	1.80 / 2.32	1.77 / 2.29	1.74 / 2.23	1.72 / 2.19	1.71 / 2.17
26	4.22 / 7.72	3.37 / 5.53	2.98 / 4.64	2.74 / 4.14	2.59 / 3.82	2.47 / 3.59	2.39 / 3.42	2.32 / 3.29	2.27 / 3.17	2.22 / 3.09	2.18 / 3.02	2.15 / 2.96	2.10 / 2.86	2.05 / 2.77	1.99 / 2.66	1.95 / 2.58	1.90 / 2.50	1.85 / 2.41	1.82 / 2.36	1.78 / 2.28	1.76 / 2.25	1.72 / 2.19	1.70 / 2.15	1.69 / 2.13

TABLE IV
(continued)

n_1 degrees of freedom (for greater mean square)

n_2	1	2	3	4	5	6	7	8	9	10	11	12	14	16	20	24	30	40	50	75	100	200	500	∞
27	4.21 / 7.68	3.35 / 5.49	2.96 / 4.60	2.73 / 4.11	2.57 / 3.79	2.46 / 3.56	2.37 / 3.39	2.30 / 3.26	2.25 / 3.14	2.20 / 3.06	2.16 / 2.98	2.13 / 2.93	2.08 / 2.83	2.03 / 2.74	1.97 / 2.63	1.93 / 2.55	1.88 / 2.47	1.84 / 2.38	1.80 / 2.33	1.76 / 2.25	1.74 / 2.21	1.71 / 2.16	1.68 / 2.12	1.67 / 2.10
28	4.20 / 7.64	3.34 / 5.45	2.95 / 4.57	2.71 / 4.07	2.56 / 3.76	2.44 / 3.53	2.36 / 3.36	2.29 / 3.23	2.24 / 3.11	2.19 / 3.03	2.15 / 2.95	2.12 / 2.90	2.06 / 2.80	2.02 / 2.71	1.96 / 2.60	1.91 / 2.52	1.87 / 2.44	1.81 / 2.35	1.78 / 2.30	1.75 / 2.22	1.72 / 2.18	1.69 / 2.13	1.67 / 2.09	1.65 / 2.06
29	4.18 / 7.60	3.33 / 5.42	2.93 / 4.54	2.70 / 4.04	2.54 / 3.73	2.43 / 3.50	2.35 / 3.33	2.28 / 3.20	2.22 / 3.08	2.18 / 3.00	2.14 / 2.92	2.10 / 2.87	2.05 / 2.77	2.00 / 2.68	1.94 / 2.57	1.90 / 2.49	1.85 / 2.41	1.80 / 2.32	1.77 / 2.27	1.73 / 2.19	1.71 / 2.15	1.68 / 2.10	1.65 / 2.06	1.64 / 2.03
30	4.17 / 7.56	3.32 / 5.39	2.92 / 4.51	2.69 / 4.02	2.53 / 3.70	2.42 / 3.47	2.34 / 3.30	2.27 / 3.17	2.21 / 3.06	2.16 / 2.98	2.12 / 2.90	2.09 / 2.84	2.04 / 2.74	1.99 / 2.66	1.93 / 2.55	1.89 / 2.47	1.84 / 2.38	1.79 / 2.29	1.76 / 2.24	1.72 / 2.16	1.69 / 2.13	1.66 / 2.07	1.64 / 2.03	1.62 / 2.01
32	4.15 / 7.50	3.30 / 5.34	2.90 / 4.46	2.67 / 3.97	2.51 / 3.66	2.40 / 3.42	2.32 / 3.25	2.25 / 3.12	2.19 / 3.01	2.14 / 2.94	2.10 / 2.86	2.07 / 2.80	2.02 / 2.70	1.97 / 2.62	1.91 / 2.51	1.86 / 2.42	1.82 / 2.34	1.76 / 2.25	1.74 / 2.20	1.69 / 2.12	1.67 / 2.08	1.64 / 2.02	1.61 / 1.98	1.59 / 1.96
34	4.13 / 7.44	3.28 / 5.29	2.88 / 4.42	2.65 / 3.93	2.49 / 3.61	2.38 / 3.38	2.30 / 3.21	2.23 / 3.08	2.17 / 2.97	2.12 / 2.89	2.08 / 2.82	2.05 / 2.76	2.00 / 2.66	1.95 / 2.58	1.89 / 2.47	1.84 / 2.38	1.80 / 2.30	1.74 / 2.21	1.71 / 2.15	1.67 / 2.08	1.64 / 2.04	1.61 / 1.98	1.59 / 1.94	1.57 / 1.91
36	4.11 / 7.39	3.26 / 5.25	2.86 / 4.38	2.63 / 3.89	2.48 / 3.58	2.36 / 3.35	2.28 / 3.18	2.21 / 3.04	2.15 / 2.94	2.10 / 2.86	2.06 / 2.78	2.03 / 2.72	1.98 / 2.62	1.93 / 2.54	1.87 / 2.43	1.82 / 2.35	1.78 / 2.26	1.72 / 2.17	1.69 / 2.12	1.65 / 2.04	1.62 / 2.00	1.59 / 1.94	1.56 / 1.90	1.55 / 1.87
38	4.10 / 7.35	3.25 / 5.21	2.85 / 4.34	2.62 / 3.86	2.46 / 3.54	2.35 / 3.32	2.26 / 3.15	2.19 / 3.02	2.14 / 2.91	2.09 / 2.82	2.05 / 2.75	2.02 / 2.69	1.96 / 2.59	1.92 / 2.51	1.85 / 2.40	1.80 / 2.32	1.76 / 2.22	1.71 / 2.14	1.67 / 2.08	1.63 / 2.00	1.60 / 1.97	1.57 / 1.90	1.54 / 1.86	1.53 / 1.84
40	4.08 / 7.31	3.23 / 5.18	2.84 / 4.31	2.61 / 3.83	2.45 / 3.51	2.34 / 3.29	2.25 / 3.12	2.18 / 2.99	2.12 / 2.88	2.07 / 2.80	2.04 / 2.73	2.00 / 2.66	1.95 / 2.56	1.90 / 2.49	1.84 / 2.37	1.79 / 2.29	1.74 / 2.20	1.69 / 2.11	1.66 / 2.05	1.61 / 1.97	1.59 / 1.94	1.55 / 1.88	1.53 / 1.84	1.51 / 1.81
42	4.07 / 7.27	3.22 / 5.15	2.83 / 4.29	2.59 / 3.80	2.44 / 3.49	2.32 / 3.26	2.24 / 3.10	2.17 / 2.96	2.11 / 2.86	2.06 / 2.77	2.02 / 2.70	1.99 / 2.64	1.94 / 2.54	1.89 / 2.46	1.82 / 2.35	1.78 / 2.26	1.73 / 2.17	1.68 / 2.08	1.64 / 2.02	1.60 / 1.94	1.57 / 1.91	1.54 / 1.85	1.51 / 1.80	1.49 / 1.78
44	4.06 / 7.24	3.21 / 5.12	2.82 / 4.26	2.58 / 3.78	2.43 / 3.46	2.31 / 3.24	2.23 / 3.07	2.16 / 2.94	2.10 / 2.84	2.05 / 2.75	2.01 / 2.68	1.98 / 2.62	1.92 / 2.52	1.88 / 2.44	1.81 / 2.32	1.76 / 2.24	1.72 / 2.15	1.66 / 2.06	1.63 / 2.00	1.58 / 1.92	1.56 / 1.88	1.52 / 1.82	1.50 / 1.78	1.48 / 1.75
46	4.05 / 7.21	3.20 / 5.10	2.81 / 4.24	2.57 / 3.76	2.42 / 3.44	2.30 / 3.22	2.22 / 3.05	2.14 / 2.92	2.09 / 2.82	2.04 / 2.73	2.00 / 2.66	1.97 / 2.60	1.91 / 2.50	1.87 / 2.42	1.80 / 2.30	1.75 / 2.22	1.71 / 2.13	1.65 / 2.04	1.62 / 1.98	1.57 / 1.90	1.54 / 1.86	1.51 / 1.80	1.48 / 1.76	1.46 / 1.72
48	4.04 / 7.19	3.19 / 5.08	2.80 / 4.22	2.56 / 3.74	2.41 / 3.42	2.30 / 3.20	2.21 / 3.04	2.14 / 2.90	2.08 / 2.80	2.03 / 2.71	1.99 / 2.64	1.96 / 2.58	1.90 / 2.48	1.86 / 2.40	1.79 / 2.28	1.74 / 2.20	1.70 / 2.11	1.64 / 2.02	1.61 / 1.96	1.56 / 1.88	1.53 / 1.84	1.50 / 1.78	1.47 / 1.73	1.45 / 1.70

n₁ degrees of freedom (for greater mean square)

n_2	1	2	3	4	5	6	7	8	9	10	11	12	14	16	20	24	30	40	50	75	100	200	500	∞
50	4.03 / 7.17	3.18 / 5.06	2.79 / 4.20	2.56 / 3.72	2.40 / 3.41	2.29 / 3.18	2.20 / 3.02	2.13 / 2.88	2.07 / 2.78	2.02 / 2.70	1.98 / 2.62	1.95 / 2.56	1.90 / 2.46	1.85 / 2.39	1.78 / 2.26	1.74 / 2.18	1.69 / 2.10	1.63 / 2.00	1.60 / 1.94	1.55 / 1.86	1.52 / 1.82	1.48 / 1.76	1.46 / 1.71	1.44 / 1.68
55	4.02 / 7.12	3.17 / 5.01	2.78 / 4.16	2.54 / 3.68	2.38 / 3.37	2.27 / 3.15	2.18 / 2.98	2.11 / 2.85	2.05 / 2.75	2.00 / 2.66	1.97 / 2.59	1.93 / 2.53	1.88 / 2.43	1.83 / 2.35	1.76 / 2.23	1.72 / 2.15	1.67 / 2.06	1.61 / 1.96	1.58 / 1.90	1.52 / 1.82	1.50 / 1.78	1.46 / 1.71	1.43 / 1.66	1.41 / 1.64
60	4.00 / 7.08	3.15 / 4.98	2.76 / 4.13	2.52 / 3.65	2.37 / 3.34	2.25 / 3.12	2.17 / 2.95	2.10 / 2.82	2.04 / 2.72	1.99 / 2.63	1.95 / 2.56	1.92 / 2.50	1.86 / 2.40	1.81 / 2.32	1.75 / 2.20	1.70 / 2.12	1.65 / 2.03	1.59 / 1.93	1.56 / 1.87	1.50 / 1.79	1.48 / 1.74	1.44 / 1.68	1.41 / 1.63	1.39 / 1.60
65	3.99 / 7.04	3.14 / 4.95	2.75 / 4.10	2.51 / 3.62	2.36 / 3.31	2.24 / 3.09	2.15 / 2.93	2.08 / 2.79	2.02 / 2.70	1.98 / 2.61	1.94 / 2.54	1.90 / 2.47	1.85 / 2.37	1.80 / 2.30	1.73 / 2.18	1.68 / 2.09	1.63 / 2.00	1.57 / 1.90	1.54 / 1.84	1.49 / 1.76	1.46 / 1.71	1.42 / 1.64	1.39 / 1.60	1.37 / 1.56
70	3.98 / 7.01	3.13 / 4.92	2.74 / 4.08	2.50 / 3.60	2.35 / 3.29	2.23 / 3.07	2.14 / 2.91	2.07 / 2.77	2.01 / 2.67	1.97 / 2.59	1.93 / 2.51	1.89 / 2.45	1.84 / 2.35	1.79 / 2.28	1.72 / 2.15	1.67 / 2.07	1.62 / 1.98	1.56 / 1.88	1.53 / 1.82	1.47 / 1.74	1.45 / 1.69	1.40 / 1.62	1.37 / 1.56	1.35 / 1.53
80	3.96 / 6.96	3.11 / 4.88	2.72 / 4.04	2.48 / 3.56	2.33 / 3.25	2.21 / 3.04	2.12 / 2.87	2.05 / 2.74	1.99 / 2.64	1.95 / 2.55	1.91 / 2.48	1.88 / 2.41	1.82 / 2.32	1.77 / 2.24	1.70 / 2.11	1.65 / 2.03	1.60 / 1.94	1.54 / 1.84	1.51 / 1.78	1.45 / 1.70	1.42 / 1.65	1.38 / 1.57	1.35 / 1.52	1.32 / 1.49
100	3.94 / 6.90	3.09 / 4.82	2.70 / 3.98	2.46 / 3.51	2.30 / 3.20	2.19 / 2.99	2.10 / 2.82	2.03 / 2.69	1.97 / 2.59	1.92 / 2.51	1.88 / 2.43	1.85 / 2.36	1.79 / 2.26	1.75 / 2.19	1.68 / 2.06	1.63 / 1.98	1.57 / 1.89	1.51 / 1.79	1.48 / 1.73	1.42 / 1.64	1.39 / 1.59	1.34 / 1.51	1.30 / 1.46	1.28 / 1.43
125	3.92 / 6.84	3.07 / 4.78	2.68 / 3.94	2.44 / 3.47	2.29 / 3.17	2.17 / 2.95	2.08 / 2.79	2.01 / 2.65	1.95 / 2.56	1.90 / 2.47	1.86 / 2.40	1.83 / 2.33	1.77 / 2.23	1.72 / 2.15	1.65 / 2.03	1.60 / 1.94	1.55 / 1.85	1.49 / 1.75	1.45 / 1.68	1.39 / 1.59	1.36 / 1.54	1.31 / 1.46	1.27 / 1.40	1.25 / 1.37
150	3.91 / 6.81	3.06 / 4.75	2.67 / 3.91	2.43 / 3.44	2.27 / 3.14	2.16 / 2.92	2.07 / 2.76	2.00 / 2.62	1.94 / 2.53	1.89 / 2.44	1.85 / 2.37	1.82 / 2.30	1.76 / 2.20	1.71 / 2.12	1.64 / 2.00	1.59 / 1.91	1.54 / 1.83	1.47 / 1.72	1.44 / 1.66	1.37 / 1.56	1.34 / 1.51	1.29 / 1.43	1.25 / 1.37	1.22 / 1.33
200	3.89 / 6.76	3.04 / 4.71	2.65 / 3.88	2.41 / 3.41	2.26 / 3.11	2.14 / 2.90	2.05 / 2.73	1.98 / 2.60	1.92 / 2.50	1.87 / 2.41	1.83 / 2.34	1.80 / 2.28	1.74 / 2.17	1.69 / 2.09	1.62 / 1.97	1.57 / 1.88	1.52 / 1.79	1.45 / 1.69	1.42 / 1.62	1.35 / 1.53	1.32 / 1.48	1.26 / 1.39	1.22 / 1.33	1.19 / 1.28
400	3.86 / 6.70	3.02 / 4.66	2.62 / 3.83	2.39 / 3.36	2.23 / 3.06	2.12 / 2.85	2.03 / 2.69	1.96 / 2.55	1.90 / 2.46	1.85 / 2.37	1.81 / 2.29	1.78 / 2.23	1.72 / 2.12	1.67 / 2.04	1.60 / 1.92	1.54 / 1.84	1.49 / 1.74	1.42 / 1.64	1.38 / 1.57	1.32 / 1.47	1.28 / 1.42	1.22 / 1.32	1.16 / 1.24	1.13 / 1.19
1000	3.85 / 6.66	3.00 / 4.62	2.61 / 3.80	2.38 / 3.34	2.22 / 3.04	2.10 / 2.82	2.02 / 2.66	1.95 / 2.53	1.89 / 2.43	1.84 / 2.34	1.80 / 2.26	1.76 / 2.20	1.70 / 2.09	1.65 / 2.01	1.58 / 1.89	1.53 / 1.81	1.47 / 1.71	1.41 / 1.61	1.36 / 1.54	1.30 / 1.44	1.26 / 1.38	1.19 / 1.28	1.13 / 1.19	1.08 / 1.11
∞	3.84 / 6.64	2.99 / 4.60	2.60 / 3.78	2.37 / 3.32	2.21 / 3.02	2.09 / 2.80	2.01 / 2.64	1.94 / 2.51	1.88 / 2.41	1.83 / 2.32	1.79 / 2.24	1.75 / 2.18	1.69 / 2.07	1.64 / 1.99	1.57 / 1.87	1.52 / 1.79	1.46 / 1.69	1.40 / 1.59	1.35 / 1.52	1.28 / 1.41	1.24 / 1.36	1.17 / 1.25	1.11 / 1.15	1.00 / 1.00

TABLE V   CRITICAL VALUES OF U IN THE MANN-WHITNEY TEST[a]

[a]Adapted and abridged from Tables 1, 3, 5, and 7 of D. Auble. Extended tables for the Mann-Whitney statistic. Bulletin of the Institute of Educational Research at Indiana University, 1953, 1 (No. 2), with permission of the author and the publisher. For additional Mann-Whitney U tables for values corresponding to other ns and other α (p) levels, see Siegel (1956).

n_1 \ n_2	9	10	11	12	13	14	15	16	17	18	19	20
1												
2	0	0	0	1	1	1	1	1	2	2	2	2
3	2	3	3	4	4	5	5	6	6	7	7	8
4	4	5	6	7	8	9	10	11	11	12	13	13
5	7	8	9	11	12	13	14	15	17	18	19	20
6	10	11	13	14	16	17	19	21	22	24	25	27
7	12	14	16	18	20	22	24	26	28	30	32	34
8	15	17	19	22	24	26	29	31	34	36	38	41
9	17	20	23	26	28	31	34	37	39	42	45	48
10	20	23	26	29	33	36	39	42	45	48	52	55
11	23	26	30	33	37	40	44	47	51	55	58	62
12	26	29	33	37	41	45	49	53	57	61	65	69
13	28	33	37	41	45	50	54	59	63	67	72	76
14	31	36	40	45	50	55	59	64	67	74	78	83
15	34	39	44	49	54	59	64	70	75	80	85	90
16	37	42	47	53	59	64	70	75	81	86	92	98
17	39	45	51	57	63	67	75	81	87	93	99	105
18	42	48	55	61	67	74	80	86	93	99	106	112
19	45	52	58	65	72	78	85	92	99	106	113	119
20	48	55	62	69	76	83	90	98	105	112	119	127

CRITICAL VALUES OF r_s, THE SPEARMAN RANK CORRELATION COEFFICIENT[a]

TABLE VI

[a]Adapted from E. G. Olds, *Distributions of sums of square of rank differences for small numbers of individuals,* Annals of Mathematical Statistics, *1938, 9, 133–148; and* from E. G. Olds, *The 5% significance levels for sums of squares of rank differences and correction,* Annals of Mathematical Statistics, *1949, 20, 117–118, by* permission of the author and the publisher.

N	Significance level (one-tailed test)	
	.05	.01
4	1.000	
5	.900	1.000
6	.829	.943
7	.714	.893
8	.643	.833
9	.600	.783
10	.564	.746
12	.506	.712
14	.456	.645
16	.425	.601
18	.399	.564
20	.377	.534
22	359	.508
24	.343	.485
26	.329	.465
28	.317	.448
30	.306	.432

TABLE VII   CRITICAL VALUES OF CHI SQUARE[a]

[a]Adapted from Table IV of Fisher, Statistical Methods for Research Workers, published by Oliver and Boyd, Ltd., Edinburgh, and by permission of the author and the publisher.

df	Level of significance for one-tailed test					
	.10	.05	.025	.01	.005	.0005
	Level of significance for two-tailed test					
	.20	.10	.05	.02	.01	.001
1	1.64	2.71	3.84	5.41	6.64	10.83
2	3.22	4.60	5.99	7.82	9.21	13.82
3	4.64	6.25	7.82	9.84	11.34	16.27
4	5.99	7.78	9.49	11.67	13.28	18.46
5	7.29	9.24	11.07	13.39	15.09	20.52
6	8.56	10.64	12.59	15.03	16.81	22.46
7	9.80	12.02	14.07	16.62	18.48	24.32
8	11.03	13.36	15.51	18.17	20.09	26.12
9	12.24	14.68	16.92	19.68	21.67	27.88
10	13.44	15.99	18.31	21.16	23.21	29.59
11	14.63	17.28	19.68	22.62	24.72	31.26
12	15.81	18.55	21.03	24.05	26.22	32.91
13	16.98	19.81	22.36	25.47	27.69	34.53
14	18.15	21.06	23.68	26.87	29.14	36.12
15	19.31	22.31	25.00	28.26	30.58	37.70
16	20.46	23.54	26.30	29.63	32.00	39.29
17	21.62	24.77	27.59	31.00	33.41	40.75
18	22.76	25.99	28.87	32.35	34.80	42.31
19	23.90	27.20	30.14	33.69	36.19	43.82
20	25.04	28.41	31.41	35.02	37.57	45.32
21	26.17	29.62	32.67	36.34	38.93	46.80
22	27.30	30.81	33.92	37.66	40.29	48.27
23	28.43	32.01	35.17	38.97	41.64	49.73
24	29.55	33.20	36.42	40.27	42.98	51.18
25	30.68	34.38	37.65	41.57	44.31	52.62
26	31.80	35.56	38.88	42.86	45.64	54.05
27	32.91	36.74	40.11	44.14	46.96	55.48
28	34.03	37.92	41.34	45.42	48.28	56.89
29	35.14	39.09	42.69	46.69	49.59	58.30
30	36.25	40.26	43.77	47.96	50.89	59.70
32	38.47	42.59	46.19	50.49	53.49	62.49
34	40.68	44.90	48.60	53.00	56.06	65.25
36	42.88	47.21	51.00	55.49	58.62	67.99
38	45.08	49.51	53.38	57.97	61.16	70.70
40	47.27	51.81	55.76	60.44	63.69	73.40
44	51.64	56.37	60.48	65.34	68.71	78.75
48	55.99	60.91	65.17	70.20	73.68	84.04
52	60.33	65.42	69.83	75.02	78.62	89.27
56	64.66	69.92	74.47	79.82	83.51	94.46
60	68.97	74.40	79.08	84.58	88.38	99.61

Answers

ANSWERS TO EXERCISES

Chapter 1

1. (a) i, (b) i, (c) e, (d) i, (e) e
2. Internal validity: d; external validity: a
3. a
4. Internal
5. See Section on characteristics of the research process.
6. Step 1, d; Step 2, l; Step 3, k; Step 4, h; Step 5, a; Step 6, i; Step 7, f; Step 8, b; Step 9, e
7. See Section 1.7.

Chapter 2

1. Problem: "The study was aimed at comparing developmental classrooms to regular classrooms in terms of both *process,* that is, the behavior of teachers presumably resulting from training, and *product,* the behavior of students presumably resulting from the behavior of teachers."
2. Problem: Example 1: Will students achieve better with homework or without homework?

   Example 2: Will students become better problem solvers if taught individually or in groups and as a function of their mental ability levels?
3. (a) Interest: This judgment is based on personal values but, considering currency (that is, current levels of interest), it is reasonably high for all three of the example problems.

   (b) Practicality: the problem in Exercise 1 rates *low* in practicality, because it requires multiple classrooms and extensive control by the researcher. A study with individual students such as Example 1 in Exercise 2 would have the greatest practicality with Example 2 in Exercise 2 falling between these extremes.
4. Developmental instruction (*input* affecting *prospective teachers*) affecting process (*instructional activity* representing *teacher-learner relationships*) to affect student achievement (*competency acquisition outcome*) and attitudes (*attitude change outcome*).
5. Example 1: Effect of homework (characteristic of instruction: *learning activity*) on student achievement (student outcome: *specific knowledge and comprehension*).

Example 2: Effect of individual versus group instruction (characteristic of instruction: *learning environment*) and mental ability (component of instruction: *student learning characteristic*) on problem-solving behavior (student outcome: *thinking and problem solving*).

6. Example 1: How does computer use versus nonuse (instruction variable) in large versus small classes (context variable) affect student learning (outcome)?
Example 2: Do teachers with more or less education (teacher variable) have differential effects on the achievement (outcome) of students with greater or lesser scholastic aptitude (student variable)?

7. Example 1: Are poor versus good study habits more likely to affect dropping out behavior by nonresident students than that by resident students?
Example 2: Are family responsibilities more likely to affect dropping out behavior by black students than that by white students?

8. Exercise 6: Example 1 offers considerably more practical value than Example 2, because it involves variables that can be manipulated by educators in carrying out instruction (that is, computer use versus nonuse and class size), but Example 2 offers somewhat higher theoretical value, because it can be tied to theories that deal with the correspondence or match between student background and teacher background.
Exercise 7: Again Example 1 has more practical value because it deals with a variable—study habits—that educators can directly affect, whereas the second example is more theoretical because it deals with the structure and culture of the family.

Chapter 3

1. To discover important variables, distinguish what has been done from what needs to be done, synthesize and gain perspective, determine and support meanings and relationships, establish the context of a problem, and establish the significance of a problem.

2. To bring a field up to date by summarizing past work, which in turn may yield useful conclusions about phenomena in the field, theoretical statements about cause and effect, and applications to practice.

3. 1 (g), 2 (f), 3 (h), 4 (e), 5 (b), 6 (a), 7 (d)

4. See the lists on pages 59 and 60.

5. Examine the *Thesaurus of ERIC Descriptors* and *Dissertation Abstracts International* to compile a list of key words; consider the potential variables included within the problem area itself. Sample descriptors: high school teaching, English education, social studies education, teacher styles, teacher attitudes.

6. Search 1: Use the five descriptors simultaneously and in various combinations to do a search of *RIE,* preferably by computer, to locate relevant unpublished sources.

Search 2: Repeat Search 1 but in *CIJE* to locate relevant journal sources. (Many centers allow you to conduct these two searches at the same time.)

Search 3: Convert descriptors to key words, and do a DATRIX search to locate relevant dissertations.

7. Select the titles that seem most relevant from the three searches, and then (1) order the relevant, unpublished, *RIE* documents in hard copy or microfiche from the ERIC Document Reproduction Service, (2) locate in your library and photocopy the relevant journal articles, and (3) order the relevant dissertations from University Microfilms.

8. A developmental instruction project was tested in Grades 1–3 in one elementary school and Grades 1–5 in a second. After 1 year of the program, comparisons with Grades 1–5 of a matched control school in the same community were made.

   Developmental teachers were found to be more flexible in their use of space and organization of classroom activities, more creative, more warm and accepting. Pupils did not differ on achievement or problem solving but developmental children had more positive (1) self-appraisals and (2) attitudes toward school than control children.

   Developmental instruction was concluded to be effective in many respects.

Chapter 4

1. (a) specific hypothesis, (b) general hypothesis, (c) observation
2. (a) general hypothesis, (b) observation, (c) specific hypothesis
3. General hypothesis: Speculates on the relationship between general classes (that is, all possible instances)
   Specific hypothesis: Speculates on the relationship between specific instances
   Observation: Identifies an event that has occurred (or been seen)
4. Children of parents in science-related occupations are more likely to choose science electives than children of parents in nonscience-related occupations.
   Children of parents in science-related occupations are less likely to choose science electives than children of parents in nonscience-related occupations.
   Children of parents in science-related occupations are as likely to choose science electives as children of parents in nonscience-related occupations.
5. Students who use this textbook will learn
         more   less   the same amount
   about research methods as compared to students who use the Brand X textbook.

6. (a) Because a child will more likely prefer one of two teachers than one of one, and two teachers means that one can be male and one female.
7. (a) deductive, (b) inductive
8. (a) Enjoyment of school by youngsters will be unrelated to their reading grade levels.
   (b) Intelligence and ordinal position of birth are unrelated; that is, first-borns and later-borns are equally intelligent.
   (c) A combination of reading readiness training and programmed reading instruction will not be more effective in teaching reading than normal classroom instruction in sight reading.

Chapter 5

1. (a) 3, (b) 5, (c) 4, (d) 1, (e) 2
2. (a) parents' occupation (science-related versus nonscience-related)
   (b) gender of student
   (c) grade level, IQ, ability
   (d) decision regarding a science elective (choosing versus not choosing)
   (e) affinity or interest through exposure
3. Examples: IQ, prior achievement in required science courses, interest test scores in science, science knowledge, age. (a) Theoretical considerations: Being smart or doing well in required science courses might influence students to elect science courses, even if their parents did not work in science fields. (b) Practical consideration: Including a moderator variable would increase the number of required subjects.
4. (a) perceptual-motor training (some versus none)
   (b) handedness (left-handed versus right-handed)
   (c) age
   (d) performance on eye-hand coordination tasks
   (e) coordination (as a property of the nervous system)
5. (a) televised feedback (present versus absent)
   (b) extent of teachers' teaching experience (much versus little)
   (c) subject matter taught (social studies only)
   (d) change in attitudes toward teaching
   (e) dissonance, self-awareness

Chapter 6

1. a
2. b, c
3. (a) *A*, (b) *C*, (c) *B*
4. (a) *C*, (b) *A*, (c) *B*

5. (a) Example: state induced by giving a person training in a course intended to increase his or her desire for success
   (b) Example: telling members of a group that test data indicate that they should all get along well
6. (a) Example: state evidenced by a person showing persistence, competitiveness, and aggressiveness in a difficult task situation
   (b) Example: state evidenced by a lack of open fighting, hostility, or disagreement and a predominance of sociability and group maintenance activity
7. (a) Example: state evidenced by a person relating fantasies of task accomplishments when confronted by an ambiguous stimulus
   (b) Example: state evidenced by group members showing many intragroup friendship choices on a sociometric measure
8. Example: As parents' income level rises, students' grade-point averages in high school also increase.
9. Example: As the number of rules and sanctions imposed by a teacher in a classroom falls, the likelihood increases that students will generate novel (uncommon) yet appropriate responses in a classroom task situation.

Chapter 7

1. b
2. c
3. 1(a) selection   2(a) instrumentation
   1(b)   2(b) mortality
   1(c) history   2(c)
   1(d) maturation   2(d) history
4. History: Use a control group, that is, equivalent subjects given nonprogrammed math instruction.
   Maturation: Use control *Ss* of the same age as experimental *Ss*.
   Testing: Administer different forms of the math achievement test for pretesting and posttesting.
   Instrumentation: Administer a standardized math achievement test.
   Selection: Randomly assign *Ss* to experimental and control groups.
   Regression: Select *Ss* whose math achievement levels cover a wide range.
   Mortality: Randomly assign *Ss* to experimental and control groups.
5. Reactive effect of testing: Administer a standardized math achievement test. Interaction effects of selection bias: Choose *Ss* with a wide range of math achievement levels.
   Reactive effect of experimental arrangements: Introduce experimental and control material as part of regular classroom activity.
   Multiple treatment interference: Isolate *Ss* from other experiments while the current one is under way.

6. History: Employ a control group of *Ss* who do not see the film. Maturation: Select experimental and control *Ss* of the same age. Selection: Randomly assign *Ss*.

7. One check would be to develop observation-based operational definitions of directive and nondirective counselors. Have trained observers listen to tapes of counseling sessions and check to see how many directive and nondirective acts each counselor makes in the two roles. Other checks are possible.

8. One approach would be to use a rating scale on which each *S* would rate his or her level of anger after the manipulation. *Ss* in the anger condition should show significantly higher ratings of anger than *Ss* in the nonanger condition. Other approaches are possible.

Chapter 8

1. (1) c, (2) a, (3) b
2. (1) c, (2) d, (3) a, (4) b
3. Example:

$$R \quad X \quad O_1$$
$$R \quad \quad\ O_2$$

$$X \cong \text{urban school experience}$$
$$O_1O_2 \cong \text{choice of teaching assignment}$$

4. Example:

$$
\begin{array}{cccc}
R & O_1 & X & Y_1 & O_5 \\
R & O_2 &   & Y_1 & O_6 \\
\hline
R & O_3 & X & Y_2 & O_7 \\
R & O_4 &   & Y_2 & O_8 \\
\end{array}
$$

$$O_1, O_2, O_3, O_4 \cong \text{math achievement pretest}$$
$$X \cong \text{programmed math instruction}$$
$$Y_1 Y_2 \cong \text{high and low math aptitude}$$
$$O_5, O_6, O_7, O_8 \cong \text{math achievement posttest}$$

5. a, d
6. b, d
7. c
8. (a) The experimenter cannot assign *Ss* to conditions. They choose their own conditions, thus creating potential selection bias.

$$
\begin{array}{ccc}
\text{(b)} \ O_1 & X & O_3 \\
\hline
O_2 &   & O_4 \\
\end{array}
$$

O_1, O_2 ≅ control variables to assess group equivalence
X ≅ urban school experience
O_3, O_4 ≅ subsequent choice of assignment

9. (a) All Ss must participate in the experiment, leaving no perfect way to control for history.

   (b) O_1 O_2 O_3 X O_4 O_5 O_6 O ≅ number of cavities
   X ≅ dental hygiene program

10. (a) Because the experimenter is not creating the broken home, he or she is selecting children from it after the fact.

    (b) C O_1 C ≅ children from broken homes
    O_2 O_1, O_2 ≅ number of demerits

11. (a) Because the extra experience and feelings of importance for being singled out might enhance development.

    (b) R X O_1 X ≅ dance program
    R H O_2 H ≅ reading program (irrelevant treatment)
    R O_3 O_1, O_2, O_3 ≅ measurements of physical and social
    skills

12. (a) Because the extra experience and feelings of importance growing out of being included in the program might contribute to an increase in verbal IQ.
    (b) Because teachers who expect the treatment to work might contribute to its working.

    (c) R O_1 X E_p O_5 O_1, O_2, O_3, O_4 ≅ pretest verbal IQ
    R O_2 X E_n O_6 H ≅ irrelevant program
    R O_3 H E_p O_7 X ≅ special program
    R O_4 H E_n O_8 E_p ≅ positive teacher expec-
    tations
    E_n ≅ neutral teacher
    expectations
    O_5, O_6, O_7, O_8 ≅ posttest verbal IQ

Chapter 9

1. (a) 2, (b) 4, (c) 1, (d) 3
2. For test-retest reliability, administer the scale to same group of Ss on two occasions. Correlate Ss' scores at Time 1 with those at Time 2. (For comparison, the split-half method involves one administration

and correlation of scores on odd-numbered items with those on even-numbered items.)

3. (a) 3, (b) 4, (c) 2, (d) 1
4. To establish concurrent validity, give the test to a sample along with a standard, widely accepted IQ test. Correlate scores on the two tests (as contrasted to relating the test score to school achievement or some other behavior with a presumed relationship to the construct of intelligence).
5. (a) 3, (b) 1, (c) 2
6. (a) 2, (b) 1, (c) 3, (d) 5, (e) 4
7. (a) 44, (b) 440, (c) 40
8. (a) 958, (b) 1,165–1,166, (c) Darwin Nelson, Michael J. Fellner, and C. L. Norrell, (d) Stoelting Co., (e) approx. 25–35 min., (f) K–2, (g) 4, (h) one form (two parts), (i) $31.00, (j) 1975–1976.
9. I would choose the Sex Knowledge Inventory, Vocabulary and Anatomy, 1977 Revision (#1117a) over the Sex Knowledge Inventory, 1979 Revision (#1117b) because the former is suitable for high school use whereas the latter is not. I would choose it over the Sexual Concerns Checklist (#111), which is a test of knowledge desired rather than knowledge acquired. (I would be concerned, however, by the datedness of the chosen instrument.)

10.

	NUMBER OF HIGH ⅓ WHO PASS	NUMBER OF LOW ⅓ WHO PASS	INDEX OF DIFFICULTY	INDEX OF DISCRIMI-NABILITY
Item 1	2	0	.50	1.00
Item 2	2	1	.75	.67
Item 3	1	1	.50	.50
Item 4	2	0	.50	1.00

Eliminate Item 3.

11. 1st, c; 2nd, f; 3rd, e; 4th, d; 5th, a; 6th, b
12. Item scores and total scores
13. Evaluation
14. .92

Chapter 10

1. c
2. a
3. (a) 4, (b) 2, (c) 5, (d) 1, (e) 3
4. (a) 4, (b) 5, (c) 7, (d) 6, (e) 1, (f) 3, (g) 2
5. (a) I, (b) Q, (c) Q, (d) Q, (e) I, (f) I
6. (a) F, (b) R, (c) C, (d) F, (e) S

7. Examples: How do you feel about procedures for ordering classroom supplies?

   What is it about the procedure that leads you to feel the way you do?

   Who do you feel is responsible for the procedure?

8. Examples: The ability of teachers to correctly follow procedures for ordering supplies is   very good   good   poor   very poor.

   I am pleased about the way teachers follow instructions for ordering supplies. TRUE or FALSE

   Which of the following groups is *least* satisfactory in following instructions for ordering supplies (check one):

   administrators   _____

   teachers   _____

   clerical staff   _____

9. male, college prep: 48   female, college prep: 40

    male, business: 12   female, business: 20

    male, vocational: 24   female, vocational: 4

    male, general: 36   female, general: 16

10. male, elementary: 6   female, elementary: 24

    male, junior high: 6   female, junior high: 9

    male, high school: 9   female, high school: 6

11. b

12. Example:

    I am conducting a study to examine the attitudes of different teachers toward problems of disciplining students and would like to enlist your cooperation. If you would fill out the two forms enclosed and return them to me in the stamped, return-addressed envelope that has been enclosed, I would be most appreciative.

    You are *not* asked to write your name on the questionnaires. Moreover, after the data are rostered by number, these questionnaires will be destroyed. No individual data will be released under any circumstances.

    The Dean of my school and my doctoral committee have endorsed this study. It is being funded under a small grant from the university. Successful completion of the study will enable me to earn my doctoral degree.

    Again, I ask for your cooperation. Studies like this enable us to learn more about the process of education.

    Thank you.

    (Note that, in order to avoid bias, the specific problem to which the study addresses itself has not been revealed.)

Chapter 11

1. c
2. a

3.
CATEGORY	SCORES
1	22, 36, 39, 40, 41
2	45, 47, 49, 50, 52
3	54, 58, 62, 67, 68
4	70, 71, 73, 74, 78
5	81, 85, 90, 92, 98

4.

S's 10	Sex	Age	Treat.	Mod.	1	2	3	4	5	6	7	8	9	10
1 2 3	4 5 6	7 8 9	10 11	12 13	14 15	16 17	18 19	20 21	22 23	24 25	26 27	28 29	30 31	32 33 34
0 1	1	2 4	1	1	4 3	1 2	3 3	0 7	1 8	9 0	4 3	3 8	1 2	1 1
0 2	2	2 0	1	2	4 0	0 9	2 4	0 2	2 4	8 0	4 1	1 9	2 4	1 3
0 3	1	2 1	1	1	3 7	0 8	4 1	1 0	1 6	6 7	5 5	2 1	2 0	0 1
.	.	.	.	.	.			.		.			.	.
2 0	2	2 2	2	2	4 1	1 9	3 1	0 9	2 9	7 3	5 5	2 9	1 4	2 1

5. Mean = 84.0, median = 84.5, sd = 5.2
6. Mean = 78.4, median = 79.5, sd = 5.6
7. $t = 3.27$, $p < .01$ ($df = 38$, two-tailed test)
8. $U = 96.5$, $p < .05$ ($n_1 = 20$, $n_2 = 20$)
9.

	1	2	
High	(9.5) 13	(9.5) 6	19
Low	(10.5) 7	(10.5) 14	21
	20	20	40

$\chi^2 = 3.61$, $p < .10$ ($df = 1$)[1]

---

[1] When computed by the $\Sigma\Sigma \dfrac{(o - e)^2}{e}$ formula, $\chi^2 = 4.92$, $p < .05$. The difference between the two χ^2 values indicates the effect of the correction for continuity built into the worksheet formula only. Note also that the same two sets of interval data when compared in interval form (t-test) differ at the .01 level, when compared in ordinal form (U-test) differ at the .05 level, and when compared in nominal form (χ^2 test with a correction for continuity) differ at the .10 level.

10.

SOURCE	df	MS	F	p
A	1	348.0	16.49	<.01
B	1	313.0	14.83	<.01
AB	1	2.5	0.12	
error	36	21.1		

11. $r_s = .83, p < .01$ ($N = 20$)
12. $r = .91, p < .01$ ($df = 8$)

Chapter 12

1. Example: An important function of the educational process in general and classroom experience in particular is to help children learn self-control and internal motivation. This might be called the *socialization function* of education. If it fails to occur, the child can expect to have difficulty in school and later life. It would be helpful to know about the kind of teaching behavior or style that is most likely to produce these socialized behaviors. Knowing this, we can train teachers in the use of such a style in order to maximize the socialization function of education.

2. Example: It was hypothesized that the ratings given each S by the school psychologist and the number of demerits each S had accumulated would be positively related. A Pearson product-moment correlation was run for the 10 Ss resulting in $r = .875$ ($df = 9$). This correlation is significant at beyond the .01 level, indicating that, as predicted, judgments of aggressiveness by a professional and actual acting out behavior were positively related. This finding provides considerable validity for the judgments of the school psychologist on the aggressiveness variable.

3. Example: It was not completely surprising to find that students assigned to high-ability groups had better attendance than those assigned to low-ability groups. Two interpretations can be offered. Perhaps high-ability youngsters are more motivated than others, this motivation accounting for their superior performance. This same motivation would also yield strong attendance. Perhaps also schools are "designed" to satisfy youngsters in high-ability groups—giving them particularly good teachers, unusual influence and privileges, and so on—thus making them more inclined to come to school than youngsters in low-ability groups whose school experiences lack these desirable features. Low-ability youngsters may also be led to believe that school will have less payoff for them than for others.

4. ANALYSIS OF VARIANCE OF STUDENTS' JUDGMENTS OF TEACHER DIRECTIVENESS AS A FUNCTION OF TEACHERS' SUBJECT AREAS (A) AND TEACHERS' PERSONALITY (B)

SOURCE	df	MS	F
A	1	504.17	45.22[a]
B	1	16.67	1.49
AB	1	0.17	0.01
error	20	11.15	

[a]$p < .01$

5. MEANS OF STUDENTS' JUDGMENTS OF TEACHER DIRECTIVENESS AS A FUNCTION OF TEACHERS' SUBJECT AREA AND PERSONALITY

	VOCATIONAL TEACHERS	NONVOCATIONAL TEACHERS	COMBINED
Abstract	53.8	44.5	49.2
Concrete	55.3	46.3	50.8
Combined	54.5[a]	45.4[a]	

[a]Significantly different, $p < .01$

6. MEANS OF STUDENTS' JUDGMENTS OF TEACHER DIRECTIVENESS AS A FUNCTION OF TEACHERS' SUBJECT AREA AND PERSONALITY

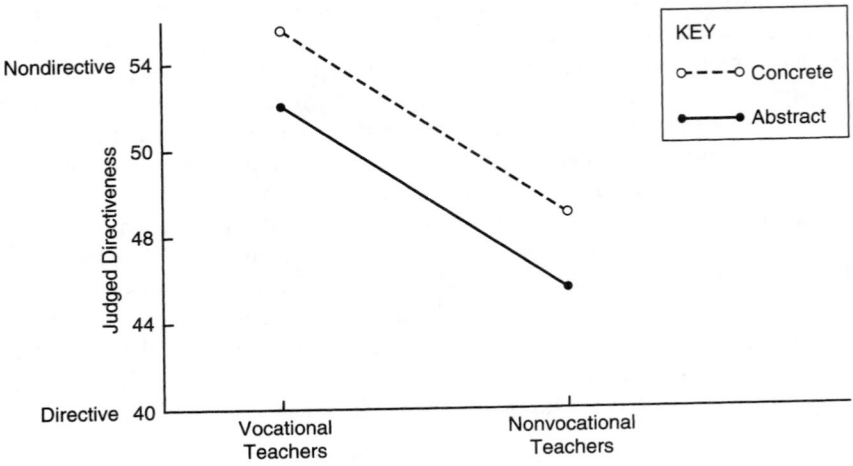

7. **Frequency Distribution of Scores on** _____
   (**N = 40**)

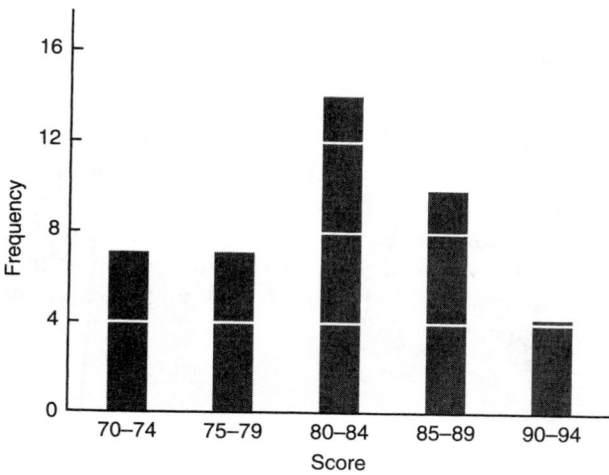

Chapter 13

1. Dependent variables were problem-solving ability, attitudes toward self, attitudes toward school, and standardized school achievement. Dependent variables closely fit the program's goals (as reflected in the last sentence of the second paragraph and the last paragraph of the write-up).
2. Reliabilities are reported as adequate, an expected consequence because all testing employed off-the-shelf instruments rather than homegrown ones.
3. The treatment was developmental instruction, patterned on the British infant school approach. It was compared to "regular classrooms."
4. Evidence was offered that developmental teachers used space more flexibly, used small-group instruction, and taught with more creativity and warmth than did regular teachers.
5. The study employed a nonequivalent control group design. By administering pretests, the researchers seem to have maintained an adequate design.
6. No moderator variable was included.
7. The report makes no mention of the statistical tests used. Analysis of variance would be a likely choice.
8. Example: The aims and objectives of this book are to enable students to design, conduct, and write research studies. A behavioral statement of these goals can take one of two forms. The first is the statement of objectives offered at the beginning of each chapter. The second is the expectation that the student could actually conduct a study, report it,

and evaluate it against the criteria set forth in the book. Measurement of the behavioral objectives set forth in the book is easily accomplished via the Competency Test Exercises at the end of each chapter. Measurement of the quality of an experiment could be accomplished by inviting a group of experts, using the worksheets in Appendix B, to evaluate each piece of research completed. A group of graduate students in education could be identified and half randomly assigned to the evaluation group, half to the control. Control *Ss* might use another book, take a course, or experience no treatment, whereas experimental *Ss* would be given the book to read. Both groups would then take all of the Competency Test Exercises (or parallel forms of each), and both groups would design, carry out, and report in writing an experiment. Experts would judge each and judgments across groups would be compared.

Chapter 14

1. L: a, c, d, f, i, k, T: b, e, g, h, j, l
2. b
3. Description: open-ended interviews of informants to ask about the whole situation. Discovery: identifying categories used by informants in making their mental maps. Classification: determining the definition of a category and its boundaries. Comparison: uncovering the relationship between categories.
4. What went on here (that is, describe the behavior)?
   Why did you react as you did?
   What effect did your behavior have on the other students?
5. What went on here (that is, describe the behavior)?
   Why did the student do what he did, and why did the teacher do what he did?
   What effect did the experience have on you?
6. Did you get what you expected? Did you like what you got?
   Did the experience change your teaching behavior?
7. Visitation schedule, interview instruments, notetaking and recording system, and observation plan
8. Developmental teaching does not require the regimentation and control of student behavior. Students in a developmental classroom do not have to follow a prescribed pattern of quietly sitting in rows (as they do in conventional classrooms).

ANSWERS TO WORKSHEETS
Sample Study III

Worksheet A: Problem Statement

1. Cite the *problem statement* as stated in study.

   The purpose of this study was to disentangle some of the controversy about the effect of teaching the initial acquisition of written words in isolation and in context.

   Does it appear on the first page?   Yes (5)   <u>No (1)</u>
   (Actually the problem statement appeared after a review of the literature.)

2. Rewrite the *problem statement* in your own words.

   Which teaching method is most effective for teaching new words to young readers: in isolation or in context?

   Was the author's version clear enough to make this task an easy one?   5   <u>4</u>   3   2   1   NA

3. Evaluate the *problem* in terms of Criteria a through e. Give both a verbal description, particularly of shortcomings, and a numerical rating.
   a. Workability
      The study seems like a practical one; the researchers were able to draw subjects from six available kindergarten classes.
      The design seemed to avoid any need for large amounts of money or time to conduct the research.   5   <u>4</u>   3   2   1   NA
   b. Critical mass
      The study consisted of 72 students from six classrooms, which seems like a typical size for this type of study. Not enough information was given to determine if this sample size is adequate for statistical methods.   5   <u>4</u>   3   2   1   NA
   c. Interest
      This study will interest many people.
   d. Theoretical value
      Use of teaching words in isolation or in context has been a controversial issue in reading for years.   <u>5</u>   4   3   2   1   NA
   e. Practical value
      These results do give specific reasons for teaching words in context in the classroom.   <u>5</u>   4   3   2   1   NA
                    Total score = 23 (out of 30)

Worksheet B: Supportive Literature

1. What, in a sentence, is the *context* of the problem?
   The study "investigates the effect of word acquisition by kindergarten children under two conditions of instruction: an isolated-word condition and a word-sentence condition."
   Is the context clear and sufficiently established?   5 <u>4</u> 3 2 1 NA

2. a. What is the magnitude of the *literature* review?
      The literature review reports the theories of the two well-established extremes on the positions investigated in the study. It also cites 20 studies that show positive findings for both sides of the controversy.   <u>5</u> 4 3 2 1 NA

   b. How empirical and up-to-date is it?
      The studies range from the years 1965 through 1980. Many of the best-known names in the field are cited.   <u>5</u> 4 3 2 1 NA

   c. Does it bear on the problem(s) of the study?
      It does bear on the problem, presenting arguments for teaching by both an isolated-word condition and a word-sentence condition.   <u>5</u> 4 3 2 1 NA

   d. Is it well-organized (introduction, subheadings, summary)?
      The article begins with the literature review, which is not identified by a heading. The introduction is adequate; the only summary mentions inconclusive and contradictory findings on this topic.   5 4 <u>3</u> 2 1 NA

   e. Try to summarize it in a sentence or two.
      Some studies support the idea that new vocabulary should be taught in isolation. Other studies support the idea that new vocabulary should be taught in context, which reinforces Goodman's argument that "syntactic and semantic cues provided by the context are vital sources of information in reading."

3. a. Do the researchers attempt to establish the *significance* of the study using argument and/or supportive literature?
      The researchers state that "previous studies in the area tend to introduce a teach/test bias, use oral rather than written contexts, and measure only immediate learning." They go on to state that "the original contribution made by this study is that all words presented to the subjects were target words in written forms. In addition the teach/test bias was eliminated and the long-term retention period extended considerably." The researchers feel that their study can end the controversy.

   b. Is the attempt convincing?   5 <u>4</u> 3 2 1 NA

   c. Summarize it in a sentence or two.
      Done under 3a.

   d. Suggest a point of significance that might be added.
      The introduction might also have considered the method in which reading is tested.

Total score = 26 (out of 30)

Worksheet C: Hypotheses

1. Where *hypotheses* cited in the study?
   No   (1)
2. Rewrite any *hypotheses* in your own words.   (Possible hypothesis)
   Kindergarten children who are instructed by presenting words in context
   will acquire given words more effectively than will children taught by
   presenting words in isolation.
3. a. The authors do not present hypotheses.   5 4 3 2 1 <u>NA</u>
   b. Is it supported by clear and understandable
      logic?   5 4 3 2 1 <u>NA</u>
   c. Is it consistent with the problem statement?   5 4 3 2 1 <u>NA</u>
   d. Is it supported by sufficient literature or
      arguments?   5 4 3 2 1 <u>NA</u>

              Total score = 1 (out of 5)

Worksheet D: Variables

1. What is the *independent variable?*
   Conditions of instruction
   Levels: 1. Isolated-word;   2. Word-sentence
2. What are the *moderator variables,* if any?
   a. Sex: male versus female
   b. Test: isolation versus sentence versus new context versus word desig-
      nation[2]
3. What are the *dependent variables?*
   I. 1. Acquisition of written words
   II. 2. Isolation test
       3. Sentence test   Short-term retention
       4. New context test
       5. Word designation test
   III. 6. Isolation test
        7. Sentence test   Long-term retention
        8. New context test
        9. Word designation test
4. What are the important *control variables?*
   1. Grade level: kindergarten only
   2. Social class (middle)
   3. Prior recognition of target words
   4. Quantity and content of instruction

---

[2] Although the four different tests represent different measures of the dependent variable, taken together they constitute a moderator variable that tests whether an instructional condition was more
effective when measured by a test using the same method as the instruction compared to a test
using a different method from the instruction.

5. What are two possible intervening variables?
   1. Semantic cues
   2. Syntactic cues
6. Did the study omit any important variables that it might have included? If so, list them and label them by type.
   1. Grade level: kindergarten versus first grade (an additional potential moderator variable)

Worksheet E: Operational Definitions

1. How did the researchers operationalize the study's *independent variable?* The researcher did not operationalize the variable; the following definitions were created from the methodology section of the article:
   Isolated-word instruction: eight target words presented in random order
   Word-sentence instruction: eight target words presented within two meaningful sentences. (Manipulation-based)
   Does each operational definition (OD) seem sufficiently operational and exclusive?   <u>5</u> 4 3 2 1 NA
2. How did the researchers operationalize each of the *moderator variables,* if any?
   Sex: (presumably by observation)
   Test: (see below)
   Does each OD seem sufficiently operational and exclusive?
   5 4 3 2 1 <u>NA</u>
3. How did the researchers operationalize each of the *dependent variables?* The researchers did not operationalize the variables; the following definitions were created from the methodology section of the article:
   Acquisition of written words: correct identification of target word on two consecutive teach/test trials
   Short-term retention: words recalled 24 hours after treatment
   Long-term retention: words recalled 3 weeks after treatment
   Isolation test: identification of words from individual word cards
   Sentence test: identification of individual words, contained in sentences
   New context test: identification of words in new sentences
   Word-designation test: identification of target words in sentences containing both target and new words
   (All are dynamic or observation-based variables.)
   Does each OD seem sufficiently operational and exclusive?
   <u>5</u> 4 3 2 1 NA
4. How did the researchers operationalize each of the important *control variables?*

Grade level: children attending kindergarten classes
Social class: residence in a middle-class area
Prior recognition of target words: correct identification of target word on preliminary screening
Quantity and content of instruction: amount of exposure to material, manner of exposure, type of verbal reinforcement
Does each OD seem sufficiently operational and exclusive?

<u>5</u> 4 3 2 1 NA

Total score = 15 (out of 15)

Worksheet F: Manipulation and Control

1. Internal Validity (certainty):
   a. Control for participant bias: The subjects were randomly assigned to one of two treatment groups.[3] No sources were uncontrolled.
      Certainty: <u>5</u> 4 3 2 1 NA
   b. Control for experience bias: Two groups received the identical content and amount of instruction but differed only in the levels of the independent variable. No sources were uncontrolled.
      Certainty: <u>5</u> 4 3 2 1 NA
2. External Validity (generality):
   a. Participant selection: All of the subjects were from middle-class areas of the Greater Vancouver School District in British Columbia, Canada. The researchers eliminated the "upper" group by omitting all the children who knew one or more of the target words from their sample. They eliminated the "lower" group by omitting all the children who were not proficient in English.
      Generalizability: 5 4 <u>3</u> 2 1 NA
   b. Experiences: The subjects received treatments and tests in individual sessions (probably not their typical classroom experience). The senior author provided all the treatments. (Her methods may differ in important ways from those of a typical classroom teacher.)
      Generalizability: 5 4 <u>3</u> 2 1 NA
3. The independent variable was conditions of instruction: isolated word (word-alone) versus word-sentence. It was manipulated by the researcher by presenting materials presented to the subjects in a way that avoided any issue regarding its success. (Ss saw words either alone or in sentences.)
                                              5 4 3 2 1 <u>NA</u>

Total score = 16 (out of 20)

---

[3] Apparently, a third group, called a *control group*, participated only in the first step of the procedure.

Worksheet G: Research Design

1. a. Diagram the study's *design* and give its name.
        Posttest only control group design. (It is drawn here for retention tests and was done two times: for short-term and long-term; for acquisition, only one O per group, and done only once.)

R	X_1	Y_1	O_1	O_2	O_3	O_4
R	X_2	Y_1	O_5	O_6	O_7	O_8
R	X_1	Y_2	O_9	O_{10}	O_{11}	O_{12}
R	X_2	Y_2	O_{13}	O_{14}	O_{15}	O_{16}

    b. What kind of design was it?
        True experimental   4
        Factorial   +1
2. Suggested moderator variable: student SES (Levels: high, low)

R	X_1	Y_1	Z_1	O_1	O_2	O_3	O_4
R	X_2	Y_1	Z_1	O_5	O_6	O_7	O_8
R	X_1	Y_1	Z_2	O_9	O_{10}	O_{11}	O_{12}
R	X_2	Y_1	Z_2	O_{13}	O_{14}	O_{15}	O_{16}
R	X_1	Y_2	Z_1	O_{17}	O_{18}	O_{19}	O_{20}
R	X_2	Y_2	Z_1	O_{21}	O_{22}	O_{23}	O_{24}
R	X_1	Y_2	Z_2	O_{25}	O_{26}	O_{27}	O_{28}
R	X_2	Y_2	Z_2	O_{29}	O_{30}	O_{31}	O_{32}

3. How else could the design be improved?
    With respect to internal validity, the design could not be improved. With respect to external validity, the population from which the sample was drawn could have been broader and the methodology carried out in a more school-like manner.
                    Total score = 5 (out of 5)

Worksheet H: Observation/Measurement of Independent/Dependent Variables

1. The dependent variables were the only ones measured:
2. For each *dependent variable* answer each of the following questions:
    a. Describe briefly how it was measured.
        The children's acquisition of the target words was measured by asking them to identify words in isolation and in the context of both familiar and unfamiliar sentences. Retention was measured by carrying out these procedures after 24 hours and again after 3 weeks.

b. How valid and reliable was its measurement as documented?
Reliability was not discussed in the article. Validity was not
discussed, but it would probably not be questioned due to the
similarity of the treatment and testing procedure which used
the same words and sentences.   5 <u>4</u> 3 2 1 NA
            Total score = 4 (out of 5)

Worksheet I: Measurement of Moderator/Control Variables

1. Moderator variable: sex
   a. It was not measured in the strict sense.   5 4 3 2 1 <u>NA</u>
2. Control variables: grade level, social class of subjects, prior recognition
   of target words, quality, and content of instruction.
   a. The only measured control variable was prior recognition of target
      words. The researchers conducted this measurement by a recognition
      test of the words in isolation, the most obvious and direct way to
      measure this variable.   <u>5</u> 4 3 2 1 NA
            Total score = 5 (out of 5)

Worksheet J: Statistical Analysis

1. Did the study apply *statistical tests* to the collected data?   <u>Yes</u> No
   a. Two-way ANOVA was used to test word acquisition.
   b. Three-way ANOVA (Test × Treatment × Sex) with repeated mea-
      sures was used to test short-term retention. A Tukey comparison was
      also run.
   c. A repeated measure analysis of variance was used to test long-term
      retention. Once again a Tukey HSD was run.
2. Did the researchers conduct the proper *statistical tests* or the most suitable ones for the design?
                                        <u>5</u> 4 3 2 1 NA
   They applied the proper statistical tests. Both the independent variable
   and the moderator variable are nominal ones, and the dependent variable is an interval one, suggesting that ANOVA would be the proper
   test.
3. Did the research report clearly describe the applications of these tests,
   and were they correctly completed?   <u>5</u> 4 3 2 1 NA
4. Should the researchers have carried out additional *statistical tests*
   or presented additional *statistical results?*   Yes <u>No</u>
5. Did the research report include a *presentation of statistical results* in
   graphic or tabular form?   <u>Yes</u> No
   An easily understood and interpreted table with the means and standard
   deviations was presented.   <u>5</u> 4 3 2 1 NA
            Total score = 15 (out of 15)

Worksheet K: Presentation and Discussion of Results

1. a. Briefly describe the *findings* of the study.
    i. *Results of word acquisition:*
        - A statistically significant difference between the two treatment methods $F(1,44) = 29.77, p < .001$
        - The word sentence group learned the eight target words in significantly fewer trials than the other group required.
        - All subjects in the WS condition reached the criterion objective, but six subjects in the WA condition did not reach that criterion on at least one word.
        - No significant sex or treatment by sex effects appeared.
    ii. *Short-term retention:*
        - The main effect of treatment was not significant: $F(1,44) = 3.33; .05 < p < .075$.
        - A significant difference appeared among tests: $F(3,132) = 34.46, p < .0001$.
        - A significant interaction emerged between tests and treatment: $F(3,132) = 32.42, p < .0001$
        - Tukey HSD comparisons showed that the mean score on the words-in-treatment-sentence test was significantly different ($p < .01$) from the means of each of the other three retention tests. This difference was caused by the high scores of the WS treatment group on the words-in-treatment-sentence test.
    iii. *Long-term retention*
        - Results revealed a significant main effect of the treatment: $F(1,44) = 5.66, p < .05$.
        - A significant difference appeared among tests: $F(1,132) = 22.87, p < .0001$.
        - A significant interaction between tests and treatment was evident: $F(3,132) = 34.79, p < .0001$
        - The results from Tukey HSD comparisons matched those for short-term retention.
    iv. Time and sex effects
        - Analysis of variance on the gain (loss) scores between the 24-hour and 3-week testing periods showed no significant differences between treatment groups for total retention.
        - All analyses conducted on retention data revealed no significant sex or treatment by sex effects.

b. Does the article include an adequate and clear *summary* of the author's *findings*?   5 <u>4</u> 3 2 1 NA

c. Were the *findings* clearly related to the study's problem and hypotheses?

They were related to the study's problem. (The report articulated no hypotheses.)   5 <u>4</u> 3 2 1 NA

2. a. Give a brief *interpretation* of the findings to indicate why they came out as they did or what they mean.

Young readers learn new vocabulary more quickly when working with the words in context. They also perform much better when also tested with the words in context. The findings may have come out as they did because of the accuracy of Goodman's theory that contextual cues provide significant information.

b. Did the authors offer and support a meaningful and convincing *interpretation* of the findings that helped you to understand those results?   5 <u>4</u> 3 2 1 NA

3. a. Briefly state a *conclusion* that could be drawn from the study and a *recommendation* based on that conclusion.

Conclusion: Context improves the efficiency of word learning. Recommendation: Young readers should be taught to read words in context.

b. Did the study's findings support meaningful *conclusions* and *recommendations,* and did the research report offer any?   5 4 <u>3</u> 2 1 NA

The researchers seemed to back off the issue at the end without giving any recommendations. They seemed to excuse themselves by stating that their "research paradigm was not a strong test." It seems that if they really wanted to settle a controversial issue, which was stated as the purpose of their study, they should have been prepared to take a stand.

Total score = 15 (out of 20)

Overall

Total score = 125 (out of 150) or 83%

The greatest strength of Sample Study III was in its literature review, design, and analysis. The researchers might have strengthened Sample Study III by articulating hypotheses, sampling from a broader population, and making more definitive recommendations.

Sample Study IV
Worksheet A: Problem Statement

1. Problem statement: "This study was initiated to determine whether CAI [computer-assisted instruction] as a supplement to traditional mathematics instruction . . . fosters gains for disadvantaged elementary school pupils in the affective as well as academic domains. Pupils' gender was included as an independent variable to provide further empirical data."
   Does it appear on the first (or second) page?   Second (3)

2. Rewritten problem statement: What is the effect of CAI on the mathematical achievement and self-concept as well as the perception of the quality of school life among disadvantaged boys and girls in third, fourth, and fifth grades?
   Was the authors' version clear enough to make this task an easy one?
                                                        5 4 3 2 1 NA

3. Evaluation of the problem:
   a. Workability: The problem was a very workable one, because programs were already in operation so the evaluation involved only testing students.   5 4 3 2 1 NA
   b. Critical mass: The problem involved a reasonably large number of schools and students.   5 4 3 2 1 NA
   c. Interest: The problem targeted an area of obvious interest to the Israeli education professors who conducted study.
   d. Theoretical value: The problem established a very limited connection with the theory of instruction or the theory of learning.   5 4 3 2 1 NA
   e. Practical value: The problem had great practical value, because it addressed possibilities for improving mathematics performance by disadvantaged learners in Israel using CAI.   5 4 3 2 1 NA
                            Total score = 24 (out of 30)

Worksheet B: Supportive Literature

1. Context of the problem: Although some research demonstrates an inverse relationship between mathematics achievement and pupil attitudes toward mathematics, CAI is an instructional practice that seems to hold promise for simultaneous enhancement of disadvantaged pupils' cognitive and affective development.
   Is the context clear and sufficiently established?   5 4 3 2 1 NA
2. a. What is the magnitude of the literature review?
      17 references.   5 4 3 2 1 NA
   b. How empirical and up-to-date is it?

More than half of the citations mention sources published
in the 1980s, and they reflect an empirical
emphasis.   <u>5</u> 4 3 2 1 NA
  c. Does it bear on the problem(s) of the study?
     Primarily on the impact of CAI on achievement.
                                            5 <u>4</u> 3 2 1 NA
  d. Is it well-organized? Yes (considering the space limitations of a
     journal article).   <u>5</u> 4 3 2 1 NA
  e. Summary of literature review: Although some evidence indicates that
     cognitive and affective outcomes cannot be simultaneously maxi-
     mized in teaching mathematics, other findings suggest such a possibil-
     ity in the context of cooperative, small-group instruction. CAI has
     been shown to be an effective tool for enhancing achievement.
3. a. Do the researchers attempt to establish the significance of the study
      using argument and/or supportive literature?
      In the introductory section, they do not. They seem to simply assume
      the study's obvious significance.   No (1)
   b. Is the attempt convincing?
      Even without speaking directly to the issue, some notion of the
      study's significance comes across.   5 4 <u>3</u> 2 1 NA
   c. Summary of the argument for the study's significance: It addresses
      the important goal of providing the kind of instruction to disadvan-
      taged students that will enable them to both learn mathematics and
      like it.
   d. A point of significance to be added: The researchers should have tried
      more explicitly to convince the reader that performance in and atti-
      tudes toward mathematics constitute an important educational prob-
      lem among disadvantaged students in Israel.
                        Total score = 28 (out of 35)

Worksheet C: Hypotheses

1. Were hypotheses cited in the study?
   "It was predicted that CAI as a supplement to traditional mathematics
   instruction would enhance pupils' mathematical self-concept . . . [and]
   would improve pupils' perceptions of school life."
   A third hypothesis, relating CAI to achievement, might have been offered in the introduction but was not. The first sentence of the discussion section did, however, mention this relationship as part of the
   study's hypotheses.   Yes (5)
2. Rewritten hypotheses: Supplementary CAI instruction in mathematics
   will enhance both the achievement and attitudes of disadvantaged
   students.
   Was the authors' version clear enough to make this task an easy one?
                                            5 <u>4</u> 3 2 1 NA

3. a. Hypothesis 1 (CAI will enhance mathematical self-concept) is a directional one.
Hypothesis 2 (CAI will enhance perceptions of school life) is a directional one.
Hypothesis 3 (CAI positively affects cognitive development) is a directional one.   <u>5</u> 4 3 2 1 NA

b. Is it clear and understandable?
The third hypothesis should have appeared in the introduction, and it should have said that CAI will enhance mathematical achievement.   5 4 <u>3</u> 2 1 NA

c. Is it consistent with the problem statement?
Yes, except for the fact that no hypotheses were offered regarding pupil gender and that the third hypothesis did not appear in the introduction.   5 <u>4</u> 3 2 1 NA

d. Is it supported by sufficient literature or arguments?
Hypotheses 1 and 2 are supported by some argument and hypothesis 3 by sufficient literature.   5 <u>4</u> 3 2 1 NA
Total score = 25 (out of 30)

Worksheet D: Variables

1. Independent variable: CAI versus no CAI
2. Moderator variables: pupil gender: boys versus girls; grade level: 3rd, 4th, 5th
3. Dependent variables: mathematics achievement; mathematical self-concept; perceptions of school life
4. Control variables: school achievement level: low (disadvantaged); cultural origin: Middle Eastern; subject matter: mathematics; hours of mathematics instruction
5. Intervening variables: student-centered versus teacher-centered instruction; nature and quality of teacher-pupil interactions
6. Other important variables: pupils' prior achievement in mathematics; pupils' prior mathematical self-concepts; pupils' prior perceptions of school life

Worksheet E: Operational Definitions

1. OD of independent variable: CAI—usage of computers in mathematics instruction in the area of drill and practice as a supplement to the regular curriculum; traditional instruction—regular classroom instruction in mathematics
Do these ODs seem sufficiently operational and exclusive?

The OD of traditional instruction is not a very operational one, perhaps because the authors felt that the operations that define traditional instruction are obvious.   5 4 <u>3</u> 2 1 NA

2. ODs of moderator variables: Pupil gender and grade level.
These ODs are, in fact, obvious.   5 4 <u>3</u> 2 1 <u>NA</u>

3. ODs of dependent variables:
Mathematics achievement: achievement in basic mathematical operations, concept comprehension, and application
Mathematical self-concept: self-evaluation of math achievement and math ability, and self-description of feelings about math
Perception of school life quality: self-description of satisfaction with school, commitment to schoolwork, attitudes toward teachers
Do these ODs seem sufficiently operational and exclusive?
                                      <u>5</u> 4 3 2 1 NA

4. ODs of control variables:
No ODs are offered, nor can any be determined, for the control variables.   5 4 3 2 <u>1</u> NA

Total score = 9 (out of 15)

Worksheet F: Manipulation and Control

1. Internal validity
   a. Participant bias: No pretest data were available on dependent measures; school equivalence was assumed on the basis of schoolwide measures of achievement levels, ethnic origins of pupils, and backgrounds of math teachers; the study did not control for pretest levels of pupils on its dependent measures.   5 4 3 <u>2</u> 1 NA
   b. Experience bias: All pupils in both conditions were taught the same content for the same amount of time; no sources seemed to be left uncontrolled.   <u>5</u> 4 3 2 1 NA
2. External validity
   a. Participant limitations: All participants were Israelis of Middle Eastern origin attending low-achieving schools.
                                      5 4 <u>3</u> 2 1 NA
   b. Experience limitations: none (The study's use of an ongoing CAI program with its normal teachers represents a strength.)   <u>5</u> 4 3 2 1 NA
3. a. Manipulation of CAI: At the time of the study, CAI was an ongoing program at the school, so it was not actually manipulated. The study's manipulation coincided with students' scheduled CAI time using a drill and practice program called TOAM.
   b. How successful was the manipulation?   5 4 3 2 1 <u>NA</u>
Total score = 15 (out of 20)

Worksheet G: Research Design

1. a. Diagram the design and give its name.

$$
\begin{array}{cccc}
\underline{X_1} & \underline{Y_1} & \underline{Z_1} & \underline{O_1} \\
\underline{X_2} & \underline{Y_1} & \underline{Z_1} & \underline{O_2} \\
\underline{X_1} & \underline{Y_2} & \underline{Z_1} & \underline{O_3} \\
\underline{X_2} & \underline{Y_2} & \underline{Z_1} & \underline{O_4} \\
\underline{X_1} & \underline{Y_1} & \underline{Z_2} & \underline{O_5} \\
\underline{X_2} & \underline{Y_1} & \underline{Z_2} & \underline{O_6} \\
\underline{X_1} & \underline{Y_2} & \underline{Z_2} & \underline{O_7} \\
\underline{X_2} & \underline{Y_2} & \underline{Z_2} & \underline{O_8} \\
\underline{X_1} & \underline{Y_1} & \underline{Z_3} & \underline{O_9} \\
\underline{X_2} & \underline{Y_1} & \underline{Z_3} & \underline{O_{10}} \\
\underline{X_1} & \underline{Y_2} & \underline{Z_3} & \underline{O_{11}} \\
X_2 & Y_2 & Z_3 & O_{12}
\end{array}
$$

X_1 = CAI; X_2 = traditional instruction
Y_1 = boys; Y_2 = girls
Z_1 = 3rd grade; Z_2 = 4th; Z_3 = 5th
Intact Group Comparison (because the treatment was already in operation, preventing the pretesting required for the nonequivalent control group design)
This design was repeated nine times, once for each of the following scores: AAT, MSC, achievement, affect, ability, QSL, SAT, COM, TCH; see Tables 2, 4, 6 in the research report.
   b. The study employed a pre-experimental, factorial design.   (2)
2. Had pretest data been available, the study might have included low versus very low achievers as a moderator variable. If pretest level had replaced pupil gender, the design would have been the same as that drawn in answer to question 1, but with the Xs preceded by Os (because it would have been a nonequivalent control group design).
3. How else could the design be improved?
   Pretesting would have made a major improvement, but this was impossible given the timing of the study.
                    Total score = 2 (out of 5)

Worksheet H: Observation/Measurement of Independent/Dependent Variables

1. a, b, c: The independent variable was not measured.
                                              5 4 3 2 1 <u>NA</u>

2. a. Measurement of dependent variables:
      Arithmetic achievement: measured by an achievement test constructed by the Israeli Ministry of Education

Mathematical self-concept: measured by a questionnaire developed for the study and requiring self-descriptions

Quality of school life: measured by a 27-item scale developed by Epstein and McPartland to measure pupils' satisfaction with school, commitment to schoolwork, and attitudes toward teachers

b. Validity and reliability:

Arithmetic Achievement Test: satisfactory reliabilities reported; the research report gives no information about content validity.

Mathematical Self-Concept Questionnaire: satisfactory reliability reported; the method of construction would support a judgment of good content validity.

Quality of School Life Scale: satisfactory reliability reported; satisfactory validity claimed   5 4 3 2 1 NA

Total score = 5 (out of 5)

Worksheet I: Measurement of Moderator/Control Variables

1. a, b, c: The study required no measurement of moderator variables for either pupil gender or grade level.

                                                    5 4 3 2 1 NA

2. a, b, c: The study reported no measurement for any control variable.   5 4 3 2 1 NA

Total score = 0 (out of 0)

Worksheet J: Statistical Analysis

1. Statistical tests used: analyses of variance

2. Did the researchers conduct the proper statistical tests or the most suitable ones for the design?   5 4 3 2 1 NA

3. Did the research report clearly describe the applications of these tests, and were they correctly completed?   5 4 3 2 1 NA

4. Should the researchers have carried out additional statistical tests or presented additional statistical results?   No

5. Did the research report include a presentation of statistical results in graphic or tabular form?   Yes, tabular

   Could it be understood and interpreted?   5 4 3 2 1 NA

Total score = 15 (out of 15)

Worksheet K: Presentation and Discussion of Results

1. a. Findings of the study: At all three grade levels and for both boys and girls, pupils in the CAI condition reported more positive perceptions of school life and scored higher on mathematics achievement than

did their peers in the traditional instruction classes. Also, the mathematical self-concepts of the CAI recipients exceeded those of traditional instruction recipients in Grades 3 and 5.

   b. Does the article include an adequate and clear summary of the findings?   <u>5</u> 4 3 2 1 NA

   c. Does it clearly relate the findings to the study's problem and hypotheses?   <u>5</u> 4 3 2 1 NA

2. a. Interpretation of the findings: CAI may have successfully maximized both cognitive and affective outcomes of mathematics instruction, because it is an inherently student-centered approach to instruction rather than a teacher-centered, whole-class approach. Also, it enables teachers to alter their usual instructional practices with entire classes. The study's results cannot be a function of differences in instructional time, because the treatments were equated on this variable.

   b. Did the authors offer and support a meaningful interpretation of the findings?   <u>5</u> 4 3 2 1 NA

3. a. Conclusion: CAI provides significant mathematics achievement gains for disadvantaged pupils without alienating them from school. Recommendation: In future research, control for pretreatment differences and pay attention to teacher-pupil and computer-pupil interactions.

   b. Did the study's findings support meaningful conclusions and recommendations, and did the research report offer any?   5 <u>4</u> 3 2 1 NA

Total score = 14 (out of 15)

Overall

Total score = 137 (out of 170) or 80%

Sample Study IV was well-organized and well-presented, and it demonstrated a highly significant outcome in favor of CAI. Its greatest weakness, which its authors acknowledged, was the lack of pretreatment measures on the dependent variable, which reduced internal validity. However, external validity was maintained.

Worksheets for Performing Statistical Tests

FIGURE I t-TEST WORKSHEET

GROUP	1	2
$N =$		
$\Sigma X =$		
$\Sigma X^2 =$		
$\overline{X} =$		

1 Calculation of group variances.

$$s_1^2 = \frac{N_1 \Sigma X_1^2 - (\Sigma X_1)^2}{N_1 (N_1 - 1)} = \underline{\hspace{3cm}} \qquad s_1^2 = \underline{\hspace{3cm}}$$

$$s_2^2 = \frac{N_2 \Sigma X_2^2 - (\Sigma X_2)^2}{N_2 (N_2 - 1)} = \underline{\hspace{3cm}} \qquad s_2^2 = \underline{\hspace{3cm}}$$

2 Calculation of t-value.

Steps

1. $\dfrac{(N_1 - 1)s_1{}^2 + (N_2 - 1)s_2{}^2}{N_1 + N_2 - 2} = \underline{\hspace{3cm}}$

2. $\dfrac{N_1 + N_2}{N_1 N_2} = \underline{\hspace{3cm}}$

3. (Step 1 $\times$ Step 2) $= \underline{\hspace{3cm}}$

4. $\sqrt{\text{Step 3}} = \underline{\hspace{3cm}}$

5. $\overline{X}_1 - \overline{X}_2 = \underline{\hspace{3cm}}$

6. $t = \dfrac{\text{Step 5}}{\text{Step 4}} = \underline{\hspace{3cm}}$ $df = N_1 + N_2 - 2 = \underline{\hspace{2cm}}$

7. Look up t value in Table II, Appendix C.* $p = \underline{\hspace{3cm}}$

*If t-value in Step 6 exceeds the table value at a specific p level, then the null hypothesis (i.e., that the means are equal) can be rejected at that p level.

CORRELATION WORKSHEET

FIGURE II

$$r = \frac{N \Sigma XY - (\Sigma X)(\Sigma Y)}{\sqrt{[N\Sigma X^2 - (\Sigma X)^2][N\Sigma Y^2 - (\Sigma Y)^2]}}$$

Formula Steps	Calculations
1. N (Number of pairs)	
2. ΣX	
3. ΣX^2	
4. ΣY	
5. ΣY^2	
6. ΣXY	
7. $N\Sigma X^2 - (\Sigma X)^2$	
8. $N\Sigma Y^2 - (\Sigma Y)^2$	
9. Step 7 X Step 8	
10. $\sqrt{\text{Step 9}}$	
11. $N\Sigma XY - (\Sigma X)(\Sigma Y)$	
12. Step 11 ÷ Step 10 = r	
13. $df = N - 2$	
14. p (from Table III, Appendix C)*	

*If r obtained in Step 12 exceeds the r given in Table III, Appendix C for df (Step 13) at a specific p level, then the null hypothesis that the variables are unrelated may be rejected at that p level.

FIGURE III   ANALYSIS OF VARIANCE ($p \times q$ FACTORIAL) WORKSHEET (WITH UNEQUAL ns)

	p_1	p_2	p_i	
q_1	$n =$ $\frac{1}{n} =$ $\Sigma X =$ $(\Sigma X)^2 =$ $\Sigma X^2 =$ $\overline{X} =$ $SS^* =$			$B_1 =$ ___
q_j				$B_j =$ ___
	$A_1 =$ _____	$A_2 =$ _____	$A_i =$ _____	

$^*SS = \Sigma X^2 - \dfrac{(\Sigma X)^2}{n}$ *(This and the above terms should be calculated for each cell.)*

$A_{1,2,i}$ = sum of means in columns 1, 2, i, respectively.

$B_{1,j}$ = sum of means in rows 1, j, respectively.

G = sum of A's = sum of B's = _____

p = number of columns = _____

q = number of rows = _____

Steps

1. Add together all the *SS*. _____ = SS_w

2. Add together all the $\dfrac{1}{n}$. _____

3. pq/Step 2 = _____ = $\tilde{n}$

4. $G^2/pq =$ _____

5. Square each A_i and add the squares together = _____ = ΣA^2

6. Step 5/q _____

(continued)

7. Square each B_j and add the squares together = _____
    $= \Sigma B^2$

8. Step 7/p _____

9. Square every $\overline{X}$ and add the squares together = _____
    $= \Sigma \overline{X}^2$

SS_A = Step 3 [Step 6 − Step 4]

SS_B = Step 3 [Step 8 − Step 4]

SS_{AB} = Step 3 [Step 9 − Step 6 − Step 8 + Step 4]

$MS_A = \dfrac{SS_A}{p-1} =$ _____

$MS_B = \dfrac{SS_B}{q-1} =$ _____

$MS_{AB} = \dfrac{SS_{AB}}{(p-1)(q-1)} =$ _____

$MS_w = \dfrac{\text{Step 1}}{(\text{Total of } n\text{'s} - pq)} =$ _____

$F_A = \dfrac{MS_A}{MS_w} =$ _____

$F_B = \dfrac{MS_B}{MS_w} =$ _____

$F_{AB} = \dfrac{MS_{AB}}{MS_w} =$ _____

From Table IV, Appendix C

df_A = $p - 1 =$ _____

df_w = total of n's $- pq =$ _____ $p =$ _____ *

df_B = $q - 1 =$ _____

df_w = _____ $p =$ _____

df_{AB} = $(p-1)(q-1) =$ _____

df_w = _____ $p =$ _____

*If an obtained F value exceeds the value given in Table IV, Appendix C (for the appropriate df's) at a specific p level, then the null hypothesis that the variables are not related can be rejected at that p level.

FIGURE IV   WORKSHEET FOR MANN-WHITNEY U-TEST

Rank all data (both groups combined)

Observation Rank Group* (in decreasing order)	Observation Rank Group	Observation Rank Group
1.	13.	25.
2.	14.	26.
3.	15.	27.
4.	16.	28.
5.	17.	29.
6.	18.	30.
7.	19.	31.
8.	20.	32.
9.	21.	33.
10.	22.	34.
11.	23.	35.
12.	24.	36.

*E = experimental group; C = control group.

If two or more scores are tied, assign each the same rank—that being the average of the ranks for the tied scores.

E score	Rank (R_1)	C score	Rank (R_2)
	$\Sigma R_1 =$ _____		$\Sigma R_2 =$ _____
	$n_1 =$ _____		$n_2 =$ _____

$$U = n_1 n_2 + \frac{n_1 (n_1 + 1)}{2} - R_1 = \underline{\hspace{2cm}}$$

$$U = n_1 n_2 + \frac{n_2 (n_2 + 1)}{2} - R_2 = \underline{\hspace{2cm}}$$

$p =$ _____ †

†Rule: Use as U whichever of the two computed U values is smaller. Look up this value in the table of critical values of U (Table V, Appendix C) to determine significance. If the smaller obtained U value is smaller than the table value at a given p level, then the difference is significant at that p level.

WORKSHEET FOR A RANK-ORDER CORRELATION (r_s)   FIGURE V

$$r_s = 1 - \frac{6 \Sigma d^2}{N^3 - N}$$

Subject or Object	Rank for Test 1 or Judge 1	Rank for Test 2 or Judge 2	Difference between Ranks (d)	d^2
(1)				
(2)				
(3)				
(4)				
(5)				
(6)				
(7)				
(8)				
(9)				
(10)				
(11)				
(12)*				

1. Σd^2 = _____

2. 6 X Step 1 = _____

3. N = number of subjects or objects = _____

4. $N^3 - N$ = _____

5. Step 2 ÷ Step 4 = _____

6. r_s = 1 — Step 5 = _____

7. p (from Table VI, Appendix C) = _____ †

*This technique can be used for any number of subjects or objects. For this illustration, N = 12.

†If r_s exceeds the table value at a given p level, then r_s is significant at that p level.

FIGURE VI   WORKSHEET FOR A CHI-SQUARE (χ^2) TEST FOR TWO INDEPENDENT SAMPLES (2×2 CONTINGENCY TABLE)

$A =$ _____	$B =$ _____	$A + B =$ _____
$C =$ _____	$D =$ _____	$C + D =$ _____

$A + C =$ _____ $B + D =$ _____ $N =$ _____

$$\chi^2 = \frac{N[(A \times D) - (B \times C) - \frac{N}{2}]^2}{(A + B)\,(C + D)\,(A + C)\,(B + D)}$$

Steps

1. $(A + B)\,(C + D)\,(A + C)\,(B + D) =$ _____
2. $A \times D =$ _____
3. $B \times C =$ _____
4. Step 2 — Step 3 = _____
5. Step 4 $- \dfrac{N}{2} =$ _____
6. (Step 5)^2 = _____
7. $N \times$ Step 6 = _____
8. Step 7 $\div$ Step 1 = χ^2 = _____

    $df = $ *(number of rows* $- 1)$ (number of columns $- 1) = (2 - 1)\,(2 - 1) = 1$

    p (from Table VII, Appendix B) = _____ *

*If the obtained χ^2 value exceeds the value given in Table VII, Appendix C, at a given p level, then the obtained χ^2 value can be considered significant at that p level.

References

American Psychological Association. (1983). *Publication manual* (3rd ed.). Washington, DC: American Psychological Association.

American Psychological Association. (1985). *Standards for educational and psychological testing.* Washington, DC: American Psychological Association.

American Psychological Association (1994). *Publication manual* (4th ed.). Washington DC: American Psychological Association.

Anderson, L. W. (1981). *Assessing affective characteristics in the schools.* Boston: Allyn & Bacon.

Bandura, A. (1986). *Social foundations of thought and action: A social cognitive theory.* Englewood Cliffs, NJ: Prentice-Hall.

Bangert-Drowns, R. L., Kulik, C-L. C., Kulik, J. A., & Morgan, M. (1991). Instructional effect of feedback in test-like events. *Review of Educational Research, 61,* 213–238.

Bean, J. P., & Metzner, B. S. (1985). A conceptual model of nontraditional undergraduate student attrition. *Review of Educational Research, 55,* 485–540.

Benware, C. A., & Deci, E. L. (1984). Quality of learning with an active versus passive motivational set. *American Educational Research Journal, 21,* 755–776.

Bloom, B. S. (1976). *Human characteristics and school learning.* New York: McGraw-Hill.

Bogdan, R. C., & Biklen, S. K. (1992). *Qualitative research in education* (2nd ed.). Boston: Allyn & Bacon.

Boggs, S. R., & Eyberg, S. (1990). Interview techniques and establishing rapport. In A. M. LaGreca (Ed.). *Through the eyes of the child* (pp. 85–108). Boston: Allyn & Bacon.

Brown, J. A. C. (1954). *The social psychology of industry.* Middlesex, England: Penguin Books.

Busch, J. W. (1985). Mentoring in graduate schools of education: Mentors' perceptions. *American Educational Research Journal, 22,* 369–388.

Butler, E. W. (1977). A comparison of the socioeconomic status and job satisfaction of male high school and community college graduates. Worcester, MA: Unpublished study.

Calfee, R. C., & Valencia, R. R. (1991). *APA guide for preparing manuscripts for journal publication.* Washington DC: American Psychological Association.

Cameron, J., & Pierce, W. D. (1994). Reinforcement, reward, and intrinsic motivation: A meta-analysis. *Review of Educational Research, 64,* 363–423.

Campbell, D. T., & Stanley, J. C. (1966). *Experimental and quasi-experimental designs for research.* Chicago: Rand McNally.

Campbell, J. P., & Dunnette, M. D. (1968). Effectiveness of T-group experiences in managerial training and development. *Psychological Bulletin, 70,* 73–104.

Campbell, W. G., & Ballou, S. V. (1990). *Form and style: Theses, reports, terms papers.* (8th ed.). Boston: Houghton Mifflin.

Casteel, C. A. (1991). Answer changing on multiple-choice test items among eighth-grade readers. *Journal of Experimental Education, 59,* 300–309.

Chi, M. T. H., DeLeeuw, N., Chiu, M., & LaVancher, C. (1994). Eliciting self-explanations improves understanding. *Cognitive Science, 18,* 439–477.

Cohen, J. (1988). *Statistical power analysis for the behavioral sciences* (2nd ed.). Hillsdale, NJ: Lawrence Erlbaum Associates.

Cohen, J. (1992). Statistical power analysis. *Current Directions in Psychological Science, 1*, 98–101.

Conoley, J. C., & Impara, J. C. (Eds.). (1995). *The twelfth mental measurements yearbook*. Lincoln, NE: Buros Institute of Mental Measurements.

Conrad, C. F., & Blackburn, R. T. (1985). Correlates of departmental quality in regional colleges and universities. *American Educational Research Journal, 22*, 279–296.

Cook, T. D., & Campbell, D. T. (1979). *Quasi-experimentation: Design and analysis issues for field settings*. Chicago: Rand McNally.

Cooper, H. M. (1982). Scientific guidelines for conducting integrative research reviews. *Review of Educational Research, 52*, 291–302.

Cruikshank, D. R. (1984). Toward a model to guide inquiry in preservice teacher education. *Journal of Teacher Education, 35* (6), 43–48.

Dobbert, M. L. (1982). *Ethnographic research: Theory and applications for modern schools and societies*. New York: Praeger.

Eisenhart, M. A., & Holland, D. C. (1983). Learning gender from peers: The role of peer groups in the cultural transmission of gender. *Human Organization, 42*, 321–332.

Ericsson, K. A., & Simon, H. A. (1993). *Protocol analysis: Verbal reports as data* (rev. ed.). Cambridge, MA: MIT Press.

Ferguson, G. A. (1981). *Statistical analysis in psychology and education* (5th ed.). New York: McGraw-Hill.

Fisher, R. A. (1948). *Statistical methods for research workers* (10th ed.). Edinburgh: Oliver and Boyd.

Forness, S. R., & Kavale, K. A. (1985). Effects of class size on attention, communication, and disruption of mildly retarded children. *American Educational Research Journal, 22*, 403–412.

Forsyth, P. B. (1976) Isolation and alienation in educational organizations. Unpublished doctoral dissertation, Rutgers University.

Friedman, G. H., Lehrer, B. E., & Stevens, J. P. (1983). The effectiveness of self-directed and lecture/discussion stress management approaches and the locus of control of teachers. *American Educational Research Journal, 20*, 563–580.

Fuchs, D., Fuchs, L. S., Power, M. H., & Dailey, A. M. (1985). Bias in the assessment of handicapped children. *American Educational Research Journal, 22*, 185–198.

Gagné, R. M. (1985). *Conditions of learning* (4th ed.). New York: Holt, Rinehart and Winston.

Gephart, W. J., & Antonoplos, D. P. (1969, June). The effects of expectancy and other research-biasing factor. *Phi Delta Kappan*, 579–583.

Ghatala, E. S., Levin, J. R., Pressley, M., & Lodico, M. G. (1985). Training cognitive strategy-monitoring in children. *American Educational Research Journal, 22*, 199–215.

Glaser, B. (1978). *Theoretical sensitivity: Advances in the methodology of grounded theory*. Mill Valley, CA: Sociology Press.

Glass, G. V. (1977). Integrating findings: The meta-analysis of research. *Review of Research in Education, 5*, 351–379.

Glass, G. V., & Hopkins, K. D. (1996). *Statistical methods in education and psychology* (3rd ed.). Englewood Cliffs, NJ: Prentice-Hall.

Glass, G. V., McGaw, B., & Smith, M. L. (1981). *Meta-analysis in social research.* Beverly Hills, CA: Sage Publications.

Goetzfried, L., & Hannafin, M. J. (1985). The effect of the locus on CAI control strategies on the learning of mathematics rules. *American Educational Research Journal, 22,* 273–278.

Guba, E. G., & Lincoln, Y. S. (1981). *Effective evaluation.* San Francisco: Jossey-Bass.

Hays, W. L. (1973). *Statistics for the social sciences* (2nd ed.). New York: Holt, Rinehart and Winston.

Helm, C. M. (1989). Effect of computer-assisted telecommunications on school attendance. *Journal of Educational Research, 82,* 362–365.

Henry, J. (1960). A cross-cultural outline of education. *Current Anthropology, 1,* 267–304.

Johnson, D. W., & Johnson, R. (1985). Classroom conflict: Controversy versus debate in learning groups. *American Educational Research Journal, 22,* 237–256.

King, A. (1990). Enhancing peer interaction and learning in the classroom through reciprocal questioning. *American Educational Research Journal, 27,* 664–687.

Klein, J. D., & Keller, J. M. (1990). Influence of student ability, locus of control, and type of instructional control on performance and confidence. *Journal of Educational Research, 83,* 140–145.

Krendl, K. A., & Broihier, M. (1992). Student responses to computers: A longitudinal study. *Journal of Educational Computing Research, 8,* 215–227.

Leonard, W. H., & Lowery, L. F. (1984). The effects of question types in textual reading upon retention of biology concepts. *Journal of Research in Science Teaching, 21,* 377–384.

Lepper, M. R., Keavney, M., & Drake, M. (1996). Intrinsic motivation and extrinsic rewards: A commentary on Cameron and Pierce's meta-analysis. *Review of Educational Research, 66,* 5–32.

McGarity, J. R., & Butts, D. P. (1984). The relationship among teacher classroom management behavior, student engagement, and student achievement of middle and high school science students of varying aptitude. *Journal of Research in Science Teaching, 21,* 55–61.

McKinney, C. W., et al. (1983). Some effects of teacher enthusiasm on student achievement in fourth grade social studies. *Journal of Educational Research, 76,* 249–253.

Mahn, C. S., & Greenwood, G. E. (1990). Cognitive behavior modification: Use of self-instruction strategies by first graders on academic tasks. *Journal of Educational Research, 83,* 158–161.

Makuch, J. R., Robillard, P. D., & Yoder, E. P. (1992). Effects of individual versus paired/cooperative computer-assisted instruction on the effectiveness and efficiency of an in-service training lesson. *Journal of Educational Technology Systems, 20,* 199–208.

Mark, J. H., & Anderson, B. D. (1985). Teacher survival rates in St. Louis, 1969–1982. *American Educational Research Journal, 22,* 413–421.

Marsh, H. W., Parker, J., & Barnes, J. (1985). Multidimensional adolescent self-concepts: Their relationship to age, sex, and academic measures. *American Educational Research Journal, 22,* 422–444.

Mevarech, Z. R., & Yisrael, R. (1985). Effects of computer-assisted mathematics instruction on disadvantaged pupils' cognitive and affective development. *Journal of Educational Research, 79,* 5–11.

O'Connor, J. F. (1995). The differential effectiveness of coding, elaborating, and outlining for learning from text. Unpublished doctoral dissertation, Florida State University, Tallahassee, FL.

Osgood, C. E., Suci, G. J., & Tannenbaum, P. H. (1957). *The measurement of meaning.* Urbana, IL: University of Illinois Press.

Patton, M. Q. (1990). *Qualitative evaluation and research methods.* Newbury Park, CA: Sage Publications.

Peterson, P. L., & Fennema, E. (1985). Effective teaching, student engagement in classroom activities, and sex-related differences in learning mathematics. *American Educational Research Journal, 22,* 309–335.

Pintrich, P. R., & De Groot, E. V. (1990). Motivational and self-regulated learning components of classroom academic performance. *Journal of Educational Psychology, 82,* 33–40.

Prater, D., & Padia, W. (1983). Effects of modes of discourse on writing performance in grades four and six. *Research in the Teaching of English, 17,* 127–134.

Ranzijn, F. J. A. (1991). The number of video examples and the dispersion of examples as instructional design variables in teaching concepts. *Journal of Experimental Education, 59,* 320–330.

Raphael, T. E., & Pearson, P. D. (1985). Increasing students' awareness of sources of information for answering questions. *American Educational Research Journal, 22,* 217–235.

Rash, J., Johnson, T. D., & Gleadow, N. (1984). Acquisition and retention of written words by kindergarten children under varying learning conditions. *Reading Research Quarterly, 19,* 452–460.

Rasinski, T. V. (1990). Effects of repeated reading and listening-while-reading on reading fluency. *Journal of Educational Research, 83,* 147–150.

Rayman, J. R., Bernard, C. B., Holland, J. L., & Barnett, D. C. (1983). The effects of a career course on undecided college students. *Journal of Vocational Behavior, 23,* 346–355.

Reiser, R. A., Tessmer, M. A., & Phelps, P. C. (1984). Adult-child interaction in children's learning from "Sesame Street." *Educational Communications and Technology, 32,* 217–223.

Roberge, J. J., & Flexner, B. K. (1984). Cognitive style, operativity and reading achievement. *American Educational Research Journal, 21,* 227–236.

Roe, A. (1966). *Psychology of occupations.* New York: Wiley.

Rosenthal, R. (1985). From unconscious experimenter bias to teacher expectancy effects. In J. B. Dusek (Ed.). *Teacher expectancies* (pp. 37–65). Hillsdale, NJ: Lawrence Erlbaum Associates.

Sahari, M., Tuckman, B. W., & Fletcher, H. J. (1996). The effect of constructing coded elaborative outlines and student generated questions on text learning. *Curriculum Forum* 6 (1), 48–59.

Schlaefli, A., Rest. J. R., & Thoma, S. J. (1985). Does moral education improve moral judgment? A meta-analysis of intervention studies using the Defining Issues Test. *Review of Educational Research, 55,* 319–352.

Siegel S. (1956). *Nonparametric statistics for the behavioral sciences.* New York: McGraw-Hill.

Slavin, R. E. (1986). Best-evidence synthesis: An alternative to meta-analytic and traditional reviews. *Educational Researcher, 15* (9), 5–11.

Slavin, R. E., & Karweit, N. L. (1984). Mastery learning and student teams: A factorial experiment in urban general mathematics classes. *American Educational Research Journal, 21,* 725–736.

Slavin, R. E., & Karweit, N. L. (1985). Effects of whole class, ability grouped, and individualized instruction on mathematics achievement. *American Educational Research Journal, 22,* 351–368.

Spradley, J. P. (1980). *Participant observation.* New York: Holt, Rinehart & Winston.

SPSS Inc. (1997). *SPSS base 7.5 for Windows: User's guide.* Chicago: SPSS Inc.

Stake, R. E. (1975). *Evaluating the arts in education: A responsive approach.* Columbus, OH: Charles E. Merrill.

Stockard, J., & Wood, J. W. (1984). The myth of female underachievement; A reexamination of sex differences in academic underachievement. *American Educational Research Journal, 21,* 825–838.

Sutton, R. E. (1991). Equity and computers in the schools: A decade of research. *Review of Educational Research, 61,* 475–504.

Taylor, B. M., & Samuels, S. J. (1983). Children's use of text structure in the recall of expository material. *American Educational Research Journal, 20,* 517–528.

Thorndike, R. L., & Hagen, E. (1991). *Measurement and evaluation in psychology and education* (5th ed.). New York: Wiley.

Tuckman, B. W. (1965). Developmental sequence in small groups. *Psychological Bulletin, 63,* 384–399.

Tuckman, B. W. (1985). *Evaluating instructional programs* (2nd ed.). Boston: Allyn & Bacon.

Tuckman, B. W. (1988). The scaling of mood. *Educational and Psychological Measurement, 48,* 419–427.

Tuckman, B. W. (1990a). Group versus goal-setting effects on the self-regulated performance of students differing in self-efficacy. *Journal of Experimental Education, 58,* 291–298.

Tuckman, B. W. (1990b). The development and concurrent validity of the Procrastination Scale. *Educational and Psychological Measurement, 51,* 473–480.

Tuckman, B. W. (1990c). A proposal for improving the quality of published research. *Educational Researcher, 19* (9), 22–25.

Tuckman, B. W. (1992a). *Educational psychology: From theory to application.* Fort Worth, TX: Harcourt Brace Jovanovich.

Tuckman, B. W. (1992b). The effect of student planning and self-competence on self-motivated performance. *Journal of Experimental Education, 60,* 119–127.

Tuckman, B. W. (1993). The coded elaborative outline as a strategy to help students learn from text. *Journal of Experimental Education, 62,* 5–13.

Tuckman, B. W. (1996a). The relative effectiveness of incentive motivation and prescribed learning strategy in improving college students' course performance. *Journal of Experimental Education, 64,* 197–210.

Tuckman, B. W. (1996b). Using spotquizzes as an incentive to motivate procrastinators to study. Paper given at the Annual Meeting of the American Educational Research Association, New York.

Tuckman, B. W., & Jensen, M. (1977). Stages of small-group development revisited. *Group and Organization Studies, 2,* 419–427.

Tuckman, B. W., & Sexton, T. L. (1990). The effect of teacher encouragement on student self-efficacy and motivation for self-regulated performance. *Journal of Social Behavior and Personality, 6,* 137–146.

Tuckman, B. W., & Trimble, S. (1997). Using tests as a performance incentive to motivate eighth-graders to study. Paper presented at the Annual Meeting of the American Psychological Association, Chicago.

Tuckman, B. W., & Waheed, M. A. (1981). Evaluating an individualized science program for community college students. *Journal of Research in Science Teaching, 18,* 489–495.

Tuckman, B. W., & Yates, D. S. (1980). Evaluating the student feedback strategy for changing teacher style. *Journal of Educational Research, 74,* 74–77.

Turner, B. A. (1981). Some practical aspects of qualitative analysis: One way of organizing the cognitive processes associated with the generation of grounded theory. *Quality and Quantity, 15,* 225–247.

U.S. Department of Health and Human Services (1991). *Code of federal regulations for the protection of human subjects.* Washington, DC: Government Printing Office.

Vockell, E. L., & Asher, W. (1974). Perceptions of document quality and use by educational decision makers and researchers. *American Educational Research Journal, 11,* 249–258.

Waite, D. (1993). Teachers in conference: A qualitative study of teacher-supervisor face-to-face interactions. *American Educational Research Journal, 30,* 675–702.

Wasson, B. B., Beare, P. L., & Wasson, J. B. (1990). Classroom behavior of good and poor readers. *Journal of Educational Research, 83,* 162–165.

Welch, W. W., & Walberg, H. J. (1970). Pretest and sensitization effects on curriculum evaluation. *American Educational Research Journal, 7,* 605–614.

Wiegmann, D. A., Dansereau, D. F., & Patterson, M. E. (1992). Cooperative learning: Effects of role playing and ability on performance. *Journal of Experimental Education, 60,* 109–116.

Wiersma, W. (1995). *Research methods in education: An introduction* (6th ed.). Boston: Allyn & Bacon.

Wilson, S. (1977). The use of ethnographic techniques in educational research. *Review of Educational Research, 47,* 245–265.

Wineburg, S. S. (1991) Historical problem solving: A study of the cognitive processes used in the evaluation of documentary and pictorial evidence. *Journal of Educational Psychology, 83,* 73–87.

Winer, B. J., Brown, D. R., & Michels, K. (1991). *Statistical principles in experimental design* (3rd ed.). New York: McGraw-Hill.

Name/Title Index

(Page numbers in italics refer to boxes, figures and tables; *n* refers to footnotes.)

SUBJECT INDEX

(Page numbers in italics refer to boxes, figures and tables; *n* refers to footnotes.)